Real-World Web Development with .NET 10

Second Edition

Build websites and services using mature and proven ASP.NET Core MVC, Web API, and Umbraco CMS

Mark J. Price

Real-World Web Development with .NET 10

Second Edition

Portfolio Director: Ashwin Nair
Relationship Lead: Suman Sen
Project Manager: Ruvika Rao
Content Engineer: Hayden Edwards
Technical Editor: Arjun Varma
Copy Editor: Safis Editing
Indexer: Tejal Soni
Proofreader: Hayden Edwards
Production Designer: Ajay Patule
Growth Lead: Priyadarshini Sharma

First published: December 2024
Second edition: December 2025

Production reference: 1251125

Published by Packt Publishing Ltd.
Grosvenor House
11 St Paul's Square
Birmingham
B3 1RB, UK.

ISBN 978-1-83588-892-6

www.packtpub.com

Contributors

About the author

Mark J. Price is a Microsoft Specialist: Programming in C# and Architecting Microsoft Azure Solutions, with over 20 years of experience. Since 1993, he has passed more than 80 Microsoft programming exams and specializes in preparing others to pass them. Between 2001 and 2003, Mark was employed to write official courseware for Microsoft in Redmond, USA. His team wrote the first training courses for C# while it was still an early alpha version. While with Microsoft, he taught "train-the-trainer" classes to get Microsoft Certified Trainers up-to-speed on C# and .NET. Mark has spent most of his career training a wide variety of students, from 16-year-old apprentices to 70-year-old retirees, with the majority being professional developers. Mark holds a BSc in Computer Science.

> *Thank you to all my readers. Your support means I get to write these books and celebrate your successes. Special thanks to the readers who give me actionable feedback via my GitHub repository and email, and interact with me and the book communities on Discord. You help make my books even better with every edition.*

About the reviewer

Giuseppe Guerra is an Italian Software Engineer focused on .NET and Azure, with several years of experience gained across various industrial sectors.

He holds a master's degree in Computer Engineering and Microsoft certifications as MCSD App Builder and Azure Developer Associate. Passionate about software and technology, he enjoys staying at the forefront of technological innovation.

Outside of work, he enjoys playing instruments and producing music. Originally from Monte Sant'Angelo, he now lives in Monopoli with his wife, Ileana.

Learn more on Discord

To join the Discord community for this book – where you can share feedback, ask questions to the author, and learn about new releases – follow this QR code:

https://packt.link/RWWD10

Table of Contents

Chapter 2: Building Websites Using ASP.NET Core MVC   71

Chapter 3: Model Binding, Validation, and Data Using EF Core   129

Chapter 15: Customizing and Extending Umbraco CMS   653

Preface

There are programming books that are thousands of pages long that aim to be comprehensive references to the C# language, the .NET libraries, and app models like websites, services, and desktop and mobile apps.

This book is different. It is concise and aims to be a brisk, fun read that is packed with practical hands-on walk-throughs of each subject. The breadth of the overarching narrative comes at the cost of some depth, but you will find many signposts to explore further if you wish.

This book is simultaneously a step-by-step guide to learning mature and proven web development using cross-platform .NET, along with the creation of websites and services that can be built with these technologies. This book is most suitable for beginners to ASP.NET Core, but you must have previous experience with C# and .NET. If you do not have this experience, I recommend my book, *C# 14 and .NET 10 - Modern Cross-Platform Development Fundamentals*.

I will point out the cool corners and gotchas of web development using.NET so that you can impress colleagues and get productive fast. Rather than slowing down and boring some readers by explaining every little thing, I will assume that you are smart enough to Google an explanation for topics that are related but not necessary to include in a beginner-to-intermediate guide that has limited space in a printed book.

Some chapters have links to additional related online-only content for those readers who would like more details. For example, *Chapter 1, Introducing Real-World Web Development Using .NET*, has an online section about web development on the client side using HTML, CSS, and JavaScript.

Who this book is for

This book is aimed at intermediate .NET developers with a good understanding of C# and .NET fundamentals. It is ideal for developers looking to expand their skills in building professional, controller-based web applications.

What this book covers

Chapter 1, Introducing Real-World Web Development Using .NET, is about introducing you to mature and proven web development with .NET. This means a set of technologies that have been refined over a decade or more with plenty of documentation, support forums, and third-party investment, including ASP.NET Core **Model-View-Controller (MVC)**, Web API services using controllers and OData, and popular frameworks like Umbraco CMS.

Chapter 2, Building Websites Using ASP.NET Core MVC, introduces building websites with a modern HTTP architecture on the server side using ASP.NET Core MVC, including the models, views, and controllers that make up the main components of an ASP.NET Core MVC project.

Chapter 3, Model Binding, Validation, and Data Using EF Core, covers model binding, model validation, and retrieving and modifying data using EF Core in an ASP.NET Core MVC website project. These concepts work together to simplify the common tasks of taking user input, processing it, and storing or retrieving data from a database.

Chapter 4, Building and Localizing Web User Interfaces, is about building web user interfaces with ASP.NET Core in more depth. You will learn more details about ASP.NET Core MVC views, Razor syntax, HTML and Tag Helpers, how to internationalize your website so that its user interface is understandable all over the world, and how to use Bootstrap for quick user interface prototyping.

Chapter 5, Authentication and Authorization, discusses authentication and authorization and how to implement them for an ASP.NET Core MVC website project. This means how to provide a web user interface for a visitor to register an account with a password, and how they can log in to access secure areas of the website.

Chapter 6, Performance and Scalability Optimization Using Caching, explains optimizing the performance and scalability of your websites and web services by using caching of various types.

Chapter 7, Web User Interface Testing Using Playwright, introduces you to web user interface testing and how to use Microsoft Playwright to write automated tests for web user interfaces.

Chapter 8, Configuring and Containerizing ASP.NET Core Projects, discusses configuring and containerizing ASP.NET Core projects.

Chapter 9, Building Web Services Using ASP.NET Core Web API, covers learning how to build web services, **AKA HTTP (Hypertext Transfer Protocol)** or **Representational State Transfer (REST)** services, using ASP.NET Core Web API with controllers. You will also learn how to try them out using tools including REST Client in VS Code and HTTP Editor in Visual Studio.

Chapter 10, Building Clients for Web Services, introduces you to how to consume web services using HTTP clients, which could be any other type of .NET app, including a website, mobile, or desktop app, or a web page using JavaScript to make HTTP calls.

Chapter 11, Testing and Debugging Web Services, introduces you to tools and techniques for testing and debugging your web services. Unit tests are good at detecting errors in business logic in a class or method, but you also need to verify that larger parts of your codebase work together with each other and external systems. This is where integration testing becomes important for web services.

Chapter 12, Building Web Services Using ASP.NET Core OData, explains OData, a standard that makes it easy to expose data via the web to make it accessible to any client that can make an HTTP request.

Chapter 13, Building Web Services Using FastEndpoints, teaches you about building web services using FastEndpoints, a popular third-party package that shuns controllers in favor of a more efficient way of defining web service endpoints.

Chapter 14, Web Content Management Using Umbraco CMS, is about building ASP.NET Core website projects that integrate with Umbraco CMS, a popular third-party web content management system.

Chapter 15, Customizing and Extending Umbraco CMS, introduces customizing and extending Umbraco CMS.

Epilogue describes your options for further study about .NET web development.

Appendix A, Answers to the Test Your Knowledge Questions, has the answers to the test questions at the end of each chapter.

Appendix B, Setting Up Your Development Environment, has step-by-step instructions for setting up your development environment. This includes a code editor such as Visual Studio or VS Code, and a database named Northwind on a database server such as SQL Server in Docker, SQL Server locally, or Azure SQL Database in the cloud.

Appendix C, Looking For Help, is all about how to find quality information about programming on the web. You will learn about Microsoft Learn documentation, including its new MCP server for integration with AI systems, getting help while coding and using dotnet commands, getting help from fellow readers in the book's Discord channel, searching the .NET source code for implementation details, and finally making the most of modern AI tools like GitHub Copilot.

The *Appendix* chapters are available to download from a link in the README file in the GitHub repository: `https://github.com/markjprice/web-dev-net10`.

You can also access a free PDF copy of the book (containing *Appendix A*, *B*, and *C*) through the following link: `https://packtpub.com/unlock`. Search for this book by name, ensure it's the correct edition, and have your purchase invoice ready.

To get the most out of this book

You can develop .NET projects using Visual Studio, VS Code, or a third-party tool like Rider. VS Code, Rider, and the command-line tools work on most operating systems, including Windows, macOS, and many varieties of Linux. Visual Studio is Windows-only because Visual Studio for Mac has been retired, does not officially support .NET 8 or later, and it reached its end of life in August 2024.

Download the example code files

You can download solutions for the step-by-step guided tasks and exercises from the GitHub repository at the following link: `https://github.com/markjprice/web-dev-net10`.

If you don't know how to download or clone a GitHub repository, then I provide instructions at the end of *Chapter 1, Introducing Real-World Web Development Using .NET*.

We also have other code bundles from our rich catalog of books and videos available at `https://github.com/PacktPublishing`. Check them out!

Conventions used

There are a number of text conventions used throughout this book.

CodeInText: Indicates code words in text, database table names, folder names, filenames, file extensions, pathnames, dummy URLs, user input, and X/Twitter handles. For example: "The Controllers, Models, and Views folders contain ASP.NET Core classes and the .cshtml files for execution on the server."

A block of code is set as follows:

```
// storing items at index positions
names[0] = "Kate";
names[1] = "Jack";
names[2] = "Rebecca";
names[3] = "Tom";
```

When we wish to draw your attention to a particular part of a code block, the relevant lines or items are set in bold:

```
// storing items at index positions
names[0] = "Kate";
names[1] = "Jack";
names[2] = "Rebecca";
names[3] = "Tom";
```

Any command-line input or output is written as follows:

```
dotnet new console
```

Bold: Indicates a new term, an important word, or words that you see on the screen. For instance, words in menus or dialog boxes appear in the text like this. For example, "Clicking on the **Next** button moves you to the next screen."

> Warnings or important notes appear like this.

> Tips and tricks appear like this.

Get in touch

Feedback from our readers is always welcome.

General feedback: If you have questions about any aspect of this book or have any general feedback, please email us at customercare@packt.com and mention the book's title in the subject of your message.

Errata: Although we have taken every care to ensure the accuracy of our content, mistakes do happen. If you have found a mistake in this book, we would be grateful if you reported this to us. Please visit http://www.packt.com/submit-errata, click **Submit Errata**, and fill in the form.

Piracy: If you come across any illegal copies of our works in any form on the internet, we would be grateful if you would provide us with the location address or website name. Please contact us at copyright@packt.com with a link to the material.

If you are interested in becoming an author: If there is a topic that you have expertise in and you are interested in either writing or contributing to a book, please visit http://authors.packt.com/.

Share Your Thoughts

Once you've read *Real-World Web Development with .NET 10, Second Edition*, we'd love to hear your thoughts! Scan the QR code below to go straight to the Amazon review page for this book and share your feedback.

https://packt.link/r/1-835-88893-3

Your review is important to us and the tech community and will help us make sure we're delivering excellent quality content.

Free benefits with your book

This book comes with free benefits to support your learning. Activate them now for instant access (see the "*How to Unlock*" section for instructions).

Here's a quick overview of what you can instantly unlock with your purchase:

Free PDF copy with appendices	Next-Gen Web-Based Reader
Free PDF copy with appendices	**Next-Gen Reader**

Access a DRM-free PDF copy of this book to read anywhere, on any device.

Unlock the book's appendices included with the free PDF.

Multi-device progress sync: Pick up where you left off, on any device.

Highlighting and notetaking: Capture ideas and turn reading into lasting knowledge.

Bookmarking: Save and revisit key sections whenever you need them.

Dark mode: Reduce eye strain by switching to dark or sepia themes.

How to Unlock

Scan the QR code (or go to packtpub.com/unlock).
Search for this book by name, confirm the edition,
and then follow the steps on the page.

*Note: Keep your invoice handy. Purchases made
directly from Packt don't require one.*

1

Introducing Real-World Web Development Using .NET

This book is about mature and proven web development with .NET. This means a set of technologies that have been refined over a decade or more with plenty of documentation, support forums, and third-party investment. These technologies are:

- **.NET:** A free, open-source developer platform from Microsoft for building and running cross-platform apps, including web, desktop, mobile, cloud, and games, using languages like C#, F#, and Visual Basic.

- **ASP.NET Core:** A set of shared components for building websites and services using .NET. This book covers a subset of its features, including the following:

  - **ASP.NET Core MVC:** An implementation of the model-view-controller design pattern for complex yet well-structured website development

  - **ASP.NET Core Web API:** For building controller-based web services that conform to the HTTP/REST service architecture conventions

  - **ASP.NET Core OData:** For building data access web services using an open standard

- **FastEndpoints:** A third-party web service platform built on ASP.NET Core.

- **Umbraco CMS:** A third-party, open-source, **content management system (CMS)** platform built on ASP.NET Core.

With these technologies, you will learn how to build cross-platform websites and web services using .NET 10.

A benefit of choosing .NET 10 is that it is a **Long-Term Support (LTS)** release, meaning it is supported for three years. .NET 10 was released in November 2025, and it will reach its end of life in November 2028. After .NET 11 is released in November 2026, you can target it, but be aware that it is a **Standard Term Support (STS)** release, and it will reach its end of life in November 2028, on the same day as .NET 10. You can learn more about STS 24-month support durations at the following link:

https://devblogs.microsoft.com/dotnet/dotnet-sts-releases-supported-for-24-months/.

Usually, the benefits of choosing the latest .NET version are performance improvements and better support for containerization in cloud hosting compared to earlier versions.

Throughout this book, I use the term **modern .NET** to refer to .NET 10 and its predecessors, like .NET 6, that derive from .NET Core. I use the term **legacy .NET** to refer to .NET Framework, Mono, Xamarin, and .NET Standard. Modern .NET is a unification of those legacy platforms and standards.

> **Who are you?** While writing this book, I have assumed that you are a .NET developer who is employed by a consultancy or a large organization. As such, you primarily work with mature and proven technologies like MVC rather than the newest shiny technologies pushed by Microsoft like Blazor. I also assume that you have little professional interest in being a web designer or content editor. You are much more concerned with how well a software product *works* rather than *looks*.

I assume you have already set up your development environment to use Visual Studio 2026, Visual Studio Code, or JetBrains Rider. Throughout this book, I will use the names **Visual Studio**, **VS Code**, and **Rider** to refer to these three code editors, respectively. If you have not set up your development environment, then you can learn how to in *Appendix B, Setting Up Your Development Environment*, or at the following link:

```
https://github.com/markjprice/web-dev-net10/blob/main/docs/ch01-setup-dev-env.md.
```

> **Warning!** Prerequisites for this book are knowledge of C# and .NET fundamentals, including how to build .NET projects with a tool like Visual Studio or the dotnet **command-line interface (CLI)**. You can learn these skills from my book, *C# 14 and .NET 10 – Modern Cross-Platform Development Fundamentals*.

I recommend that you work through this and subsequent chapters sequentially because later chapters will reference projects in earlier chapters, and you will build up sufficient knowledge and skills to tackle the more challenging problems in later chapters. For example, a section in this chapter will walk you through creating a pair of class libraries that define a database entity model that will be used in subsequent chapters.

In this chapter, we will cover the following topics:

- Introducing this book and its siblings
- Understanding ASP.NET Core
- Making good use of the GitHub repository for this book
- Structuring projects and managing packages
- Building an entity model for use in the rest of the book
- Looking for help
- Using future versions of .NET with this book
- Understanding web development

Free Benefits with Your Book

Your purchase includes a free PDF copy of this book (containing *Appendix A, B,* and *C*), along with other exclusive benefits. Check the *Free Benefits with Your Book* section in the Preface to unlock them instantly and maximize your learning experience.

Introducing this book and its siblings

Before we dive in, let's set the context by understanding that this is one of four books about .NET 10 that I have written that cover almost everything a beginner to .NET needs to know.

This book is the second of a quartet of books that completes your learning journey through .NET 10:

1. The first book, *C# 14 and .NET 10 – Modern Cross-Platform Development Fundamentals*, covers the fundamentals of the C# language, the .NET libraries, and using modern ASP.NET Core, Blazor, and Minimal API web services for web development. It is designed to be read linearly because skills and knowledge from earlier chapters build up and are needed to understand later chapters.

2. The second book (the one you're reading now), *Real-World Web Development with .NET 10*, covers mature and proven web development technologies like ASP.NET Core MVC and controller-based Web API web services, as well as OData, FastEndpoints, and Umbraco CMS for building real-world web projects on .NET 10. You will learn how to test your web services using xUnit and test the user interfaces of your websites using Playwright, and then how to containerize your projects ready for deployment.

3. The third book, *Apps and Services with .NET 10*, covers data using SQL Server, Dapper, and EF Core, as well as more specialized .NET libraries like internationalization and popular third-party packages including Serilog and Noda Time. You will learn how to build native **ahead-of-time** (**AOT**)-compiled services with ASP.NET Core Minimal API web services and how to improve performance, scalability, and reliability using caching, queues, and background services. You will implement modern services using GraphQL, gRPC, and SignalR. Finally, you will learn how to build graphical user interfaces for websites, desktop, and mobile apps with .NET MAUI, Avalonia, and Blazor.

4. The fourth book, *Tools and Skills for .NET 10*, covers important tools and skills that a professional .NET developer should have. These include design patterns and solution architecture, debugging, memory analysis, all the important types of testing, whether it be unit, integration, performance, or web user interface testing, and then topics for testing cloud-native solutions on your local computer, like containerization, Docker, and Aspire. Finally, we will look at how to prepare for an interview to get the .NET developer career that you want.

A summary of the .NET 10 quartet and their most important topics is shown in *Figure 1.1:*

C# language, including new C# 14 features, debugging, unit testing, and object-oriented programming.

.NET libraries, including number types, text, regular expressions, collections, file I/O, and data with EF Core and SQLite.

Modern websites and web services with ASP.NET Core, Blazor, and Minimal API web services.

Mature websites using ASP.NET Core MVC and Umbraco CMS, including defining routes, controllers, models, and views.

Mature web services using Web API controllers, OData, and FastEndpoints, including authentication, authorization, and integration testing.

Caching, web testing, configuration, and containerizing for deployment.

Modern apps: .NET MAUI mobile apps, Avalonia desktop apps, and Blazor WebAssembly web apps.

Modern services: Minimal API web services, caching, queuing, GraphQL, gRPC, and SignalR.

Libraries: Popular third-party packages, integrating LLMs and MCP, and internationalization.

Data: SQL Server, ADO.NET SqlClient, Dapper, and EF Core.

Tools: IDEs, debugging, memory analysis, and AI assistants.

Libraries: Cryptography, multi-tasking and concurrency.

Tests: Unit, integration, performance, security, and web.

Develop: Docker and .NET Aspire.

Design: Patterns, principles, software and solution architecture.

Career: Teamwork and interviews.

Figure 1.1: Companion books for learning .NET for beginner-to-intermediate readers

Now, let's review some of the history of web development using .NET, which means learning about one of its most important platforms, ASP.NET Core.

Understanding ASP.NET Core

To understand ASP.NET Core, it is useful to first see where it came from.

A brief history of ASP.NET Core

ASP.NET Core is part of a 30-year history of Microsoft technologies used to build websites and services that work with data that have evolved over the decades:

- **ActiveX Data Objects (ADO)** was released in 1996 and was Microsoft's attempt to provide a single set of **Component Object Model (COM)** components for working with data. With the release of .NET Framework in 2002, an equivalent was created named **ADO.NET**, which is still today the fastest method to work with data in .NET with its core classes, DbConnection, DbCommand, and DbDataReader. ORMs like EF Core use ADO.NET internally. For example, EF Core for SQL Server references the Microsoft.Data.SqlClient package that implements ADO.NET for SQL Server. Even if you don't use the rest of ADO.NET, its classes, like SqlConnectionBuilder, can be used to dynamically and safely construct connection strings to SQL Server databases.

- **Active Server Pages (ASP)** was released in 1996 and was Microsoft's first attempt at a platform for dynamic server-side execution of website code. The file extension for the page files is .asp. I include this bullet so that you understand where the ASP initialism comes from because it is still used today in modern ASP.NET Core.

- **ASP.NET Web Forms** was released in 2002 with .NET Framework and was designed to enable non-web developers, such as those familiar with Visual Basic, to quickly create websites by dragging and dropping visual components and writing event-driven code in Visual Basic or C#, as shown in *Figure 1.2*. Web Forms page files have the `.aspx` file extension. Web Forms is not available on modern .NET, and it should be avoided for new web projects, even with .NET Framework, due to limitations on cross-platform compatibility and modern development practices.

- **Windows Communication Foundation (WCF)** was released in 2006 and enables developers to build SOAP and REST services. SOAP is powerful but complex, so it should be avoided in new projects unless you need advanced features, such as distributed transactions and complex messaging topologies. SOAP is still widely used in existing enterprise solutions, so you may come across it. I would be interested in hearing from you about this, since I am considering adding a chapter in a future edition of this book if there is enough interest.

- **ASP.NET MVC** was released in 2009 to cleanly separate the concerns of web developers between the **models**, which temporarily store the data; the **views**, which present the data using various formats in the UI; and the **controllers**, which fetch the model and pass it to a view. This separation enables improved reuse and unit testing, and fits more naturally with web development without hiding the reality with an additional complex layer of event-driven user interface.

- **ASP.NET Web API** was released in 2012 and enables developers to create HTTP services (a.k.a. REST services) that are simpler and more scalable than SOAP services.

- **ASP.NET SignalR** was released in 2013 and enables real-time communication for websites by abstracting underlying technologies and techniques, such as WebSockets and long polling. This enables website features such as live chat or updates to time-sensitive data, such as stock prices, across a wide variety of web browsers, even when they do not support an underlying technology such as WebSockets, as described at the following link: `https://websockets.spec.whatwg.org/`.

- **ASP.NET Core** was released in 2016 and combines modern implementations of .NET Framework technologies such as MVC, Web API, and SignalR with alternative technologies such as Razor Pages, gRPC, and Blazor, all running on modern .NET. Therefore, ASP.NET Core can execute cross-platform. ASP.NET Core has many project templates to get you started with its supported technologies. Over the past decade, the ASP.NET Core team has greatly improved performance and reduced memory footprint to make it the best platform for cloud computing. In some ways, Blazor is a return to Web Forms-style user interface development, as shown in *Figure 1.2*:

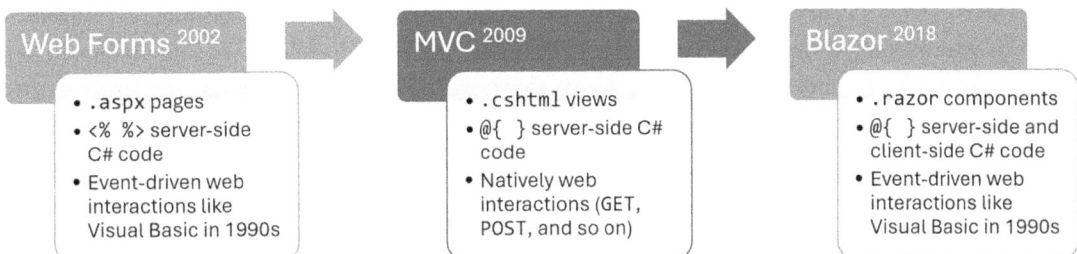

Web Forms 2002	MVC 2009	Blazor 2018
• `.aspx` pages • `<% %>` server-side C# code • Event-driven web interactions like Visual Basic in 1990s	• `.cshtml` views • `@{ }` server-side C# code • Natively web interactions (GET, POST, and so on)	• `.razor` components • `@{ }` server-side and client-side C# code • Event-driven web interactions like Visual Basic in 1990s

Figure 1.2: Evolution of web user interface technologies in .NET

> **Good practice:** Choose ASP.NET Core to develop websites and web services because it includes web-related technologies that are mature, proven, and cross-platform.

Classic ASP.NET versus modern ASP.NET Core

Until modern .NET, ASP.NET was built on top of a large assembly in .NET Framework named `System.Web.dll`, and it was tightly coupled to Microsoft's Windows-only web server named **Internet Information Services (IIS)**. Over the years, this assembly has accumulated a lot of features, many of which are not suitable for modern cross-platform development.

ASP.NET Core is a major redesign of ASP.NET. It removes the dependency on the `System.Web.dll` assembly and IIS and is composed of modular lightweight packages, just like the rest of modern .NET. You can develop and run ASP.NET Core applications cross-platform on Windows, macOS, and Linux. Microsoft has even created a cross-platform, super-performant web server named **Kestrel**. Using IIS as the web server on Windows is still supported by ASP.NET Core if preferred.

Kestrel is mostly open source. However, it depends on some underlying components and infrastructure that are not fully open source. Kestrel's open-source components include:

- The core Kestrel server is open source, and its source code is available on GitHub under the ASP.NET repository. You can explore, modify, and even contribute to it: `https://github.com/dotnet/aspnetcore/tree/main/src/Servers/Kestrel`.
- Kestrel is part of the ASP.NET Core ecosystem, which is entirely open source under the .NET Foundation: `https://github.com/dotnet/aspnetcore`.
- Kestrel uses the .NET Sockets API for its transport layer, whose implementation is open source.

Kestrel's non-open-source components include:

- Some lower-level networking optimizations and APIs in Windows, which Kestrel can take advantage of, are not open source. For example, some of the advanced socket APIs are part of Windows' closed-source infrastructure.
- While the .NET runtime is largely open source, there are some proprietary components or dependencies, especially when running on Windows, that are not open source. This would include some optimizations and integrations specific to Microsoft's cloud infrastructure or networking stack that are baked into Kestrel's performance characteristics when running on Windows.
- If you're using Kestrel hosted in Azure, some integration points, telemetry, and diagnostic services are proprietary. For example, Azure-specific logging, application insights, and security features (though not strictly part of Kestrel itself) are not fully open source.

Also, note that a non-open-source alternative to Kestrel is HTTP.sys. This is a Windows-specific HTTP server, and it is closed source. Applications can use HTTP.sys for edge cases requiring Windows authentication or other Windows-specific networking features, but this is outside of Kestrel itself.

Building websites using ASP.NET Core

Websites are made up of multiple web pages loaded statically from the filesystem or generated dynamically by a server-side technology such as ASP.NET Core. A web browser makes GET requests using **Uniform Resource Locators (URLs)** that identify each page and can manipulate data stored on the server using POST, PUT, and DELETE requests.

With many websites, the web browser is treated as a presentation layer, with almost all the processing performed on the server side. Some JavaScript might be used on the client side to implement form validation warnings and some presentation features, such as carousels.

ASP.NET Core provides multiple technologies for building the user interface for websites:

- **ASP.NET Core Razor Pages** is a simple way to dynamically generate HTML for small websites.
- **ASP.NET Core MVC** is an implementation of the **Model-View-Controller** (**MVC**) design pattern that is popular for developing complex websites. Microsoft's first implementation of MVC on .NET was in 2009, so it is more than 15 years old now. Its APIs are stable, it has plentiful documentation and support, and many third parties have built powerful products and platforms on top of it and controller-based Web APIs. MVC is designed to work with the HTTP request/response model instead of hiding it, so that you are encouraged to embrace the nature of web development rather than pretending it doesn't exist, which can store up worse problems in the future.
- **Blazor** lets you build user interface components using C# and .NET instead of a JavaScript-based UI framework like Angular, React, and Vue. Early versions of Blazor required a developer to choose a **hosting model**. The **Blazor WebAssembly** hosting model runs your code in the browser like a JavaScript-based framework would. The **Blazor Server** hosting model runs your code on the server and updates the web page dynamically using SignalR. Introduced with .NET 8 is a unified, full-stack hosting model that allows individual components to execute either on the server or client side, or even to adapt dynamically at runtime.

So which should you choose?

> *"Blazor is now our recommended approach for building web UI with ASP.NET Core, but neither MVC nor Razor Pages are now obsolete. Both MVC & Razor Pages are mature, fully supported, and widely used frameworks that we plan to support for the foreseeable future. There is also no requirement or guidance to migrate existing MVC or Razor Pages apps to Blazor. For existing, well-established MVC-based projects, continuing to develop with MVC is a perfectly valid and reasonable approach." – Dan Roth*

You can see Dan Roth's original comment post at the following link: https://github.com/dotnet/aspnetcore/issues/51834#issuecomment-1913282747. Dan Roth is the Principal Product Manager on the ASP.NET team, so he knows the future of ASP.NET Core better than anyone else: https://devblogs.microsoft.com/dotnet/author/danroth27/.

I agree with the quote by Dan Roth. For me, there are two main choices:

- For real-world websites and web services using mature and proven web development, choose controller-based ASP.NET Core MVC and Web API. For even more productivity, you can layer on top third-party platforms, for example, a .NET CMS like Umbraco. All these technologies are covered in this book.

- For websites and web services using modern web development, choose Blazor for the web user interface and Minimal APIs for the web service. Choosing these is more of a risk because their APIs are still changing, as they are relatively new. These technologies are covered in my other books, *C# 14 and .NET 10 – Modern Cross-Platform Development Fundamentals* and *Apps and Services with .NET 10.*

Much of ASP.NET Core is shared across these two choices anyway, so you will only need to learn about those shared components once, as shown in *Figure 1.3*:

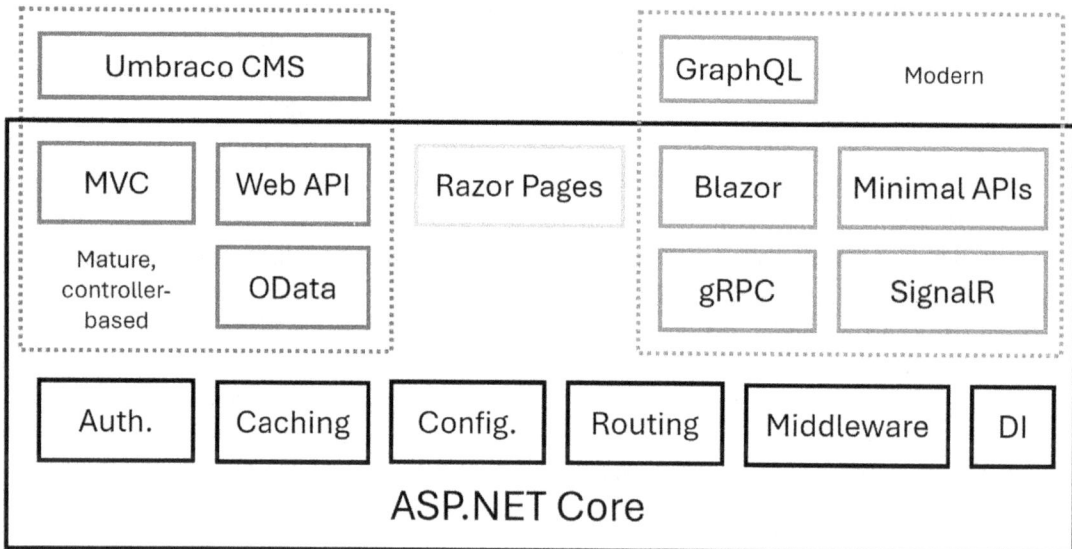

Figure 1.3: Modern or mature controller-based (and shared) ASP.NET Core components

JetBrains did a survey of 26,348 developers from all around the world and asked about web development technologies and ASP.NET Core usage by .NET developers. The results showed that most .NET developers still use mature and proven controller-based technologies like MVC and Web API. The newer technologies, like Blazor, were far behind. A chart from the report is shown in *Figure 1.4*:

Which ASP.NET Core technologies do you use?

This question was shown only to respondents who reported using ASP.NET Core.

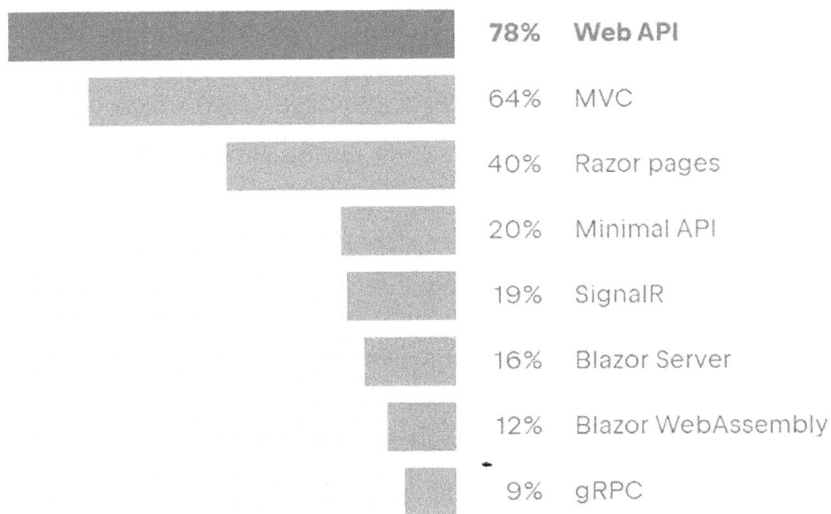

78%	**Web API**
64%	MVC
40%	Razor pages
20%	Minimal API
19%	SignalR
16%	Blazor Server
12%	Blazor WebAssembly
9%	gRPC

Figure 1.4: The State of Developer Ecosystem 2023 – ASP.NET Core

It is also interesting to see which JavaScript libraries and cloud host providers are used by .NET developers. For example, 18% use React, 15% use Angular, and 9% use Vue, and all have dropped by a few percent since the previous year. I speculate that this is due to a shift to Blazor instead. For cloud hosting, 24% use Azure, and 12% use AWS. This makes sense for .NET developers since Microsoft puts more effort into supporting .NET developers on its cloud platform.

> You can read more about the JetBrains report, *The State of Developer Ecosystem 2023*, and see the results of the ASP.NET Core question at `https://www.jetbrains.com/lp/devecosystem-2023/csharp/#csharp_asp_core`.

In summary, C# and .NET can be used on both the server side and the client side to build websites, as shown in *Figure 1.5*:

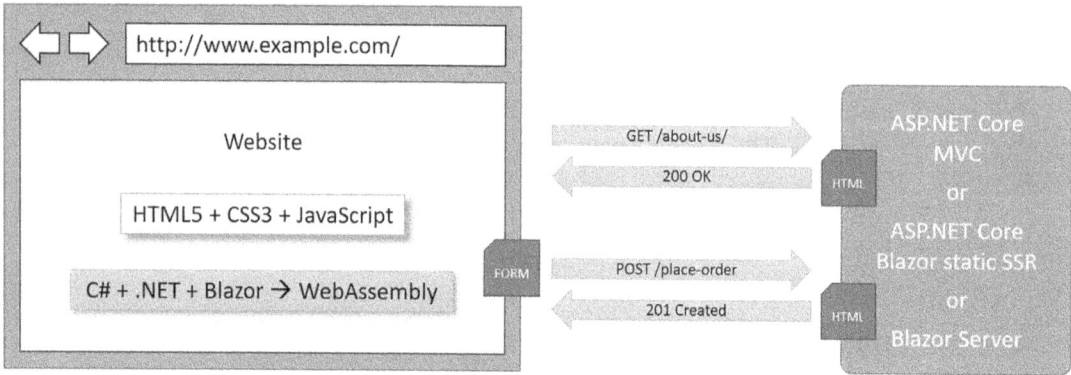

Figure 1.5: The use of C# and .NET to build websites on both the server and client side

To summarize what's new in ASP.NET Core for its mature and proven controller-based technologies, let's end this section with another quote from Dan Roth:

> *"We're optimizing how static web assets are handled for all ASP.NET Core apps so that your files are pre-compressed as part of publishing your app. For API developers we're providing built-in support for OpenAPI document generation." – Dan Roth*

Comparison of file types used in ASP.NET Core

It is useful to summarize the file types used by these technologies because they are similar but different. If you do not understand some subtle but important differences, it can cause much confusion when trying to implement your own projects. Please note the differences in *Table 1.1*:

Technology	Special filename	File extension	Directive
Razor View (MVC)		`.cshtml`	
Razor Layout		`.cshtml`	
Razor View Start	`_ViewStart`	`.cshtml`	
Razor View Imports	`_ViewImports`	`.cshtml`	
Razor Component (Blazor)		`.razor`	
Razor Component (Blazor with page routing)		`.razor`	`@page "<path>"`
Razor Component Imports (Blazor)	`_Imports`	`.razor`	
Razor Page		`.cshtml`	`@page`

Table 1.1: Comparison of file types used in ASP.NET Core

Directives like @page are added to the top of a file's contents.

If a file does not have a special filename, then it can be named anything. For example, you might create a Razor View named Customer.cshtml, or you might create a Razor Layout named _MobileLayout. cshtml.

> The naming convention for shared Razor files, like layouts and partial views, is to prefix with an underscore, _. For example, _ViewStart.cshtml, _Layout.cshtml, or _Product. cshtml (this might be a partial view for rendering a product).

A Razor Layout file like _MyCustomLayout.cshtml is identical to a Razor View. What makes the file a layout is being set as the Layout property of another Razor file, as shown in the following code:

```
@{
    Layout = "_MyCustomLayout"; // File extension is not needed.
}
```

> **Warning!** Be careful to use the correct file extension and directive at the top of the file, or you will get unexpected behavior.

Building websites using a content management system

Most websites have a lot of content, and if developers had to be involved every time some content needed to be changed, that would not scale well. Almost no real-world website built with .NET only uses ASP.NET Core. A professional .NET web developer, therefore, needs to learn about other platforms built on top of ASP.NET Core.

A CMS enables CMS administrators to define content structure and templates to provide consistency and good design while making it easy for a non-technical content owner to manage the actual content. They can create new pages or blocks of content, and update existing content, knowing it will look great for visitors with minimal effort.

There are a multitude of CMSs available for all web platforms, like WordPress for PHP or Django for Python. CMSs that support modern .NET include Optimizely Content Cloud, Umbraco, Piranha, and Orchard Core.

The key benefit of using a CMS is that it provides a friendly content management user interface. Content owners log in to the website and manage the content themselves. The content is then rendered and returned to visitors using ASP.NET Core MVC controllers and views, or via web service endpoints, known as a **headless CMS**, to provide that content to "heads" implemented as mobile or desktop apps, in-store touchpoints, or clients built with JavaScript frameworks or Blazor.

This book covers the world's most popular .NET CMS, Umbraco, in *Chapter 14, Web Content Management Using Umbraco CMS*, and *Chapter 15, Customizing and Extending Umbraco CMS*. The quantifiable evidence – usage statistics from BuiltWith, GitHub activity, download numbers, community engagement, and search trends – all point to Umbraco as the most popular .NET-based CMS worldwide. You can see a list of almost 100,000 websites built using Umbraco at the following link: `https://trends.builtwith.com/websitelist/Umbraco/Historical`.

Umbraco is open source and hosted on GitHub. It has over 2.7k forks and 4.4k stars on its main repository, found at the following link: `https://github.com/umbraco/Umbraco-CMS`.

The active developer community and constant updates indicate its popularity among developers. Umbraco has reported more than six million downloads of its CMS, which is a significant metric compared to competitors in the .NET CMS space.

> You can learn more about alternative .NET CMSs in the GitHub repository at `https://github.com/markjprice/web-dev-net10/blob/main/docs/book-links.md#other-net-content-management-systems`.

Building web applications using SPA frameworks

Web applications are often built using technologies known as **Single-Page Application** (SPA) frameworks, such as Blazor, Angular, React, Vue, or a proprietary JavaScript library. They can make requests to a backend web service to get more data when needed and post updated data using common serialization formats such as XML and JSON. The canonical examples are Google web apps like Gmail, Maps, and Docs.

With a web application, the client side uses JavaScript frameworks or Blazor to implement sophisticated user interactions, but most of the important processing and data access still happens on the server side because the web browser has limited access to local system resources.

JavaScript is loosely typed and is not designed for complex projects, so most JavaScript libraries these days use TypeScript, which adds strong typing to JavaScript and is designed with many modern language features for handling complex implementations.

The .NET SDK has project templates for JavaScript and TypeScript-based SPAs, but we will not spend any time learning how to build JavaScript and TypeScript-based SPAs in this book.

If you are interested in building SPAs with an ASP.NET Core backend, Packt has other books that you might be interested in, as shown in the following list:

- *ASP.NET Core 8 and Angular – Sixth Edition*: Full-stack web development with ASP.NET Core 8 and Angular: `https://www.amazon.com/ASP-NET-Core-Angular-Full-stack-development/dp/1805129937/`
- *ASP.NET Core 5 and React*: Full-stack web development using .NET 5, React 17, and TypeScript 4, 2nd Edition: `https://www.amazon.com/ASP-NET-Core-React-Full-stack-development-ebook/dp/B08KYKNGCC/`

- *ASP.NET Core and Vue.js*: Build real-world, scalable, full-stack applications using Vue.js 3, Type-Script, .NET 5, and Azure: `https://www.amazon.com/ASP-NET-Core-Vue-js-real-world-applications-ebook/dp/B08QTVV8RK/`

Building web and other services

In this book, you will learn how to build a controller-based web service using **ASP.NET Core Web API**, and then how to call that web service from an ASP.NET Core MVC website.

There are no formal definitions, but services are sometimes described based on their complexity:

- **Service**: All functionality needed by a client app in one monolithic service.
- **Microservice**: Multiple services that each focus on a smaller set of functionalities. They are often deployed using **containerization**, which we will cover in *Chapter 8, Configuring and Containerizing ASP.NET Core Projects*.
- **Nanoservice**: A single function provided as a service. Unlike services and microservices that are hosted 24/7/365, nanoservices are often inactive until called upon to reduce resources and costs.

Cloud providers and deployment tools

These days, websites and web services are often deployed to cloud providers like Microsoft Azure or Amazon Web Services. Hundreds of different tools are used to perform the deployments, like Azure Pipelines or Octopus Deploy.

Cloud providers and deployment tools are out of the scope for this book because there are too many choices, and I don't want to force anyone to learn about or pay for cloud hosting that they will never use for their own projects. Instead, this book covers containerization using Docker in *Chapter 8, Configuring and Containerizing ASP.NET Core Projects*. Once you have containerized an ASP.NET Core project, it is easy to deploy it to any cloud provider using any deployment or production management tool.

We have now reviewed the important technologies used for web development with .NET. Now, let's make sure that you know how to get the solutions for all the coding tasks in this book if you get stuck.

Making good use of the GitHub repository for this book

Git is a commonly used source code management system. **GitHub** is a company, website, and desktop application that makes it easier to manage Git. Microsoft purchased GitHub in 2018, so it will continue to get closer integration with Microsoft tools.

I created a GitHub repository for this book, and I use it for the following:

- To store the solution code for the book that can be maintained after the print publication date
- To provide extra materials that extend the book, like errata fixes, small improvements, lists of useful links, and optional sections about topics that cannot fit in the printed book
- To provide a place for readers to get in touch with me if they have issues with the book

> **Good practice:** I strongly recommend that all readers review the errata, improvements, post-publication changes, and common errors pages before attempting any coding task in this book. You can find them at the following link: `https://github.com/markjprice/web-dev-net10/blob/main/docs/errata/README.md`.

Understanding the solution code on GitHub

You can complete all the coding tasks just from reading this book because all the code is shown in the pages. You do not need to download or clone the solution code to complete this book. The solution code is provided in the GitHub repository only so that you can view it if you get stuck working from the book, and to save you time from entering long files yourself. It is also more reliable to copy from an actual code file than from a PDF or other e-book format.

> This book uses the new `.slnx` format solution files. You can learn about them at the following link: `https://github.com/markjprice/cs14net10/blob/main/docs/ch01-solution-evolution.md`.

The solution code in the GitHub repository for this book can be opened with any of the following code editors:

- **Visual Studio or Rider:** Open the `MatureWeb.slnx` solution file.
- **VS Code:** Open the `MatureWeb` folder.

All the chapters in this book share a single solution file named `MatureWeb.slnx`.

All the code solutions can be found at the following link:

`https://github.com/markjprice/web-dev-net10/tree/main/code`.

> If you are new to .NET development, then the GitHub repository has step-by-step instructions for three code editors (Visual Studio, VS Code, and Rider), along with additional screenshots: `https://github.com/markjprice/web-dev-net10/tree/main/docs/code-editors/`.

Downloading the solution code from the GitHub repository

If you just want to download all the solution files without using Git, click the green **Code** button and then select **Download ZIP**, as shown in *Figure 1.6*:

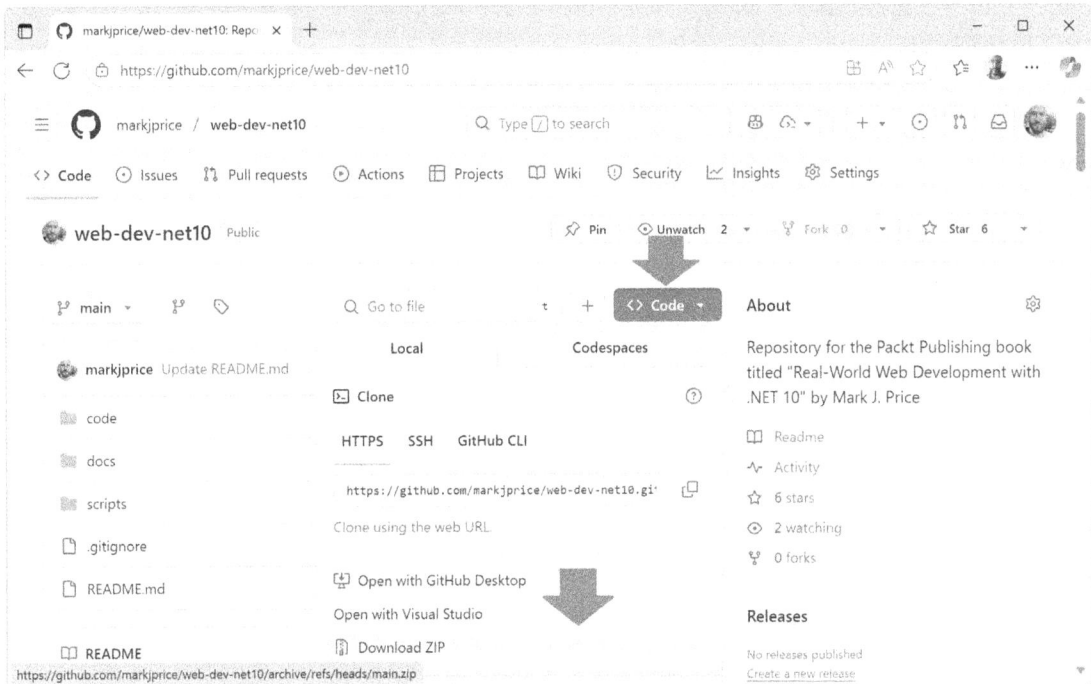

Figure 1.6: Downloading the repository as a ZIP file

Good practice: It is best to clone or download the code solutions to a short folder path, like `C:\web-dev-net10\` or `C:\book\`, to avoid build-generated files exceeding the maximum path length. You should also avoid special characters like #. For example, do not use a folder name like `C:\C# projects\`. That folder name might work for a simple console app project, but once you start adding features that automatically generate code, you are likely to have strange issues. Keep your folder names short and simple.

Cloning the book solution code repository

You do not need to clone the book solution code repository because all the code you need is in the book, and you can enter it all yourself, which is the best way to learn. But I also recommend cloning the solution so that you can refer to it while you create your own projects as you follow the instructions in this book.

If you want to clone the book solution code repository, then you can create an empty folder and in that folder, enter the appropriate Git command at any command prompt or terminal window:

```
git clone https://github.com/markjprice/web-dev-net10.git
```

> Note that cloning all the solutions for all the chapters will take a minute or so, so please be patient.

Now that you have downloaded or cloned the code solutions for all the tasks in this book, let's review how to structure the projects that you create yourself and how to manage the packages that add common functionality to your projects.

Structuring projects and managing packages

How should you structure your projects? In this book, we will build multiple projects using different technologies that work together to provide a single solution.

With large, complex solutions, it can be difficult to navigate through all the code. So, the primary reason to structure your projects is to make it easier to find components. It is good to have an overall name for your solution that reflects the application or solution.

We will build multiple projects for a fictional company named **Northwind**. We will name the solution MatureWeb and use the name Northwind as a prefix for all the project names.

There are many ways to structure and name projects and solutions, for example, using a folder hierarchy as well as a naming convention. If you work in a team, make sure you know how your team does it.

Structuring projects in a solution

It is good to have a naming convention for your projects in a solution so that any developer can tell what each one does instantly. A common choice is to use the type of project, for example, a class library, console app, website, and so on.

Since you might want to run multiple web projects at the same time, and they will be hosted on a local web server, we need to differentiate each project by assigning different port numbers for its endpoints for both HTTP and HTTPS.

Commonly assigned local port numbers are 5000 for HTTP and 5001 for HTTPS. We will use a numbering convention of 5<chapter>0 for HTTP and 5<chapter>1 for HTTPS. For example, for an ASP.NET Core MVC website project that we will create in *Chapter 2*, we will assign 5020 for HTTP and 5021 for HTTPS.

We will therefore use the following project names and port numbers, as shown in *Table 1.2*:

Name	Ports	Description
Northwind.Common	N/A	A class library project for common types, like interfaces, enums, classes, records, and structs, is used across multiple projects.
Northwind.EntityModels	N/A	A class library project for common EF Core entity models. Entity models are often used on both the server and client side, so it is best to separate dependencies on specific database providers.
Northwind.DataContext	N/A	A class library project for the EF Core database context with dependencies on specific database providers.
Northwind.UnitTests	N/A	An xUnit test project for the solution.
Northwind.Mvc	HTTP 5020, HTTPS 5021	An ASP.NET Core project for complex websites that uses a mixture of static HTML files and MVC Razor Views.
Northwind.WebApi	HTTP 5090, HTTPS 5091	An ASP.NET Core project for a Web API, a.k.a. HTTP service. A good choice for integrating with websites because it can use any .NET app, JavaScript library, or Blazor to interact with the service.

Table 1.2: Example project names for various project types

Structuring folders in a project

In ASP.NET Core projects, organizing the project structure is vital for maintainability and scalability. Two popular approaches are organizing by technological concerns and using feature folders.

Folder structure based on technological concerns

In this approach, folders are structured based on the type of components, such as Controllers, Models, Views, Services, and so on, as shown in the following output:

```
/Controllers
  ShoppingCartController.cs
  CatalogController.cs
/Models
  Product.cs
  ShoppingCart.cs
/Views
  /ShoppingCart
    Index.cshtml
    Summary.cshtml
  /Catalog
    Index.cshtml
```

```
      Details.cshtml
/Services
  ProductService.cs
  ShoppingCartService.cs
```

There are pros and cons to the technical concerns approach, as shown in the following list:

- **Pro – Familiarity:** This structure is common and well-documented, and many sample projects use it, making it easier for developers to understand.

- **Pro – IDE support:** SDKs and IDEs assume this structure and may provide better support and navigation for it.

- **Con – Scalability:** As the project grows, finding related files can become difficult since they are spread across multiple folders.

- **Con – Cross-cutting concerns:** Managing cross-cutting concerns like logging and validation can become cumbersome.

The .NET SDK project templates use this technological concerns approach to folder structure. This means that many organizations use it by default despite it not being the best approach for their needs.

Folder structure based on features

In this approach, folders are organized by features or vertical slices, grouping all related files for a specific feature together, as shown in the following output:

```
/Features
  /ShoppingCart
    ShoppingCartController.cs
    ShoppingCartService.cs
    ShoppingCart.cs
    Index.cshtml
    Summary.cshtml
  /Catalog
    CatalogController.cs
    ProductService.cs
    Product.cs
    Index.cshtml
    Details.cshtml
```

There are pros and cons to the feature folders approach, as shown in the following list:

- **Pro – Modularity:** Each feature is self-contained, making it easier to manage and understand. Adding new features is straightforward and doesn't affect the existing structure. Easier to maintain since related files are located together.

- **Pro – Isolation:** It helps in isolating different parts of the application, promoting better test-ability and refactoring.

- • **Con – Learning curve:** It is less familiar to some developers, requiring a learning curve.
- • **Con – Code duplication:** There is a potential for code duplication if not managed properly.

Feature folders are a common choice for modular monolith architecture. It makes it easier to later split the feature out into a separate project for deployment.

Feature folders align well with the principles of **Vertical Slice Architecture (VSA)**. VSA focuses on organizing code by features or vertical slices, each slice handling a specific business capability end-to-end. This approach often includes everything from the UI layer down to the data access layer for a given feature in one place, as described in the following key points:

- • Each slice represents an end-to-end implementation of a feature.
- • VSA promotes loose coupling between features, making the application more modular and easier to maintain.
- • Each slice is responsible for a single feature or use case, which fits well with SOLID's **Single Responsibility Principle (SRP)**.
- • VSA allows for features to be developed, tested, and deployed independently, which is beneficial for microservices or distributed systems.

Folder structure summary

Both organizational techniques have their merits, and the choice depends on the specific needs of your project. Technological concerns organization is straightforward and familiar, but can become unwieldy as the project grows. Feature folders, while potentially introducing a learning curve, offer better modularity and scalability, aligning well with the principles of VSA.

Feature folders are particularly advantageous in larger projects or those with distributed teams, as they promote better organization and isolation of features, leading to improved maintainability and flexibility in the long run.

Central package management

By default, with the .NET SDK CLI and most code editor-created projects, if you need to reference a NuGet package, you add the reference to the package name and version directly in the project file, as shown in the following markup:

```
<ItemGroup>
  <PackageReference Include="Microsoft.EntityFrameworkCore.SqlServer"
                    Version="10.0.0" />
  ...
</ItemGroup>
```

Central Package Management (CPM) is a feature that simplifies the management of NuGet package versions across multiple projects and solutions within a directory hierarchy. This is particularly useful for large solutions with many projects, where managing package versions individually can become cumbersome and error-prone.

Features and benefits of CPM

The key features and benefits of CPM include:

- **Centralized control:** CPM allows you to define package versions in a single file, typically `Directory.Packages.props`, which is placed in the root directory of a directory hierarchy that contains all your solutions and projects. This file centralizes the version information for all NuGet packages used across the projects in your solutions.

- **Consistency:** It ensures consistent package versions across multiple projects. By having a single source of truth for package versions, it eliminates discrepancies that can occur when different projects specify different versions of the same package.

- **Simplified updates:** Updating a package version in a large solution becomes straightforward. You update the version in the central file, and all projects referencing that package automatically use the updated version. This significantly reduces the maintenance overhead.

- **Reduced redundancy:** It removes the need to specify package versions in individual project files (`.csproj`). This makes project files cleaner and easier to manage, as they no longer contain repetitive version information.

> **Good practice:** It is important to regularly update NuGet packages and their dependencies to address security vulnerabilities.

Defining project properties to reuse version numbers

Microsoft packages usually have the same number each month, like 10.0.2 in February, 10.0.3 in March, and so on. You can define properties at the top of your `Directory.Packages.props` file, and then reference these properties throughout the file. This approach keeps package versions consistent and makes updates easy.

For example, in your `Directory.Packages.props` file, at the top of the file, within a `<ProjectGroup>` tag, define your custom property and then reference it for the package version, as shown in the following markup:

```
<Project>
  <PropertyGroup>
    <MicrosoftPackageVersion>10.0.2</MicrosoftPackageVersion>
  </PropertyGroup>

  <ItemGroup>
    <PackageVersion Include="Microsoft.EntityFrameworkCore"
                Version="$(MicrosoftPackageVersion)" />
    <PackageVersion Include="Microsoft.Extensions.Logging"
                Version="$(MicrosoftPackageVersion)" />
    <!-- Add more Microsoft packages as needed. -->
```

```
    </ItemGroup>

    <!-- Other packages with specific versions. -->
    <ItemGroup>
      <PackageVersion Include="Newtonsoft.Json" Version="13.0.4" />
    </ItemGroup>
  </Project>
```

Note the following about the preceding configuration:

- **Define a property**: In the `<PropertyGroup>` element, the line `<MicrosoftPackageVersi on>10.0.2</MicrosoftPackageVersion>` defines the property. This value can be changed once at the top of the file, and all references will update automatically.
- **Reference the property**: Use the syntax `$(PropertyName)` to reference the defined property. All occurrences of `$(MicrosoftPackageVersion)` will resolve to the version number that you set.

When the monthly update rolls around, for example, from 10.0.2 to 10.0.3, you only have to update this number once.

You might want separate properties for related packages if they differ in version number, such as:

```
<AspNetCorePackageVersion>10.0.3</AspNetCorePackageVersion>
<EFCorePackageVersion>10.1.2</EFCorePackageVersion>
```

This allows independent updates if packages diverge in their release cycles or versions later.

After making changes, at the terminal or command prompt, run the following command:

```
dotnet restore
```

This will verify the correctness of your references and quickly alert you if you've introduced errors. By adopting this pattern combined with CPM, you simplify version management, reduce redundancy, and make your projects easier to maintain over time.

> **Good practice:** Choose clear and consistent property names, like `MicrosoftPackageVersion` or `AspNetCorePackageVersion`, to easily distinguish between different package ecosystems. Check your `Directory.Packages.props` file into source control. Regularly update and test after changing versions to ensure compatibility.

Configuring CPM for this book's projects

Let's set up CPM for a solution that we will use throughout the rest of the chapters in this book. We will define item groups for the following packages:

- **EF Core**: SQLite for authentication and SQL Server for a fictional company database
- **Testing**: .NET test SDK, xUnit, and Playwright for web UI testing
- **ASP.NET Core**: EF Core, Identity, and testing integration

- **Caching:** Hybrid cache
- **Web Services:** OpenAPI, JWT bearer authentication
- **OData:** For OData web services
- **FastEndpoints:** For FastEndpoints web services
- **Umbraco:** CMS

Let's go:

1. Create a new folder named `web-dev-net10` that we will use for all the code in this book. For example, on Windows, create a folder: `C:\web-dev-net10`.
2. In the `web-dev-net10` folder, create a new folder named `MatureWeb`.
3. In the `MatureWeb` folder, create a new file named `Directory.Packages.props`. At the command prompt or terminal, you can optionally use the following command: `dotnet new packagesprops`

> To save you time manually typing this large file, you can download it at the following link: `https://github.com/markjprice/web-dev-net10/blob/main/code/MatureWeb/Directory.Packages.props`.

4. In `Directory.Packages.props`, modify its contents, as shown in the following markup:

```
<Project>

  <PropertyGroup>

<ManagePackageVersionsCentrally>true</ManagePackageVersionsCentrally>
    <Net10>10.0.0</Net10>
  </PropertyGroup>

  <ItemGroup Label="For EF Core.">
    <PackageVersion Include="Microsoft.EntityFrameworkCore.SqlServer"
                Version="$(Net10)" />
    <PackageVersion Include="Microsoft.EntityFrameworkCore.Sqlite"
                Version="$(Net10)" />
    <PackageVersion Include="Microsoft.EntityFrameworkCore.Design"
                Version="$(Net10)" />
    <PackageVersion Include="Microsoft.EntityFrameworkCore.Tools"
                Version="$(Net10)" />
  </ItemGroup>

  <ItemGroup Label="For testing.">
    <PackageVersion Include="coverlet.collector"
                Version="6.0.4" />
```

```
        <PackageVersion Include="Microsoft.NET.Test.Sdk"
                    Version="18.0.1" />
    <PackageVersion Include="xunit" Version="2.9.3" />
    <PackageVersion Include="xunit.runner.visualstudio"
                    Version="3.1.6" />
    <PackageVersion Include="Microsoft.Playwright"
                    Version="1.56.0" />
    <PackageVersion Include="NSubstitute" Version="5.3.0" />
  </ItemGroup>

  <ItemGroup Label="For ASP.NET Core websites.">
    <PackageVersion Include=
      "Microsoft.AspNetCore.Diagnostics.EntityFrameworkCore"
      Version="$(Net10)" />
    <PackageVersion Include=
      "Microsoft.AspNetCore.Identity.EntityFrameworkCore"
      Version="$(Net10)" />
    <PackageVersion Include="Microsoft.AspNetCore.Identity.UI"
                    Version="$(Net10)" />
    <PackageVersion Include="Microsoft.AspNetCore.Mvc.Testing"
                    Version="$(Net10)" />
  </ItemGroup>

  <ItemGroup Label="For caching.">
    <PackageVersion Include="Microsoft.Extensions.Caching.Hybrid"
                    Version="$(Net10)" />
  </ItemGroup>

  <ItemGroup Label="For ASP.NET Core web services.">
    <PackageVersion Include="Microsoft.AspNetCore.OpenApi"
                    Version="$(Net10)" />
    <PackageVersion Include="Scalar.AspNetCore"
                    Version="2.10.3" />
    <PackageVersion Include="Refit" Version="8.0.0" />
    <PackageVersion Include="Refit.HttpClientFactory"
                    Version="8.0.0/>
    <PackageVersion Include=
      "Microsoft.AspNetCore.Authentication.JwtBearer"
      Version="$(Net10)" />
    <PackageVersion Include="Asp.Versioning.Mvc"
                    Version="8.1.0" />
```

```xml
        <PackageVersion Include="Asp.Versioning.Mvc.ApiExplorer"
                        Version="8.1.0" />
    </ItemGroup>

    <ItemGroup Label="For OData web services.">
        <PackageVersion Include="Microsoft.AspNetCore.OData"
                        Version="9.4.1" />
    </ItemGroup>

    <ItemGroup Label="For FastEndpoints web services.">
        <PackageVersion Include="FastEndpoints" Version="7.1.0" />
        <PackageVersion Include="FluentValidation" Version="12.1.0" />
        <PackageVersion Include="Microsoft.AspNetCore.JsonPatch"
                        Version="$(Net10)" />
        <PackageVersion Include=
            "Microsoft.AspNetCore.JsonPatch.SystemTextJson"
            Version="$(Net10)" />
    </ItemGroup>

    <ItemGroup Label="For Umbraco CMS.">
        <PackageVersion Include="Umbraco.Cms" Version="17.0.0" />
        <PackageVersion Include="Microsoft.ICU.ICU4C.Runtime"
                        Version="72.1.0.3" />
    </ItemGroup>

</Project>
```

Warning! The `<ManagePackageVersionsCentrally>` element and its true value must all go on one line. Also, you cannot use floating wildcard version numbers like `10.0-*` as you can in an individual project. Wildcards are useful to automatically get the latest patch version, for example, monthly package updates on Patch Tuesday. But with CPM, you must manually update the versions.

For any projects that we add underneath the folder containing this file, we can reference the packages without explicitly specifying the version, as shown in the following markup:

```xml
<ItemGroup>
  <PackageReference Include="Microsoft.EntityFrameworkCore.SqlServer" />
  <PackageReference Include="Microsoft.EntityFrameworkCore.Design" />
</ItemGroup>
```

CPM good practice

You should regularly review and update the package versions in the `Directory.Packages.props` file to ensure that you are using the latest stable releases with important bug fixes and performance improvements.

> **Good practice:** I recommend that you set a monthly event in your calendar for the second Wednesday of each month. This will occur after the second Tuesday of each month, which is Patch Tuesday, when Microsoft releases bug fixes and patches for .NET and related packages.

For example, in December 2025, there are likely to be patch versions, so you can go to the NuGet page for each of your packages. You can then update individual package versions if necessary, for example, as shown in the following markup:

```
<ItemGroup Label="For EF Core.">
  <PackageVersion Include="Microsoft.EntityFrameworkCore.SqlServer"
                  Version="10.0.1" />
```

Or, if you have defined custom properties referenced by multiple packages, update those version numbers, as shown in the following markup:

```
<PropertyGroup>
  <ManagePackageVersionsCentrally>true</ManagePackageVersionsCentrally>
  <Net10>10.0.1</Net10>
```

Before updating package versions, check for any breaking changes in the release notes of the packages. Test your solution thoroughly after updating to ensure compatibility.

Educate your team and document the purpose and usage of the `Directory.Packages.props` file to ensure everyone understands how to manage package versions centrally.

In each individual project file, you can override an individual package version by using the `VersionOverride` attribute on a `<PackageReference />` element, as shown in the following markup:

```
<PackageReference Include="Microsoft.EntityFrameworkCore.SqlServer"
                  VersionOverride="10.0.0" />
```

This can be useful if a newer version introduces a regression bug, so you can force the use of an older version without the bug until the bug is fixed in a later patch version.

> You can learn more about CPM at the following link: https://learn.microsoft.com/en-us/nuget/consume-packages/central-package-management.

Package source mapping

If you use CPM and you have more than one package source configured for your code editor, as shown in *Figure 1.7*, then you will see NuGet warning NU1507. For example, if you have both the default package source (`https://api.nuget.org/v3/index.json`) and a custom package source configured:

```
There are 2 package sources defined in your configuration. When using central
package management, please map your package sources with package source mapping
(https://aka.ms/nuget-package-source-mapping) or specify a single package
source. The following sources are defined: https://api.nuget.org/v3/index.json,
https://northwind.com/packages/.
```

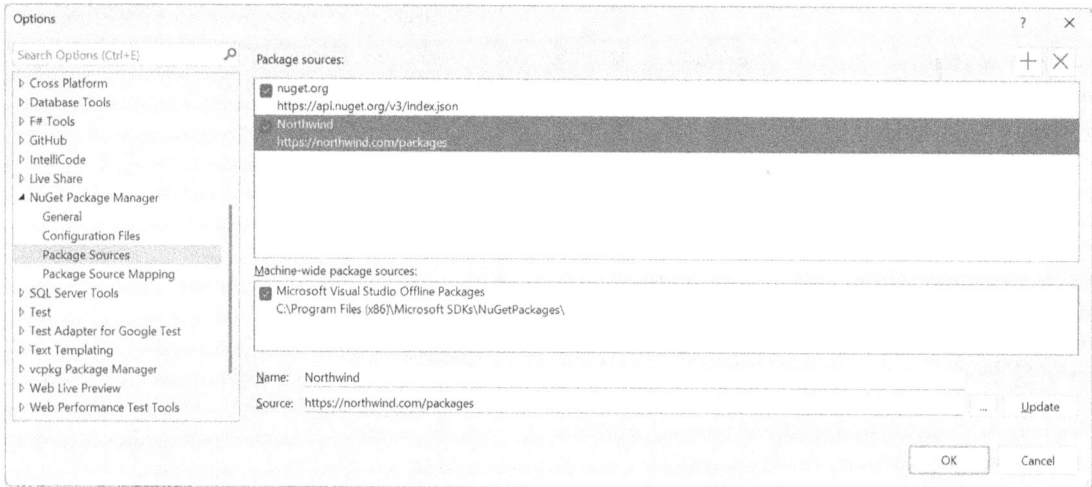

Figure 1.7: Visual Studio with two NuGet package sources configured

> The NU1507 warning reference page can be found at the following link: `https://learn.microsoft.com/en-us/nuget/reference/errors-and-warnings/nu1507`.

Package Source Mapping (PSM) can help safeguard your software supply chain if you use a mix of public and private package sources, as in the preceding example.

By default, NuGet will search all configured package sources when it needs to download a package. When a package exists on multiple sources, it may not be deterministic which source the package will be downloaded from. With PSM, you can filter, per package, which source(s) NuGet will search.

PSM is supported by Visual Studio 2022, .NET 6 and later, and NuGet 6 and later. Older tooling will ignore the PSM configuration.

To enable PSM, you must have a `nuget.config` file.

> **Good practice:** Create a `nuget.config` file at the root of your source code directory hierarchy.

In a PSM file, there are two parts: defining package sources and mapping package sources to packages. All requested packages must map to one or more sources by matching a defined package pattern. In other words, once you have defined a `packageSourceMapping` element, you must explicitly define which sources every package (including transitive packages) will be restored from.

For example, if you want most packages to be sourced from the default `nuget.org` site, but there are some private packages that must be sourced from your organization's website, you would define the two package sources and set the mapping (assuming all your private packages are named `Northwind.Something`), as shown in the following markup:

```xml
<?xml version="1.0" encoding="utf-8"?>
<configuration>
  <!-- <clear /> ensures no additional sources are inherited from another
config file. -->
  <packageSources>
    <clear />
    <!-- key can be any identifier for your source. -->
    <add key="nuget.org" value="https://api.nuget.org/v3/index.json" />
    <add key="Northwind" value="https://northwind.com/packages" />
  </packageSources>

  <!-- All packages sourced from nuget.org except Northwind packages. -->
  <packageSourceMapping>
    <!-- key value for <packageSource> should match key values from
<packageSources> element -->
    <packageSource key="nuget.org">
      <package pattern="*" />
    </packageSource>
    <packageSource key="Northwind">
      <package pattern="Northwind.*" />
    </packageSource>
  </packageSourceMapping>
</configuration>
```

Let's create a nuget.config file for all the solutions and projects in this book that will use nuget.org as the source for all packages:

1. In the MatureWeb folder, create a new file named nuget.config. At the command prompt or terminal, you can use the following command: dotnet new nugetconfig

2. In nuget.config, modify its contents, as shown in the following markup:

```xml
<?xml version="1.0" encoding="utf-8"?>
<configuration>
  <!-- <clear /> ensures no additional sources are inherited from another
config file. -->
  <packageSources>
    <clear />
    <!-- key can be any identifier for your source. -->
    <add key="nuget.org" value="https://api.nuget.org/v3/index.json" />
  </packageSources>

  <!-- All packages sourced from nuget.org. -->
  <packageSourceMapping>
    <!-- key value for <packageSource> should match key values from
<packageSources> element -->
    <packageSource key="nuget.org">
      <package pattern="*" />
    </packageSource>
  </packageSourceMapping>
</configuration>
```

3. Save changes.

> You can learn more about nuget.config at the following link: https://learn.microsoft.com/en-us/nuget/reference/nuget-config-file.
>
> You can learn more about PSM at the following link: https://learn.microsoft.com/en-us/nuget/consume-packages/package-source-mapping.

Treating warnings as errors

By default, compiler warnings may appear if there are potential problems with your code when you first build a project, but they do not prevent compilation, and they are hidden if you rebuild. Warnings are given for a reason, so ignoring warnings encourages poor development practices.

Some developers would prefer to be forced to fix warnings, so .NET provides a project setting to do this, as shown highlighted in the following markup:

```
<PropertyGroup>
  <OutputType>Exe</OutputType>
  <TargetFramework>net10.0</TargetFramework>
  <ImplicitUsings>enable</ImplicitUsings>
  <Nullable>enable</Nullable>
  <TreatWarningsAsErrors>true</TreatWarningsAsErrors>
</PropertyGroup>
```

I have enabled the option to treat warnings as errors in (almost) all the solutions in the GitHub repository.

If you find that you get too many errors after enabling this, you can disable specific warnings by using the <WarningsNotAsErrors> element with a comma-separated list of warning codes, as shown highlighted in the following markup:

```
<TreatWarningsAsErrors>true</TreatWarningsAsErrors>
<WarningsNotAsErrors>0219,CS8981</WarningsNotAsErrors>
```

> You can learn more about controlling warnings as errors at the following link: https://learn.microsoft.com/en-us/dotnet/csharp/language-reference/compiler-options/errors-warnings#warningsaserrors-and-warningsnotaserrors.

Now that we have reviewed how to structure projects and manage packages in your projects, we will create some projects to define some sample data that we will then use throughout the rest of the book.

Building an entity model for use in the rest of the book

Websites and web services usually need to work with data in a relational database or another data store. There are several technologies that could be used, from lower-level ADO.NET to higher-level EF Core, but we will use EF Core since it is flexible and more familiar to .NET developers.

In this section, we will define an EF Core entity data model for a database named Northwind stored in SQL Server. It will be used in most of the projects that we create in subsequent chapters.

Northwind database SQL scripts

The script for SQL Server creates 13 tables as well as related views and stored procedures. The SQL scripts are found at the following link:

https://github.com/markjprice/web-dev-net10/tree/main/scripts/sql-scripts.

I recommend that in your web-dev-net10 folder, you create a sql-scripts folder and copy all the SQL scripts to that local folder.

There are multiple SQL scripts to choose from, as described in the following list:

- `Northwind4SqlServerContainer.sql` script: To use SQL Server on a local computer in a container system like Docker. The script creates the Northwind database. It does not drop the database if it already exists because the Docker container should be empty anyway, as a fresh one can be spun up each time. Instructions to install Docker and set up a SQL Server image and container are in the next section of this book. This is my recommendation for using SQL Server in this book.

- `Northwind4SqlServerLocal.sql` script: To use SQL Server on a local Windows or Linux computer. The script checks if the Northwind database already exists and, if necessary, drops (deletes) it before creating it. Instructions to install SQL Server Developer Edition (free) on your local Windows computer can be found in the GitHub repository for this book at the following link: `https://github.com/markjprice/web-dev-net10/blob/main/docs/sql-server/README.md`.

- `Northwind4SqlServerCloud.sql` script: To use SQL Server with an Azure SQL Database resource created in the Azure cloud. You will need an Azure account; these resources cost money as long as they exist! The script does not drop or create the Northwind database because you should manually create the Northwind database using the Azure portal user interface. The script only creates the database objects, including the table structure and data.

Before you can execute any of these SQL scripts, you need a SQL Server instance. My recommendation is to use Docker and a container, so that's what we will cover in the next section. If you prefer a local or cloud SQL Server, then you can skip this next section.

Installing Docker and an SQL Server container image

Docker provides a consistent environment across development, testing, and production, minimizing the "it works on my machine" issue. Docker containers are more lightweight than traditional virtual machines, making them faster to start up and less resource-intensive.

Docker containers can run on any system with Docker installed, making it easy to move databases between environments or across different machines. You can quickly spin up a SQL database container with a single command, making setup faster and more reproducible. Each database instance runs in its own container, ensuring that it is isolated from other applications and databases on the same machine.

You can install Docker on any operating system and use a container that has SQL Server installed. For personal, educational, and small business use, Docker Desktop is free to use. It includes the full set of Docker features, including container management and orchestration. The Docker CLI and Docker Engine are open source and free to use, allowing developers to build, run, and manage containers.

Docker also has paid tiers that offer additional features, such as enhanced security, collaboration tools, more granular access control, priority support, and higher rate limits on Docker Hub image pull.

The Docker image we will use has SQL Server 2025 hosted on Ubuntu 22.04. It is supported with Docker Engine 1.8 or later.

Let's install Docker and set up the SQL image and container now:

1. Install Docker Desktop from the following link: `https://docs.docker.com/engine/install/`.

2. Start Docker Desktop, which could take a few minutes on the initial start, as shown in *Figure 1.8*:

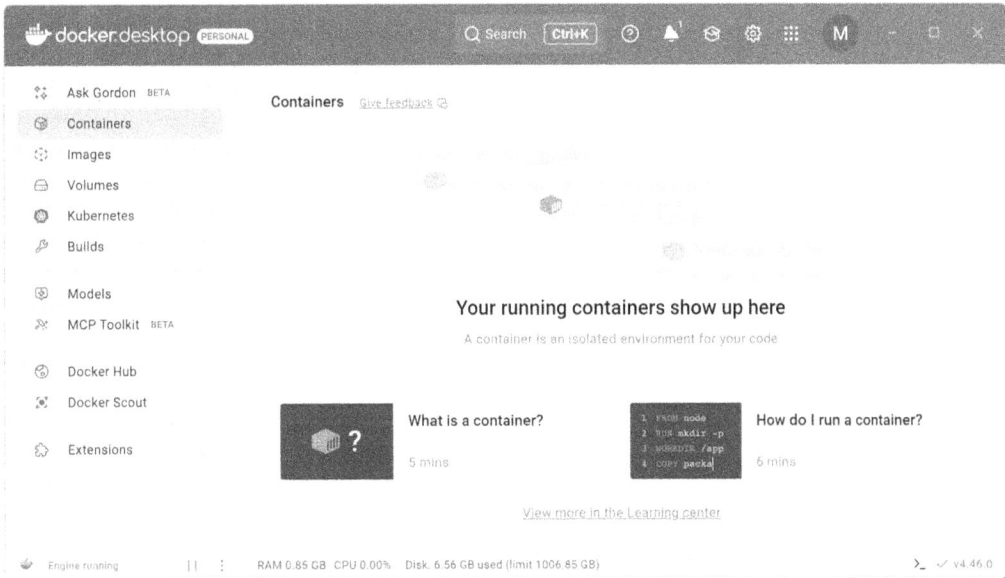

Figure 1.8: Docker Desktop on Windows

3. At the command prompt or terminal, pull down the latest container image for SQL Server 2025, as shown in the following command:

```
docker pull mcr.microsoft.com/mssql/server:2025-latest
```

> Unfortunately, the recent SQL Server images from Microsoft only support x64 architecture. If you want to use an image that runs without emulation on ARM CPUs, for example, if you have a Surface Laptop 7 or Mac, then you can use a minimal edition of SQL Server known as Azure SQL Edge that runs on either x64 or ARM64, with a minimum of 1 GB RAM on the host. But Azure SQL Edge is no longer supported by Microsoft, so use it at your own risk. I think that it's fine for learning purposes, but do not use unsupported software in production. To pull the Azure SQL Edge image, enter the following command: `docker pull mcr.microsoft.com/azure-sql-edge:latest`

4. Wait for the image as it is downloading, and then note the results, as shown in the following output:

```
2025-latest: Pulling from mssql/server
a7f551132cc7: Pull complete
d39c64e0c073: Pull complete
04a0776f5c78: Pull complete
Digest:
sha256:e2e5bcfe395924ff49694542191d3aefe86b6b3bd6c024f9ea01bf5a8856c56e
Status: Downloaded newer image for mcr.microsoft.com/mssql/server:2025-latest
```

Running the SQL Server container image

You can create a container from the image and run it in a single `docker run` command with the following options:

- `--cap-add SYS_PTRACE`: This grants the container the `SYS_PTRACE` capability allows debugging tools (like `strace` or certain profilers) to attach to processes within the container. Microsoft recommends this for enabling debugging or diagnostic tools inside the container, but it's not strictly necessary for normal SQL Server operation.

- `-e 'ACCEPT_EULA=1'` or `-e "ACCEPT_EULA=1"`: This sets an environment variable to accept the SQL Server **End User License Agreement** (**EULA**). If you don't provide this, the container will exit immediately with a message saying you must accept the EULA.

- `-e 'MSSQL_SA_PASSWORD=s3cret-Ninja'` or `-e "MSSQL_SA_PASSWORD=s3cret-Ninja"`: This sets an environment variable to set the SQL Server `sa` (system administrator) account's password. The password must be at least eight characters long and contain characters from three of the following four sets: uppercase letters, lowercase letters, digits, and symbols. Otherwise, the container cannot set up the SQL Server engine and will fail. `s3cret-Ninja` satisfies those rules (lowercase, number, hyphen, uppercase), but feel free to use your own password if you wish.

- `-p 1433:1433`: This maps a port from the container to the host. 1433 is the default port for SQL Server. This allows applications on the host to connect to SQL Server inside the container as if it were running natively.

- `--name nw-container`: This gives the container a custom name. This is optional, but if you don't set a name, a random one will be assigned for you, like `frosty_mirzakhani`.

- `-d`: This runs the container in detached mode (in the background). Without it, Docker would run the container in the foreground, tying up your terminal or command prompt window.

- `mcr.microsoft.com/mssql/server:2025-latest`: This specifies the image to run. `mcr.microsoft.com` is Microsoft's official container registry. `mssql/server` is the SQL Server on Linux container image. `2025-latest` is the tag for the latest build of SQL Server 2025.

Now that you understand what you are about to do, we can run the image:

1. At the command prompt or terminal, run the container image for SQL Server with a strong password, and name the container `nw-container`, as shown in the following command:

```
docker run --cap-add SYS_PTRACE -e 'ACCEPT_EULA=1' -e 'MSSQL_SA_
PASSWORD=s3cret-Ninja' -p 1433:1433 --name nw-container -d mcr.microsoft.
com/mssql/server:2025-latest
```

> **Warning!** The preceding command must be entered all on one line, or the container will not be started up correctly. In particular, the container might start up, but without a password set, and therefore, later, you won't be able to connect to it! All command lines used in this book can be found and copied from the following link: `https://github.com/markjprice/web-dev-net10/blob/main/docs/command-lines.md`. Also, different operating systems may require different quote characters, or none at all. To set the environment variables, you should be able to use either straight single-quotes or straight double-quotes. If the logs show that you did not accept the license agreement, then try the other type of quotes.

> If running the container image at the command prompt fails for you, see the next section, titled *Running a container using the user interface*.

2. If your operating system firewall blocks access, then allow access.

3. In Docker Desktop, in the **Containers** section, confirm that the image is running, as shown in *Figure 1.9*:

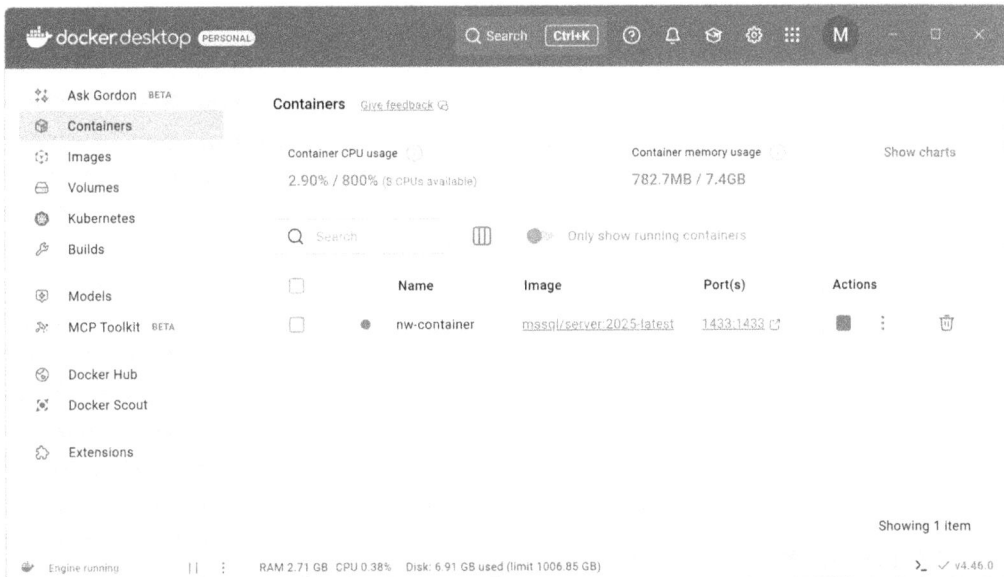

Figure 1.9: SQL Server container running in Docker Desktop on Windows

You might assume that the link in the **Port(s)** column is clickable and will navigate to a working website. But that container image only has SQL Server in it. SQL Server is listening on that port and can be connected to using a TCP address, not an HTTP address, so Docker is misleading you! There is no web server listening on port 1433, so a web browser that makes a request to `http://localhost:1433` will get a **This page isn't working** error. This is expected behavior because a database server is not a web server. Many containers in Docker do host a web server, and in those scenarios, having a convenient clickable link is useful. But Docker has no idea which containers have web servers and which do not. All it knows is what ports are mapped from internal ports to external ports. It is up to the developer to know if those links are useful.

4. At the command prompt or terminal, ask Docker to list all containers, both running and stopped, as shown in the following command:

```
docker ps -a
```

5. Note the container STATUS is Up 53 seconds and listening externally on port 1433, which is mapped to its internal port 1433, as shown highlighted in the following output:

```
CONTAINER ID    IMAGE                                    COMMAND
CREATED         STATUS          PORTS                           NAMES
183f02e84b2a    mcr.microsoft.com/ mssql/server:2025-latest    "/opt/mssql/
bin/perm…"     8 minutes ago   Up 53 seconds   1401/tcp, 0.0.0.0:1433-
>1433/tcp    nw-container
```

> You can learn more about the `docker ps` command at `https://docs.docker.com/engine/reference/commandline/ps/`.

Running a container using the user interface

If you successfully ran the SQL Server container, then you can skip this section and continue with the next section, titled *Connecting to SQL Server in a Docker container*.

If entering a command at the prompt or terminal fails for you, try following these steps to use the user interface:

1. In Docker Desktop, navigate to the **Images** tab.
2. In the **mcr.microsoft.com/mssql/server** row, in the **Actions** column, click the **Run** button.
3. In the **Run a new container** dialog box, expand **Optional settings**, and complete the configuration, as shown in *Figure 1.10* and in the following items:

    •   **Container name:** nw-container, or leave blank to use a random name.
    •   **Ports:** Enter 1433 to map to **:1433/tcp**.
    •   **Volumes:** Leave empty.

- **Environment variables** (click + to add a second one):

  - Enter ACCEPT_EULA with the value Y (or 1).
  - Enter MSSQL_SA_PASSWORD with the value s3cret-Ninja.

4. Click **Run**.

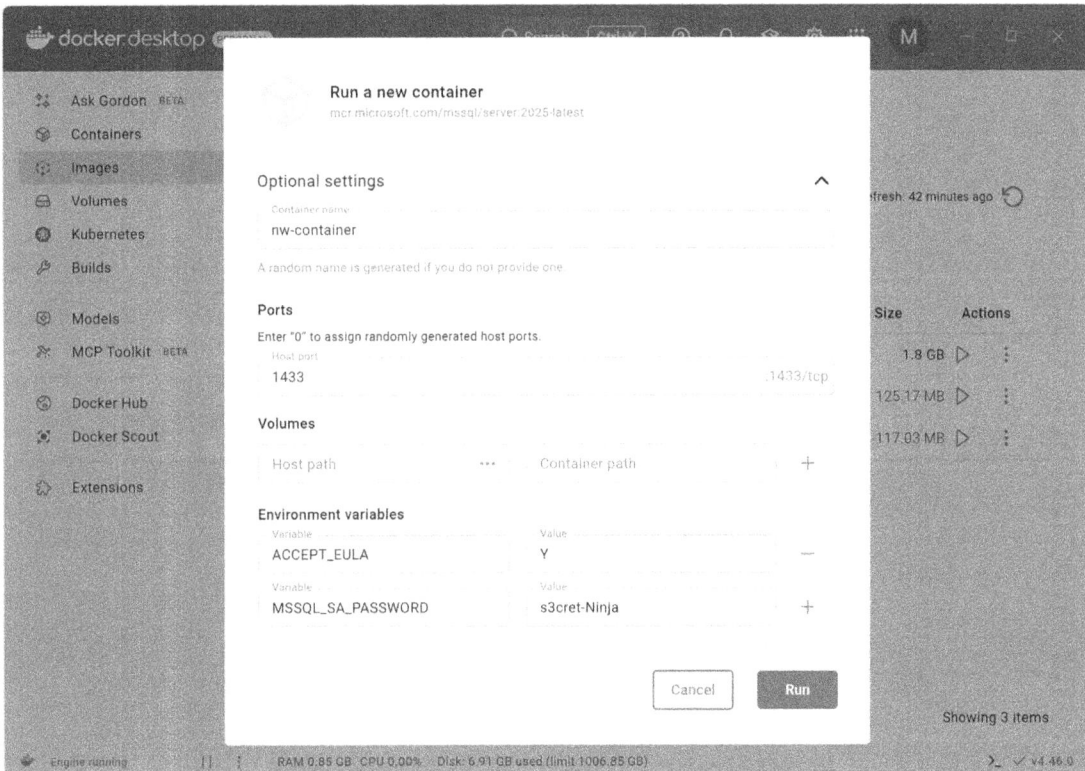

Figure 1.10: Running a container for SQL Server with the user interface

Connecting to SQL Server in a Docker container

Use your preferred database tool to connect to SQL Server in the Docker container. Some common database tools are shown in the following list:

- Windows only:

  - **SQL Server Management Studio (SSMS)**: The most popular and comprehensive tool for managing SQL Server databases. Free to download from Microsoft.

  - **SQL Server Data Tools (SSDT)**: Integrated into Visual Studio and free to use, SSDT provides database development tools for designing, deploying, and managing SQL Server databases.

- Cross-platform for Windows, macOS, Linux:

  - **VS Code's MS SQL extension**: Query execution, IntelliSense, database browsing, and connection to SQL Server databases.

Some notes about the database connection string for SQL Server in a container:

- **Data Source**, a.k.a. **Server Name:** `tcp:127.0.0.1,1433`
- **Authentication:** You must use **SQL Server Authentication**, a.k.a. **SQL Login**. That is, you must supply a username and password. The SQL Server image has the `sa` user already created, and you had to give it a strong password when you ran the container. We chose the password `s3cret-Ninja`.
- You must select the **Trust server certificate** checkbox.
- Optionally, you might want to save your password for future use.
- **Initial Catalog**, a.k.a. **database:** `master` or leave blank. (We will create the Northwind database using a SQL script, so we do not specify that as the database name yet.)

> **Warning!** If you already have SQL Server installed locally, and its services are running, then it will be listening to port **1433**, and it will take priority over any Docker-hosted SQL Server services that are also trying to listen on port **1433**. You will need to stop the local SQL Server before being able to connect to any Docker-hosted SQL Server services. You can do this using Windows Services: in the **Services (Local)** list, right-click **SQL Server (MSSQLSERVER)** and choose **Stop**. (This can take a few minutes, so be patient.) You can also right-click and choose **Properties** and then set **Startup type** to **Manual**, as shown in *Figure 1.11* (it defaults to **Automatic**, so if you restart Windows, it will be running again). Or change the port number(s) for either the local or Docker-hosted SQL Server services so that they do not conflict.

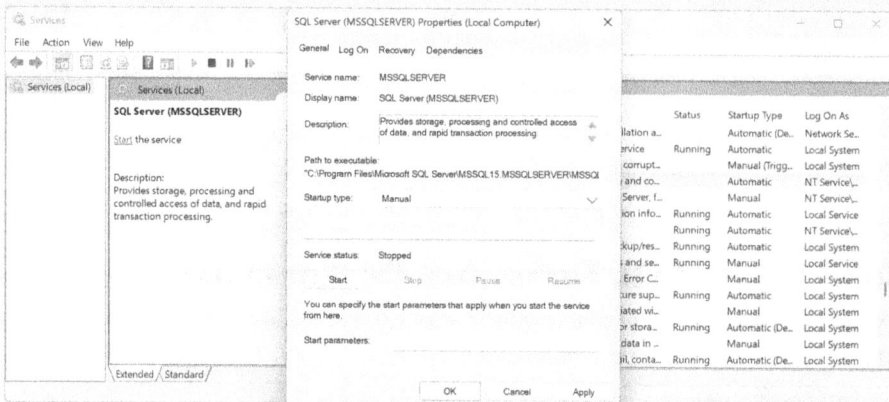

Figure 1.11: SQL Server service properties

> I have created a troubleshooting guide if you have trouble connecting: `https://github.com/markjprice/web-dev-net10/blob/main/docs/errata/sql-container-issues.md`.

Connecting from Visual Studio

To connect to SQL Server using Visual Studio:

1.   In Visual Studio, navigate to **View | Server Explorer**.

2.   In the **Server Explorer** mini-toolbar, click the **Connect to Database...** button.

3.   If prompted to **Change Data Source**, then choose **Microsoft SQL Server**.

4.   Enter the connection details, as shown in *Figure 1.12*:

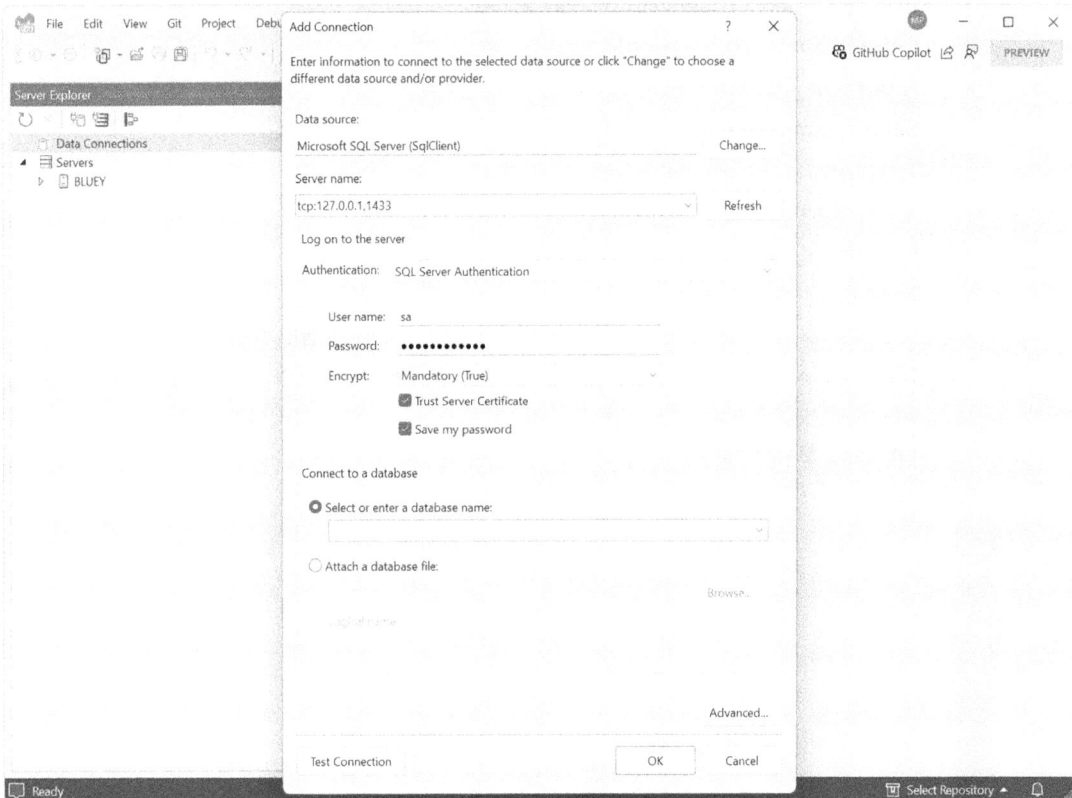

Figure 1.12: Connecting to your SQL Server in a container from Visual Studio

Warning! If you get the error **Login failed for user 'sa'**, then the most likely causes are either that the password was not set correctly when you ran the Docker container, or you are connecting to a different SQL Server, for example, a local one instead of the one in the container.

Connecting from VS Code

To connect to SQL Server in a container using VS Code, follow these steps:

1. In VS Code, navigate to the **SQL Server** extension. Note that the `mssql` extension might take a few minutes to initialize the first time.

2. In the **SQL** extension, click **Add Connection....**

3. In the **Connect to Database** pane, enter the connection details, as shown in *Figure 1.13*:

    *   **Profile Name:** `SQL Server in Container`
    *   **Connection Group:** <Default>
    *   **Input type: Parameters**
    *   **Server name:** `tcp:127.0.0.1,1433`
    *   **Trust server certificate:** Selected
    *   **Authentication type: SQL Login**
    *   **User name:** `sa`
    *   **Password:** `s3cret-Ninja`
    *   **Save Password:** Cleared (or selected for convenience during learning)
    *   **Database name:** `master` or leave blank (we will create the Northwind database using a SQL script, so we do not specify that as the database name yet)
    *   **Encrypt: Mandatory**

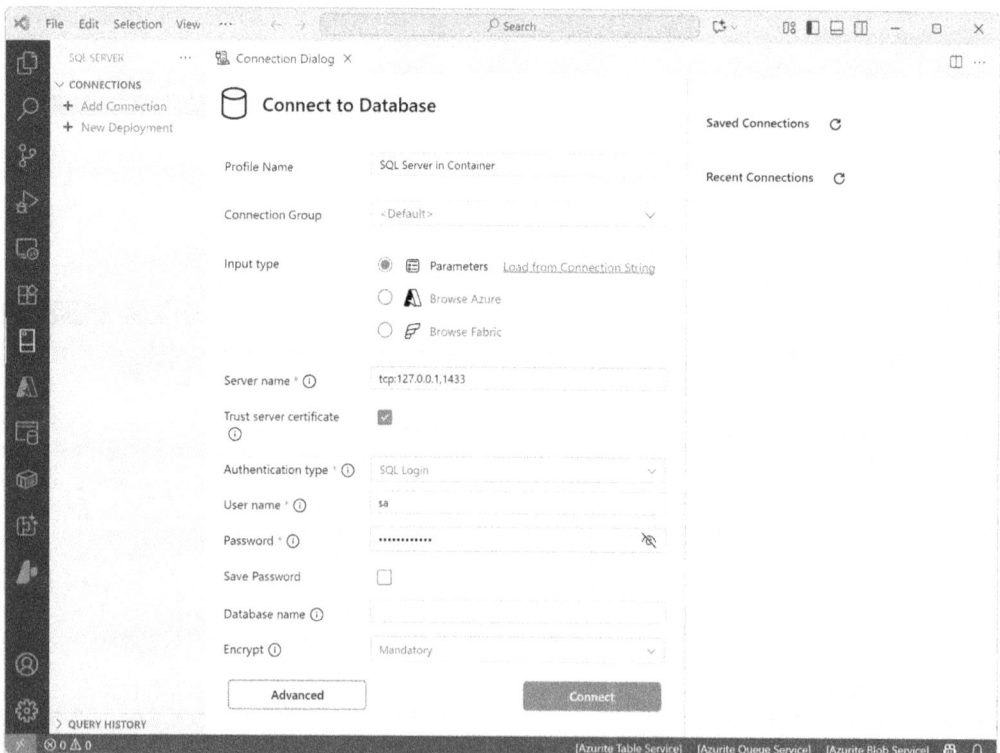

Figure 1.13: Connecting to your SQL Server in a container from VS Code

4. Click **Connect** and then note the success notification message.

Creating the Northwind database using a SQL script

Now you can use your preferred code editor (or database tool) to execute the SQL script to create the Northwind database in SQL Server in a container:

1. Open the `Northwind4SqlServerContainer.sql` file. Note that this file does not know about the **Server Explorer** connection to the SQL Server database.

2. Connect the file to the SQL Server database. For example, in Visual Studio, right-click in the script file, navigate to **Connection** | **Connect...**, and then fill in the dialog box as before.

3. Execute the SQL script:

   - If you are using Visual Studio, right-click in the script file, select **Execute**, and then wait to see the **Command completed successfully** message.

   - If you are using VS Code, right-click in the script file, select **Execute Query**, select the **SQL Server in a Container** connection profile, and then wait to see the **Commands completed successfully** message.

4. Refresh the data connection:

   - If you are using Visual Studio, then in **Server Explorer**, right-click **Tables** and select **Refresh**.

   - If you are using VS Code, then right-click the **SQL Server in a Container** connection profile and choose **Refresh**.

5. Expand **Databases**, expand **Northwind**, and then expand **Tables**.

6. Note that 13 tables have been created, for example, `Categories`, `Customers`, and `Products`. Also note that dozens of views and stored procedures have also been created, as shown in *Figure 1.14*:

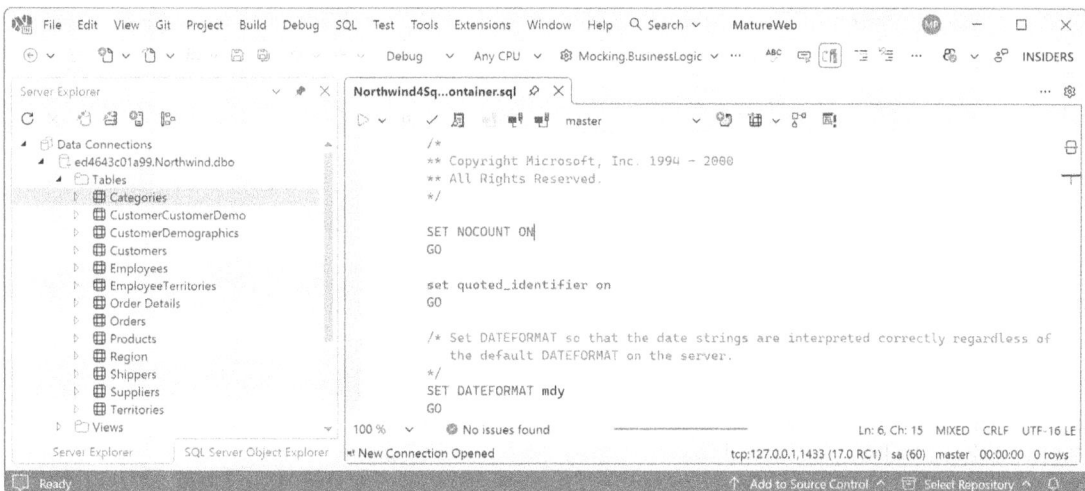

Figure 1.14: Northwind database created by SQL script in Visual Studio Server Explorer

You now have a running instance of SQL Server containing the Northwind database that you can connect to from your ASP.NET Core projects.

You will want to keep the container while you work through all the chapters in this book. You can stop and start the container whenever you want, and the database will persist. Eventually, once you have finished this book, you might want to delete the container. This will also delete the database, so if you recreate the container, you will need to rerun the SQL script to recreate the Northwind database.

Removing Docker resources

When you have completed all the chapters in the book, or you plan to use a local SQL Server or Azure SQL Database in the cloud instead of a SQL Server container, and you want to remove all the Docker resources that it uses, then either use the Docker Desktop user interface or follow these steps at the command prompt or terminal:

1. At the command prompt or terminal, stop the nw-container container, as shown in the following command:

    ```
    docker stop nw-container
    ```

2. At the command prompt or terminal, remove the nw-container container, as shown in the following command:

    ```
    docker rm nw-container
    ```

    > **Warning!** Removing the container will delete all data inside it.

3. At the command prompt or terminal, remove the image to release its disk space, as shown in the following command:

    ```
    docker rmi mcr.microsoft.com/mssql/server:2025-latest
    ```

Setting up the EF Core CLI tool

The .NET CLI tool named dotnet can be extended with capabilities useful for working with EF Core. It can perform design-time tasks like creating and applying migrations from an older model to a newer model and generating code for a model from an existing database.

The dotnet-ef command-line tool is not automatically installed. You must install this package as either a **global** or **local** tool. If you have already installed an older version of the tool, then you should update it to the latest version:

1. At a command prompt or terminal, check if you have already installed dotnet-ef as a global tool, as shown in the following command:

    ```
    dotnet tool list --global
    ```

2. Check in the list if an older version of the tool has been installed, like the one for .NET 9, as shown in the following output:

```
Package Id          Version         Commands
------------------------------------
dotnet-ef           9.0.0           dotnet-ef
```

3. If an old version is installed, then update the tool, as shown in the following command:

```
dotnet tool update --global dotnet-ef
```

4. If it is not already installed, then install the latest version, as shown in the following command:

```
dotnet tool install --global dotnet-ef
```

If necessary, follow any OS-specific instructions to add the `dotnet tools` directory to your `PATH` environment variable, as described in the output of installing the `dotnet-ef` tool.

By default, the latest **general availability (GA)** release of .NET will be used to install the tool. To explicitly set a version, for example, to use a preview, add the `--version` switch. For example, to update to the latest .NET 11 preview or release candidate version (which will be available from February 2026 to October 2026), use the following command with a version wildcard:

```
dotnet tool update --global dotnet-ef --version 11.0-*
```

Once the .NET 11 GA release happens in November 2026, you can just use the command without the `--version` switch to upgrade.

You can also remove the tool, as shown in the following command:

```
dotnet tool uninstall --global dotnet-ef
```

Creating a class library for entity models

You will now define entity data models in a class library so that they can be reused in other types of projects, including client-side app models.

> **Good practice:** You should create a separate class library project for your entity data models from the class library for your database context. This allows easier sharing of the entity models between backend web servers and frontend desktop, mobile, and Blazor clients, while only the backend needs to reference the database context class library.

We will automatically generate some entity models using the EF Core command-line tool:

1. Use your preferred code editor to create a new project and solution, as defined in the following list:

    *   **Project template: Class Library** / `classlib`
    *   **Project file and folder:** `Northwind.EntityModels`
    *   **Solution file and folder:** `MatureWeb`

> **Good practice:** You should target .NET 10 (LTS) or a later version for all the projects in this book, but you should be consistent. If you choose to target later versions like .NET 11 for the class libraries, then target .NET 11 for the later MVC and Web API projects too. This does not mean that you can download or clone the solution projects and then only change the target framework from `net10.0` to `net11.0` and it will work. What I mean is that you can choose to target .NET 11 when you create all the projects. Some of the project templates will change between .NET 10 and .NET 11, especially the Aspire templates. Just changing the target version after project creation might not be enough.

2. In the `Northwind.EntityModels.csproj` project file, add package references for the SQL Server database provider and EF Core design-time support, as shown in the following markup:

```
<ItemGroup>
  <PackageReference Include="Microsoft.EntityFrameworkCore.SqlServer" />
  <PackageReference Include="Microsoft.EntityFrameworkCore.Design">
    <PrivateAssets>all</PrivateAssets>
    <IncludeAssets>runtime; build; native; contentfiles; analyzers;
buildtransitive</IncludeAssets>
  </PackageReference>
</ItemGroup>
```

3. Delete the `Class1.cs` file.

4. Build the `Northwind.EntityModels` project to restore packages.

5. Make sure that the SQL Server container is running because you are about to connect to the server and its Northwind database.

6. At a command prompt or terminal, in the `Northwind.EntityModels` project folder (the folder that contains the `.csproj` project file), generate entity class models for all tables, as shown in the following command:

```
dotnet ef dbcontext scaffold "Data Source=tcp:127.0.0.1,1433;Initial
Catalog=Northwind;User Id=sa;Password=s3cret-Ninja;TrustServerCertificat
e=true;"
Microsoft.EntityFrameworkCore.SqlServer
--namespace Northwind.EntityModels --data-annotations
```

Note the following:

- The command to perform: `dbcontext scaffold`
- The connection string: `"Data   Source=tcp:127.0.0.1,1433;Initial Catalog=Northwind;User Id=sa;Password= s3cret-Ninja;TrustServerCertificate=true;"`
- The database provider: `Microsoft.EntityFrameworkCore.SqlServer`

- The namespace: `--namespace Northwind.EntityModels`
- To use data annotations as well as the Fluent API: `--data-annotations`

> **Warning!** `dotnet-ef` commands must be entered all on one line and in a folder that contains a project, or you will see the following error: `No project was found. Change the current working directory or use the --project option.` Remember that all command lines can be found at and copied from the following link: `https://github.com/markjprice/web-dev-net10/blob/main/docs/command-lines.md`.

If you are using a local instance of SQL Server, then you can use the following command:

```
dotnet ef dbcontext scaffold "Data Source=.;Initial
Catalog=Northwind;Integrated Security=true;TrustServerCertificate=true;"
Microsoft.EntityFrameworkCore.SqlServer
--namespace Northwind.EntityModels --data-annotations
```

Note the different data source and authentication in the connection string: `"Data Source=.;Initial Catalog=Northwind;Integrated Security=true;TrustServerCertificate=true;"`

Creating a class library for a database context

You will now define a database context class library:

1. Add a new project to the solution, as defined in the following list:

    - **Project template: Class Library** / `classlib`
    - **Project file and folder:** `Northwind.DataContext`
    - **Solution file and folder:** `MatureWeb`

2. In the `Northwind.DataContext` project, statically and globally import the `Console` class, add a package reference to the EF Core data provider for SQL Server, and add a project reference to the `Northwind.EntityModels` project, as shown in the following markup:

    ```
    <ItemGroup Label="To simplify use of WriteLine.">
      <Using Include="System.Console" Static="true" />
    </ItemGroup>

    <ItemGroup Label="Versions are set at solution-level.">
      <PackageReference Include="Microsoft.EntityFrameworkCore.SqlServer" />
    </ItemGroup>

    <ItemGroup>
      <ProjectReference
        Include="..\Northwind.EntityModels\Northwind.EntityModels.csproj" />
    </ItemGroup>
    ```

> 🔆 **Warning!** The path to the project reference should not have a line break in your project file.

3. In the `Northwind.DataContext` project, delete the `Class1.cs` file.
4. Build the `Northwind.DataContext` project to restore packages.
5. In the `Northwind.DataContext` project, add a class named `NorthwindContextLogger.cs`.
6. Modify its contents to define a static method named `WriteLine` that appends a string to the end of a text file named `northwindlog-<date_time>.txt` on the desktop, as shown in the following code:

```
using static System.Environment;

namespace Northwind.EntityModels;

public class NorthwindContextLogger
{
  public static void WriteLine(string message)
  {
    string folder = Path.Combine(GetFolderPath(
      SpecialFolder.DesktopDirectory), "book-logs");

    if (!Directory.Exists(folder))
      Directory.CreateDirectory(folder);

    string dateTimeStamp = DateTime.Now.ToString("yyyyMMdd_HHmmss");

    string path = Path.Combine(folder,
      $"northwindlog-{dateTimeStamp}.txt");

    StreamWriter textFile = File.AppendText(path);
    textFile.WriteLine(message);
    textFile.Close();
  }
}
```

> 📝 Although the project name (and therefore default assembly name) is `Northwind.DataContext`, to simplify usage of the data context class, we have defined it in the same namespace as the related models: `Northwind.EntityModels`.

7. Move the `NorthwindContext.cs` file from the `Northwind.EntityModels` project/folder to the `Northwind.DataContext` project/folder.

> **Warning!** In Visual Studio Solution Explorer, if you drag and drop a file between projects, it will be copied. If you hold down *Shift* while dragging and dropping, it will be moved. In VS Code EXPLORER, if you drag and drop a file between projects, it will be moved. If you hold down *Ctrl* while dragging and dropping, it will be copied.

8. In `NorthwindContext.cs`, note that the second constructor can have `options` passed as a parameter, which allows us to override the default database connection string in any projects, such as websites, that need to work with the Northwind database, as shown in the following code:

```
public NorthwindContext(
  DbContextOptions<NorthwindContext> options)
  : base(options)
{
}
```

9. In `NorthwindContext.cs`, both constructors give dozens of warnings, one for each of its `DbSet<T>` properties that represent tables and views, because they are marked as not nullable, and the compiler does not know that EF Core will automatically instantiate them all, so they will never actually be null. We can hide these warnings by disabling warning code CS8618 just for those two constructors, as shown in the following code:

```
public partial class NorthwindContext : DbContext
{
#pragma warning disable CS8618
  public NorthwindContext()
#pragma warning restore CS8618
  {
  }

#pragma warning disable CS8618
  public NorthwindContext(DbContextOptions<NorthwindContext> options)
#pragma warning restore CS8618
      : base(options)
  {
  }
```

Good practice: We could simplify the code by disabling that warning code once at the top of the file and not restoring it anywhere in that file, but it is safer to re-enable warning codes in case you encounter more instances that you do need to handle differently.

You can learn more about this warning code at the following link: `https://learn.microsoft.com/en-us/dotnet/csharp/language-reference/compiler-messages/nullable-warnings#nonnullable-reference-not-initialized`.

10. In `NorthwindContext.cs`, in the `OnConfiguring` method, remove the compiler `#warning` about the connection string and then add statements to dynamically build a database connection string for SQL Server in a container, as shown in the following code:

```
protected override void OnConfiguring(
  DbContextOptionsBuilder optionsBuilder)
{
  if (!optionsBuilder.IsConfigured)
  {
    SqlConnectionStringBuilder builder = new();

    builder.DataSource = "tcp:127.0.0.1,1433"; // SQL Server in
container.
    builder.InitialCatalog = "Northwind";
    builder.TrustServerCertificate = true;
    builder.MultipleActiveResultSets = true;

    // Because we want to fail faster. Default is 15 seconds.
    builder.ConnectTimeout = 3;

    // SQL Server authentication.
    builder.UserID = Environment.GetEnvironmentVariable("MY_SQL_USR");
    builder.Password = Environment.GetEnvironmentVariable("MY_SQL_PWD");

    optionsBuilder.UseSqlServer(builder.ConnectionString);

    optionsBuilder.LogTo(NorthwindContextLogger.WriteLine,
      new[] { Microsoft.EntityFrameworkCore
      .Diagnostics.RelationalEventId.CommandExecuting });
  }
}
```

11. In the `Northwind.DataContext` project, add a class named `NorthwindContextExtensions.cs`. Modify its contents to define an extension method that adds the Northwind database context to a collection of dependency services, as shown in the following code:

```
using Microsoft.Data.SqlClient; // To use SqlConnectionStringBuilder.
using Microsoft.EntityFrameworkCore; // To use UseSqlServer.
using Microsoft.Extensions.DependencyInjection; // To use
IServiceCollection.

namespace Northwind.EntityModels;

public static class NorthwindContextExtensions
{
  /// <summary>
  /// Adds NorthwindContext to the specified IServiceCollection. Uses the
SqlServer database provider.
  /// </summary>
  /// <param name="services">The service collection.</param>
  /// <param name="connectionString">Set to override the default.</param>
  /// <returns>An IServiceCollection that can be used to add more
services.</returns>
  public static IServiceCollection AddNorthwindContext(
    this IServiceCollection services, // The type to extend.
    string? connectionString = null)
  {
    if (connectionString is null)
    {
      SqlConnectionStringBuilder builder = new();

      builder.DataSource = "tcp:127.0.0.1,1433"; // SQL Server in
container.
      builder.InitialCatalog = "Northwind";
      builder.TrustServerCertificate = true;
      builder.MultipleActiveResultSets = true;

      // Because we want to fail faster. Default is 15 seconds.
      builder.ConnectTimeout = 3;

      // SQL Server authentication.
      builder.UserID = Environment.GetEnvironmentVariable("MY_SQL_USR");
      builder.Password = Environment.GetEnvironmentVariable("MY_SQL_
PWD");
```

```
      connectionString = builder.ConnectionString;
    }

    services.AddDbContext<NorthwindContext>(options =>
    {
      options.UseSqlServer(connectionString);
      options.LogTo(NorthwindContextLogger.WriteLine,
        new[] { Microsoft.EntityFrameworkCore
          .Diagnostics.RelationalEventId.CommandExecuting });
    },
    // Register with a transient lifetime to avoid concurrency
    // issues with Blazor Server projects.
    contextLifetime: ServiceLifetime.Transient,
    optionsLifetime: ServiceLifetime.Transient);

    return services;
  }
}
```

12. Build the two class libraries and fix any compiler errors.

> There is duplicate code in these two classes because the `NorthwindContext` class and its extensions are written to allow developers to instantiate the context class directly as well as via the extension method. They can also override the connection string or choose to accept defaults.

Setting the user and password for SQL Server authentication

If you are using SQL Server authentication (i.e., you must supply a user and password), then complete the following steps:

1. In the `Northwind.DataContext` project, note the statements that set `UserId` and `Password`, as shown in the following code:

    ```
    // SQL Server authentication.
    builder.UserId = Environment.GetEnvironmentVariable("MY_SQL_USR");
    builder.Password = Environment.GetEnvironmentVariable("MY_SQL_PWD");
    ```

2. Set the two environment variables at the command prompt or terminal, as shown in the following commands:

    *   On Windows:

    ```
    setx MY_SQL_USR <your_user_name>
    setx MY_SQL_PWD <your_password>
    ```

- On macOS and Linux:

```
export MY_SQL_USR=<your_user_name>
export MY_SQL_PWD=<your_password>
```

> Unless you set a different password, `<your_user_name>` will be `sa`, and `<your_password>` will be `s3cret-Ninja`.

3. You **must** restart any command prompts, terminal windows, and applications like Visual Studio for this change to take effect.

> **Good practice:** Although you could define the two environment variables in the `launchSettings.json` file of an ASP.NET Core project, you must then be extremely careful not to include that file in a GitHub repository! You can learn how to ignore files in Git at `https://docs.github.com/en/get-started/getting-started-with-git/ignoring-files`.

Registering dependency services

You can register dependency services with different lifetimes, as shown in the following list:

- **Transient:** These services are created each time they're requested. Transient services should be lightweight and stateless.
- **Scoped:** These services are created once per client request and are disposed of; then the response returns to the client.
- **Singleton:** These services are usually created the first time they are requested and then shared, although you can provide an instance at the time of registration, too.

In this book, you will use all three types of lifetime.

By default, a `DbContext` class is registered using the `Scope` lifetime, meaning that multiple threads can share the same instance. But `DbContext` does not support multiple threads. If more than one thread attempts to use the same `NorthwindContext` class instance at the same time, then you will see the following runtime exception thrown: `A second operation started on this context before a previous operation completed. This is usually caused by different threads using the same instance of a DbContext. However, instance members are not guaranteed to be thread-safe.`

This happens in Blazor projects with components set to run on the server side because, whenever interactions on the client side happen, a SignalR call is made back to the server, where a single instance of the database context is shared between multiple clients. This issue does not occur if a component is set to run on the client side.

Improving the class-to-table mapping

We will make some small changes to improve the entity model mapping and validation rules for SQL Server.

> Remember that all code is available in the GitHub repository for the book. Although you will learn more by typing the code yourself, you never have to. Go to the following link and press . (or change .com to .dev manually) to get a live code editor in your browser: https://github.com/markjprice/web-dev-net10.

We will add a regular expression to validate that a `CustomerId` value is exactly five uppercase letters:

1. In `Customer.cs`, add a regular expression to validate its primary key, `CustomerId`, to only allow five uppercase Western characters, as shown highlighted in the following code:

   ```
   [Key]
   [StringLength(5)]
   [RegularExpression("[A-Z]{5}")]
   public string CustomerId { get; set; } = null!;
   ```

2. In `Customer.cs`, add the `[Phone]` attribute to its `Phone` property, as shown highlighted in the following code:

   ```
   [StringLength(24)]
   [Phone]
   public string? Phone { get; set; }
   ```

   The `[Phone]` attribute adds the following to the rendered HTML: `type="tel"`. On a mobile phone, this makes the keyboard use the phone dialer instead of the normal keyboard.

3. In `Order.cs`, decorate the `CustomerId` property with the same regular expression to enforce five uppercase characters.

Testing the class libraries using xUnit

xUnit is a popular unit testing framework for .NET applications. It was created by the original inventor of NUnit and is designed to be more modern, extensible, and aligned with .NET development practices.

Several benefits of using xUnit are shown in the following list:

- xUnit is open source and has a strong community and active development team behind it. This makes it more likely that it will stay up to date with the latest .NET features and best practices. xUnit benefits from a large and active community, which means many tutorials, guides, and third-party extensions are available for it.
- xUnit uses a more simplified and extensible approach compared to older frameworks. It encourages the use of custom test patterns and less reliance on setup and teardown methods, leading to cleaner test code.

- Tests in xUnit are configured using .NET attributes, which makes the test code easy to read and understand. It uses [Fact] for standard test cases and [Theory] with [InlineData], [ClassData], or [MemberData] for parameterized tests, enabling data-driven testing. This makes it easier to cover many input scenarios with the same test method, enhancing test thoroughness while minimizing effort.

- xUnit includes an assertion library that allows for a wide variety of assertions out of the box, making it easier to test a wide range of conditions without having to write custom test code. It can also be extended with popular assertion libraries, like FluentAssertions, that allow you to articulate test expectations with human-readable reasons.

- By default, xUnit supports parallel test execution within the same test collection, which can significantly reduce the time it takes to run large test suites. This is particularly beneficial in continuous integration environments where speed is critical. However, if you run your tests in a memory-limited **Virtual Private Server** (VPS), then that impacts how much data the server can handle at any given time and how many applications or processes it can run concurrently. In this scenario, you might want to disable parallel test execution. Memory-limited VPS instances are typically used as cheap testing environments.

- xUnit offers precise control over the test lifecycle with setup and teardown commands through the use of the constructor and destructor patterns and the IDisposable interface, as well as with the [BeforeAfterTestAttribute] for more granular control.

Now let's build some unit tests to ensure the class libraries are working correctly.

Let's write the tests:

1. Use your preferred coding tool to add a new **xUnit Test Project [C#]** / xunit project named Northwind.UnitTests to the MatureWeb solution.

2. In the Northwind.UnitTests project, make changes as described in the following bullets, and as shown in the following configuration:

   - Delete the version numbers specified for the testing packages in the project file. (Visual Studio and other code editors will give errors if you have projects that should use CPM but specify their own package versions without using the VersionOverride attribute.)

   - Add a project reference to the Northwind.DataContext project:

   ```
   <ItemGroup>
     <PackageReference Include="coverlet.collector" />
     <PackageReference Include="Microsoft.NET.Test.Sdk" />
     <PackageReference Include="xunit" />
     <PackageReference Include="xunit.runner.visualstudio" />
   </ItemGroup>

   <ItemGroup>
     <ProjectReference
       Include="..\Northwind.DataContext\Northwind.DataContext.csproj" />
   </ItemGroup>
   ```

> 💡 **Warning!** The project reference must go all on one line with no line break.

3. Build the `Northwind.UnitTests` project to build referenced projects.
4. Rename `UnitTest1.cs` to `EntityModelTests.cs`.
5. Modify the contents of the file to define two tests, the first to connect to the database and the second to confirm there are eight categories in the database, as shown in the following code:

```
using Northwind.EntityModels; // To use NorthwindContext.

namespace Northwind.UnitTests;

public class EntityModelTests
{
  [Fact]
  public void DatabaseConnectTest()
  {
    using NorthwindContext db = new();
    Assert.True(db.Database.CanConnect());
  }

  [Fact]
  public void CategoryCountTest()
  {
    using NorthwindContext db = new();
    int expected = 8;
    int actual = db.Categories.Count();
    Assert.Equal(expected, actual);
  }

  [Fact]
  public void ProductId1IsChaiTest()
  {
    using NorthwindContext db = new();
    string expected = "Chai";
    Product? product = db.Products.Find(keyValues: 1);
    string actual = product?.ProductName ?? string.Empty;
    Assert.Equal(expected, actual);
  }
}
```

6. Run the unit tests:

   - If you are using Visual Studio, then navigate to **Test** | **Run All Tests**, and then view the results in **Test Explorer**.

   - If you are using VS Code, then in the `Northwind.UnitTests` project's **TERMINAL** window, run the tests, as shown in the following command: `dotnet test`. Alternatively, use the **TESTING** window if you have installed the C# Dev Kit.

7. Note that the results should indicate that three tests were run, and all passed, as shown in *Figure 1.15*:

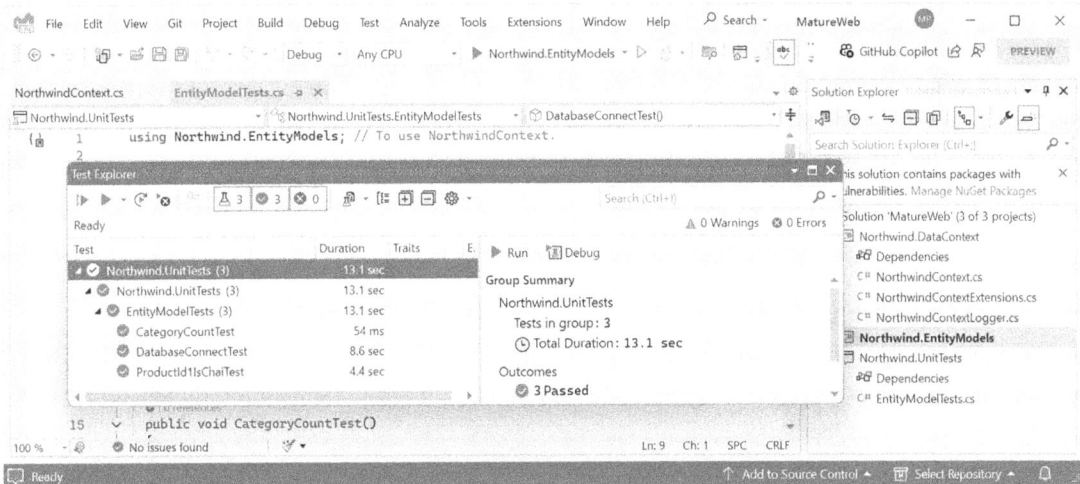

Figure 1.15: Three successful unit tests ran

If any of the tests fail, then try to fix the issue.

For example, you might see the following exception:

```
System.ArgumentNullException : Value cannot be null. (Parameter 'User ID')
```

This occurs when the code tries to read the environment variable, but it has not been set. If you executed the commands to set the environment variables, then to fix the problem, restart Visual Studio and any terminal and command prompt windows. This will allow them to access the environment variables.

Now that we have built an entity model to use to work with sample data in all the projects in this book, let's end this chapter by looking at where you can get help when you get stuck.

Looking for help

This section is about how to find quality information about programming on the web. You will learn about Microsoft Learn documentation, including its new MCP server for integration with AI systems, getting help while coding and using `dotnet` commands, getting help from fellow readers in the book's Discord channel, searching the .NET source code for implementation details, and finally, making the most of modern AI tools like GitHub Copilot.

This is useful information that all readers should know and refer to throughout reading any of my .NET 10 books, especially if you are new to .NET.

This section has been made into a separate *Appendix C*, both to make it reusable in all four of my .NET 10 books, and to avoid wasting pages in the print book for those readers who have already read it from one of the other books.

An online Markdown version of *Appendix C* is available in the book's GitHub repository at the following link: `https://github.com/markjprice/markjprice/blob/main/articles/getting-help.md`. Since this is hosted in my personal GitHub account, I can keep it updated more frequently throughout the three-year support period of .NET 10.

As part of this book's free exclusive benefits, you can also access a PDF version of the book, which includes *Appendix C*. You can unlock it and the other benefits at the following link: `https://packtpub.com/unlock`, then search for this book by name. Ensure it's the correct edition. Have your purchase invoice ready before you start.

Now let's review two of the most important topics in *Appendix C*, Microsoft's official documentation and its MCP server, and how to ask for help in this book's Discord channel.

Microsoft Learn documentation and its MCP server

The definitive resource for getting help with Microsoft developer tools and platforms is in the technical documentation on Microsoft Learn, and you can find it at the following link: `https://learn.microsoft.com/en-us/docs`.

> *"One of the most ambitious and impactful projects our engineers have built recently is Ask Learn, an API that provides generative AI capabilities to Microsoft Q&A." – Bob Tabor, Microsoft's Skilling organization*

You can read about Ask Learn at the following link:

`https://devblogs.microsoft.com/engineering-at-microsoft/how-we-built-ask-learn-the-rag-based-knowledge-service/`.

Microsoft has also created an MCP server for its official documentation so that chatbots can be configured to use the official documentation as a tool in their responses. The MCP server is accessible to any code editor or tool that supports the **Model Context Protocol** (**MCP**) using the following endpoint:

`https://learn.microsoft.com/api/mcp`

You can install it for VS Code and Cursor using the following link: `https://github.com/MicrosoftDocs/mcp?tab=readme-ov-file#-installation--getting-started`.

For Visual Studio, at the time of writing in June 2025, you must configure it manually using the following steps:

1. In the `MatureWeb` folder, create a file named `.mcp.json`.

2. In the `.mcp.json` file, define the endpoint for the Microsoft Docs MCP server, as shown in the following JSON:

```
{
  "servers": {
    "microsoft.docs.mcp": {
      "type": "http",
      "url": "https://learn.microsoft.com/api/mcp"
    }
  }
}
```

3. In Visual Studio, make sure the `MatureWeb` solution is open in **Solution Explorer**.

4. In the toolbar, click **GitHub Copilot**, and then navigate to **Settings | Options....** You must be logged in with your GitHub account to see this option.

5. In the **Options** dialog box, in the **GitHub | Copilot** section, select the **Enable Agent mode in the chat pane** and **Enable MCP server integration in agent mode** checkboxes.

6. Open the **GitHub Copilot Chat** window.

7. At the bottom of the chat window, select **Agent** mode, and then select the tool named `microsoft_docs_search`, as shown in *Figure 1.16*:

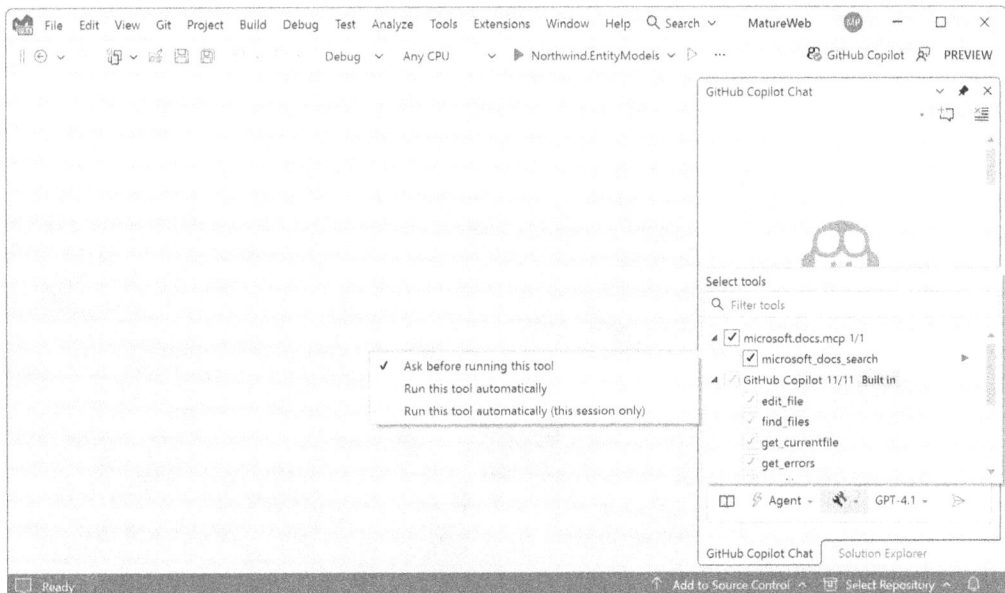

Figure 1.16: Configuring Copilot Chat tools

8. Optionally, click the right-pointing black arrow to customize options like setting the tool to ask you before running, as shown in *Figure 1.16*.

9. Select a model like **GPT-4.1** or **Claude Sonnet 3.7**. Some models, like **Gemini 2.5 Pro**, might require additional configuration.

10. Ask what the Northwind.UnitTests project does, as shown in the following query:

```
What does the Northwind.UnitTests project do?
```

11. Note the response (the response you get will be different since LLMs are non-deterministic):

```
5 references
Read 5 code snippets for 'test', 'unit test', ...
The Northwind.UnitTests project is a test project that uses the xUnit
framework to perform unit and integration tests on the Northwind
application. Specifically, it tests the Northwind.EntityModels and
Northwind.DataContext projects. The tests include:
•    Verifying that the database connection can be established.
•    Checking that the number of categories in the database matches the
expected count.
•    Ensuring that the product with ID 1 is named "Chai".
The project references xUnit and related test packages, and it depends on
the Northwind.DataContext project for database access. These tests help
ensure that the application's data access layer is functioning correctly.
```

12. Ask for important details about the int data type in the official documentation, as shown in the following query:

```
What remarks about int are in the docs?
```

13. When the model tries to use the MCP server, click **Allow this time**. Other options include **Always allow**, **Allow in this solution**, and **Deny**.

14. Note the response:

```
Here are some key remarks about int in the official documentation:
•    int in C# is a 32-bit signed integer, represented by System.Int32,
with a value range from -2,147,483,648 to 2,147,483,647.
•    int is an immutable value type.
•    Integer division truncates the result, and the remainder can be
obtained with the % operator.
•    int has minimum and maximum limits; exceeding these causes overflow
or underflow, wrapping the value.
•    int is a value type (struct) and derives from System.Object.
•    Type conversions involving int may require explicit casting, and
overflow can occur if the value is out of range.
```

You can read more about the Microsoft Learn MCP server at the following link: `https://github.com/MicrosoftDocs/mcp`.

Getting help on Discord and other chat forums

Asking questions in programming forums and Discord channels is an art as much as it is a science. To maximize your chances of receiving a helpful answer, there's a blend of clarity, specificity, and community awareness that you should aim for.

Here are some tips for asking questions:

- **Ask in a public channel, not in private:** Please do not direct message an author with a question or a friend request. Remember, every question asked and answered builds the collective knowledge and resourcefulness of the whole community. Asking in public also allows other readers to help you, not just the author. The community that Packt and I have built around my books is friendly and smart. Let us *all* help you.

- **Research before asking:** It's important to look for answers yourself before turning to the community. Use search engines, official documentation, and the search function within the forum or Discord server. This not only respects the community's time but also helps you learn more effectively. Another place to look first is the errata and improvements section of the book, found at the following link: `https://github.com/markjprice/web-dev-net10/blob/main/docs/errata/README.md`.

- **Be specific and concise:** Clearly state what you're trying to achieve, what you've tried so far, and where you're stuck. A concise question is more likely to get a quick response.

- **Specify the book location:** If you are stuck on a particular part of the book, specify the page number and section title so that others can look up the context of your question.

- **Show your work:** Demonstrating that you've made an effort to solve the problem yourself not only provides context but also helps others understand your thought process and where you might have gone down the wrong path.

- **Prepare your question:** Avoid too broad or vague questions. Screenshots of errors or code snippets (with proper formatting) can be very helpful.

Oddly, I've been seeing more and more examples of readers taking photos of their screens and posting those. These are harder to read and limited in what they can show. It's better to copy and paste the text of your code or the error message so that others can copy and paste it themselves. Alternatively, at least take a high-resolution screenshot instead of a photo with your phone camera at a jaunty angle!

- **Format your code properly**: Most forums and Discord servers support code formatting using Markdown syntax. Use formatting to make your code more readable. For example, surround code keywords in single backticks, like `public void`, and surround code blocks with three backticks with optional language code, as shown in the following code:

```cs
using static System.Console;
WriteLine("This is C# formatted code.");
```

> **Good practice:** After the three backticks that start a code block in Markdown, specify a language short name like `cs`, `csharp`, `js`, `javascript`, `json`, `html`, `css`, `cpp`, `xml`, `mermaid`, `python`, `java`, `ruby`, `go`, `sql`, `bash`, or `shell`.

> To learn how to format text in Discord channel messages, see the following link: `https://support.discord.com/hc/en-us/articles/210298617-Markdown-Text-101-Chat-Formatting-Bold-Italic-Underline`.

- **Be polite and patient**: Remember, you're asking for help from people who are giving their time voluntarily. A polite tone and patience while waiting for a response go a long way. Channel participants are often in a different time zone, so you may not see your question answered until the next day.
- **Be ready to actively participate**: After asking your question, stay engaged. You might receive follow-up questions for clarification. Responding promptly and clearly can significantly increase your chances of getting a helpful answer. When I ask a question, I set an alarm for three hours later to go back and see if anyone has responded. If there hasn't been a response yet, then I set another alarm for 24 hours later.

Incorporating these approaches when asking questions not only increases your likelihood of getting a useful response but also contributes positively to the community by showing respect for others' time and effort.

> **Good practice:** Never just say "Hello" as a message on any chat system. You can read why at the following link: `https://nohello.net/`. Similarly, don't ask to ask: `https://dontasktoask.com/`.

Using future versions of .NET with this book

Microsoft is expected to release .NET 11 at the .NET Conf 2026 on Tuesday, November 10, 2026. Many readers will want to use this book with .NET 11 and future versions of .NET, so this section explains how.

.NET 11 is likely to be available in preview from February 2026, or you can wait for the final version in November 2026.

> **Warning!** Once you install a .NET 11 SDK, it will be used by default for all .NET projects unless you override it using a `global.json` file. You can learn more about doing this at the following link: `https://learn.microsoft.com/en-us/dotnet/core/tools/global-json`.

You can easily continue to target the .NET 10 runtime while installing and using future C# compilers, as shown in *Figure 1.17* and illustrated in the following list:

1. **November 2025 onward**: Install .NET SDK 10.0.100 or later and use it to build projects that target .NET 10 and use the C# 14 compiler by default. Every month, update to .NET 10 SDK patches on the development computer and update to .NET 10 runtime patches on any deployment computers.

2. **February to October 2026**: Optionally, install .NET SDK 11 previews each month to explore the new C# 15 language and .NET 11 library features. Note that you won't be able to use new library features while targeting .NET 10.

3. **November 2026 onward**: Install .NET SDK 11.0.100 or later and use it to build projects that continue to target .NET 10 and use the C# 15 compiler for its new features. You will be using a fully supported SDK and a fully supported runtime. You can also use new features in EF Core 11 because it will continue to target .NET 10.

4. **February to October 2027**: Optionally, install .NET 12 previews to explore new C# 16 language and .NET 12 library features. Start planning if any new libraries and ASP.NET Core features in .NET 11 and .NET 12 can be applied to your .NET 10 projects when you are ready to migrate.

5. **November 2027 onward**: Install .NET 12.0.100 SDK or later and use it to build projects that target .NET 10 and use the C# 16 compiler.

6. You could migrate your .NET 10 projects to .NET 12 since .NET 12 is an LTS release. You have until November 2028 to complete the migration when .NET 10 reaches end-of-life.

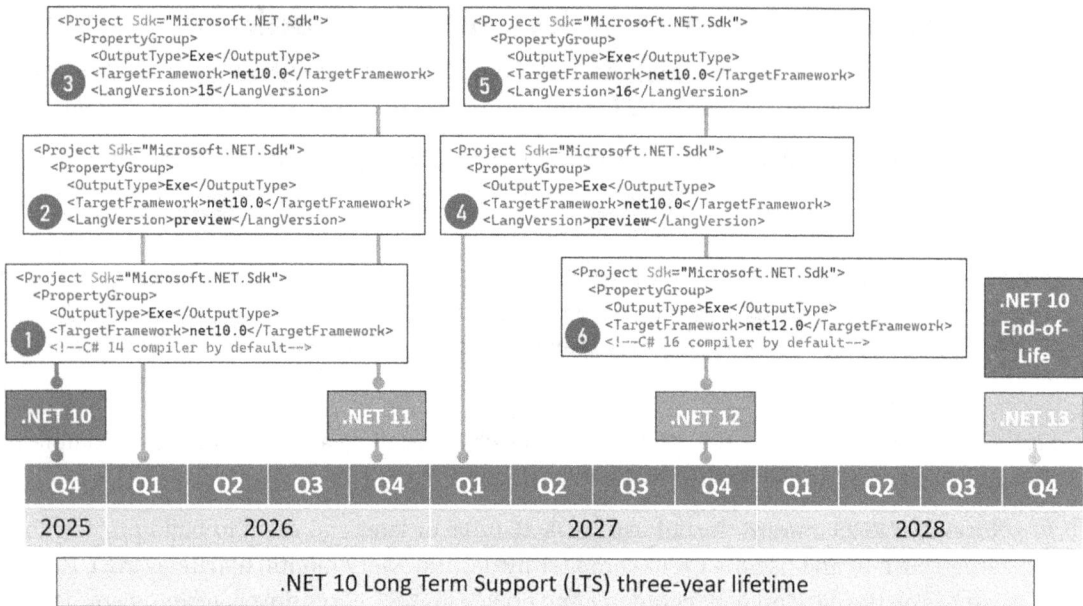

Figure 1.17: Targeting .NET 10 for long-term support while using the latest C# compilers

When deciding to install a .NET SDK, remember that the latest is used by default to build any .NET projects. Once you've installed a .NET 11 SDK preview, it will be used by default for all projects, unless you force the use of an older, fully supported SDK version like 10.0.100 or a later patch.

To gain the benefits of whatever new features are available in C# 15, while still targeting .NET 10 for long-term support, modify your project file, as shown highlighted in the following markup:

```
<Project Sdk="Microsoft.NET.Sdk">

  <PropertyGroup>
    <OutputType>Exe</OutputType>
    <TargetFramework>net10.0</TargetFramework>
    <LangVersion>15</LangVersion> <!--Requires .NET 11 SDK GA-->
    <ImplicitUsings>enable</ImplicitUsings>
    <Nullable>enable</Nullable>
  </PropertyGroup>
</Project>
```

Good practice: Use a GA SDK release like .NET 11 to use new compiler features while still targeting older but longer supported versions of .NET like .NET 10.

Understanding web development

Developing for the web means developing with the **Hypertext Transfer Protocol (HTTP)**, so we will start by reviewing this important foundational technology.

Understanding the Hypertext Transfer Protocol

To communicate with a web server, the client, also known as the **user agent**, makes calls over the network using HTTP. As such, HTTP is the technical underpinning of the web. So when we talk about websites and web services, we mean that they use HTTP to communicate between a client (often a web browser) and a server.

A client makes an HTTP request to a resource, such as a page, uniquely identified by a URL, and the server sends back an HTTP response, as shown in *Figure 1.18*:

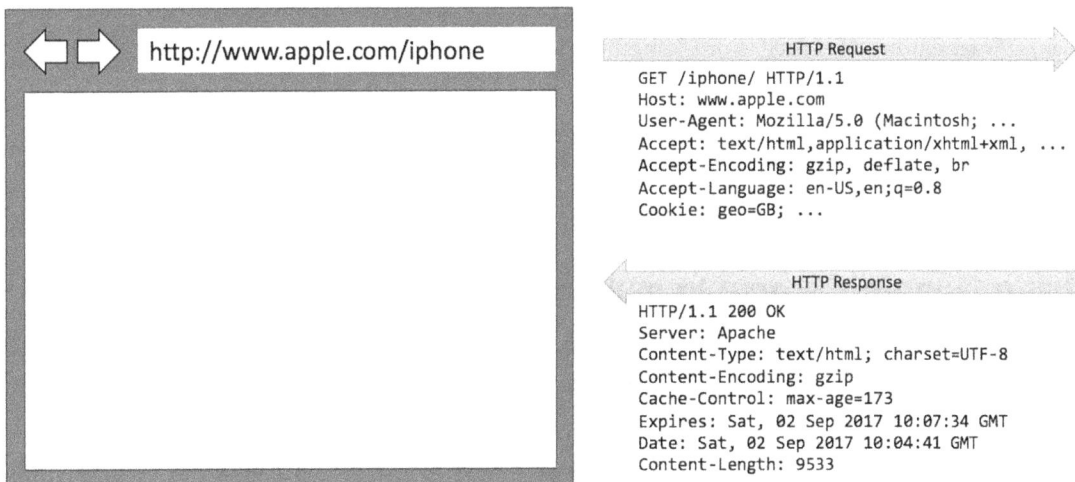

Figure 1.18: An HTTP request and response

You can use Google Chrome and other browsers to record requests and responses.

> **Good practice:** Google Chrome is currently used by about two-thirds of website visitors worldwide, and it has powerful, built-in developer tools, so it is a good first choice for trying out your websites. Try out your websites with Chrome and at least two other browsers, for example, Firefox and Safari for macOS and iPhone, respectively. Microsoft Edge switched from using Microsoft's own rendering engine to using Chromium in 2019, so it is less important to try out with it, although some say Edge has the best developer tools. If Microsoft's Internet Explorer is used at all, it tends to be mostly inside organizations for intranets.

Understanding the components of a URL

A URL is made up of several components:

- **Scheme**: `http` (clear text) or `https` (encrypted).

- **Domain**: For a production website or service, the **Top-Level Domain** (TLD) might be `example.com`. You might have subdomains such as `www`, `jobs`, or `extranet`. During development, you typically use `localhost` for all websites and services.

- **Port number**: For a production website or service, use `80` for `http` and `443` for `https`. These port numbers are usually inferred from the scheme. During development, other port numbers are commonly used, such as `5000`, `5001`, and so on, to differentiate between websites and services that all use the shared domain `localhost`.

- **Path**: A relative path to a resource, for example, `/customers/germany`.

- **Query string**: A way to pass parameter values, for example, `?country=Germany&searchtext=shoes`.

- **Fragment**: A reference to an element on a web page using its `id` value, for example, `#toc`.

> A URL is a subset of a **Uniform Resource Identifier** (URI). A URL specifies where a resource is located and how to get it. A URI identifies a resource either by the URL or **Uniform Resource Name** (URN).

Using Google Chrome to make HTTP requests

Let's explore how to use Google Chrome to make HTTP requests:

1. Start Google Chrome.

2. Navigate to **More tools | Developer tools**.

3. Click the **Network** tab, and Chrome should immediately start recording the network traffic between your browser and any web servers (note the red circle), as shown in *Figure 1.19*:

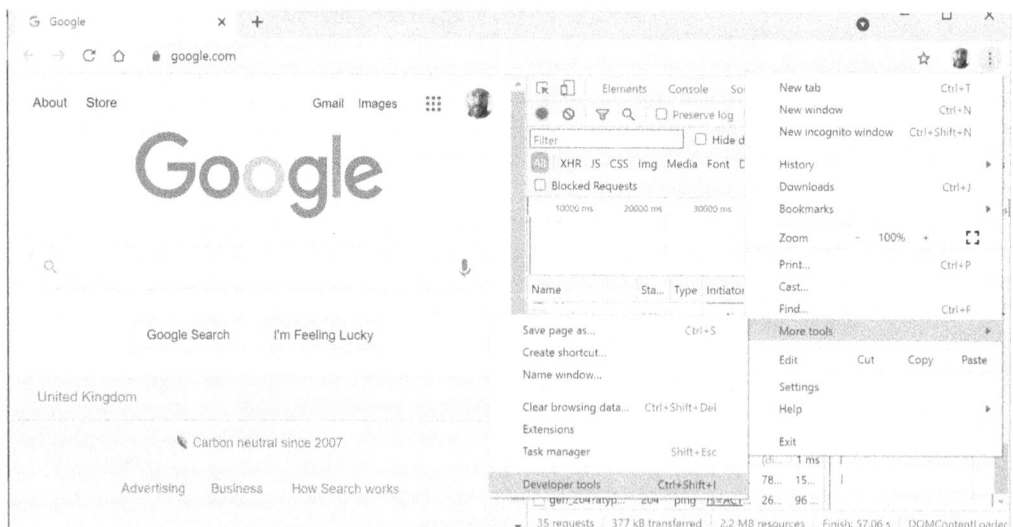

Figure 1.19: Chrome Developer tools recording network traffic

4. In Chrome's address box, enter the address of Microsoft's website for learning ASP.NET, which is the following URL: `https://dotnet.microsoft.com/en-us/learn/aspnet`.

5. In **Developer Tools**, in the list of recorded requests, scroll to the top and click on the first entry, the row where **Type** is **document**, as shown in *Figure 1.20*:

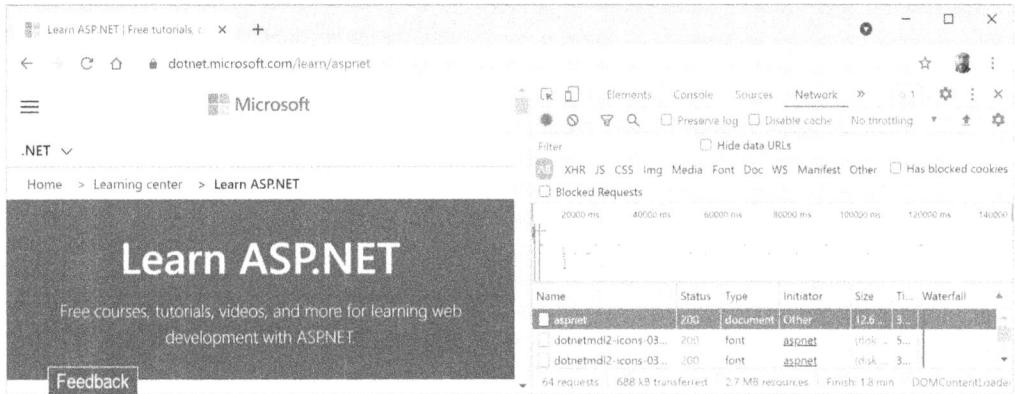

Figure 1.20: Recorded requests in Developer Tools

6. On the right-hand side, click on the **Headers** tab, and you will see details about **Request Headers** and **Response Headers**, as shown in *Figure 1.21*:

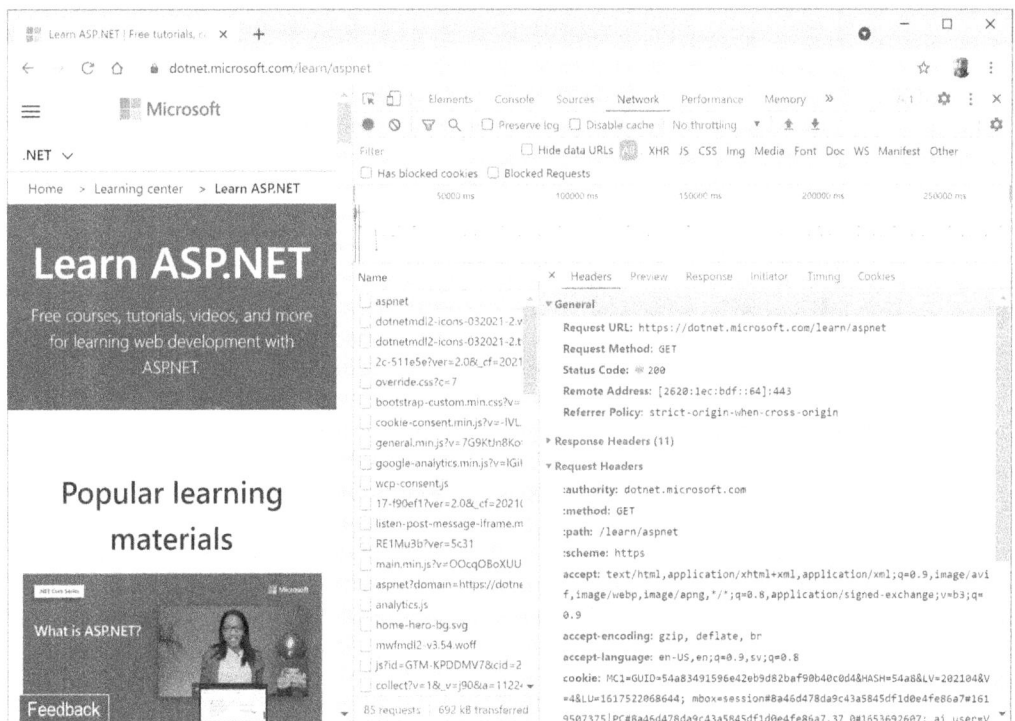

Figure 1.21: Request and response headers

Note the following aspects:

- **Request Method** is GET. Other HTTP methods that you could see here include POST, PUT, DELETE, HEAD, and PATCH.
- **Status Code** is 200 OK. This means that the server found the resource that the browser requested and has returned it in the body of the response. Other status codes that you might see in response to a GET request include 301 Moved Permanently, 400 Bad Request, 401 Unauthorized, and 404 Not Found.
- **Request Headers** sent by the browser to the web server include:
  - accept, which lists what formats the browser accepts. In this case, the browser is saying it understands HTML, XHTML, XML, and some image formats, but it will accept all other files (*/*). Default weightings, also known as quality values, are 1.0. XML is specified with a quality value of 0.9, so it is less preferable than HTML or XHTML. All other file types are given a quality value of 0.8, so they are the least preferred.
  - accept-encoding, which lists what compression algorithms the browser understands, in this case, GZIP, DEFLATE, and Brotli.
  - accept-language, which lists the human languages it would prefer the content to use, in this case, US English, which has a default quality value of 1.0; any dialect of English, which has an explicitly specified quality value of 0.9; and then any dialect of Swedish, which has an explicitly specified quality value of 0.8.
- **Response Headers** (content-encoding), which tells me that the server has sent back the HTML web page response compressed using the gzip algorithm, as it knows that the client can decompress that format. (This is not visible in *Figure 12.9* because there is not enough space to expand the **Response Headers** section.)

7. Close Chrome.

Understanding client-side web development technologies

When building websites, a developer needs to know more than just C# and .NET. On the client (that is, in the web browser), you will use a combination of the following technologies:

- **HTML5:** This is used for the content and structure of a web page.
- **CSS3:** This is used for the styles applied to elements on the web page.
- **JavaScript:** This is used to code any business logic needed on the web page, for example, validating form input or making calls to a web service to fetch more data needed by the web page.

Although HTML5, CSS3, and JavaScript are the fundamental components of frontend web development, there are many additional technologies that can make frontend web development more productive, including:

- **Bootstrap,** the world's most popular frontend open-source toolkit
- **SASS** and **LESS,** CSS preprocessors for styling

- Microsoft's **TypeScript** language for writing more robust code
- JavaScript libraries such as **Angular**, **jQuery**, **React**, and **Vue**

All these higher-level technologies ultimately translate or compile to the underlying three core technologies, so they work across all modern browsers.

As part of the build and deploy process, you will likely use technologies such as:

- **Node.js**, a framework for server-side development using JavaScript
- **Node Package Manager** (**npm**) and **Yarn**, both client-side package managers
- **webpack**, a popular module bundler and a tool for compiling, transforming, and bundling website source files

Practicing and exploring

Test your knowledge and understanding by answering some questions, getting some hands-on practice, and exploring this chapter's topics with deeper research.

Exercise 1.1 – Online material

If you have any issues with the code or content of this book, or general feedback or suggestions for me for future editions, then please read the following short article:

`https://github.com/markjprice/web-dev-net10/blob/main/docs/ch01-issues-feedback.md`.

One of the best sites for learning client-side web development is W3Schools, found at `https://www.w3schools.com/`.

A summary of what's new with ASP.NET Core 10 can be found at the following link:

`https://learn.microsoft.com/en-us/aspnet/core/release-notes/aspnetcore-10.0`.

If you need to decide between ASP.NET Core web UIs, check this link:

`https://learn.microsoft.com/en-us/aspnet/core/tutorials/choose-web-ui`.

You can learn about ASP.NET Core best practices at the following link:

`https://learn.microsoft.com/en-us/aspnet/core/fundamentals/best-practices`.

Exercise 1.2 – Practice exercises

The following practice exercises help you to explore the topics in this chapter more deeply.

How is this website so fast!?

If you care about the performance of your websites, instead of worrying about what the best web development framework to use is, learn about how the common web technologies like HTTP, HTML, CSS, and JavaScript work and how to optimize them. A deep understanding of this will provide 99% of the improvements.

As a quick introduction to what I mean, watch this 14-minute video by Wes Bos to learn how a commercial website selling 700,000 products is so fast, and note that you can use all the techniques regardless of the web development framework you use: `https://www.youtube.com/watch?v=-Ln-8QM8KhQ`.

Some of the techniques the website uses:

- **Server-rendered HTML:** "They are server-rendering all their HTML. They are not using any JavaScript framework." ASP.NET Core MVC is optimized to do this, so you will see how to do server-rendered HTML in this book.
- **Prefetching HTML:** "They are also prefetching HTML."
- **CDN caching:** "They are also using caching pretty aggressively."
- **Client caching with service worker:** "They are caching it both on a CDN around the world, but they also are caching it in your browser using something called a service worker. And what that allows us to do is you can intercept requests with a service worker and then serve up the cached version. That's especially helpful for offline."
- **Preloading assets:** "These `<link rel="preload">` tells the browser, hey, I'm going to need their logo, and these are all web fonts."
- **Critical CSS:** "You're not finding any link tags that load in CSS. What they're doing here is they are loading their CSS in a style tag before you even get to the body. As soon as this HTML is rendered to the page, the browser already knows what CSS to apply to it, and you're not going to get any weird page jank."
- **Largest Contentful Paint** (LCP): "174 ms is good." This is due to them using critical CSS.
- **Fixed-size images:** "They have fixed widths and heights for their actual images, and what that allows you to do is, if the browser doesn't know how large an image is going to be, it's going to give it zero pixels by zero pixels, and then it downloads and then it has to push down the content, that's another re-render. But if you explicitly give it a spot, you don't get any jank."
- **JavaScript:** "They split up the JavaScript by page."
- **jQuery and YUI:** "A wicked fast website does not matter what framework or whatever you're using. You can be using 15-year-old tech."

I am considering adding a chapter about client-side web techniques like these to the next edition, even though they are not .NET-specific. Please give me feedback in the Discord channel or GitHub repository for the book.

Troubleshooting web development

It is common to have temporary issues with web development because there are so many moving parts. Sometimes, variations of the classic "turn it off and on again" can fix these!

1. Delete the project's `bin` and `release` folders.
2. Restart the web server to clear its caches.
3. Reboot the computer.

Exercise 1.3 – Test your knowledge

Try to answer the following questions, remembering that although most answers can be found in this chapter, you should do some online research or code writing to answer others:

1. What was the name of Microsoft's first dynamic server-side-executed web page technology, and why is it still useful to know this history today?
2. What are the names of two Microsoft web servers?
3. What are some differences between a microservice and a nanoservice?
4. What is Blazor?
5. What was the first version of ASP.NET Core that could not be hosted on .NET Framework?
6. What is a user agent?
7. What impact does the HTTP request-response communication model have on web developers?
8. Name and describe four components of a URL.
9. What capabilities does Developer Tools give you?
10. What are the three main client-side web development technologies, and what do they do?

Know your webbreviations

What do the following web abbreviations stand for, and what do they do?

1. URI
2. URL
3. WCF
4. TLD
5. API
6. SPA
7. CMS
8. Wasm
9. SASS
10. REST

Exercise 1.4 – Explore topics

Use the links on the following page to learn more details about the topics covered in this chapter:

`https://github.com/markjprice/web-dev-net10/blob/main/docs/book-links.md#chapter-1---` `introducing-real-world-web-development-using-net`.

Summary

In this chapter, you have:

- Been introduced to some of the technologies that you can use to build websites and web services using C# and .NET
- Reviewed options for structuring ASP.NET Core projects
- Reviewed how to get help and download code solutions for this book
- Created class libraries to define an entity data model for working with the Northwind database using SQL Server

In the next chapter, you will learn the details about how to build a basic website using ASP.NET Core MVC.

Learn more on Discord

To join the Discord community for this book – where you can share feedback, ask questions to the author, and learn about new releases – follow this QR code:

`https://packt.link/RWWD10`

Join .NETPro — It's Free

Staying sharp in .NET takes more than reading release notes. It requires real-world tips, proven patterns, and scalable solutions. That's what .NETPro, Packt's new newsletter, is all about.

Scan the QR code or visit the link to subscribe:

`https://landing.packtpub.com/dotnetpronewsletter/`

2

Building Websites Using ASP.NET Core MVC

This chapter is about building websites with a modern HTTP architecture on the server side using ASP.NET Core **model-view-controller** (**MVC**), including the models, views, and controllers that make up the main components of an ASP.NET Core MVC project, and how to customize your website.

ASP.NET Core MVC is one of the most powerful and flexible frameworks for building dynamic, data-driven websites and web applications. MVC separates your application's logic, user interface, and data handling into distinct layers. This structure makes it easier to manage complex projects, reuse code, and keep your applications maintainable as they grow.

You'll learn how to create a fully functioning website using ASP.NET Core MVC, starting from the ground up. We'll begin by setting up a new project and walking through its structure so you understand where everything fits. From there, we'll explore how models represent your data, how controllers handle requests and coordinate application logic, and how views generate the HTML your users interact with.

This chapter will cover the following topics:

- Setting up an ASP.NET Core MVC website
- Exploring an ASP.NET Core MVC website
- Customizing an ASP.NET Core MVC website

Setting up an ASP.NET Core MVC website

The **MVC** design pattern is useful for complex websites, where a formal structure is needed to manage that complexity. ASP.NET Core MVC uses technologies like Razor syntax, but allows a cleaner separation of responsibilities, sometimes called technical concerns, as shown in the following list:

- **Models**: Classes that represent the data entities and view models used on the website.
- **Views**: Razor Views are `.cshtml` files that render data in view models into HTML for a dynamically generated web page.

> 🔆 **Warning!** When creating a Razor View, you must *not* use the @page directive at the top of the file! If you do, then you have created a *Razor Page* and this behaves differently. For example, the controller will not pass the model and it will be null, throwing a NullReferenceException when you try to access any of its members.

- **Controllers:** Classes that execute code when an HTTP request arrives at the web server. The controller methods usually instantiate a view model and pass that to a view in order to generate an HTTP response. This is returned to the web browser or other client that made the original request.

In the following subsections, you will review how an HTTP request is processed by ASP.NET Core MVC, create an ASP.NET Core MVC project, review how authentication works, including the identity database, configure port numbers, and review how files are managed in an ASP.NET Core project.

Example of an HTTP request processing

Let's review a simplified diagram to understand how these components work together to process an incoming HTTP request and send back an outgoing HTTP response, as shown in *Figure 2.1*:

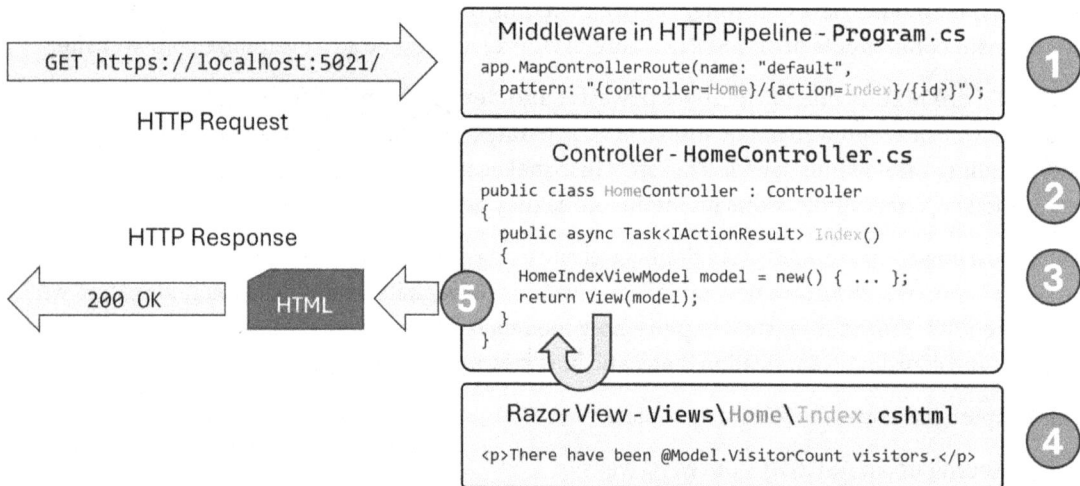

Figure 2.1: An ASP.NET Core MVC website responding to an HTTP request

The HTTP request is processed as labeled in *Figure 2.1* and as described in the following steps:

1. **Route:** In Program.cs, there is a block of statements that configures the HTTP pipeline. A default route is configured so that if no relative path is specified, it assumes a controller name of **Home** (with a class name of HomeController) and an action method name of Index. If a relative path is specified, for example, /Products/Detail/3, then the controller name would be **Products** (with a class name of ProductsController), an action method name of Details, and an id parameter value of 3.

2. **Controller:** In `<controller>Controller.cs`, the controller class is instantiated and the action method is called. If the method has parameters, they are set automatically from parameters in the HTTP request. These can come from the route path, query string, and any posted `<form>` element or uploaded file.

3. **Model:** The action method constructs an instance of the appropriate model and passes it to a view.

4. **View:** The appropriate view renders the model into a response format, typically HTML, but could be anything, like an image, PDF, JSON, or XML.

5. **Response:** The controller returns the rendered view to the HTTP pipeline as a response, including a status code like `200 OK` or `400 Bad Request`.

> The MVC design pattern, as implemented in ASP.NET Core MVC, might have been better named **Route-Controller-Model-View (RCMV)** to match the order of the components that are used in the process. But MVC sounds better.

The best way to understand using the MVC design pattern is to see a working example.

Creating an ASP.NET Core MVC website

You will use a project template to create an ASP.NET Core MVC website project that has a database for authenticating and authorizing users using individual accounts. A visitor to the website can register their email, set a password, and then log in to the website using those credentials.

Visual Studio defaults to using SQL Server LocalDB for the accounts database. VS Code (or more accurately, the `dotnet` CLI tool) uses SQLite by default, and you can specify a switch to use SQL Server LocalDB instead.

Let's see the ASP.NET Core MVC project template and its authentication accounts database in action:

1. Use your preferred code editor to open the `MatureWeb` solution.

2. Add an MVC website project with authentication accounts stored in a local database, as defined in the following list:

   - Project template: **ASP.NET Core Web App (Model-View-Controller) [C#]** / `mvc`
   - Project file and folder: `Northwind.Mvc`
   - Solution file and folder: `MatureWeb`
   - Framework: **.NET 10.0 (Long Term Support)**
   - **Authentication type: Individual Accounts** / `--auth Individual`
   - **Configure for HTTPS:** Selected
   - **Enable container support:** Cleared
   - **Do not use top-level statements:** Cleared

For VS Code, in the MatureWeb solution folder, use dotnet new mvc --auth Individual -o Northwind.Mvc and dotnet sln add Northwind.Mvc.

For Rider, right-click the MatureWeb solution, navigate to **Add | New Project...**, and in the **New Project** dialog box, select **ASP.NET Core Web Application**, for **Type**, select **Web App (Model-View-Controller)**, and for **Auth**, select **Individual authentication**, and then click **Create**.

Warning! If you are using a Windows ARM machine, like the Surface Laptop 7 that I used to write this book, then you might also want to use this CLI command to create the project because SQL Server LocalDB does not work properly on ARM!

3. Set Northwind.Mvc as your startup project.

4. In the Northwind.Mvc.csproj project file, remove the Version attributes in <PackageReference> elements because they are set in the solution-level Directory.Packages.props file, as shown in the following configuration:

```
<ItemGroup>
  <PackageReference Include="Microsoft.AspNetCore.Diagnostics.
EntityFrameworkCore" />
  <PackageReference Include="Microsoft.AspNetCore.Identity.
EntityFrameworkCore" />
  <PackageReference Include="Microsoft.AspNetCore.Identity.UI" />
  <PackageReference Include="Microsoft.EntityFrameworkCore.SqlServer" />
  <PackageReference Include="Microsoft.EntityFrameworkCore.Tools" />
</ItemGroup>
```

5. Add an element to import the System.Console class globally and statically, as shown in the following markup:

```
<ItemGroup Label="To simplify use of WriteLine.">
  <Using Include="System.Console" Static="true" />
</ItemGroup>
```

6. If you are using Visual Studio, in **Solution Explorer**, toggle **Show All Files**. If you are using Rider, then hover the cursor over the **Solution** pane, and then click the eyeball icon. If you are using VS Code, then all folders and files are already visible.

7. Expand the obj folder, expand the Debug folder, expand the net10.0 folder, select the Northwind. Mvc.GlobalUsings.g.cs file, and note how the implicitly imported namespaces include all the ones for a console app or class library, as well as some ASP.NET Core ones, such as Microsoft. AspNetCore.Builder, as shown in the following code:

```
// <autogenerated />
global using global::Microsoft.AspNetCore.Builder;
global using global::Microsoft.AspNetCore.Hosting;
global using global::Microsoft.AspNetCore.Http;
global using global::Microsoft.AspNetCore.Routing;
global using global::Microsoft.Extensions.Configuration;
global using global::Microsoft.Extensions.DependencyInjection;
global using global::Microsoft.Extensions.Hosting;
global using global::Microsoft.Extensions.Logging;
global using global::System;
global using global::System.Collections.Generic;
global using global::System.IO;
global using global::System.Linq;
global using global::System.Net.Http;
global using global::System.Net.Http.Json;
global using global::System.Threading;
global using global::System.Threading.Tasks;
global using static global::System.Console;
```

8. Close the file and collapse the obj folder.

9. Build the Northwind.Mvc project.

10. At the command prompt or terminal, use the help switch to see other options for this project template, as shown in the following command:

```
dotnet new mvc --help
```

11. Note the results, as shown in the following partial output:

```
ASP.NET Core Web App (Model-View-Controller) (C#)
Author: Microsoft
Description: A project template for creating an ASP.NET Core application
with example ASP.NET Core MVC Views and Controllers. This template can
also be used for RESTful HTTP services.
```

There are many options, especially related to authentication, as shown in *Table 2.1*:

Switches	Description
`-au` or `--auth`	The type of authentication to use:
	`None` (default): This choice also allows you to disable HTTPS.
	`Individual`: Individual authentication that stores registered users and their passwords in a database (SQLite by default). We will use this in the project we create for this chapter.
	`IndividualB2C`: Individual authentication with Azure AD B2C.
	`SingleOrg`: Organizational authentication for a single tenant.
	`MultiOrg`: Organizational authentication for multiple tenants.
	`Windows`: Windows authentication. Mostly useful for intranets.
`-uld` or `--use-local-db`	To use SQL Server LocalDB instead of SQLite. This option only applies if `--auth Individual` or `--auth IndividualB2C` is specified. The value is an optional bool with a default of `false`.
`-rrc` or `--razor-runtime-compilation`	This determines if the project is configured to use Razor runtime compilation in Debug builds. This can improve the performance of the startup process during debugging because it can defer the compilation of Razor Views. The value is an optional bool with a default of `false`.
`-f` or `--framework`	The target framework for the project. Values can be `net10.0` (default), `net9.0`, or `net8.0`. Older versions than those are no longer supported.

Table 2.1: Additional switches for the dotnet new mvc project template

Creating the authentication database for SQL Server LocalDB

If you created the MVC project using Visual Studio, or you used dotnet new mvc with the `-uld` or `--use-local-db` switch, then the database for authentication and authorization will be stored in SQL Server LocalDB. But the database itself does not exist yet.

If you created the MVC project using dotnet new or Rider, then the database for authentication and authorization will be stored in SQLite, and the file has already been created, named `app.db`.

The connection string for the authentication database is named `DefaultConnection`, and it is stored in the `appsettings.json` file in the root folder for the MVC website project.

For SQLite, see the following setting:

```
{
  "ConnectionStrings": {
    "DefaultConnection": "DataSource=app.db;Cache=Shared"
  },
```

If you created the MVC project using Visual Studio, then let's create its authentication database now by following a few simple steps:

1. In the `Northwind.Mvc` project, in `appsettings.json`, note the database connection string named `DefaultConnection`, as shown highlighted in the following configuration:

```
{
  "ConnectionStrings": {
    "DefaultConnection": "Server=(localdb)\\mssqllocaldb;Database=aspnet-
Northwind.Mvc-440bc3c1-f7e7-4463-99d5-896b6a6500e0;Trusted_
Connection=True;MultipleActiveResultSets=true"
  },
  "Logging": {
    "LogLevel": {
      "Default": "Information",
      "Microsoft.AspNetCore": "Warning"
    }
  },
  "AllowedHosts": "*"
}
```

> Your database name will use the pattern `aspnet-[ProjectName]-[GUID]` and have a different GUID value from the example above.

2. At a command prompt or terminal, in the `Northwind.Mvc` folder, enter the command to run database migrations so that the database used to store credentials for authentication is created, as shown in the following command:

```
dotnet ef database update
```

3. Note the database is created with tables like `AspNetRoles`, as shown in the following partial output:

```
Build started...
Build succeeded.
info: Microsoft.EntityFrameworkCore.Infrastructure[10403]
      Entity Framework Core 10.0.0 initialized 'ApplicationDbContext'
using provider 'Microsoft.EntityFrameworkCore.SqlServer:10.0.0' with
options: None
info: Microsoft.EntityFrameworkCore.Database.Command[20101]
      Executed DbCommand (129ms) [Parameters=[], CommandType='Text',
CommandTimeout='60']
      CREATE DATABASE [aspnet-Northwind.Mvc-440bc3c1-f7e7-4463-99d5-
896b6a6500e0];
```

```
...
info: Microsoft.EntityFrameworkCore.Database.Command[20101]
      Executed DbCommand (3ms) [Parameters=[], CommandType='Text',
CommandTimeout='30']
      CREATE TABLE [AspNetRoles] (
          [Id] nvarchar(450) NOT NULL,
          [Name] nvarchar(256) NULL,
          [NormalizedName] nvarchar(256) NULL,
          [ConcurrencyStamp] nvarchar(max) NULL,
          CONSTRAINT [PK_AspNetRoles] PRIMARY KEY ([Id])
      );
...
info: Microsoft.EntityFrameworkCore.Database.Command[20101]
      Executed DbCommand (8ms) [Parameters=[], CommandType='Text',
CommandTimeout='30']
      INSERT INTO [__EFMigrationsHistory] ([MigrationId],
[ProductVersion])
      VALUES (N'00000000000000_CreateIdentitySchema', N'10.0.0');
```

> **Warning!** SQL Server LocalDB is not yet supported on Windows ARM. According to Microsoft employee Drew Skwiers-Koballa, *"Connectivity to SQLLocalDB on arm64 remains on our roadmap, but we do not have a release that I can commit to at this time. We understand that connecting to LocalDB dramatically simplifies the SQL projects development process. You may find installing SQL Server Developer edition on the local arm64 Windows machine for developer purposes to be a suitable workaround."* The comment is at the following link: https://developercommunity.visualstudio.com/t/Unable-to-load-the-SQLUserInstanced11/10188568#T-N10695492.

> If you get an error because SQL Server LocalDB is not installed, you can install it manually using the instructions at the following link: https://learn.microsoft.com/en-us/sql/database-engine/configure-windows/sql-server-express-localdb.

Changing the port numbers and starting the website

By default, the project template assigns random port numbers to host the website. The port numbers could conflict with other port numbers used on your computer, so it is good practice to manually set them.

Let's review the behavior of the default ASP.NET Core MVC website project template:

1. In the Northwind.Mvc project/folder, expand the folder named Properties, open the file named launchSettings.json, and note the profiles named http and https. They have randomly assigned port numbers that you will change in the next step, so for now, just note their locations, as shown highlighted in the following configuration:

```
{
  "$schema": "http://json.schemastore.org/launchsettings.json",
  "profiles": {
    "http": {
      "commandName": "Project",
      "dotnetRunMessages": true,
      "launchBrowser": true,
      "applicationUrl": "http://localhost:5122",
      "environmentVariables": {
        "ASPNETCORE_ENVIRONMENT": "Development"
      }
    },
    "https": {
      "commandName": "Project",
      "dotnetRunMessages": true,
      "launchBrowser": true,
      "applicationUrl": "https://localhost:7155;http://localhost:5122",
      "environmentVariables": {
        "ASPNETCORE_ENVIRONMENT": "Development"
      }
    }
  }
}
```

The launchSettings.json file is only for use during development. It has no effect on the build process. It is not deployed with the compiled website project, so it has no effect on the production runtime. It is only processed by code editors like Visual Studio and Rider to set up environment variables and define URLs for the web server to listen on when the project is started by a code editor. In *Chapter 8, Configuring and Containerizing ASP.NET Core Projects*, you will learn about how to set options like these and how to containerize a project ready for deployment to production.

2. In `launchSettings.json`, change the configured port numbers for the `https` profile, as shown highlighted in the following configuration:

```
"applicationUrl": "https://localhost:5021;http://localhost:5020",
```

> The order of URLs in this setting is important. The first URL will be used by default, and the second will only be used as a fallback.

3. Save the changes to the `launchSettings.json` file.

4. Start the `Northwind.Mvc` website using the `https` launch profile without debugging:

    *   If you are using Visual Studio, in the toolbar, select the **https** profile, select **Google Chrome** as the **Web Browser**, and then start the project without debugging.
    *   If you are using VS Code, start the project with the `https` launch profile, as shown in the following command: `dotnet run --launch-profile https`, and then start Chrome.
    *   If you are using Rider, navigate to **Run | Edit Configurations...**, and in the **Run/Debug Configurations** dialog box, select **Northwind.Mvc: https**. At the bottom of the dialog box, to the right of the **After launch** checkbox, select **Chrome** and then click **OK**. Navigate to **Run | Run 'Northwind.Web: https'**.

    > **Good practice:** When you start a project in Visual Studio, you can choose whether to attach a debugger or not. If you do not need to debug, then it is better not to attach one because attaching a debugger requires more resources and slows everything down. Attaching a debugger also limits you to only starting one project. If you want to run more than one project, each with a debugger attached, then you must start multiple instances of Visual Studio. In the toolbar, click the green outline triangle button (to the right of **https** in the top bar) to start without debugging, instead of the green solid triangle button (to the left of **https** in the top bar), unless you need to debug.
    >
    > Another reason to start without debugging is that if you start a console app with the debugger attached, it will automatically close the console window before you can read it. To disable this behavior, navigate to **Tools | Options | Debugging | General** and clear the **Automatically close the console when debugging stops** check box.

5. On Windows, if you see a **Windows Security Alert** saying **Windows Defender Firewall has blocked some features of this app**, then click the **Allow access** button.

6. The first time you start a secure website, you might be prompted that your project is configured to use SSL, and to avoid warnings in the browser, you can choose to trust the self-signed certificate that ASP.NET Core has generated. Click **Yes**. When you see the **Security Warning** dialog box, click **Yes** again.

7. At the command prompt or terminal, note that the MVC website is hosted on the two URLs that we specified, as shown in the following output:

```
info: Microsoft.Hosting.Lifetime[14]
      Now listening on: https://localhost:5021
info: Microsoft.Hosting.Lifetime[14]
      Now listening on: http://localhost:5020
info: Microsoft.Hosting.Lifetime[0]
      Application started. Press Ctrl+C to shut down.
info: Microsoft.Hosting.Lifetime[0]
      Hosting environment: Development
info: Microsoft.Hosting.Lifetime[0]
      Content root path: C:\web-dev-net10\MatureWeb\Northwind.Mvc
```

> Visual Studio will also start your chosen browser automatically and navigate to the first URL. If you are using VS Code, you will have to start Chrome manually.

8. Leave the Kestrel web server running in the command prompt or terminal.

9. In Chrome, open **Developer Tools** and select the **Network** tab.

10. Navigate to http://localhost:5020/ and note the following, as shown in *Figure 2.2*:

    • Requests for HTTP on port 5020 are automatically redirected to HTTPS on port 5021.

    • The top navigation menu with links to **Home**, **Privacy**, **Register**, and **Login**. If the view-port width is 575 pixels or less, then the navigation collapses into a hamburger menu.

    • The title of the website, **Northwind.Mvc**, shown in the header and footer:

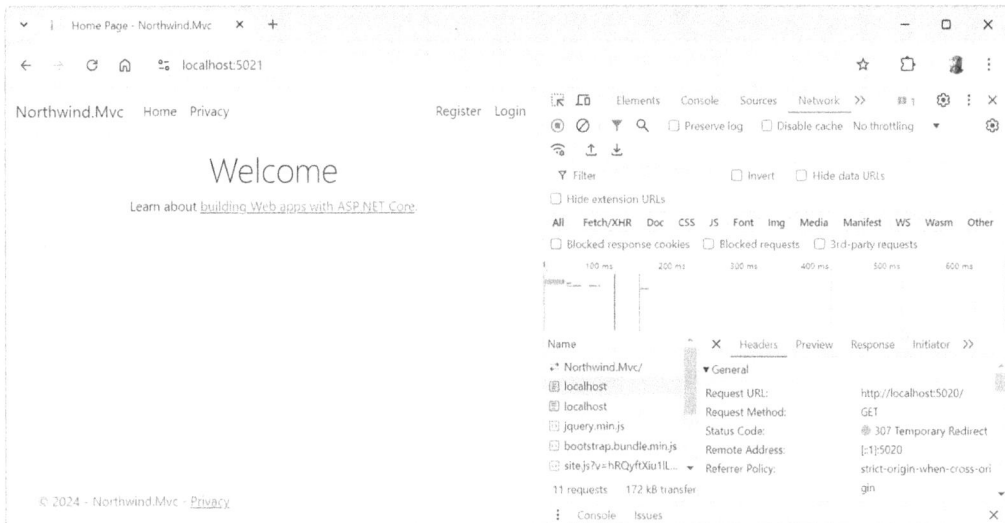

Figure 2.2: The ASP.NET Core MVC project template website home page

11. Leave the browser running.

Understanding browser requests during development

In **Developer Tools**, we can see all the requests made by the browser. Some will be requests that you expect, for example:

- **localhost:** This is the request for the home page in the website project. For our current project, the address will be `http://localhost:5020/` or `https://localhost:5021/`.

- **bootstrap.min.css:** This is the request for Bootstrap's styles. We added a reference to this on the home page, so the browser then made this request for the stylesheet.

Some of the requests are made only during development and are determined by the code editor that you use. You can usually ignore them if you see them in **Developer Tools**. For example:

- **browserLink** and **aspnetcore-browser-refresh.js:** These are requests injected dynamically by Visual Studio to connect the browser to Visual Studio for debugging and Hot Reload. For example, `https://localhost:5021/_vs/browserLink` and `https://localhost:5021/_framework/aspnetcore-browser-refresh.js`. These features can cause problems with the `MapStaticAssets` feature of ASP.NET Core 9 and later, as I will describe later in this chapter.

- **negotiate?requestUrl, connect?transport, abort?Transport**, and so on: These are additional requests used to connect Visual Studio with the browser.

- **Northwind.Mvc/:** This is a secure WebSockets request related to SignalR used to connect Visual Studio with the browser: `wss://localhost:44396/Northwind.Web/`.

Now that you have seen how to set up a basic MVC website, let's review how it implements visitor registration.

Exploring visitor registration

By default, passwords must have at least one non-alphanumeric character, at least one digit (0-9), and at least one uppercase letter (A-Z). I use `Pa$$w0rd` in scenarios like this when I am just exploring.

The MVC project template follows best practices for **double-opt-in (DOI)**, meaning that after filling in an email and password to register, an email is sent to the email address, and the visitor must click a link in that email to confirm that they want to register.

We have not yet configured an email provider to send that email, so we must simulate that step:

1. In Chrome, close the **Developer Tools** pane so that you have more space to interact with the website UI.

2. In the top navigation menu, click **Register**.

3. On the **Register**, **Create a new account** page, enter an email and password (twice), and then click the **Register** button. (I used `test@example.com` and `Pa$$w0rd`.)

4. On the **Register confirmation** page, read the note telling you how to read the documentation to enable real email confirmation, and then click the link labeled **Click here to confirm your account**.

5. Note that you are redirected to a **Confirm email** web page that you can customize. By default, the **Confirm email** page just says **Thank you for confirming your email**. You can click the **x** to close the information box.

6. In the top navigation menu, click **Login**, enter your email and password (note that there is an optional checkbox to remember you, and there are links if the visitor has forgotten their password or wants to register as a new visitor), and then click the **Log in** button.

7. In the top navigation menu, click your email address (for me, it was labeled **Hello test@example.com!**). This will navigate to an account management page. Note that you can set a phone number, change your email address, change your password, enable two-factor authentication (if you add an authenticator app), and download and delete your personal data. This last feature is good for compliance with legal regulations like the European GDPR.

8. Close Chrome and shut down the web server by pressing *Ctrl + C* in the command prompt or terminal that is hosting your website.

> If you do want to implement better email testing without sending actual emails, a popular choice is Mailpit, "a small, fast, low memory, zero-dependency, multi-platform email testing tool & API for developers," which you can read about at the following link: https://mailpit.axllent.org/.

Now that you have created an ASP.NET Core MVC project, let's review its structure.

Reviewing an MVC website project structure

In your code editor, in Visual Studio **Solution Explorer** (toggle on **Show All Files**), VS Code **EXPLORER**, or Rider, hover your mouse in the **Solution** pane, click the eyeball icon, and then review the structure of an MVC website project. We will look in more detail at some of these parts later, but for now, note the following in *Figure 2.3*:

Figure 2.3: Visual Studio Solution Explorer view of an MVC project

1. `Properties`: This folder contains a configuration file for **Internet Information Services (IIS)** or IIS Express on Windows and for launching the website during development named `launchSettings.json`. This file is only used on the local development machine and is not deployed to your production website.

2. `wwwroot`: This folder contains static content used by the website. For example, you should put images and other static file resources like PDF documents here or in a subfolder.

    - `css`: This folder contains a stylesheet for the website project.
    - `js`: This folder contains a JavaScript file for the website project.
    - `lib`: This folder contains client-side libraries like Bootstrap and jQuery.
    - `favicon.ico`: This file is shown on tabs by browsers.

3. `Areas`: This folder contains nested folders and a file needed to integrate your website project with **ASP.NET Core Identity**, which is used for authentication.

4. `Controllers`: This folder contains C# classes that have methods (known as actions) that fetch a model and pass it to a view, for example, `HomeController.cs`.

5. `Data`: This folder contains **Entity Framework Core** (**EF Core**) migration classes used by the ASP.NET Core Identity system to provide data storage for authentication and authorization, for example, `ApplicationDbContext.cs`.

6. `Models`: This folder contains C# classes that represent all of the data gathered together by a controller and passed to a view, for example, `ErrorViewModel.cs`.

7. `Views`: This folder contains the `.cshtml` Razor files that combine HTML and C# code to dynamically generate HTML responses:

    - `Home`: This subfolder contains Razor files for the home and privacy pages.
    - `Shared`: This subfolder contains Razor files for the shared layout, an error page, and two partial views for logging in and validation scripts.
    - `_ViewImports`: This file imports common namespaces used in all views, like Tag Helpers.
    - `_ViewStart`: This file sets the default layout.

8. `app.db`: This is the SQLite database that stores registered visitors. (If you used SQL Server LocalDB, then it will not be needed.)

9. `appsettings.json` and `appsettings.Development.json`: These files contain settings that your website can load at runtime, for example, the database connection string for the ASP.NET Core Identity system and logging levels. These settings can be overridden by other mechanisms like environment variables, application secrets, and command-line arguments. You will learn details about how to control settings like these in *Chapter 8, Configuring and Containerizing ASP.NET Core Projects*.

10. `Program.cs`: This file defines a hidden `Program` class that contains the `<Main>$` entry point. It builds a pipeline for processing incoming HTTP requests and hosts the website using default options like configuring the Kestrel web server and loading `appsettings`. It adds and configures services that your website needs, for example, ASP.NET Core Identity for authentication, SQLite or SQL Server for identity data storage, and so on, and routes for your application.

11. `Northwind.Mvc.csproj`: This file contains project settings like the use of the web .NET SDK, an entry for SQLite to ensure that the `app.db` file is copied to the website's output folder, and a list of NuGet packages that your project requires, including EF Core and ASP.NET Core Identity packages. To edit it with Visual Studio, double-click the project name.

12. `Northwind.Mvc.csproj.user`: This file contains Visual Studio session settings for remembering options. For example, which launch profile was selected, like `https`. Visual Studio hides this file, and it should not normally be included in source code control because it is specific to an individual developer.

Now that you have reviewed the structure of an ASP.NET Core MVC project, let's review the identity database used to authenticate website visitors.

Reviewing the ASP.NET Core Identity database

When creating the ASP.NET Core MVC website project, if you choose to enable authentication using individual accounts, then you need a database to store the user accounts, including emails and passwords. This could be a local SQLite database file or a SQL Server database. By default, the SQL Server database will use SQL Server LocalDB as the database server, but you can configure the database connection string to use a remote or cloud SQL Server instead.

> **Good practice:** Most ASP.NET Core MVC projects need to connect to other databases too. For example, our project connects to the Northwind database. Although, by default, the tables needed by ASP.NET Core Identity are stored in their own database, you could add those tables to an existing database like Northwind. This could simplify deployments by having a single database for everything needed by the MVC project, instead of multiple separate databases.

Open `appsettings.json` to find the connection string used for the ASP.NET Core Identity database, as shown highlighted for SQL Server LocalDB in the following markup:

```
{
  "ConnectionStrings": {
    "DefaultConnection": "Server=(localdb)\\mssqllocaldb;Database=aspnet-
Northwind.Mvc-2F6A1E12-F9CF-480C-987D-FEFB4827DE22;Trusted_
Connection=True;MultipleActiveResultSets=true"
  },
  "Logging": {
    "LogLevel": {
      "Default": "Information",
      "Microsoft.AspNetCore": "Warning"
    }
  },
  "AllowedHosts": "*"
}
```

If you used SQL Server LocalDB for the identity data store, then you can use **Server Explorer** to connect to the database. You can copy parts of the connection string, like the data source or server name, from the `appsettings.json` file. Remember to remove the second backslash between (`localdb`) and `mssqllocaldb`.

You can then see the tables that the ASP.NET Core Identity system uses to register users and roles, including the `AspNetUsers` table used to store the registered visitor, as shown in *Figure 2.4*:

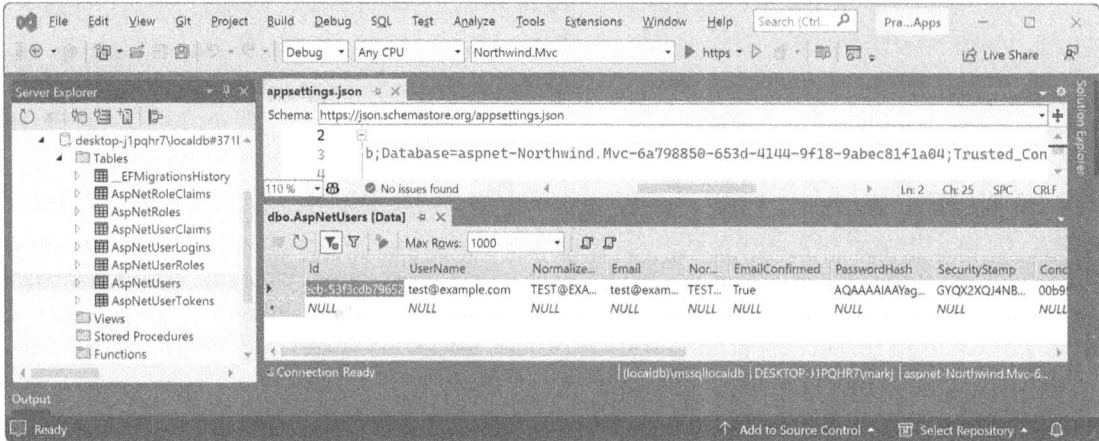

Figure 2.4: The AspNetUsers table with the registered user

Installing SQLiteStudio

You can use a cross-platform graphical database manager named **SQLiteStudio** to easily manage SQLite databases:

1. Navigate to the following link, `https://sqlitestudio.pl`, and then download and install the application.
2. Start **SQLiteStudio**.
3. Navigate to **Database | Add a database**.
4. For **File**, browse for and select `app.db`.
5. In the **Databases** pane, double-click **AspNetUsers** and then select the **Data** tab.

Configuring files included in an ASP.NET Core project

Until now, most of our projects have been simple console apps and class libraries with a few C# class files. By default, when we compiled those projects, all `.cs` files in the project folder or subfolders were automatically included in the build at compile time.

ASP.NET Core projects get more complicated. There are many more file types; some of them can be compiled at runtime instead of compile time, and some of them are just content that does not need to be compiled but does need to be deployed along with the compiled assemblies.

You can control how files are processed during a build, and which are included or excluded from a deployment, by putting elements in the project file. These are processed by **MS Build** and other tools during builds and deployments.

You declare items in the project file as child elements of an `<ItemGroup>` element. For example:

```
<--Include the greet.proto file in the build process.-->
<ItemGroup>
  <Protobuf Include="Protos\greet.proto" GrpcServices="Server" />
</ItemGroup>

<--Remove the stylecop.json file from the build process.-->
<ItemGroup>
  <None Remove="stylecop.json" />
</ItemGroup>

<--Include the stylecop.json file in the deployment.-->
<ItemGroup>
  <AdditionalFiles Include="stylecop.json" />
</ItemGroup>
```

You can have as many `<ItemGroup>` elements as you want, so it is good practice to use them to logically divide elements by type. They are merged automatically by build tools.

Usually, you manually add these elements when you know you need to use them, but unfortunately, Visual Studio and other code editors sometimes mess things up by trying to be helpful.

For example, you might have added a new Razor Page file in the `Pages` folder named `index.cshtml`. You start the web server, but the page does not appear. Or, you are working on a GraphQL service, and you add a file named `seafoodProducts.graphql`. But when you run the GraphQL tool to auto-generate client-side proxies, it fails.

These are both common indications that your code editor has decided that the new file should not be part of the project. It has automatically added an element to the project file to remove the file from the build process without telling you.

To solve this type of problem, review the project file for unexpected entries, like the following, and delete them:

```
<ItemGroup>
  <Content Remove="Pages\index.cshtml" />
</ItemGroup>
<ItemGroup>
  <GraphQL Remove="seafoodProducts.graphql" />
</ItemGroup>
```

Good practice: When using tools that automatically "fix" problems without telling you, review your project file for unexpected elements when unexpected results happen.

You can read more about managing MS Build items at the following link: `https://learn.microsoft.com/en-us/visualstudio/msbuild/msbuild-items`.

Project file build actions

As we have just seen, it is important that ASP.NET Core developers understand how project build actions affect compilation.

All files in a .NET SDK project have a build action. Most are set implicitly based on their file extension. You can override the default behavior by explicitly setting a build action. You can do this either by directly editing the `.csproj` project file or by using your code editor's **Properties** window, as shown in *Figure 2.5*:

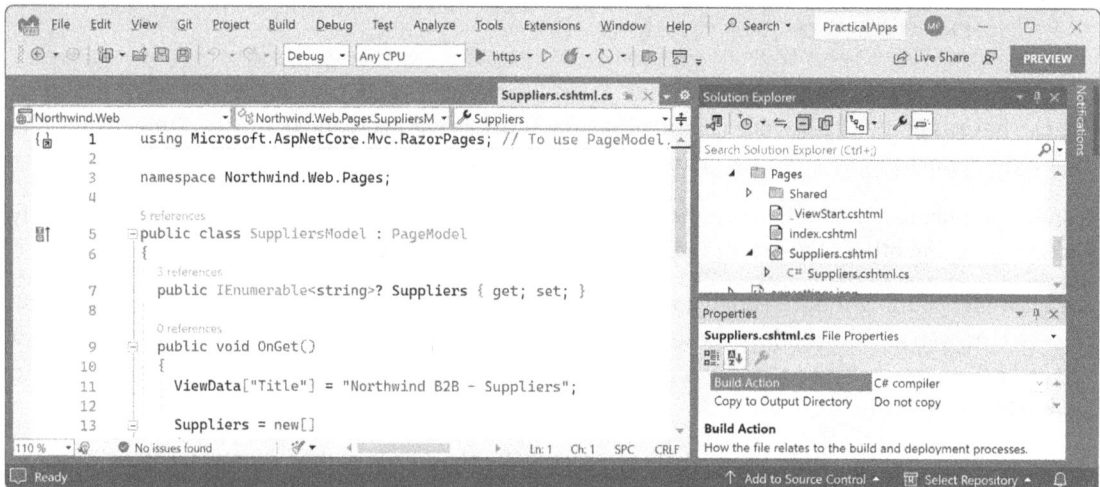

Figure 2.5: The properties of Suppliers.cshtml.cs show its default build action is C# compiler

Common build actions for ASP.NET Core project files are shown in *Table 13.1*:

Build action	Description
AdditionalFiles	This provides inputs to analyzers to verify code quality.
Compile or **C# compiler**	This is passed to the compiler as a source file.
Content	This is included as part of the website when it's deployed.
Embedded Resource	This is passed to the compiler as a resource to be embedded in the assembly.
None	This is not part of the build. This value can be used for documentation and other files that should not be deployed with the website.

Table 13.1: Common build actions for ASP.NET Core project files

You can learn more about build actions and .csproj entries at the following link: https://learn.microsoft.com/en-us/visualstudio/ide/build-actions.

We've spent a lot of time reviewing what the ASP.NET Core MVC project template provides us by default. Now let's explore how all its components fit together in more detail and extend the project with our own project items, including controllers, models, and views.

Exploring an ASP.NET Core MVC website

Let's walk through the parts that make up a modern ASP.NET Core MVC website.

.NET 5 and earlier ASP.NET Core project templates used both a Program class and a Startup class to separate initialization and configuration, but with .NET 6 and later, Microsoft encourages putting everything in a single Program.cs file. I mention this because you might work on existing projects that use the older style. At the end of this chapter, you will find an online section that explains how this works.

ASP.NET Core MVC initialization

Appropriately enough, we will start by exploring the MVC website's default initialization and configuration:

1. In Program.cs, note that it can be divided into four important sections from top to bottom. As you review the sections, you might want to add regions and comments to remind yourself of what each section is used for.

2. The first section imports some namespaces (and optionally you can add a #region to make each section collapsible), as shown in the following code:

```
#region Import namespaces.

using Microsoft.AspNetCore.Identity; // To use IdentityUser.
using Microsoft.EntityFrameworkCore; // To use UseSqlServer method.
using Northwind.Mvc.Data; // To use ApplicationDbContext.

#endregion
```

Remember that, by default, many other namespaces are imported using the implicit usings feature of .NET 6 and later. Build the project and then the globally imported namespaces can be found in the following file: obj\Debug\net10.0\Northwind.Mvc.GlobalUsings.g.cs.

3.   The second section creates and configures a web host builder that does the following:

- It registers an application database context using SQL Server or SQLite. The database connection string is loaded from the appsettings.json file.

- It adds ASP.NET Core Identity for authentication and configures it to use the application database.

- It adds support for MVC controllers with views, as shown in the following code:

```
#region Configure the host web server including services.


var builder = WebApplication.CreateBuilder(args);


// Add services to the container.
var connectionString = builder.Configuration
  .GetConnectionString("DefaultConnection") ??
  throw new InvalidOperationException(
    "Connection string 'DefaultConnection' not found.");


builder.Services.AddDbContext<ApplicationDbContext>(options =>
  options.UseSqlServer(connectionString)); // Or UseSqlite.


builder.Services.AddDatabaseDeveloperPageExceptionFilter();


builder.Services.AddDefaultIdentity<IdentityUser>(options =>
  options.SignIn.RequireConfirmedAccount = true)
  .AddEntityFrameworkStores<ApplicationDbContext>();


builder.Services.AddControllersWithViews();


var app = builder.Build();


#endregion
```

4.   Note the builder object has two commonly used properties that are complex objects in their own right, Configuration and Services:

- Configuration contains merged values from all the places you could set configuration: appsettings.json, environment variables, command-line arguments, and so on.

- Services is a collection of registered dependency services.

The call to `AddDbContext` is an example of registering a dependency service. ASP. NET Core implements the **dependency injection** (**DI**) design pattern so that other components, like controllers, can request needed services through their constructors. Developers register those services in this section of `Program.cs`.

5. The third section configures the HTTP pipeline through which requests and responses flow in and out. It configures a relative URL path to run database migrations if the website runs in development, or a friendlier error page and **HTTP Strict Transport Security** (**HSTS**) for production. HTTPS redirection, static files, routing, and ASP.NET Identity are enabled, and an MVC default route and Razor Pages are configured, as shown in the following code:

```
#region Configure the HTTP request pipeline.

if (app.Environment.IsDevelopment())
{
  app.UseMigrationsEndPoint();
}
else
{
  app.UseExceptionHandler("/Home/Error");
  // The default HSTS value is 30 days. You may want to change this for
  production scenarios, see https://aka.ms/aspnetcore-hsts.
  app.UseHsts();
}

app.UseHttpsRedirection();
app.UseRouting();
app.UseAuthorization();
app.MapStaticAssets();

app.MapControllerRoute(
  name: "default",
  pattern: "{controller=Home}/{action=Index}/{id?}")
  .WithStaticAssets();

app.MapRazorPages()
  .WithStaticAssets();

#endregion
```

Note the following about the preceding code:

- The `MapStaticAssets` and `WithStaticAssets` methods were introduced with .NET 9. They compress static assets in the `wwwroot` folder and allow MVC and Razor Pages to reference the optimized assets.

- Arguably the most important method in this section of `Program.cs` is `MapControllerRoute`, which maps a default route for use by MVC. This route is very flexible because it will map to almost any incoming URL, as you will see in the next topic.

- Although we will not create any Razor Pages in this book, we need to leave the method call that maps Razor Page support because our MVC website uses ASP.NET Core Identity for authentication and authorization, and that uses a Razor class library containing Razor Pages for its UI components, like visitor registration and login.

6. The fourth and final section has a thread-blocking method call that runs the website and waits for incoming HTTP requests to respond to, as shown in the following code:

```
#region Start the host web server listening for HTTP requests.


app.Run(); // This is a thread-blocking call.


#endregion
```

In this section, you noted the `MapStaticAssets` method. Let's dig deeper into what it does.

What does MapStaticAssets do?

ASP.NET Core 9 introduced the `MapStaticAssets` method that automatically compresses the static files, which reduces bandwidth requirements. For ASP.NET Core 8 and earlier, you must call the `UseStaticFiles` method instead. You can learn more at the following link: https://learn.microsoft.com/en-us/aspnet/core/release-notes/aspnetcore-9.0#optimizing-static-web-asset-delivery.

`MapStaticAssets` works by integrating build and publish-time processes to gather data about all the static resources in an application. This data is then used by the runtime library to serve these files efficiently to the browser.

While `MapStaticAssets` can often directly replace `UseStaticFiles`, it is specifically optimized for serving assets known to the app at build and publish time. For assets served from other locations, such as disk or embedded resources, `UseStaticFiles` should still be used.

`MapStaticAssets` provides the following benefits compared to `UseStaticFiles`:

- Build time compression for all the assets in the app:

  - `gzip` during development and `gzip` + `brotli` during publishing.
  - All assets are compressed with the goal of reducing the size of the assets to the minimum.

- The ETags for each resource are the Base64-encoded string of the SHA-256 hash of the content. This ensures that the browser only redownloads a file if its contents have changed.

As an example, *Table 2.2* shows the original and compressed sizes using the Fluent UI Blazor components library, with a total of 478 KB uncompressed and 84 KB compressed:

File	Original	Compressed	% Reduction
fluent.js	384	73	80.99%
fluent.css	94	11	88.30%
Total	478	84	82.43%

Table 2.2: How MapStaticAssets compresses Fluent UI Blazor components

MapStaticAssets compresses files during the build process. This is why you must rebuild your project if you add, modify, or remove files in wwwroot. If you do not rebuild, the compression process does not happen, and there will be a mismatch between the files in wwwroot and what is expected by the previously built project. In the output window, ASP.NET Core will write warnings about which files are mismatched, but it will allow your project to run, and you will experience unexpected behavior.

But MapStaticAssets does have a problem if you use some features of Visual Studio and you need to serve static web pages like index.html. By default, static assets are put in the wwwroot folder. Imagine that you have added some stylesheets (.css), some images (.jpeg), and some static web pages (.html) to the wwwroot folder or subfolders. If you run the website and navigate to one of the static web pages, the browser never downloads the web page, so it looks blank and spins forever. The Developer Tools console shows Failed to load resource: net::ERR_CONTENT_DECODING_FAILED. If you request a stylesheet or image, it displays correctly.

MapStaticAssets has an issue with working with static HTML files when you have Visual Studio features like Browser Link and Hot Reload.

This is because those features intercept requests for HTML files and inject <script> elements to enable their features, as shown in *Figure 2.6*. But the MapStaticAssets feature has already compressed those files during the build process, and therefore those Visual Studio features are "corrupting" the stream and the browser cannot decode them!

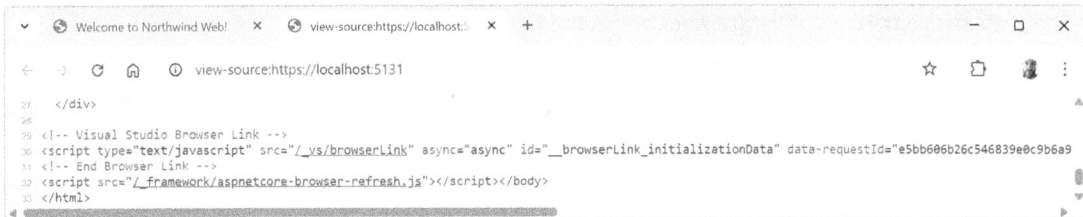

Figure 2.6: Scripts injected by Visual Studio features

Any system attempting to dynamically inject some script or other elements into the compressed file at runtime will cause problems during decompression because it has literally "corrupted" the response stream! To fix the issue, you would need to do one of the following (each has pros and cons, so there is no good fix, just choices with trade-offs):

- Disable the Visual Studio browser refresh and Hot Reload/Browser Link features by setting the **Auto build and refresh option** drop-down listbox to **None** and the **CSS Hot Reload** drop-down listbox to **Disabled** (and anything else that dynamically modifies the response stream), as shown in *Figure 2.7*:

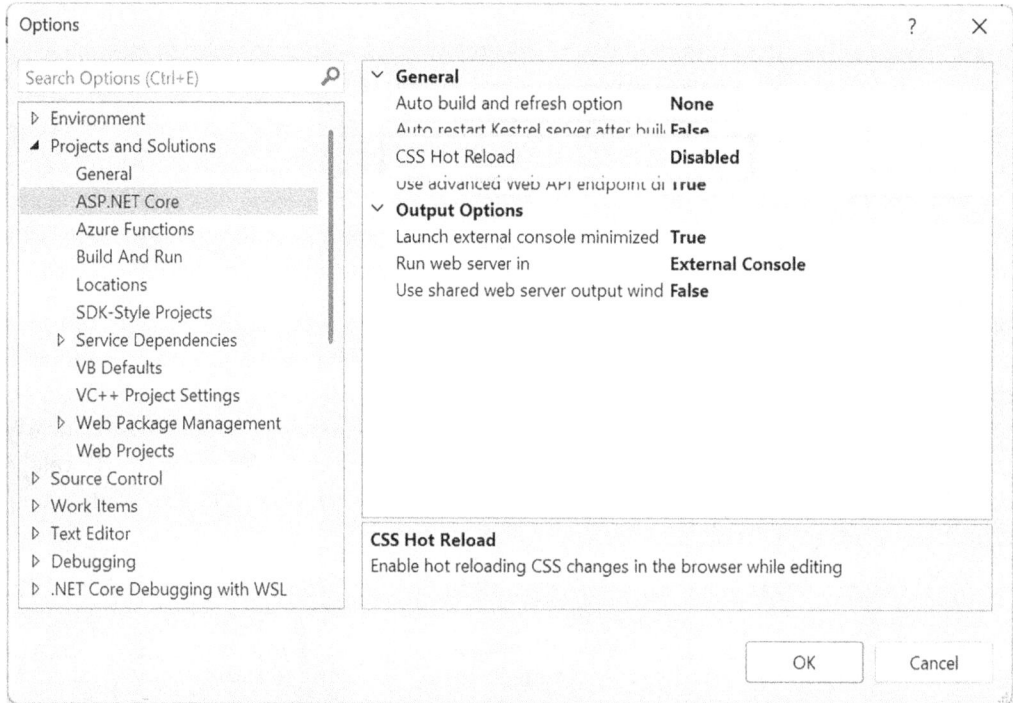

Figure 2.7: Disabling Visual Studio browser refresh and Hot Reload/Browser Link features

- Do not use static HTML files. You can map an endpoint and return raw HTML instead. But this means your HTML files are not compressed.
- Switch back to the non-compressed static file process by replacing `MapStaticAssets` with `UseStaticFiles`. But this means all your static files are not compressed.

Since the most common issue is caused by Visual Studio features, if you do not use Visual Studio, then you can use `MapStaticAssets` without worrying. And Visual Studio only injects its scripts during development, not production. So, in production, you can use `MapStaticAssets` without worrying at all. But you may have a scenario where some other system dynamically injects into HTML pages in production, and in those scenarios, you will need to consider disabling `MapStaticAssets` for HTML files.

At this point, `MapStaticAssets` is not the only method that you might be curious to learn more about.

What does UseMigrationsEndPoint do?

What does the `UseMigrationsEndPoint` extension method do? You could read the official documentation, but it does not help much, as you can see at the following link: `https://learn.microsoft.com/en-us/dotnet/api/microsoft.aspnetcore.builder.migrationsendpointextensions.usemigrationsendpoint`.

For example, although you can learn that this method activates an endpoint that lets you apply database migrations via HTTP requests during development by triggering EF Core migrations from the browser rather than needing a CLI command, it does not tell us what relative URL path it defines by default.

Effectively, it gives you a way to hit a URL like /Migrations or whatever the default path is, and the middleware will try to apply any pending migrations to your database. It's a quick and dirty way to keep your dev environment in sync without running `dotnet ef database update` manually.

Luckily, ASP.NET Core is open-source, so we can read the source code and discover what it does. You can find the source code for the relative path used by the `UseMigrationsEndPoint` extension method at the following link: `https://github.com/dotnet/aspnetcore/blob/main/src/Middleware/Diagnostics.EntityFrameworkCore/src/MigrationsEndPointOptions.cs#L18`.

> **Good practice:** Get into the habit of exploring the source code for ASP.NET Core to understand how it works.

Controlling the hosting environment

In ASP.NET Core 5 and earlier, the project template sets a rule to say that while in development mode, any unhandled exceptions will be shown in the browser window for the developer to see the details of the exception, as shown in the following code:

```
if (app.Environment.IsDevelopment())
{
  app.UseDeveloperExceptionPage();
}
```

With ASP.NET Core 6 and later, this code is executed automatically, so it is no longer included in the project template `Program.cs` source code.

How does ASP.NET Core know when we are running in development mode so that the `IsDevelopment` method returns `true`, and this extra code executes to set up the developer exception page? Let's find out.

ASP.NET Core can read from settings files and environment variables to determine what hosting environment to use, for example, `DOTNET_ENVIRONMENT` or `ASPNETCORE_ENVIRONMENT`.

You can override these settings during local development:

1. In the Northwind.Mvc folder, expand the folder named Properties and open the file named launchSettings.json. Note the https launch profile sets the environment variable for the hosting environment to Development, as shown highlighted in the following configuration:

```
"https": {
    "commandName": "Project",
    "dotnetRunMessages": true,
    "launchBrowser": true,
    "applicationUrl": "https://localhost:5021;http://localhost:5020",
    "environmentVariables": {
        "ASPNETCORE_ENVIRONMENT": "Development"
    }
},
```

2. Change the ASPNETCORE_ENVIRONMENT environment variable from Development to Production.

3. If you are using Visual Studio, optionally, change launchBrowser to false to prevent Visual Studio from automatically launching a browser. This setting is ignored when you start a website project using dotnet run or Rider.

4. In Program.cs, after the call to MapRazorPages, add a call to the MapGet method, as shown in the following code:

```
app.MapGet("/env", () =>
    $"Environment is {app.Environment.EnvironmentName}");
```

5. Start the website project using the https launch profile and note that the hosting environment is Production, as shown in the following output:

```
info: Microsoft.Hosting.Lifetime[0]
      Hosting environment: Production
```

6. In Chrome, navigate to https://localhost:5021/env and note that the plain text is Environment is Production.

7. Shut down the web server.

8. In launchSettings.json, change the environment variable back to Development.

> You can learn more about environments at the following link: https://learn.microsoft.com/en-us/aspnet/core/fundamentals/environments.

One of the first components of an ASP.NET Core MVC website that processes an incoming HTTP request is a route. You can have hundreds of routes defined in your website project, but the most important is the default route.

The default MVC route

The responsibility of a route is to discover the name of a controller class to instantiate and an action method to execute, with an optional `id` parameter to pass into the method that will generate an HTTP response.

A default route is configured for MVC, as shown in the following code:

```
app.MapControllerRoute(
  name: "default",
  pattern: "{controller=Home}/{action=Index}/{id?}");
```

The route pattern has parts in curly brackets {} called **segments**, and they are like named parameters of a method. The value of these segments can be any `string`. Segments in URLs are not case-sensitive.

The route pattern looks at any URL path requested by the browser and matches it to extract the name of a `controller`, the name of an `action`, and an optional `id` value (the `?` symbol makes it optional).

If the user hasn't entered these names, it uses the defaults of `Home` for the controller and `Index` for the action (the = assignment sets a default for a named segment).

Table 2.3 contains example URLs and how the default route would work out the names of a controller and action:

URL	Controller	Action	ID
`/`	Home	Index	
`/Muppet`	Muppet	Index	
`/Muppet/Kermit`	Muppet	Kermit	
`/Muppet/Kermit/Green`	Muppet	Kermit	Green
`/Products`	Products	Index	
`/Products/Detail`	Products	Detail	
`/Products/Detail/3`	Products	Detail	3

Table 2.3: Example URLs mapped via the default route (all but two ID values are blank)

Controllers and actions

In MVC, the C stands for *controller*. As you saw in *Figure 2.1*, the incoming request is handled by the configured HTTP request pipeline, then by a route handler, and then by a controller, which creates a model and passes it to a view. The letters MVC are not in the order of processing, and there is more to MVC than just models, views, and controllers.

The responsibilities of a controller

The responsibilities of a controller are as follows:

- Identify the services that the controller needs to be in a valid state and to function properly in their class constructors.
- Use the action name to identify a method to execute.
- Extract parameters from the HTTP request.
- Use the parameters to fetch any additional data needed to construct a view model and pass it to the appropriate view for the client. For example, if the client is a web browser, then a view that renders HTML would be most appropriate. Other clients might prefer alternative renderings, like document formats such as a PDF file or an Excel file, or data formats like JSON or XML.
- Return the results from the view to the client as an HTTP response with an appropriate status code.

> **Good practice:** Controllers should be *thin*, meaning they only perform the above-listed activities but do not implement any business logic. All business logic should be implemented in services that the controller calls when needed.

Routing to controllers

From the route and an incoming URL, ASP.NET Core knows the name of the controller; so, it will then look for a class that is decorated with the [Controller] attribute or derives from a class decorated with that attribute. For example, the Microsoft-provided class named ControllerBase, as shown in the following code:

```
namespace Microsoft.AspNetCore.Mvc
{
  //
  // Summary:
  // A base class for an MVC controller without view support.
  [Controller]
  public abstract class ControllerBase
  {
...
```

The ControllerBase class

As you can see in the XML comment in the previous code block, ControllerBase does not support views. It is used for creating web services, as you will see in *Chapter 9, Building Services Using ASP.NET Core Web API*.

ControllerBase has many useful properties for working with the current HTTP context, as shown in *Table 2.4*:

Property	Description
Request	Just the HTTP request, for example, headers, query string parameters, the body of the request as a stream that you can read from, the content type and length, and cookies.
Response	Just the HTTP response, for example, headers, the body of the response as a stream that you can write to, the content type and length, status code, and cookies. There are also delegates like OnStarting and OnCompleted that you can hook a method up to.
HttpContext	Everything about the current HTTP context, including the request and response, information about the connection, a collection of features that have been enabled on the server with middleware, and a User object for authentication and authorization.

Table 2.4: Useful properties for working with the current HTTP context

The Controller class

Microsoft provides another class named Controller that your classes can inherit from if they need view support, as shown in the following code:

```
namespace Microsoft.AspNetCore.Mvc
{
  //
  // Summary:
  // A base class for an MVC controller with view support.
  public abstract class Controller : ControllerBase,
    IActionFilter, IFilterMetadata, IAsyncActionFilter, IDisposable
  {
  ...
```

`Controller` has many useful properties for working with views, as shown in *Table 2.5*:

Property	Description
ViewData	A dictionary in which the controller can store key/value pairs that is accessible in a view. The dictionary's lifetime is only for the current request/response.
ViewBag	A dynamic object that wraps the `ViewData` to provide a friendlier syntax for setting and getting dictionary values.
TempData	A dictionary in which the controller can store key/value pairs that is accessible in a view. The dictionary's lifetime is for the current request/response and the next request/response for the same visitor session. This is useful for storing a value during an initial request, responding with a redirect, and then reading the stored value in the subsequent request.

Table 2.5: Useful properties for working with views

`Controller` also has many useful methods for working with views, as shown in *Table 2.6*:

Method	Description
View	This returns a `ViewResult` after executing a view that renders a full response, for example, a dynamically generated web page. The view can be selected using a convention or be specified with a string name. A model can be passed to the view.
PartialView	This returns a `PartialViewResult` after executing a view that is part of a full response, for example, a dynamically generated chunk of HTML. The view can be selected using a convention or be specified with a string name. A model can be passed to the view.
ViewComponent	This returns a `ViewComponentResult` after executing a component that dynamically generates HTML. The component must be selected by specifying its type or its name. An object can be passed as an argument.
Json	This returns a `JsonResult` containing a JSON-serialized object. This can be useful for implementing a simple web API as part of an MVC controller that primarily returns HTML for a human to view.

Table 2.6: Useful methods for working with views

Reviewing the project template controller

Let's review the controller used to generate the home, privacy, and error pages:

1. Expand the `Controllers` folder.
2. Open the file named `HomeController.cs`.
3. Note, as shown in the following code, that:

    •   Extra namespaces are imported, which I have added comments to in order to show which types they are needed for.

    •   All three action methods call a method on the base class named `View` and return the results as an `IActionResult` interface to the client.

- The `Error` action method passes a view model into its view with a request ID used for tracing. The error response will not be cached:

```
using Microsoft.AspNetCore.Mvc; // To use Controller,
IActionResult.
using Northwind.Mvc.Models; // To use ErrorViewModel.
using System.Diagnostics; // To use Activity.

namespace Northwind.Mvc.Controllers;

public class HomeController : Controller
{
  public IActionResult Index()
  {
    return View();
  }

  public IActionResult Privacy()
  {
    return View();
  }

  [ResponseCache(Duration = 0,
    Location = ResponseCacheLocation.None,
    NoStore = true)]
  public IActionResult Error()
  {
    return View(new ErrorViewModel { RequestId =
      Activity.Current?.Id ?? HttpContext.TraceIdentifier });
  }
}
```

If the visitor navigates to a path of / or /Home, then it is the equivalent of /Home/Index because those were the default names for the controller and action in the default route.

The view search path convention

The `Index` and `Privacy` methods are identical in implementation, yet they return different web pages. This is because of **conventions**. The call to the `View` method looks at different paths for the Razor file to generate the web page.

Let's deliberately break one of the page names so that we can see the paths searched by default:

1. In the `Northwind.Mvc` project, expand the `Views` folder and then the `Home` folder.
2. Rename the `Privacy.cshtml` file to `Privacy2.cshtml`.

3. Start the `Northwind.Mvc` website project using the `https` launch profile.

4. Start Chrome, navigate to `https://localhost:5021/`, click **Privacy**, and note the paths that are searched for a view to render the web page (including in `Shared` folders for MVC views and Razor Pages) in the exception in both the browser and the command prompt or terminal output, as shown in *Figure 2.8*:

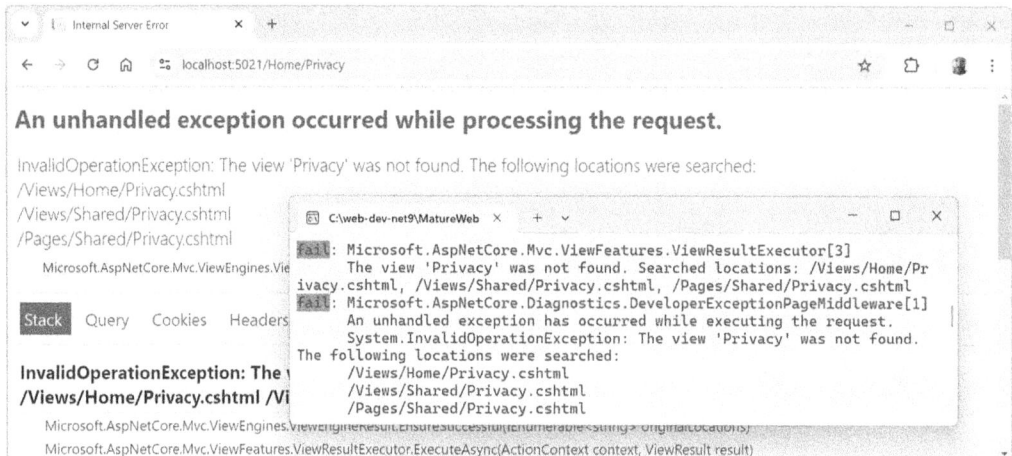

Figure 2.8: An exception showing the default search path for views

5. Close Chrome and shut down the web server.

6. Rename the `Privacy2.cshtml` file back to `Privacy.cshtml`.

You have now seen the view search path convention, as shown in the following list:

*   Specific Razor View: `/Views/{controller}/{action}.cshtml`
*   Shared Razor View: `/Views/Shared/{action}.cshtml`
*   Shared Razor Page: `/Pages/Shared/{action}.cshtml`

> **Good practice:** In *Chapter 4, Building and Localizing Web User Interfaces*, you will implement feature folders. For these to work, you override the search paths by explicitly specifying the path to Razor Views for a feature because they will not be stored under the `Views` folder, as shown in the preceding convention.

Logging using the dependency service

You have just seen that some errors are caught and written to the console. You can write your own messages to the console in the same way by using the logger:

1. In the `Controllers` folder, in `HomeController.cs`, declare a private field to store a logger, and set it in a constructor using dependency injection, as shown in the following code:

```
private readonly ILogger<HomeController> _logger;

public HomeController(ILogger<HomeController> logger)
{
  _logger = logger;
}
```

2. In the `Index` method, add statements before the `return` statement to use the logger to write some messages of various levels to the console, as shown highlighted in the following code:

```
public IActionResult Index()
{
  _logger.LogError("This is a serious error (not really!)");
  _logger.LogWarning("This is your first warning!");
  _logger.LogWarning("Second warning!");
  _logger.LogInformation("I am in the Index method of the
HomeController.");

  return View();
}
```

3. Start the `Northwind.Mvc` website project using the `https` launch profile.

4. Start Chrome and navigate to the home page of the website.

5. At the command prompt or terminal, note the messages, as shown in the following output:

```
fail: Northwind.Mvc.Controllers.HomeController[0]
      This is a serious error (not really!)
warn: Northwind.Mvc.Controllers.HomeController[0]
  This is your first warning!
warn: Northwind.Mvc.Controllers.HomeController[0]
  Second warning!
info: Northwind.Mvc.Controllers.HomeController[0]
  I am in the Index method of the HomeController.
```

6. Close Chrome and shut down the web server.

7. Now that you've seen what the different logging levels look like in output, comment out the four logging statements so they do not clutter the output from now on.

You can learn a lot more about ASP.NET Core logging at the following link: `https://learn.microsoft.com/en-us/aspnet/core/fundamentals/logging/`

As you have now seen, routes and controllers handle the flow of requests in an ASP.NET Core MVC project, but they don't manage data directly. To work effectively, controllers rely on models, classes that represent the data your website uses and the rules that govern it. Models provide the structure for storing, validating, and manipulating information, whether it comes from a database, an API, or user input. Let's now explore how models are defined, how they interact with controllers and views, and how they make it easier to keep your project's data organized and consistent.

Using entity and view models

In MVC, the **M** stands for *model*. Models represent the data required to respond to a request. There are two types of models commonly used:

- **Entity models** represent entities in a database like SQL Server or SQLite. Based on the request, one or more entities might need to be retrieved from data storage. Entity models are defined using classes since they might need to change and then be used to update the underlying data store.

- All the data that we want to show in response to a request is the **MVC model**, sometimes called a **view model**, because it is a model that is passed into a view for rendering into a response format like HTML or JSON. View models should be immutable, so they are commonly defined using C# `record` types. For example, the following HTTP `GET` request might mean that the browser is asking for the product details page for product number 3: `http://www.example.com/products/details/3`. The controller would need to use the ID route value 3 to retrieve the entity for that product and pass it to a view that can then turn the model into HTML for display in a browser.

Controllers (and their action methods) actually do things, like make decisions, using business logic; so, they have responsibilities. Models are just dumb structures that hold data. They don't decide or do anything, so they don't have responsibilities. Views just convert that data into some other format. They should not have any complex business logic in them either.

View model example

Imagine that when a user comes to our website, we want to show them a carousel of categories, a list of products, and a count of the number of visitors we have had this month.

EF Core is a natural way to get real data onto a website. In *Chapter 1, Introducing Real-World Web Development Using .NET*, you created a pair of class libraries: one for the entity models and one for the Northwind database context, using the SQL Server data provider. You will now use them in your website project.

Functionality, such as EF Core database contexts, that is needed by an ASP.NET Core project should be registered as a dependency service during website startup. The code in the GitHub repository solution and below uses SQL Server.

Let's see how:

1. In the `Northwind.Mvc` project, add a project reference to `Northwind.DataContext`, as shown in the following markup:

    ```
    <ItemGroup>
      <ProjectReference Include=
        "..\Northwind.DataContext\Northwind.DataContext.csproj" />
    </ItemGroup>
    ```

2. Build the `Northwind.Mvc` project to compile its dependencies and copy the assemblies to the MVC project's `bin` folder.

3. In `appsettings.json`, add a connection string for the Northwind database using SQL Server, as shown highlighted in the following markup:

    ```
    {
      "ConnectionStrings": {
        "DefaultConnection": "...",
        "NorthwindConnection": "Server=tcp:127.0.0.1,1433;Database=Northwind;
    MultipleActiveResultSets=true;TrustServerCertificate=true;"
      },
    ```

    > **Warning!** Modify the connection string to match wherever your Northwind database is. For example, in SQL Server in a container or local SQL Server Developer edition. If you have to use SQL Server authentication, never store the user and password in this file! You will follow good practice by setting them from environment variables in code.

4. In `Program.cs`, import the namespace to work with your entity model types, as shown in the following code:

    ```
    using Northwind.EntityModels; // To use AddNorthwindContext method.
    using Microsoft.Data.SqlClient; // To use SqlConnectionStringBuilder.
    ```

5. Before the `builder.Build` method call, add statements to load the appropriate connection string, and then register the `Northwind` database context, as shown in the following code:

    ```
    string? sqlServerConnection = builder.Configuration
      .GetConnectionString("NorthwindConnection");

    if (sqlServerConnection is null)
    {
      WriteLine("Northwind database connection string is missing from
    configuration!");
    }
    else
    ```

```
{
    // If you are using SQL Server authentication then disable
    // Windows Integrated authentication and set user and password.
    SqlConnectionStringBuilder sql = new(sqlServerConnection);

    sql.IntegratedSecurity = false;
    sql.UserID = Environment.GetEnvironmentVariable("MY_SQL_USR");
    sql.Password = Environment.GetEnvironmentVariable("MY_SQL_PWD");

    builder.Services.AddNorthwindContext(sql.ConnectionString);
}
```

6. In the `Models` folder, add a class file named `HomeIndexViewModel.cs`.

> **Good practice:** Although the `ErrorViewModel` class created by the MVC project template does not follow this convention, I recommend that you use the naming convention `{Controller}{Action}ViewModel` for your view model classes.

7. In `HomeIndexViewModel.cs`, add statements to define a record that has three properties for a count of the number of visitors, and lists of categories and products, as shown in the following code:

```
using Northwind.EntityModels; // To use Category, Product.

namespace Northwind.Mvc.Models;

public record HomeIndexViewModel(int VisitorCount,
    IList<Category> Categories, IList<Product> Products);
```

8. In `HomeController.cs`, import the `Northwind.EntityModels` namespace, as shown in the following code:

```
using Northwind.EntityModels; // To use NorthwindContext.
```

9. Add a field to store a reference to a `Northwind` instance and initialize it in the constructor, as shown highlighted in the following code:

```
public class HomeController : Controller
{
    private readonly ILogger<HomeController> _logger;
    private readonly NorthwindContext _db;

    public HomeController(ILogger<HomeController> logger,
```

```
    NorthwindContext db)
  {
    _logger = logger;
    _db = db;
  }
```

> ASP.NET Core will use constructor parameter injection to pass an instance of the
> NorthwindContext database context using the connection string you specified
> in Program.cs.

10. In the Index action method, after the statements that write to the log, create an instance of
the view model for this method, simulating a visitor count using the Random class to generate
a number between 1 and 1,000, and using the Northwind database to get lists of categories
and products and then pass the model to the view, as shown highlighted in the following code:

```
HomeIndexViewModel model = new
(
  VisitorCount: Random.Shared.Next(1, 1001),
  Categories: _db.Categories.ToList(),
  Products: _db.Products.ToList()
);

return View(model); // Pass the model to the view.
}
```

Remember the view search convention: When the View method is called in a controller's action method, ASP.NET Core MVC looks in the Views folder for a subfolder with the same name as the current
controller, that is, Home. It then looks for a file with the same name as the current action, that is, Index.
cshtml. It will also search for views that match the action method name in the Shared folder and for
Razor Pages in the Pages folder.

Complex object models

Your models can be as complex as you need, as long as they are serializable. Types like string, int,
float, and other simple types do not require any additional setup as they are inherently serializable.

A class or record can easily define an object graph like a User combined with multiple Modules, as
shown in the following code:

```
record Module(string ModuleName, [other serializable properties]);
record User(string UserName, List<Module> UserModules, [other serializable
properties])
```

So, you've now seen that models define the data your website project works with, but on their own, they don't control how that data is presented to users. That's where views come in. Views are responsible for transforming the information provided by controllers and models into HTML that users can see and interact with in the browser. Views focus entirely on the user interface, keeping presentation concerns separate from the website's business logic and data structures. Let's see how views are created, how they use Razor syntax to combine C# with HTML, and how they work with models to deliver dynamic, data-driven web pages.

Implementing views

In MVC, the **V** stands for *view*. The responsibility of a view is to transform a model into HTML or other formats.

There are multiple **view engines** that could be used to do this. The default view engine is called **Razor**, and it uses the @ symbol to indicate server-side code execution.

Let's modify the home page view to render the lists of categories and products:

1. Expand the Views folder, and then expand the Home folder.

2. In Index.cshtml, note the block of C# code wrapped in @{ }. This will execute first and can be used to store data that needs to be passed into a shared layout file, like the title of the web page, as shown in the following code:

    ```
    @{
        ViewData["Title"] = "Home Page";
    }
    ```

3. Note the static HTML content in the <div> element that uses Bootstrap for styling, for example, class="text-center":

    > **Good practice:** As well as defining your own styles, base your styles on a common library, such as Bootstrap, that implements responsive design. We will cover Bootstrap basics in *Chapter 4, Building and Localizing Web User Interfaces*, in the section titled *Prototyping with Bootstrap*.

    *   Just as with Razor Pages, there is a file named _ViewStart.cshtml that gets executed by the View method. It is used to set defaults that apply to all views.

    *   For example, it sets the Layout property of all views to a shared layout file, as shown in the following markup:

    ```
    @{
        Layout = "_Layout";
    }
    ```

4. In the Views folder, in _ViewImports.cshtml, note that it imports some namespaces and then adds the ASP.NET Core Tag Helpers, as shown in the following code:

```
@using Northwind.Mvc
@using Northwind.Mvc.Models
@addTagHelper *, Microsoft.AspNetCore.Mvc.TagHelpers
```

5. In the Shared folder, open the _Layout.cshtml file.

6. Note that the title is being read from the ViewData dictionary that was set earlier in the Index.cshtml view, as shown in the following markup:

```
<title>@ViewData["Title"] - Northwind.Mvc</title>
```

7. Note the rendering of links to support Bootstrap, a site stylesheet, and styles specific to this project, where ~ means the wwwroot folder, as shown in the following markup:

```
<link rel="stylesheet"
  href="~/lib/bootstrap/dist/css/bootstrap.min.css" />
<link rel="stylesheet" href="~/css/site.css" asp-append-version="true" />
<link rel="stylesheet" href="~/Northwind.Mvc.styles.css"
  asp-append-version="true" />
```

> The ASP.NET Core MVC project template uses a local copy of Bootstrap version 5.3.3. This might have been updated to a later version by the time you read this.

8. Note the rendering of a navigation bar in the header, as shown in the following markup:

```
<body>
  <header>
    <nav class="navbar ...">
```

9. Note the rendering of a collapsible <div> containing a partial view for logging in, and hyperlinks to allow users to navigate between pages using ASP.NET Core Tag Helpers with attributes like asp-controller and asp-action, as shown in the following markup:

```
<div class=
  "navbar-collapse collapse d-sm-inline-flex justify-content-between">
    <ul class="navbar-nav flex-grow-1">
      <li class="nav-item">
        <a class="nav-link text-dark" asp-area=""
          asp-controller="Home" asp-action="Index">Home</a>
      </li>
      <li class="nav-item">
        <a class="nav-link text-dark"
```

```
              asp-area="" asp-controller="Home"
              asp-action="Privacy">Privacy</a>
      </li>
    </ul>
    <partial name="_LoginPartial" />
  </div>
```

> The <a> elements use Tag Helper attributes named asp-controller and asp-action to specify the controller name and action name that will execute when the link is clicked on. If you want to navigate to a feature in a Razor class library, then you use asp-area to specify the feature name.

10. Note the rendering of the body inside the <main> element, as shown in the following markup:

```
<div class="container">
  <main role="main" class="pb-3">
    @RenderBody()
  </main>
</div>
```

> The RenderBody method injects the contents of a specific Razor View for a page like the Index.cshtml file at that point in the shared layout.

11. Note the rendering of <script> elements at the bottom of the page so that it does not slow down the display of the page, and that you can add your own script blocks into an optional defined section named scripts, as shown in the following markup:

```
<script src="~/lib/jquery/dist/jquery.min.js"></script>
<script src="~/lib/bootstrap/dist/js/bootstrap.bundle.min.js">
</script>
<script src="~/js/site.js" asp-append-version="true"></script>
@await RenderSectionAsync("Scripts", required: false)
```

12. In _LoginPartial.cshtml, note that the login functionality is implemented using the ASP.NET Core Identity system as Razor Pages using an asp-area named Identity, as shown in the following markup:

```
@using Microsoft.AspNetCore.Identity
@inject SignInManager<IdentityUser> SignInManager
@inject UserManager<IdentityUser> UserManager
<ul class="navbar-nav">
  @if (SignInManager.IsSignedIn(User))
  {
```

```
    <li class="nav-item">
      <a class="nav-link text-dark" asp-area="Identity"
         asp-page="/Account/Manage/Index" title="Manage">
      Hello @User.Identity?.Name!</a>
    </li>
    <li class="nav-item">
      <form class="form-inline" asp-area="Identity"
            asp-page="/Account/Logout"
            asp-route-returnUrl="@Url.Action("Index", "Home",
            new { area = "" })">
        <button type="submit" class="nav-link btn
  btn-link text-dark">Logout</button>
      </form>
    </li>
  }
  else
  {
    <li class="nav-item">
      <a class="nav-link text-dark" asp-area="Identity"
         asp-page="/Account/Register">Register</a>
    </li>
    <li class="nav-item">
      <a class="nav-link text-dark" asp-area="Identity"
         asp-page="/Account/Login">Login</a>
    </li>
  }
</ul>
```

13. In _ValidationScriptsPartial.cshtml, note this partial view has references to a pair of jQuery scripts for performing validation, as shown in the following markup:

```
<script src="~/lib/jquery-validation/dist/jquery.validate.min.js">
</script>
<script src="~/lib/jquery-validation-unobtrusive/jquery.validate.
unobtrusive.min.js"></script>
```

> **Good practice:** If you create a Razor View that uses a model with validation attributes like [Required] and [StringLength], then add this partial view to the Scripts block to enable validation on the client side by the browser, as shown in the following markup:
>
> ```
> @section Scripts {
>   <partial name="_ValidationScriptsPartial" />
> }
> ```

How cache busting with Tag Helpers works

When `asp-append-version` is specified with a `true` value in a `<link>`, `<img>`, or `<script>` element, the Tag Helper for that tag type is invoked.

They work by automatically appending a query string value named `v` that is generated from a SHA256 hash of the referenced source file, as shown in the following example generated output:

```
<script src="~/js/site.js?v=Kl_dqr9NVtnMdsM2MUg4qthUnWZm5T1fCEimBPWDNgM">
</script>
```

> You can see this for yourself in the current project because the `_Layout.cshtml` file has the `<script src="~/js/site.js" asp-append-version="true"></script>` element.

If even a single byte within the `site.js` file changes, then its hash value will be different, and therefore if a browser or CDN is caching the script file, then it will bust the cached copy and replace it with the new version.

The `src` attribute must be set to a static file stored on the local web server, usually in the wwwroot folder, but you can configure additional locations. Remote references are not supported.

Now that you've seen more detail about how controllers, models, and views work together to provide the functionality of a website, let's see some examples of how you might customize the project by defining styles, adding images, defining your own views, designing your controllers, applying cross-functional filters, temporarily storing data while processing a request, and handling configuration.

Customizing an ASP.NET Core MVC website

Now that you've reviewed the structure of a basic MVC website, you will customize and extend it. You have already registered an EF Core model for the Northwind database, so the next task is to output some of that data on the home page.

Defining a custom style

The home page will show a list of the 77 products in the Northwind database. To make efficient use of space, we want to show the list in three columns. To do this, we need to customize the stylesheet for the website:

1. In the wwwroot\css folder, open the site.css file.
2. At the bottom of the file, add a new style that will apply to an element with the `product-columns` ID, as shown in the following code:

    ```
    #product-columns
    {
      column-count: 3;
    }
    ```

Setting up the category images

The Northwind database includes a table of eight categories, but they do not have images, and websites look better with some colorful pictures:

1. In the `wwwroot` folder, create a folder named `images`.
2. In the `images` folder, add eight image files named `category1.jpeg`, `category2.jpeg`, and so on, up to `category8.jpeg`.

> You can download images from the GitHub repository for this book at the following link: `https://github.com/markjprice/web-dev-net10/tree/main/code/images/Categories`.

Razor syntax and expressions

Before we customize the home page view, let's review an example Razor file that has a model of data that it needs to render into HTML. We are doing this now so that you avoid common mistakes.

The file has an initial Razor code block that instantiates an order with the price and quantity, and then outputs information about the order on the web page, as shown in the following markup:

```
@{
  Order order = new()
  {
    OrderId = 123,
    Product = "Sushi",
    Price = 8.49M,
    Quantity = 3
  };
}
<div>Your order for @order.Quantity of @order.Product has a total cost of $@
order.Price * @order.Quantity</div>
```

The preceding Razor file would result in the following incorrect output:

```
Your order for 3 of Sushi has a total cost of $8.49 * 3
```

Although Razor markup can include the value of any single property using the `@object.property` syntax, you should wrap expressions in parentheses, as shown in the following markup:

```
<div>Your order for @order.Quantity of @order.Product has a total cost of $@
(order.Price * order.Quantity)</div>
```

The preceding Razor expression results in the following correct output:

```
Your order for 3 of Sushi has a total cost of $25.47
```

Defining a typed view

To improve the IntelliSense when writing a view, you can define what type the view can expect using an @model directive at the top:

1. In the Views folder, in _ViewImports.cshtml, add a statement to import the EF Core entity models for all Razor Views, as shown in the following code:

    ```
    @using Northwind.EntityModels
    ```

2. In the Views\Home folder, open Index.cshtml.

3. At the top of the file, add statements to set the model type to use the HomeIndexViewModel, as shown in the following code:

    ```
    @model HomeIndexViewModel
    ```

    Now, whenever we type Model in this view, our code editor will know the correct type for the model and will provide IntelliSense for it.

    While entering code in a view, remember the following:

    - Declare the type for the model using @model (with a lowercase m).
    - Interact with the instance of the model using @Model (with an uppercase M).

    Let's continue customizing the view for the home page.

4. In the initial Razor code block, add a statement to declare a string variable for the current item, as shown highlighted in the following markup:

    ```
    @{
        ViewData["Title"] = "Home Page";
        string currentItem = "";
    }
    ```

5. Under the existing <div> element, after its closing </div>, add new markup to output categories in a carousel and products as an unordered list, as shown in the following markup:

    > Instead of typing all this markup yourself, you can copy and paste it from the solution file in the GitHub repository at the following link: https://github.com/ markjprice/web-dev-net10/blob/main/code/MatureWeb/Northwind.Mvc/ Views/Home/Index.cshtml.

    ```
    @if (Model is not null)
    {
    <div id="categories" class="carousel slide" data-bs-ride="carousel"
      data-bs-interval="3000" data-keyboard="true">
      <ul class="carousel-indicators">
      @for (int c = 0; c < Model.Categories.Count; c++)
    ```

```
{
   if (c == 0)
   {
      currentItem = "active";
   }
   else
   {
      currentItem = "";
   }
   <li data-bs-target="#categories" data-bs-slide-to="@c"
class="@currentItem"></li>
 }
 </ul>
 <div class="carousel-inner">
 @for (int c = 0; c < Model.Categories.Count; c++)
 {
   if (c == 0)
   {
      currentItem = "active";
   }
   else
   {
      currentItem = "";
   }
   <div class="carousel-item @currentItem">
      <img class="d-block w-100" src=
"~/images/category@(Model.Categories[c].CategoryId).jpeg"
alt="@Model.Categories[c].CategoryName" />
      <div class="carousel-caption d-none d-md-block">
         <h2>@Model.Categories[c].CategoryName</h2>
         <h3>@Model.Categories[c].Description</h3>
         <p>
            <a class="btn btn-primary" href="/home/categorydetail/
@Model.Categories[c].CategoryId">View</a>
         </p>
      </div>
   </div>
 }
 </div>
 <a class="carousel-control-prev" href="#categories"
role="button" data-bs-slide="prev">
   <span class="carousel-control-prev-icon"
```

```
  aria-hidden="true"></span>
    <span class="sr-only">Previous</span>
  </a>
  <a class="carousel-control-next" href="#categories"
 role="button" data-bs-slide="next">
    <span class="carousel-control-next-icon" aria-hidden="true"></span>
    <span class="sr-only">Next</span>
  </a>
</div>
}
<div class="row">
  <div class="col-md-12">
    <h1>Northwind</h1>
    <p class="lead">
      We have had @Model?.VisitorCount visitors this month.
    </p>
    @if (Model is not null)
    {
    <h2>Products</h2>
    <div id="product-columns">
      <ul class="list-group">
      @foreach (Product p in @Model.Products)
      {
        <li class="list-group-item d-flex justify-content-between align-
items-start">
          <a asp-controller="Home" asp-action="ProductDetail"
            asp-route-id="@p.ProductId" class="btn btn-outline-primary">
          <div class="ms-2 me-auto">@p.ProductName</div>
          <span class="badge bg-primary rounded-pill">
            @(p.UnitPrice is null ? "zero" : p.UnitPrice.Value.
ToString("C"))
          </span>
        </a>
      </li>
      }
      </ul>
    </div>
    }
  </div>
</div>
```

While reviewing the preceding Razor markup, note the following:

- Rider might tell you that `Model` is never `null`, so you do not need to check for `null`. Visual Studio will warn you the opposite, which is why I put in the `null` check. Unfortunately, it is a common programmer error to pass an object for the model that is `null`.

- It is easy to mix static HTML elements such as `<ul>` and `<li>` with C# code to output the carousel of categories and the list of product names.

- The `<div>` element with the `id` attribute of `product-columns` will use the custom style that we defined earlier, so all the content in that element will be displayed in three columns.

- The `<img>` element for each category uses parentheses around a Razor expression to ensure that the compiler does not include the `.jpeg` as part of the expression, as shown in the following markup: `"~/images/category@(Model.Categories[c].CategoryID).jpeg"`.

- The `<a>` elements for the product links use Tag Helpers to generate URL paths. Clicks on these hyperlinks will be handled by the `HomeController` and its `ProductDetail` action method. This action method does not exist yet, but you will add it later in this chapter. The ID of the product is passed as a route segment named `id`, as shown in the following URL path for Ipoh Coffee: `https://localhost:5021/Home/ProductDetail/43`.

Now, we are ready to see the results of our customizations.

Testing the home page with categories

Let's see the result of our customized home page:

1. Start Docker and the `nw-container` container.

2. Start the `Northwind.Mvc` website project using the `https` launch profile.

3. Note the home page has a rotating carousel showing categories (when your mouse is over the carousel, it stops on the current category, otherwise it animates automatically), a random number of visitors, and a list of products in three columns, as shown in *Figure 2.9*:

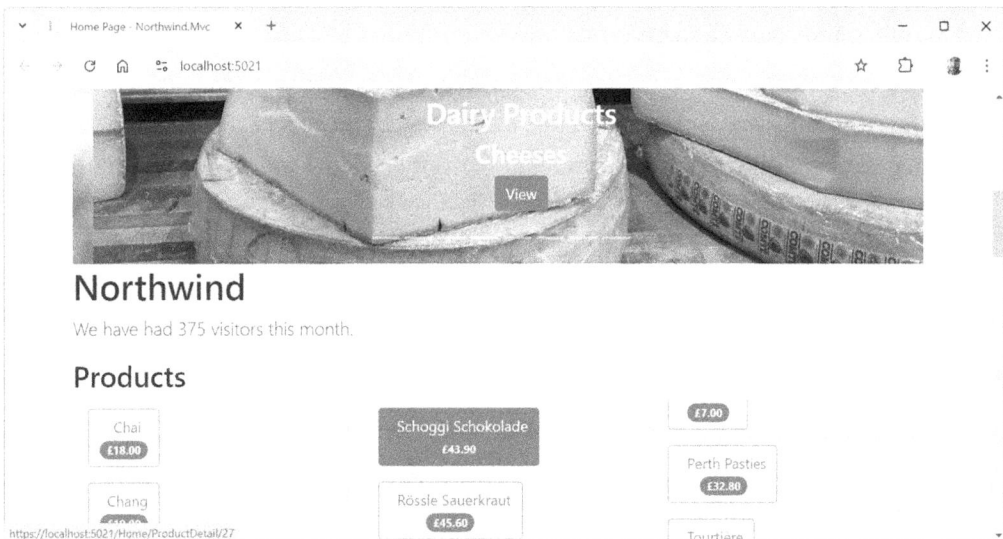

Figure 2.9: The updated Northwind MVC website home page

> For now, clicking on any of the categories or product links gives **404 Not Found**. You will fix this in the next chapter.

4. Close Chrome and shut down the web server.

Designing controllers and action methods

Designing controllers and action methods in ASP.NET Core requires careful thought about maintainability, readability, separation of concerns, and future extensibility. You could implement an entire website with extremes: either the "God Controller" (one controller with hundreds of action methods) or the "Nano Controller" (separate controllers with one action method each). Both are problematic, and good practice usually lies in a pragmatic middle ground.

Organize by resource, not by verb

Each controller should represent a single resource or functional area. For example:

- `ProductController`
- `UserController`
- `CustomerController`

This aligns with RESTful design and keeps things predictable. Each controller should handle actions that are cohesively related. Ideally, one controller per entity or bounded context. Think of a controller like a class in OOP: it should do one thing well.

Limit the number of action methods per controller

There's no fixed rule, but once a controller starts getting more than 10–15 actions, it's a sign you might need to split it. You could do so by:

- Sub-resource: `ProductInventoryController`, `ProductReviewsController`
- Use case: `AdminProductsController`, `PublicProductsController`
- Separate query (read) from command (write): `ProductsQueryController` for `GET` actions, `ProductsCommandController` for `POST/PUT/DELETE`. But only do this if your app's complexity warrants it. Don't over-engineer by applying this to everything.

Other good practices include keeping action methods thin. Business logic should be in separate services retrieved via dependency injection.

Cross-functional filters

When you need to add some functionality to multiple controllers and actions, you can use existing filters or define your own filters that are implemented as an attribute class.

Filters can be applied at the following levels:

- At the action level, by decorating an action method with the attribute. This will only affect that one action method. An example is the `[Route]` attribute that you will see in the next section.

- At the controller level, by decorating the controller class with the attribute. This will affect all methods of the controller.
- At the global level, by adding the attribute type to the `Filters` collection of the `MvcOptions` instance, which can be used to configure MVC when calling the `AddControllersWithViews` method, as shown in the following code:

```
builder.Services.AddControllersWithViews(options =>
  {
    options.Filters.Add(typeof(MyCustomFilter));
  });
```

Using a filter to define a custom route

You might want to define a simplified route for an action method instead of using the default route.

For example, showing the privacy page currently requires the following URL path, which specifies both the controller and action: `https://localhost:5021/home/privacy`

We could make the route simpler, as shown at the following link: `https://localhost:5021/private`

Let's see how to do that:

1. In `HomeController.cs`, add an attribute to the `Privacy` method to define a simplified route, as shown highlighted in the following code:

```
[Route("private")]
public IActionResult Privacy()
```

2. Start the `Northwind.Mvc` website project using the `https` launch profile.
3. In the address bar, enter the following URL path, and note that the simplified path shows the **Privacy** page: `https://localhost:5021/private`.

> The ASP.NET Core routing system is smart enough that the **Privacy** item in the navigation menu also uses the new route.

4. Close Chrome and shut down the web server.

Temporarily storing data

You often need to temporarily store data in a shared location that can then be accessed in other components of the website. This allows one part of the website to share data with another. For example, a specific page could share data with a layout for it to render, or one page could share data with another.

There are two useful dictionaries that you can write and read to:

- ViewData: This dictionary exists during the lifetime of a single HTTP request. A component of the website, like middleware or a controller, can store some data in it that can then be read by another component of the website, like a view or a shared layout, which executes later in that same request process. It is named ViewData because it is mostly used to store information that will later be needed for rendering in a Razor View.

- TempData: This dictionary exists during the lifetime of an HTTP request and the next HTTP request from the same browser. This allows a part of the website, like a controller, to store some data in it, respond to the browser with a redirect, and then another part of the website can read the data on the second request. Only the browser that made the original request can access this data.

Let's take a look at an example of each dictionary.

Example request using ViewData

For example, a typical ViewData scenario is shown in *Figure 2.10* and includes the following steps:

1. A browser makes a request for a page like the home page.
2. Middleware could store some information about the request in the ViewData dictionary.
3. The controller could store some data needed by the request, like a list of categories, in the ViewData dictionary.
4. The action method could store its title in the ViewData dictionary.
5. The shared layout could read the title from the ViewData dictionary and render it in the <title> element in the <head> section of the web page.
6. The view could read the information about the request and the data from the ViewData dictionary and render it in appropriate elements of the web page.
7. The web page is returned as HTML to the browser.

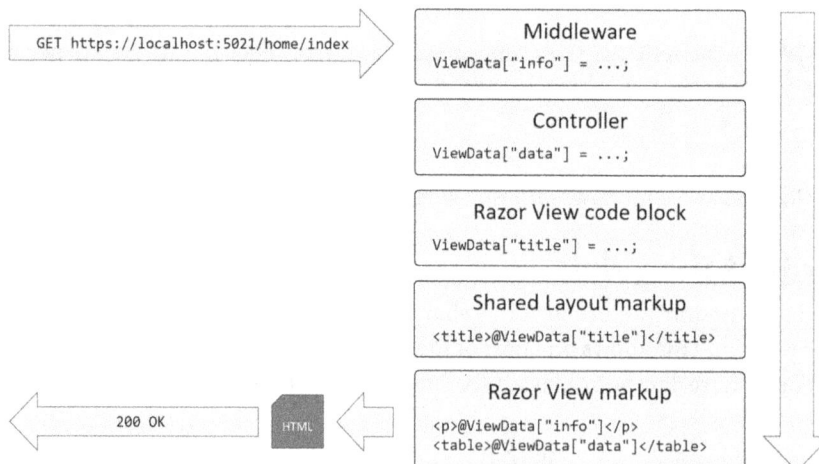

Figure 2.10: Using ViewData to share information during a single request

Example request using TempData

For example, a typical `TempData` scenario is shown in *Figure 2.11* and includes the following steps:

1. A browser makes a request for a page like the home page.
2. Middleware or a controller could store some information about the request in the `TempData` dictionary and then respond with status code 307 to tell the browser to make a second request.
3. The browser makes a second request, for example, for the page of orders.
4. A controller could read the data stored in `TempData` to process the request.
5. A Razor View or Razor Layout could read the data stored in `TempData` and render it to HTML.

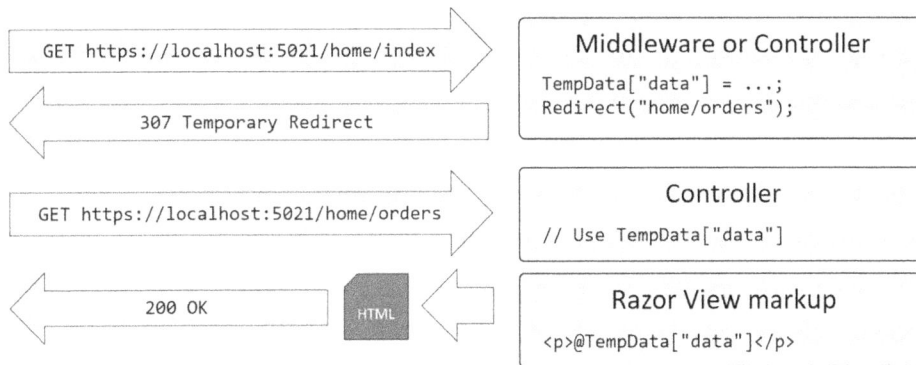

Figure 2.11: Using TempData to share information between two requests

After seeing how to temporarily store data during a request, let's end this chapter by looking at some good practices for initializing an ASP.NET Core project by separating the configuration of the HTTP pipeline and hosting in a web server.

Separating configuration and hosting

You may have heard of a file named `Startup.cs` or seen it in some ASP.NET Core projects. In ASP.NET Core 1.x – 5.x, Microsoft separated website configuration from its hosting.

`Program.cs` was used as the entry point for the website and to set up the host (web server), as shown in the following code:

```
public class Program
{
  public static void Main(string[] args)
  {
    CreateHostBuilder(args).Build().Run();
  }

  public static IHostBuilder CreateHostBuilder(string[] args) =>
    Host.CreateDefaultBuilder(args)
      .ConfigureWebHostDefaults(webBuilder =>
```

```
      {
        webBuilder.UseStartup<Startup>();
      });
  }
```

Everything else was delegated to the Startup.cs file. It had two methods to configure the dependency services and to configure the HTTP pipeline, as shown in the following code:

```
public class Startup
{
  public void ConfigureServices(IServiceCollection services)
  {
    services.AddControllers();
    // other DI registrations
  }

  public void Configure(IApplicationBuilder app, IWebHostEnvironment env)
  {
    if (env.IsDevelopment())
    {
      app.UseDeveloperExceptionPage();
    }

    app.UseRouting();

    app.UseEndpoints(endpoints =>
    {
      endpoints.MapControllers();
    });
  }
}
```

The Startup class followed a familiar model seen in OWIN, Katana, and even Java Spring's ApplicationContext. The framework looked for Startup.ConfigureServices and Startup.Configure by convention, but you could replace or extend it. By isolating DI setup in ConfigureServices and HTTP pipeline middleware setup in Configure, these were easier to mock, override, and unit test.

Starting with ASP.NET Core 6, they dropped this in favor of just a Program.cs because:

- Two separate files, with multiple indirection layers felt verbose, especially for newcomers.
- Beginners struggled to find "where the app starts" or "where the controller is wired up."
- Settings were initialized in one file, read in another, and injected elsewhere.
- To support truly minimal apps, the framework needed a more composable model.

Today, the design is much simpler, as shown in the following code:

```
var builder = WebApplication.CreateBuilder(args);

builder.Services.AddControllers(); // DI here

var app = builder.Build();

app.UseRouting(); // Middleware here
app.MapControllers(); // Endpoints here

app.Run();
```

The benefits of this are:

- Everything is in one place, with easy-to-follow top-down execution.
- You don't have to create `Startup.cs`, though you still can.
- Small services and microservices can be written in 10 lines of code.
- Roslyn analyzers and code generators have fewer moving parts to worry about.

The move to the single-file minimal hosting model is a good call for new projects. It's readable, compact, and works seamlessly with Minimal API web services. But for large-scale enterprise apps, the `Startup.cs` model arguably remains more organized, especially if you're already structuring by features and layering your services cleanly.

Separating using extension methods

In fact, you can still adopt a hybrid approach by using `Program.cs` only as a shell and move complex service registration and middleware setup to extension methods (`AddMyAppServices`, `UseMyAppPipelines`, and so on). That gives you both structure and modern simplicity.

Already, our `Program.cs` is getting cluttered. In the region that configures the host web server, including services, we have several statements that configure the database for ASP.NET Core Identity, and several statements that configure the database for Northwind.

Let's create some extension methods to do that now:

1. In the `Northwind.Mvc` project, create a folder named `Extensions`.
2. In `Extensions`, add a new file named `WebApplicationBuilderExtensions.cs`.
3. In `WebApplicationBuilderExtensions.cs`, define a class to add two extension methods to the `WebApplicationBuilder` class, as shown in the following code:

```
namespace Northwind.Mvc.Extensions;

public static class WebApplicationBuilderExtensions
{
  public static WebApplicationBuilder AddIdentityDatabase(
```

```
    this WebApplicationBuilder builder)
  {
    return builder;
  }

  public static WebApplicationBuilder AddNorthwindDatabase(
    this WebApplicationBuilder builder)
  {

    return builder;
  }
}
```

> **Good practice:** Extension methods for configuring ASP.NET Core should usually
> return the same type that they extend so that the method calls can be chained if
> the developer using them wishes.

4. Cut and paste blocks of statements from `Program.cs` to `WebApplicationBuilderExtensions.`
    `cs`, as described in the following bullets and as shown in the following code:

    *   The import namespaces to the top of the file.
    *   The statements to configure the Identity database to the `AddIdentityDatabase` method.
    *   The statements to configure the Northwind database to the `AddNorthwindDatabase`
        method.

```
#region Import namespaces.

using Microsoft.AspNetCore.Identity;
using Microsoft.EntityFrameworkCore;
using Northwind.Mvc.Data;
using Northwind.EntityModels; // To use AddNorthwindContext method.
using Microsoft.Data.SqlClient; // To use SqlConnectionStringBuilder.

#endregion

public static class WebApplicationBuilderExtensions
{
  public static WebApplicationBuilder AddIdentityDatabase(
    this WebApplicationBuilder builder)
  {
    var connectionString = builder.Configuration
      .GetConnectionString("DefaultConnection") ??
```

```
      throw new InvalidOperationException(
      "Connection string 'DefaultConnection' not found.");

    builder.Services.AddDbContext<ApplicationDbContext>(options =>
      options.UseSqlServer(connectionString));

    builder.Services.AddDatabaseDeveloperPageExceptionFilter();

    builder.Services.AddDefaultIdentity<IdentityUser>(options =>
      options.SignIn.RequireConfirmedAccount = true)
        .AddEntityFrameworkStores<ApplicationDbContext>();

    return builder;
  }

  public static WebApplicationBuilder AddNorthwindDatabase(
    this WebApplicationBuilder builder)
  {
    string? sqlServerConnection = builder.Configuration
      .GetConnectionString("NorthwindConnection");

    if (sqlServerConnection is null)
    {
      WriteLine("Northwind database connection string is missing from
configuration!");
    }
    else
    {
      // If you are using SQL Server authentication then disable
      // Windows Integrated authentication and set user and password.
      SqlConnectionStringBuilder sql = new(sqlServerConnection);

      sql.IntegratedSecurity = false;
      sql.UserID = Environment.GetEnvironmentVariable("MY_SQL_USR");
      sql.Password = Environment.GetEnvironmentVariable("MY_SQL_PWD");

      builder.Services.AddNorthwindContext(sql.ConnectionString);
    }

    return builder;
  }
}
```

5. In `Program.cs`, at the top of the file, import the extensions namespace, as shown in the following code:

    ```
    // To use AddIdentityDatabase and AddNorthwindDatabase methods.
    using Northwind.Mvc.Extensions;
    ```

6. In `Program.cs`, make calls to the two extension methods, as shown in the following code:

    ```
    #region Configure the host web server including services.

    var builder = WebApplication.CreateBuilder(args);

    // Add services to the container.

    builder.AddIdentityDatabase();

    builder.Services.AddControllersWithViews();

    builder.AddNorthwindDatabase();

    var app = builder.Build();

    #endregion
    ```

7. Build and run the website to make sure it still works as before.

Practicing and exploring

Test your knowledge and understanding by answering some questions, getting some hands-on practice, and exploring this chapter's topics with deeper research.

Exercise 2.1 – Online material

If you need to maintain ASP.NET Core projects that were built using .NET 5 or earlier, then they will use an additional file along with `Program.cs`: a file named `Startup.cs`. I have written an online section about this, found at the following link: `https://github.com/markjprice/web-dev-net10/blob/main/docs/ch02-startup.md`.

The official documentation for ASP.NET Core MVC is found at the following link: `https://learn.microsoft.com/en-us/aspnet/core/mvc/overview`.

Exercise 2.2 – Practice exercises

The following practice exercises help you to explore the topics in this chapter more deeply.

Practice unit testing MVC controllers

Controllers are where the business logic of your website runs, so it is important to test the correctness of that logic using unit tests. Write some unit tests for `HomeController`.

You can read more about how to unit test controllers at the following link:

`https://learn.microsoft.com/en-us/aspnet/core/mvc/controllers/testing`.

Exercise 2.3 — Test your knowledge

Answer the following questions:

1. What do the files with the special names _ViewStart and _ViewImports do when created in the `Views` folder?
2. What are the names of the three segments defined in the default ASP.NET Core MVC route, what do they represent, and which are optional?
3. What does `UseMigrationsEndPoint` do?
4. In a shared layout file like `_Layout.cshtml`, how do you output the content of the current view?
5. In a shared layout file like `_Layout.cshtml`, how do you output a section that the current view can supply content for, and how does the view supply the contents for that section?
6. When calling the `View` method inside a controller's action method, what paths are searched for the view by convention?
7. How does cache busting with Tag Helpers work?
8. Why might you enable Razor Pages even if you are not creating any yourself?
9. How does ASP.NET Core MVC identify classes that can act as controllers?
10. In what ways does ASP.NET Core MVC make it easier to test a website?

Exercise 2.4 — Explore topics

Use the links on the following page to learn more about the topics covered in this chapter: `https://github.com/markjprice/web-dev-net10/blob/main/docs/book-links.md#chapter-2---building-websites-using-aspnet-core-mvc`.

Summary

In this chapter, you learned how to build simple ASP.NET Core MVC websites using the HTTP pipeline, routes, models, views, and controllers, as summarized in the following list:

- **HTTP pipeline:** A sequence of middleware components that process HTTP requests and responses, allowing for handling tasks like routing, authentication, and exception handling. You will learn more details about customizing the HTTP pipeline in *Chapter 8, Configuring and Containerizing ASP.NET Core Projects*.
- **Routes:** These define URL patterns in ASP.NET Core that map incoming HTTP requests to corresponding controllers and actions for processing.

- **Controllers:** These act as intermediaries between models and views in ASP.NET Core, handling user input, updating models, and returning views or other types of responses like JSON.
- **Models:** These represent the data in ASP.NET Core applications and are used to manage and manipulate data, often interacting with a database.
- **Views:** These are responsible for rendering the UI, typically using Razor templates to generate dynamic HTML content based on data from the models.

In the next chapter, you will learn how to perform model binding, model validation, and retrieving and modifying data using EF Core.

3

Model Binding, Validation, and Data Using EF Core

This chapter is about model binding, model validation, and retrieving and modifying data using **Entity Framework (EF) Core** in an ASP.NET Core MVC website project. These concepts work together to simplify the common tasks of taking user input, processing it, and storing or retrieving data from a database.

Model binding is at the heart of how ASP.NET Core MVC applications interact with user input. When a user submits a form, the data in that form needs to be mapped to the models (objects or classes) in your application. Model binding automates this process, converting incoming HTTP request data like form fields, query strings, and route data into C# objects that your application can work with.

Model validation ensures that the data coming into your application meets the defined rules before it is processed or saved. In ASP.NET Core MVC, this is often achieved by decorating your models with data annotations like `[Required]`, `[StringLength]`, or custom validation attributes. This maintains the integrity of the data your application deals with, especially when it interacts with a database.

ASP.NET Core's model validation is tightly integrated with model binding, meaning that as soon as the data is bound to your model, the framework will automatically validate it. This is especially useful for quickly validating user inputs and ensuring that only clean, safe, and correct data is passed further into your business logic or database operations.

EF Core is an **Object-Relational Mapper (ORM)** that abstracts away much of the complexity involved in querying, updating, and managing a relational database. Instead of writing raw SQL queries, EF Core allows you to work with your data using strongly-typed C# objects called entities, which represent the tables in your database.

EF Core integrates with ASP.NET Core in a way that supports dependency injection, allowing your `DbContext` to be injected into your controllers. This ensures that each controller action method can easily retrieve or modify data. When working with EF Core, it also takes care of tasks like change tracking (knowing which objects have been modified), cascading deletes, and even complex relationships like one-to-many or many-to-many associations between tables.

Imagine you are creating a blog website. Users might fill out a form to submit new blog posts. Model binding automatically maps the form data to a Post object, which is then validated to ensure that, for example, the title isn't empty and the content isn't too long. Once validated, EF Core takes over, saving the new Post object to the database without the need to write any SQL queries.

This chapter will cover the following topics:

- Model binding and validation
- Using EF Core with ASP.NET Core
- Improving scalability using asynchronous tasks

> All solution code is available in the GitHub repository for this book. This chapter adds code to the following project: `https://github.com/markjprice/web-dev-net10/tree/main/code/MatureWeb/Northwind.Mvc`.

Model binding and validation

Model binding and validation are features of ASP.NET Core MVC that help simplify getting data from HTTP requests like GET or POST and ensure it meets specific criteria before processing.

How model binding works

Model binding is the process by which data from HTTP requests, like form fields, query strings, route data, or the body of a POST or PUT request, is automatically mapped to .NET models. This allows you to work with strongly typed objects in the controllers instead of dealing with raw HTTP data.

When an HTTP request is received, ASP.NET Core inspects the request data and attempts to bind it to the parameters of the action method or the properties of a model object. For example, if you have a form that posts data to a controller action, the fields in the form are automatically mapped to the parameters of that action or a model class, as long as the names match.

ASP.NET Core is capable of binding complex objects that have properties matching the incoming data. For example, if you have a User class with properties like Name, Email, and Address, the framework can automatically bind incoming data to these properties.

You can also create custom model binders to handle more complex scenarios or specific data transformations, but that is beyond the scope of this book.

How validation rules are defined

Validation ensures that the data received through model binding meets specific business rules or requirements before the application processes it. Validation is typically performed on models, where attributes are used to enforce rules.

ASP.NET Core uses data annotations on model properties to specify validation rules. For example, [Required], [StringLength(100)], and [Range(18, 99)] are common data annotations that enforce validation rules like non-nullability, maximum string length, and numeric ranges, respectively.

When a model is bound, ASP.NET Core automatically checks if it meets the specified validation rules. If the model is invalid, the framework adds error messages to the ModelState, which can then be checked in the controller to determine how to proceed.

In addition to data annotations, developers can implement custom validation logic by creating custom validation attributes or by implementing the IValidatableObject interface in their models, allowing for more complex validation scenarios.

ASP.NET Core MVC supports client-side validation using JavaScript. Validation attributes are rendered as data-* attributes on form fields, and JavaScript libraries can use these attributes to provide immediate feedback to users without requiring a round-trip to the server.

Let's see some practical examples, starting with passing (and validating) parameters using route values, and later by using query string and form values.

Passing parameters using a route value

One way to pass a simple parameter is to use the id segment defined in the default route:

1. In the Northwind.Mvc project, in HomeController, import the namespace for calling the Include extension method so that we can get related entities, as shown in the following code:

```
using Microsoft.EntityFrameworkCore; // To use Include method.
```

2. Add an action method named ProductDetail, as shown in the following code:

```
public IActionResult ProductDetail(int? id)
{
  if (!id.HasValue)
  {
    return BadRequest("You must pass a product ID in the route, for
example, /Home/ProductDetail/21");
  }

  Product? model = _db.Products.Include(p => p.Category)
    .SingleOrDefault(p => p.ProductId == id);

  if (model is null)
  {
    return NotFound($"ProductId {id} not found.");
  }
  return View(model); // Pass model to view and then return result.
}
```

Note the following about the preceding code:

- This method uses a feature of ASP.NET Core called **model binding** to automatically match the `id` value passed in the route to the parameter named `id` in the method.

- Inside the method, we check to see whether `id` does not have a value, and if so, we call the `BadRequest` method to return a `400` status code with a custom message explaining the correct URL path format.

- Otherwise, we can connect to the database and try to retrieve a product using the `id` value and include the related category information so we can see its name.

- If we find a product, we pass it to a view; otherwise, we call the `NotFound` method to return a `404` status code and a custom message explaining that a product with that ID was not found in the database. The view then renders the passed model into HTML, which is then returned in an HTTP response from the web server to the browser.

3. In the `Views\Home` folder, add a new Razor View file named `ProductDetail.cshtml`. (In Visual Studio, the item template is named **Razor View – Empty**. At the command prompt or terminal, enter `dotnet new view -n ProductDetail`.)

> **Warning!** Be careful not to add a Razor Page. If you do, then the file will have an `@page` directive at the top, which will prevent the model from being passed from the controller to the view, and you will get a `NullReferenceException`.

4. Modify the contents to render a product using Razor expressions and an HTML definition list, `<dl>`, with terms, `<dt>`, and definitions, `<dd>`, as shown in the following markup:

```
@model Northwind.EntityModels.Product
@{
   ViewData["Title"] = $"Product Detail - {Model.ProductName}";
}
<h2>Product Detail</h2>
<hr />
<div>
  <dl>
    <dt>Product Id</dt>
    <dd>@Model.ProductId</dd>
    <dt>Product Name</dt>
    <dd>@Model.ProductName</dd>
    <dt>Category</dt>
    <dd>@Model.CategoryId - @Model.Category?.CategoryName</dd>
    <dt>Unit Price</dt>
    <dd>@(Model.UnitPrice is null ? "zero" :
          Model.UnitPrice.Value.ToString("C"))</dd>
```

```
        <dt>Units In Stock</dt>
        <dd>@Model.UnitsInStock</dd>
      </dl>
    </div>
```

5. Start the `Northwind.Mvc` project using the `https` launch profile.

6. When the home page appears with the list of products, click on one of them, for example, the second product, **Chang**.

7. Note the URL path in the browser's address bar, the page title shown in the browser tab, and the product details page, as shown in *Figure 3.1*:

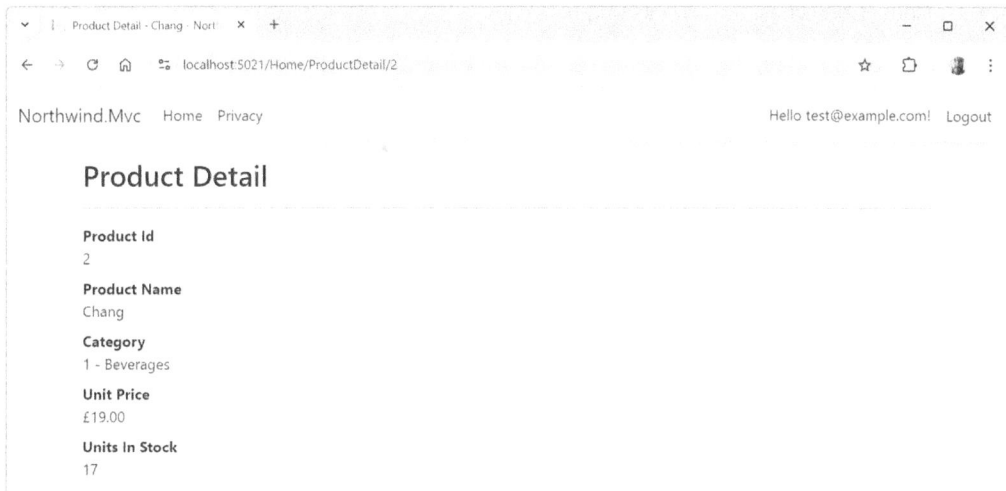

Figure 3.1: The product details page for Chang

8. View **Developer Tools**.

9. Edit the URL in the address box of Chrome to request a product ID that does not exist, like 99, and note the `404 Not Found` status code and custom error response.

10. Close Chrome and shut down the web server.

Model binders in detail

Model binders are a powerful yet easy way to set parameters of action methods based on values passed in an HTTP request, and the default one does a lot for you. After the default route identifies a controller class to instantiate and an action method to call, if that method has parameters, then those parameters need to have values set.

Model binders do this by looking for parameter values passed in the HTTP request as any of the following types of parameters:

*   **Route parameter,** like id, as we used in the previous section, as shown in the following URL path: `/Home/ProductDetail/2`

*   **Query string parameter,** as shown in the following URL path: `/Home/ProductDetail?id=2`

- **Form input parameter**, as shown in the following markup:

```
<form action="post" action="/Home/ProductDetail">
  <input type="text" name="id" value="2" />
  <input type="submit" />
</form>
```

Model binders can populate almost any type:

- Simple types, like `int`, `string`, `DateTime`, and `bool`
- Complex types defined by `class`, `record`, or `struct`
- Collection types, like arrays and lists

The process of model binding can cause errors, for example, data type conversions or validation errors if the model has been decorated with validation rules. What data has been bound, and any binding or validation errors are stored in `ControllerBase.ModelState`.

> **Good practice:** Data validation is not just about complying with business rules. It is also important for security. A lack of validation opens the door to various types of attacks that can compromise the integrity, confidentiality, and availability of your system. For example, it helps prevent SQL injection and **Cross-Site Scripting (XSS)** attacks.

Disambiguating action methods

When you have a `<form>` element in an ASP.NET Core MVC view, by default, when you trigger the form to submit, you will "post back" to the same route and its associated action method that was used to generate the view and its form. But you will want to process the contents of the form that was submitted and, therefore, execute a different action method.

For example, a `HomeController` that allows the visitor to add new products to a database with an action method to initially generate the view with its form might look like the following code:

```
public IActionResult AddProduct()
{
  return View(); // The page with a blank product form to fill in and submit.
}
```

And the action method to process the submitted form might look like the following code:

```
public IActionResult AddProduct(Product productToAdd)
{
  // Code to insert the product into the database.

  return View(); // Show success or failure.
}
```

Although the C# compiler can differentiate between the two AddProduct methods by noting that the signatures are different, from the point of view of routing an HTTP request, both methods are potential matches for the route /home/addproduct.

We need an HTTP-specific way to disambiguate the action methods. We could do this by creating different names for the actions, but we want to reuse the same action method name for both since they work together. To specify that one method should be used for a specific HTTP verb, like GET, POST, DELETE, and so on, you decorate the action method with one of the following attributes: [HttpGet], [HttpPost], [HttpDelete], and so on.

Let's create a somewhat artificial example to illustrate what can be achieved using the default model binder and what we can do with the model state by applying some validation rules to the bound model and showing invalid data messages in the view:

1. In the Models folder, add a new file named Thing.cs. This will represent an entity model.

2. Modify the contents to define a record with three properties: a nullable integer named Id, a string named Color, and a string named Email, each with appropriate validation attributes, as shown in the following code:

    ```
    // To use [Range], [Required], [EmailAddress].
    using System.ComponentModel.DataAnnotations;

    namespace Northwind.Mvc.Models;

    public record Thing(
      [Range(1, 10)] int? Id,
      [Required] string? Color,
      [EmailAddress] string? Email
    );
    ```

3. In the Models folder, add a new class file named HomeModelBindingViewModel.cs. This will represent a view model.

4. Modify its contents to define a record with properties to store the bound model, a flag to indicate that there are errors, and a sequence of error messages, as shown in the following code:

    ```
    namespace Northwind.Mvc.Models;

    public record HomeModelBindingViewModel(
      Thing Thing,
      bool HasErrors,
      IEnumerable<string> ValidationErrors);
    ```

5. In HomeController, add two new action methods, one to show a page with a form and one to display a thing with a parameter using your new model type, as shown in the following code:

```
// This action method will handle GET and other requests except POST.
public IActionResult ModelBinding()
{
  return View(); // The page with a form to submit.
}


[HttpPost] // This action method will handle POST requests.
public IActionResult ModelBinding(Thing thing)
{
  HomeModelBindingViewModel model = new(
    Thing: thing, HasErrors: !ModelState.IsValid,
    ValidationErrors: ModelState.Values
      .SelectMany(state => state.Errors)
      .Select(error => error.ErrorMessage)
  );
  return View(model); // Show the model bound thing.
}
```

> The first ModelBinding action method will implicitly be used for all other types of HTTP requests, like GET, PUT, DELETE, and so on, because the second ModelBinding action method is decorated with [HttpPost].

> **Good practice:** While the preceding code passes the validation errors to the view for display, alternatives would be to call a method like BadRequest or Problem to return an HTTP error status code with details of the problem. You will see more alternatives like these later in this section.

6. In the Views\Home folder, add a new **Razor View – Empty** file named ModelBinding.cshtml.

7. Modify its contents, as shown in the following markup:

```
@model HomeModelBindingViewModel
@{
  ViewData["Title"] = "Model Binding Demo";
}
<h1>@ViewData["Title"]</h1>
<div>
  Enter values for your thing in the following form:
</div>
<form method="POST" action="/home/modelbinding?id=3">
```

```
    <input name="color" value="Red" />
    <input name="email" value="test@example.com" />
    <input type="submit" />
</form>
@if (Model is not null)
{
<h2>Submitted Thing</h2>
<hr />
<div>
    <dl class="dl-horizontal">
      <dt>Model.Thing.Id</dt>
      <dd>@Model.Thing.Id</dd>
      <dt>Model.Thing.Color</dt>
      <dd>@Model.Thing.Color</dd>
      <dt>Model.Thing.Email</dt>
      <dd>@Model.Thing.Email</dd>
    </dl>
</div>
    @if (Model.HasErrors)
    {
    <div>
      @foreach(string errorMessage in Model.ValidationErrors)
      {
        <div class="alert alert-danger" role="alert">@errorMessage</div>
      }
    </div>
    }
}

@* The following is required to enable validation. *@
@section Scripts {
  <partial name="_ValidationScriptsPartial" />
}
```

8. In the Views\Shared folder, in _Layout.cshtml, after the **Home** navigation menu item, add a menu item for **Model Binding**, as shown highlighted in the following markup:

```
<li class="nav-item">
  <a class="nav-link text-dark" asp-area="" asp-controller="Home" asp-
action="Index">Home</a>
</li>
```

```
<li class="nav-item">
  <a class="nav-link text-dark" asp-area="" asp-controller="Home"
    asp-action="ModelBinding">Model Binding</a>
</li>
```

9. Start the `Northwind.Mvc` website project using the `https` launch profile.

10. In the top navigation menu, click **Model Binding**.

11. On the **Model Binding Demo** page, click the **Submit** button. Note the value for the `Id` property is set from the query string parameter in the `action` attribute of the form (`?id=3`), and the values for the color and email properties are set from the form input elements, as shown in *Figure 3.2*:

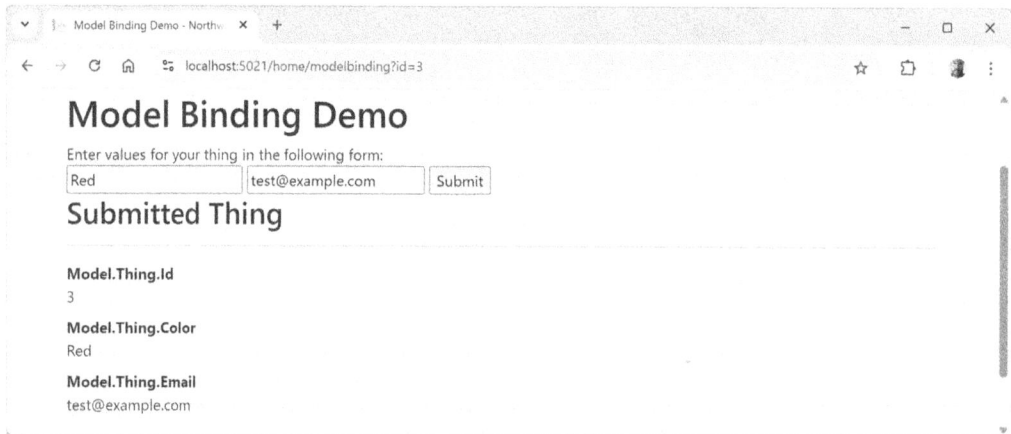

Figure 3.2: The Model Binding Demo page

12. Close Chrome and shut down the web server.

Passing a route parameter

Now we will set the property using a route parameter:

1. In the `Views\Home` folder, in `ModelBinding.cshtml`, modify the action for the form to pass the value of 2 as an MVC route parameter, as shown in the following markup:

```
<form method="POST" action="/home/modelbinding/2?id=3">
```

2. Start the `Northwind.Mvc` website project using the `https` launch profile.

3. On the home page, click **Model Binding**.

4. Click the **Submit** button, and note that the value for the `Id` property is set from the route parameter.

5. Close Chrome and shut down the web server.

Passing a form parameter

Now we will set the property using a form parameter:

1. In the `Views\Home` folder, in `ModelBinding.cshtml`, modify the action for the form to pass the value of 1 as a form element parameter, as shown highlighted in the following markup:

```
<form method="POST" action="/home/modelbinding/2?id=3">
  <input name="id" value="1" />
  <input name="color" value="Red" />
  <input name="email" value="test@example.com" />
  <input type="submit" />
</form>
```

2. Start the `Northwind.Mvc` website project using the `https` launch profile.

3. On the home page, click **Model Binding**.

4. Click the **Submit** button, and note that the values for all the properties are set from the form element parameters.

> **Good practice:** If you have multiple parameters with the same name, then remember that form parameters have the highest priority and query string parameters have the lowest priority for automatic model binding.

5. Enter an `Id` value of 13, clear the **Color** textbox, delete the @ from the email address, click the **Submit** button, and note the error messages, as shown in *Figure 3.3*:

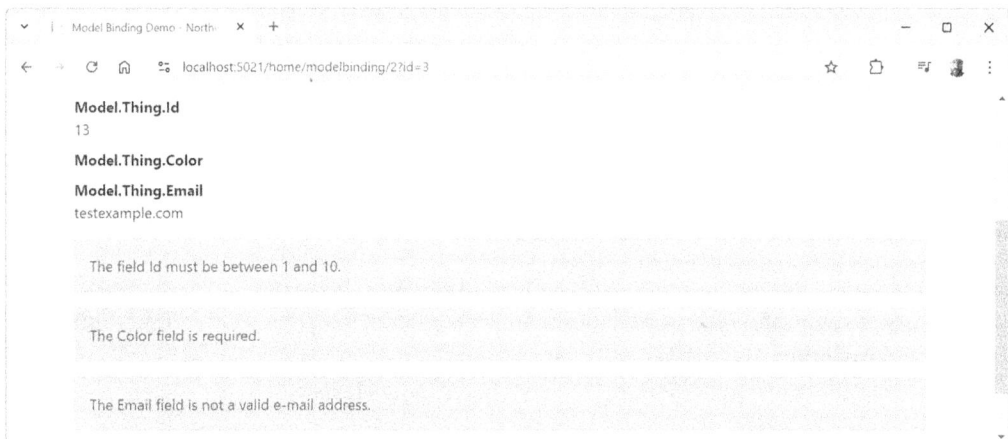

Figure 3.3: The Model Binding Demo page with field validations

6. Close Chrome and shut down the web server.

> **Good practice:** What regular expression does Microsoft use for the implementation of the `EmailAddress` validation attribute? Find out at the following link: `https://github.com/microsoft/referencesource/blob/5697c29004a34d80acdaf5742d7e699022c64ecd/System.ComponentModel.DataAnnotations/DataAnnotations/EmailAddressAttribute.cs#L54`.

You can summarize model binding as shown in *Figure 3.4*:

```
app.MapControllerRoute(name: "default",
    pattern: "{controller=Home}/{action=Index}/{id?}");
```

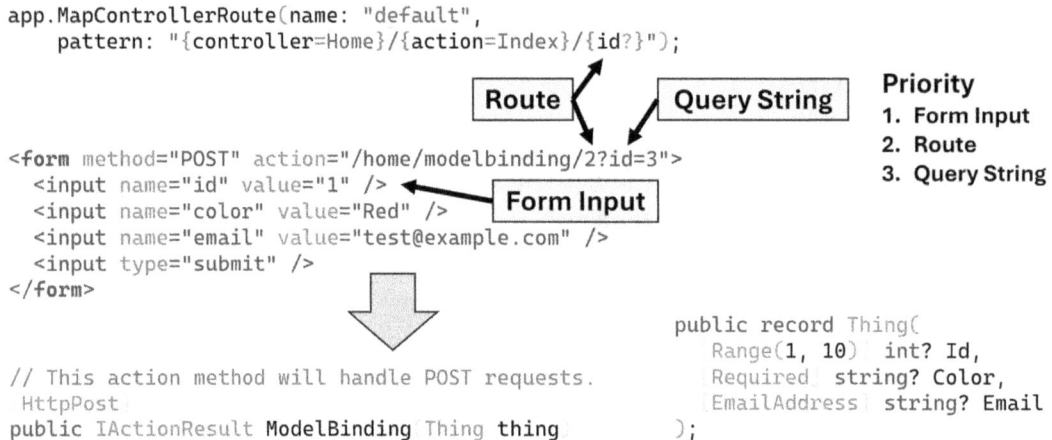

```
<form method="POST" action="/home/modelbinding/2?id=3">
  <input name="id" value="1" />
  <input name="color" value="Red" />
  <input name="email" value="test@example.com" />
  <input type="submit" />
</form>
```

```
// This action method will handle POST requests.
 HttpPost
public IActionResult ModelBinding Thing thing
```

```
public record Thing(
    Range(1, 10) int? Id,
    Required string? Color,
    EmailAddress string? Email
);
```

Priority
1. Form Input
2. Route
3. Query String

Figure 3.4: Summary of model binding

The model binder in ASP.NET Core can do a lot for you automatically, but at the cost of potentially opening your website to attacks. Let's review a common attack that takes advantage of easy model binding so that you can mitigate it.

Avoiding over-posting, a.k.a. mass assignment attacks

Over-posting, also known as mass assignment, is a vulnerability where an attacker sends unexpected data in an HTTP request that might map to properties of your model that were not meant to be exposed or modified. This can happen when an attacker manipulates form fields or query parameters to include additional data not meant to be bound.

For example, imagine a model representing a user profile with fields like `Username`, `Email`, and `IsAdmin`. If your form is only intended to update the `Username` and `Email`, but you inadvertently expose the `IsAdmin` field to model binding because you've declared the parameter to be a `UserProfile` object, an attacker could include that field in the request, potentially elevating their privileges.

To defend against over-posting, ASP.NET Core MVC's model binding and validation should be fine-tuned:

- Use custom models (rather than directly exposing your domain models) to ensure that only the fields you intend to update are bindable.
- Apply validation attributes and explicitly define which properties can be bound in the controller using the `[Bind]` attribute, further reducing the risk of over-posting.

- Implement data annotations that restrict which fields can be updated by which users, depending on their roles or permissions.

By combining model validation with proper model binding techniques, you can significantly reduce the risk of mass assignment attacks.

Returning HTTP error status codes

In ASP.NET Core, a controller action method can return error HTTP status codes using several methods. These methods are built into the `ControllerBase` class, and they allow you to return standardized error responses with appropriate HTTP status codes, like `400 Bad Request`, `404 Not Found`, or `500 Internal Server Error`.

Here are some of the key methods you can use in a controller action method to return error HTTP status codes.

BadRequest

This returns a `400 Bad Request` status code. It's typically used when the request is malformed or contains invalid data. This is useful in scenarios like validation errors or missing required fields in a POST request:

- `BadRequest()`: Returns `400 Bad Request` without a body
- `BadRequest(object error)`: Returns `400 Bad Request` with an error message or an object containing details of the error

An example is shown in the following code:

```
public IActionResult CreateUser(UserDto user)
{
  if (!ModelState.IsValid)
  {
    return BadRequest(ModelState); // 400 Bad Request with validation errors.
  }
  // Rest of the logic
}
```

NotFound

This returns a `404 Not Found` status code. It's used when a resource requested by the client cannot be found. This is common in `GET` requests where the requested item doesn't exist:

- `NotFound()`: Returns `404 Not Found` without a body
- `NotFound(object value)`: Returns `404 Not Found` with a custom error message or an object detailing the issue

An example is shown in the following code:

```
public IActionResult GetUserById(int id)
{
  UserDto user = _userService.GetUserById(id);

  if (user is null)
  {
    return NotFound(); // 404 Not Found.
  }
  return View(user); // 200 OK with rendered view.
}
```

Unauthorized

This returns a 401 Unauthorized status code. It indicates that the client needs to authenticate to access the resource. It's typically used when an authentication mechanism is required but not provided or invalid:

- Unauthorized(): Returns 401 Unauthorized without a body
- Unauthorized(object value): Returns 401 Unauthorized with additional details about the error

An example is shown in the following code:

```
public IActionResult GetProtectedResource()
{
  if (!User.Identity.IsAuthenticated)
  {
    return Unauthorized(); // 401 Unauthorized.
  }
  // Access protected resource.
}
```

Forbid

This returns a 403 Forbidden status code. It's used when the client is authenticated but does not have the necessary permissions to access the resource.

An example is shown in the following code:

```
public IActionResult DeleteUser(int id)
{
  if (!User.HasClaim("Admin", "true"))
  {
    return Forbid(); // 403 Forbidden
  }
  // Delete user logic
}
```

Conflict

This returns a `409 Conflict` status code. It's used when there is a conflict with the current state of the resource, for example, if two clients are attempting to update the same resource simultaneously.

UnprocessableEntity

This returns a `422 Unprocessable Entity` status code. It's used when the request is well formed but the data can't be processed, usually due to semantic errors, like validation failures. This status code is often used in cases where `400 Bad Request` doesn't fully capture the nature of the issue.

StatusCode

This allows you to return any HTTP status code manually. It's useful when you need to return a custom status code that isn't covered by the built-in methods or when you need to handle a specific HTTP response outside the common scenarios:

- `StatusCode(int statusCode)`: Returns the specified status code without a body
- `StatusCode(int statusCode, object value)`: Returns the specified status code along with a message or object

An example is shown in the following code:

```
public IActionResult SomeAction()
{
  // Custom Logic
  return StatusCode(418, "I'm a teapot");
}
```

Problem

This returns a generic error response with a `500 Internal Server Error` by default, but can be customized for any status code. It returns a standardized response body using the Problem Details format, which is useful for conveying rich error information in a structured way:

- `Problem()`: Returns a `500 Internal Server Error` with a standardized Problem Details body
- `Problem(string detail, string instance = null, int? statusCode = null, string title = null, string type = null)`: Allows customization of the Problem Details response

An example is shown in the following code:

```
public IActionResult SomeAction()
{
  try
  {
    // Some logic that may throw an exception
  }
  catch (Exception ex)
```

```
  {
    return Problem(detail: ex.Message, statusCode: 500);
  }
}
```

ValidationProblem

This returns a `400 Bad Request` with a standardized validation error response. It's used to return validation errors in a standardized way when model validation fails:

- `ValidationProblem()`: Returns a `400 Bad Request` with validation Problem Details
- `ValidationProblem(ValidationProblemDetails problemDetails)`: Returns a `400 Bad Request` with custom Problem Details

By using these methods, you can handle various error cases in a structured, consistent manner, ensuring that clients receive meaningful and accurate HTTP status codes that reflect the nature of any issues.

Now that you've seen how model binding and validation work, let's get more practical and see how ASP.NET Core can integrate with databases using an EF Core entity model.

Modifying data using EF Core and ASP.NET Core

In *Chapter 2*, *Building Websites Using ASP.NET Core MVC*, you learned how to configure EF Core with ASP.NET Core and register a database context as a dependency service. You then used it to retrieve categories and products for display on the home page.

Now, let's see how to use EF Core to retrieve data to display on a web page, and to modify data to perform inserts, updates, and deletes.

Displaying Northwind suppliers

We will follow good practice and create a separate controller for suppliers, and then a page to display Northwind suppliers:

1. In the `Models` folder, create a new class named `SuppliersIndexViewModel.cs`. This will contain a sequence of suppliers to display in an HTML table in a Razor View.

2. Modify the contents, as shown in the following code:

   ```
   using Northwind.EntityModels; // To use Supplier.

   namespace Northwind.Mvc.Models;

   public record SuppliersIndexViewModel(IEnumerable<Supplier>? Suppliers);
   ```

3. In the `Controllers` folder, create a new controller named `SuppliersController.cs`. (The Visual Studio project item template is named **MVC Controller - Empty**.)

4. In `SuppliersController.cs`, add a constructor to get an instance of the Northwind database context using dependency injection, and then in the `Index` action method, write statements to retrieve all suppliers from the `Suppliers` property of the database context, sorted by country and then company name, as shown in the following code:

```
using Microsoft.AspNetCore.Mvc; // To use Controller, IActionResult.
using Northwind.EntityModels; // To use NorthwindContext.
using Northwind.Mvc.Models; // To use SuppliersIndexViewModel.

namespace Northwind.Mvc.Controllers;

public class SuppliersController : Controller
{
  private readonly NorthwindContext _db;

  public SuppliersController(NorthwindContext db)
  {
    _db = db;
  }

  public IActionResult Index()
  {
    SuppliersIndexViewModel model = new(_db.Suppliers
      .OrderBy(c => c.Country)
      .ThenBy(c => c.CompanyName));

    return View(model);
  }
}
```

Good practice: We have used constructor parameter injection to get an instance of the Northwind database context. This is good if all action methods use the dependency service. If only one action method needs a dependency service, then it is better to use method parameter injection. If you do this, to indicate that the parameter should not participate in model binding, you must decorate it with the `[FromServices]` attribute. But later, we will add more action methods that also need the Northwind database context, so we have used constructor parameter injection.

5. In the `Views` folder, create a folder named `Suppliers`.
6. In `Views\Suppliers`, create a **Razor View – Empty** named `Index.cshtml`.

7. Modify the contents of `Index.cshtml` to render multiple columns for each supplier, as shown in the following markup:

```html
@model SuppliersIndexViewModel
<div class="row">
  <h1 class="display-2">Suppliers</h1>
  <a class="btn btn-outline-primary"
     asp-controller="Suppliers" asp-action="Add">Add New Supplier</a>
  <table class="table">
    <thead class="thead-inverse">
      <tr>
        <th>Company Name</th>
        <th>Country</th>
        <th>Phone</th>
        <th>Actions</th>
      </tr>
    </thead>
    <tbody>
    @if (Model.Suppliers is not null)
    {
      @foreach(Supplier s in Model.Suppliers)
      {
        <tr>
          <td>@s.CompanyName</td>
          <td>@s.Country</td>
          <td>@s.Phone</td>
          <td>
            <a asp-controller="Suppliers" asp-action="Edit"
               asp-route-id="@s.SupplierId">Edit</a>
            <a asp-controller="Suppliers" asp-action="Delete"
               asp-route-id="@s.SupplierId">Delete</a>
          </td>
        </tr>
      }
    }
    </tbody>
  </table>
</div>
```

8. In the `Views\Shared` folder, in `_Layout.cshtml`, after the **Model Binding** navigation menu item, add one for **Suppliers**, as shown highlighted in the following markup:

```
<li class="nav-item">
  <a class="nav-link text-dark" asp-area="" asp-controller="Home" asp-
  action="ModelBinding">Model Binding</a>
</li>
<li class="nav-item">
  <a class="nav-link text-dark" asp-area="" asp-controller="Suppliers"
    asp-action="Index">Suppliers</a>
</li>
```

9. Start the website using the `https` launch profile and go to the website home page.

10. In the top navigation menu, click **Suppliers**, and note that the suppliers are retrieved from the Northwind database. Also, note that they are sorted first by country and then by company name, as shown in *Figure 3.5*:

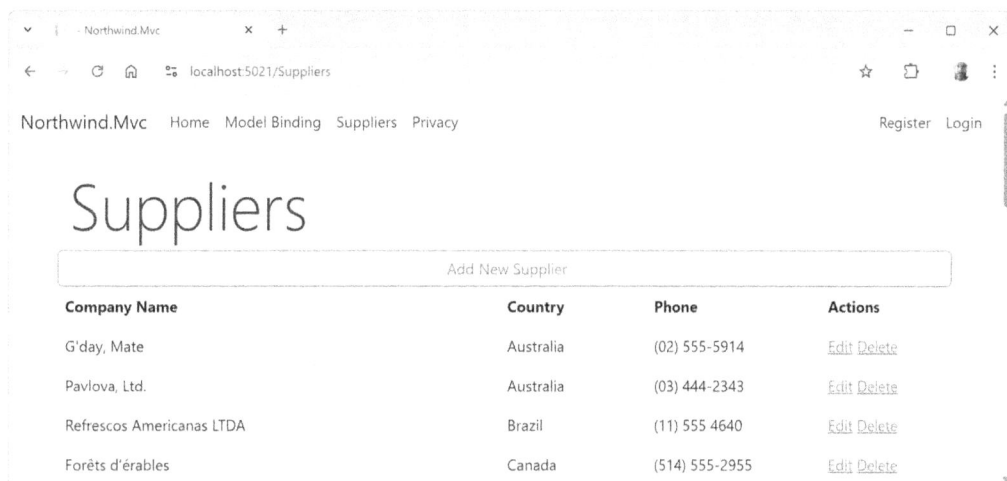

Figure 3.5: The Suppliers table loaded from the Northwind database

11. Close Chrome and shut down the web server.

Inserting, updating, and deleting suppliers

Next, we will create some action methods and Razor Views to define a form that a visitor can fill in and submit to insert a new supplier, and to update or delete an existing supplier.

Since we are enabling a visitor to manipulate data, we should implement authentication and authorization before we deploy this functionality into production. You will learn how to do this in *Chapter 5, Authentication and Authorization*. For now, we are just going to implement the data access functionality and make sure that it works locally on your development machine.

To perform these operations, you create pairs of action methods:

- First, create a GET action method and view to show a web page containing a form where the user can enter details for a new supplier, edit the details of an existing supplier, or see a read-only view of the details for an existing supplier, and then a button to submit the data.
- Second, create a POST action method to perform the add, update, or delete operation, and if successful, redirect to the page of suppliers to review the change, or, if an error occurs, then back to the single supplier page to try again.

In a RESTful API design:

- POST is typically used for creating resources.
- PUT is used for updating resources.
- DELETE is used for deleting resources.

HTML forms inherently support only two HTTP methods: GET and POST. They do not natively support PUT, DELETE, or other HTTP methods. This limitation means that when you need to use PUT or DELETE to update or delete, you cannot specify these methods directly in the <form> element.

A convention in ASP.NET Core MVC is to simulate these methods using POST, often with the help of a hidden input field called _method or specifying the action in the path, like /suppliers/edit and /suppliers/delete.

Let's create some action methods and Razor Views to define a form that a visitor can fill in and submit to insert a new supplier, and update or delete an existing supplier:

1. In the Models folder, create a new class named SupplierViewModel.cs. This will contain a single supplier and information about the success or failure of changes to affected entities, like inserts, updates, and deletes.

2. Modify the contents, as shown in the following code:

```
using Northwind.EntityModels; // To use Supplier.

namespace Northwind.Mvc.Models;

public record SupplierViewModel(
  int EntitiesAffected, Supplier? Supplier);
```

3. In the Controllers folder, in SuppliersController.cs, add a GET action method to retrieve a single supplier using a unique supplier ID and allow it to be edited, as shown in the following code:

```
// GET: /suppliers/edit/{id}
public IActionResult Edit(int? id)
{
  Supplier? supplierInDb = _db.Suppliers.Find(id);
```

```
    SupplierViewModel model = new(
        supplierInDb is null ? 0 : 1, supplierInDb);

    // Views\Suppliers\Edit.cshtml
    return View(model);
}
```

4. In `Views\Suppliers`, create a **Razor View – Empty** named `Edit.cshtml`.

5. In `Edit.cshtml`, add common Microsoft Tag Helpers so that we can use the `asp-for` Tag Helper on this Razor View. Add a form to edit a supplier, and use the `asp-for` Tag Helper to bind the `CompanyName`, `Country`, and `Phone` properties of the `Supplier` class to the input box, as shown in the following markup:

```
@addTagHelper *, Microsoft.AspNetCore.Mvc.TagHelpers
@model SupplierViewModel
<div class="row">
  <p>Edit the details for this supplier:</p>
  <form method="post">
    @Html.AntiForgeryToken()
    <div><input asp-for="Supplier.SupplierId" hidden /></div>
    <div><input asp-for="Supplier.CompanyName" /></div>
    <div><input asp-for="Supplier.Country" /></div>
    <div><input asp-for="Supplier.Phone" /></div>
    <input type="submit" value="Save Changes"
            class="btn btn-outline-primary" />
    <a href="/Home/Suppliers"
            class="btn btn-outline-secondary">Cancel</a>
  </form>
</div>
@section Scripts {
  @{
    await Html.RenderPartialAsync("_ValidationScriptsPartial");
  }
}
```

While reviewing the preceding markup, note the following:

*   The `<form>` element with a `POST` method is ordinary HTML, so an `<input type="submit" />` element inside it will make an HTTP `POST` request back to the current path with values of any other elements inside that form.

- The `Html.AntiForgeryToken()` method makes it easy to mitigate **Cross-Site Request Forgery (CSRF)** attacks using ASP.NET Core MVC. If you need to integrate client-side technologies like AJAX, Angular, or React, then there are extra steps required. This is beyond the scope of this book, but you can learn more at the following link: `https://learn.microsoft.com/en-us/aspnet/core/security/anti-request-forgery#javascript-ajax-and-spas`.

- An `<input>` element with a Tag Helper named `asp-for` enables data binding to the model for the Razor View.

> **Warning!** Code editors can be overzealous with null warnings. If you get them in the model binding expressions, you can apply the null-forgiving operator, as shown in the following code expression: `Model.Supplier!.CompanyName`.

6. In the `Controllers` folder, in `SuppliersController.cs`, add an action method to update a supplier, as shown in the following code:

```
// POST: /suppliers/edit
// Body: Supplier
// Updates an existing supplier.
[HttpPost]
[ValidateAntiForgeryToken]
public IActionResult Edit(Supplier supplier)
{
  int affected = 0;

  if (ModelState.IsValid)
  {
    Supplier? supplierInDb = _db.Suppliers.Find(supplier.SupplierId);

    if (supplierInDb is not null)
    {
      supplierInDb.CompanyName = supplier.CompanyName;
      supplierInDb.Country = supplier.Country;
      supplierInDb.Phone = supplier.Phone;
      /*
      // Other properties not in the HTML form.
      supplierInDb.ContactName = supplier.ContactName;
      supplierInDb.ContactTitle = supplier.ContactTitle;
      supplierInDb.Address = supplier.Address;
      supplierInDb.City = supplier.City;
      supplierInDb.Region = supplier.Region;
```

```
        supplierInDb.PostalCode = supplier.PostalCode;
        supplierInDb.Fax = supplier.Fax;
        */
        affected = _db.SaveChanges();
      }
    }

    SupplierViewModel model = new(
      affected, supplier);

    if (affected == 0) // Supplier was not updated.
    {
      // Views\Suppliers\Edit.cshtml
      return View(model);
    }
    else // Supplier was updated; show in table.
    {
      return RedirectToAction("Index");
    }
  }
```

7. In the `Controllers` folder, in `SuppliersController.cs`, add an action method to retrieve a single supplier using a unique supplier ID and allow it to be deleted, as shown in the following code:

```
// GET: /suppliers/delete/{id}
public IActionResult Delete(int? id)
{
  Supplier? supplierInDb = _db.Suppliers.Find(id);

  SupplierViewModel model = new(
    supplierInDb is null ? 0 : 1, supplierInDb);

  // Views\Suppliers\Delete.cshtml
  return View(model);
}
```

8. In `Views\Suppliers`, create a **Razor View – Empty** named `Delete.cshtml`.

9. In `Delete.cshtml`, add common Microsoft Tag Helpers so that we can use the `asp-for` Tag Helper on this Razor View, display a supplier, and use the `asp-for` Tag Helper to bind the `CompanyName`, `Country`, and `Phone` properties of the `Supplier` class to the labels, as shown in the following markup:

```
@addTagHelper *, Microsoft.AspNetCore.Mvc.TagHelpers
@model SupplierViewModel
<div class="row">
  <p>Are you sure that you want to delete this supplier?</p>
  <form method="post">
    @Html.AntiForgeryToken()
    <div><input asp-for="Supplier.SupplierId" hidden /></div>
    <div><input asp-for="Supplier.CompanyName" readonly /></div>
    <div><input asp-for="Supplier.Country" readonly /></div>
    <div><input asp-for="Supplier.Phone" readonly /></div>
    <input type="submit" value="Delete" />
    <a href="Suppliers">Cancel</a>
  </form>
</div>
```

10. In the `Controllers` folder, in `SuppliersController.cs`, add an action method to delete a supplier, as shown in the following code:

```
// POST: /suppliers/delete/{id}
// Removes an existing supplier.
[HttpPost("/suppliers/delete/{id:int?}")]
[ValidateAntiForgeryToken]
// C# won't allow two methods with the same name and signature.
public IActionResult DoTheDelete(int? id)
{
  int affected = 0;

  Supplier? supplierInDb = _db.Suppliers.Find(id);

  if (supplierInDb is not null)
  {
    _db.Suppliers.Remove(supplierInDb);
    affected = _db.SaveChanges();
  }

  SupplierViewModel model = new(
    affected, supplierInDb);
```

```
      if (affected == 0) // Supplier was not deleted.
      {
        // Views\Suppliers\Delete.cshtml
        return View(model);
      }
      else
      {
        return RedirectToAction("Index");
      }
    }
```

11. In the `Controllers` folder, in `SuppliersController.cs`, add an action method to allow a visitor to enter details for a new supplier and then insert it, as shown in the following code:

```
// GET: /suppliers/add
public IActionResult Add()
{
  SupplierViewModel model = new(
    0, new Supplier());

  // Views\Suppliers\Add.cshtml
  return View(model);
}
```

12. In `Views\Suppliers`, create a **Razor View – Empty** named `Add.cshtml`.

13. In `Add.cshtml`, add common Microsoft Tag Helpers so that we can use the `asp-for` Tag Helper on this Razor View, display a supplier, and use the `asp-for` Tag Helper to bind the `CompanyName`, `Country`, and `Phone` properties of the `Supplier` class to the text boxes, as shown in the following markup:

```
@addTagHelper *, Microsoft.AspNetCore.Mvc.TagHelpers
@model SupplierViewModel
<div class="row">
  <p>Enter details for a new supplier:</p>
  <form method="POST">
    @Html.AntiForgeryToken()
    <div><input asp-for="Supplier.CompanyName"
                placeholder="Company Name" /></div>
    <div><input asp-for="Supplier.Country"
                placeholder="Country" /></div>
    <div><input asp-for="Supplier.Phone"
                placeholder="Phone" /></div>
    <input type="submit" value="Insert" class="btn btn-outline-primary"
  />
```

```
      <a href="/Home/Suppliers" class="btn btn-outline-secondary">Cancel</
a>
    </form>
  </div>
  @section Scripts {
    @{
      await Html.RenderPartialAsync("_ValidationScriptsPartial");
    }
  }
}
```

14. In the `Controllers` folder, in `SuppliersController.cs`, add an action method to insert a new supplier, as shown in the following code:

```
// POST: /suppliers/add
// Body: Supplier
// Inserts a new supplier.
[HttpPost]
[ValidateAntiForgeryToken]
public IActionResult Add(Supplier supplier)
{
  int affected = 0;

  if (ModelState.IsValid)
  {
    _db.Suppliers.Add(supplier);
    affected = _db.SaveChanges();
  }

  SupplierViewModel model = new(
    affected, supplier);

  if (affected == 0) // Supplier was not added.
  {
    // Views\Suppliers\Add.cshtml
    return View(model);
  }
  else
  {
    return RedirectToAction("Index");
  }
}
```

Manually trying to insert, update, and delete data

In the real world, you would create automated tests for functionality like inserting, updating, and deleting data. You will learn how to do this in *Chapter 7, Web User Interface Testing Using Playwright*. For now, we will just manually try those actions out on your local machine to manipulate the Northwind suppliers:

1. Start the website using the `https` launch profile and navigate to the website home page.
2. Click **Suppliers**, click **Add New Supplier**, and enter Bob's Burgers, USA, and (603) 555-4567, as shown in *Figure 3.6*:

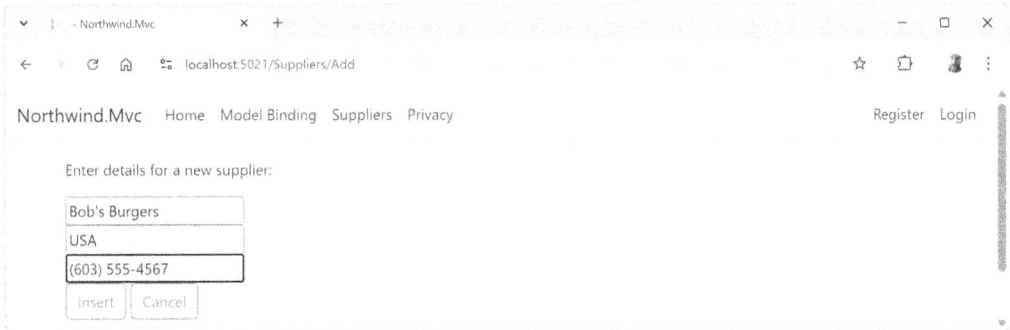

Figure 3.6: Entering details for a new supplier

3. Click **Insert** and note that you are redirected to the **Suppliers** page.
4. On the **Suppliers** page, scroll down to the bottom of the table where the USA suppliers are sorted and note that the new supplier has been added, as shown in *Figure 3.7*:

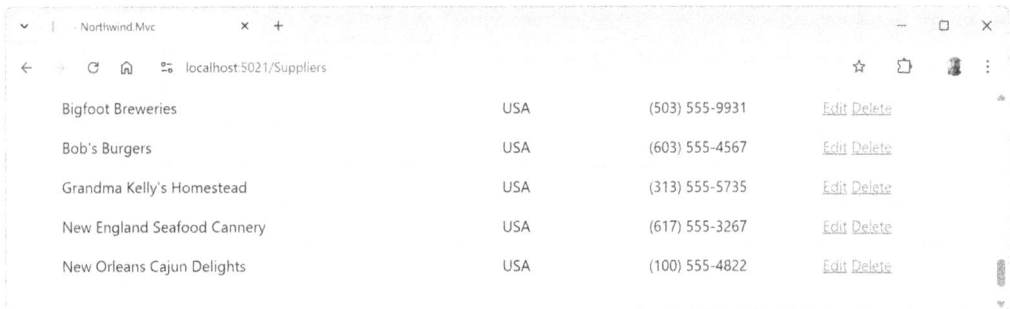

Figure 3.7: The new supplier in the table

5. In the **Bob's Burgers** row, click **Edit**.
6. Change the last digit of the phone number from 7 to 8, and then click **Save Changes**.
7. In the **Bob's Burgers** row, note that the phone has been updated, and then click **Delete**.
8. Confirm that you are about to delete the **Bob's Burgers** supplier entity, and then click **Delete**.
9. On the **Suppliers** page, scroll down to the bottom of the table where the USA suppliers are sorted, and note that the **Bob's Burgers** supplier has been deleted.
10. Optionally, review the logged SQL statements in the command prompt or terminal.
11. Close Chrome and shut down the web server.

Protecting against CSRF attacks

The `Html.AntiForgeryToken()` method protects your websites from CSRF attacks. It generates an anti-forgery token that is used to ensure that form submissions or other types of requests to the server are made by an authenticated user from the same site, rather than a malicious third party.

How CSRF attacks work

A CSRF attack tricks an authenticated user into performing actions on a site without their knowledge. For instance, if a user is logged in to their bank's website and unknowingly clicks on a malicious link, a request might be sent to the bank, performing an action like transferring funds. Since the request comes from the user's authenticated session, the server processes it, thinking it is legitimate.

How anti-forgery tokens prevent CSRF

Anti-forgery tokens mitigate CSRF attacks by ensuring that any request made to your server originates from a legitimate form submission on your site, rather than from an external source. The token mechanism is based on the principle that an attacker cannot easily obtain or replicate the token embedded in legitimate requests.

The `Html.AntiForgeryToken()` method generates a pair of tokens:

- **Cookie token:** A token is generated and stored in an HTTP cookie (on the client side, named `.AspNetCore.AntiForgery`). This cookie is tied to the user's session and is sent along with every HTTP request made to the server.

- **Form token:** Another token is generated and inserted into the form as a hidden field. This token is embedded within the HTML of the form and gets sent to the server when the form is submitted, as shown in the following code:

  ```
  <input type="hidden" name="__RequestVerificationToken"
    value="token_value_here" />
  ```

Both tokens are cryptographically linked and validated against each other on the server.

When the form is submitted, both the cookie token and the form token (hidden field) are sent to the server. The server then validates these tokens to ensure they match and were generated by the same user session. If the tokens do not match, the request is rejected, preventing CSRF attacks.

How to use Html.AntiForgeryToken()

You should include `@Html.AntiForgeryToken()` inside form elements that perform actions requiring protection against CSRF, as shown in the following markup:

```
<form asp-action="PostData" method="post">
  @Html.AntiForgeryToken()
  <input type="text" name="data" />
  <button type="submit">Submit</button>
</form>
```

The anti-forgery token is automatically validated on the server if you are using ASP.NET Core MVC. By default, ASP.NET Core includes an anti-forgery validation filter in all controllers that have [HttpPost] methods. The framework automatically checks for the presence of the anti-forgery token in incoming requests.

The validation ensures that the request originated from the same user session that received the page and not from a third-party site:

- If the tokens match, the request is allowed to proceed.
- If the tokens don't match or are missing, the request is rejected with an HTTP 400 Bad Request response, protecting against CSRF.

If you want to explicitly ensure that anti-forgery validation is enforced in specific actions, you can use the [ValidateAntiForgeryToken] attribute in your controller actions, as shown in the following code:

```
[HttpPost]
[ValidateAntiForgeryToken]
public IActionResult PostData(string data)
{
  // The request will only reach here if the anti-forgery token is valid.
  return Ok();
}
```

Querying a database and using display templates

In previous examples, we defined a view model that contained properties for every value that needed to be rendered in the view. In this example, there will be two values: a list of products and the price the visitor entered. To avoid having to define a class or record for the view model, we will pass the list of products as the model and store the maximum price in the ViewData collection.

Let's create a new action method that can have a query string parameter passed to it and use that to query the Northwind database for products that cost more than a specified price:

1. In HomeController.cs, add a new action method, as shown in the following code:

    ```
    public IActionResult ProductsThatCostMoreThan(decimal? price)
    {
      if (!price.HasValue)
      {
        return BadRequest("You must pass a product price in the query string,
    for example, /Home/ProductsThatCostMoreThan?price=50");
      }

      IEnumerable<Product> model = _db.Products
        .Include(p => p.Category)
        .Include(p => p.Supplier)
    ```

```
      .Where(p => p.UnitPrice > price);

  if (!model.Any())
  {
    return NotFound(
      $"No products cost more than {price:C}.");
  }

  // Format currency using web server's culture.
  ViewData["MaxPrice"] = price.Value.ToString("C");

  // We can override the search path convention.
  return View("Views/Home/CostlyProducts.cshtml", model);
}
```

Good practice: One of the benefits of using an EF Core model to interact with our database is that it helps prevent SQL injection by parameterizing queries.

2. In the Views\Home folder, add a new file named CostlyProducts.cshtml.
3. Modify the contents to render zero, one, or more products as an HTML table, including the category name, supplier company name, product name, unit price, and the number of units in stock for each product, as shown in the following code:

```
@model IEnumerable<Product>
@{
  string title =
    $"Products That Cost More Than {ViewData["MaxPrice"]}";
  ViewData["Title"] = title;
}
<h2>@title</h2>
@if (Model is null)
{
  <div>No products found.</div>
}
else
{
  <table class="table">
    <thead>
      <tr>
        <th>Category Name</th>
```

```
      <th>Supplier's Company Name</th>
      <th>Product Name</th>
      <th>Unit Price</th>
      <th>Units In Stock</th>
    </tr>
  </thead>
  <tbody>
  @foreach (Product p in Model)
  {
    <tr>
      <td>
        @if (p.Category is not null)
        {
          @Html.DisplayFor(modelItem => p.Category.CategoryName);
        }
      </td>
      <td>
        @if (p.Supplier is not null)
        {
          @Html.DisplayFor(modelItem => p.Supplier.CompanyName);
        }
      </td>
      <td>
        @Html.DisplayFor(modelItem => p.ProductName)
      </td>
      <td>
        @Html.DisplayFor(modelItem => p.UnitPrice)
      </td>
      <td>
        @Html.DisplayFor(modelItem => p.UnitsInStock)
      </td>
    </tr>
  }
  <tbody>
</table>
}
```

4. In the Views\Home folder, open Index.cshtml.

5. Add the following form element below the visitor count and above the rendering of the products. This will provide a form for the user to enter a price. The user can then click **Submit** to call the action method that shows only products that cost more than the entered price:

```
<p class="lead">
  We have had @Model?.VisitorCount visitors this month.
</p>

<h3>Query products by price</h3>
<form asp-action="ProductsThatCostMoreThan" method="GET">
  <input name="price" placeholder="Enter a product price" />
  <input type="submit" />
</form>

@if (Model is not null)
```

6. Start the `Northwind.Mvc` website project using the `https` launch profile.
7. On the home page, enter a price in the form, for example, `50`, and then click on **Submit**.
8. Note the table of the products that cost more than the price that you entered, as shown in *Figure 3.8*:

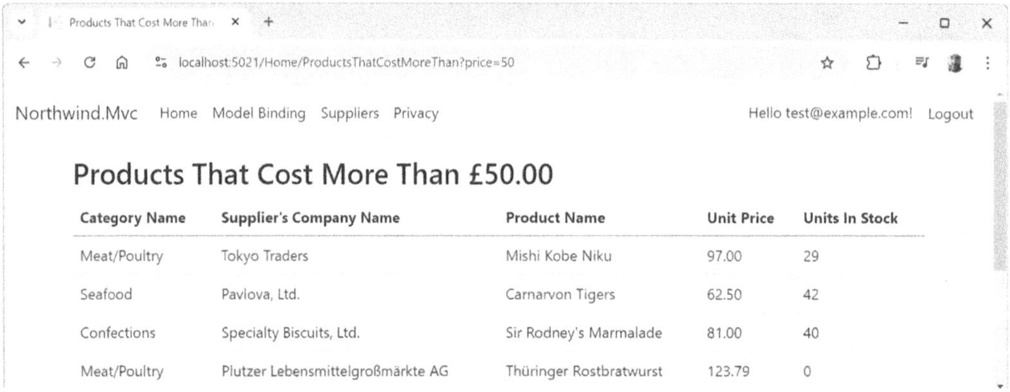
Products That Cost More Than
localhost:5021/Home/ProductsThatCostMoreThan?price=50
Northwind.Mvc
Home
Model Binding
Suppliers
Privacy
Hello test@example.com!
Logout
Products That Cost More Than £50.00
Category Name | Supplier's Company Name | Product Name | Unit Price | Units In Stock
Meat/Poultry | Tokyo Traders | Mishi Kobe Niku | 97.00 | 29
Seafood | Pavlova, Ltd. | Carnarvon Tigers | 62.50 | 42
Confections | Specialty Biscuits, Ltd. | Sir Rodney's Marmalade | 81.00 | 40
Meat/Poultry | Plutzer Lebensmittelgroßmärkte AG | Thüringer Rostbratwurst | 123.79 | 0

Figure 3.8: A filtered list of products that cost more than £50

9. Close Chrome and shut down the web server.

Method spoofing

In an ASP.NET Core MVC project, the use of `<form method="post">` for updating or deleting an entity is primarily due to limitations of HTML and the way the HTTP methods are handled by browsers and the ASP.NET Core framework.

As a reminder, HTML forms inherently support only two HTTP methods: `GET` and `POST`. They do not natively support `PUT`, `DELETE`, or other HTTP methods. This limitation means that when you need to use `PUT` or `DELETE`, you cannot specify these methods directly in the `<form>` element.

In a RESTful API design:

- POST is typically used for creating resources.
- PUT is used for updating resources.
- DELETE is used for deleting resources.

However, since HTML forms cannot use PUT or DELETE, the convention in ASP.NET Core MVC is to simulate (or "spoof") these methods using POST, often with the help of a hidden input field called _method.

ASP.NET Core supports method spoofing to work around this limitation. Here's how it works:

- In <form method="post">, you include a hidden input field named _method.
- The _method field specifies the actual HTTP method (PUT or DELETE).
- When the form is submitted, ASP.NET Core interprets the _method value automatically and routes the request accordingly.

An example is shown in the following markup:

```
<form method="post" action="/suppliers/delete">
  <input type="hidden" name="_method" value="DELETE" />
  <button type="submit">Delete</button>
</form>
```

ASP.NET Core MVC middleware can handle method spoofing by checking the _method parameter in the request body. This enables the framework to correctly route the request to an action that expects a PUT or DELETE method.

Using POST with method spoofing ensures that operations like updating or deleting entities are not performed accidentally or maliciously via simple URL manipulations (as could happen with GET requests). POST requests typically require deliberate user actions, such as clicking a button, which adds a layer of security.

Suppose you have an action in your SuppliersController, as shown in the following code:

```
[HttpDelete]
public IActionResult Delete(int id)
{
  // Code to delete the supplier.

  return RedirectToAction("Index");
}
```

You would write the form in your Razor View as shown in the following markup:

```
<form method="post" action="/suppliers/delete">
  <input type="hidden" name="_method" value="DELETE" />
  <input type="hidden" name="id" value="123" />
  <button type="submit">Delete</button>
</form>
```

This approach allows the form to simulate a DELETE request, and ASP.NET Core will correctly route it to the Delete action method.

You've now implemented a complete example of inserting, updating, and deleting data using ASP.NET Core MVC integrated with EF Core and a SQL Server database. Accessing data is often a source of performance problems with websites, so the last topic we will look at in this chapter is how to use threads to improve the scalability of your ASP.NET Core MVC projects.

Improving scalability using asynchronous tasks

When building a desktop or mobile app, multiple tasks (and their underlying threads) can be used to improve responsiveness, because while one thread is busy with the task, another can handle interactions with the user.

Tasks on a web server

Tasks can be useful on the server side too, especially with websites that work with files, or request data from a store or a web service that could take a while to respond. But they are detrimental to complex calculations that are CPU-bound, so leave these to be processed synchronously as normal.

When a request handler performs I/O tasks like database queries, file access, or HTTP calls, use the asynchronous APIs so the thread can return to the pool while the OS completes the I/O task. That increases throughput because the freed thread can run other requests. By contrast, async doesn't speed up CPU-bound calculations; on servers, keep them synchronous or run them in a separate service or queue.

In ASP.NET Core, each request initially runs on a thread-pool thread. If you call synchronous I/O, that thread is blocked and can't serve other requests. Enough blocking can cause thread-pool starvation and timeouts. With proper async/await, the handler yields while waiting, and the thread goes back to the pool, improving scalability.

You can't just crank up the thread count and call it a day. Extra threads burn memory and CPU. On Windows, the stack reservation per thread is around 1 MB by default; on many Linux systems, it's substantially larger. Also, the .NET ThreadPool grows adaptively using a hill-climbing algorithm, not at a fixed "one every two seconds" rate; growth is typically much faster.

Bottom line: for web apps, use async for I/O paths, avoid blocking calls, and don't rely on Task.Run to make CPU-bound work scale.

> **Good practice:** Make your controller action methods asynchronous, as described at the following link: https://learn.microsoft.com/en-us/aspnet/core/fundamentals/best-practices#avoid-blocking-calls.

Making controller action methods asynchronous

It is easy to make an existing action method asynchronous.

> In an earlier task, you imported the `Microsoft.EntityFrameworkCore` namespace so that you could use the `Include` extension method. You are about to use another extension method that requires that namespace to be imported.

Let's go:

1. In `HomeController.cs`, modify the `Index` action method to be asynchronous and await the calls to asynchronous methods to get the categories and products, as shown highlighted in the following code:

```
public async Task<IActionResult> Index()
{
  /*
  _logger.LogError("This is a serious error (not really!)");
  _logger.LogWarning("This is your first warning!");
  _logger.LogWarning("Second warning!");
  _logger.LogInformation("I am in the Index method of the
HomeController.");
  */

  HomeIndexViewModel model = new
  (
    VisitorCount: Random.Shared.Next(1, 1001),
    Categories: await _db.Categories.ToListAsync(),
    Products: await _db.Products.ToListAsync()
  );

  return View(model); // Pass the model to the view.
}
```

2. Modify the `ProductDetail` action method in a similar way, as shown highlighted in the following code:

```
public async Task<IActionResult> ProductDetail(int? id,
```

3. In the `ProductDetail` action method, await the calls to asynchronous methods to get the product, as shown highlighted in the following code:

```
Product? model = await _db.Products.Include(p => p.Category)
  .SingleOrDefaultAsync(p => p.ProductId == id);
```

4. Start the `Northwind.Mvc` website project using the `https` launch profile.

5. Note that the functionality of the website is the same, but trust that it will now scale better.

6. Close Chrome and shut down the web server.

Practicing and exploring

Test your knowledge and understanding by answering some questions, getting some hands-on practice, and exploring this chapter's topics with deeper research.

Exercise 3.1 – Online material

Microsoft has an official tutorial series, *ASP.NET Core MVC with EF Core - tutorial series*, available at the following link: https://learn.microsoft.com/en-us/aspnet/core/data/ef-mvc/.

Exercise 3.2 – Practice exercises

The following practice exercises help you to explore the topics in this chapter more deeply.

Practice implementing MVC by implementing a category detail page

The Northwind.Mvc project has a home page that shows categories, but when the **View** button is clicked, the website returns a 404 Not Found error, for example, for the following URL:

https://localhost:5021/home/categorydetail/1.

Extend the Northwind.Mvc project by adding the ability to show a detail page for a category.

For example, add an action method to the HomeController class, as shown in the following code:

```
public async Task<IActionResult> CategoryDetail(int? id)
{
  if (!id.HasValue)
  {
    return BadRequest("You must pass a category ID in the route, for example, /
Home/CategoryDetail/6");
  }

  Category? model = await _db.Categories.Include(p => p.Products)
    .SingleOrDefaultAsync(p => p.CategoryId == id);

  if (model is null)
  {
    return NotFound($"CategoryId {id} not found.");
  }
  return View(model); // Pass model to view and then return result.
}
```

And create a view that matches the name `CategoryDetail.cshtml`, as shown in the following markup:

```
@model Category
@{
  ViewData["Title"] = "Category Detail - " + Model.CategoryName;
}
<h2>Category Detail</h2>
<div>
  <dl class="dl-horizontal">
    <dt>Category Id</dt>
    <dd>@Model.CategoryId</dd>
    <dt>Category Name</dt>
    <dd>@Model.CategoryName</dd>
    <dt>Products</dt>
    <dd>@Model.Products.Count</dd>
    <dt>Description</dt>
    <dd>@Model.Description</dd>
  </dl>
</div>
```

Exercise 3.3 — Test your knowledge

Answer the following questions:

1. What does the default model binder do, and what data types can it handle?
2. How do you specify validation rules for ASP.NET Core model binding?
3. Where can you find any validation errors caused during model binding?
4. What is over-posting, aka. a mass assignment attack?
5. When should you return a `401 Unauthorized` status code, and when should you return a `403 Forbidden` status code?
6. To allow a user to insert an entity like a `Customer`, why do you typically define a pair of action methods, `GET` and `POST`, and what do they do?
7. How does a CSRF attack work?
8. What should you do to prevent CSRF attacks in an ASP.NET Core project?
9. What are two ways to get data into a view?
10. How do you make an action method asynchronous?

Exercise 3.4 — Explore topics

Use the links on the following page to learn more about the topics covered in this chapter:

https://github.com/markjprice/web-dev-net10/blob/main/docs/book-links.md#chapter-3---model-binding-validation-and-data-using-ef-core.

Summary

In this chapter, you learned how to bind models to data in an HTTP request, validate those models, and use EF Core to manipulate data.

In the next chapter, you will learn how to build web user interfaces with ASP.NET Core, including more details about views, Razor syntax, HTML, and Tag Helpers, and how to internationalize your website.

Learn more on Discord

To join the Discord community for this book – where you can share feedback, ask questions to the author, and learn about new releases – follow this QR code:

```
https://packt.link/RWWD10
```

Join .NETPro – It's Free

Staying sharp in .NET takes more than reading release notes. It requires real-world tips, proven patterns, and scalable solutions. That's what .NETPro, Packt's new newsletter, is all about.

Scan the QR code or visit the link to subscribe:

```
https://landing.packtpub.com/dotnetpronewsletter/
```

4

Building and Localizing Web User Interfaces

This chapter looks into building web user interfaces with ASP.NET Core in more depth. You will learn more details about ASP.NET Core MVC views, Razor syntax, HTML and Tag Helpers, how to internationalize your website so that its user interface is understandable all over the world, and how to use Bootstrap for quick **user interface** (UI) prototyping.

Razor is a view engine in ASP.NET Core that allows developers to define dynamic web user interfaces using a clean, HTML-friendly syntax. Razor Views combine C# logic with HTML to create rich, data-driven pages. One of Razor's core features is its ability to use shared layouts, which are templates that provide a consistent structure and design across multiple pages of an application. Shared layouts typically include common elements such as headers, footers, navigation bars, and styles, making it easy to maintain a cohesive look and feel throughout the site. Developers can define a layout once and then reuse it across different views by specifying it in the `_ViewStart.cshtml` file or directly within individual Razor Views. This approach promotes **DRY (Don't Repeat Yourself)** principles and simplifies future updates to the user interface, as changes to the layout propagate across all views that use it.

Tag Helpers simplify the way developers interact with HTML elements and Razor Views. They provide a way to encapsulate C# logic and apply it directly to HTML tags, making the code more intuitive and less verbose. For example, the built-in `asp-for` Tag Helper binds form input elements to model properties, reducing boilerplate code and minimizing errors. This modularity not only enhances the flexibility of web interfaces but also aligns well with the MVC architecture, where keeping concerns separate is key to building maintainable, testable applications.

In today's globalized world, creating applications that are accessible and usable by people from different cultural and linguistic backgrounds is increasingly important. ASP.NET Core offers decent localization and globalization support, enabling developers to build web user interfaces that can adapt to different languages, time zones, and regional formats. **Localization** involves translating and formatting user interface elements, such as dates, numbers, and strings, according to the user's culture settings, while **globalization** ensures that the application is designed to support multiple languages and cultures from the start. ASP.NET Core uses resource files (`.resx`) to store localized content and offers middleware for detecting the user's culture based on browser preferences or other factors.

This chapter will cover the following topics:

- Defining web user interfaces with Razor Views
- Defining web user interfaces with Tag Helpers
- Localizing web user interfaces with ASP.NET Core
- Prototyping with Bootstrap

Defining web user interfaces with Razor Views

Let's review how we can build the user interface of a web page in a modern ASP.NET Core MVC website.

Using shared layouts with Razor Views

Most websites have more than one page. If every page had to contain all of the boilerplate markup that is currently in `Index.cshtml`, that would become a pain to manage. So, ASP.NET Core has a feature named **layouts**. These can reduce code duplication and improve maintainability.

To use layouts, we must create a Razor file to define the default layout for all Razor Views and store it in a `Shared` folder so that it can be easily found by convention. The name of this file can be anything, because we will specify it, but `_Layout.cshtml` is good practice. We must also have a specially named file to set the default layout file for all Razor Views. This file *must* be named `_ViewStart.cshtml`.

The `_ViewStart.cshtml` file is used to define settings or behaviors, like layout assignment, that should apply to all views in the directory it resides in and in any subdirectories. You typically have one `_ViewStart.cshtml` file in the root `Views` folder, which is global and applies to all views unless overridden. For example, this file might set a default layout for the entire project.

If you place another `_ViewStart.cshtml` file in a specific folder, such as `Views/Home` or `Views/Products`, this file will override the settings from the global `_ViewStart.cshtml` file, but only for the views within that directory and its subdirectories. This allows for different layouts or behaviors for different parts of the site.

If a directory-specific `_ViewStart.cshtml` file does not define all the settings or behaviors found in the global `_ViewStart.cshtml` file, then those settings are inherited from the global file. For example, if the `_ViewStart.cshtml` in a specific directory does not specify a layout, it will still inherit the layout defined in the global `_ViewStart.cshtml`.

You can also create as many alternative layout files as you like, and a Razor View can explicitly specify that it wants to use that layout. You can also nest layouts for even more power and flexibility.

Let's see how the default layout works and how to override it:

1. In the `Views` folder, note the file named `_ViewStart.cshtml`. (The Visual Studio project item template is named **Razor View Start** if you need to create one in the future.)
2. Note the `_ViewStart.cshtml` file content, as shown in the following markup:

```
@{
  Layout = "_Layout";
}
```

3. In the Views folder, note the folder named Shared.

4. In the Shared folder, note the file named _Layout.cshtml. (The Visual Studio item template is named **Razor Layout** if you need to create one in the future.)

5. Note the content of _Layout.cshtml, as shown in the following markup:

```
<!DOCTYPE html>
<html lang="en">
<head>
  <meta charset="utf-8" />
  <meta name="viewport" content="width=device-width, initial-scale=1.0"
/>
  <title>@ViewData["Title"] - Northwind.Mvc</title>
  <script type="importmap"></script>
  <link rel="stylesheet" href="~/lib/bootstrap/dist/css/bootstrap.min.
css" />
  <link rel="stylesheet" href="~/css/site.css" asp-append-version="true"
/>
  <link rel="stylesheet" href="~/Northwind.Mvc.styles.css" asp-append-
version="true" />
</head>
<body>
  <header>
    <nav class="navbar navbar-expand-sm navbar-toggleable-sm navbar-light
bg-white border-bottom box-shadow mb-3">
      <div class="container-fluid">
        <a class="navbar-brand" asp-area="" asp-controller="Home" asp-
action="Index">Northwind.Mvc</a>
        <button class="navbar-toggler" type="button" data-
bs-toggle="collapse" data-bs-target=".navbar-collapse" aria-
controls="navbarSupportedContent"
 aria-expanded="false" aria-label="Toggle navigation">
          <span class="navbar-toggler-icon"></span>
        </button>
        <div class="navbar-collapse collapse d-sm-inline-flex justify-
content-between">
          <ul class="navbar-nav flex-grow-1">
            <li class="nav-item">
              <a class="nav-link text-dark" asp-area="" asp-
controller="Home" asp-action="Index">Home</a>
            </li>
            <li class="nav-item">
              <a class="nav-link text-dark" asp-area="" asp-
controller="Home" asp-action="ModelBinding">Model Binding</a>
```

```
          </li>
          <li class="nav-item">
            <a class="nav-link text-dark" asp-area="" asp-
controller="Suppliers" asp-action="Index">Suppliers</a>
          </li>
          <li class="nav-item">
            <a class="nav-link text-dark" asp-area="" asp-
controller="Home" asp-action="Privacy">Privacy</a>
          </li>
        </ul>
        <partial name="_LoginPartial" />
      </div>
    </div>
  </nav>
</header>
<div class="container">
  <main role="main" class="pb-3">
    @RenderBody()
  </main>
</div>
<footer class="border-top footer text-muted">
  <div class="container">
    &copy; 2025 - Northwind.Mvc - <a asp-area="" asp-controller="Home"
asp-action="Privacy">Privacy</a>
  </div>
</footer>
<script src="~/lib/jquery/dist/jquery.min.js"></script>
<script src="~/lib/bootstrap/dist/js/bootstrap.bundle.min.js"></script>
<script src="~/js/site.js" asp-append-version="true"></script>
@await RenderSectionAsync("Scripts", required: false)
</body>
</html>
```

While reviewing the preceding markup, note the following:

- `<title>` is set dynamically using server-side code by reading from a dictionary named `ViewData`. This is a simple way to pass data between different parts of an ASP.NET Core website. In this case, the `title` value will be set in the `controller` action method and then output in the shared layout. You learned about the `ViewData` and `TempData` dictionaries in *Chapter 2, Building Websites Using ASP.NET Core MVC*.

- `@RenderBody()` marks the insertion point for the view being requested.

- At the bottom of the layout is a script to implement some cool features of Bootstrap, such as a carousel of images.

- After the `<script>` elements for Bootstrap, we have defined a section named `Scripts` so that a Razor View can optionally inject additional scripts that it needs.

6. In the `Views` folder, in `_ViewStart.cshtml`, add some comments and add a statement to set a default page title if a specific MVC view does not set one for itself, as shown highlighted in the following code:

```
@{
  // Set a default layout for all views in this folder hierarchy.
  Layout = "_Layout";

  // Set a default title for all views in this folder hierarchy,
  // if one has not already been set.
  ViewData["Title"] ??= "Northwind MVC";
}
```

7. Save changes to the file.

Defining views with HTML Helper methods

While creating a view for ASP.NET Core MVC, you can use the `Html` object and its methods to generate markup. When Microsoft first introduced ASP.NET MVC in 2009, these HTML Helper methods were the way to programmatically render HTML. Modern ASP.NET Core retains these HTML Helper methods for backward compatibility and provides Tag Helpers that are usually easier to read and write in most scenarios.

> **Good practice:** Use Tag Helpers wherever possible, but remember that there are notable situations where Tag Helpers cannot be used, like in Razor components, primarily because Tag Helpers and Razor components are fundamentally different technologies with distinct rendering mechanisms and purposes. The key difference is that Razor components deal with interactive UIs and dynamic rendering through the component model, where changes to the user interface are handled reactively.

Some useful methods include the following:

- `ActionLink`: Use this to generate an anchor `<a>` element that contains a URL path to the specified controller and action. For example, `Html.ActionLink(linkText: "Binding", actionName: "ModelBinding", controllerName: "Home")` would generate `<a href="/home/modelbinding">Binding</a>`. You can achieve the same result using the anchor tag helper `<a asp-action="ModelBinding" asp-controller="Home">Binding</a>`.

- `AntiForgeryToken`: Use this inside a `<form>` to insert a `<hidden>` element containing an anti-forgery token that will be validated when the form is submitted.

- `Display` and `DisplayFor`: Use these to generate HTML markup for the expression relative to the current model using a display template. There are built-in display templates for .NET types, and custom templates can be created in the `DisplayTemplates` folder. The folder name is case-sensitive on case-sensitive filesystems.

- `DisplayForModel`: Use this to generate HTML markup for an entire model instead of a single expression.

- `Editor` and `EditorFor`: Use these to generate HTML markup for the expression relative to the current model using an editor template. There are built-in editor templates for .NET types that use `<label>` and `<input>` elements, and custom templates can be created in the `EditorTemplates` folder. The folder name is case-sensitive on case-sensitive filesystems.

- `EditorForModel`: Use this to generate HTML markup for an entire model instead of a single expression.

- `TextBox`, `DropDownList`, `CheckBox`, and so on: Use these to generate specific types of input controls.

- `Encode`: Use this to safely encode an object or string into HTML. For example, the string value `"<script>"` would be encoded as `"&lt;script&gt;"`. This is not normally necessary since the Razor @ symbol encodes string values by default.

- `Raw`: Use this to render a string value *without* encoding it as HTML.

- `PartialAsync` and `RenderPartialAsync`: Use these to generate HTML markup for a partial view. You can optionally pass a model and view data.

HTML Helper methods are mostly a legacy way to render HTML in a Razor View. Now let's review the modern, simpler way: Tag Helpers.

Defining web user interfaces with Tag Helpers

Tag Helpers make it easier to make HTML elements dynamic. The markup is cleaner and easier to read, edit, and maintain than if you use HTML Helpers.

However, Tag Helpers do not completely replace HTML Helpers because there are some things that can only be achieved with HTML Helpers, like rendering output that contains multiple nested tags. Tag Helpers also cannot be used in Razor components. So, you must learn how to use HTML Helpers and treat Tag Helpers as an optional choice that is better in some scenarios.

Tag Helpers are especially useful for **Front End (FE)** developers who primarily work with HTML, CSS, and JavaScript because the FE developer does not have to learn C# syntax. Tag Helpers just use what look like normal HTML attributes on elements. The attribute names and values can also be selected from IntelliSense if your code editor supports that; both Visual Studio and VS Code do.

Comparing HTML Helpers and Tag Helpers

For example, to render a linkable hyperlink to a controller action, you could use an HTML Helper method, as shown in the following markup:

```
@Html.ActionLink("View our privacy policy.", "Privacy", "Home")
```

To make it clearer how it works, you could use named parameters, as shown in the following code:

```
@Html.ActionLink(linkText: "View our privacy policy.",
  action: "Privacy", controller: "Home")
```

But using a Tag Helper would be even clearer and cleaner for someone who works more with HTML than C#, as shown in the following markup:

```
<a asp-action="Privacy" asp-controller="Home">View our privacy policy.</a>
```

All three examples above generate the same rendered HTML element, as shown in the following markup:

```
<a href="/home/privacy">View our privacy policy.</a>
```

In the next few sections, we will review some of the more common Tag Helpers:

- Anchor Tag Helper
- Cache Tag Helper
- Environment Tag Helper
- Forms-related Tag Helpers

Exploring the Anchor Tag Helper

The Anchor Tag Helper enhances the standard HTML anchor (`<a ... ></a>`) tag by adding new attributes that understand routing in an ASP.NET Core MVC project, so you can more flexibly set what the link should be without hardcoding the URL. For example, you can specify the controller and action method, and the `href` will be generated automatically. Let's see it in action with some examples.

First, we will create three clickable hyperlinks styled as buttons to view the home page with all orders, the orders for a single customer, and the orders in a single country. This will allow us to see the basics of creating links to controllers and actions, as well as passing parameters using a route parameter and arbitrary query string parameters.

Let's explore these examples of the Anchor Tag Helper:

1. In the `Views` folder, in `_ViewImports.cshtml`, note the `@addTagHelper` directive that adds the ASP.NET Core Tag Helpers, as shown highlighted in the following code:

    ```
    @using Northwind.Mvc
    @using Northwind.Mvc.Models
    @addTagHelper *, Microsoft.AspNetCore.Mvc.TagHelpers
    @using Northwind.EntityModels
    ```

    > You could create your own Tag Helpers, and you would have to register them in the same way. But this is beyond the scope of this book, so if you want to learn how, you can read the following documentation: https://learn.microsoft.com/en-us/aspnet/core/mvc/views/tag-helpers/authoring.

2. In the `Views/Home` folder, in `Privacy.cshtml`, at the bottom of the file, add markup to define a paragraph with clickable hyperlinks styled as buttons using the `<a>` tag, as shown in the following markup:

```
<p>
  <a asp-controller="Home" asp-action="Orders"
     class="btn btn-primary" role="button">Orders</a>
  <a asp-controller="Home"
     class="btn btn-outline-primary" role="button">This Page</a>
  <a asp-controller="Home" asp-action="Orders" asp-route-id="ALFKI"
     class="btn btn-outline-primary" role="button">
     Orders for Alfreds Futterkiste</a>
  <a asp-controller="Home" asp-action="Orders" asp-route-country="Brazil"
     class="btn btn-outline-primary" role="button">Orders in Brazil</a>
</p>
```

> If you set a controller name without an action name, then it defaults to the current action, in this case, `Privacy`. The `asp-route-{parametername}` attribute can use any arbitrary parameter name. In the code example above, we use `id` and `country`. The ID will map to the route parameter with the same name. `country` is not a route parameter, so it will be passed as a query string.

3. In the `Controllers` folder, in `HomeController.cs`, create an `Orders` action method with two optional parameters to pass a customer ID and the name of a country, and write a LINQ query to use them to filter orders if they are set, as shown in the following code:

```
public IActionResult Orders(
  string? id = null, string? country = null)
{
  // Start with a simplified initial model.
  IEnumerable<Order> model = _db.Orders
    .Include(order => order.Customer)
    .Include(order => order.OrderDetails);

  // Add filtering based on parameters.
  if (id is not null)
  {
    model = model.Where(order => order.Customer?.CustomerId == id);
  }
  else if (country is not null)
  {
    model = model.Where(order => order.Customer?.Country == country);
  }
```

```
    // Add ordering and make enumerable.
    model = model
      .OrderByDescending(order => order.OrderDetails
        .Sum(detail => detail.Quantity * detail.UnitPrice))
      .AsEnumerable();

    return View(model);
  }
```

4. In the Views\Home folder, add a new **Razor View – Empty** file named Orders.cshtml.

5. In Orders.cshtml, add statements to render the orders in an HTML table, as shown in the following markup:

```
@model IEnumerable<Order>
@{
  ViewData["Title"] = "Orders";
}
<div class="text-center">
  <h1 class="display-4">@ViewData["Title"]</h1>
  <table class="table table-bordered table-striped">
    <thead>
      <tr>
        <th>Order ID</th>
        <th>Order Date</th>
        <th>Company Name</th>
        <th>Country</th>
        <th>Item Count</th>
        <th>Order Total</th>
      </tr>
    </thead>
    <tbody>
      @foreach (Order order in Model)
      {
        <tr>
          <td>@order.OrderId</td>
          <td>@order.OrderDate?.ToString("D")</td>
          <td>@order.Customer?.CompanyName</td>
          <td>@order.Customer?.Country</td>
          <td>@order.OrderDetails.Count()</td>
          <td>@order.OrderDetails.Sum(detail => detail.Quantity * detail.
UnitPrice).ToString("C")</td>
```

```
          </tr>
        }
      </tbody>
    </table>
  </div>
```

6. Start the `Northwind.Mvc` website project with the `https` profile.

7. View **Developer Tools** and click the **Elements** tab.

8. On the home page, click **Privacy** to navigate to that page, and note the buttons, including their raw HTML that shows the `href` attribute paths that were generated by the Anchor Tag Helper, as shown in Figure *4.1*:

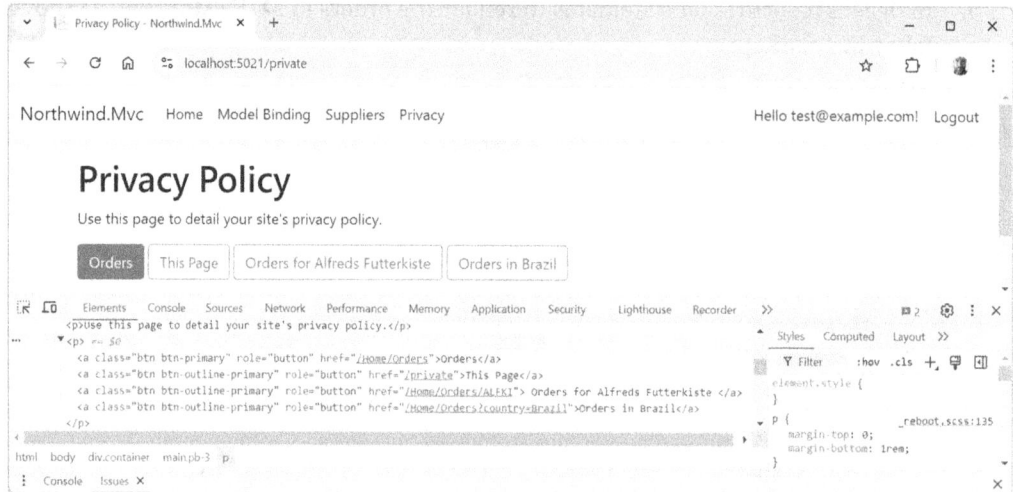

Figure 4.1: Hyperlinks styled as buttons generated by the Anchor Tag Helper

9. Click each button and then come back to the **Privacy Policy** page to make sure they work correctly.

10. Close the browser and shut down the web server.

11. In the `Views/Home` folder, in `Orders.cshtml`, at the end of the table of orders, add an anchor tag to indicate the end of the orders table, as shown highlighted in the following markup:

```
    </table>
    <a id="endOfTable" />
  </div>
```

12. In the `Views/Home` folder, in `Privacy.cshtml`, after the existing anchor tags, add another one to link to the anchor with an `id` of `endOfTable` by setting the `asp-fragment` attribute, as shown in the following markup:

```
<a asp-controller="Home" asp-action="Orders" asp-fragment="endOfTable"
    class="btn btn-outline-primary">Orders (end of table)</a>
```

13. Modify the second anchor tag to explicitly set the protocol to use `https`, as shown highlighted in the following markup:

```
<a asp-controller="Home" asp-protocol="https"
   class="btn btn-outline-primary">This Page</a>
```

14. In the `Controllers` folder, in `HomeController.cs`, add an action method named `Shipper`. Give it a parameter to receive a **Shipper** entity and then pass it to the view, as shown in the following code:

```
public IActionResult Shipper(Shipper shipper)
{
  return View(shipper);
}
```

> This action method can respond to any method of request, for example, `GET` or `POST`. With a `GET` request, the shipper entity would be passed as query string key-value pairs. With a `POST` request, the shipper entity would be passed in the body.

15. In the `Controllers` folder, in `HomeController.cs`, in the `Privacy` action method, make the method asynchronous and then add statements to get the first shipper and store its properties in `ViewData` to pass them to the view, as shown highlighted in the following code:

```
[Route("private")]
public async Task<IActionResult> Privacy()
{
  // Construct a dictionary to store properties of a shipper.
  Dictionary<string, string>? keyValuePairs = null;

  // Find the shipper with ID of 1.
  Shipper? shipper1 = await _db.Shippers.FindAsync(1);

  if (shipper1 is not null)
  {
    keyValuePairs = new()
    {
      { "ShipperId", shipper1.ShipperId.ToString() },
      { "CompanyName", shipper1.CompanyName },
      { "Phone", shipper1.Phone ?? string.Empty }
    };
  }

  ViewData["shipper1"] = keyValuePairs;
```

```
      return View();
  }
```

16. In the Views/Home folder, add an empty Razor View named Shipper.cshtml.

17. Modify the contents, as shown in the following markup:

```
@model Shipper
@{
  ViewData["Title"] = "Shippers";
}
<h1>@ViewData["Title"]</h1>
<div>
  <div class="mb-3">
    <label for="shipperIdInput" class="col-sm-2 col-form-label">Shipper
Id</label>
    <div class="col-sm-10">
      <input type="number" class="form-control"
             id="shipperIdInput" value="@Model.ShipperId">
    </div>
  </div>
  <div class="mb-3">
    <label for="companyNameInput"
           class="col-sm-2 col-form-label">Company Name</label>
    <div class="col-sm-10">
      <input class="form-control" id="companyNameInput"
             value="@Model.CompanyName">
    </div>
  </div>
  <div class="mb-3">
    <label for="phoneInput" class="col-sm-2 col-form-label">Phone</label>
    <div class="col-sm-10">
      <input class="form-control" id="phoneInput" value="@Model.Phone">
    </div>
  </div>
</div>
```

18. In the Views/Home folder, in Privacy.cshtml, after the existing anchor tags, add another one to pass the dictionary to the current page, as shown in the following markup:

```
<a asp-controller="Home" asp-action="Shipper" asp-all-route-data=
   "@ViewData["shipper1"] as IDictionary<string, string>"
   class="btn btn-outline-primary">Shipper</a>
```

> Passing a complex object as a query string like this quickly hits the limit of about 1,000 characters for a URL. To send larger objects, you should use POST instead of GET by using a <form> element instead of an anchor tag <a>.

19. If your database server is not running, for example, because you are hosting it in Docker, a virtual machine, or in the cloud, then make sure to start it.

20. Start the Northwind.Mvc website project.

21. View **Developer Tools** and click **Elements**.

22. On the home page, click **Privacy** to navigate to that page and note the buttons, including their raw HTML that shows the href attribute paths that were generated by the Anchor Tag Helper, as shown in Figure *4.2*:

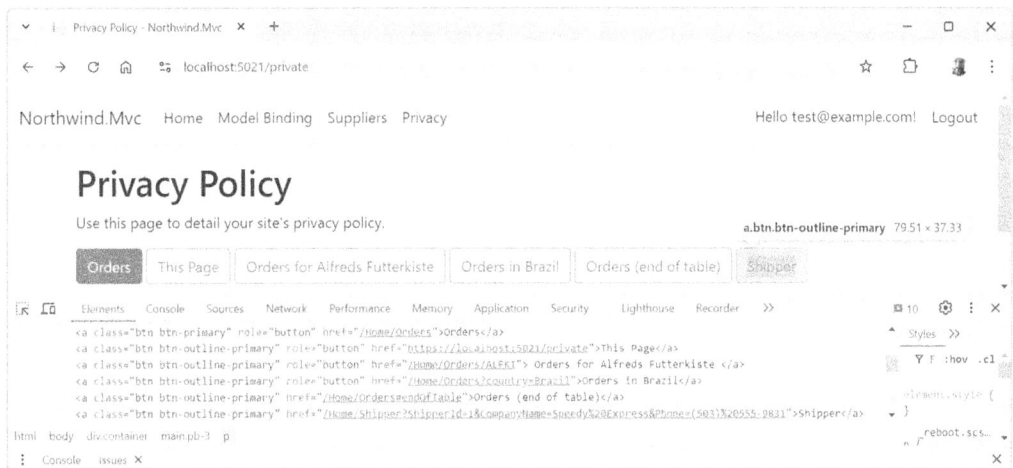

Figure 4.2: Using a fragment and passing a complex object using query string parameters

> A side benefit of specifying the protocol with asp-protocol="https" in *Step 13* is that the generated URL must include the protocol, domain, and any port number, as well as the relative path, so it is a convenient way to get an absolute URL instead of the default relative path URL, as shown in the second link above.

23. Click the **Orders (end of table)** button and note that the browser navigates to the home page and then jumps to the end of the **Orders** table.

24. Go back to the **Privacy** page, click the **Shipper** button, and note that the shipper details are pre-entered into the **Shipper** form.

25. Close the browser and shut down the web server.

Exploring the Cache Tag Helpers

The Cache and Distributed Cache Tag Helpers improve the performance of your web pages by caching their content using the in-memory or registered distributed cache provider, respectively. We will cover reading and writing objects to these caches in more detail in *Chapter 6, Performance and Scalability Optimization Using Caching*. For now, we will see how to store fragments of HTML for a view in those caches.

The Distributed Cache Tag Helper inherits from the same base class as the Cache Tag Helper. All of the Cache Tag Helper attributes are available to the Distributed Tag Helper, so in this section, we will only see examples of the Cache Tag Helper since the Distributed Cache Tag Helper is identical except for where the data is cached.

An in-memory cache is best for a single web server or a web server farm with session affinity enabled. Session affinity means that subsequent requests from the same browser are served by the same web server. A distributed cache is best for a web server farm or in a cloud provider like Azure.

> You can register providers for SQL Server, Redis, or NCache, or create your own custom provider, as you can learn about at the following link: https://learn.microsoft.com/en-us/aspnet/core/performance/caching/distributed#establish-distributed-caching-services.

Attributes that can be applied to the Cache Tag Helper include:

- enabled: The default value is true. This exists so that you can include the <cache> element in the markup but decide at runtime if it should be enabled or not.
- expires-after: A TimeSpan value to expire after. The default is 00:20:00, meaning 20 minutes.
- expires-on: A DateTimeOffset value to expire at. No default.
- expires-sliding: A TimeSpan value to expire after if the value has not been accessed during that time. This is useful when storing database entities that cost a lot to create and have varied popularity. The popular entities will stay cached if they continue to be accessed. Less popular entities will drop out. No default.
- vary-by-{type}: These attributes allow multiple different cached versions based on different values for {type}, including an HTTP header value, the browser type, a user, a route, a cookie, a query string value, or a custom value.

Let's see an example of the Cache Tag Helper:

1. In the Views/Home folder, in Index.cshtml, below the **Welcome** heading and above the **Learn about** paragraph, add <div> elements to define a Bootstrap row with two columns that show the current UTC date and time twice, once live and then once cached, as shown in the following markup:

```
<div class="row">
  <div class="col">
    <h2>Live</h2>
```

```
        <p class="alert alert-info">
        UTC: @DateTime.UtcNow.ToLongDateString() at
            @DateTime.UtcNow.ToLongTimeString()
        </p>
    </div>
    <div class="col">
        <h2>Cached</h2>
        <p class="alert alert-secondary">
          <cache>
            UTC: @DateTime.UtcNow.ToLongDateString() at
                @DateTime.UtcNow.ToLongTimeString()
          </cache>
        </p>
    </div>
</div>
```

> The Distributed Cache Tag Helper uses the tag `<distributed-cache>` instead of `<cache>`.

2. Start the `Northwind.Mvc` website project.
3. Refresh the home page several times over several seconds and note that the left-hand time is always refreshed to show the live time, and the right-hand time is cached (for 20 minutes by default), as shown in *Figure 4.3*:

Figure 4.3: Live and cached UTC times

4. Close the browser and shut down the web server.
5. In the `Views/Home` folder, in `Index.cshtml`, modify the `<cache>` element to expire after 10 seconds, as shown highlighted in the following markup:

```
<cache expires-after="@TimeSpan.FromSeconds(10)">
```

6. Start the `Northwind.Mvc` website project.

7. Refresh the home page several times over several seconds and note that the left-hand time is always refreshed to show the live time, and the right-hand time is cached for 10 seconds before it then refreshes.

8. Close the browser and shut down the web server.

Exploring the Environment Tag Helper

The Environment Tag Helper renders its content only if the current environment matches one of the values in a comma-separated list of names. This is useful if you want to render some content like instructions to a tester when hosted in a staging environment, or content like customer-specific information that developers and testers do not need to see while hosted in the production environment.

As well as a `names` attribute to set the comma-separated list of environments, you can also use `include` (works the same as `names`) and `exclude` (renders for all environments *except* the ones in the list).

> **Warning!** We are about to simulate a production environment while executing a development build. This requires an extra step to manually tell the static assets system used by the `MapStaticAssets` method to read the environment from the current configuration. If we don't do this, when we simulate the production environment, static assets like stylesheets will not be found, and the website will lose formatting.

Let's see an example:

1. In `Program.cs`, import the namespace for manually configuring static assets, as shown in the following code:

   ```
   // To use StaticWebAssetsLoader.
   using Microsoft.AspNetCore.Hosting.StaticWebAssets;
   ```

2. In `Program.cs`, after creating the `builder`, configure static assets to read the current environment from the configuration, as shown in the following code:

   ```
   // Enable switching environments (Development, Production) during
   development.
   StaticWebAssetsLoader.UseStaticWebAssets(
     builder.Environment, builder.Configuration);
   ```

3. In the `Views/Home` folder, in `Privacy.cshtml`, inject the dependency service for the web host environment, as shown in the following code:

   ```
   @inject IWebHostEnvironment webhost
   ```

4. After the `<h1>` heading, add two `<environment>` elements, the first to show output only for developers and testers, and the second to show output only for product visitors, as shown in the following markup:

```
<environment names="Development,Staging">
  <div class="alert alert-warning">
    <h2>Attention developers and testers</h2>
    <p>
      This is a warning that only developers and testers will see.
      Current environment:
      <span class="badge bg-warning">@webhost.EnvironmentName</span>
    </p>
  </div>
</environment>
<environment names="Production">
  <div class="alert alert-info">
    <h2>Welcome, visitor!</h2>
    <p>
      This is information that only a visitor to the production website
      will see. Current environment:
      <span class="badge bg-info">@webhost.EnvironmentName</span>
    </p>
  </div>
</environment>
```

5. Start the `Northwind.Mvc` website project.

6. Navigate to the **Privacy** page, and note the message for developers and testers, as shown in *Figure 4.4*:

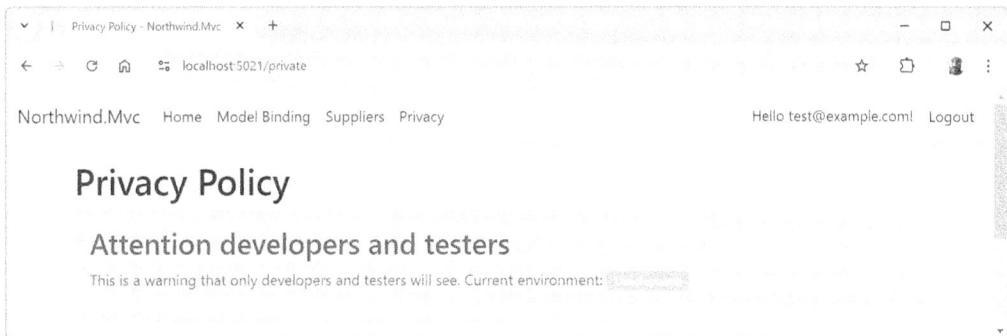

Figure 4.4: The Privacy page in the Development environment

7. Close the browser and shut down the web server.

8. In the `Properties` folder, in `launchSettings.json`, for the `https` profile, change the environment setting to `Production`, as shown highlighted in the following JSON:

```
"https": {
  ...
  "environmentVariables": {
  "ASPNETCORE_ENVIRONMENT": "Production"
  }
},
```

9. Save changes to `launchSettings.json`.

10. Start the `Northwind.Mvc` website project.

11. Navigate to the **Privacy** page, and note the message for public visitors, as shown in *Figure 4.5*:

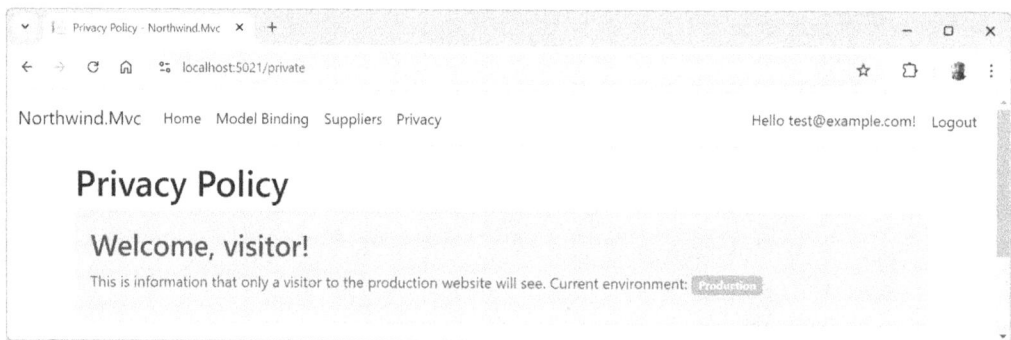

Figure 4.5: The Privacy page in the Production environment

12. Close the browser and shut down the web server.

13. In the `Properties` folder, in `launchSettings.json`, for the `https` profile, change the environment setting back to `Development`.

> Related to the Environment Tag Helper is the concept of environment-specific configuration settings. This is achieved through a naming convention for `appsettings.json` files. If you include an environment name in the filename, then that settings file will only be processed for that environment. For example, `appsettings.Development.json` will only be processed when the environment is set to `Development`.

Exploring Forms-related Tag Helpers

Forms-related Tag Helpers generate the `<form>` element's `action` attribute for an MVC controller action or named route. Like the Anchor Tag Helper, you can pass parameters using the `asp-route-<parametername>` attribute. They also generate a hidden verification token to prevent cross-site request forgery. You must apply the `[ValidateAntiForgeryToken]` attribute to the HTTP POST action method to properly use this feature.

The Label and Input Tag Helpers bind labels and inputs to properties on a model. They can then generate the id, name, and for attributes automatically, as well as adding validation attributes and messages.

Let's see an example of a form for entering shipper information:

1. In the Views/Home folder, in Shipper.cshtml, duplicate the existing markup that outputs shipper details, wrap it in a <form> element that uses the Form Tag Helper, and modify the <label> and <input> elements to use the Label and Input Tag Helpers, as shown highlighted in the following markup:

```
@model Shipper
@{
  ViewData["Title"] = "Shipper";
}
<h1>@ViewData["Title"]</h1>
<h2>Without Form Tag Helper</h2>
<div>
  <div class="mb-3">
    <label for="shipperIdInput" class="col-sm-2 col-form-label">Shipper
ID</label>
    <div class="col-sm-10">
      <input type="number" class="form-control" id="shipperIdInput"
 value="@Model.ShipperId">
    </div>
  </div>
  <div class="mb-3">
    <label for="companyNameInput" class="col-sm-2 col-form-label">Company
Name</label>
    <div class="col-sm-10">
      <input class="form-control" id="companyNameInput"
 value="@Model.CompanyName">
    </div>
  </div>
  <div class="mb-3">
    <label for="phoneInput" class="col-sm-2 col-form-label">Phone</label>
    <div class="col-sm-10">
      <input class="form-control" id="phoneInput" value="@Model.Phone">
    </div>
  </div>
</div>
<h2>With Form Tag Helper</h2>
<form asp-controller="Home" asp-action="ProcessShipper" role="form">
  <div class="mb-3">
    <label asp-for="ShipperId" class="col-sm-2 col-form-label"></label>
```

```
      <div class="col-sm-10">
        <input asp-for="ShipperId" class="form-control">
      </div>
    </div>
    <div class="mb-3">
      <label asp-for="CompanyName" class="col-sm-2 col-form-label"></label>
      <div class="col-sm-10">
        <input asp-for="CompanyName" class="form-control">
      </div>
    </div>
    <div class="mb-3">
      <label asp-for="Phone" class="col-sm-2 col-form-label"></label>
      <div class="col-sm-10">
        <input asp-for="Phone" class="form-control">
      </div>
    </div>

    <div class="mb-3">
      <div class="col-sm-10">
        <input type="submit" class="form-control">
      </div>
    </div>
  </form>
```

> When you use the `asp-*` attributes on a `<form>` element, the Tag Helper will automatically add a `method="post"` to the form so that it can post back to the controller action.

> **Warning!** The Label Tag Helper is not self-closing, so you cannot use `<label asp-for="ShipperId" class="form-label" />`. The Label Tag Helper will use the property names from the model as the labels in the form, so it will use `ShipperId` and `CompanyName` by default. In *Step 3*, you will override this behavior. As a general rule, assume that all Tag Helpers that are containers for other elements like `<label>`, `<script>`, `<cache>`, and so on cannot be self-closing.

2. In the `Controllers` folder, in `HomeController.cs`, add an action method named `ProcessShipper`. Give it a parameter to receive a shipper entity and then return it as a JSON document using the `Json` method, as shown in the following code:

```
[HttpPost]
[ValidateAntiForgeryToken]
```

```
public IActionResult ProcessShipper(Shipper shipper)
{
  return Json(shipper);
}
```

3. In the Northwind.EntityModels project, in the Shipper.cs class, decorate the ShipperId and CompanyName properties with the [Display] attribute, as shown highlighted in the following code:

```
public partial class Shipper
{
  [Key]
  [Display(Name = "Shipper ID")] // Used by the Label Tag Helper.
  public int ShipperId { get; set; }

  [StringLength(40)]
  [Display(Name = "Company Name")] // Used by the Label Tag Helper.
  public string CompanyName { get; set; } = null!;
```

Trying out the form

Now we can try out the form:

1. Start the Northwind.Mvc website project.

2. Navigate to the **Privacy** page, and then click the **Shipper** button.

3. On the **Shipper** page, right-click, select **View page source**, and note the different HTML output for the form generated by the Form, Input, and Label Tag Helpers, including a hidden element named __RequestVerificationToken, as shown in the following markup:

```
<h2>With Form Tag Helper</h2>
<form role="form" action="/Home/ProcessShipper" method="post">
  <div class="mb-3">
    <label class="col-sm-2 col-form-label" for="ShipperId">Shipper ID</label>
    <div class="col-sm-10">
      <input class="form-control" type="number" data-val="true"
             data-val-required="The Shipper ID field is required."
             id="ShipperId" name="ShipperId" value="1">
      <input name="__Invariant" type="hidden" value="ShipperId" />
    </div>
  </div>
  <div class="mb-3">
    <label class="col-sm-2 col-form-label" for="CompanyName">Company Name</label>
```

```
    <div class="col-sm-10">
      <input class="form-control" type="text" data-val="true" data-val-
length="The field Company Name must be a string with a maximum length
of 40." data-val-length-max="40" data-val-required="The Company Name
field is required." id="CompanyName" maxlength="40" name="CompanyName"
value="Speedy Express">
    </div>
  </div>
  <div class="mb-3">
    <label class="form-label" for="Phone">Phone</label>
    <div class="col-sm-10">
      <input class="form-control" type="text" data-val="true" data-
val-length="The field Phone must be a string with a maximum length of
24." data-val-length-max="24" id="Phone" maxlength="24" name="Phone"
value="(503) 555-9831">
    </div>
  </div>
  <div class="mb-3">
    <input type="submit" class="form-control">
  </div>
</div>
<input name="__RequestVerificationToken" type="hidden"
value="CfDJ8NTt08jabvBCqd1P4J-HCq3X9CDrTPjBphdDdVmG6UT0GFBJk1w7F1OLmNT-
jEGjlGIjfV3kmNUaofOAxlGgiZJwbAR73g-QgFw8oFV_0vjlo45t9dL9E1l1hZzjLXtj8B
7ysDkCYcm8W9zS0T7V3R0" /></form>
```

4. In the form, change the shipper ID and company name, noting that attributes like `maxlength="40"` prevent a company name longer than 40 characters, and `type="number"` only allows numbers for the shipper ID.

5. Click the **Submit** button and note the JSON document returned, as shown in the following output:

```
{"shipperId":1,"companyName":"Speedy Express","phone":"(503)
555-9831","orders":[]}
```

6. Close the browser and shut down the web server.

You've seen that Tag Helpers enable server-side code to participate in creating and rendering HTML elements in Razor files. Now let's look at how to make your web user interfaces work well worldwide.

Localizing web user interfaces with ASP.NET Core

Let's look at an important intermediate-level topic that is often overlooked when building websites for the World Wide Web: supporting all the world's languages and cultures. In this section, we will look at how to localize a website that uses ASP.NET Core.

Working with cultures

Internationalization is the process of enabling your code to run correctly all over the world. It has two parts, **globalization** and **localization**, and both of them are about working with cultures.

Globalization is about writing your code to accommodate multiple languages and region combinations. The combination of a language and a region is known as a culture. It is important for your code to know both the language and region because, for example, the date and currency formats are different in Quebec and Paris, despite them both using the French language.

There are **International Organization for Standardization (ISO)** codes for all culture combinations. For example, in the code da-DK, da indicates the Danish language and DK indicates the Denmark region, and in the code fr-CA, fr indicates the French language and CA indicates the Canada region.

> ISO is not an acronym. ISO is a reference to the Greek word *isos* (which means *equal*). You can see a list of ISO culture codes at the following link: https://lonewolfonline.net/list-net-culture-country-codes/.

Localization is about customizing the user interface to support a language, for example, changing the label of a button to **Close** (en) or **Fermer** (fr). Since localization is more about the language, it doesn't always need to know about the region, although, ironically enough, the words *standardization* (en-US) and *standardisation* (en-GB) suggest otherwise.

> **Good practice:** I am not a professional translator of software user interfaces, so take all examples in this chapter as general guidance. My research into French user interface labeling common practice led me to the following links, but it would be best to hire a professional if you are not a native language speaker: https://french.stackexchange.com/questions/12969/translation-of-it-terms-like-close-next-search-etc and https://www.linguee.com/english-french/translation/close+button.html.

Localizing your user interface

A localized application is divided into two parts:

- An assembly containing code that is the same for all locales and contains resources for when no other resource file is found. This is said to support invariant culture.

- One or more assemblies that contain the user interface resources, which are different for different locales. These are known as **satellite assemblies**.

This model allows the initial application to be deployed with default invariant resources, and over time, additional satellite assemblies can be deployed as the resources are translated. In the coding task, you will add resources to the ASP.NET Core MVC project that compile to an embedded invariant culture (English) and satellite assemblies for French (Neutral), French (France), and English (British). To add more cultures in the future, just follow the same steps.

User interface resources include any text for messages, logs, dialog boxes, buttons, labels, or even file-names of images, videos, and so on. Resource files are XML files with the `.resx` extension. The filename includes a culture code, for example, `PacktResources.en-GB.resx` or `PacktResources.da-DK.resx`.

If a resource file or individual entry is missing, the automatic culture fallback search path for resources goes from a specific culture (language and region) to a neutral culture (language only) to an invariant culture (supposedly independent but, basically, US English). If the current thread culture is `en-AU` (Australian English), then it will search for the resource file in the following order:

1. Australian English: `PacktResources.en-AU.resx`
2. Neutral English: `PacktResources.en.resx`
3. Invariant: `PacktResources.resx`

Web user interface localization

To localize Razor Views in ASP.NET Core MVC websites, there are some built-in types like `IStringLocalizer` and `IHtmlLocalizer` for loading string values from resource files easily.

As well as localizing `string` values into languages like French and Spanish using `IStringLocalizer`, you can localize HTML content using `IHtmlLocalizer`, but this should be used with care. Usually, HTML markup should be the same for all locales. For MVC views, you can use `IViewLocalizer`.

But how does ASP.NET Core know which culture, and therefore language, to use?

Request localization means that the browser can request what culture it prefers in the following ways:

- Add a query string parameter, for example, `?culture=en-US&ui-culture=en-US`.
- Send a cookie with the request, for example, `c=en-US|uic=en-US`.
- Set an HTTP header, for example, `Accept-Language:  en-US,en;q=0.9,fr-FR;q=0.8,fr;q=0.7,en-GB;q=0.6`.

To enable request localization, call the `UseRequestLocalization` method when you configure the HTTP request pipeline in `Program.cs`. This tells ASP.NET Core to look for these requests and to automatically change the current thread that is processing that request (and only that request; no one else's requests) to use the appropriate culture to format data and load resource values.

Creating resource files

Let's create some resource files to localize the web user interface of the **Orders** page into American English, British English, and French, and then globalize data like dates and currency values:

1. In the `Northwind.Mvc` project, add a new folder named `Resources`. This is the default name for the folder that localizer services look in for `*.resx` resource files.
2. In `Resources`, add a new folder named `Views`.
3. In `Views`, add a new folder named `Home`.

How you create resource files (`*.resx`) depends on your code editor.

> To save you from doing this task manually, you can just copy the `.resx` files from the GitHub repository found in the folder at the following link: `https://github.com/markjprice/web-dev-net10/tree/main/code/MatureWeb/Northwind.Mvc/Resources/Views/Home`.

> **Warning!** If you do copy the resource files from the GitHub repository, then Visual Studio's **Resource Explorer** may show a warning for every file: `{culture} may have security considerations`. You will need to close Visual Studio, unblock the files by right-clicking them in **File Explorer** and choosing **Properties**, then click **Unblock** and **OK**, and then restart Visual Studio.

If you are using Visual Studio

You can use a special project item type and editor:

1. In the `Resources\Views\Home` folder, add a file type of **Resources File** named `Orders.resx`.
2. In `Orders.resx`, click the green plus icon + (**Add Resource** *Ctrl + Shift + A*) to open the **Add New Resource To Orders** dialog box, define a **Name** and **Value** of `Company Name`, leave the **Comment** blank, and then click **Add**, as shown in *Figure 4.6*:

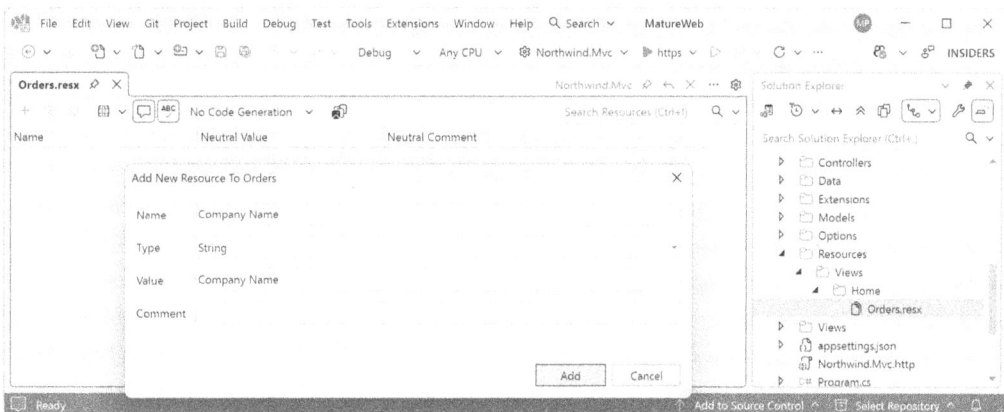

Figure 4.6: Using the Resources File editor to add a localized label

3. Define six more **Name** and **Value** entries, as shown in the following list and in *Figure 4.7*:

    *   `Country`
    *   `Item Count`
    *   `Order Date`
    *   `Order ID`
    *   `Order Total`
    *   `Orders`

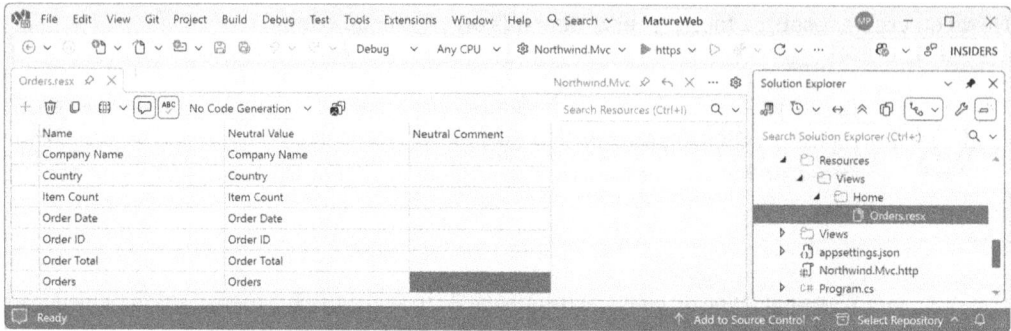

Figure 4.7: Using the Resources File editor to define more localized labels

> Rider has its own resource file editor that combines all `.resx` files in one experience as a grid. Each language has its own column, side by side. To get the same experience in Visual Studio, you must use version 17.11 or later. In earlier versions of Visual Studio, you had to edit each `.resx` file individually.

4. Copy and paste the file and rename it `Orders.en-GB.resx`.

> **Warning!** You must not change any of the entries in the **Name** column because these are used to look up localized values for all languages! You can only change the entries in the **Value** or **Comment** column.

5. Open `Orders.en-GB.resx`. Toggle the **Show Neutral Comment Column** to hide that column. Note that you can see the **Neutral Value** as well as **en-GB (English (United Kingdom))** in side-by-side columns, and then modify `Orders` to `Orders (UK)`, as shown in *Figure 4.8*:

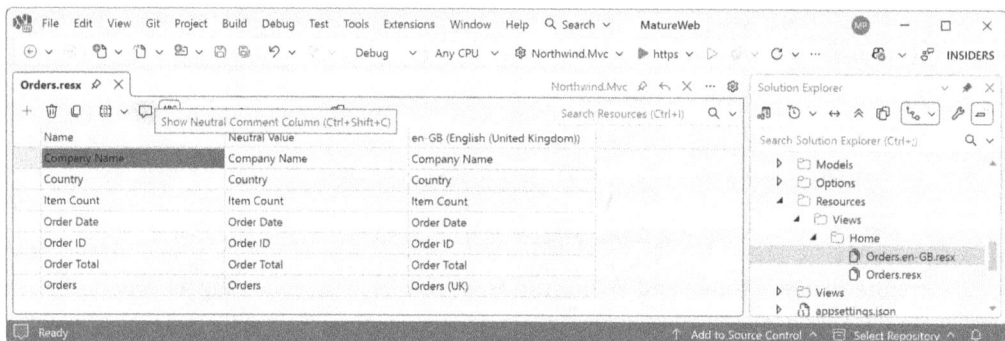

Figure 4.8: Editing a UK resource value

6. Copy and paste the `Orders.resx` file and rename it `Orders.fr-FR.resx`.

7. In `Orders.fr-FR.resx`, modify the value column to use French. (See the step-by-step instructions in the next section on VS Code for the translations.)

8. Copy and paste the file and rename it `Orders.fr.resx`.

9. In `Orders.fr.resx`, modify the last value to be `Commandes (Neutral French)`.

10. Your `Orders.resx` should now look like *Figure 4.9*:

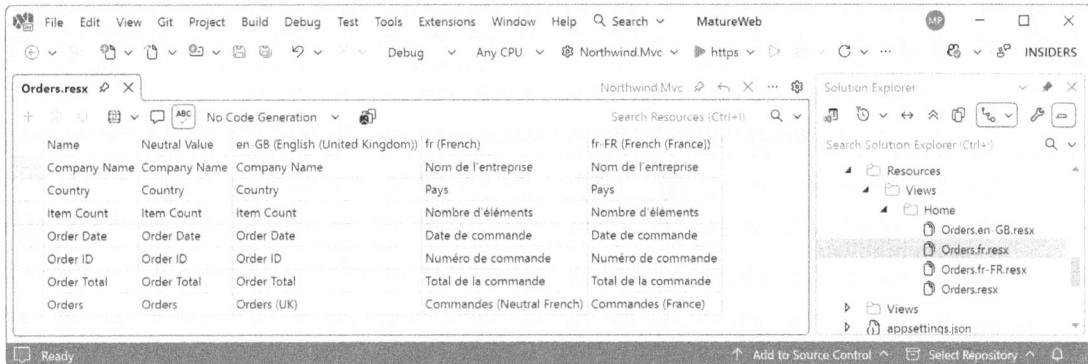

Figure 4.9: The complete resources

If you are using VS Code

You will have to edit the file without a special editor:

1. In `Resources\Views\Home`, add a new file named `Orders.resx`.

2. Modify the contents to contain neutral (American English) language resources, as shown in the following markup:

```xml
<?xml version="1.0" encoding="utf-8"?>
<root>
  <data name="Company Name" xml:space="preserve">
    <value>Company Name</value>
  </data>
  <data name="Country" xml:space="preserve">
    <value>Country</value>
  </data>
  <data name="Item Count" xml:space="preserve">
    <value>Item Count</value>
  </data>
  <data name="Order Date" xml:space="preserve">
    <value>Order Date</value>
  </data>
  <data name="Order ID" xml:space="preserve">
    <value>Order ID</value>
  </data>
  <data name="Order Total" xml:space="preserve">
    <value>Order Total</value>
  </data>
```

```
    <data name="Orders" xml:space="preserve">
      <value>Orders</value>
    </data>
  </root>
```

3. Copy and paste the file and rename it `Orders.en-GB.resx`.

4. In `Orders.en-GB.resx`, modify `Orders` to `Orders (UK)`. This is so we can see a difference.

5. Copy and paste the file and rename it `Orders.fr-FR.resx`.

6. In `Orders.fr-FR.resx`, modify the `value` element to use French, but do not change the `name`, as shown highlighted in the following markup:

```xml
<?xml version="1.0" encoding="utf-8"?>
<root>
  <data name="Company Name" xml:space="preserve">
    <value>Nom de l'entreprise</value>
  </data>
  <data name="Country" xml:space="preserve">
    <value>Pays</value>
  </data>
  <data name="Item Count" xml:space="preserve">
    <value>Nombre d'éléments</value>
  </data>
  <data name="Order Date" xml:space="preserve">
    <value>Date de commande</value>
  </data>
  <data name="Order ID" xml:space="preserve">
    <value>Numéro de commande</value>
  </data>
  <data name="Order Total" xml:space="preserve">
    <value>Total de la commande</value>
  </data>
  <data name="Orders" xml:space="preserve">
    <value>Commandes (France)</value>
  </data>
</root>
```

7. Copy and paste the file and rename it `Orders.fr.resx`.

8. In `Orders.fr.resx`, modify the last value to be `Commandes (Neutral French)`.

Before we implement our views to use these resource files, let's take a brief diversion to see some other resource file tools and how to manage complex web projects with many resource files.

Other resource file tools

You can use tools like **ResX Resource Manager** (found at the following link: `https://dotnetfoundation.org/projects/resx-resource-manager`) to create many more `.resx` files, compile them into satellite assemblies, and then deploy them to users without needing to recompile the original project.

> **Good practice:** Consider whether your application needs to be internationalized, and plan for that before you start coding! Think about all the data that will need to be globalized (date formats, number formats, and sorting text behavior). Write down all the pieces of text in the user interface that will need to be localized.

Microsoft has an online tool (found at the following link: `https://learn.microsoft.com/en-us/globalization/reference/microsoft-language-resources`) that can help you translate text in your user interfaces.

Managing resource files

The process of translating an application into multiple languages can become quite complex, especially as the number of supported languages increases.

Here are some key strategies for managing localization files effectively:

- Using a **version control system** (**VCS**), such as Git, is a natural part of managing any software project, including those with multiple language translations. The key to using version control effectively for localization is to treat `.resx` files just like any other source code. Consider creating feature branches when making significant localization changes for a particular language. Translators or localization teams can work on those branches independently of the main codebase. Once translations are completed and reviewed, the branch can be merged into the main branch.

- For large-scale projects, or when working with external translators, dedicated localization tools can vastly improve the workflow. These tools typically provide user-friendly interfaces for translators, offer version control, and streamline the process of adding new translations. Crowdin (`https://crowdin.com/`), Transifex (`https://www.transifex.com/`), and Phrase (`https://phrase.com/`) are popular tools that provide a user interface for translators to work on `.resx` files.

- To streamline the localization process and reduce the manual overhead, you can adopt continuous localization, which aligns with the principles of **Continuous Integration** (**CI**) and **Continuous Deployment** (**CD**). As part of your CI/CD pipeline, you can run automated tests to ensure that all strings have translations in all supported languages. This ensures that missing translations don't make it to production.

Now that we have reviewed how to manage resource files, let's move on to using them to localize your Razor Views.

Localizing Razor Views with an injected view localizer

Now we can continue with these steps for both code editors to localize a Razor View with an injected view localizer:

1. In the `Views/Home` folder, in `Orders.cshtml`, import the namespace for working with localization, inject the `IViewLocalizer` service, and make changes to use the labels in the view model, as shown highlighted in the following markup:

```
@using Microsoft.AspNetCore.Mvc.Localization
@model IEnumerable<Order>
@inject IViewLocalizer Localizer
@{
    ViewData["Title"] = Localizer["Orders"];
}
<div class="text-center">
    <h1 class="display-4">@ViewData["Title"]</h1>
    <table class="table table-bordered table-striped">
        <thead>
            <tr>
                <th>@Localizer["Order ID"]</th>
                <th>@Localizer["Order Date"]</th>
                <th>@Localizer["Company Name"]</th>
                <th>@Localizer["Country"]</th>
                <th>@Localizer["Item Count"]</th>
                <th>@Localizer["Order Total"]</th>
            </tr>
        </thead>
```

> **Good practice:** Key values like `"Order ID"` are used to look up the localized values. If a value is missing, then it returns the key as a default. It is good practice to therefore use keys that also work as a good fallback, which is why I used US English proper titles with spaces as the keys above and in the `.resx` files.

2. In `Program.cs`, before the call to `AddControllersWithViews`, add a statement to add localization and set the path to find resource files to the `Resources` folder, and after the call to `AddControllersWithViews`, append a call to add view localization, as shown highlighted in the following code:

```
builder.Services.AddLocalization(
    options => options.ResourcesPath = "Resources");

builder.Services.AddControllersWithViews()
    .AddViewLocalization();
```

3. In the `Extensions` folder, add a new class named `WebApplicationExtensions.cs`.

4. In `WebApplicationExtensions.cs`, add statements to declare four cultures that we will support: US English, British English, neutral French, and French in France. Then, create a new localization options object and add those cultures as supported for both localization of user interfaces (`UICultures`) and globalization of data values like dates and currency (`Cultures`), as shown in the following code:

```
namespace Northwind.Mvc.Extensions;

public static class WebApplicationExtensions
{
  public static WebApplication UseNorthwindLocalization(this
WebApplication app)
  {
    string[] cultures = { "en-US", "en-GB", "fr", "fr-FR" };

    RequestLocalizationOptions localizationOptions = new();

    // cultures[0] will be "en-US"
    localizationOptions.SetDefaultCulture(cultures[0])
      // Set globalization of data formats like dates and currencies.
      .AddSupportedCultures(cultures)
      // Set localization of user interface text.
      .AddSupportedUICultures(cultures);

    app.UseRequestLocalization(localizationOptions);

    return app;
  }
}
```

5. In `Program.cs`, in the region to configure the HTTP request pipeline, before the check for the development environment, call the extension method, as shown highlighted in the following code:

```
app.UseNorthwindLocalization();

if (app.Environment.IsDevelopment())
```

6. Start the `Northwind.Mvc` website project using the `https` profile.

7. In Chrome, navigate to **Settings**.

8. In the **Search settings** box, type `lang`, and note that you will find the **Preferred languages** section, as shown in *Figure 4.10*:

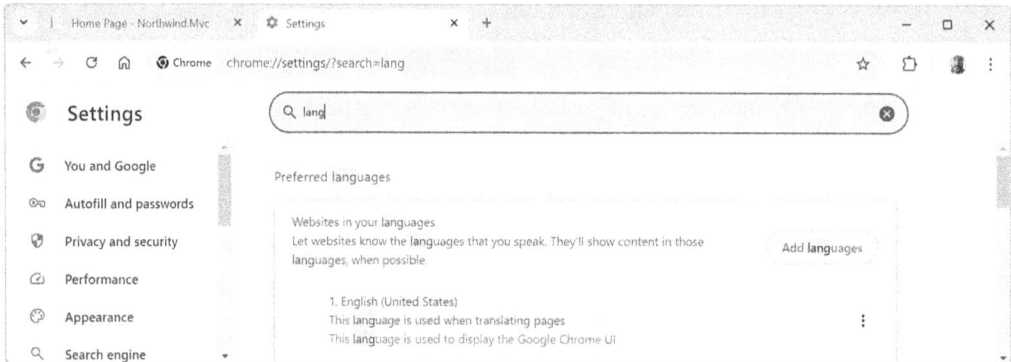

Figure 4.10: Searching Chrome Settings for the Preferred languages section

> **Warning!** If you are using a localized version of Chrome (in other words, its user interface is in your local language, like French), then you will need to search for the word "language" in your own language. (Although "language" in French is "langue," so entering "lang" will still work. But in Spanish, you would need to search for "idioma.")

9. Click **Add languages**, search for `french`, select both **French - francais** and **French (France) – francais (France)**, and then click **Add**.

> **Warning!** If you are using a localized version of Chrome, then you will need to search for the word "French" in your own language. For example, in Spanish, it would be "Francés," and in Welsh, it would be "Ffrangeg."

10. Add **English (United States)** and **English (United Kingdom)** if you do not have them on the list already.
11. In the dots ... menu to the right of **French (France)**, click **Move to the top**, and confirm that it is at the top of your list of languages.
12. Close the **Settings** tab.
13. In the top navigation menu, click **Privacy**.
14. On the **Privacy** page, click **Orders**.

15. In Chrome, perform a hard reload/refresh (for example, hold down *Ctrl* and click the **Refresh** button), and note the home page now uses localized labels and French formats for dates and currency, as shown in *Figure 4.11*:

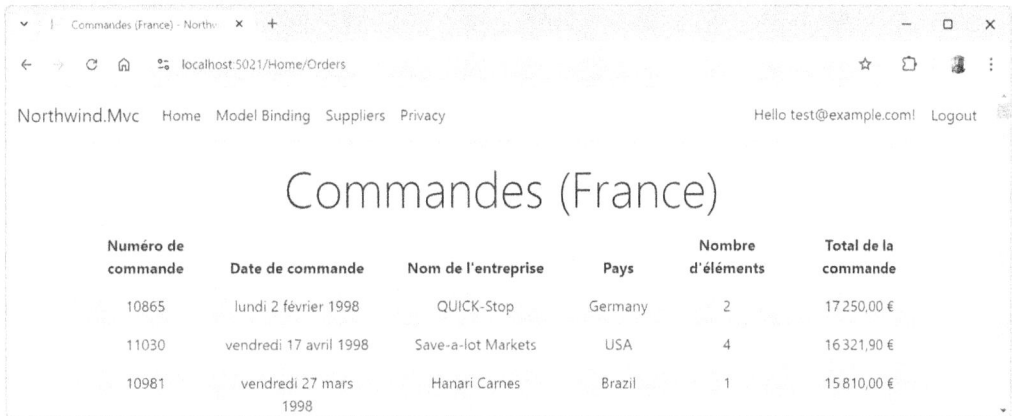

Figure 4.11: The Orders table localized and globalized into French in France

16. Repeat the above steps for the other languages, for example, **English (United Kingdom)**.

17. View **Developer Tools,** and note the request headers have been set with British English (en-GB) first, as shown in *Figure 4.12*:

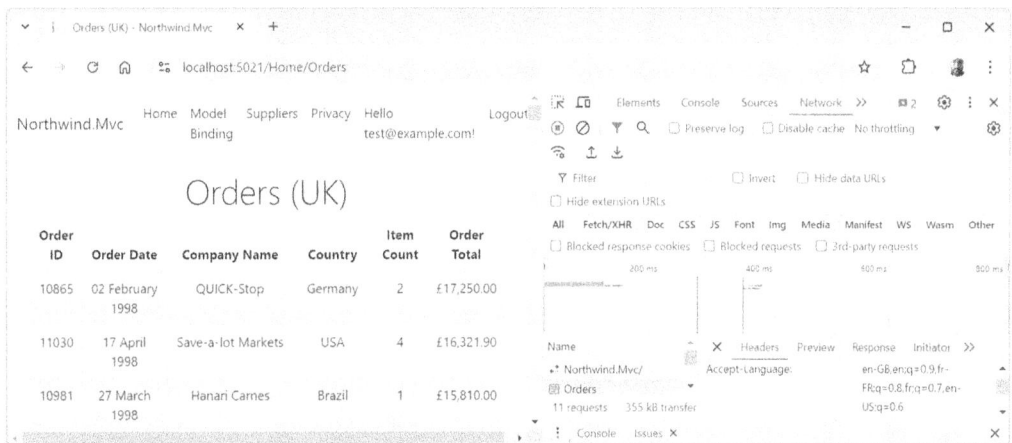

Figure 4.12: Orders localized and globalized into British English due to the Accept-Language: en-GB header

18. Close the browser and shut down the web server.

Understanding the Accept-Language header

Earlier in this section, you saw that the `Accept-Language` header in HTTP requests is used by the client web browser to tell the server which languages it prefers for the content it requests. This allows web servers and applications to serve localized or translated content based on the user's language preferences.

You might wonder how the `Accept-Language` header works. It can be confusing when you look at a typical value, as shown in the following example:

```
Accept-Language: en-US,en;q=0.9,fr-FR;q=0.8,fr;q=0.7,en-GB;q=0.6
```

The `Accept-Language` header uses commas as separators between culture codes. Each culture code can be neutral (just a language) or specific (language and region), and each can have a **quality value** (q) between 0.0 and 1.0 (the default value if it is not explicitly specified). A higher q value indicates a stronger preference for that language.

The preceding `Accept-Language` header example should therefore be read as follows:

- `en-US`: English language in the United States ranked highest at 1.0 (if q not explicitly set)
- `en;q=0.9`: English language anywhere in the world ranked at 0.9
- `fr-FR;q=0.8`: French language in France ranked at 0.8
- `fr;q=0.7`: French language anywhere in the world ranked at 0.7
- `en-GB;q=0.6`: English language in the United Kingdom ranked lowest at 0.6

So that's the basics of localization. You can see that doing it properly can be a lot of work, but to market to the world, it's often a necessity.

You've already been using Bootstrap to apply aesthetic styling to your website. Let's now take some time to see why Bootstrap is popular, why you typically do not use it for branded public websites, and how to use it in practice in more detail.

Prototyping with Bootstrap

Bootstrap is the world's most popular framework for building responsive, mobile-first websites. It combines CSS stylesheets with JavaScript libraries to implement its functionality. It is a good choice for prototyping a website UI, although, before going public, you might want to hire a web designer to build a custom Bootstrap theme or replace it with a completely custom set of CSS stylesheets to give your website a distinct brand.

Bootstrap can be divided into four parts:

- **Layout:** The layout system in Bootstrap provides a responsive grid system, flexible containers, and powerful utilities for creating structured, adaptive designs that adjust seamlessly across various screen sizes and devices.

- **Content:** The content section of Bootstrap includes a variety of pre-styled HTML elements like typography, images, and tables, ensuring a consistent and polished look for textual and visual content across your web pages.

- **Components:** Bootstrap's components are reusable, pre-built UI elements such as buttons, navigation bars, modals, and forms, designed to enhance functionality and user experience with minimal coding effort.

- **Utilities:** Utilities in Bootstrap offer a range of CSS classes that provide quick, low-level control over common styling tasks like spacing, alignment, display, and visibility, allowing easy customization and fine-tuning of your designs.

You do not need to implement all these features; you can use only the parts you need. Let's look at some of the most commonly used and important features.

Breakpoints and containers

The first thing to understand about Bootstrap is its predefined **breakpoints.** In Bootstrap, a breakpoint is a specific viewport width at which the layout and design of a web page change to provide the best user experience for different screen sizes. Breakpoints are predefined screen widths, as shown in the following list:

- X-small (no inline suffix): <576px
- Small (sm): >=576px
- Medium (md): >=768px
- Large (lg): >=992px
- Extra large (xl): >=1200px
- Extra extra large (xxl): >=1400px

Containers are the foundation of the Bootstrap grid layout system that are used to wrap and align your content within a web page. Containers are essential because they provide consistent horizontal padding and control the maximum width of your content at different breakpoints. Think of a container as the frame within which Bootstrap's grid system and other components work. Without containers, your layout can stretch awkwardly or look misaligned on larger screens.

Imagine you have a `<div>` element that uses the Bootstrap `container` class, as shown in the following markup:

```
<div class="container">
  Some content.
</div>
```

As you can see in *Table 2.6*, when the width of the browser is less than 576 pixels, the <div> will stretch to fill 100% of the available width. When the width of the browser is greater than or equal to 576 pixels, the width of the <div> becomes fixed at 540 pixels until the width of the browser is greater than or equal to 768 pixels, at which point the width of the <div> becomes fixed at 720 pixels. This repeats as the width of the browser increases; at each breakpoint, the fixed width of the <div> snaps to a larger value.

	X-Small	Small	Medium	Large	Extra large	XXL
	<576px	**>=576px**	**>=768**	**>=992px**	**>=1200px**	**>=1400px**
`.container`	100%	540px	720px	960px	1140px	1320px
`.container-sm`	100%	540px	720px	960px	1140px	1320px
`.container-md`	100%	100%	720px	960px	1140px	1320px
`.container-lg`	100%	100%	100%	960px	1140px	1320px
`.container-xl`	100%	100%	100%	100%	1140px	1320px
`.container-xxl`	100%	100%	100%	100%	100%	1320px
`.container-fluid`	100%	100%	100%	100%	100%	100%

Table 2.6: Bootstrap container widths

Now imagine that you now have a <div> element that uses the container-lg class, as shown in the following markup:

```
<div class="container-lg">
  Some content.
</div>
```

As you can see in the table above, when the width of the browser is less than 992 pixels, the <div> will always take up 100% of the available browser width. At 992 pixels and above, the <div> width snaps to the breakpoints 960px, 1140px, and 1320px.

If you use the class container-fluid, the <div> always takes up 100% of the available width.

Rows and columns

A Bootstrap container can be divided into rows and columns, for example, one row with three columns, as shown in the following markup:

```
<div class="container">
  <div class="row">
    <div class="col">
      Column
    </div>
    <div class="col">
      Column
```

```
      </div>
      <div class="col">
        Column
      </div>
    </div>
  </div>
```

If you use the col class, then each column will have equal width. But each row is also divided into 12 virtual columns. If you specify a number suffix between 1 and 12, then that column will use that number of twelfths, and the others will divide the rest equally. For example, you could say the left column should use two twelfths, the right column should use four twelfths, and the middle column should use the rest, as shown in the following markup:

```
<div class="container">
  <div class="row">
    <div class="col-2">
      Column
    </div>
    <div class="col">
      Column
    </div>
    <div class="col-4">
      Column
    </div>
  </div>
</div>
```

> The grid system is powerful but can get complicated quickly. To learn more, you can visit the following link: https://getbootstrap.com/docs/5.3/layout/grid/.

Color themes

Bootstrap has eight built-in color themes in addition to the default (black on white), as shown in the following list and *Figure 4.13*:

- primary: Bright blue theme. For example, white text on a bright blue background, or bright blue text and outline on a white background.
- secondary: Gray theme. For example, white text on a gray background, or gray text and outline on a white background.
- success: Green theme. For example, white text on a dark green background, or dark green text and outline on a white background.

- danger: Red theme. For example, white text on a red background, or red text and outline on a white background.
- warning: Yellow theme. For example, black text on a yellow background, or yellow text and outline on a white background.
- info: Light blue theme. For example, black text on a light blue background, or light blue text and outline on a white background.
- light: Light gray theme. For example, black text on a light gray background, or light gray text and outline on a white background.
- dark: Dark gray theme. For example, white text on a dark gray background, or dark gray text and outline on a white background.

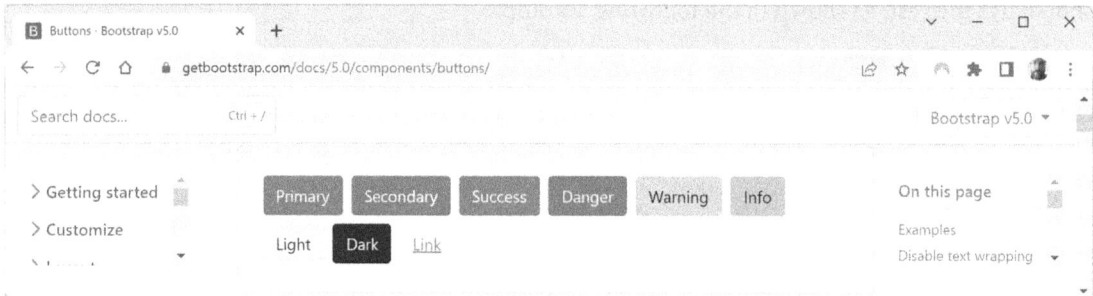

Figure 4.13: Bootstrap color themes

These color themes apply to almost all components, as a `class` attribute of the tag in the form of `{component type}-{theme name}`. For example, to apply the `primary` color theme to a button, you would use `class="btn-primary"`. For text, you would use `class="text-primary"`.

Tables

Bootstrap styles for tables are not automatically applied. You must opt in by applying the `table` class. You can then apply additional style classes:

- table: This is required to enable table styling.
- table-primary, table-warning, and so on: Alternative enabling of table styling with a color theme.
- table-sm: To use half the default padding so the table is more compact.
- table-striped: Add zebra-striping to any table row within the `<tbody>`.
- table-hover: Enable a hover state to change highlights as the mouse moves over table rows within a `<tbody>`.
- table-bordered: Add a border on all sides of the table and its cells.

Let's see an example, as shown in the following markup:

```
<table class="table table-striped table-hover table-bordered">
  <thead>
    <tr>
```

```
          <th>
            ...
        </thead>
        <tbody>
          <tr>
            <td>
              ...
        </tbody>
      </table>
```

The contents in cells in `<thead>` align to the bottom by default. The contents in cells in `<tbody>` align to the top by default. Override these defaults and control other alignment by using the following classes:

- `align-top`: Align the contents of the row or cell to the top.
- `vertical-align-middle`: Align the contents of the row or cell to the middle vertically.
- `align-bottom`: Align the contents of the row or cell to the bottom.
- `align-left`: Align the contents of the row or cell to the left.
- `align-middle`: Align the contents of the row or cell to the middle horizontally.
- `align-right`: Align the contents of the row or cell to the right.

Buttons and links

Bootstrap has button styles that can be applied to actual `<button>` and `<input type="button">` elements as well as hyperlinks, as shown in the following markup:

```
<button class="btn btn-primary" type="button">Click Me</button>
<input class="btn btn-primary" type="button" value="Click Me">
<a class="btn btn-primary" href="#" role="button">Click Me</a>
```

All three elements above will look like a bright blue button with the label **Click Me**.

If you do not want the text in the button label to wrap, add the `text-nowrap` class.

Use `btn-outline-primary` (or any of the other color themes) to have more subtle styling that uses the color for the outline and text with a white background until the mouse hovers over the button.

You can adjust the size of the button by adding `btn-sm` to make it smaller or `btn-lg` to make it larger.

Badges

Badges are used to show small pieces of information, like the number of unread messages. For example:

```
<button type="button" class="btn btn-primary">
  Messages <span class="badge bg-secondary">4</span>
</button>
```

You can reposition the badge and use the `rounded-pill` class to turn the default rectangle badge into a circular one, like most apps do, to show the number of unread notifications or messages inside a red circle:

```
<button type="button" class="btn btn-primary position-relative">
  Messages
  <span class="position-absolute top-0 start-100 translate-middle
 badge rounded-pill bg-danger">
    12 <span class="visually-hidden">unread messages</span>
  </span>
</button>
```

You can use a more rounded corner to turn a badge into a pill, as shown in the following markup and *Figure 4.14*:

```
<span class="badge rounded-pill bg-primary">Primary</span>
<span class="badge rounded-pill bg-secondary">Secondary</span>
<span class="badge rounded-pill bg-success">Success</span>
<span class="badge rounded-pill bg-danger">Danger</span>
<span class="badge rounded-pill bg-warning text-dark">Warning</span>
<span class="badge rounded-pill bg-info text-dark">Info</span>
<span class="badge rounded-pill bg-light text-dark">Light</span>
<span class="badge rounded-pill bg-dark">Dark</span>
```

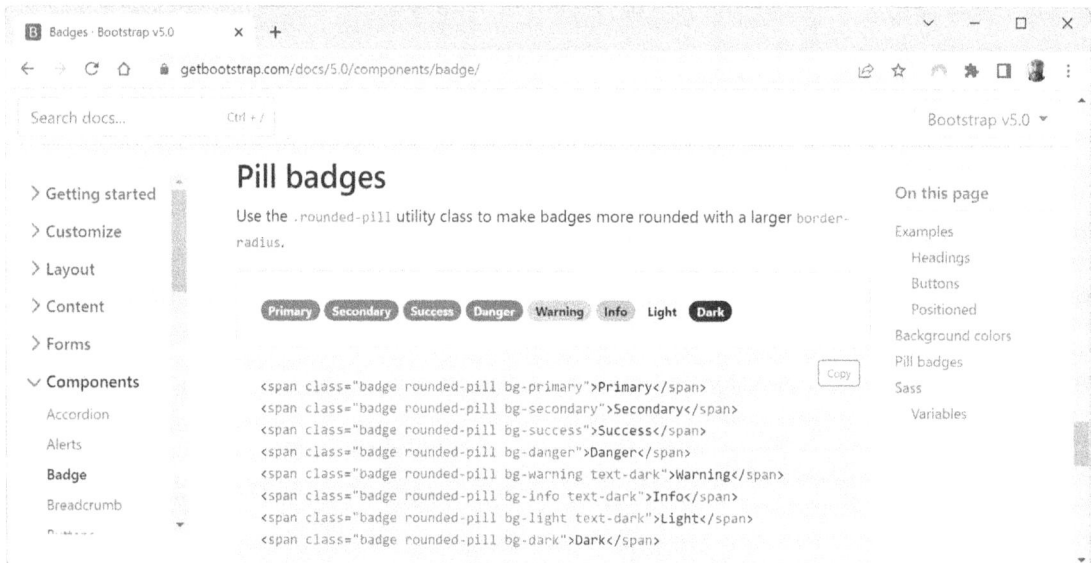

Figure 4.14: Pill badges using Bootstrap

Alerts

You will often need to show messages to website visitors. Alerts must use one of the eight color themes. Any links within the alert element should use the `alert-link` class. The contents can be plain text or use additional elements like headings, as shown in the following markup:

```
<div class="alert alert-success" role="alert">
  <h4 class="alert-heading">Order was accepted.</h4>
  <p>To view the order, click <a href="#" class="alert-link">here</a>.</p>
</div>
```

> For more examples of alerts, for example, adding icons inside the alert, see the official documentation at the following link: https://getbootstrap.com/docs/5.3/components/alerts/#icons.

Should you use Bootstrap?

Bootstrap is like Marmite. Some developers love it; some hate it.

Good reasons to use Bootstrap include:

- It saves time.
- It is customizable.
- It is open source.
- It is well documented officially and has lots of answers about it on sites like Stack Overflow.

But implementing Bootstrap without care has the following negatives:

- Your website will look generic.
- It is heavy compared to a hand-crafted solution.

> **Good practice:** As well as defining your own styles, base your styles on a common library, such as Bootstrap, that implements responsive design. However, if you are building a website that needs a distinct identity or brand, make sure you use its theming support. Do not just accept the defaults.

Practicing and exploring

Test your knowledge and understanding by answering some questions, getting some hands-on practice, and exploring this chapter's topics with deeper research.

Exercise 4.1 – Online material

Official documentation for ASP.NET Core MVC views can be found at the following link:

`https://learn.microsoft.com/en-us/aspnet/core/mvc/views/overview`.

Partial views are an effective way to break up large markup files into smaller components. You can learn about partial views at the following link:

`https://learn.microsoft.com/en-us/aspnet/core/mvc/views/partial`.

Layouts in ASP.NET Core are documented at the following link:

`https://learn.microsoft.com/en-us/aspnet/core/mvc/views/layout`.

The following is a Razor syntax reference:

`https://learn.microsoft.com/en-us/aspnet/core/mvc/views/razor`.

Exercise 4.2 – Practice exercises

The following practice exercises help you to explore the topics in this chapter more deeply.

Practice creating a custom Tag Helper

A Tag Helper is any class that implements the `ITagHelper` interface. When you write your own Tag Helper, it is usually derived from the `TagHelper` class because that gives you access to a minimal implementation with the `Process` method.

Complete the following online tutorial to learn how to build your own Tag Helper:

`https://learn.microsoft.com/en-us/aspnet/core/mvc/views/tag-helpers/authoring`.

Practice building UIs with Bootstrap

Create a new ASP.NET Core MVC project named `ExploringBootstrap`. Add views that implement the following Bootstrap features:

- Accordion: `https://getbootstrap.com/docs/5.3/components/accordion/`
- Cards: `https://getbootstrap.com/docs/5.3/components/card/`
- Carousel: `https://getbootstrap.com/docs/5.3/components/carousel/`
- Navbar: `https://getbootstrap.com/docs/5.3/components/navbar/`
- Popovers: `https://getbootstrap.com/docs/5.3/components/popovers/`
- Toast: `https://getbootstrap.com/docs/5.3/components/toasts/`
- Tooltips: `https://getbootstrap.com/docs/5.3/components/tooltips/`

Exercise 4.3 – Test your knowledge

Answer the following questions:

1. What is the advantage of declaring a strongly typed Razor View, and how do you do it?

2. How do you enable Tag Helpers in a view?

3. What are the pros and cons of HTML Helper methods compared to Tag Helpers?

4. How can a browser request a preferred language for localization?

5. How do you localize text in a view?

6. What is the prefix for attributes recognized by Tag Helpers?

7. How can you pass a complex object as a query string parameter?

8. How can you control how long the contents of the `<cache>` element are cached for?

9. What is the `<environment>` element used for?

10. What is Bootstrap, and what is a good reason to use it?

Exercise 4.4 – Explore topics

Use the links on the following page to learn more about the topics covered in this chapter:

```
https://github.com/markjprice/web-dev-net10/blob/main/docs/book-links.md#chapter-4---
building-and-localizing-web-user-interfaces.
```

Summary

In this chapter, you learned how to build user interfaces using ASP.NET Core MVC. You learned about:

- ASP.NET Core Razor Views and Razor syntax
- HTML Helpers and Tag Helpers
- Localizing an ASP.NET Core website

You also learned about Bootstrap, which is great for rapid prototyping or internal websites that do not need distinct branding.

In the next chapter, you will learn how to secure your websites using authentication and authorization.

5

Authentication and Authorization

Authentication verifies a user's identity, typically through a login process, while authorization determines what actions or resources the authenticated user is allowed to access. This is essential for protecting sensitive data, ensuring privacy, and maintaining the overall security of the website, preventing unauthorized access or misuse.

Authentication and authorization are important for any website because they ensure that only legitimate users can access the system and that each user has the appropriate permissions. Most public websites have pages that should be public to everyone anonymously, and some pages that should only be accessed by known users with the appropriate permission.

There are two types of web development projects that you will likely want to secure: websites for humans to interact with and web services for code to interact with.

This chapter is about authentication and authorization and how to implement them for an ASP.NET Core MVC website project. This means how to provide a web user interface for a visitor to register an account with a password, and how they can log in to access secure areas of the website.

Later, in *Chapter 9, Building Web Services Using ASP.NET Core Web API*, you will learn how to implement authentication and authorization for ASP.NET Core Web API web service projects. This means learning how to provide endpoints to request authentication tokens to then enable calls to secure endpoints of a web service.

This chapter will cover the following topics:

- Introducing authentication and authorization
- Securing controller action methods using filters

Introducing authentication and authorization

Authentication and authorization are two concepts in web application security, often used together but with distinct purposes, as described in the following list:

- **Authentication, AKA "who are you?"**: This is the process of verifying the identity of a user. When a user attempts to log in to an application, the system checks whether the credentials, for example, username and password, provided by the user match those stored in the system. Successful authentication confirms that the user is who they claim to be.

  Once authentication has occurred, a system often provides the client with a token that the client can submit with future requests to avoid having to re-authenticate each time. These tokens can be HTTP cookies, JSON, or some other format like **JWT (JSON Web Token)** that can encapsulate additional claims.

- **Authorization, AKA "what can you do?"**: Once the user is authenticated, authorization determines what resources or actions the user is allowed to access within the application. For instance, an authenticated user might have permission to view their account information, but they might not have permission to access administrative features. Authorization is often based on role or group membership rather than permissions assigned to an individual account.

Key concepts of authentication and authorization

You should be familiar with several concepts and techniques related to authentication and authorization, particularly in the context of ASP.NET Core. In this section, I will introduce or remind you of some of those key concepts, and if and when needed, I will cover more details at the appropriate points throughout the book.

Identity management

A key technology for authentication is identity management. This involves understanding how to manage user identities, including the use of **ASP.NET Core Identity**, which provides a framework for managing users, passwords, roles, claims, tokens, and more. You will learn more details about this topic in this chapter and in *Chapter 9, Building Web Services Using ASP.NET Core Web API*. There are many third-party choices as well, and you can optionally complete a tutorial for one of them, Auth0, in the practice section at the end of this chapter.

Authentication schemes

Different methods can be used for authentication, such as cookies, JWT, OAuth2, OpenID Connect, and so on. A developer should understand when and how to use these schemes based on the application's requirements. You will learn more details about this topic in *Chapter 9, Building Web Services Using ASP.NET Core Web API*.

Role-based and claims-based authorization

ASP.NET Core supports role-based and claims-based authorization. Role-based is simpler, where users are granted roles, for example, Administrator, Salesperson, or Visitor. Claims-based is more flexible, allowing finer-grained control based on specific claims, for example, permission to edit a particular table or record in a database. For example, only members of the finance department might be given access to aggregate financial data. You will learn more details about this topic later in this chapter.

Security best practices

It is important for a .NET developer to understand security best practices like hashing passwords, which ASP.NET Core Identity handles by default, enforcing HTTPS, implementing secure cookie practices, regular software updates, using secure HTTP headers (**CSP**), input validation, and mitigating common vulnerabilities such as SQL injection, **Cross-Site Scripting (XSS)**, and **Cross-Site Request Forgery (CSRF)**.

For example, you learned how to mitigate SQL injection and CSRF attacks in *Chapter 3, Model Binding, Validation, and Data Using EF Core*.

Cookie-based authentication

Cookie-based authentication works by storing a session identifier or authentication token inside an HTTP cookie on the user's browser. Every time the user makes a request to the server, the browser automatically sends this cookie, allowing the server to recognize the user and verify their identity.

Cookie-based authentication can be vulnerable to several security risks if not properly handled. Here are some potential vulnerabilities and best practices associated with using cookies for authentication:

- **XSS**: If an attacker can inject malicious scripts into your website, they may access cookies stored in the user's browser, especially if the cookies aren't marked as HttpOnly. This allows attackers to steal session cookies and impersonate users.

- **CSRF**: CSRF attacks trick users into unknowingly making requests on a website where they are authenticated. If cookies are automatically sent with every request, attackers could exploit this to perform actions on behalf of the user.

- **Cookie Theft via Insecure Transmission**: Without enforcing secure transmission (using the Secure flag), cookies can be transmitted over unencrypted HTTP connections, making them vulnerable to **man-in-the-middle (MITM)** attacks where attackers can intercept the cookies.

- **Session Hijacking**: If session cookies are not properly protected, an attacker may steal them and hijack an authenticated session, potentially gaining unauthorized access to the application.

- **Persistent Cookie Vulnerabilities**: Persistent cookies that remain on the user's device beyond the session can be exploited if a device is lost or shared, allowing unauthorized access if not properly protected.

Due to the preceding potential vulnerabilities, I recommend the following best practices:

- **Use the HttpOnly Flag:** The HttpOnly flag prevents client-side JavaScript from accessing cookies. This significantly reduces the risk of XSS attacks being able to steal session cookies:

  ```
  options.Cookie.HttpOnly = true;
  ```

- **Set the SameSite Attribute:** The SameSite attribute helps prevent CSRF attacks by ensuring cookies are only sent in first-party contexts or when users explicitly navigate to your website. Setting SameSite=Strict provides the highest level of protection, but SameSite=Lax can offer a balance between security and usability for many applications:

  ```
  options.Cookie.SameSite = SameSiteMode.Strict;
  ```

- **Use the Secure Flag:** Mark cookies with the Secure flag to ensure they are only transmitted over HTTPS, preventing them from being sent over insecure HTTP connections. This protects cookies from being intercepted by attackers in transit:

  ```
  options.Cookie.SecurePolicy = CookieSecurePolicy.Always;
  ```

- **Implement Short Session Expiration:** Limit the lifespan of authentication cookies by setting a short expiration time to reduce the window of opportunity for attackers if a session is hijacked. Avoid persistent cookies unless absolutely necessary:

  ```
  options.Cookie.Expiration = TimeSpan.FromMinutes(30);
  ```

- **Regenerate Session Cookies on Authentication:** Always regenerate session cookies after a user authenticates (after login) to prevent session fixation attacks, where an attacker forces a user to use a known session ID.

- **Enable Multi-Factor Authentication (MFA):** Combining cookie-based authentication with MFA adds an extra layer of security by requiring users to provide a second form of verification beyond the password, even if the cookie is compromised.

- **Use Strong, Random Session IDs:** Ensure that session IDs stored in cookies are randomly generated and sufficiently long, making them difficult to guess or brute-force.

- **Restrict Cookie Scope:** Limit the scope of cookies by setting the Domain and Path attributes appropriately. For example, restrict cookies to only be sent on specific subdomains or paths, reducing the risk of accidental or malicious exposure:

  ```
  options.Cookie.Domain = "yourdomain.com";
  options.Cookie.Path = "/secure-path";
  ```

You've now seen that cookie-based authentication is a popular method for managing user sessions, and it is the default for ASP.NET Core Identity. But keep in mind that it comes with potential vulnerabilities that should be addressed. Now, let's review some good practices for passwords.

Password verifier good practices

Authentication systems include password verifiers that check a password entered during user registration. For example, the following is true of password verifiers that follow good practices:

- **SHALL** require passwords to be a minimum of eight characters in length.
- **SHOULD** require passwords to be a minimum of 15 characters in length.
- **SHALL NOT** impose composition rules like requiring mixtures of different character types.
- **SHALL NOT** require users to change passwords periodically.
- **SHALL** force a password change if there is evidence of compromise of the authenticator.

> **Good practice:** The latest recommendations can be found at `https://pages.nist.gov/800-63-4/sp800-63b.html#passwordver`.

Now, let's get practical and see how to implement authentication and authorization.

Implementing authentication and authorization

When implementing authentication and authorization in an ASP.NET Core MVC project, for your future reference, here are the essential steps and considerations:

> **Warning!** You do not need to complete these steps now! I am documenting them here as a reference. Most of the steps have already been completed for you in your ASP.NET Core MVC project because you enabled authentication in the project template.

1. Start by adding ASP.NET Core Identity to your ASP.NET Core project. If you use the MVC project template, it does this for you. At the command prompt or terminal, to add ASP.NET Core Identity with its EF Core store provider to an existing project, use the following command:

```
dotnet add package Microsoft.AspNetCore.Identity.EntityFrameworkCore
```

> While EF Core is the most common choice for ASP.NET Core Identity, the framework is flexible enough to work with a wide range of data stores, from traditional relational databases to modern NoSQL solutions and even custom store provider implementations. Community-maintained store providers are available at
>
> `https://github.com/dotnet/AspNetCore/tree/main/src/Identity#community-maintained-store-providers`.

2. Define an ASP.NET Core Identity database context class file named `ApplicationDbContext.cs`, as shown in the following code:

```
public class ApplicationDbContext : IdentityDbContext<IdentityUser>
{
  public ApplicationDbContext(
    DbContextOptions<ApplicationDbContext> options) : base(options)
  {
  }
}
```

If you use the ASP.NET Core MVC project template, then this will be done for you. You will find the `ApplicationDbContext.cs` file in the `Data` folder. The code solution is found at the following link: `https://github.com/markjprice/web-dev-net10/blob/main/code/MatureWeb/Northwind.Mvc/Data/ApplicationDbContext.cs`.

Optionally, you can customize this class by adding additional properties and methods to manage your application's specific data needs alongside user identity information.

3. In `Program.cs`, configure ASP.NET Core Identity by adding an EF Core database context for the store provider and configuring the default identity user class in the dependency services collection, and then enabling authentication and authorization in the HTTP pipeline, as shown highlighted in the following code:

```
var builder = WebApplication.CreateBuilder(args);

builder.Services.AddDbContext<ApplicationDbContext>(options =>
  options.UseSqlServer(builder.Configuration
  .GetConnectionString("DefaultConnection")));

builder.Services.AddDefaultIdentity<IdentityUser>(options =>
  options.SignIn.RequireConfirmedAccount = true)
  .AddEntityFrameworkStores<ApplicationDbContext>();

builder.Services.AddControllersWithViews();

var app = builder.Build();

app.UseAuthentication(); // Enable authentication middleware.
app.UseAuthorization(); // Enable authorization middleware.
```

Note the following about the preceding code:

- `AddDbContext<ApplicationDbContext>()` registers the `ApplicationDbContext` class as a database context, just as you might for the `Northwind` database. `UseSqlServer` specifies using SQL Server as the underlying data store. The connection string is retrieved from the configuration using the name `"DefaultConnection"`. At this point, the code has no connection with ASP.NET Core Identity.
- `AddDefaultIdentity<IdentityUser>()` configures ASP.NET Core Identity with the default `IdentityUser` class for user accounts.
- `SignIn.RequireConfirmedAccount = true` enforces an additional security measure by requiring users to confirm their email address before logging in.
- `AddEntityFrameworkStores<ApplicationDbContext>()` connects the database context to ASP.NET Core Identity.

> If you use the ASP.NET Core MVC project template, then this will be done for you. The code solution is found at the following link: `https://github.com/markjprice/web-dev-net10/blob/main/code/MatureWeb/Northwind.Mvc/Program.cs`.

4. Decorate classes and methods with the `[Authorize]` attribute to protect controllers or routes, for example, as shown in the following code:

```
[Authorize(Roles = "Admin")]
public IActionResult AdminOnly()
{
    return View();
}
```

> Authorization based on role membership is just one type of authorization. You can implement custom attributes with any business logic you need. For example, you could define authorization based on the visitor's age, as shown at `https://learn.microsoft.com/en-us/aspnet/core/security/authorization/iard`.

5. ASP.NET Core Identity uses cookie authentication by default. Optionally, customize the cookie behavior, for example, change the path to login, and the path to a route that shows when access is denied, as shown in the following code:

```
builder.Services.ConfigureApplicationCookie(options =>
{
    options.LoginPath = "/Account/Login";
    options.AccessDeniedPath = "/Account/AccessDenied";
});
```

The default login page is implemented as a Razor Page, as shown at the following link: `https://github.com/dotnet/aspnetcore/blob/main/src/Identity/UI/src/Areas/Identity/Pages/V5/Account/Login.cshtml`.

The default access denied page is also implemented as a Razor Page, as shown at the following link: `https://github.com/dotnet/aspnetcore/blob/main/src/Identity/UI/src/Areas/Identity/Pages/V5/Account/AccessDenied.cshtml`.

6. Implement login and logout actions in your controller, as shown in the following code:

```
public async Task<IActionResult> Login(LoginViewModel model)
{
  if (ModelState.IsValid)
  {
    var result = await _signInManager.PasswordSignInAsync(
      model.Username, model.Password, model.RememberMe,
      lockoutOnFailure: false);

    if (result.Succeeded)
    {
      return RedirectToAction("Index", "Home");
    }
    ModelState.AddModelError(string.Empty, "Invalid login attempt.");
  }
  return View(model);
}

public async Task<IActionResult> Logout()
{
  await _signInManager.SignOutAsync();
  return RedirectToAction("Index", "Home");
}
```

If you use the MVC project template, then this will be done for you by the Razor Pages provided by the `Microsoft.AspNetCore.Identity.UI` package, so you will not see this code in an MVC project by default. You can see the code to log in at the following link: `https://github.com/dotnet/aspnetcore/blob/main/src/Identity/UI/src/Areas/Identity/Pages/V5/Account/Login.cshtml.cs#L120`.

7.   Create users and roles, and then assign roles to users. Add claims to users. This could be scripted or via a custom user interface as part of the ASP.NET Core project.

Defining policies

As well as simple role-based authorization, you might want to define **policies** for more complex requirements. Policies encapsulate a set of requirements or conditions that must be met for access to be granted. For example, an employee might need to be a "Manager," a member of the "HR" department, and under the age of 60, and they must only access the page during working hours.

Policy-based authorization in ASP.NET Core provides flexibility to create complex authorization rules tailored to specific application needs. Whether you require role-based, claim-based, or more custom requirements, policies allow you to encapsulate and manage these rules effectively.

When configuring authorization, you can implement policies, for example, to require membership of a role like Admin, as shown in the following code:

```
builder.Services.AddAuthorization(options =>
{
  options.AddPolicy("RequireAdministratorRole", policy =>
    policy.RequireRole("Admin"));
});
```

You can create policies for specific business logic, as shown in the following code:

```
builder.Services.AddAuthorization(options =>
{
  options.AddPolicy("Over18Only", policy =>
    policy.RequireClaim("Age", "Over18"));
});
```

You can implement custom authorization handlers when you need to implement complex logic that can't be captured by simple policies or roles, as shown in the following code:

```
public class MinimumAgeHandler : AuthorizationHandler<MinimumAgeRequirement>
{
  protected override Task HandleRequirementAsync(
    AuthorizationHandlerContext context,
    MinimumAgeRequirement requirement)
  {
    // Custom logic here.
    return Task.CompletedTask;
  }
}
```

External authentication

ASP.NET Core Identity supports external authentication providers like Google, Facebook, and Microsoft. This is useful for several reasons:

- **Streamlined User Experience:** Many users already have accounts with these providers, so allowing them to sign in with existing credentials eliminates the need to create new accounts, reducing friction during the registration and login process.

- **Improved Security:** External providers often offer more robust security measures than many custom authentication systems. For example, Google and Microsoft use advanced security practices, such as MFA, regular vulnerability patches, and large-scale monitoring, which can give your users better protection than a home-grown system.

- **Trust and Familiarity:** Many users feel more comfortable using authentication providers they already know and trust. This can boost confidence in your application, as users don't have to worry about creating and storing another password or trusting a smaller, less familiar system with their personal information.

- **Faster Onboarding:** New users can quickly register and start using the application, as the process is simplified to a few clicks when using an existing account from Google, Facebook, or Microsoft. This removes the need for email verification steps and other traditional registration hurdles.

To integrate with external authentication providers like Google, you first need to register with their account system. This will provide you with a unique client identifier and a client secret.

Next, you must reference the appropriate package, like `Microsoft.AspNetCore.Authentication.Google`, and then configure the provider in `Program.cs`, as shown in the following code:

```
builder.Services.AddAuthentication()
  .AddGoogle(options =>
  {
    options.ClientId = "GoogleClientId";
    options.ClientSecret = "GoogleClientSecret";
  });
```

Tutorials to walk you through integrating with various external authentication providers can be found at the following links:

- Google: `https://learn.microsoft.com/en-us/aspnet/core/security/authentication/social/google-logins`
- Facebook: `https://learn.microsoft.com/en-us/aspnet/core/security/authentication/social/facebook-logins`
- Microsoft: `https://learn.microsoft.com/en-us/aspnet/core/security/authentication/social/microsoft-logins`

Securing APIs with JWT

You will learn more about securing web services in *Chapter 9, Building Web Services Using ASP.NET Core Web API,* but let's briefly introduce you to one of the most important concepts.

If your application includes APIs, securing them with **JWTs (JSON Web Tokens)** is a common practice.

JWTs are a compact, URL-safe means of representing claims between two parties. They consist of three parts: header, payload, and signature, encoded in base64:

- The header contains metadata.
- The payload contains claims (for example, user info and permissions)
- The signature ensures the token's integrity.

JWTs are self-contained, meaning all the information needed to verify the user is in the token itself, reducing the need for server-side session storage. They also use digital signatures to verify that the token hasn't been tampered with, ensuring the integrity of the data.

Plus, JWTs are compact and can be easily transmitted via URLs, headers, or in the body of HTTP requests.

Since JWTs are stateless and transmitted in a compact format, they are ideal for distributed systems, mobile apps, and APIs, allowing secure, token-based communication between different services or platforms. Since they are stateless, JWTs help scale applications by reducing the server's burden of storing session data, making them ideal for cloud-based or microservice architectures.

You configure JWTs in `Program.cs`, as shown in the following code:

```
builder.Services.AddAuthentication(JwtBearerDefaults.AuthenticationScheme)
  .AddJwtBearer(options =>
  {
    options.TokenValidationParameters = new TokenValidationParameters
    {
      ValidateIssuer = true,
      ValidateAudience = true,
      ValidateLifetime = true,
      ValidateIssuerSigningKey = true,
      ValidIssuer = Configuration["Jwt:Issuer"],
      ValidAudience = Configuration["Jwt:Audience"],
      IssuerSigningKey = new SymmetricSecurityKey(
        Encoding.UTF8.GetBytes(Configuration["Jwt:Key"]))
    };
  });
```

You can learn about all the dozens of properties that can be set depending on your specific scenario at the following link: https://learn.microsoft.com/en-us/dotnet/api/microsoft.identitymodel.tokens.tokenvalidationparameters.

Now, let's add authorization to our MVC website project by securing some of its functionality provided by some of its action methods.

Securing controller action methods using filters

You might want to ensure that one particular action method of a controller class can only be called by members of certain security roles. You do this by decorating the method with the [Authorize] attribute, as described in the following list:

- [Authorize]: Only allow authenticated (non-anonymous, logged-in) visitors to access this action method.
- [Authorize(Roles = "Sales,Marketing")]: Only allow visitors who are members of the specified role(s) to access this action method.

Let's see an example:

1. In HomeController.cs, import the namespace for working with authorization, as shown in the following code:

```
using Microsoft.AspNetCore.Authorization; // To use [Authorize].
```

2. Add an attribute to the ModelBinding method to only allow access to logged-in users who are members of a group/role named Administrators, as shown highlighted in the following code:

```
[Authorize(Roles = "Administrators")]
public IActionResult ModelBinding()
```

3. Start **Docker Desktop** and the nw-container container.

4. Start the Northwind.Mvc project website using the https profile.

5. If you are logged in (for example, you might have selected the **Remember me?** check box), then in the top navigation menu, on the far-right side, click **Logout**.

6. In the top navigation menu, click **Model Binding** and note that you are automatically redirected to the login page because this page requires authorization. Therefore, you must first be authenticated so the system then knows what permissions you have.

7. Enter your email and password.

8. Click **Log in** and note the message, **Access denied - You do not have access to this resource.** (As mentioned earlier in this chapter, this user interface is provided by a Razor Page in the Microsoft.AspNetCore.Identity.UI package.)

9. Close Chrome and shut down the web server.

Now that we have configured the ModelBinding action method to authorize only members of the Administrators role, we will need to enable role management and add ourselves to the Administrators role.

Enabling role management and creating a role programmatically

By default, role management is not enabled in an ASP.NET Core MVC project, so we must first enable it before creating roles. Then, we will create a controller that will programmatically create an Administrators role (if it does not already exist) and assign our test user to that role:

1. In the Extensions folder, in WebApplicationBuilderExtensions.cs, in the setup of ASP.NET Core Identity and its database, add a call to AddRoles to enable role management, as shown highlighted in the following code:

```
services.AddDefaultIdentity<IdentityUser>(
  options => options.SignIn.RequireConfirmedAccount = true)
  .AddRoles<IdentityRole>() // Enable role management.
  .AddEntityFrameworkStores<ApplicationDbContext>();
```

2. In the Controllers folder, add an empty controller class named RolesController.cs and modify its contents, as shown in the following code:

> The complete file can be found at the following link: https://github.com/markjprice/web-dev-net10/blob/main/code/MatureWeb/Northwind.Mvc/Controllers/RolesController.cs.

```
using Microsoft.AspNetCore.Identity; // To use RoleManager, UserManager.
using Microsoft.AspNetCore.Mvc; // To use Controller, IActionResult.

namespace Northwind.Mvc.Controllers;

public class RolesController : Controller
{
  private string AdminRole = "Administrators";
  private string UserEmail = "test@example.com";
  private readonly RoleManager<IdentityRole> _roleManager;
  private readonly UserManager<IdentityUser> _userManager;
  private readonly ILogger<RolesController> _logger;

  public RolesController(ILogger<RolesController> logger,
    RoleManager<IdentityRole> roleManager,
    UserManager<IdentityUser> userManager)
  {
    _logger = logger;
```

```csharp
    _roleManager = roleManager;
    _userManager = userManager;
}

private void LogIdentityResult(
    IdentityResult result, string message)
{
    if (result.Succeeded)
    {
        _logger.LogInformation(message);
    }
    else
    {
        foreach (IdentityError error in result.Errors)
        {
            _logger.LogError(error.Description);
        }
    }
}

public async Task<IActionResult> Index()
{
    if (!(await _roleManager.RoleExistsAsync(AdminRole)))
    {
        await _roleManager.CreateAsync(new IdentityRole(AdminRole));
    }

    IdentityUser? user = await _userManager.FindByEmailAsync(UserEmail);

    if (user == null)
    {
        user = new();
        user.UserName = UserEmail;
        user.Email = UserEmail;

        IdentityResult result = await _userManager.CreateAsync(
            user, "Pa$$w0rd");

        LogIdentityResult(result,
            $"User {user.UserName} created successfully."); }
    }
```

```
              if (!user.EmailConfirmed)
              {
                string token = await _userManager
                  .GenerateEmailConfirmationTokenAsync(user);

                IdentityResult result = await _userManager
                  .ConfirmEmailAsync(user, token);

                LogIdentityResult(result,
                  $"User {user.UserName} email confirmed successfully.");
              }

              if (!(await _userManager.IsInRoleAsync(user, AdminRole)))
              {
                IdentityResult result = await _userManager
                  .AddToRoleAsync(user, AdminRole);

                LogIdentityResult(result,
                  $"User {user.UserName} added to {AdminRole} successfully.");
              }
              return Redirect("/");
          }
      }
```

Note the following, which explains all the code in the preceding `RolesController.cs` file. You should go through the code line by line, matching the following bullet descriptions:

- Two fields for the name of the role and the email of the user.
- The constructor gets and stores the registered user and role manager dependency services.
- If the `Administrators` role does not exist, we use the role manager to create it.
- We try to find a test user by its email, create it if it does not exist, and then assign the user to the `Administrators` role.
- Since the website uses DOI, we must generate an email confirmation token and use it to confirm the new user's email address.
- Success messages and any errors are written out to the console.
- You will automatically be redirected to the home page.

3. Start the `Northwind.Mvc` website project using the `https` profile.
4. Click **Model Binding** and note that you are redirected to the login page.
5. Enter your email and password. (I used `test@example.com` and `P@$$w0rd`.)
6. Click **Log in** and note that you are denied access to the **Model Binding** page as before.

7. Click **Home**.

8. In the address bar, manually enter `roles` as a relative URL path, as shown at `https://localhost:5021/roles`.

9. At the command prompt or terminal that is hosting the web server, note the logged `INSERT INTO [AspNetUserRoles]` statement and the success message written to the console, as shown in *Figure 5.1* and in the following output:

```
User test@example.com added to Administrators successfully.
```

```
C:\web-dev-net10\MatureWeb\Northwind.Mvc\bin\Debug\net10.0\Northwind.Mvc.exe    ×    + ∨                        —    □    ×
info: Microsoft.EntityFrameworkCore.Database.Command[20101]
      Executed DbCommand (5ms) [Parameters=[@p0='?' (Size = 450), @p1='?' (Size = 450), @p16='?' (Size = 450), @p2='?' (
DbType = Int32), @p3='?' (Size = 4000), @p17='?' (Size = 4000), @p4='?' (Size = 256), @p5='?' (DbType = Boolean), @p6='?
' (DbType = Boolean), @p7='?' (DbType = DateTimeOffset), @p8='?' (Size = 256), @p9='?' (Size = 256), @p10='?' (Size = 40
00), @p11='?' (Size = 4000), @p12='?' (DbType = Boolean), @p13='?' (Size = 4000), @p14='?' (DbType = Boolean), @p15='?'
(Size = 256)], CommandType='Text', CommandTimeout='30']
      SET NOCOUNT ON;
      INSERT INTO [AspNetUserRoles] ([RoleId], [UserId])
      VALUES (@p0, @p1);
      UPDATE [AspNetUsers] SET [AccessFailedCount] = @p2, [ConcurrencyStamp] = @p3, [Email] = @p4, [EmailConfirmed] = @p
5, [LockoutEnabled] = @p6, [LockoutEnd] = @p7, [NormalizedEmail] = @p8, [NormalizedUserName] = @p9, [PasswordHash] = @p1
0, [PhoneNumber] = @p11, [PhoneNumberConfirmed] = @p12, [SecurityStamp] = @p13, [TwoFactorEnabled] = @p14, [UserName] =
@p15
      OUTPUT 1
      WHERE [Id] = @p16 AND [ConcurrencyStamp] = @p17;
info: Northwind.Mvc.Controllers.RolesController[0]
      User test@example.com added to Administrators successfully.  ⬅
```

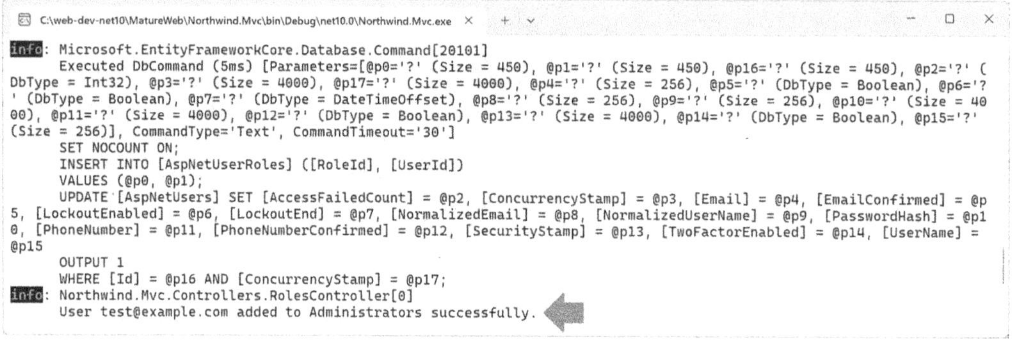

Figure 5.1: Output from adding the user to the Administrators role

> If you did not register yourself as `test@example.com`, then you will also see the message `User test@example.com created successfully.`

10. Click **Logout**, because you must log out and back in to load your role memberships when they are created after you have already logged in.

11. Try accessing the **Model Binding** page again, enter the email for the new user that was programmatically created, for example, `test@example.com`, and their password, and then click **Log in**. You should now have access.

12. Close Chrome and shut down the web server.

Cross-functional filters

When you need to add some functionality to multiple controllers and actions, you can use or define your own filters that are implemented as an attribute class. Filters allow you to run code before or after certain stages in the request processing pipeline. They provide a mechanism to add cross-cutting concerns like authentication, authorization, logging, error handling, and more.

Filters can be applied at the following levels:

- At the action level, by decorating an action method with the attribute. This will only affect the one action method.

- At the controller level, by decorating the controller class with the attribute. This will affect all methods of the controller.

- At the global level, by adding the attribute type to the `Filters` collection of the `MvcOptions` instance that can be used to configure MVC when calling the `AddControllersWithViews` method, as shown in the following code:

```
builder.Services.AddControllersWithViews(options =>
  {
    options.Filters.Add(typeof(MyCustomFilter));
  });
```

Filters execute in a specific order, both before and after the action method is executed. The order of filter execution is determined by its type, as described in the following list:

1. **Authorization Filters**: a class that implements `IAuthorizationFilter`.
2. **Resource Filters**: a class that implements `IResourceFilter`.
3. **Action Filters**: a class that implements `IActionFilter`.
4. **Exception Filters**: a class that implements `IExceptionFilter`.
5. **Result Filters**: a class that implements `IResultFilter`.

Filters are called in two phases:

- **Before Action Execution**: Filters are executed in the preceding order before the action method.
- **After Action Execution**: Filters are executed in the reverse order after the action method completes.

Authorization filter (IAuthorizationFilter)

This runs first in the filter pipeline to ensure the user is authorized to access the resource. It executes before anything else in the pipeline, even before model binding. If the user is unauthorized, the rest of the pipeline is skipped.

A common use case is to validate that a user has the necessary permissions or roles, as shown in the following code:

```
public class CustomAuthorizationFilter : IAuthorizationFilter
{
  public void OnAuthorization(AuthorizationFilterContext context)
  {
    if (!context.HttpContext.User.Identity.IsAuthenticated)
    {
      context.Result = new UnauthorizedResult();
    }
  }
}
```

The benefit is that they ensure that authorization logic is applied early, preventing unnecessary resource consumption, like model binding and action execution, for unauthorized users.

Resource filter (IResourceFilter)

This handles resource-related concerns before and after the action. It can be used to short-circuit the request processing pipeline, such as caching responses. They run after authorization filters but before model binding and action execution.

A common use case is to implement caching, or modify the request or response before entering the action, as shown in the following code:

```
public class CustomResourceFilter : IResourceFilter
{
  public void OnResourceExecuting(ResourceExecutingContext context)
  {
    // Logic before the action execution like checking cache.
  }
  public void OnResourceExecuted(ResourceExecutedContext context)
  {
    // Logic after the action execution like storing result in cache.
  }
}
```

The benefit is that they improve performance by handling resource-based logic like caching or request manipulation before heavy processing begins.

Action filter (IActionFilter)

This executes logic before and after the action method execution. It runs after the resource filter and before the result filters. It can modify the parameters passed to the action or the action result.

Common use cases include logging action execution, modifying input data, or altering the action result, as shown in the following code:

```
public class CustomActionFilter : IActionFilter
{
  public void OnActionExecuting(ActionExecutingContext context)
  {
    // Logic before the action executes like logging or modifying parameters.
  }

  public void OnActionExecuted(ActionExecutedContext context)
  {
    // Logic after the action executes like logging or modifying the result.
  }
}
```

The benefit is they are useful for logging, validating, or modifying the flow based on the action's input or output.

Exception filter (IExceptionFilter)

This handles exceptions thrown during the execution of an action or the result. It only runs if an unhandled exception occurs in the pipeline. If the exception is caught, it can modify or handle the error response.

To indicate that your filter has handled an exception, set the `ExceptionContext.ExceptionHandled` property to `true`.

A common use case is to centralize exception handling, logging, and custom error responses, as shown in the following code:

```
public class CustomExceptionFilter : IExceptionFilter
{
  public void OnException(ExceptionContext context)
  {
    // Logic to handle exceptions like logging or returning a custom error
response.
    context.Result = new ObjectResult("Something went wrong")
      { StatusCode = 500 };

    context.ExceptionHandled = true;
  }
}
```

The benefit is that they provide a centralized location for handling exceptions, preventing the need for a `try-catch` block in every controller action, and allowing consistent error responses.

Result filter (IResultFilter)

This executes logic before and after the result is returned, for example, a view or a JSON response. They run after the action method execution but before the result is processed.

A common use case is to modify the result, like a view, or apply additional processing to the response before it's returned to the client, as shown in the following code:

```
public class CustomResultFilter : IResultFilter
{
  public void OnResultExecuting(ResultExecutingContext context)
  {
    // Logic before the result executes like modifying the result.
  }

  public void OnResultExecuted(ResultExecutedContext context)
  {
    // Logic after the result executes like logging or altering the response.
  }
}
```

The benefit is that they allow final adjustments to the response before it is sent to the client, such as adding response headers or modifying the result.

Common benefits of all filters

There are several benefits that come from using any filter:

- **Separation of Concerns**: Filters help keep your controller actions clean by separating cross-cutting concerns like logging, authentication, and error handling from the business logic of your application.

- **Reusability**: Filters can be applied globally, to controllers, or specific actions, making them easy to reuse across different parts of the application.

- **Maintainability**: Centralizing logic like authorization, error handling, and caching in filters simplifies maintenance since you can update logic in one place rather than across multiple actions.

- **Consistency**: Filters ensure that important logic like authorization or logging is applied consistently across your application, reducing the chance of missing critical operations in certain actions or controllers.

In summary, filters provide a clean, flexible way to handle cross-cutting concerns like authorization, logging, exception handling, and more. They execute in a well-defined order, allowing for precise control over the flow of requests and responses.

Practicing and exploring

Test your knowledge and understanding by answering some questions, getting some hands-on practice, and exploring this chapter's topics with deeper research.

Exercise 5.1 – Online material

You can learn how to build your own custom store provider for ASP.NET Core Identity at the following link:

`https://learn.microsoft.com/en-us/aspnet/core/security/authentication/identity-custom-storage-providers`.

Exercise 5.2 – Practice exercises

The following practice exercises help you to explore the topics in this chapter more deeply.

Auth0 integration

Auth0 is an identity management platform that simplifies the process of implementing authentication and authorization for your applications. It provides secure and scalable identity solutions, allowing developers to manage user logins, **single sign-on (SSO)**, **multi-factor authentication (MFA)**, passwordless authentication, and more, without having to write complex authentication logic from scratch.

ASP.NET Core MVC developers often need to handle user authentication and authorization securely, and Auth0 abstracts much of this complexity. Instead of manually writing code to manage user sessions, password storage, and token-based authentication, you can offload these tasks to Auth0, which already follows best security practices.

Auth0 supports various identity providers like social logins (Google, Facebook, GitHub, etc.), enterprise logins (LDAP and Active Directory), and custom databases. This allows ASP.NET Core developers to integrate a wide range of authentication methods without having to deal with different protocols and providers manually.

Auth0 uses secure, token-based authentication protocols such as OAuth 2.0 and OpenID Connect. These standards make it easier to build secure APIs and enable secure communication between the frontend and backend services. ASP.NET Core MVC developers can easily integrate these protocols through Auth0's SDKs and middleware.

Auth0 offers SDKs and libraries specifically designed to work with ASP.NET Core MVC, making it relatively straightforward to implement authentication using middleware like OpenID Connect or JwtBearer. Auth0 also provides comprehensive documentation, code samples, and tutorials, making integration easier for developers who are not experts in identity management.

You can walk through a tutorial showing how to integrate Auth0 with ASP.NET Core MVC at the following link:

```
https://github.com/auth0/auth0-dotnet-templates/blob/main/docs/auth0webapp.md.
```

Exercise 5.3 — Test your knowledge

Answer the following questions:

1. How many characters long should a password be, and should it contain special characters?
2. How frequently should passwords be changed?
3. What are three authentication schemes?
4. Which external authentication providers are supported by ASP.NET Core Identity?
5. How can you significantly reduce the risk of XSS attacks being able to steal session cookies?
6. What are some of the security vulnerabilities of cookies?
7. Why might you enable Razor Pages even if you are not creating any yourself?
8. How can you customize the user interface provided by ASP.NET Core Identity, for example, the login form?
9. What dependency service should you use to programmatically register a visitor to your website?
10. What are the five types of ASP.NET Core filters, and in what order do they execute?

Exercise 5.4 — Explore topics

Use the links on the following page to learn more about the topics covered in this chapter:

```
https://github.com/markjprice/web-dev-net10/blob/main/docs/book-links.md#chapter-5---
authentication-and-authorization.
```

Summary

In this chapter, you learned how to secure an ASP.NET Core MVC website. You learned about the following:

- Key concepts about authentication and authorization.
- How to implement basic authentication and authorization in an ASP.NET Core MVC website project.
- How to secure controllers and action methods using authorization filters.
- How to build custom filters for other purposes.

In the next chapter, you will learn how to optimize the performance and scalability of your websites and web services by using caching of various types.

6

Performance and Scalability Optimization Using Caching

This chapter is about optimizing the performance and scalability of your websites and web services by using caching of various types.

Scalability in an ASP.NET Core project refers to the system's ability to handle increased load, typically in terms of more users, more requests, or higher data throughput, without compromising performance. A scalable system can adjust to changing demands, whether through vertical or horizontal scaling:

- **Vertical scaling**: Adding more resources to the same machine
- **Horizontal scaling**: Adding more machines to a system

Caching is a technique that directly impacts scalability. By caching frequently accessed data or computation results, you reduce the number of times expensive operations, like database calls or complex calculations, need to be performed. This reduces the load on your backend resources, such as databases and application servers, and speeds up response times for users.

In a scalable system, caching minimizes unnecessary resource consumption. Proper use of caching can help prevent bottlenecks as the number of concurrent users grows. Caching strategies can reduce the amount of processing per request, lowering latency and decreasing server load, thereby improving the overall ability of the system to scale.

This chapter will cover the following topics:

- Introducing caching with ASP.NET Core
- Output caching
- Object caching
- More techniques to improve scalability

Introducing caching with ASP.NET Core

Caching can enable our systems to copy some data from a remote data center to a local data center, or from a server or disk to memory. Caches store data as key-value pairs.

However, one of the hardest parts of caching is getting the balance right between storing enough data and keeping it fresh. The more data we copy, the more resources we use. We also need to consider how we will keep the copies synchronized with the original data.

General caching guidelines

Caching works best with data that costs a lot to generate and does not change often.

Follow these guidelines when caching:

- Your code should never depend on cached data. It should always be able to get the data from the original source when the data is not found in the cache.
- Wherever you cache data (in-memory or in a database), it is a limited resource, so deliberately limit the amount of data cached and for how long by implementing expirations and size limits. You should monitor cache hits (when data is successfully found in the cache) to obtain the right balance for your specific scenarios.

In the coding tasks in this section, you will implement these guidelines.

Cache invalidation

In ASP.NET Core, cache invalidation refers to the process of expiring or removing cached data when it becomes stale or is no longer valid. It's a critical aspect of caching because stale data can lead to bugs, inconsistencies, or user confusion.

ASP.NET Core provides a flexible caching infrastructure, and different invalidation strategies can be applied depending on the type of cache in use, for example, in-memory caching, distributed caching, or response caching.

Let's review the three common cache invalidation strategies in ASP.NET Core:

- **Time-based expiration (absolute and sliding expiration)**: Time-based expiration automatically removes cache entries after a set period. Use this when data is valid for a specific amount of time, such as news headlines or API data fetched every 10 minutes.
- **Dependency-based invalidation:** In this approach, you invalidate the cache based on a dependency, typically by using a `CancellationToken`. This is useful when cache entries are tied to some external event, like a file change, database update, or application state change. Use this when cache entries should be invalidated based on an external trigger.
- **Manual invalidation (explicit removal)**: Sometimes you need to explicitly remove or overwrite a cache entry, for example, after saving new data or handling an admin update. Use this when the cache is invalidated by a user action, such as editing or deleting content.

For distributed caching, invalidation must be managed more deliberately, often by setting expiration or managing cache keys in a central store like Redis. ASP.NET Core's `IResponseCaching` middleware uses time-based expiration and cache headers, and is more appropriate for HTTP responses.

When caching complex objects, ensure that changes in reference data properly trigger invalidation.

Don't overuse caching. Premature caching can make bugs harder to diagnose, especially when data inconsistencies creep in.

Reviewing types of caching

Let's start by reviewing the caching technologies built into ASP.NET Core. *Figure 6.1* shows a summary diagram of types and locations of caching in an ASP.NET Core MVC project:

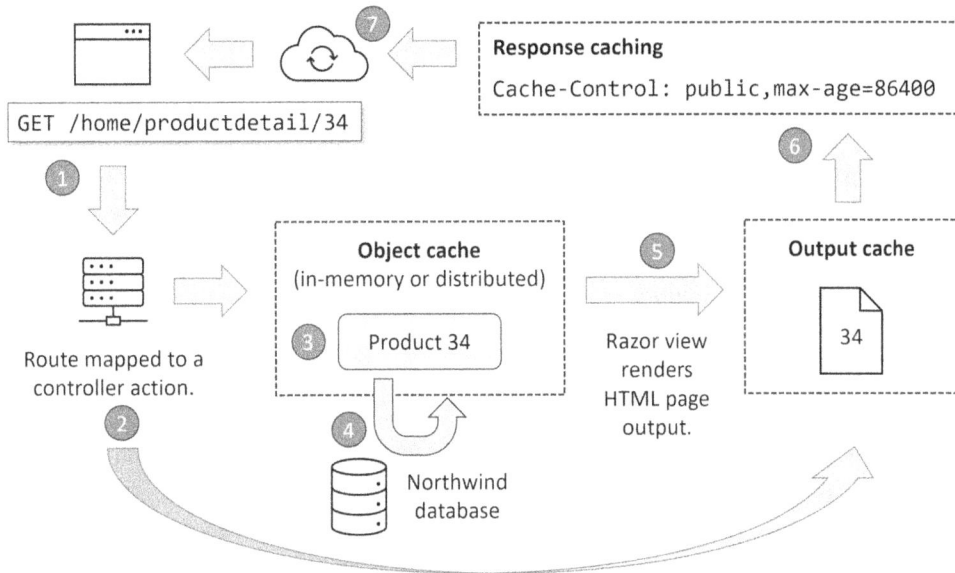

Figure 6.1: Types and locations for caching

Let's review a scenario. The numbered bullets match the numbered labels in *Figure 6.1*:

1. A web browser requests the product detail page for the product with an ID of 34 from an MVC website using the following relative path: `/home/productdetail/34`.

2. On the web server, the output caching system looks in the output cache to see if that web page already exists with a match on its route. If not, the request is mapped to the appropriate controller class and action method and the `id` value 34 is passed in as a parameter.

3. The action method implementation looks in the object cache to see if that entity already exists. The object cache has multiple implementations to choose from: in-memory, distributed, and, in .NET 9 or later, a hybrid cache that automatically uses the best of both.

4. If not, it is retrieved from the database and stored in the object cache.

5. The action method passes the product entity to the appropriate Razor View, which renders it into an HTML page and stores it in the output cache.

6. The action method adds response caching headers to the response before returning it.

7. Any intermediaries, as well as the web browser, can read the HTTP response headers and cache them if allowed.

On the next request, caching at various levels could improve matters:

1. The web browser might have the page in its local cache due to response caching. No further action is required. If not, a request is made to the web server. If intermediaries like a **content delivery network (CDN)** were allowed to cache the response, then they could return it to the browser without needing to forward the request to the web server.

2. If a request arrives at the web server, and the page is in the output cache, the action method processing can be bypassed, and the page is immediately returned with new response headers set.

Caching HTTP responses for websites

To improve response times and scalability, you might want to try to cache the HTTP response that is generated by an action method by decorating the method with the [ResponseCache] attribute. This tells intermediaries like CDNs and the web browser itself how long they should cache the response by adding HTTP headers to the response, like Cache-Control directives.

The Cache-Control directive is important for the following reasons:

*   **Improving performance:** By caching static or semi-static resources, you can reduce latency and server load, allowing quicker delivery of content to users.

*   **Reducing server load:** Serving resources from the client's cache or a CDN decreases the number of requests that your server has to handle, allowing it to focus on more complex or personalized tasks.

*   **Ensuring freshness:** It allows precise control over how resources are cached, so users always get the most up-to-date version of resources or personalized content without unnecessary validation requests.

*   **Security:** By using directives like no-store, you can prevent sensitive information from being stored anywhere, ensuring better protection of personal data.

Common Cache-Control directives

Common Cache-Control directives include:

*   public: This indicates that the response can be cached by any caching mechanism, including browser, proxy, CDN, and so on. This is good practice for resources that are static or don't require restricted access.

*   private: The response is specific to an individual visitor and should not be cached by shared caches like proxies or CDNs. However, the client may cache it. This is good practice for resources like personalized pages or user-specific data.

*   no-cache: This instructs the client and any intermediary to always revalidate the response with the server before using a cached copy. It does not mean "don't cache" but rather "don't use it without checking with the server first." It is useful for ensuring that content is always fresh while still allowing caching for potential revalidation.

*   no-store: This completely prevents the client or any intermediary from caching the response. It will not store it at all. This is good practice for resources that include sensitive data, like bank account information, where you don't want it to be stored anywhere.

- `max-age=<seconds>`: This defines the maximum amount of time (in seconds) that a resource is considered fresh. Once the `max-age` has passed, the client will revalidate the resource with the server. For example, `Cache-Control: max-age=3600` says that the resource will be considered fresh for one hour (3600 seconds).

- `s-maxage=<seconds>`: Similar to `max-age`, but applies only to shared caches, like proxies or CDNs. If both are specified, this overrides `max-age` for these caches. For example, this option is useful for having different caching rules for public CDNs compared to browsers.

- `must-revalidate`: This instructs caches that once the resource becomes stale after `max-age` expires, it must be revalidated with the server before serving it again. This ensures that clients don't use outdated resources without explicit validation.

- `proxy-revalidate`: Similar to `must-revalidate`, but only applies to shared caches, like proxies.

- `no-transform`: This prevents any intermediary, like a proxy, from altering the content or its encoding, for example, compressing it. This is important when you want to ensure that responses are delivered exactly as they were originally generated.

- `immutable`: This tells the client that the resource will never change, so it doesn't need to revalidate it even after the `max-age` expires. This is good practice for static assets, like images or CSS files, that are versioned in their URL and don't need to be revalidated.

- `stale-while-revalidate=<seconds>`: This allows the client to use a stale resource while asynchronously checking in the background whether a new version exists. This helps reduce perceived latency. For example, `Cache-Control: stale-while-revalidate=60` allows serving stale data for 60 seconds while fetching fresh data.

- `stale-if-error=<seconds>`: If the origin server is unavailable, this directive allows the cache to serve stale content for a specified time period. For example, `Cache-Control: stale-if-error=300` allows the serving of stale content for up to five minutes in case of errors.

These options are often combined. For example, a common HTTP response header for static assets, like images or CSS files, that rarely changes, as shown in the following example:

```
Cache-Control: public, max-age=31536000, immutable
```

The resource will be publicly cacheable, fresh for one year, and marked as immutable to signal it will not change.

> **Good practice:** Response caching is only advisory. You cannot force other systems to cache if you do not control them. Keep in mind that any response caching you configure could be ignored. However, response caching is often the most important type of caching to enable in real-life web development. Organizations often find that up to 90% of client requests to their websites and services can be handled by CDN caching. Only 1 in 10 requests actually need to hit their web servers and use resources. Look at how well your CDN caches are configured before wasting time optimizing your code or database queries. Since you could be using any third-party CDN, I do not cover how to do this in this book.

Now that you understand the theory of the `Cache-Control` directive, let's see how you actually set it in an ASP.NET Core project.

Controlling Cache-Control directives in ASP.NET Core

You indicate where the response should be cached and for how long by setting parameters in the [ResponseCache] attribute, as shown in *Table 6.1*:

Parameter	Description
Duration	This sets the max-age HTTP response header measured in seconds. Common good practice values are 3600 (one hour) and 86400 (one day). Note that this sets a maximum cached time, not a guaranteed duration.
Location	This sets the Cache-Control HTTP response header to one of the following: public, private, or no-cache. The value must be one of the ResponseCacheLocation values: Any (meaning public), Client (meaning private), or None (meaning no-cache).
NoStore	If true, this ignores Duration and Location and sets the Cache-Control HTTP response header to no-store.

Table 6.1: ResponseCache attribute parameters

Exploring Cache-Control directives

Let's see a practical example:

1. In the Northwind.Mvc project, add a folder named Constants.
2. In the Constants folder, add a class named DurationInSeconds.cs.
3. In DurationInSeconds.cs, define constants for setting durations in seconds, as shown in the following code:

```
namespace Northwind.Mvc;

public static class DurationInSeconds
{
  public const int TenSeconds = 10;
  public const int HalfMinute = 30;
  public const int OneMinute = 60;
  public const int TenMinutes = 600;
  public const int HalfHour = 1_800;
  public const int OneHour = 3_600;
  public const int EightHours = 28_800;
  public const int HalfDay = 43_200;
  public const int OneDay = 86_400;
  public const int OneWeek = 604_800;
}
```

4. In `HomeController.cs`, add an attribute to the `Index` method to cache the response for 10 seconds on the browser or any proxies between the server and browser, as shown highlighted in the following code:

```
[ResponseCache(Duration = DurationInSeconds.TenSeconds,
  Location = ResponseCacheLocation.Any)]
public IActionResult Index()
```

5. In `Views\Home`, in `Index.cshtml`, after the **Welcome** heading, add a paragraph to output the current time in long format to include seconds, as shown in the following markup:

```
<p class="alert alert-primary">@DateTime.Now.ToLongTimeString()</p>
```

6. Start the `Northwind.Mvc` website project using the `https` launch profile.

7. Note the time on the home page, as shown in *Figure 6.2*:

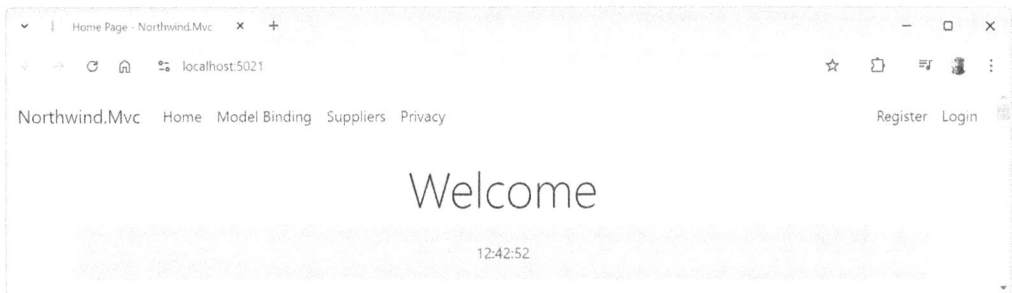

Figure 6.2: The current time on the home page

8. View **Developer Tools**, select the **Network** tab, select the **localhost** request, refresh the page, and note the `Cache-Control` response header, as shown in the following output:

```
Cache-Control: public,max-age=10
```

Seeing the effect of Cache-Control directives

Now, let's navigate back and forth between different pages so we can see the effect of this `Cache-Control` directive in different scenarios:

1. Click **Register** so that you leave the home page.

> **Warning!** Do *not* click the **Reload the page** button as this will override the cache and refresh the page with a new request to the web server.

2. Click **Home** and note that the time on the home page is the same because a cached version of the page is used.

3. Click **Register**. Wait at least 10 seconds.

4. Click **Home** and note that the time has now updated.

5. Click **Log in**, enter your email and password, and then click **Log in**.

6. Note the time on the home page.

7. Click **Model Binding**.

8. Click **Home** and note that the page is not cached.

9. View the console and note the warning message explaining that your caching has been over-ridden because the visitor is logged in. Also note that in this scenario, ASP.NET Core uses anti-forgery tokens and they should not be cached:

```
warn: Microsoft.AspNetCore.Antiforgery.DefaultAntiforgery[8]
      The 'Cache-Control' and 'Pragma' headers have been overridden
and set to 'no-cache, no-store' and 'no-cache' respectively to prevent
caching of this response. Any response that uses antiforgery should not
be cached.
```

10. Close Chrome and shut down the web server.

Summary of caching types

We have summarized the different types of caching in *Table 6.2*:

Type	Where	How to enable and configure
Response	Browser, CDN	Decorate the action method with the [`ResponseCache`] attribute.
Output	Web server	Call the `UseOutputCaching`, `AddOutputCaching`, and `CacheOutput` methods in `Program.cs`.
Object	Web server, other processes	Multiple implementations are available: in-memory, distributed, and hybrid. Multiple versions of distributed implementation are also available, including Redis and SQL Server. You will learn about them later in this chapter.

Table 6.2: Comparing types of caching

You've been introduced to the main types of caching and seen some examples of response caching, so let's now dive in deeper to another common type, output caching.

Output caching

Output caching middleware was introduced with ASP.NET Core 7, and it can be used in all types of ASP.NET Core projects.

Output caching endpoints

Output caching stores dynamically generated responses on the server so that they do not have to be regenerated for another request. This can improve performance.

Let's see it in action with examples of applying output caching to some endpoints:

1. In the `Northwind.Mvc` project, at the top of `Program.cs`, import the name for our class of duration constants, as shown in the following code:

```
using Northwind.Mvc; // To use DurationInSeconds.
```

2. In `Program.cs`, before the call to `Build`, add statements to add the output cache middleware and override the default expiration timespan to make it only 10 seconds, as shown highlighted in the following code:

```
builder.Services.AddOutputCache(options =>
{
  options.DefaultExpirationTimeSpan =
    TimeSpan.FromSeconds(DurationInSeconds.TenSeconds);
});

var app = builder.Build();
```

> **Good practice:** The default expiration timespan if you call `AddOutputCache` without configuring options is one minute. Think carefully about what the duration should be based on your website's typical visitor behavior.

3. In `Program.cs`, add statements before the call to map controllers to use the output cache, as shown highlighted in the following code:

```
app.UseOutputCache();

app.MapControllerRoute(
    name: "default",
    pattern: "{controller=Home}/{action=Index}/{id?}");
```

4. In `Program.cs`, add statements after the call to map Razor Pages to create two endpoints that respond with plain text, one that is not cached and one that uses the output cache, as shown highlighted in the following code:

```
app.MapRazorPages()
  .WithStaticAssets();

app.MapGet("/notcached", () => DateTime.Now.ToString());
app.MapGet("/cached", () => DateTime.Now.ToString()).CacheOutput();
```

5. In `appsettings.Development.json`, add a log level of `Information` for the output caching middleware, as shown highlighted in the following configuration:

    ```json
    {
      "Logging": {
        "LogLevel": {
          "Default": "Information",
          "Microsoft.AspNetCore": "Warning",
          "Microsoft.AspNetCore.OutputCaching": "Information"
        }
      }
    }
    ```

6. Start the `Northwind.Mvc` website project using the `https` launch profile.

7. Arrange the browser and command prompt or terminal window so that you can see both.

8. In the browser, make sure that you are not logged in because that would disable caching.

9. Navigate to `https://localhost:5021/notcached`, and note that nothing is written to the command prompt or terminal.

10. In the browser, click the **Reload this page** button several times and note that the time is always updated because it is not served from the output cache.

11. In the browser, navigate to `https://localhost:5021/cached`, and note that messages are written to the console or terminal to tell you that you have made a request for a cached resource, but it does not have anything in the output cache, so it has now cached the output, as shown in the following output:

    ```
    info: Microsoft.AspNetCore.OutputCaching.OutputCacheMiddleware[7]
          No cached response available for this request.
    info: Microsoft.AspNetCore.OutputCaching.OutputCacheMiddleware[9]
          The response has been cached.
    ```

12. In the browser, click the **Refresh** button several times and note that the time is not updated, and an output caching message tells you that the value was served from the cache, as shown in the following output:

    ```
    info: Microsoft.AspNetCore.OutputCaching.OutputCacheMiddleware[5]
          Serving response from cache.
    ```

13. Continue refreshing until 10 seconds have passed, and note that messages are written to the command prompt or terminal to tell you that the cached output has been updated.

14. Close the browser and shut down the web server.

Output caching MVC views

Now, let's see how we can output cache an MVC view:

1. In the Views\Home folder, in ProductDetail.cshtml, add a paragraph <p> to show the current time, as shown highlighted in the following markup:

    ```
    <h2>Product Detail</h2>
    <p class="alert alert-success">@DateTime.Now.ToLongTimeString()</p>
    ```

2. Start the Northwind.Mvc website project using the https launch profile.

3. Arrange the browser and command prompt or terminal window so that you can see both.

4. On the home page, scroll down and then select one of the products.

5. On the product detail page, note the current time, and then refresh the page and note that the time updates every second.

6. Close the browser and shut down the web server.

7. In Program.cs, at the end of the call to map controllers, add a call to the CacheOutput method, as shown highlighted in the following code:

    ```
    app.MapControllerRoute(
        name: "default",
        pattern: "{controller=Home}/{action=Index}/{id?}")
      .WithStaticAssets()
    .CacheOutput();
    ```

8. Start the Northwind.Mvc website project using the https launch profile and arrange the browser window and command prompt or terminal window so that you can see both.

9. On the home page, scroll down, select one of the products, and note that the product detail page is not in the output cache, so SQL commands are executed to get the data. Then, once the Razor View generates the page, it is stored in the cache, as shown in the following output:

    ```
    info: Microsoft.AspNetCore.OutputCaching.OutputCacheMiddleware[7]
          No cached response available for this request.
    dbug: 20/09/2025 17:23:02.402 RelationalEventId.CommandExecuting[20100]
    (Microsoft.EntityFrameworkCore.Database.Command)
          Executing DbCommand [Parameters=[@__id_0='?' (DbType = Int32)],
    CommandType='Text', CommandTimeout='30']
          SELECT "p"."ProductId", "p"."CategoryId", "p"."Discontinued",
    "p"."ProductName", "p"."QuantityPerUnit", "p"."ReorderLevel",
    "p"."SupplierId", "p"."UnitPrice", "p"."UnitsInStock",
    "p"."UnitsOnOrder", "c"."CategoryId", "c"."CategoryName",
    "c"."Description", "c"."Picture"
          FROM "Products" AS "p"
          LEFT JOIN "Categories" AS "c" ON "p"."CategoryId" =
    "c"."CategoryId"
    ```

```
      WHERE "p"."ProductId" = @__id_0
      LIMIT 2
info: Microsoft.EntityFrameworkCore.Database.Command[20101]
      Executed DbCommand (7ms) [Parameters=[@__id_0='?' (DbType =
Int32)], CommandType='Text', CommandTimeout='30']
      SELECT "p"."ProductId", "p"."CategoryId", "p"."Discontinued",
"p"."ProductName", "p"."QuantityPerUnit", "p"."ReorderLevel",
"p"."SupplierId", "p"."UnitPrice", "p"."UnitsInStock",
"p"."UnitsOnOrder", "c"."CategoryId", "c"."CategoryName",
"c"."Description", "c"."Picture"
      FROM "Products" AS "p"
      LEFT JOIN "Categories" AS "c" ON "p"."CategoryId" =
"c"."CategoryId"
      WHERE "p"."ProductId" = @__id_0
      LIMIT 2
info: Microsoft.AspNetCore.OutputCaching.OutputCacheMiddleware[9]
      The response has been cached.
```

10. On the product detail page, note the current time, and then refresh the page and note that the whole page, including the time and product detail data, is served from the output cache, as shown in the following output:

```
info: Microsoft.AspNetCore.OutputCaching.OutputCacheMiddleware[5]
      Serving response from cache.
```

11. Keep refreshing until 10 seconds have passed and note that the page is then regenerated from the database and the current time is shown.

12. In the browser address bar, change the product ID number to a value between 1 and 77 to request a different product, and note that the time is current, and therefore a new cached version has been created for that product ID because the ID is part of the relative path.

13. Refresh the browser and note that the time is cached (and therefore the whole page is).

14. In the browser address bar, change the product ID number to a value between 1 and 77 to request a different product, and note that the time is current, and therefore a new cached version has been created for that product ID because the ID is part of the relative path.

15. In the browser address bar, change the product ID number back to the previous ID and note that the page is still cached with the time that the previous page was first added to the output cache.

16. Close the browser and shut down the web server.

Varying output cached data by query string

If a value is different in the relative path, then output caching automatically treats the request as a different resource and so caches different copies for each, including differences in any query string parameters. Consider the following URLs:

- `https://localhost:5021/Home/ProductDetail/12`
- `https://localhost:5021/Home/ProductDetail/29`
- `https://localhost:5021/Home/ProductDetail/12?color=red`
- `https://localhost:5021/Home/ProductDetail/12?color=blue`

All four requests will have their own cached copy of their own page. If the query string parameters have no effect on the generated page, then that is a waste.

Let's see how we can fix this problem. We will start by disabling varying the cache by query string parameter values, and then implement some page functionality that uses a query string parameter:

1. In `Program.cs`, in the call to `AddOutputCache`, set the default expiration to 10 seconds and add a statement to define a named policy to disable varying by query string parameters, as shown highlighted in the following code:

   ```
   builder.Services.AddOutputCache(options =>
   {
     options.DefaultExpirationTimeSpan =
       TimeSpan.FromSeconds(DurationInSeconds.TenSeconds);

     options.AddPolicy("views", p => p.SetVaryByQuery(""));
   });
   ```

   > Named output cache policies mean that it is possible to define multiple caching policies in the `AddOutputCache` method and then apply the most suitable one to each specific endpoint, as you will do in the next step.

2. In `Program.cs`, in the call to `CacheOutput` for MVC, specify the named policy, as shown in the following code:

   ```
   app.MapControllerRoute(
       name: "default",
       pattern: "{controller=Home}/{action=Index}/{id?}")
     .WithStaticAssets()
     .CacheOutput(policyName:"views");
   ```

3. In `ProductDetail.cshtml`, modify the `<p>` that outputs the current time to set its alert style based on a value stored in the `ViewData` dictionary, as shown highlighted in the following markup:

```
<p class="alert alert-@ViewData["alertstyle"]">
  @DateTime.Now.ToLongTimeString()</p>
```

4. In the `Controllers` folder, in `HomeController.cs`, in the `ProductDetail` action method, store a query string value in the `ViewData` dictionary, as shown in the following code:

```
public IActionResult ProductDetail(int? id,
  string alertstyle = "success")
{
  ViewData["alertstyle"] = alertstyle;
```

5. Start the `Northwind.Mvc` website project using the `https` launch profile.

6. Arrange the browser and command prompt or terminal window so that you can see both.

7. On the home page, scroll down, select one of the products, and note that the color of the alert is green because the `alertstyle` defaults to `success`.

8. In the browser address bar, append a query string parameter, `?alertstyle=warning`, and note that it is ignored because the same cached page is returned.

> The preceding step (and other steps in this task) must be completed within 10 seconds to see the effect. You might want to read through all the steps first, then go through the whole process.

9. In the browser address bar, change the product ID number to a value between 1 and 77 to request a different product and append a query string parameter, `?alertstyle=warning`. Note that the alert is yellow because it is treated as a new request.

10. In the browser address bar, append a query string parameter, `?alertstyle=info`, and note that it is ignored because the same cached page is returned.

11. Close the browser and shut down the web server.

12. In `Program.cs`, in the call to `AddPolicy`, set `alertstyle` as the only named parameter to vary by for query string parameters, as shown highlighted in the following code:

```
options.AddPolicy("views", p => p.SetVaryByQuery("alertstyle"));
```

13. Start the `Northwind.Mvc` website project using the `https` launch profile.

14. Repeat the steps above to confirm that requests for different `alertstyle` values do have their own cached copies, but any other query string parameter would be ignored.

15. Close the browser and shut down the web server.

Disabling output caching to avoid confusion

Before we continue, let's disable view output caching; otherwise, you are likely to be confused by the website behavior if or when you forget caching is enabled!

1. In `Program.cs`, disable the output caching by commenting out the call to `CacheOutput`, as shown highlighted in the following code:

    ```
    app.MapControllerRoute(
        name: "default",
        pattern: "{controller=Home}/{action=Index}/{id?}")
      .WithStaticAssets();
    // .CacheOutput(policyName: "views");
    ```

2. Save the changes.

You've now seen output caching in action. Let's move on to object caching.

Object caching

Object caching refers to the practice of temporarily storing objects or data in memory to improve the performance and scalability of a website or web service by reducing redundant data retrieval and computation.

In-memory and distributed caching work with any type of app or service, using any transport technology, because all the magic happens on the server.

By caching frequently accessed or expensive-to-create data, you can reduce the load on your database or other backend services, minimize response times, and improve the overall user experience.

Common use cases for object caching include the following:

*   **Expensive database queries**: Cache the result of complex or frequently accessed database queries. You will do this for the Northwind MVC website home page that currently accesses the SQL Server database on every request. Even with output caching enabled, that is only currently cached for 30 seconds.
*   **External service calls**: Cache responses from external APIs to reduce latency and cost.
*   **Computed data**: Store results of computationally expensive operations.

Caching objects using in-memory caching

The `IMemoryCache` interface represents a cache that uses local web server memory. The `Microsoft.Extensions.Caching.Memory` package has a modern implementation of `IMemoryCache`. Avoid the older `System.Runtime.Caching`.

> **Good practice:** If you have multiple servers hosting your web service or website, then you must enable "sticky sessions." This means that an incoming request from a client or visitor will be directed to the same server as previous requests from that client or visitor, allowing the request to find the correct cached data in that server's memory.

Expirations for in-memory caching

When you add an object to a cache, you should set an expiration. There are two types, absolute and sliding, and you can set one or the other, both, or neither:

- **Absolute expiration:** This is a fixed date/time, for example, 1 a.m. on December 24, 2023. When the date/time is reached, the object is evicted. To use this, set the `AbsoluteExpiration` property of a cache entry to a `DateTime` value. Choose this if you need to guarantee that at some point, the data in the cache will be refreshed.

- **Sliding expiration:** This is a time span, for example, 20 seconds. When the time span expires, the object is evicted. However, whenever an object is read from the cache, its expiration is reset for another 20 seconds. This is why it is described as *sliding*. A common duration for a **content management system (CMS)**, where content like a web page is loaded from a database, is 12 hours. Content frequently viewed by visitors, like the home page, is then likely to remain in memory. To use this, set the `SlidingExpiration` property of a cache entry to a `TimeSpan` value. Choose this if it is acceptable for data to potentially never be refreshed. A good CMS will have an additional mechanism to reliably force a refresh when new content is published, but this functionality is not built into .NET caching.

- **Both expirations:** If you only set a sliding expiration, an object may stay in the cache forever, so you might also want to set the `AbsoluteExpirationRelativeToNow` property to a `TimeSpan` further in the future, after which the object would definitely be evicted. Choose this if you want the "best of both worlds."

- **Never:** You can set a cache entry to have a priority of `CacheItemPriority.NeverRemove`.

You can also configure a method to call back to when an object is evicted from the cache. This allows you to execute some business logic to decide if you want to add the object back into the cache, perhaps after refreshing it from the original data source. You do this by calling the `RegisterPostEvictionCallback` method.

> **Good practice:** Sizes of objects in the cache are defined using custom units. If you store simple `string` values, then you could use the length of the `string`. If you don't know the size, you could just use 1 unit for each entry to simply limit the number of entries.

Exploring in-memory object caching

Let's explore the in-memory cache:

1. In the Northwind.Mvc project, in Program.cs, import the namespace to work with the in-memory cache, as shown in the following code:

   ```
   using Microsoft.Extensions.Caching.Memory; // To use IMemoryCache and so
   on.
   ```

2. In Program.cs, after the call to CreateBuilder, in the section for configuring services, register an implementation for the in-memory cache, configured to store a maximum of 50 products, as shown in the following code:

   ```
   builder.Services.AddSingleton<IMemoryCache>(new MemoryCache(
     new MemoryCacheOptions
     {
       TrackStatistics = true,
       SizeLimit = 50 // Products.
     }));
   ```

3. In HomeController.cs, import the namespace to work with the in-memory cache, as shown in the following code:

   ```
   using Microsoft.Extensions.Caching.Memory; // To use IMemoryCache.
   ```

4. In HomeController.cs, declare some fields to store the in-memory cache and a key prefix for the products, as shown in the following code:

   ```
   private readonly IMemoryCache _memoryCache;
   private const string ProductKey = "PROD";

   public HomeController(ILogger<HomeController> logger,
     NorthwindContext db, IMemoryCache memoryCache)
   {
     _logger = logger;
     _db = db;
     _memoryCache = memoryCache;
   }
   ```

5. In HomeController.cs, in the ProductDetail action method, add statements to try to get the product from the cache, and if it is not cached, get it from the database and set it in the cache, using a sliding expiration of 10 seconds, as highlighted in the following code:

```
public async Task<IActionResult> ProductDetail(int? id,
   string alertstyle = "success")
{
  ViewData["alertstyle"] = alertstyle;

  if (!id.HasValue)
  {
    return BadRequest("You must pass a product ID in the route, for
example, /Home/ProductDetail/21");
  }

  // Try to get the cached product.
  if (!_memoryCache.TryGetValue($"{ProductKey}{id}",
    out Product? model))
  {
    // If the cached value is not found, get the value from the database.
    model = await _db.Products.Include(p => p.Category)
      .SingleOrDefaultAsync(p => p.ProductId == id);

    if (model is null)
    {
      return NotFound($"ProductId {id} not found.");
    }

    MemoryCacheEntryOptions cacheEntryOptions = new()
    {
      SlidingExpiration = TimeSpan.FromSeconds(DurationInSeconds.
TenSeconds),
      Size = 1 // product
    };
    _memoryCache.Set($"{ProductKey}{id}", model, cacheEntryOptions);
  }
  MemoryCacheStatistics? stats = _memoryCache.GetCurrentStatistics();

  _logger.LogInformation($"Memory cache. Total hits: {stats?
    .TotalHits}. Estimated size: {stats?.CurrentEstimatedSize}.");

  return View(model); // Pass model to view and then return result.
}
```

6. Start the `Northwind.Mvc` project using the `https` profile.

7. Arrange the windows so that you can see the command prompt or terminal at the same time as the web page.

8. Click on a product, like **Chai**, and then at the command prompt or terminal, note in the output that EF Core executes a SQL statement to get the product, the total hit counter is zero, and one product has now been cached, as shown in the following output:

```
info: Northwind.Mvc.Controllers.HomeController[0]
      Memory cache. Total hits: 0. Estimated size: 1.
```

9. Click **Reload this page** within 10 seconds, and continue to click it a few more times:

   - Note that EF Core does not need to re-execute the SQL statement because the product is cached, and if something reads them within a 10-second sliding expiration, they will stay in memory forever.
   - Note the total hit counter for the cache increments each time the product is found in the object cache, as shown in the following output:

```
info: Northwind.Mvc.Controllers.HomeController[0]
      Memory cache. Total hits: 1. Estimated size: 1.
info: Northwind.Mvc.Controllers.HomeController[0]
      Memory cache. Total hits: 2. Estimated size: 1.
info: Northwind.Mvc.Controllers.HomeController[0]
      Memory cache. Total hits: 3. Estimated size: 1.
```

10. Wait at least 10 seconds.

11. Click **Reload this page**, and note in the output that EF Core executes a SQL statement to get the product because it has not been read within the 10-second sliding expiration window.

12. View some other product detail pages and note that the estimated size of the object cache increases as more products are added to it.

13. Close the browser and shut down the web server.

You have now seen how easy it is to use an in-memory cache for objects. Using a distributed cache to store objects is just as easy, although you must make sure your objects are serializable.

Caching objects using distributed caching

Distributed caches have benefits over in-memory caches. Objects stored in a distributed cache:

- Are consistent across requests to multiple servers
- Survive server restarts and service deployments
- Do not waste local server memory
- Are stored in a shared area; so, in a server farm scenario with multiple servers, you do not need to enable sticky sessions

Warning! A disadvantage of distributed caches is that in-memory caches can store any object, but a distributed cache can only store byte arrays. Your object needs to be serialized and sent across a network to the remote cache.

Microsoft provides the `IDistributedCache` interface with pre-defined methods to manipulate items in any distributed cache implementation. The methods are:

- `Set` or `SetAsync`: To store an object in the cache
- `Get` or `GetAsync`: To retrieve an object from the cache
- `Remove` or `RemoveAsync`: To remove an object from the cache
- `Refresh` or `RefreshAsync`: To reset the sliding expiration for an object in the cache

There are many implementations of distributed caching to choose from, including the following:

- SQL Server: `https://learn.microsoft.com/en-us/aspnet/core/performance/caching/distributed#distributed-sql-server-cache`
- Redis: `https://learn.microsoft.com/en-us/aspnet/core/performance/caching/distributed#distributed-redis-cache`
- NCache: `http://www.alachisoft.com/ncache/aspnet-core-idistributedcache-ncache.html`

We will use the **distributed memory cache**, which is a Microsoft built-in implementation of `IDistributedCache` that stores items in memory on the server where the service runs.

It is not an actual distributed cache, but it is useful for scenarios like unit testing, where you want to remove the dependency on yet another external service, or while learning, as we are doing in this book.

Later, you only need to change the configured distributed cache, not the service implementation code that uses it, because all interactions go through the registered `IDistributedCache` implementation.

Let's go!

1. In the `Northwind.Mvc` project, in `Program.cs`, after the call to `CreateBuilder`, in the section for configuring services, register the implementation for the distributed memory cache, as shown in the following code:

   ```
   builder.Services.AddDistributedMemoryCache();
   ```

2. In `HomeController.cs`, import the namespace for working with a distributed cache implementation and serialized JSON, as shown in the following code:

   ```
   using Microsoft.Extensions.Caching.Distributed; // To use
   IDistributedCache.
   using System.Text.Json; // To use JsonSerializer.
   ```

3. In `HomeController.cs`, declare some fields to store the distributed cache implementation and an item key for categories, as highlighted in the following code:

```
private readonly IDistributedCache _distributedCache;
private const string CategoriesKey = "CATEGORIES";

public HomeController(ILogger<HomeController> logger,
  NorthwindContext db, IMemoryCache memoryCache,
  IDistributedCache distributedCache)
{
  _logger = logger;
  _db = db;
  _memoryCache = memoryCache;
  _distributedCache = distributedCache;
}
```

4. In `HomeController.cs`, add a private method to get the categories from the database as a list collection, and set it in the distributed cache, using a sliding expiration of 1 minute and an absolute expiration of 20 minutes, and return them, as shown in the following code:

```
private async Task<List<Category>> GetCategoriesFromDatabaseAsync()
{
  List<Category> cachedValue = await _db.Categories.ToListAsync();

  DistributedCacheEntryOptions cacheEntryOptions = new()
  {
    // Allow readers to reset the cache entry's lifetime.
    SlidingExpiration = TimeSpan.FromMinutes(1),
    // Set an absolute expiration time for the cache entry.
    AbsoluteExpirationRelativeToNow = TimeSpan.FromMinutes(20),
  };

  byte[]? cachedValueBytes =
    JsonSerializer.SerializeToUtf8Bytes(cachedValue);

  await _distributedCache.SetAsync(CategoriesKey,
    cachedValueBytes, cacheEntryOptions);

  return cachedValue;
}
```

5. In `HomeController.cs`, in the `Index` action method, add statements to try to get the cached categories, and if not cached, get them from the database. If a `byte` array is found in the cache, try to deserialize it into a list of categories, but if that fails too, get the categories from the database, as highlighted in the following code:

```csharp
[ResponseCache(Duration = DurationInSeconds.TenSeconds,
  Location = ResponseCacheLocation.Any)]
public async Task<IActionResult> Index()
{
  /*
  _Logger.LogError("This is a serious error (not really!)");
  _Logger.LogWarning("This is your first warning!");
  _Logger.LogWarning("Second warning!");
  _Logger.LogInformation("I am in the Index method of the
HomeController.");
  */

  // Try to get the cached value.
  List<Category>? cachedValue = null;

  byte[]? cachedValueBytes =
    await _distributedCache.GetAsync(CategoriesKey);

  if (cachedValueBytes is null)
  {
    cachedValue = await GetCategoriesFromDatabaseAsync();
  }
  else
  {
    cachedValue = JsonSerializer
      .Deserialize<List<Category>>(cachedValueBytes);

    if (cachedValue is null)
    {
      cachedValue = await GetCategoriesFromDatabaseAsync();
    }
  }

  HomeIndexViewModel model = new
  (
    VisitorCount: Random.Shared.Next(1, 1001),
    Categories: cachedValue ?? new List<Category>(),
```

```
    Products: await _db.Products.ToListAsync()
  );

  return View(model); // Pass the model to the view.
}
```

> Unlike the in-memory cache, which can store any live object, objects stored in distributed cache implementations must be serialized into `byte` arrays because they need to be transmittable across networks.

6. Start the `Northwind.Mvc` project using the `https` profile.

7. Arrange the windows so that you can see the command prompt or terminal at the same time as the web page, and note in the output that EF Core executes a SQL statement to get the categories to show on the home page.

8. Click **Reload this page** within one minute, continue to click it a few more times, and note that EF Core does not need to re-execute the SQL statement because the categories are cached. EF Core continues to execute the SQL statement to get the products.

9. Close the browser and shut down the web server.

You have now implemented both in-memory and distributed object caching. Wouldn't it be nice not to have to choose? Wouldn't it be nice to have object caching that is smart enough to use the best of both automatically? Well, now you can.

Hybrid object caching

The `HybridCache` API, introduced in preview with ASP.NET Core 9, addresses some limitations found in the `IDistributedCache` and `IMemoryCache` APIs. As an abstract class with a default implementation, `HybridCache` efficiently manages most tasks related to storing and retrieving data from the cache.

The key points about hybrid caching are shown in the following list:

- **Unified API:** It provides a single interface for both in-memory (aka in-process) and distributed (aka out-of-process) object caching. `HybridCache` can seamlessly replace any existing `IDistributedCache` and `IMemoryCache` usage. It always uses the in-memory cache initially, and when an `IDistributedCache` implementation is available, `HybridCache` leverages it for secondary caching. This dual-level caching approach combines the speed of in-memory caching with the durability of distributed or persistent caching.

- **Stampede protection:** `HybridCache` prevents cache stampedes, which occur when a frequently used cache entry is invalidated, causing multiple requests to try to repopulate it simultaneously. `HybridCache` merges concurrent operations, ensuring all requests for the same response wait for the first request to complete.

- **Configurable serialization:** HybridCache allows for configurable serialization during service registration, supporting both type-specific and generalized serializers via the WithSerializer and WithSerializerFactory methods, which are chained from the AddHybridCache call. By default, it manages string and byte[] internally and utilizes System.Text.Json for other types. It can be configured to use other serializers, such as Protobuf or XML.

> Although HybridCache was introduced in preview with .NET 9, its package targets .NET Standard 2.0, so it can be used with older versions of .NET, even including .NET Framework 4.6.2 or later. The HybridCache package reached general availability in March 2025 with version 9.3 (previous versions were all previews): https://devblogs.microsoft.com/dotnet/hybrid-cache-is-now-ga/.

Now that you've learned the concepts and basic implementation options for caching, let's create a data repository for a customer's page that caches entities to improve performance and scalability.

Creating data repositories with caching for entities

Defining and implementing a data repository to provide CRUD operations is good practice. We will create a data repository for the Customers table in Northwind. There are only 91 customers in this table, so we will cache a copy of the whole table in memory to improve scalability and performance when reading customer records.

> **Good practice:** In a real web service, you should use a distributed cache like Redis, an open-source data structure store that can be used as a high-performance, high-availability database, cache, or message broker. You can learn about this at the following page: https://learn.microsoft.com/en-us/aspnet/core/performance/caching/distributed.

HybridCache automatically switches between in-memory and distributed cache types.

> You can learn more about HybridCache at the following page: https://learn.microsoft.com/en-us/aspnet/core/performance/caching/hybrid.

We will follow a modern good practice and make the repository API asynchronous. It will be instantiated by an endpoint using parameter injection, so a new instance is created to handle every HTTP request. It will use a singleton instance of the hybrid cache.

Enabling hybrid caching in the MVC project

Let's enable hybrid caching in the MVC project:

1. In the `Northwind.Mvc.csproj` project file, add a package reference for hybrid caching, as shown in the following markup:

    ```
    <PackageReference Include="Microsoft.Extensions.Caching.Hybrid" />
    ```

2. Build the `Northwind.Mvc` project to restore packages.

3. In `Program.cs`, import the namespace for working with a hybrid cache, as shown in the following code:

    ```
    using Microsoft.Extensions.Caching.Hybrid; // To use
    HybridCacheEntryOptions.
    ```

4. In `Program.cs`, after the call to `CreateBuilder`, in the section for configuring services, register the hybrid cache service with a default cache entry duration of 60 seconds overall, and 30 seconds for local in-memory caching, as shown in the following code:

    ```
    builder.Services.AddHybridCache(options =>
    {
      options.DefaultEntryOptions = new HybridCacheEntryOptions
      {
        Expiration = TimeSpan.FromSeconds(DurationInSeconds.OneMinute),
        LocalCacheExpiration = TimeSpan.FromSeconds(DurationInSeconds.
    HalfMinute)
      };
    });
    ```

Adding a class library to implement a data repository

Next, we will create the data repository in a separate class library so that we can reuse it in *Chapter 9, Building Web Services Using ASP.NET Core Web API*, as well as in the current MVC project:

1. In the `MatureWeb` solution, add a new **Class Library** / `classlib` project named `Northwind.Repositories`.

2. In the `Northwind.Repositories.csproj` project file, add a reference to the Northwind database context project, as shown in the following markup:

    ```
    <ItemGroup>
      <ProjectReference Include=
        "..\Northwind.DataContext\Northwind.DataContext.csproj" />
    </ItemGroup>
    ```

3. Delete the file named `Class1.cs`.

4. Build the `Northwind.Repositories` project to build dependencies.

5. In the `Northwind.Repositories` project, add a new interface file named `ICustomerRepository.cs` and a class file named `CustomerRepository.cs`.

6. In `ICustomerRepository.cs`, define an interface with five CRUD methods, as shown in the following code:

```
using Northwind.EntityModels; // To use Customer.

namespace Northwind.Repositories;

public interface ICustomerRepository
{
  Task<Customer?> CreateAsync(Customer c);
  Task<Customer[]> RetrieveAllAsync();
  Task<Customer?> RetrieveAsync(string id,
    CancellationToken token);
  Task<Customer?> UpdateAsync(Customer c);
  Task<bool?> DeleteAsync(string id);
}
```

7. In `CustomerRepository.cs`, define a class that will implement the interface and use the hybrid cache (its methods will be implemented over the next few steps, so for now, ignore the errors you will be shown), as shown in the following code:

```
using Microsoft.EntityFrameworkCore.ChangeTracking; // To use
EntityEntry<T>.
using Northwind.EntityModels; // To use Customer.
using Microsoft.EntityFrameworkCore; // To use ToArrayAsync.
using Microsoft.Extensions.Caching.Hybrid; // To use HybridCache.

namespace Northwind.Repositories;

public class CustomerRepository : ICustomerRepository
{
  private readonly HybridCache _cache;

  // Use an instance data context field because it should not be
  // cached due to the data context having internal caching.
  private NorthwindContext _db;

  public CustomerRepository(NorthwindContext db,
    HybridCache hybridCache)
  {
    _db = db;
```

```
  _cache = hybridCache;
  }
}
```

8. Implement the `RetrieveAllAsync` method to always read the latest customers from the database, as shown in the following code:

```
public Task<Customer[]> RetrieveAllAsync()
{
  return _db.Customers.ToArrayAsync();
}
```

9. Implement the `RetrieveAsync` method to get the customer from the cache if possible or from the data model and set it in the cache for next time, as shown in the following code:

```
public async Task<Customer?> RetrieveAsync(string id,
  CancellationToken token = default)
{
  id = id.ToUpper(); // Normalize to uppercase.

  return await _cache.GetOrCreateAsync(
    key: id, // Unique key to the cache entry.
    factory: async cancel => await _db.Customers
      .FirstOrDefaultAsync(c => c.CustomerId == id, token),
    cancellationToken: token);
}
```

10. Implement the `CreateAsync` method, as shown in the following code:

```
public async Task<Customer?> CreateAsync(Customer c)
{
  c.CustomerId = c.CustomerId.ToUpper(); // Normalize to uppercase.

  // Add to database using EF Core.
  EntityEntry<Customer> added =
    await _db.Customers.AddAsync(c);

  int affected = await _db.SaveChangesAsync();

  if (affected == 1)
  {
    // If saved to database then store in cache.
    await _cache.SetAsync(c.CustomerId, c);
    return c;
  }
}
```

```
    return null;
  }
```

> The return value of the EF Core DbSet<Customer>.AddAsync method is an EntityEntry<Customer>. The code stores this in a local variable named added but we do not do anything with it. We could simplify the code by not defining and setting the added variable, but a reason you might want the local variable is to discover database-assigned values like an identifier. The Customers table uses a five-character text value for its primary key column that must be supplied by client code before adding to the database, so it's not necessary in this scenario. But if we were adding a new entity to the Shippers table, which has an auto-incrementing integer primary key column (or any other database-assigned value like a GUID or calculated value), then we could use the local added variable to read that assigned value, as shown in the following code: int assignedShipperId = added.Entity.ShipperId;. You can learn more at the following page: https://learn.microsoft.com/en-us/ef/core/change-tracking/entity-entries.

11. Implement the UpdateAsync method to update the database and, if successful, then update the cached customer as well, as shown in the following code:

```
public async Task<Customer?> UpdateAsync(Customer c)
{
  c.CustomerId = c.CustomerId.ToUpper();

  _db.Customers.Update(c);

  int affected = await _db.SaveChangesAsync();

  if (affected == 1)
  {
    await _cache.SetAsync(c.CustomerId, c);
    return c;
  }
  return null;
}
```

12. Implement the delete method to delete the customer from the database and, if successful, then remove the cached customer as well, as shown in the following code:

```
public async Task<bool?> DeleteAsync(string id)
{
  id = id.ToUpper();
```

```
Customer? c = await _db.Customers.FindAsync(id);

if (c is null) return null;

_db.Customers.Remove(c);

int affected = await _db.SaveChangesAsync();

if (affected == 1)
{
  await _cache.RemoveAsync(c.CustomerId);
  return true;
}

return false;
}
```

13. In the Northwind.Mvc.csproj project file, add a reference to the Northwind repositories project, as shown highlighted in the following markup:

```
<ItemGroup>
  <ProjectReference Include=
  "..\Northwind.DataContext\Northwind.DataContext.csproj" />
  <ProjectReference Include=
    "..\Northwind.Repositories\Northwind.Repositories.csproj" />
</ItemGroup>
```

14. Build the Northwind.Mvc project to build dependencies.

Configuring the customer repository

Now you will register a scoped dependency service implementation for the repository when the MVC website starts up, and then use constructor parameter injection to get it in a new controller for working with customers. It will have five action methods to perform CRUD operations on customers, including two GET methods (for all customers or one customer), POST (create), PUT (update), and DELETE:

1. In the Northwind.Mvc project, in Program.cs, import the namespace for working with our customer repository, as shown in the following code:

```
using Northwind.Repositories; // To use ICustomerRepository.
```

2. In Program.cs, add a statement before the call to the Build method, which will register the CustomerRepository for use at runtime as a scoped dependency, as shown in the following code:

```
builder.Services.AddScoped<ICustomerRepository,
  CustomerRepository>();
```

Good practice: Our repository uses a database context that is registered as a scoped dependency. You can only use scoped dependencies inside other scoped dependencies, so we cannot register the repository as a singleton. You can read more about this at the following page: `https://learn.microsoft.com/en-us/dotnet/core/extensions/dependency-injection#scoped`.

3. In the `Northwind.Mvc` project, in the `Controllers` folder, add a new empty controller class named `CustomersController.cs`.

4. In `CustomersController.cs`, add statements to define a controller with an `Index` action method that responds to HTTP `GET` requests for all customers or customers within a specified country in a simplified route, and a `Detail` action method that responds with a single customer based on its ID, as shown in the following code:

```
using Microsoft.AspNetCore.Mvc; // To use ProblemDetails.
using Northwind.EntityModels; // To use Customer.
using Northwind.Repositories; // To use ICustomerRepository.

namespace Northwind.Mvc.Controllers;

public class CustomersController : Controller
{
  private readonly ICustomerRepository _repo;

  public CustomersController(ICustomerRepository customerRepository)
  {
    _repo = customerRepository;
  }

  [Route("Customers/{country?}")]
  public async Task<IActionResult> Index(
    string? country = null)
  {
    IEnumerable<Customer> model = await _repo.RetrieveAllAsync();

    if (!string.IsNullOrWhiteSpace(country))
    {
      model = model.Where(customer => customer.Country == country);
    }

    return View(model);
  }
}
```

```
      [Route("Customers/Detail/{id}")]
      public async Task<IActionResult> Detail(string id)
      {
        Customer? model = await _repo.RetrieveAsync(id, default);

        return View(model);
      }
    }
```

5. In the Views folder, create a folder named Customers.

6. In the Customers folder, create a **Razor View – Empty** file named Index.cshtml.

7. In Index.cshtml, add Razor statements to render the customers into an HTML table with columns for Customer ID, Company Name, Contact Name, City, and Country, as shown in the following markup:

```
@model IEnumerable<Customer>
@{
  ViewData["Title"] = "Customers";
}
<div class="text-center">
  <h1 class="display-4">@ViewData["Title"]</h1>
  <table class="table table-bordered table-striped">
    <thead>
      <tr>
        <th>Customer ID</th>
        <th>Company Name</th>
        <th>Contact Name</th>
        <th>City</th>
        <th>Country</th>
      </tr>
    </thead>
    <tbody>
      @foreach (Customer customer in Model)
      {
        <tr>
          <td>
            <a href="/customers/detail/@customer.CustomerId">
              @customer.CustomerId</a></td>
          <td>@customer.CompanyName</td>
          <td>@customer.ContactName</td>
          <td>@customer.City</td>
```

```
            <td>
              <a href="/customers?country=@customer.Country">
                @customer.Country</a></td>
          </tr>
        }
      </tbody>
    </table>
  </div>
```

8. In the Customers folder, create a **Razor View – Empty** file named Detail.cshtml.

9. In Detail.cshtml, add Razor statements to render a customer, including Customer ID, Company Name, Contact Name, City, and Country, as shown in the following markup:

```
@model Customer
<div class="container">
  <div class="card shadow-sm rounded-4">
    <div class="card-body">
      <div class="row g-4 align-items-center">
        <div class="col-md-2 text-center">
          <img src="https://placebear.com/100/100" class="rounded-circle
img-fluid" alt="Customer Avatar">
        </div>
        <div class="col-md-10">
          <h4 class="mb-1">@Model.ContactName</h4>
          <p class="mb-0 text-muted">Customer ID: <strong>#@Model.
CustomerId</strong></p>
          <span class="badge bg-success">Active</span>
        </div>
      </div>
      <hr class="my-4">
      <div class="row">
        <div class="col-md-6 mb-3">
          <h6 class="text-uppercase text-muted">Contact</h6>
          <p class="mb-1"><strong>Title:</strong> @Model.ContactTitle</p>
          <p class="mb-1"><strong>Phone:</strong> @Model.Phone</p>
        <p class="mb-1"><strong>Fax:</strong> @Model.Fax</p>
      </div>
        <div class="col-md-6 mb-3">
          <h6 class="text-uppercase text-muted">Address</h6>
          <p class="mb-1">@Model.CompanyName</p>
          <p class="mb-1">@Model.City</p>
          <p class="mb-1">@Model.Region</p>
```

```
                <p class="mb-1">@Model.PostalCode</p>
                <p class="mb-1">@Model.Country</p>
              </div>
            </div>
          </div>
        </div>
      </div>
```

> I have used the website placebear.com to serve random images of bears for the contact photo. Alternatives include placehold.co, picsum.photos, dummyimage.com, and placekitten.com.

10. In the Views\Shared folder, in _Layout.cshtml, add a menu item to navigate to the customer's home page, as shown in the following markup:

```
<li class="nav-item">
  <a class="nav-link text-dark" asp-area=""
     asp-controller="Customers" asp-action="Index">Customers</a>
</li>
```

11. Start the Northwind.Mvc website project using the https profile.
12. On the home page, click **Customers**, and note the table of 91 customers in all countries.
13. In the browser address bar, append /USA to the end of the path, press *Enter*, and note that the table is limited to customers in the USA.
14. Press the browser back button to return to the full list of customers.
15. Click one of the country names in the Country column of the table, like Argentina, and note that the table is now limited to customers in Argentina.
16. Click one of the customer IDs, and note the detail page for that customer.
17. Close Chrome and shut down the web server.

When an HTTP request is received by the website, it will create an instance of the Controller class, call the appropriate action method, return the response as an HTML page generated by the appropriate Razor View, and release the resources used by the controller, including the repository and its database context.

If you use Chrome to try out your ASP.NET Core projects, it has some behavior that developers should know about to avoid frustration.

Clearing Chrome's address bar autocomplete

If you've already entered a country name with the wrong case, then if you try to enter that same country name with the correct case, Chrome will auto-convert it back to the wrong-cased entry!

This has been a well-known annoyance in the web developer community for many years but the Chrome team don't seem minded to fix it.

To allow you to re-enter a country with its correct casing, in Chrome, navigate to **History** (or press *Ctrl + H*), find the wrong-cased entry, click its **...** menu on the right, and then select **Remove from history**.

Designing for case sensitivity

If you want to be able to do case-insensitive queries, then the most efficient solution is to enable case-insensitive text comparison for the `Country` column in the `Customers` table. Then you could use `uk` or `france` or `gErmAny` in the queries.

If you cannot change the database, then you could force the country search value and country column values to be uppercase or lowercase on both sides. But beware, because "while it may be tempting to use `string.ToLower` to force a case-insensitive comparison in a case-sensitive database, doing so may prevent your application from using indexes." You can read more about how to handle case-sensitivity in EF Core at the following page: `https://learn.microsoft.com/en-us/ef/core/miscellaneous/collations-and-case-sensitivity`.

Casing depends on need. For faster searches, you would use case sensitivity, which is why the `Country` column uses that in Microsoft's example Northwind database. What we have built at this point in the book is an API for code to call. An end user is never going to type a country name into the address bar of the browser, so you do not need to worry about incorrect casing. Instead, you would build a website UI that can make sure the user picks a country name that exists in the table column and has the correct casing.

For case-insensitive searches using standard SQL features without losing the speed of indexed searches, you could store the original content in mixed/proper case for display, and also store a normalized version (for example, in all lowercase) in another column for searching/sorting/indexing, and convert the user's search input text into matching lowercase at runtime for comparison. This gives the best of both worlds at the expense of needing more storage space.

Or for a proper full-text case-insensitive search on larger amounts of more varied text, like a product description, you would implement the **full-text search** (FTS) capabilities available in SQL Server. Each database has its own FTS product.

So far in this chapter, we have focused on using caching to improve performance and scalability. Now let's briefly introduce some other techniques.

More techniques to improve scalability

Scalability in ASP.NET Core is all about ensuring that your application can handle increased load by efficiently managing resources. In-memory and distributed caching play a role in scaling by reducing the need for expensive operations.

Other techniques, like asynchronous programming, load balancing, and database optimization, all contribute to making an ASP.NET Core application more scalable. Combining these strategies with cloud-native tools, like auto-scaling and CDNs, ensures your application can grow with demand while maintaining high performance.

Horizontal scaling with load balancing

This technique distributes incoming requests across multiple application instances. You can set up load balancing using tools like NGINX, Azure Load Balancer, or AWS Elastic Load Balancing. This helps distribute traffic and avoid overloading any single instance.

Asynchronous programming

Using `async` and `await` in ASP.NET Core ensures that your application does not block threads while waiting for I/O-bound operations, such as database calls or API requests. This helps optimize the use of server resources and improves concurrency, which is crucial when scaling.

At the end of this chapter, there is an optional practice about improving scalability by understanding and implementing async action methods.

Database optimizations

There are a few database techniques that can improve scalability:

- **Database indexing**: Properly index your database to improve the speed of queries and reduce the load on the database server. Slow database queries are often a bottleneck in scalability.
- **Connection pooling**: Use database connection pooling to minimize the overhead of opening and closing database connections.
- **Read replicas**: Use database replication strategies to offload read-heavy operations to read replicas while leaving write operations on the primary database.

Message queues and background services

Offload heavy or long-running tasks to background services using message queues, like Azure Service Bus, RabbitMQ, or Kafka. This allows your web servers to quickly respond to user requests without waiting for background tasks to complete.

Auto-scaling in the cloud

Use cloud services such as Azure App Service or AWS Elastic Beanstalk, which automatically scale your application instances based on traffic. This auto-scaling feature allows the infrastructure to dynamically add or remove servers to meet current demand.

CDN

Use a CDN to offload static content like images, CSS, and JavaScript libraries to edge servers that are geographically closer to users. This reduces the load on your web server and improves performance for end users. Azure CDN or Cloudflare are commonly used solutions.

Health checks and monitoring

Regularly monitor your application performance and set up health checks to ensure that your instances are running optimally. ASP.NET Core has built-in health check middleware that helps with monitoring and reporting the health of your services, which is crucial for identifying bottlenecks or issues early.

Practicing and exploring

Test your knowledge and understanding by answering some questions, getting some hands-on practice, and exploring this chapter's topics with deeper research.

Exercise 6.1 – Online material

"What are the best practices for optimizing content delivery using Cloudflare's CDN? Any tips for improving website performance?":

```
https://community.cloudflare.com/t/what-are-the-best-practices-for-optimizing-content-
delivery-using-cloudflares-cdn-any-tips-for-improving-website-performance/557911
```

Exercise 6.2 – Practice exercises

The following practice exercises help you to explore the topics in this chapter more deeply.

Practicing improving scalability by understanding and implementing async action methods

Almost a decade ago, Stephen Cleary wrote an excellent article for MSDN Magazine explaining the scalability benefits of implementing async action methods for ASP.NET. The same principles apply to ASP.NET Core, but even more so because, unlike the old ASP.NET, as described in the article, ASP.NET Core supports asynchronous filters and other components.

Read the article at the following link:

```
https://learn.microsoft.com/en-us/archive/msdn-magazine/2014/october/async-programming-
introduction-to-async-await-on-asp-net.
```

Exercise 6.3 – Test your knowledge

Answer the following questions:

1. How can you instruct the visitor's browser to cache the response for 24 hours?
2. What is the difference between the `max-age=<seconds>` and `s-maxage=<seconds>` directives?
3. When is it important to use the `NoStore` parameter on the `[ResponseCache]` attribute?
4. How do you set the default expiration time for output caching?
5. How do you enable output caching for an endpoint defined using `MapGet`?
6. Why might you need to set both a sliding and an absolute expiration for object caching?
7. What are some benefits of distributed object caching compared to in-memory object caching?
8. What is hybrid object caching?
9. What are some non-caching techniques to improve the scalability of a website?
10. What is a CDN, and what are its benefits for a website?

Exercise 6.4 – Explore topics

Use the following link to learn more about the topics covered in this chapter:

```
https://github.com/markjprice/web-dev-net10/blob/main/docs/book-links.md#chapter-6---
performance-and-scalability-optimization-using-caching.
```

Summary

In this chapter, you learned about the various types of caching, including HTTP response caching, output caching, and in-memory or distributed object caching, as well as, new in .NET 9, hybrid caching, to get the best of both worlds.

Always remember that caching works best with data that (a) costs a lot to generate and (b) does not change often.

Follow these guidelines when caching:

- Your code should never depend on cached data. It should always be able to get the data from the original source when the data is not found in the cache.
- Wherever you cache data (in-memory or in a database), it is a limited resource, so deliberately limit the amount of data cached and for how long by implementing expirations and size limits.

In the next chapter, you will learn how to write automated tests of web user interfaces using Playwright.

Learn more on Discord

To join the Discord community for this book – where you can share feedback, ask questions to the author, and learn about new releases – follow this QR code:

```
https://packt.link/RWWD10
```

Join .NETPro — It's Free

Staying sharp in .NET takes more than reading release notes. It requires real-world tips, proven patterns, and scalable solutions. That's what .NETPro, Packt's new newsletter, is all about.

Scan the QR code or visit the link to subscribe:

`https://landing.packtpub.com/dotnetpronewsletter/`

7

Web User Interface Testing Using Playwright

Testing modern web applications is more challenging than ever. Web user interfaces are dynamic, interactive, and expected to work consistently across multiple devices and browsers. Ensuring a smooth user experience requires verifying not just individual components but also complete user flows, such as signing in, placing orders, or updating account details.

By focusing on automating key user flows, balancing between automated and manual testing, and addressing cross-browser compatibility, developers can significantly enhance the reliability and quality of their web UI. Manual testing alone is rarely enough to catch subtle bugs or performance issues, especially in large, complex applications.

This chapter introduces you to web user interface testing and how to use Microsoft Playwright to write automated tests for web user interfaces. Playwright is a powerful testing framework that makes it easier to simulate real-world user interactions, test across multiple browsers, and debug test failures effectively.

This chapter covers the following topics:

- Introducing web user interface testing
- Testing web user interfaces using Playwright
- Interacting with a web user interface
- Generating tests with the Playwright Inspector

Introducing web user interface testing

Web UI testing helps to improve the functionality, usability, and performance of a web application from the end-user's perspective. Before diving into practical examples using Playwright, let's make sure you have a good grounding in the general fundamentals.

Types of web UI testing

There are several approaches to web UI testing, each serving different purposes:

- **Manual testing:** This involves human testers interacting with the website and verifying that the UI behaves as expected. This is often useful for exploratory or visual testing. Manual testing can be time-consuming, but an experienced human tester can improve the quality of your website better than any automated testing.

- **Automated UI testing:** This involves scripts or tools to automate the interaction with the UI. For example, filling in forms, clicking buttons, selecting from drop-down lists, and so on. Automation is particularly useful for regression testing and ensuring that rapid changes do not break the UI. This type of testing is the main focus of this chapter. For those unfamiliar, regression testing is a type of software testing performed to ensure that new changes, such as bug fixes, feature enhancements, or code refactoring, haven't introduced new defects or broken existing functionality in an application. The goal is to verify that the software still works as expected after updates.

- **Visual regression testing:** This ensures that the appearance of the UI remains consistent. Tools compare screenshots or DOM snapshots of a page before and after changes, raising alerts if something looks different.

A wide variety of tools are available for automating UI tests, including:

- **Selenium:** One of the most popular tools for automating browsers. It supports multiple languages like C#, Python, and Java. However, Selenium tests can be flaky due to reliance on timing and browser inconsistencies.

- **Playwright** and **Puppeteer:** Newer headless browser testing frameworks that are generally more stable and offer features like parallel test execution and direct browser control.

- **Cypress:** Popular for UI testing, offering great speed and reliability by running directly in the browser. It's known for having a user-friendly API and detailed debugging tools.

- **TestCafe:** Another modern tool for UI testing, known for not requiring WebDriver and running tests on multiple browsers.

> **WebDriver** is a W3C-standardized API for automating and controlling web browsers. It allows developers and testers to simulate real user interactions like clicking buttons, entering text, navigating pages, and verifying content, without manually using the browser. It's most commonly associated with Selenium WebDriver, but the standard itself is supported by all major browsers, including Chrome, Firefox, Edge, and Safari.

What should you test in a web UI?

One of the most important decisions is about what you should test in a web UI. There is likely to be an unending list of potential UI interactions that you could test. Let's review what you should prioritize:

- **Layout and design:** Make sure elements like buttons, text boxes, images, and other UI components are properly aligned and visible on different screen sizes and browsers.

- **Functionality**: Validate that UI controls, like buttons, links, and forms, are working correctly, interacting with the backend properly, and triggering the right actions.

- **Cross-browser compatibility**: Ensure the application works across different browsers, like Chrome, Firefox, Safari, and Edge, and across different browser versions.

- **Responsive design:** Test how the UI adapts to different screen resolutions and devices, including desktops, tablets, and smartphones.

- **User workflow:** Validate that user flows, like login, checkout, and visitor registration, are intuitive and error-free.

- **Accessibility:** Ensure that the UI is accessible to users with disabilities by following standards like **Web Content Accessibility Guidelines** (**WCAG**). Tools like Axe or WAVE can help automate this.

Challenges and good practices with web UI testing

Most developers find that web UI testing is more challenging than other types of testing, for example, unit testing, for the following reasons:

- **Flakiness:** Automated UI tests can be brittle due to timing issues, changing UI elements, or dependencies on external services like APIs that you have no control over and could change at any moment. For example, a temporarily slow network could make a button appear later than expected, causing tests to fail. This can be extremely frustrating and can make some developers give up on web UI testing altogether. Don't give up hope!

- **Dynamic content:** Modern web apps often load content dynamically, which can make them harder to test reliably. Synchronizing test scripts with the UI, for example, waiting for elements to appear or certain actions to complete, is a key technique that, when implemented, will make your tests more reliable and less frustrating.

- **Test maintenance:** Changes in the UI often break tests, requiring constant updates. You can keep your tests more maintainable by using stable locators like unique IDs or named CSS classes, and avoiding hardcoded wait times.

- **Speed:** Automated UI tests can be slower compared to unit or integration tests since they simulate full user interactions and render the UI. Balancing between UI and non-UI tests is important to optimize feedback loops.

To deal with these challenges, there are some good practices that you should follow:

- **Start small:** Don't test everything through the UI. UI tests should focus on high-level, critical user interactions like the login and checkout process (because these are often how your website pays for itself). For internal logic, rely on unit and integration tests to cover business rules. You shouldn't need to test internal logic via UI tests.

- **Use stable locators:** Selectors like IDs and data attributes like `data-testid` are more stable than CSS or XPath locators, which may change more frequently.

- **Test in multiple browsers:** Unless your website is only used within your organization and it dictates the web browser used, it is important to run your tests across different browsers to catch issues that may only appear in specific environments. You can use data about actual visitors' browsers to prioritize which browsers it is most important to support. Different geographic regions can have very different browser usage. It's best not to assume what your website's visitors prefer.

- **Accessibility and usability testing:** Automated tools can check for accessibility issues, but manual review is still required for subjective aspects like usability. Ensure that the application is navigable using a keyboard, that alt text is provided for images, and that the contrast ratio is sufficient for visually impaired users.

- **Mock dependencies:** If external services are causing problems for your UI tests, then isolate the tests by using mock servers or stubs. Doing so will improve test reliability and speed.

- **Parallelize tests:** Use parallel execution to speed up the test suite, especially with cloud-based solutions like BrowserStack or Sauce Labs, which support running tests on multiple devices concurrently.

- **Continuous integration** (CI): Integrate UI tests into your CI pipeline so that they run automatically on every code commit or pull request. This helps catch UI issues early and ensures that tests are run consistently.

- **Handling test data:** Make sure that test environments are reset between test runs to avoid polluted data. Also, ensure that the test data used reflects real-life scenarios so you catch edge cases.

The roles of developers and testers

The roles of developers and testers in web UI testing are distinct but complementary. They need to work together to ensure that the user interface functions correctly, looks good, and provides a seamless experience.

Developers and web UI testing

Developers are primarily responsible for writing unit tests and integration tests that focus on the code behind the UI. While these tests don't test the UI directly, they ensure that the business logic and underlying components work as expected. These types of testing are summarized in the following list:

- **Unit tests:** Developers write tests for individual components or pieces of logic in isolation. For instance, a developer might test that a form validation function works correctly, independent of how it's displayed in the UI.

- **Integration tests:** Developers also write tests that check interactions between different components or services, ensuring that data flows correctly from the backend to the UI.

In some teams, developers contribute directly to UI testing by writing automated scripts that simulate user interactions with the UI.

Developers typically focus on writing scripts that perform key user flows like login, form submission, or navigating between pages. Developers ensure that UI tests are part of the CI pipeline. Developers also refactor tests when the UI changes or by adding new test cases when new features are introduced.

To make the UI easier to test, developers can create stable CSS selectors, IDs, or custom attributes, like adding a `data-testid` attribute for important elements. This helps testers or automated test scripts locate elements more reliably, especially when UI designs change.

Developers may also add test hooks or specific test-friendly functionality to allow easier automation. For instance, they might expose certain states or data specifically for testing purposes.

They need to work closely with testers to understand edge cases and user behaviors that need to be tested. They need to quickly fix any bugs or issues found during testing and deploy patches or improvements based on test feedback.

Developers are responsible for debugging UI defects found during testing. When a tester finds an issue, like a button not responding, alignment issues, or functionality that breaks on certain browsers, then the developer investigates the root cause. This could be a frontend code issue involving HTML, CSS, and JavaScript, a backend data issue, or an integration problem.

Testers and web UI testing

Testers play a role in manual testing by interacting directly with the web application as an end user would. They focus on:

- **Usability**: Ensuring that the UI is intuitive and user-friendly
- **Functionality**: Verifying that all UI elements like buttons, forms, and links behave as expected
- **Cross-browser and cross-device compatibility**: Manually checking that the application works across different browsers, like Chrome, Firefox, Edge, and Safari, and across devices, like desktops, tablets, and phones
- **Visual testing**: Ensuring that the layout, fonts, colors, and overall design are consistent with the design specifications

Testers may use exploratory testing techniques to find edge cases or unexpected behavior that automated scripts might not catch. Experience really matters with manual testing, so hire the best.

Testers also write and maintain automated UI tests. They usually focus on automating critical user flows like login, checkout, and form submissions to ensure that these workflows work with each release. They often manage regression testing by running automated tests to ensure that changes or new features don't break existing functionality.

Even when they don't write the scripts themselves, testers have primary responsibility for designing test cases based on:

- **User stories or requirements**: Ensuring that each piece of functionality works as intended
- **Common user scenarios**: Focusing on what real users will do on the platform, ensuring that typical and edge-case flows work as expected
- **Negative testing**: Trying to break the system with unexpected inputs, such as entering invalid data or trying to perform actions that should be restricted, like submitting a form with missing fields

Testers evaluate the accessibility of the web UI, ensuring that it meets WCAG. For example, testers will:

- Check whether the application is navigable using just the keyboard (without a mouse).
- Ensure that screen readers can interpret the content.
- Verify contrast ratios, color choices, and font sizes to ensure that the UI is usable by people with visual impairments.

Automated tools like Axe or WAVE can be used for basic accessibility checks, but manual review is often necessary to evaluate usability from an accessibility perspective.

Testers document and communicate defects found during both manual and automated testing. Their bug reports need to be clear and reproducible by providing enough information for developers to reproduce the issue. They also need to indicate whether the bug is a critical failure, a minor glitch, or something in between, to help developers focus on the most pressing issues first.

Collaboration between developers and testers

Of course, developers and testers need to work closely together. Developers and testers need strong communication, especially during the development lifecycle, to ensure that features are fully tested and that bugs are addressed efficiently.

Both developers and testers should collaborate to set up a robust CI/CD pipeline where automated tests run on every code change, providing quick feedback and ensuring a stable UI. In Agile teams, developers and testers work in close-knit sprints, where testers validate features as soon as they are developed, and both roles participate in sprint planning, daily standups, and retrospectives.

By dividing responsibilities in this way, developers and testers can work together to build and maintain a high-quality web UI that is functional, responsive, and user-friendly across all environments and devices.

Real-life applications of web user interface testing

Web UI testing has proven to be vital in various real-life scenarios across industries, preventing software defects and enhancing user experiences. The following examples illustrate how UI testing ensures the reliability, usability, and overall quality of web applications.

E-commerce websites: preventing cart and checkout failures

UI testing can simulate a user's shopping experience from product selection to payment, ensuring that forms are correctly submitted, payments are processed, and orders are confirmed. Automated UI tests catch errors in the checkout form or payment integration early, preventing loss of revenue due to broken transactions. Visual regression testing can also ensure that product images, buttons, and banners display correctly, maintaining trust in the brand.

Companies like Amazon and Walmart use automated UI testing for complex scenarios involving dynamic content, promotions, multiple payment gateways, and global users. Missing a bug in these areas could cause millions of dollars in lost revenue or damage user trust.

Financial applications: ensuring data integrity and accuracy

UI testing ensures that all forms accept the correct input, calculations are accurate, and reports generated match expected outcomes. It can also test responsiveness, ensuring that critical financial data appears correctly on different screen sizes and browsers. Testing user inputs, error messages, and data display can prevent financial applications from producing inaccurate results, which could lead to serious trust issues or even regulatory penalties.

Companies like Intuit (the makers of TurboTax and QuickBooks) rely on extensive UI testing to ensure that users can input financial data correctly and that their dashboards display the correct information. A UI bug in such tools could lead to wrong tax calculations or financial decisions.

Healthcare portals: guaranteeing user and data safety

Automated UI tests can simulate user actions like booking appointments, filling in medical forms, and reviewing personal records. UI testing ensures that the app functions correctly, and visual tests can ensure that sensitive medical data is displayed securely and properly across browsers. Catching booking bugs before release prevents patient frustration and reduces the need for manual corrections. Secure and stable UI testing can also help healthcare portals comply with HIPAA or other data protection regulations.

Platforms like Epic Systems or MyChart must perform extensive UI and functional testing, as errors could not only affect appointment scheduling but also patient privacy and compliance with healthcare regulations. A simple UI failure could expose sensitive medical data, leading to lawsuits or fines.

Banking applications: avoiding security and transaction errors

UI tests simulate core banking actions such as logging in, viewing account balances, transferring money, and paying bills. Cross-browser and cross-device testing are essential to ensure these actions work flawlessly across different user environments. Regular UI testing catches issues that could prevent users from accessing their accounts or completing essential tasks, thereby avoiding costly support interventions and frustrated customers.

Banks like Chase or Wells Fargo need robust UI testing because any downtime or malfunction in essential features like transfers or bill payments can damage trust and result in financial and reputational loss. Additionally, security-related UI elements (such as password fields and two-factor authentication) must function properly to avoid security vulnerabilities.

Government and public sector: ensuring accessibility compliance

Government websites are often required to meet accessibility standards, such as WCAG 2.1. UI testing that incorporates accessibility checks ensures the website is usable by people with various disabilities. By catching accessibility issues during testing, the organization avoids potential lawsuits and fines while ensuring that the service is accessible to all citizens.

Websites like irs.gov and gov.uk must go through extensive UI and accessibility testing to ensure that people of all abilities can navigate their services. Governments are often legally bound to ensure that services are usable for people with disabilities, and testing helps prevent non-compliance.

SaaS platforms: preventing downtime and data loss

UI testing verifies that critical user actions such as saving, editing, and deleting data work as intended. It can simulate complex user workflows that include data inputs, modifications, and integrations with third-party APIs. UI testing prevents breaking changes from reaching production, avoiding costly incidents where users might lose data or be unable to access key features.

Salesforce and HubSpot depend heavily on automated UI testing to ensure that their complex dashboards function correctly and that integrations with third-party tools work without issues. Any UI malfunction could disrupt entire sales teams or customer service operations, leading to client dissatisfaction.

Travel and booking platforms: ensuring smooth transactions

UI testing validates dynamic features such as calendars, maps, and real-time availability checks. Cross-device testing ensures that the booking process works smoothly on both desktop and mobile interfaces. By catching UI issues early, the platform prevents customers from abandoning their bookings due to frustrating interactions or display problems.

Companies like Expedia and Airbnb depend on thorough UI testing to ensure that their booking and search interfaces are fast, responsive, and work across multiple devices and browsers. Any defect could lead to user frustration and result in lost revenue.

Now that you've been introduced to the important concepts and real-world benefits of thorough web UI testing, let's see some practical examples of how to test web user interfaces using Playwright.

Testing web user interfaces using Playwright

Playwright is an open-source framework for the automated testing of websites and web apps across various browsers. Playwright was developed by Microsoft and is maintained as an open-source project. The development of Playwright is primarily driven by Microsoft engineers, many of whom previously worked on Puppeteer, a similar web testing tool developed by Google.

Playwright is hosted on GitHub under the Microsoft organization, which actively maintains it and releases updates. Here is the GitHub link: `https://github.com/microsoft/playwright`.

While it's an open-source project and contributions can come from the wider community, the core direction and development are controlled by Microsoft. Playwright is a part of Microsoft's broader strategy to improve developer tools, especially for testing modern web applications.

A developer who understands browser architecture, especially its main components like the renderer process, browser process, network stack, and JavaScript engine, can write far more efficient, reliable, and debuggable Playwright tests, so let's start by reviewing modern browser components.

Modern browser components

When we talk about "browsers" like Chrome, Edge, Safari, or Firefox, we're really talking about bundles of several cooperating components: engines, UI shells, and platform integration layers. It's useful to understand how modern browsers are architected and what terms like *Chromium*, *WebKit*, *Blink*, and *Gecko* actually mean.

The modern browser stack

Every modern browser is conceptually made up of five core subsystems:

1. User interface:

    - The visible browser window, tabs, menus, address bar, bookmarks, and so on.
    - Each vendor builds its own: for example, Chrome's UI shell, Edge's Fluent shell, Opera's custom interface.
    - Not standardized or shared between browsers that use the same engine.

2. Browser engine:

    - Manages communication between the UI and the rendering engine
    - Responsible for navigation, history, permissions, and resource loading
    - Example: Chromium's Browser Process or Safari's Browser Daemon

3. Rendering engine:

    - Parses HTML and CSS, constructs the DOM and render trees, computes layouts, and paints the final pixels
    - Examples: Blink (used by Chromium-based browsers), WebKit (used by Safari), and Gecko (used by Firefox)

4. JavaScript engine:

    - Executes JS code, JIT-compiles scripts, manages garbage collection, and runs the event loop
    - Examples: V8 (Chrome, Edge, Opera), JavaScriptCore/Nitro (Safari), and SpiderMonkey (Firefox)

5. Networking, storage, and multimedia layers:

    - Networking stack (HTTP/2, QUIC, DNS, cache)
    - Persistent storage (cookies, IndexedDB, localStorage)
    - Audio/video pipelines and codecs
    - Sandboxing and process isolation (critical for security)

Key browser engines and projects

The big three modern rendering engines are shown in *Table 7.1*:

Engine	Used by	Derived from	JS engine	Maintained by
Blink	Chrome, Edge, Opera, Brave, and Vivaldi	Forked from WebKit in 2013	V8	Google
WebKit	Safari (and some embedded browsers)	Original KHTML (Konqueror)	JavaScriptCore	Apple
Gecko	Firefox	Independent (from Netscape)	SpiderMonkey	Mozilla

Table 7.1: Big three modern rendering engines

Chromium versus Blink

Chromium is often confused with Blink, but they are not the same. Chromium is the entire open-source browser project Google maintains. It includes:

- The UI (Omnibox, tab management, and so on)
- The networking stack (Chromium's own implementation of HTTP and QUIC)
- The sandboxing model
- The rendering engine (Blink)
- The JavaScript engine (V8)
- Platform integrations (printing, GPU acceleration, etc.)

So, Blink is just one subsystem inside Chromium, specifically the rendering/layout engine. Browsers like Edge, Brave, and Opera all take Chromium, modify the UI layer, change telemetry or feature flags, and release their own builds. But they're still powered by Blink + V8.

WebKit and Safari

WebKit was originally created by Apple in 2002 as a fork of KDE's KHTML and KJS (Konqueror's HTML and JS engines). Later, Google forked WebKit into Blink in 2013. WebKit today is composed of:

- **WebCore:** The layout and rendering engine
- **JavaScriptCore (JSC):** The JavaScript runtime
- **WebKit layer:** The glue between the engine and the OS/browser UI (used in Safari and iOS)

Apple's Safari adds iCloud integration, Apple Pay, Reading List, and so on, strict privacy controls (Intelligent Tracking Prevention), and tight macOS/iOS integration. And due to Apple's App Store policies, all iOS browsers (even Chrome and Firefox for iPhone) are forced to use WebKit under the hood.

Now that we've reviewed the main browser components, let's see what Playwright can do with browsers to automate user interface testing.

What can Playwright do?

Playwright enables developers and testers to write scripts that simulate user interactions with web pages. These interactions can include anything from navigating pages, filling out forms, and clicking buttons to more complex scenarios like handling **single-page applications (SPAs)**, web components, and even file downloads and uploads.

The most popular browsers to test with are WebKit, Firefox, Google Chrome, Microsoft Edge, and other Chromium-based browsers. Playwright uses open-source Chromium builds. The Chromium project is ahead of the branded browsers, so when the latest branded release is Google Chrome *N*, Playwright already supports Chromium *N+1*, which will be released in branded browsers a few weeks later.

Playwright's Firefox version uses the most recent Firefox stable build. Playwright's WebKit version uses the most recent WebKit trunk build before it is used in Apple Safari and other WebKit-based browsers. Playwright doesn't work with the branded version of Firefox or Safari since they rely on patches.

Playwright can operate against branded browsers available on your computer. In particular, the current Playwright version will support the stable and Beta channels of these browsers, for example, to configure Microsoft Edge, as shown in the following markup:

```xml
<?xml version="1.0" encoding="utf-8"?>
<RunSettings>
  <Playwright>
    <BrowserName>chromium</BrowserName>
    <LaunchOptions>
      <Channel>msedge</Channel>
    </LaunchOptions>
  </Playwright>
</RunSettings>
```

To ensure that Playwright can recognize this configuration, you should place this file in the root folder of your test project (the same directory as your test project file, like `.csproj` for .NET projects) or in a dedicated folder for test settings. Typically, this file should be named something like `Playwright.runsettings` or `test.runsettings`.

If you're running tests via the command line, you can specify the run settings as shown in the following command:

```
dotnet test --settings Playwright.runsettings
```

When running a test project, you can then specify the browser and channel, as shown in the following command:

```
dotnet test -- Playwright.BrowserName=chromium Playwright.LaunchOptions.
Channel=msedge
```

Different browsers can render web pages differently due to variations in their underlying engines. By specifying the browser, developers can ensure that their applications work correctly across multiple browsers. This helps in catching browser-specific issues early in the development process. Specifying the channel is particularly useful for ensuring compatibility with the latest browser features or with certain versions that users might still be using.

Some bugs may only appear in certain browsers or channels. By explicitly specifying these in tests, developers can catch and address browser-specific bugs, enhancing the overall reliability and user experience of the web application.

You can run Playwright tests against multiple browsers at once. You can specify multiple browsers using command-line arguments, although this approach is less common than using a configuration file. By default, Playwright runs tests in parallel. When configured to run against multiple browsers, it will parallelize the tests across those browsers as well. This can significantly speed up the testing process and provide comprehensive coverage quickly.

Playwright also has specific packages that integrate with NUnit and MSTest. For other testing systems, like xUnit, or if you just want to write tests in a console app, then you can just reference the main Playwright package, as we will do in the step-by-step task for this chapter.

> The Playwright website and documentation can be found at the following link: `https://playwright.dev/dotnet/`.

Benefits for .NET developers

For .NET developers, Playwright offers a comprehensive set of benefits that can streamline the development and testing processes, including those shown in the following list:

- **Cross-browser support:** Playwright supports testing across all modern browsers, including Chrome, Firefox, Safari, and Edge. This is particularly beneficial for ensuring application compatibility and performance across different user environments without having to manually test each browser.

- **Rich set of APIs:** Playwright provides a rich set of APIs for automating web interactions, including support for modern web features like web components, shadow DOM, and asynchronous operations. This allows for more sophisticated and accurate tests that closely mimic real user behavior.

- **Speed and reliability:** Playwright tests are designed to be fast and reliable. Its architecture minimizes flakiness and improves test stability, which is crucial for agile development and fast iteration cycles.

- **Headless mode:** Playwright can run browsers in headless mode, meaning the browser is invisible, which is faster and uses less memory than a full browser UI, making it ideal for automated test pipelines and CI systems. While Selenium supports headless mode, Playwright's implementation is more optimized, resulting in faster execution times.

- **Parallel test execution**: Playwright supports running tests in parallel, significantly reducing the time required to execute extensive test suites. This feature is incredibly beneficial in a CI/CD environment, where speed and efficiency are paramount.

Playwright and alternatives

There are several alternatives to Playwright that .NET developers might consider, including the two main competitors, Selenium and Puppeteer. Let's review their pros and cons compared to Playwright.

Selenium

One of the most well-known and widely used tools for web application testing, Selenium offers a mature ecosystem and extensive browser support. However, it may be slower and less efficient than Playwright in some scenarios, especially with modern web applications.

For example, Playwright automatically waits for elements to be ready before performing actions on them. This reduces flakiness and the need for explicit waits or sleep commands, which are more common in Selenium scripts and can slow down test execution.

Parallelization is more sophisticated in Playwright compared to Selenium, which tends to be slower due to its architecture and the overhead of the WebDriver protocol.

SPAs rely heavily on JavaScript for rendering content dynamically; Playwright can interact with these apps more seamlessly because it was designed to work with modern JavaScript frameworks and handle the complexity of client-side navigation better than Selenium.

Selenium requires different WebDriver implementations for each browser, adding complexity and potential inconsistency.

You can view the Selenium developer website at the following link: `https://www.selenium.dev/`.

Puppeteer

Developed by the Chrome DevTools team, Puppeteer is another popular choice for browser automation, primarily focused on Chrome and Chromium-based browsers. While it offers a similar feature set to Playwright, it lacks native support for other browsers like Firefox and Safari.

You can view the Puppeteer developer website at the following link: `https://pptr.dev/`.

Both of these tools have their strengths and weaknesses, and the best choice depends on the specific needs of your project, including the browsers you need to support, the complexity of your web application, and your development environment.

The biggest benefit of Selenium over Playwright is its mature ecosystem and extensive community support. Selenium has been around since 2004, making it one of the oldest and most widely adopted web automation tools. This long history means it has a well-established ecosystem, with extensive documentation, numerous tutorials, and a vast array of third-party tools and integrations.

Playwright

Playwright, with its comprehensive browser support and .NET integration, represents a compelling option for .NET developers looking for a modern and efficient way to automate their web application testing.

The next few sections contain reference tables for the common types and the common testing and locating methods provided by Playwright when writing UI tests. I recommend scanning the information to get a brief idea of what's available, and then move on to the next section, where you will see some practical code examples. That's when the information in the tables will make more sense, and you can return to them as a reference.

Common Playwright testing types

Playwright provides some useful types to test the user interface of a website. Some of the most common are described in *Table 7.2*, and you will use all of them in the coding tasks later in this chapter:

Type	Description
`IPlaywright`	Represents the Playwright system. Has properties like `Chromium`, `Firefox`, and `Webkit` that represent browsers, and properties like `Selectors` that configure how you can select elements on a web page to automate testing.
`IBrowser`	Represents a web browser. Has properties like `Contexts`, `IsConnected`, `BrowserType`, and `Version`. Has methods like `NewContextAsync` and `NewPageAsync`.
`IBrowserContext`	Represents a browser session. A good practice is to create a browser context and then create a page within that context. Cookies and cached objects are not shared between contexts. Has properties like `APIRequest` and `Pages`. Has methods like `NewPageAsync`, `AddCookiesAsync`, `CookiesAsync`, and `StorageStateAsync`. The `SetGeolocationAsync` and `SetOfflineAsync` methods can be used to simulate those features.
`IResponse`	Represents an HTTP response from the web server. Has properties like `Headers`, `Ok`, `Status`, and `StatusText`. Has methods like `BodyAsync`, `JsonAsync`, and `TextAsync` to get the body of the response.
`IPage`	Represents a web page. Each page belongs to a browser context, a.k.a. session, and shares its cookies and cache.
`ILocator`	Represents one or more HTML elements within a web page.

Table 7.2: Common Playwright testing types

For example, imagine you want to write a web UI test to perform the following actions:

1. Create an instance of Playwright.
2. Launch the Chromium browser.
3. Create a new browser session.
4. Create a new page.
5. Navigate to your locally hosted website's home page.

6.   Get an element on the page using its `data-testid` attribute value.

You would write statements to automate Playwright types, as shown in the following code:

```
using IPlaywright? playwright = await Playwright.CreateAsync();
IBrowser browser = await playwright.Chromium.LaunchAsync();
IBrowserContext session = await browser.NewContextAsync();
IPage page = await session.NewPageAsync();
IResponse response = await page.GotoAsync("https://localhost:5021/");
// Could check response.Ok or response.Status.
ILocator element = page.GetByTestId("visitor_count");
```

Common Playwright testing methods

Playwright provides some useful methods to automate and test a web page represented by an `IPage` instance, as described in *Table 7.3*:

IPage method	Description
GotoAsync, GoBackAsync, GoForwardAsync	Navigates to the specified resource or navigates back and forward. Returns an `IResponse` instance. You saw a call to GotoAsync in the preceding code example.
ContentAsync	Gets the full HTML content of the page.
TitleAsync	Gets the page title.

Table 7.3: Common Playwright page automation methods

Common Playwright locator methods

Playwright provides some useful methods to get one or more elements on a web page, and they all return an `ILocator` instance, as described in *Table 7.4*:

Method	Description
GetByRole	Match elements based on accessibility role. Specify the role and additional values, as shown in the following code: `GetByRole(AriaRole.Heading, new() { Name = "Sign up" }))`. These roles and values select the following element: `<h3>Sign up</h3>`, or `GetByRole(AriaRole.Button, new() { Name = "Sign in" })`. This element will, in turn, select the following element: `<button>Sign in</button>`.
GetByLabel	Use to fill in input fields in a form. For example, `GetByLabel("Password"). FillAsync("secret")` would fill the following element: `<label>Password <input type="password" /></label>`.
GetByPlaceholder	Also useful to fill in input fields in a form. For example, `GetByPlaceholder("name@example.com").FillAsync("playwright@ microsoft.com")` would fill the following element: `<input type="email" placeholder="name@example.com" />`.

`GetByTestId`	Test IDs are specified by adding the `data-testid` attribute to an element. You saw a call to `GetByTestId` in the preceding code example.
`GetByText`	Find an element by the text it contains, like `<div>`, `<span>`, `<p>`, and so on.
`GetByTitle`	Locate an element with a matching title attribute. For example, use `GetByTitle("Unread messages")` to locate `<span title='Unread messages'>3</span>`.
`GetByAltText`	You can locate an image based on the text alternative. For example, `GetByAltText("playwright logo")` would find the following image: `<img alt="playwright logo" src="/img/playwright-logo.svg" width="100" />`.
`Locator`	Return an `ILocator` instance that matches the specified CSS or XPath selector specified using `css=` or `xpath=`, although these prefixes are optional. This should be avoided in favor of one of the `GetBy...` methods. CSS and XPath selectors are less resilient to changes.
`And, Or`	Combine multiple locators into a Boolean matching expression.
`First, Last, Nth`	Return the first, last, or *n*th element when there are multiple matches. But avoid these methods because, when your page changes in the future, Playwright may click on an element you did not intend.

Table 7.4: Common Playwright locator methods

Good practice: Use role locators to locate elements as much as possible because it is the closest way to how users and assistive technology perceive the page.

Common Playwright locator automation methods

Playwright provides some useful methods for testing part of a page using an `ILocator` instance, and most will throw an exception if more than one element is matched by the locator, as described in *Table 7.5*:

ILocator method	Description
`CheckAsync, UncheckAsync`	Selects or clears a checkbox or a radio button
`SelectOptionAsync`	Selects an option in a list box
`ClickAsync`	Clicks a button or other element
`DblClickAsync`	Double-clicks a button or other element
`FillAsync`	Fills an input element like a text box
`FocusAsync`	Sets the focus to an element
`HoverAsync`	Hovers the mouse pointer over an element

PressAsync	Presses a key in the element
PressSequentiallyAsync	Presses a sequence of keys in the element
ScreenshotAsync	Takes a screenshot of the element
ScrollIntoViewIfNeededAsync	Scrolls the viewport to show the element
SelectTextAsync	Selects text within an element
TapAsync	Taps on an element

Table 7.5: Common Playwright locator automation methods

Warning! All operations on locators that imply a single DOM element will throw an exception if more than one element matches. For example, if you have a locator that matches all buttons and call ClickAsync, then an exception is thrown.

You can learn more about locators at the following link: https://playwright.dev/dotnet/docs/locators.

Disposing of Playwright objects

Should unit tests that use Playwright implement IDisposable and call Dispose on the browser object variable? The short answer is: don't implement IDisposable for Playwright tests.

The long answer is that Playwright's .NET objects (IPlaywright, IBrowser, IBrowserContext, and IPage) are asynchronous disposables, so you should either use await using or your test framework's async lifecycle hooks.

Also, don't dispose of the browser per test; reuse a browser and create a fresh context per test for isolation.

Why not IDisposable?

IBrowser and other Playwright classes implement IAsyncDisposable, not IDisposable. If you stick cleanup into Dispose(), you can't properly await async teardown, which risks leaks and flaky tests. Use DisposeAsync() or await using.

Playwright's guidance is to reuse a browser and isolate tests with new browser contexts. That model lines up with async disposal of contexts/pages rather than synchronous disposal on the test class.

Recommended patterns

Use IAsyncLifetime on the test class or a fixture, as shown in the following code:

```
public class UiTests : IAsyncLifetime
{
  private IPlaywright _pw = default!;
  private IBrowser _browser = default!;

  public async Task InitializeAsync()
  {
    _pw = await Playwright.CreateAsync();
    _browser = await _pw.Chromium.LaunchAsync(new() { Headless = true });
  }

  public async Task DisposeAsync()
  {
    await _browser.DisposeAsync(); // or CloseAsync.
    _pw?.Dispose(); // IPlaywright implements IDisposable.
  }

  [Fact]
  public async Task HomePage_Loads()
  {
    await using var context = await _browser.NewContextAsync();
    var page = await context.NewPageAsync();
    await page.GotoAsync("https://example.com");
    // assertions...
  }
}
```

xUnit runs a new instance per test, calling InitializeAsync and then DisposeAsync, which lets you await cleanup correctly.

If you're using Playwright's test runner integrations, inherit the provided base classes. They manage a shared browser and give you an isolated page per test; you focus on test logic, not wiring and disposal.

What to dispose of and when:

- **Per test:** Create a new BrowserContext and close or dispose of it after the test. This gives clean cookies and storage and avoids state bleed.
- **Per class/collection/worker:** Launch and reuse a single IBrowser for speed; close or dispose of it in async teardown.

If you manually close the browser, close contexts first so page-close events fire cleanly.

Anti-patterns to avoid

Do not implement IDisposable on the test class to clean up Playwright resources. It's synchronous and doesn't await async teardown. Prefer IAsyncLifetime with async teardown.

Do not use using var on IPlaywright during setup, which goes out of scope while tests still run. That prematurely tears down the connection.

Do not launch and dispose of the browser for every test. It's slow and unnecessary; contexts provide the isolation you actually need.

Reviewing the website before testing

Playwright enables a wide range of automated testing scenarios, from basic navigations to complex user interactions and validations. In this first step-by-step task, we will walk through some key pages and functionality to understand what we want to test.

Let's get started:

1. Start the Northwind.Mvc project using the https profile without debugging.
2. If a browser is not started automatically, then start your preferred browser, navigate to https://localhost:5021/, and scroll down the home page to show the visitor count and products, as shown in *Figure 7.1*:

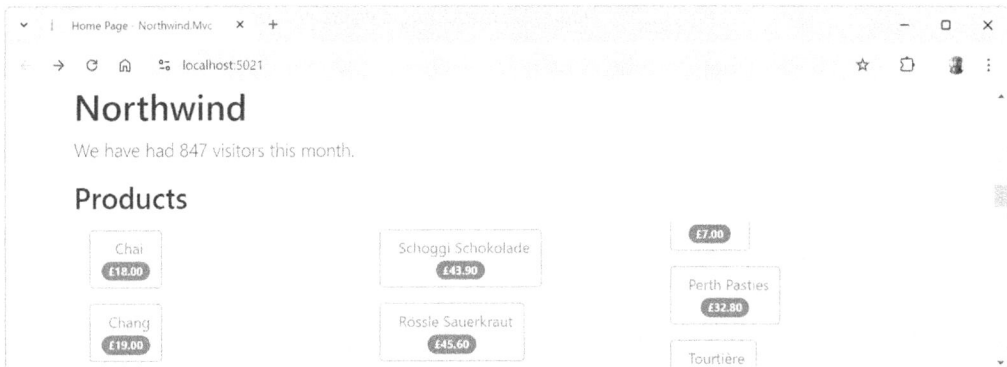

Figure 7.1: The Northwind.Mvc home page, showing visitors and products

3. Right-click in the middle of the page, select **View page source**, and note the <title> element in <head>, as shown highlighted in the following markup:

```
<!DOCTYPE html>
<html lang="en">
<head>
    <meta charset="utf-8" />
    <meta name="viewport" content="width=device-width, initial-scale=1.0"
/>
    <title>Home Page - Northwind.Mvc</title>
...
```

4. Close the page source tab.

5. Right-click in the middle of the visitor count, select **Inspect**, and note the <p> for showing the number of visitors, as shown highlighted in the following markup and in *Figure 7.2*:

```
<div class="col-md-12">
   <h1>Northwind</h1>
   <p class="lead">We have had 847 visitors this month.</p>
</div>
```

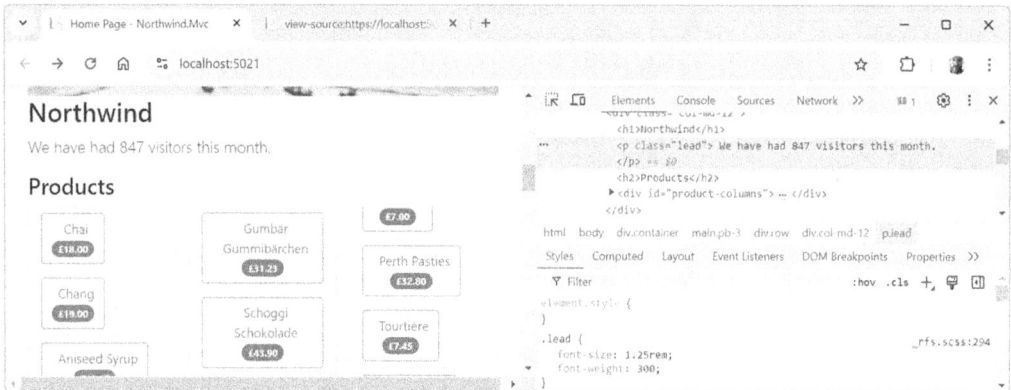

Figure 7.2: Inspecting a visitor count

6. Scroll up to the **Query products by price** section above the category photos, right-click the input box, select **Inspect**, and note the two <input> elements in the <form> element, as shown in the following markup and in *Figure 7.3*:

```
<h3>Query products by price</h3>
<form method="GET" action="/Home/ProductsThatCostMoreThan">
   <input name="price" placeholder="Enter a product price" />
   <input type="submit" />
</form>
```

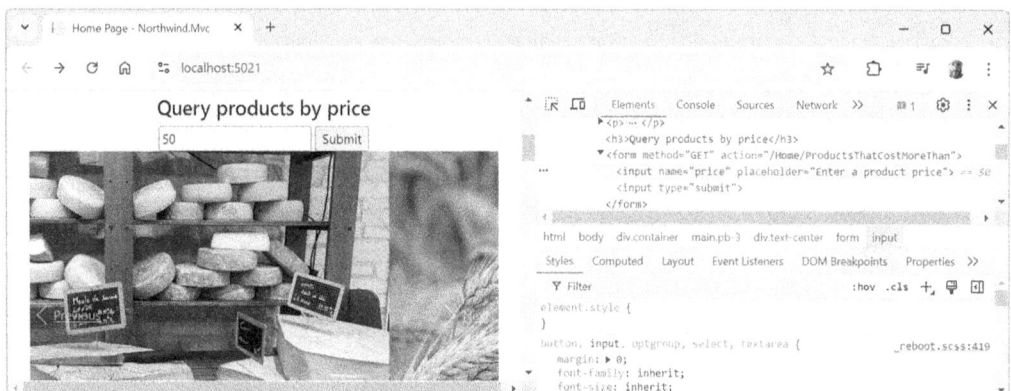

Figure 7.3: Inspecting the form to filter products by price

Good practice: Elements that we might want to automate, like the `<input>` text box, should have a `data-testid` attribute set to a unique value. If you have no control over the markup, then you can use less optimal techniques to find and automate page elements.

7. Close the browser's inspection pane.

8. At the top of the home page, in the navigation menu, click **Login**.

9. Right-click the **Email** label, select **Inspect,** and note the two labels, two inputs, and the button to log in, as shown in the following markup and in *Figure 7.4*:

```html
<form id="account" method="post" novalidate="novalidate">
  <h2>Use a local account to log in.</h2>
  <hr>
  <div class="form-floating mb-3">
    <input class="form-control valid" autocomplete="username" aria-required="true" placeholder="name@example.com" type="email" data-val="true" data-val-email="The Email field is not a valid e-mail address." data-val-required="The Email field is required." id="Input_Email" name="Input.Email" value="" aria-describedby="Input_Email-error" aria-invalid="false">
    <label class="form-label" for="Input_Email">Email</label>
    <span class="text-danger field-validation-valid" data-valmsg-for="Input.Email" data-valmsg-replace="true"></span>
  </div>
  <div class="form-floating mb-3">
    <input class="form-control valid" autocomplete="current-password" aria-required="true" placeholder="password" type="password" data-val="true" data-val-required="The Password field is required." id="Input_Password" name="Input.Password" aria-describedby="Input_Password-error" aria-invalid="false">
    <label class="form-label" for="Input_Password">Password</label>
    <span class="text-danger field-validation-valid" data-valmsg-for="Input.Password" data-valmsg-replace="true"></span>
  </div>
  ...
  <button id="login-submit" type="submit" class="w-100 btn btn-lg btn-primary">Log in</button>
```

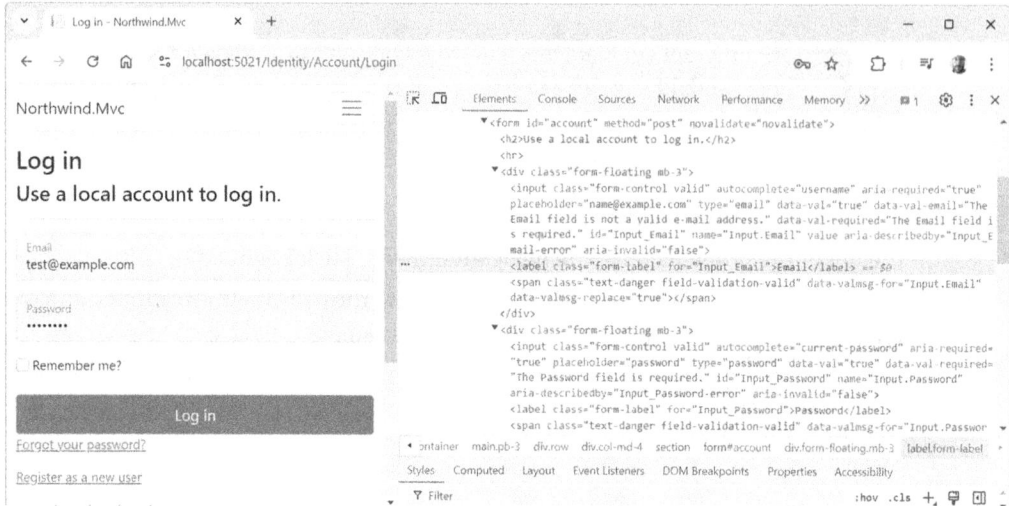

Figure 7.4: Inspecting the login form

10. Close the browser and shut down the web server. You can do this at the command prompt or terminal by pressing *Ctrl + C*.

Let's review some common examples of tests that developers often automate using Playwright, starting with basic website navigation.

Testing page navigation and title verification

A fundamental test case is to navigate to a web page and verify its title to ensure the correct page is loaded. To do this, we will use all the types in *Table 7.2* and some of the methods like `TitleAsync` in *Table 7.3*. This test can be used as a **smoke test** for website availability and correct routing.

Let's go:

1. Use your preferred code editor to add a new **xUnit Test Project [C#]** / xunit project named `Northwind.WebUITests` to the `MatureWeb` solution. For example, at the command prompt or terminal in the `MatureWeb` folder, enter the following commands:

```
dotnet new xunit -o Northwind.WebUITests
dotnet sln add Northwind.WebUITests
```

2. In the `Northwind.WebUITests.csproj` project file, remove the version numbers from all package references and add a reference to the Playwright package, as shown highlighted in the following markup:

```
<ItemGroup>
  <PackageReference Include="coverlet.collector" />
  <PackageReference Include="Microsoft.NET.Test.Sdk" />
  <PackageReference Include="xunit" />
  <PackageReference Include="xunit.runner.visualstudio" />
  <PackageReference Include="Microsoft.Playwright" />
</ItemGroup>
```

3. Build the `Northwind.WebUITests` project to restore packages.

4. Navigate to `Northwind.WebUITests\bin\Debug\net10.0` and, at the command prompt or terminal, install browsers for Playwright to automate, as shown in the following command:

```
pwsh playwright.ps1 install
```

> **Warning!** If you get the error, `The command "pwsh" is not recognized.`, then the most likely problem is that PowerShell is not installed properly on your computer (meaning not installed at all, or installed but not set up, so it is not found from the command prompt). For some readers, the following command might fix the issue:
>
> `dotnet tool update --global PowerShell`
>
> Instructions to install PowerShell on Windows, Linux, and macOS are found at the following link: `https://learn.microsoft.com/en-us/powershell/scripting/install/installing-powershell`.
>
> Some of the answers here might help: *getting started instructions dont work #1865*, `https://github.com/microsoft/playwright-dotnet/issues/1865`.

> Playwright needs special versions of browser binaries to operate. You must use the Playwright PowerShell script to install these browsers. If you have issues, you can learn more at the following link: `https://playwright.dev/dotnet/docs/browsers`.

5. Note that Playwright downloads its own copies of Chrome, Firefox, and WebKit, as shown in the following output:

```
Downloading Chromium 136.0.7103.25 (playwright build v1169) from https://
playwright.azureedge.net/builds/chromium/1169/chromium-win64.zip
136.2 MiB [====================] 100% 0.0s
Chromium 125.0.6422.26 (playwright build v1169) downloaded to C:\Users\
markj\AppData\Local\ms-playwright\chromium-1169
Downloading FFMPEG playwright build v1011 from https://playwright.
azureedge.net/builds/ffmpeg/1011/ffmpeg-win64.zip
1.4 MiB [====================] 100% 0.0s
FFMPEG playwright build v1011 downloaded to C:\Users\markj\AppData\Local\
ms-playwright\ffmpeg-1011
Downloading Firefox 137.0 (playwright build v1482) from https://
playwright.azureedge.net/builds/firefox/1482/firefox-win64.zip
84.8 MiB [====================] 100% 0.0s
Firefox 137.0 (playwright build v1482) downloaded to C:\Users\markj\
AppData\Local\ms-playwright\firefox-1449
Downloading Webkit 18.4 (playwright build v2158) from https://playwright.
azureedge.net/builds/webkit/2158/webkit-win64.zip
```

```
48.5 MiB [=====================] 100% 0.0s
Webkit 18.4 (playwright build v2158) downloaded to C:\Users\markj\
AppData\Local\ms-playwright\webkit-2158
```

> **Warning!** If you do not run this script, then when you try to run Playwright tests, they will fail, and you will see the following message in the test output: Looks like Playwright was just installed or updated. Please run the following command to download new browsers: pwsh bin/Debug/netX/ playwright.ps1 install.

6. In the `Northwind.WebUITests` project, rename `UnitTest1.cs` to `MvcWebUITests.cs`.

7. In `MvcWebUITests.cs`, define a class with a method to set up Playwright to use Chromium, and a test method that will confirm that the home page is returned successfully (the page is not null and the request for it returned a 200 OK status code), then check that the title of the home page is the text that we expect, and finally, ask Playwright to take a screenshot and save it to the desktop so that we can see the home page as it appeared during the test, as shown in the following code:

```csharp
using Microsoft.Playwright; // To use Playwright, IBrowser, and so on.

namespace Northwind.WebUITests;

public class MvcWebUITests: IAsyncLifetime
{
  // Class lifetime objects.
  private IPlaywright _pw = default!;
  private IBrowser? _browser = default!;

  // Test lifetime objects.
  private IBrowserContext? _session;
  private IPage? _page;
  private IResponse? _response;

  public async Task InitializeAsync()
  {
    _pw = await Playwright.CreateAsync();
    _browser = await _pw.Chromium.LaunchAsync(
      new BrowserTypeLaunchOptions { Headless = false });
  }

  public async Task DisposeAsync()
  {
```

```
    await _browser.DisposeAsync(); // or CloseAsync.
    _pw.Dispose(); // IPlaywright implements IDisposable.
  }

  private async Task GotoHomePage()
  {
    _session = await _browser.NewContextAsync();
    _page = await _session.NewPageAsync();
    _response = await _page.GotoAsync("https://localhost:5021/");
  }

  private async void CleanUpSession()
  {
    if (_session is not null)
    {
      await _session.DisposeAsync();
      _session = null;
    }
    _page = null;
    _response = null;
  }b

  [Fact]
  public async Task HomePage_Title()
  {
    // Arrange: Navigate to home page.
    await GotoHomePage(playwright);

    if (_page is null)
    {
      throw new NullReferenceException("Home page not found.");
    }

    string actualTitle = await _page.TitleAsync();

    // Assert: Navigating to home page worked and its title is as
expected.
    string expectedTitle = "Home Page - Northwind.Mvc";
    Assert.NotNull(_response);
    Assert.True(_response.Ok);
    Assert.Equal(expectedTitle, actualTitle);
```

```
// Universal sortable ("u") format: 2009-06-15 13:45:30Z
// : and spaces will cause problems in a filename
// so replace them with dashes.
string timestamp = DateTime.Now.ToString("u")
  .Replace(":", "-").Replace(" ", "-");

await _page.ScreenshotAsync(new PageScreenshotOptions
{
  Path = Path.Combine(Environment.GetFolderPath(
    Environment.SpecialFolder.Desktop),
    $"homepage-{timestamp}.png")
});

CleanUpSession();
  }
}
```

> **Good practice:** Instead of a test method decorated with [Fact], in a real-life test, you could make the method parameterized and decorate it with [Theory] so that you can run the test multiple times with different parameter values for different pages and titles (and even browsers).

8. Start the Northwind.Mvc project using the https profile without debugging.

9. Navigate to **Test | Run All Tests** to run the test, and note that the result is that it passes. You will note that the Chrome browser briefly appears on your screen.

10. On your desktop, open the image and confirm that it is a screenshot of the home page.

11. In MvcWebUITests.cs, in the GotoHomePage method, change the browser to Headless, as shown highlighted in the following code:

```
browser = await playwright.Chromium.LaunchAsync(
  new BrowserTypeLaunchOptions { Headless = true });
```

> You could also just call the LaunchAsync method without passing a BrowserTypeLaunchOptions object because Headless defaults to true.

12. Run the test again and note that the result is that it passes. This time, the browser does not appear, and the test executes faster.

Now let's try some more complex yet common examples.

Interacting with a web user interface

Common web user interface interactions include selecting items from drop-down lists, clicking elements like buttons and icons, filling in and submitting forms, and validating that elements contain specific text or are visible to the visitor.

Filling in input boxes and clicking elements

A good practice is to add the data-testid attribute with a unique value to identify elements on a page that will participate in UI tests.

> **Good practice:** There is some debate about whether to strip the data-testid attributes out in production, often as an automated part of the build process. My recommendation is to keep them in production unless you have a concrete reason to remove them. If you remove attributes only in production, you're no longer testing the exact thing you ship. Teams have hit CI failures because selectors exist in dev builds but not in prod builds. They have negligible overhead since they're tiny strings. They don't affect SEO or runtime meaningfully. If you run end-to-end checks against the live site, having durable selectors in the live DOM is useful and reduces flakiness.

The Northwind MVC website home page shows a visitor count, and it allows the visitor to filter the products by entering a number and clicking a button. Let's use the GetByTestId method in *Table 7.4* to automate this. We will start by adding a data-testid attribute to the elements we want to locate:

1. In the Northwind.Mvc project, in the Views\Home folder, in Index.cshtml, wrap the visitor count in a `<span>` element with a unique attribute, as shown in the following markup:

```
We have had <span data-testid="visitor_count">
@Model?.VisitorCount</span> visitors this month.
```

2. In Index.cshtml, in the `<form>` element for filtering products, add unique attributes to the input box for the price and the submit button, as shown in the following markup:

```
<form asp-action="ProductsThatCostMoreThan" method="GET">
  <input name="price" placeholder="Enter a product price"
        data-testid="price" />
  <input type="submit" data-testid="submit_price" />
</form>
```

3. In `MvcWebUITests.cs`, statically import the `Assertions` class so that we can use its `Expect` method, as shown in the following code:

```
using static Microsoft.Playwright.Assertions; // To use Expect.
```

4. In `MvcWebUITests.cs`, add a test to check that the visitor count is an integer and is visible to the visitor, as shown in the following code:

```
[Fact]
public async Task HomePage_VisitorCount()
{
  // Arrange: Navigate to home page.
  await GotoHomePage(playwright);

  // The best way to select the element is to use its data-testid.
  ILocator? element = _page?.GetByTestId("visitor_count");

  string? countText = null;

  if (element is not null)
  {
    // The text content might contain whitespace like \n so
    // we must trim that away.
    countText = (await element.TextContentAsync())?.Trim();
  }

  bool isInteger = int.TryParse(countText, out int count);

  // Assert: Visitor count is as expected.
  Assert.True(isInteger);
  Assert.True(count >= 1 && count <= 1000);

  await Expect(element).ToBeVisibleAsync();

  CleanUpSession();
}
```

5. In `MvcWebUITests.cs`, add a test to check that the filtering products feature works correctly, as shown in the following code:

```
[Fact]
public async Task HomePage_FilterProducts()
{
  // Arrange: Navigate to home page.
```

```
await GotoHomePage(playwright);

if (_page is null)
{
  throw new NullReferenceException("Home page not found.");
}

// Set the price input box to 60.
ILocator price = _page.GetByTestId("price");
await price.FillAsync("60");

// Click the submit button to apply the filter.
ILocator submit = _page.GetByTestId("submit_price");
await submit.ClickAsync();
string actualTitle = await _page.TitleAsync();

// Assert: Navigating to products page worked.
string expectedTitle = "Products That Cost More Than $60.00 -
Northwind.Mvc";
Assert.NotNull(_response);
Assert.True(_response.Ok);
Assert.Equal(expectedTitle, actualTitle);

string timestamp = DateTime.Now.ToString("u")
  .Replace(":", "-").Replace(" ", "-");

await _page.ScreenshotAsync(new PageScreenshotOptions
{
  Path = Path.Combine(Environment.GetFolderPath(
    Environment.SpecialFolder.Desktop),
    $"products-60-{timestamp}.png")
});

  CleanUpSession();
}
```

6. Start the Northwind.Mvc project using the https profile without debugging.

7. In **Test Explorer**, right-click on **Northwind.WebUITests** and select **Run**, or press *Ctrl + R, T*, (or run all tests), and note that they all succeed and the screenshot shows the five matching products correctly, as shown in *Figure 7.5*:

Northwind.Mvc   Home   Model Binding   Suppliers   Customers   Privacy   Register   Login

Products That Cost More Than $60.00

Category Name	Supplier's Company Name	Product Name	Unit Price	Units In Stock
Meat/Poultry	Tokyo Traders	Mishi Kobe Niku	97.00	29
Seafood	Pavlova, Ltd.	Carnarvon Tigers	62.50	42
Confections	Specialty Biscuits, Ltd.	Sir Rodney's Marmalade	81.00	40
Meat/Poultry	Plutzer Lebensmittelgroßmärkte AG	Thüringer Rostbratwurst	123.79	0
Beverages	Aux joyeux ecclésiastiques	Côte de Blaye	263.50	17

Figure 7.5: Screenshot of filtered products taken by Playwright

Form submission, authentication, and validation

Automating form submissions and validating the responses or resulting actions is a common scenario for testing web applications. Playwright can fill out forms, click **Submit** buttons, and verify whether the submission leads to the expected outcome, such as a thank you page, a validation error, or the creation of a new database record.

Testing user authentication flows, including login and logout functionality, is another common use case. Playwright can simulate a user logging in to an application, performing actions as an authenticated user, and then logging out, as shown in the following code:

```
// Navigate to log in page.
await page.GotoAsync("https://example.com/login");
await page.FillAsync("input#username", "dummyuser");
await page.FillAsync("input#password", "123456");
await page.ClickAsync("button#login");

// Verify login was successful by checking for a logout button
// and a welcome message.
bool isLoggedIn = await page.IsVisibleAsync("button#logout");
Assert.True(isLoggedIn);
string successMessage = await page.InnerTextAsync("div.success");
Assert.Equal("Welcome, Dummy!", successMessage);

// Perform actions as logged-in user and then log out.
...
await page.ClickAsync("button#logout");
```

Responsive design testing

Testing your web user interfaces for how well they implement responsive design is important in modern web development. Let's review some common scenarios.

Emulating screen sizes

With Playwright, you can test how your application behaves on different screen sizes, which is essential for ensuring a good user experience across devices, like making sure that an important section is visible to mobile visitors, as shown in the following code:

```
await page.SetViewportSizeAsync(640, 480); // Set to a mobile view.
await page.GotoAsync("https://example.com");
bool isLoggedIn = await page.IsVisibleAsync("div#importantSection");
Assert.True(isLoggedIn);
```

You can set the viewport back to desktop size, as shown in the following code:

```
await page.SetViewportSizeAsync(1920, 1080); // Set to a desktop view
```

Emulating devices

You can emulate specific devices when you create a browser context, as shown in the following code:

```
browser = await playwright.Chromium.LaunchAsync(
  new BrowserTypeLaunchOptions { Headless = false });
BrowserNewContextOptions iphone13 = playwright.Devices["iPhone 13"];
IBrowserContext context = await browser.NewContextAsync(iphone13);
```

Emulating locale, time zone, and geolocation

You can emulate the device locale and time zone, as shown in the following code:

```
BrowserNewContextOptions options = new()
{
  Locale = "de-DE", // Accept-Language header.
  TimezoneId = "Europe/Berlin"
};
IBrowserContext context = await browser.NewContextAsync(options);
```

> Valid time zones for Chromium are documented at the following link: `https://source.chromium.org/chromium/chromium/deps/icu.git/+/faee8bc70570192d82d2978a71e2a615788597d1:source/data/misc/metaZones.txt`.

You can grant geolocation permissions and set geolocation to a specific area, as shown in the following code:

```
BrowserNewContextOptions options = new()
{
  Permissions = [ "geolocation" ],
  Geolocation = new() { Longitude = 41.890221F, Latitude = 12.492348F }
};
IBrowserContext context = await browser.NewContextAsync(options);
```

If you need to dynamically change the geolocation, then you can call a method, as shown in the following code:

```
await context.SetGeolocationAsync(new()
  { Longitude = 48.858455F, Latitude = 2.294474F });
```

Emulating dark mode and color schemes

You can emulate dark mode, as shown in the following code:

```
BrowserNewContextOptions options = new()
  { ColorScheme = ColorScheme.Dark };
IBrowserContext context = await browser.NewContextAsync(options);
```

If you need to dynamically change the color mode, then you can call a method on a page, as shown in the following code:

```
await page.EmulateMediaAsync(new()
  { ColorScheme = ColorScheme.Dark });
```

Customizing the user agent, disabling JavaScript, and going offline

Not all clients are commonly used web browsers. For example, some are web crawlers and bots indexing the web or consuming web content to feed **large language models** (**LLMs**). Some browsers have JavaScript disabled, and this can severely affect many modern websites that rely on JavaScript. Many parts of the world have unreliable internet connectivity, so it is useful to test how your website would behave during a disruption.

Playwright configuration options to simulate these scenarios include customizing the user agent, disabling JavaScript, and going offline, as shown in the following code:

```
BrowserNewContextOptions options = new()
{
  UserAgent = "My User Agent",
  JavaScriptEnabled = false,
  Offline = true
};
IBrowserContext context = await browser.NewContextAsync(options);
```

You can learn more about emulation at the following link: `https://playwright.dev/dotnet/docs/emulation`.

SPAs and dynamic content

Playwright excels in handling complex web applications that use JavaScript heavily for dynamic content loading, SPAs, and AJAX calls. You can wait for elements to become visible or load, or for network requests to complete before proceeding with tests, as shown in the following code:

```
await page.GotoAsync("https://example.com/spa");
await page.ClickAsync("button#loadData");

// Wait for data to load.
await page.WaitForSelectorAsync("div.dataLoaded");
string loadedData = await page.InnerTextAsync("div.dataLoaded");
```

SPAs built with frameworks like Angular, React, Vue, and Blazor are out of scope for this book, so I won't be showing any more detailed examples of testing them with Playwright.

Now let's see how you can get Playwright to generate the testing code for you.

Generating tests with the Playwright Inspector

Code generation with Playwright for .NET is a super cool feature that can significantly speed up your test automation workflow. Code generation is like having a personal assistant who watches over your shoulder as you browse through your web application and automatically writes the test scripts for you. In essence, it's a way to automate the automation, which is meta in a good way.

The Playwright Inspector tool allows you to create comprehensive test scripts in a fraction of the time it would take to write them manually. It captures user interactions with high precision, reducing the chance of errors that can occur when writing tests by hand. Even if you're new to test automation, you can get started quickly. It's also a great way to learn how Playwright structures its tests by examining the generated code.

As you navigate through your application, Playwright records your actions, like clicks, text inputs, and navigations, and then generates the corresponding C# test code in real time. Once you're done, you can stop the code generation tool, and it will output the generated script. You can then review this code, make any necessary adjustments, and integrate it into your test suite.

After integrating the generated code into your project, you can run your tests using the Playwright test runner, ensuring that your application behaves as expected across different browsers and devices. The generated code is a great starting point, but don't be afraid to refine and customize it to better suit your testing needs.

Let's see it in action:

1. If you previously stopped the web service, then start the `Northwind.Mvc` project using the `https` profile without debugging.

2. In the `Northwind.WebUITests` project folder, at the command prompt or terminal, enter the following command to start the code generator:

```
pwsh bin/Debug/net10.0/playwright.ps1 codegen https://localhost:5021/
```

3. Note that two application windows will open, one for the special version of the Chromium browser, which has a "Chrome" icon in shades of blue, and one for **Playwright Inspector**, which has a pair of colorful actor masks, as shown in *Figure 7.6*:

Figure 7.6: The Playwright Inspector and Chromium icons in the Windows taskbar

4. In the **Chromium** window, note that it has a floating toolbar with buttons for **Record**, **Pick locator**, **Assert visibility**, **Assert text**, **Assert value**, and **Assert snapshot**, and when you move your mouse cursor over an element on the page, like the price input box that applies a filter to products, it suggests a locator to select that element, as shown in *Figure 7.7*:

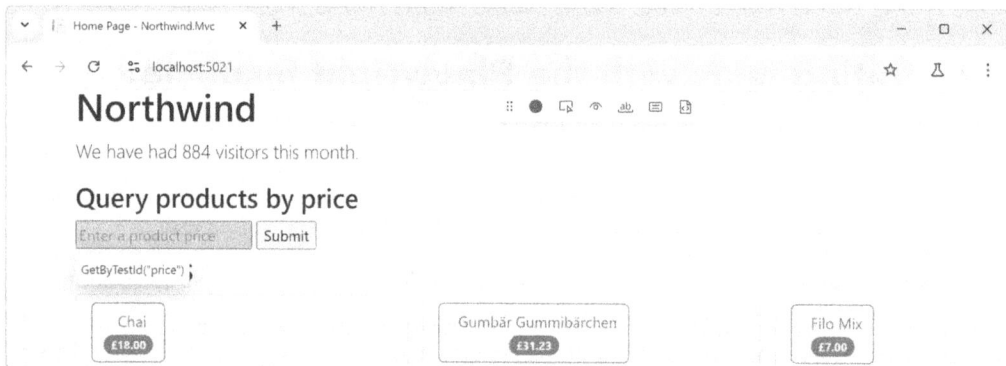

Figure 7.7: Chromium with the Playwright Inspector toolbar

5. In the **Playwright Inspector** window, note the initial C# code to automate the browser test; in the top-right corner is a drop-down list of targets that can be set to any of multiple languages and testing frameworks like **.NET C# Library** or **NUnit**, or **Node.js Test Runner**, as shown in *Figure 7.8*:

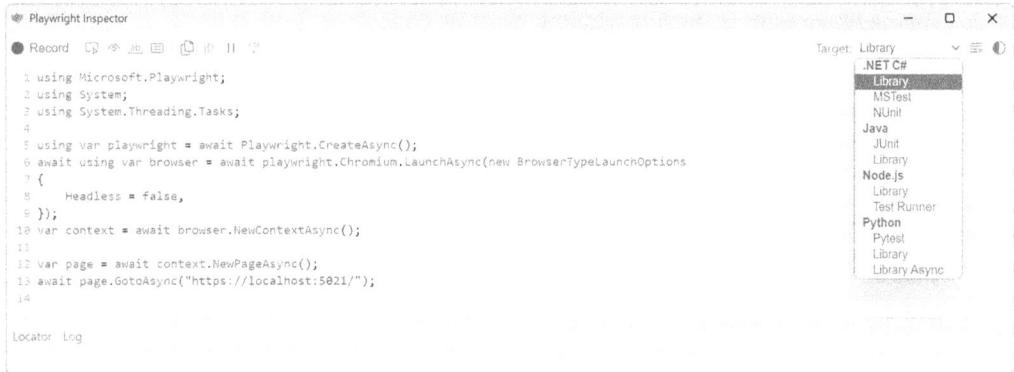

Figure 7.8: The Playwright Inspector showing initial C# code to automate the browser test

> **Warning!** When the **Record** button is red, you are recording. When the **Record** button is black, you are *not* recording. The Playwright Inspector starts recording automatically.

6. Switch to the Chromium browser window.

7. Optionally, arrange the two application windows to be side by side and both visible so that you can see the code written for you as you perform actions in the Chromium browser window.

8. On the website home page, in the top navigation, click **Login** and note that a new statement is written for you to select, and then click that element, as shown in the following code:

```
await page.GetByRole(AriaRole.Link, new() { Name = "Login"
}).ClickAsync();
```

9. In the **Email** box, enter test@example.com.

10. In the **Password** box, enter Pa$$w0rd.

11. Click the **Log in** button.

12. On the home page, in the toolbar, click **Assert text**.

13. Click **Hello test@example.com!**.

14. In the **Assert that element contains text** pop-up window, note the value Hello test@example.com!, and in the top-right corner, click the **Accept** tick icon to accept that text.

15. On the website home page, in the top navigation, click **Logout**.

16. On the toolbar, click the red **Record** button to stop recording.

17. In the **Playwright Inspector** window, note the code:

```
using Microsoft.Playwright;
using System;
using System.Threading.Tasks;

using var playwright = await Playwright.CreateAsync();

await using var browser = await playwright.Chromium.LaunchAsync(
  new BrowserTypeLaunchOptions
{
    Headless = false,
});
var context = await browser.NewContextAsync();

var page = await context.NewPageAsync();
await page.GotoAsync("https://localhost:5021/");
await page.GetByRole(AriaRole.Link, new() { Name = "Log in"
}).ClickAsync();
await page.GetByRole(AriaRole.TextBox, new() { Name = "Email"
}).ClickAsync();
await page.GetByRole(AriaRole.TextBox, new() { Name = "Email"
}).FillAsync("test@example.com");
await page.GetByRole(AriaRole.TextBox, new() { Name = "Email"
}.PressAsync("Tab");
await page.GetByRole(AriaRole.TextBox, new() { Name = "Password"
}).FillAsync("Pa$$w0rd");
await page.GetByRole(AriaRole.Button, new() { Name = "Log in"
}).ClickAsync();
await Expect(page.GetByRole(AriaRole.Navigation)).
ToContainTextAsync("Hello test@example.com!");
await page.GetByRole(AriaRole.Button, new() { Name = "Logout"
}).ClickAsync();
```

> Note the assertion, like await Expect(page.GetByRole(AriaRole.Navigation)).
> ToContainTextAsync("Hello test@example.com!");.

18. You can now copy and paste this code into your test project and edit it to remove unnecessary statements, like clicking on text boxes or pressing the *Tab* key, as shown in the following code:

```
// This statement is not needed.
await page.GetByRole(AriaRole.TextBox, new() { Name = "Email"
}).ClickAsync();

// This statement is not needed.
await page.GetByRole(AriaRole.TextBox, new() { Name = "Email"
}).PressAsync("Tab");
```

> Your code could be different because you are unlikely to have followed all the steps exactly as I did.

You can start the Playwright Inspector with emulation options like setting a viewport size, as shown in the following command:

```
pwsh bin/Debug/net10.0/playwright.ps1 codegen --viewport-size=800,600 https://
localhost:5021/
```

You could emulate a device, as shown in the following command:

```
pwsh bin/Debug/net10.0/playwright.ps1 codegen --device="iPhone 13" https://
localhost:5021/
```

> Learn more about code generation with the Playwright Inspector at the following link: https://playwright.dev/dotnet/docs/codegen.

Practicing and exploring

Test your knowledge and understanding by answering some questions, getting some hands-on practice, and exploring the topics covered in this chapter with deeper research.

Exercise 7.1 — Online-only material

You can read the official documentation for Playwright for .NET at the following link:

https://playwright.dev/dotnet/docs/intro.

The Playwright Community page has links to their Discord channel and other useful places like videos on conference talks, live streams, features and releases, and their YouTube channel:

https://playwright.dev/dotnet/community/welcome.

Search using the **Playwright** tag on Stack Overflow for commonly asked questions with good answers:

`https://stackoverflow.com/tags/playwright`.

Exercise 7.2 – Practice exercises

If you are done with Playwright and you want to remove the special browsers (`chromium`, `firefox`, and `webkit`) of the current Playwright installation, then run the Playwright PowerShell script with the `uninstall` option, as shown in the following command:

```
pwsh bin/Debug/net10.0/playwright.ps1 uninstall
```

To remove browsers of other Playwright installations as well, add the `--all` switch, as shown in the following command:

```
pwsh bin/Debug/net10.0/playwright.ps1 uninstall --all
```

Exercise 7.3 – Test your knowledge

Answer the following questions. If you get stuck, try googling the answers, while remembering that if you get totally stuck, the answers are in the appendix:

1. What browsers does Playwright use when running its tests?
2. What are the main interfaces that represent important objects when writing tests for Playwright?
3. Using Playwright, what are some methods to get one or more elements on a web page?
4. What happens if more than one element matches and you call a method that implies a single DOM element, like `ClickAsync`?
5. What does the Playwright Inspector do?

Exercise 7.4 – Explore topics

Use the links on the following page to learn more details about the topics covered in this chapter:

`https://github.com/markjprice/web-dev-net10/blob/main/docs/book-links.md#chapter-7---web-user-interface-testing-using-playwright`.

Summary

In this chapter, you learned:

*   Important concepts about web UI testing, including the roles that developers and testers play in the testing process
*   How to test a web user interface using Playwright
*   How to generate tests with the Playwright Inspector

In the next chapter, you will learn how to configure and containerize ASP.NET Core projects ready for deployment.

Get This Book's PDF Version and Exclusive Extras

Scan the QR code (or go to `packtpub.com/ unlock`). Search for this book by name, confirm the edition, and then follow the steps on the page.

Note: Keep your invoice handy. Purchases made directly from Packt don't require one.

8

Configuring and Containerizing ASP.NET Core Projects

Now that we have built a website that reads and writes to a database, implemented security and caching, and tested the user interface, we will look at how to configure and containerize ASP.NET Core projects.

Modern ASP.NET Core applications are rarely simple, single-project solutions. Instead, they often involve multiple services, APIs, databases, and background processes that must work together seamlessly. To build reliable, maintainable applications, developers need to understand how to configure the components that make up their solution, manage dependencies effectively, and set up an HTTP request pipeline that ensures performance, security, and scalability.

In this chapter, you'll learn how to configure dependency services using ASP.NET Core's built-in dependency injection framework. You'll see how to register services, manage lifetimes, and control how your application resolves and uses them at runtime. We'll then move on to configuring the HTTP pipeline, where middleware components are arranged to handle requests and responses in a structured, predictable way.

You'll also explore configuration options and learn how to manage app settings across multiple environments without hardcoding values or duplicating configuration. From there, we'll cover containerizing ASP.NET Core projects, enabling you to package applications with all their dependencies and run them consistently across different machines and platforms.

Finally, we'll introduce Aspire, a framework for orchestrating multi-project solutions. You'll learn how Aspire simplifies development and testing when working with complex systems that include multiple services, APIs, and depend0encies.

> Aspire 13 is polyglot (meaning it supports multiple languages), so Aspire orchestrates apps in C#, Java, Python, JavaScript, TypeScript, Go, and more. It is more than just a .NET feature now so the branding drops ".NET" from the old name, ".NET Aspire". The new official website for Aspire can be found at the following link: https://aspire.dev/.

This chapter will cover the following topics:

- Configuring dependency services
- Configuring the HTTP pipeline
- Configuring options
- Containerizing ASP.NET Core projects
- Orchestrating projects using Aspire

Configuring dependency services

We will start by reviewing how to register dependency services and configure dependency injection.

Introducing dependency injection

Dependency injection (DI) is a design pattern used to implement **inversion of control (IoC)** to resolve dependencies in a program. Traditionally, the flow of control is dictated by your code, as it makes calls to reusable libraries or frameworks to use their functionality. IoC inverts this control so that the framework controls it instead.

ASP.NET Core uses DI for IoC extensively. The framework controls the flow of request processing, and the developer's code is executed in response to specific events like HTTP GET or POST requests.

The main idea of DI is to decouple the creation of an object's dependencies from its own behavior, which allows for more modular, testable, and maintainable code. Instead of objects creating dependencies themselves using the new operator, they are injected with their dependencies at runtime, often by an external framework or container.

For example, in *Figure 8.1*, on the left, you can see a statement that directly instantiates a calculator that implements an interface, and on the right, you can see a statement that requests the registered calculator from a service container:

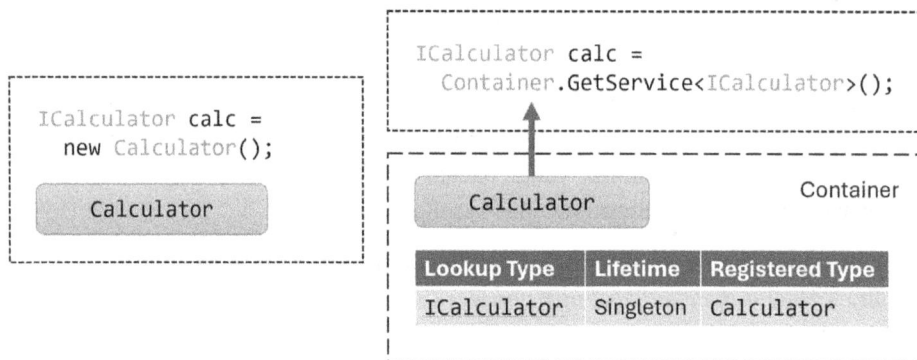

Figure 8.1: Comparing object creation directly with using a DI container

The use of the service container allows us to swap out the registered implementation class and even change its scope without changing the code. The service container is responsible for creating and managing the lifetime of services, aka dependency objects.

Why use DI?

The most common reasons for using DI are shown in the following list:

- **Decoupling**: DI helps in decoupling components and their dependencies, making a system more modular with independent components. When software is divided into modules, changes can be made to individual parts without affecting the entire system. This makes it easier to update, fix bugs, and add new features. Modularity enforces a clear structure, making it easier for developers to understand and navigate the codebase. This reduces the learning curve for new developers joining the project.

- **Testability**: By injecting dependencies, it becomes easier to replace real dependencies with mocks or stubs during testing. Modules can be tested independently from the rest of the application. This makes it easier to identify and fix issues, as tests can be run on smaller, more manageable pieces of code. When an issue arises, debugging is simplified because the problem can often be isolated to a specific module so you don't have to comb through the entire codebase.

- **Flexibility**: Changes in dependencies or their configurations have minimal impacts on the client code. Modularity allows flexible architecture designs where modules can be easily added, removed, or replaced as needed. By encapsulating functionality within modules, it is easier to ensure that the internal workings of a module are hidden from other parts of an application, promoting better data integrity and reducing unintended side effects.

- **Maintainability**: With dependencies being centralized, updates and maintenance become more manageable. Different developers or teams can work on separate modules simultaneously without interfering with each other. This parallel development can significantly speed up the development process. Teams can progress independently on their modules, making it easier to manage large projects with multiple moving parts.

Injection mechanisms of DI in .NET

Imagine that we have an interface and an implementation, as shown in the following code:

```
public interface INotificationService
{
  void Notify(string message);
}

public class NotificationService : INotificationService
{
  public void Notify(string message)
  {
    // Send notification.
  }
}
```

There are primarily three ways to inject dependencies into other components that depend on them:

- **Constructor injection:** Dependencies are provided through a class constructor, as shown in the following code. This is the best practice, since it enables the easiest mocking of services during testing:

```
public class DataService
{
  private readonly INotificationService _service;

  // Constructor Injection
  public DataService(INotificationService service)
  {
    _service = service;
  }

  public void ProcessData(string data)
  {
    // Process data and send it using the notification service.
    _service.Notify(data);
  }
}
```

- **Property injection:** Dependencies are set on public properties of the class, as shown in the following code. Property injection is useful when the dependency is optional or when the dependency might change during the lifetime of an object. It provides more flexibility compared to constructor injection:

```
public class DataService
{
  // Property Injection
  public INotificationService Service { get; set; }

  public void ProcessData(string data)
  {
    // Process data and send it using the notification service.
    Service.Notify(data);
  }
}
```

- **Method injection:** Dependencies are provided through method parameters, as shown in the following code. This approach is suitable for dependencies that are only needed for a specific method. This keeps the rest of the class clean and focused on its core responsibilities:

```
public class DataService
{
  // ...other code.

  // Method Injection
  public void ProcessData(string data, INotificationService service)
  {
    // Process data and send it using the notification service.
    service.Notify(data);
  }
}
```

Examples in modern .NET

.NET includes built-in support for DI, making it straightforward to implement DI patterns in your applications. Let's look at an ASP.NET Core constructor injection example.

Constructor injection example

Suppose you have an `IEmailService` interface and an `EmailService` implementation. You want to inject this service into a consumer class, `UserRegistrationController`, that allows a user to register themselves with your website. The interface, class, and controller are shown in the following code:

```
public interface IEmailService
{
  void SendEmail(string to, string subject, string body);
}

public class EmailService : IEmailService
{
  public void SendEmail(string to, string subject, string body)
  {
    // Implementation to send an email.
  }
}

public class UserRegistrationController
{
  private readonly IEmailService _emailService;
```

```
    public UserRegistrationController(IEmailService emailService)
    {
      _emailService = emailService;
    }

    public void SendUserConfirmationEmail(string userId)
    {
      // Use _emailService to send an email to the user.
      // Code not shown because it will vary based on specific email service.
      ...
    }
}
```

In the ASP.NET Core project dependency services configuration section in `Program.cs`, you would register your dependencies, as highlighted in the following code:

```
var builder = WebApplication.CreateBuilder(args);

// Add services to the container.
builder.Services.AddControllersWithViews();
builder.Services.AddSingleton<IEmailService, EmailService>();

// Other service registrations.

var app = builder.Build();
```

This setup tells the .NET DI container to inject an instance of `EmailService` whenever an `IEmailService` is required using any method of injection, including constructor injection.

Property injection example

Property injection is commonly achieved using third-party libraries or custom solutions because ASP. NET Core does not have native support for property injection. It's generally used in scenarios where constructor injection is not feasible or when optional dependencies are involved.

For example, in Autofac 7.0 or later, all required properties are automatically resolved, in a similar manner to constructor parameters, as shown in the following code:

```
public class NorthwindService
{
  // These properties will be automatically set by Autofac.
  public required ILogger Logger { protected get; init; }
  public required IConfigReader ConfigReader { protected get; init; }
  // More implementation.
}
```

All required properties of the component must be resolvable services; otherwise, an exception will be thrown when trying to resolve the component.

You would then need to use Autofac to register the services, as shown in the following code:

```
ContainerBuilder builder = new();

builder.RegisterType<NorthwindService>();
builder.RegisterType<ConsoleLogger>().As<ILogger>();
builder.RegisterType<ConfigReader>().As<IConfigReader>();

var container = builder.Build();
```

> Autofac is an alternative third-party DI/IoC container. You can learn more about it at the following page: https://autofac.org/.

Method injection example

Method injection is typically used when a specific method in a class requires a dependency but the rest of the class does not. For example, the Index action method might need an instance of the database context but the other methods do not, as shown in the following code:

```
public class SuppliersController : Controller
{
  public IActionResult Index([FromServices] NorthwindContext db)
  {
    SuppliersIndexViewModel model = new(db.Suppliers
      .OrderBy(c => c.Country)
      .ThenBy(c => c.CompanyName));

    return View(model);
  }

  // Other action methods that do not use NorthwindContext.
}
```

It's not as commonly used as constructor injection but can be useful in certain scenarios, especially with Minimal API web services, which do not use classes with constructors, as shown in the following code:

```
app.MapGet("/weather", (IWeatherService weatherService) =>
{
  return Results.Ok(new { Weather = weatherService.GetWeather() });
});
```

In the `MapGet` method, the `IWeatherService` parameter in the lambda expression indicates that this dependency should be provided by the DI container. The DI container automatically resolves the `IWeatherService` and injects it into the handler method.

Dependency graphs and service resolution

It is common to use DI in a chained fashion. Each requested dependency, like `WorkerService`, requests its own dependencies, like `ILogger`. The container finds the required dependencies in its graph of services and returns the fully resolved service.

The set of dependencies that must be resolved is referred to as a dependency tree, dependency graph, or object graph, as shown in *Figure 8.2*:

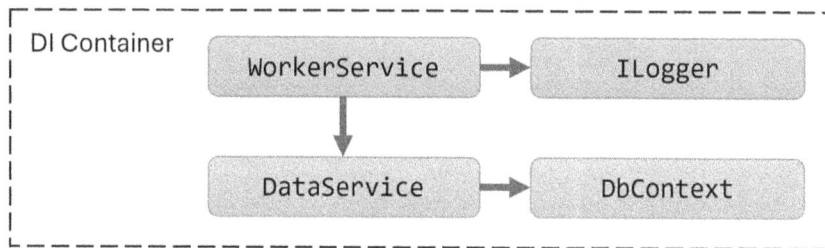

Figure 8.2: DI container and a dependency tree or graph

In *Figure 8.2*, the DI container manages the dependencies. `WorkerService` is a service that depends on other services. `ILogger` is a dependency that is required by `WorkerService`. `DataService` is another dependency that might be needed by `WorkerService` or other services. `DbContext` is a dependency required by `DataService`.

The arrow from `WorkerService` to `ILogger` shows that `WorkerService` depends on `ILogger`. The DI container resolves `WorkerService` and in the process resolves its dependencies, like `ILogger` and `DataService`, which in turn might have their own dependencies, like `DbContext`. This chained resolution ensures that all dependencies are fully resolved and injected where needed.

Registering dependency service lifetimes

You can register dependency services with different lifetimes, as shown in the following list:

- **Transient**: These services are created each time they're requested. Transient services should be lightweight and stateless. Use for lightweight, stateless services where a new instance is required for each operation, such as utility or helper services.

- **Scoped**: For ASP.NET Core projects, these services are created once per client request and are disposed of when the response returns to the client. For other types of projects, like console apps, you need to define a scope manually. You can also create custom additional scopes in ASP.NET Core projects if needed. Use them when you need a separate instance of a service for each request; they are useful for services that interact with per-request data, such as database contexts.

- **Singleton:** These services are usually created the first time they are requested and then shared, although you can provide an instance at the time of registration too. Use when you need a single instance of a service for an entire application's lifetime, typically for shared resources or configurations.

Choosing the right service lifetime ensures that resources are used efficiently and that your application behaves correctly, with services being instantiated and disposed of at the appropriate times.

In this chapter, you will use all three types of lifetimes, which are controlled by a service scope.

When are exceptions thrown?

When resolving dependencies in a DI container, several scenarios can lead to exceptions being thrown. Understanding these scenarios can help you diagnose and fix issues related to dependency resolution. Here are some common scenarios:

- **Service not registered:** If a service is not registered with the DI container, attempting to resolve it will result in an exception – for example: `InvalidOperationException: Unable to resolve service for type 'IMyService' while attempting to activate 'MyComponent'`.
- **Circular dependency:** A circular dependency occurs when two or more components or projects depend on each other in a way that creates a loop. If there is a circular dependency, the DI container cannot resolve the services and will throw an exception – for example: `InvalidOperationException: A circular dependency was detected for the service of type 'ServiceA'`.
- **Missing constructor:** If a service requires a constructor with parameters that cannot be resolved by the DI container, it will throw an exception – for example: `InvalidOperationException: Unable to resolve service for type 'NonRegisteredDependency' while attempting to activate 'MyService'`.
- **Wrong lifetime configuration:** If services are registered with incompatible lifetimes, for example, a scoped service depending on a transient service in a singleton context, this can lead to exceptions or unexpected behavior. This may not throw an exception immediately but can lead to issues like `ObjectDisposedException` when the scoped service is disposed of while still referenced by the singleton.
- **Multiple implementations:** If multiple implementations of a service are registered without specifying which one to use, the DI container may throw an exception or resolve the wrong implementation – for example: `InvalidOperationException: Multiple constructors accepting all given argument types have been found in type 'MyService2'. There should only be one applicable constructor`.
- **Invalid service descriptor:** If a service is registered with an invalid descriptor, such as using a type that does not implement the interface, it can lead to exceptions – for example: `InvalidOperationException: Type 'MyService' does not implement interface 'IMyService'`.

Dependency resolution exceptions can arise from various misconfigurations. Understanding these scenarios helps developers better configure their DI containers and debug issues more effectively.

Registering services for features using extension methods

With a complex ASP.NET Core project, you are likely to need to register many related services for each feature of the website or web service in `Program.cs`, as shown in the following code:

```
builder.Services.AddScoped<IShoppingCart, InMemoryShoppingCart>();
builder.Services.AddScoped<ICustomerAccount, CustomerAccount>();
builder.Services.AddScoped<IUserRegistration, UserRegistration>();
```

It is good practice to define an extension method to group all these registrations, as shown in the following code:

```
public static class ServiceCollectionExtensions
{
  public static IServiceCollection AddNorthwindFeatures(
    this IServiceCollection services)
  {
    services.AddScoped<IShoppingCart, InMemoryShoppingCart>();
    services.AddScoped<ICustomerAccount, CustomerAccount>();
    services.AddScoped<IUserRegistration, UserRegistration>();
    return services;
  }
}
```

This will simplify the statements in `Program.cs`, as shown in the following code:

```
builder.Services.AddNorthwindFeatures();
```

The ASP.NET Core team does this themselves with methods like `AddControllersWithViews`.

When you cannot use constructor injection

If you are building ASP.NET Core MVC or controller-based Web API projects, then your controller classes can use constructor injection to get registered services, just like any other class. But there are other situations where you cannot use constructor injection to get registered services, as it forces a scoped service to behave like a singleton, which throws a runtime exception.

There are several situations in ASP.NET Core where using constructor injection may not be appropriate or possible. These scenarios typically arise when the service lifetimes are incompatible, or the context in which the service is needed does not support constructor injection. Here are some of those situations:

- **Background services**, such as those derived from `BackgroundService` or `IHostedService`, are typically singleton services. Injecting scoped services via the constructor is not appropriate due to their singleton nature. Injecting scoped services into background services via the constructor can cause them to be treated as singletons, leading to issues with resource management and state handling. The solution is to create a scope with the `IServiceScopeFactory.CreateScope()` API, as described at the following page: https://learn.microsoft.com/en-us/dotnet/core/extensions/scoped-service.

- **Tag Helpers** are created per view instance, and injecting services via the constructor is not supported. Constructor injection is not feasible because Tag Helpers are not managed by the DI container in the same way that controllers or other services are. The solution is to use property injection with the [ViewContext] attribute.
- **Filters** can be registered globally, per-controller, or per-action. Filters registered as singleton services cannot depend on scoped services directly via constructor injection. The solution is to use the ServiceFilter or TypeFilter attributes, or the DI container within the filter's methods.

Constructor injection is not always feasible, particularly when dealing with middleware, background services, Tag Helpers, and filters. In these cases, method injection, property injection, or resolving services within the method scope are the preferred approaches to ensure that services are correctly instantiated and managed according to their intended lifetimes.

Let's look at one of these scenarios in more detail: dealing with middleware.

Using scoped services in middleware

Although singletons can be passed in the constructor to middleware, to use scoped and transient services in middleware, you should inject a service into the middleware's Invoke or InvokeAsync method, as shown in the following code:

```
public class NorthwindMiddleware
{
  private readonly RequestDelegate _next;
  private readonly ILogger _logger;
  private readonly ISingletonService _singleton;

  // Singleton services can use constructor injection.
  public MyMiddleware(RequestDelegate next,
    ILogger<MyMiddleware> logger,
    ISingletonService singleton)
  {
    _logger = logger;
    _singleton = singleton;
    _next = next;
  }

  public async Task InvokeAsync(HttpContext context,
    // Transient and scoped services must use method injection.
    ITransientService transient, IScopedService scoped)
  {
    _logger.LogInformation("Transient: " + transient.ProductId);
    _logger.LogInformation("Scoped: " + scoped.ProductId);
    _logger.LogInformation("Singleton: " + _singleton.ProduceId);
```

```
    await _next(context);
  }
}
```

You will see more examples of middleware later in this chapter.

Resolving services at startup

To resolve a scoped service when an ASP.NET Core project starts, you must define a scope, as shown in the following code:

```
using Packt.Shared; // To use INorthwindService.

WebApplicationBuilder builder = WebApplication.CreateBuilder(args);

builder.Services.AddScoped<INorthwindService, NorthwindService>();

WebApplication app = builder.Build();

using (IServiceScope scope = app.Services.CreateScope())
{
  INorthwindService service = scope.ServiceProvider
    .GetRequiredService<INorthwindService>();
  // Use the service here.
}

app.MapGet("/", () => "Hello World!");

app.Run();
```

In the rest of the project, for example, in a controller class or Razor component, a service scope will be created automatically to handle each incoming HTTP request.

As well as constructor injection, you can get the services container from the current HTTP context, as shown in the following code:

```
IServiceProvider services = HttpContext.RequestServices;
```

DI and MVC controller action methods

If you are building controller-based MVC websites or Web API services, then there are alternative techniques to constructor injection.

You can use action method injection using attributes like [FromServices] and [FromKeyedServices].

First, register the services as normal, as shown in the following code:

```
builder.Services.AddSingleton<IOrderProcessor, OrderProcessor>();
builder.Services.AddKeyedSingleton<ICache, BigCache>("big");
```

Then, decorate action method parameters with attributes, as shown in the following code:

```
public IActionResult SubmitOrder([FromServices] IOrderProcessor processor)
{
  // Use processor.
}

public ActionResult<object> GetCatalog([FromKeyedServices("big")] ICache cache)
{
  return cache.Get("catalog");
}
```

DI and MVC views

To inject a service into an MVC Razor View, use the `@inject` directive, as shown in the following code:

```
@inject NorthwindService nw
```

Disposing of services

If a service implements `IDisposable`, then the container calls the `Dispose` method for the services that it creates automatically. You should never explicitly dispose of a service created by the container yourself because you do not know what the dependency tree or graph looks like, and just because you don't need a service anymore does not mean that it's not needed by other services. You also do not know what lifetime it has been registered with. If you dispose of it, other services are likely to fail.

However, if you use the technique of manually creating an instance of a service and passing that to the container, then you will have to dispose of it manually, as shown in the following code:

```
// The service is manually instantiated so must be manually disposed.
builder.Services.AddSingleton(new NorthwindService());
```

Best practices for DI

You should use best practices when implementing DI, as shown in the following list:

- **Prefer constructor injection:** This makes the dependencies of your class explicit and ensures that your class is always in a valid state.
- **Use interfaces for dependencies:** This makes it easier to swap implementations without changing the consuming class.

- **Avoid the service locator pattern:** This is when your code explicitly gets a service inside its implementation using `IServiceProvider.GetService<T>()` and similar methods. This is bad practice because it hides class dependencies, making the code harder to understand and maintain, and tests cannot mock the dependency or replace it when needed.

- **Keep scopes and lifetimes in mind:** Be aware of the scope and, therefore, lifetime of your dependencies to avoid memory leaks or unintended behavior.

DI in .NET simplifies managing dependencies, leading to cleaner, more maintainable code. By leveraging the built-in DI container in .NET, developers can focus more on business logic rather than the intricacies of object creation and management.

Configuring the HTTP pipeline

Now that we have reviewed how dependency services are registered and retrieved using dependency injection, let's have a look at related topics, including endpoint routing and how to configure the HTTP pipeline in ASP.NET Core.

Understanding endpoint routing

Endpoint routing is designed to enable better interoperability between frameworks that need routing, such as Razor Pages, MVC, or Web API services, and middleware that needs to understand how routing affects them, such as localization, authorization, and so on.

Endpoint routing gets its name because it represents the route table as a compiled tree of endpoints that can be walked efficiently by the routing system. One of the biggest improvements is the performance of routing and action method selection.

Benefits of endpoint routing

Endpoint routing is a significant improvement over the previous routing system used pre-ASP.NET Core 2.2. In previous versions, routing was decentralized across MVC controllers, Razor Pages, and middleware. Endpoint routing unifies the routing system across the entire project, allowing you to define all routes in one place.

One of the main goals of endpoint routing was to enhance performance. In earlier versions, routing and middleware pipelines were distinct processes, which added overhead. Endpoint routing integrates routing earlier in the request pipeline, allowing ASP.NET Core to make routing decisions before running middleware.

Prior to endpoint routing, it wasn't easy to route directly to middleware. Endpoint routing allows you to define routes that go directly to middleware, bypassing the MVC controller mechanism if needed. This opens up a lot of flexibility for lightweight APIs, where full controller logic might not be necessary.

In previous routing systems, routing was often tightly coupled with MVC and controllers. Endpoint routing decouples routing from the MVC framework, allowing you to route to anything, including Razor Pages, gRPC, SignalR, and even custom endpoints.

Endpoint routing has improved support for attribute routing, making it easier to handle complex routing scenarios with attributes on controllers and actions. It simplifies and optimizes how attributes are processed, allowing better route resolution.

Endpoint routing introduces a more powerful model for extensibility. For example, you can attach metadata to routes, allowing you to define things like policies, authorization requirements, or caching strategies directly on the route.

Endpoint routing provides a more efficient way of routing by using asynchronous matching and execution. This makes routing more performant and scalable in high-concurrency applications.

Endpoint routing supports complex routing scenarios by allowing you to apply constraints, policies, and filters to routes easily. This includes things like route parameters, versioning, and localization.

Reviewing the default endpoint routing configuration

Review the statements in `Program.cs` in a freshly created ASP.NET Core MVC project template without authentication, as shown in the following code:

```
var builder = WebApplication.CreateBuilder(args);

// Add services to the container.
builder.Services.AddControllersWithViews();

var app = builder.Build();

// Configure the HTTP request pipeline.
if (!app.Environment.IsDevelopment())
{
  app.UseExceptionHandler("/Home/Error");
  // The default HSTS value is 30 days. You may want to change this for
production scenarios, see https://aka.ms/aspnetcore-hsts.
  app.UseHsts();
}

app.UseHttpsRedirection();
app.UseRouting();
app.UseAuthorization();
app.MapStaticAssets();

app.MapControllerRoute(
  name: "default",
  pattern: "{controller=Home}/{action=Index}/{id?}")
  .WithStaticAssets();

app.Run();
```

The web application `builder` registers services that can then be retrieved when the functionality they provide is needed using dependency injection. The naming convention for a method that registers a service is `AddService`, where `Service` is the service name, for example, `AddControllersWithViews`.

Common methods for registering dependencies

Common methods that register dependency services, including services that combine other method calls that register services, are shown in *Table 8.1*:

Method	Services that it registers
`AddMvcCore`	Minimum set of services necessary to route requests and invoke controllers. Most websites will need more configuration than this.
`AddAuthorization`	Authentication and authorization services.
`AddDataAnnotations`	MVC data annotations service.
`AddCacheTagHelper`	MVC cache Tag Helper service.
`AddRazorPages`	Razor Pages, including the Razor View engine. Commonly used in simple website projects. It calls the following additional methods: `AddMvcCore` `AddAuthorization` `AddDataAnnotations` `AddCacheTagHelper`
`AddApiExplorer`	Web API explorer service.
`AddCors`	**Cross-origin resource sharing (CORS)** support for enhanced security.
`AddFormatterMappings`	Mappings between a URL format and its corresponding media type.
`AddControllers`	Controller services but not services for views or pages. Commonly used in ASP.NET Core Web API projects. It calls the following additional methods: `AddMvcCore` `AddAuthorization` `AddDataAnnotations` `AddCacheTagHelper` `AddApiExplorer` `AddCors` `AddFormatterMappings`
`AddViews`	Support for `.cshtml` views including default conventions.
`AddRazorViewEngine`	Support for the Razor View engine including processing the @ symbol.

`AddControllersWithViews`	Controller, view, and page services. Commonly used in ASP.NET Core MVC website projects. It calls the following additional methods:
	`AddMvcCore`
	`AddAuthorization`
	`AddDataAnnotations`
	`AddCacheTagHelper`
	`AddApiExplorer`
	`AddCors`
	`AddFormatterMappings`
	`AddViews`
	`AddRazorViewEngine`
`AddMvc`	Similar to `AddControllersWithViews`, but you should only use it for backward compatibility.
`AddDbContext<T>`	Your `DbContext` type and its optional `DbContextOptions<TContext>`.
`AddNorthwindContext`	A custom extension method we created to make it easier to register the `NorthwindContext` class for SQL Server.

Table 8.1: Common methods that register dependency services

Common methods for registering middleware

Key middleware extension methods used in the default endpoint routing configuration code include the following:

- `UseHsts`: Adds middleware for using HSTS, which adds the `Strict-Transport-Security` header.

> **HTTP Strict Transport Security (HSTS)** is a simple and widely supported standard to protect visitors by ensuring that their browsers always connect to a website over HTTPS. You can learn more at the following page: `https://en.wikipedia.org/wiki/HTTP_Strict_Transport_Security`.

- `UseHttpsRedirection`: Adds middleware for redirecting HTTP requests to HTTPS, so in our code a request for `http://localhost:5020` would receive a `307` response telling the browser to request `https://localhost:5021`.
- `UseDefaultFiles`: Adds middleware that enables default file mapping on the current path, so in our code, it would identify files such as `index.html` or `default.html`.
- `UseStaticFiles`: Adds middleware that looks in `wwwroot` for static files to return in the HTTP response. This is used by ASP.NET Core project templates for .NET 8 and earlier.
- `MapStaticAssets`: Adds middleware that looks in `wwwroot` for static files to return in the HTTP response. This is used by ASP.NET Core project templates for .NET 9 and later.

- **MapRazorPages**: Adds middleware that will map URL paths such as /suppliers to a Razor Page file in the /Pages folder named suppliers.cshtml and return the results as the HTTP response.

- **MapGet**: Adds middleware that will map URL paths such as /hello to an inline delegate that writes plain text directly to the HTTP response. You will see a similar example that registers an inline delegate with the Use method in the next section.

- **UseRouting**: Adds middleware that defines a point in the pipeline where routing decisions are made and must be combined with a call to UseEndpoints where the processing is then executed.

- **UseEndpoints**: Adds middleware to execute to generate responses from decisions made earlier in the pipeline.

Configuring endpoint routing

Endpoint routing is the default for all ASP.NET Core projects, so you have been seeing examples of it in all the projects we have created so far in this book. For more complex scenarios than we have seen so far, endpoint routing can use a pair of calls to the UseRouting and UseEndpoints methods:

- **UseRouting** marks the pipeline position where a routing decision is made.

- **UseEndpoints** marks the pipeline position where the selected endpoint is executed.

Middleware such as the localization that runs in between these methods can see the selected endpoint and switch to a different endpoint if necessary.

Endpoint routing uses the same route template syntax that has been used in ASP.NET MVC since 2010 with .NET Framework 4 and the [Route] attribute introduced with ASP.NET MVC 5 in 2013.

Setting up the HTTP pipeline

After building the web application and its services, the next statements configure the HTTP pipeline through which HTTP requests and responses flow in and out. The pipeline is made up of a connected sequence of delegates that can perform processing and then decide to either return a response themselves or pass processing on to the next delegate in the pipeline. Responses that come back can also be manipulated.

Remember that delegates define a method signature that a delegate implementation can plug into. The delegate for the HTTP request pipeline is simple, as shown in the following code:

```
public delegate Task RequestDelegate(HttpContext context);
```

You can see that the input parameter is an HttpContext. This provides access to everything you might need to process the incoming HTTP request, including the URL path, query string parameters, cookies, and user agent.

These delegates are often called **middleware** because they sit in between the browser client and the website or web service.

Middleware delegates are configured using one of the following methods or a custom method that calls them itself:

- Run: Adds a middleware delegate that terminates the pipeline by immediately returning a response instead of calling the next middleware delegate.
- Map: Adds a middleware delegate that creates a branch in the pipeline when there is a matching request usually based on a URL path like /hello.
- Use: Adds a middleware delegate that forms part of the pipeline so it can decide if it wants to pass the request to the next delegate in the pipeline. It can modify the request and response before and after the next delegate.

For convenience, there are many extension methods that make it easier to build the pipeline, for example, UseMiddleware<T>, where T is a class that has:

- A constructor with a RequestDelegate parameter that will be passed to the next pipeline component
- An Invoke method with an HttpContext parameter and returns a Task

> You saw an example of this use of middleware in the earlier section titled *Using scoped services in middleware*.

Visualizing the HTTP pipeline

The HTTP request and response pipeline can be visualized as a sequence of request delegates, called one after the other in a chain or pipeline, as shown in the simplified diagram shown in *Figure 8.3*, which excludes some middleware delegates, such as UseHsts and MapGet:

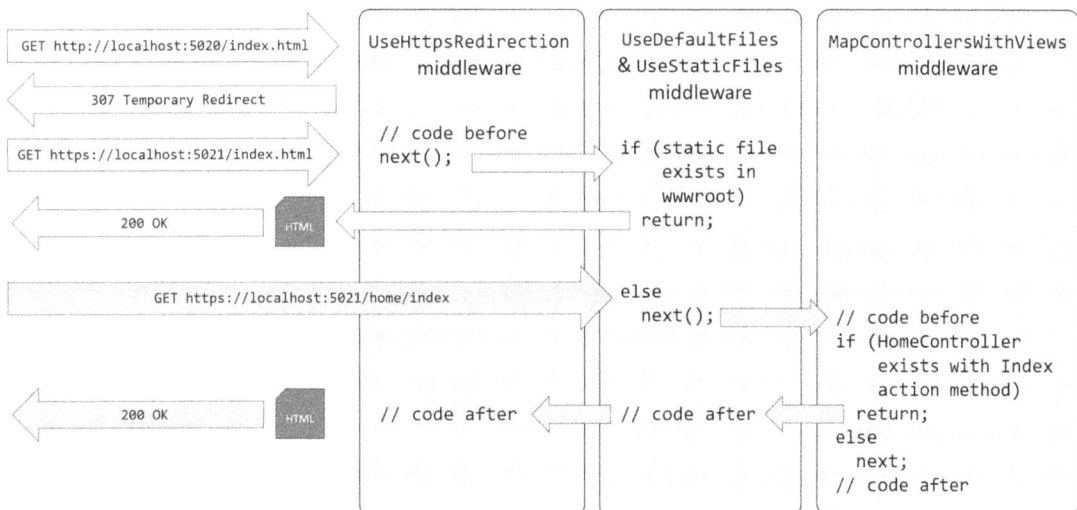

Figure 8.3: The HTTP request and response pipeline

The diagram shows two HTTP requests, as described in the following list:

- First, in yellow, an HTTP request is made for the static file index.html. The first middleware to process this request is HTTPS redirection, which detects that the request is not for HTTPS and responds with a 307 status code and the URL for the secure version of the resource. The browser then makes another request using HTTPS, which gets past the HTTPS redirection middleware and is passed on to the UseDefaultFiles and MapStaticAssets middleware (or UseStaticFiles middleware). This finds a matching static file in the wwwroot folder and returns it.

- Second, in blue, an HTTPS request is made for the relative path /home/index. The request uses HTTPS, so the HTTPS redirection middleware passes it through to the next middleware component. No matching static file path is found in the wwwroot folder, so the static files middleware passes the request through to the next middleware in the pipeline. A match is found in the Controllers folder for the HomeController class and its Index action method. The controller class is instantiated and its action method is executed, which passes a model to the Views\Home\Index.cshtml view that generates an HTML page that is returned as the HTTP response along with a 200 OK status code. Any code in the middleware that is part of the pipeline could make changes to this HTTP response as it flows back through if needed, although in this scenario, none of it does.

To better understand the flow through the HTTP pipeline, let's now add an anonymous inline delegate as middleware and then see when it executes.

Implementing an anonymous inline delegate as middleware

A delegate can be specified as an inline anonymous method. We will register one that plugs into the pipeline after routing decisions for endpoints have been made. It will output which endpoint was chosen, as well as handling one specific route: /bonjour. If that route is matched, it will respond with plain text, without calling any further into the pipeline to find a match:

1. In the Northwind.Mvc project, in the Extensions folder, in WebApplicationExtensions.cs, add a method to use an anonymous method as a middleware delegate, as shown in the following code:

```
public static WebApplication UseRouteLoggerAndBonjourEndpoint(
  this WebApplication app)
{
  // Implementing an anonymous inline delegate as middleware
  // to intercept HTTP requests and responses.
  app.Use(async (HttpContext context, Func<Task> next) =>
  {
    WriteLine($"Request: {context.Request.Method} {context.Request.
Path}");
    RouteEndpoint? rep = context.GetEndpoint() as RouteEndpoint;

    if (rep is not null)
```

```
    {
      WriteLine($"Endpoint: {rep.DisplayName}");
      WriteLine($"Route: {rep.RoutePattern.RawText}");
    }

    if (context.Request.Path == "/bonjour")
    {
      // In the case of a match on URL path, this becomes a terminating
      // delegate that returns so does not call the next delegate.
      await context.Response.WriteAsync("Bonjour Monde!");
      return;
    }

    // We could modify the request before calling the next delegate.
    // Call the next delegate in the pipeline.
    await next();

    // The HTTP response is now being sent back through the pipeline.
    // We could modify the response at this point before it continues.
  });
}
```

> **Warning!** You must add your delegate after the call to `UseRouting` or the `GetEndpoint()` method will return `null`!

2. In `Program.cs`, in the region that configures the HTTP pipeline, before the call to `MapControllerRoute`, add a statement to call the `UseRouteLoggerAndBonjour`, as shown in the following code:

```
app.UseRouteLoggerAndBonjourEndpoint();
```

3. Start the `Northwind.Mvc` website project using the `https` launch profile.

4. Arrange your terminal and the browser window so that you can see both.

5. In Chrome, navigate to `https://localhost:5021/`, look at the console output, and note that there was a match on an endpoint route `/`; it was processed as `/home/index`, due to default values in the default MVC route, and the `Index` action method in the `HomeController` class was executed to return the response, as shown in the following output:

```
Request: GET /
Endpoint: Northwind.Mvc.Controllers.HomeController.Index (Northwind.Mvc)
Route: {controller=Home}/{action=Index}/{id?}
```

6. Note that requests for static assets like `images/category1.jpeg` and `css/site.css` are also output by our custom middleware.

7. Navigate to `https://localhost:5021/suppliers` and note that you can see that there was a match on an endpoint route `/Suppliers`, and the `SuppliersController` and its `Index` method were executed to return the response, as shown in the following output:

```
Request: GET /Suppliers
Endpoint: Northwind.Mvc.Controllers.SuppliersController.Index (Northwind.
Mvc)
Route: {controller=Home}/{action=Index}/{id?}
```

8. Navigate to `https://localhost:5021/bonjour` and note that the request was logged but there is no output written about the endpoint because there was no matching endpoint route. Instead, our delegate matched on `/bonjour`, wrote the plain text `Bonjour Monde!` directly to the response stream, and returned with no further processing, so the browser rendered the plain text.

9. Close Chrome and shut down the web server.

> You can learn more about the HTTP pipeline and middleware order at the following page: `https://learn.microsoft.com/en-us/aspnet/core/fundamentals/middleware/#middleware-order`.

You've now seen how to configure the HTTP pipeline. The next topic we will look at is the best way to configure options for your web development projects.

Configuring options

Every web development project will have its own specific set of custom options. A simple project may not need any options. A complex project may need hundreds of options. What the options are is completely dependent on your specific web development project. This section is about how you can configure those options, not what the options themselves are.

Configuration in ASP.NET Core is designed to be flexible, allowing you to load settings from various sources, such as JSON files, environment variables, and command-line arguments. It can be accessed using the `IConfiguration` interface, which allows you to retrieve configuration values easily.

Configuration sources

ASP.NET Core can load configuration from multiple sources, as shown in *Table 8.2*:

Source	Description
`appsettings.json` file	The most common source for configuration, typically containing environment-specific settings.
Environment variables	Useful for settings that vary by environment, especially in containerized or cloud environments.
Command-line arguments	Allows passing configuration settings via the command line during application startup.
Secrets manager	Used primarily in development to store sensitive data.
Custom providers	You can create your own configuration providers to load settings from custom sources like databases or APIs.

Table 8.2: Configuration sources

Configuration classes and interfaces

In `Program.cs`, everything starts with a `WebApplicationBuilder`, as shown in the following code:

```
var builder = WebApplication.CreateBuilder(args);
```

I like to explicitly specify the type of the `builder` variable, as shown in the following code:

```
WebApplicationBuilder builder = WebApplication.CreateBuilder(args);
```

This class has properties to configure the setup of the environment, services, configuration, logging, and the web server and host, and a method to build everything into a web application, as shown in the following code:

```
namespace Microsoft.AspNetCore.Builder;

public sealed class WebApplicationBuilder : IHostApplicationBuilder
{
  public IWebHostEnvironment Environment { get; }
  public IServiceCollection Services { get; }
  public ConfigurationManager Configuration { get; }
  public ILoggingBuilder Logging { get; }
  public IMetricsBuilder Metrics { get; }
  public ConfigureWebHostBuilder WebHost { get; }
  public ConfigureHostBuilder Host { get; }
  public WebApplication Build();
}
```

So far in our Northwind.Mvc project, we have mostly added and configured dependency services in the Services collection. Now, we will look at the Configuration property.

How to manually set up configuration

Configuration in ASP.NET Core is set up in the Program.cs file using the ConfigurationManager class (which implements the IConfigurationBuilder interface), as shown in the following code:

```
namespace Microsoft.Extensions.Configuration;

public sealed class ConfigurationManager : IConfiguration,
  IConfigurationBuilder, IConfigurationManager,
  IConfigurationRoot, IDisposable
{
  public ConfigurationManager();
  public string? this[string key] ...
  public IList<IConfigurationSource> Sources { get; }
  public void Dispose();
  public IEnumerable<IConfigurationSection> GetChildren();
  public IConfigurationSection GetSection(string key);
}
```

Note the indexer this[string key] to quickly access configuration settings by their key, and the GetSection method to extract sections by their key from configuration files.

The IConfigurationBuilder interface is extended by many built-in and third-party packages to enable configuration with extension methods, as shown in the following code:

```
namespace Microsoft.Extensions.Configuration;

public interface IConfigurationBuilder
{
  ...
  IConfigurationRoot Build();
}

public static class FileConfigurationExtensions
{
  public static IConfigurationBuilder SetBasePath(
    this IConfigurationBuilder builder, string basePath);
  ...
}

public static class JsonConfigurationExtensions
```

```
{
  public static IConfigurationBuilder AddJsonFile(
    this IConfigurationBuilder builder, string path,
    bool optional, bool reloadOnChange);
  ...
}

public static class CommandLineConfigurationExtensions
{
  public static IConfigurationBuilder AddCommandLine(
    this IConfigurationBuilder configurationBuilder, string[] args);
  ...
}
```

An instance of `ConfigurationManager` is available as the `Configuration` property of the `WebApplicationBuilder` class.

Here's an example of manually setting up configuration to load options from a JSON file, environment variables, and command-line arguments:

```
WebApplicationBuilder builder = WebApplication.CreateBuilder(args);

// Add configuration sources.
builder.Configuration
  .SetBasePath(Directory.GetCurrentDirectory())
  .AddJsonFile("appsettings.json", optional: false, reloadOnChange: true)
  .AddJsonFile($"appsettings.{builder.Environment.EnvironmentName}.json",
    optional: true, reloadOnChange: true)
  .AddEnvironmentVariables()
  .AddCommandLine(args);

var app = builder.Build();
```

Note the following in the preceding code:

- `SetBasePath` sets the base path for the configuration files.
- `AddJsonFile` loads the configuration from `appsettings.json` and an optional environment-specific JSON file. For example, during development, it would load `appsettings.Development.json`.
- `AddEnvironmentVariables` loads configuration from environment variables.
- `AddCommandLine` allows configuration via command-line arguments.

The preceding setup is not needed if you use the default `WebApplication.CreateBuilder`. You can learn more about what this does for you by default at the following page: `https://learn.microsoft.com/en-us/aspnet/core/fundamentals/configuration/#default-application-configuration-sources`.

Understanding IConfiguration and IConfigurationRoot

Both `IConfiguration` and `IConfigurationRoot` are interfaces that are used to manage configuration settings, but they serve slightly different purposes and are used in different contexts. Understanding the distinction between them can help you better structure and manage configuration in your applications.

IConfiguration for combined settings from all providers

`IConfiguration` represents a key-value pair collection of all configuration settings across many providers. It is commonly used throughout an application and it allows hierarchical configuration, meaning you can have nested configurations that are accessible via key paths.

For example, `IConfiguration` is injected into a controller, and it is used to retrieve a value from the configuration and pass it as the model of a view, as shown in the following code:

```
public class MyController
{
  private readonly IConfiguration _configuration;

  public MyController(IConfiguration configuration)
  {
    _configuration = configuration;
  }

  public void Index()
  {
    string model = $"Setting1: {_configuration["MySettings:Setting1"]}";
    View(model);
  }
}
```

The setting itself could be set in any of the configured source providers, from a JSON file to command-line arguments.

IConfigurationRoot for more advanced scenarios

IConfigurationRoot extends the IConfiguration interface with additional capabilities. Specifically, it represents the root of the configuration hierarchy and includes methods to reload and access underlying providers. It is typically used internally by the framework or in advanced scenarios where you need to manage configuration providers directly.

While IConfiguration is what most developers interact with, IConfigurationRoot is used when you need to programmatically manage the configuration's lifecycle, such as reloading configuration or accessing specific configuration providers, as shown in the following code:

```
ConfigurationBuilder builder = new()
  .SetBasePath(Directory.GetCurrentDirectory())
  .AddJsonFile("appsettings.json", optional: false, reloadOnChange: true)
  .AddEnvironmentVariables();

IConfigurationRoot configurationRoot = builder.Build();

// Reload the configuration.
configurationRoot.Reload();

// Accessing the reloaded configuration data.
string settingValue = configurationRoot["MySettings:Setting1"];
Console.WriteLine($"Setting1: {settingValue}");
```

To summarize:

- IConfiguration is a more general interface that can be used throughout the application to access configuration data. IConfiguration is typically injected into services and used to access configuration settings. In practice, IConfiguration is what you'll interact with most of the time.
- IConfigurationRoot is the specific implementation that serves as the root of the configuration system, managing the lifecycle and underlying providers. IConfigurationRoot is usually handled during the configuration setup phase in the Program.cs, where you might need to interact with the configuration in more advanced ways, such as reloading the configuration dynamically. IConfigurationRoot provides the Reload() method, which allows you to reload the configuration from the sources. This is particularly useful when using configuration sources that may change at runtime, like JSON files with reloadOnChange set to true.

As illustrated in a coding task in the next section, when an IConfigurationRoot service is not configured, it is often possible to cast from IConfiguration.

Showing providers and settings

Now, let's see some example code that will show the provider sources for configuration and any settings that have been configured:

1. In the `Northwind.Mvc` project, in the `Models` folder, add a new class file named `ConfigIndexViewModel.cs`.

2. In `ConfigIndexViewModel.cs`, define a record with a `Providers` property to store the sources of configuration, and a `Settings` property as a string dictionary, as shown in the following code:

```
namespace Northwind.Mvc.Models;

public record ConfigIndexViewModel(
  IEnumerable<string?> Providers,
  IDictionary<string, string?> Settings);
```

3. In the `Controllers` folder, add an empty controller class named `ConfigController.cs`.

4. In `ConfigController.cs`, define a class with an `Index` action method to show the sources of configuration, as shown in the following code:

```
using Microsoft.AspNetCore.Mvc;
using Northwind.Mvc.Models; // To use ConfigIndexViewModel.

namespace Northwind.Mvc.Controllers;

public class ConfigController : Controller
{
  private readonly IConfigurationRoot _configRoot;

  public ConfigController(IConfiguration config)
  {
    // No service is registered for IConfigurationRoot but
    // one is registered for IConfiguration and it also
    // implements IConfigurationRoot.
    _configRoot = (IConfigurationRoot)config;
  }

  public IActionResult Index()
  {
    ConfigIndexViewModel model = new(
      Providers: _configRoot.Providers
        .Select(provider => provider.ToString()),
      Settings: _configRoot.AsEnumerable().ToDictionary());
```

```
      return View(model);
    }
  }
```

5. If you are using Visual Studio, then right-click in View(model), select **Add View...**, select **Razor View – Empty**, and click **Add**. Visual Studio will create a view named Index.cshtml in a new folder named Config in the Views folder. If you are using VS Code, then you'll have to do this manually.

6. In the Views\Config folder, in Index.cshtml, add statements to output the providers in a table, as shown in the following markup:

```
@model ConfigIndexViewModel
@{
  ViewData["Title"] = "Configuration";
}
<div class="text-center">
  <h1 class="display-4">@ViewData["Title"]</h1>
  <h2>Providers</h2>
  <table class="table table-bordered table-striped">
    <thead>
      <tr>
        <th>Provider</th>
      </tr>
    </thead>
    <tbody>
      @foreach (string? provider in Model.Providers)
      {
        <tr>
          <td>@provider</td>
        </tr>
      }
    </tbody>
  </table>
  <h2>Settings</h2>
  <dl>
    @foreach (KeyValuePair<string, string?> setting in Model.Settings)
    {
      <dt>@setting.Key</dt>
      <dd>@setting.Value</dd>
    }
  </dl>
</div>
```

7. In the `Views\Shared` folder, in `_Layout.cshtml`, add a menu item for the configuration page, as shown in the following markup:

```
<li class="nav-item">
  <a class="nav-link text-dark" asp-area="" asp-controller="Config"
 asp-action="Index">Config</a>
</li>
```

Trying out the configuration web page

Now we can start the website to see the results:

1. Start the `Northwind.Mvc` website project using the `https` launch profile.
2. Navigate to the **Config** page and note the table of providers showing sources of configuration, including environment variables and JSON files, as shown in *Figure 8.4*:

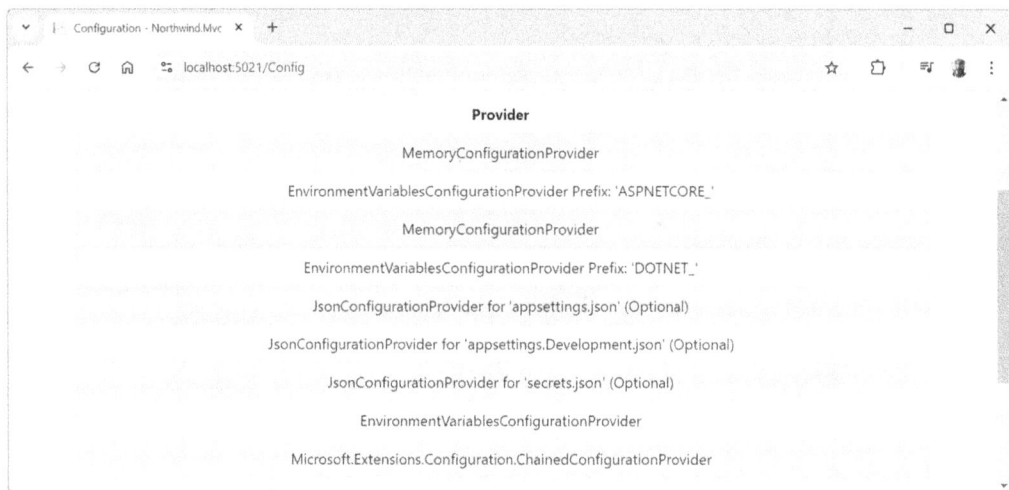

Figure 8.4: Providers table showing sources of configuration

3. Note the table of settings, including logging levels that come from `appsettings.Development.json`, as shown in *Figure 8.5*, and that match the contents of the file:

```
{
  "Logging": {
    "LogLevel": {
      "Default": "Information",
      "Microsoft.AspNetCore": "Warning",
      "Microsoft.AspNetCore.OutputCaching": "Information"
    }
  }
}
```

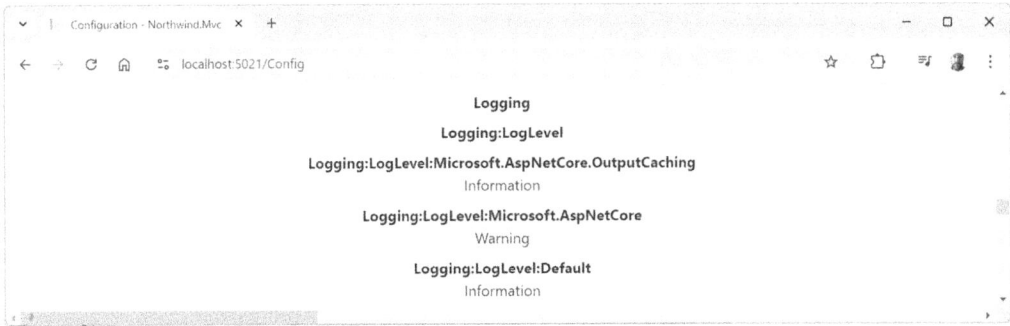

Figure 8.5: Settings from appsettings.Development.json

Most of these settings come from environment variables, including ones you set yourself, like MY_SQL_USR and MY_SQL_PWD. Use your browser find feature (*Ctrl +* *F*) to find text like ConnectionStrings, LogLevel, or MY_SQL_PWD in the web page.

4. Also note in the table of settings database connection strings that come from appsettings. json, as shown in *Figure 8.6*, and that match the contents of the file:

```
{
  "ConnectionStrings": {
    "DefaultConnection": "DataSource=app.db;Cache=Shared",
    "NorthwindConnection": "Server=tcp:127.0.0.1,1433;Database=Northwind;
                            MultipleActiveResultSets=true;
                            TrustServerCertificate=true;"
  },
  "Logging": {
    "LogLevel": {
      "Default": "Information",
      "Microsoft.AspNetCore": "Warning"
    }
  },
  "AllowedHosts": "*"
}
```

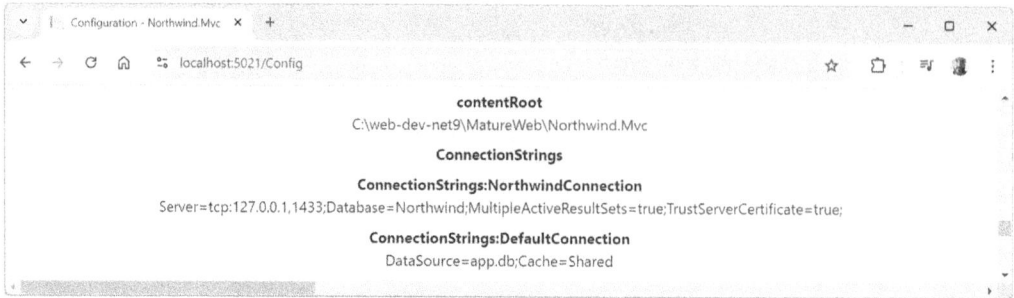

Figure 8.6: Database connection strings from appsettings.json

5. Close Chrome and shut down the web server.

Showing specific settings

Now let's highlight specific settings that we might want to note easily:

1. In the Models folder, in ConfigIndexViewModel.cs, add two properties to store the Identity database connection string and the output caching logging level, as shown highlighted in the following code:

```
namespace Northwind.Mvc.Models;

public record ConfigIndexViewModel(
  IEnumerable<string?> Providers,
  IDictionary<string, string?> Settings,
  string OutputCachingLoggingLevel,
  string IdentityConnectionString
);
```

2. In the Controllers folder, in ConfigController.cs, set the two properties in the model, as highlighted in the following code:

```
ConfigIndexViewModel model = new(
  Providers: _configRoot.Providers
    .Select(provider => provider.ToString()),
  Settings: _configRoot.AsEnumerable().ToDictionary(),
  OutputCachingLoggingLevel: _configRoot[
    "Logging:LogLevel:Microsoft.AspNetCore.OutputCaching"]
    ?? "Not found.",
  IdentityConnectionString: _configRoot[
    "ConnectionStrings:DefaultConnection"]
    ?? "Not found."
);
```

3. In the Views\Config folder, in Index.cshtml, immediately after the **Settings** heading and before the definitions list `<dl>`, output the two properties, as shown in the following markup:

```
<div class="alert alert-primary" role="alert">
  <dl>
    <dt>Output caching logging level</dt>
    <dd>@Model.OutputCachingLoggingLevel</dd>
    <dt>Identity connection string</dt>
    <dd>@Model.IdentityConnectionString</dd>
  </dl>
</div>
```

4. Start the Northwind.Mvc website project using the https launch profile.

5. Navigate to the **Config** page and note the two highlighted settings, as shown in *Figure 8.7*:

Figure 8.7: Providers table showing two highlighted settings

Configuration overriding in production deployments

Configuration overriding is particularly useful in cloud environments, where you need different configurations for development, testing, and production environments.

Remember that configuration is hierarchical and supports multiple sources, like appsettings.json and appsettings.{Environment}.json (for example, appsettings.Production.json), environment variables, command-line arguments, and Azure Key Vault or other external configuration providers (for cloud environments).

When the website project starts, it reads configuration settings from all available sources in the order they are added. By default, ASP.NET Core loads the configuration in a specific order, allowing later sources to override earlier ones.

Environment variables are often the preferred method for overriding configurations in cloud deployments because they are easy to change without altering the application itself, which is especially useful for containerized and serverless systems. By default, ASP.NET Core includes environment variables as a configuration source, so an explicit AddEnvironmentVariables() call is optional unless you're customizing the configuration setup.

ASP.NET Core maps environment variables to configuration settings using a specific naming convention. The default settings in JSON files use a hierarchical structure (sections and subsections). Environment variables use a colon (:) or double underscore (__) to represent the hierarchy.

For example, given the following `appsettings.json` file:

```
{
  "Logging": {
    "LogLevel": {
      "Default": "Information",
      "Microsoft": "Warning"
    }
  }
}
```

You can override this configuration to set the default logging level from `Information` to `Debug` by using the following environment variable:

```
Logging:LogLevel:Default=Debug
```

Now let's see how configuration overriding works specifically with Docker and Kubernetes.

Configuration overriding in Docker

In a Docker container, you would typically set the environment variable in the Docker container or the container orchestration system, like Kubernetes, as shown in the following Dockerfile:

```
FROM mcr.microsoft.com/dotnet/aspnet:10.0 AS base
WORKDIR /app
# Set environment variable to override configuration.
ENV Logging__LogLevel__Default=Debug
COPY . .
ENTRYPOINT ["dotnet", "YourApp.dll"]
```

Environment variables are especially useful in cloud scenarios for the following reasons:

- **Configuration per environment**: Cloud environments often differ in configuration needs. For example, you might have different logging levels, database connection strings, or API keys for development, staging, and production environments. Using environment variables makes it easy to adjust these settings without modifying the code or even the configuration files.

- **Security**: Sensitive information like database passwords, API keys, or connection strings can be stored securely in environment variables. This keeps them out of version control instead of committing them in `appsettings.json`, and they can be managed by cloud platforms securely by using features like Azure Key Vault and AWS Secrets Manager.

- **Containerized applications:** Containers like Docker are designed to be immutable. Changing configuration should not involve rebuilding the image. Instead, you can inject configuration through environment variables at runtime, via either the Docker CLI or orchestrators like Kubernetes, which support setting environment variables for Pods and containers.

- **Serverless platforms:** In serverless platforms such as Azure Functions or AWS Lambda, you don't control the underlying infrastructure, so environment variables offer a straightforward way to modify the configuration between deployments without modifying the code.

Configuration overriding in Kubernetes

In Kubernetes, you can set environment variables at the Pod level in your `deployment.yaml` file:

```
apiVersion: apps/v1
kind: Deployment
metadata:
  name: myapp-deployment
spec:
  replicas: 1
  template:
    spec:
      containers:
      - name: myapp
        image: myapp:latest
        env:
        - name: Logging__LogLevel__Default
          value: Debug
        - name: ConnectionStrings__MyDatabase
          value: "Server=prod-db-server;Database=mydb;User
Id=myuser;Password=mypassword;"
```

In the preceding example, the `Logging:LogLevel:Default` and `ConnectionStrings:MyDatabase` values will be overridden by the environment variables, allowing Kubernetes to inject cloud-specific configuration.

Using environment variables to override configuration in cloud deployments is one of the most flexible and secure approaches to managing settings. It keeps sensitive data out of source control, makes it easy to apply configuration changes without rebuilding or redeploying your application, and works seamlessly across containers, serverless environments, and more traditional cloud-based VMs.

By using environment variables, you create a more portable and maintainable application that's easier to configure per environment and scale in cloud platforms.

Loading configuration using the Options pattern

ASP.NET Core promotes the use of the **Options pattern** to manage settings. This involves binding sections of your configuration to strongly typed classes, which are then injected into services or controllers. This pattern provides type safety and IntelliSense, making it easier to manage and use configuration settings.

Let's implement this pattern in our MVC project:

1. In the `Northwind.Mvc` project, in `appsettings.json`, add a new section for a couple of settings related to the website, as highlighted in the following markup:

    ```json
    {
      ...,
      "Northwind": {
        "SiteTitle": "Northwind B2B",
        "PagerSize": 20
      }
    }
    ```

2. In the `Northwind.Mvc` project, add a new folder named `Options`.

3. In the `Options` folder, add a new class file to represent these settings named `NorthwindOptions.cs`, as shown in the following code:

    ```csharp
    namespace Northwind.Mvc.Options;

    public class NorthwindOptions
    {
      public string SiteTitle { get; set; } = "Missing title.";
      public int PagerSize { get; set; } = 10;
    }
    ```

4. In `Program.cs`, import the namespace to use the `NorthwindOptions` class, as shown in the following code:

    ```csharp
    using Northwind.Mvc.Options; // To use NorthwindOptions.
    ```

5. In `Program.cs`, after the call to `CreateBuilder`, in the section to add services to the container, bind the `Northwind` section of the configuration to the `NorthwindOptions` class, as shown in the following code:

    ```csharp
    builder.Services.Configure<NorthwindOptions>(builder
      .Configuration.GetSection("Northwind"));
    ```

6. In the `Models` folder, in `ConfigIndexViewModel.cs`, add another property to store the options, as highlighted in the following code:

```
using Northwind.Mvc.Options; // To use NorthwindOptions.

namespace Northwind.Mvc.Models;

public record ConfigIndexViewModel(
  IEnumerable<string?> Providers,
  IDictionary<string, string?> Settings,
  string OutputCachingLoggingLevel,
  string IdentityConnectionString,
  NorthwindOptions Options
);
```

7. In the `Controllers` folder, in `ConfigController.cs`, import the namespaces to use the `IOptions<T>` interface and `NorthwindOptions` class, as shown in the following code:

```
using Microsoft.Extensions.Options; // To use IOptions<T>.
using Northwind.Mvc.Options; // To use NorthwindOptions.
```

8. In `ConfigController.cs`, to access the configured options in a service, you inject `IOptions<NorthwindOptions>` into the constructor, as highlighted in the following code:

```
public class ConfigController : Controller
{
  private readonly IConfigurationRoot _configRoot;
  private readonly NorthwindOptions _options;

  public ConfigController(IConfiguration config,
    IOptions<NorthwindOptions> options)
  {
    // No service is registered for IConfigurationRoot but
    // one is registered for IConfiguration and it also
    // implements IConfigurationRoot.
    _configRoot = (IConfigurationRoot)config;
    _options = options.Value;
  }

  public IActionResult Index()
  {
    ConfigIndexViewModel model = new(
      Providers: _configRoot.Providers
        .Select(provider => provider.ToString()),
```

```
        Settings: _configRoot.AsEnumerable().ToDictionary(),
        OutputCachingLoggingLevel: _configRoot[
            "Logging:LogLevel:Microsoft.AspNetCore.OutputCaching"]
            ?? "Not found.",
        IdentityConnectionString: _configRoot[
            "ConnectionStrings:DefaultConnection"]
            ?? "Not found.",
        Options: _options
    );

    return View(model);
  }
}
```

9. In `Views\Config`, in `Index.cshtml`, after the `<h1>` element, show the options in the view, as shown in the following code:

```html
<h2>Northwind Options</h2>
<div class="alert alert-danger" role="alert">
  <dl>
    <dt>Site title</dt>
    <dd>@Model.Options.SiteTitle</dd>
    <dt>Pager size</dt>
    <dd>@Model.Options.PagerSize</dd>
  </dl>
</div>
```

10. Start the `Northwind.Mvc` website project using the `https` launch profile.

11. Click **Config**, and note the options displayed, as shown in *Figure 8.8*:

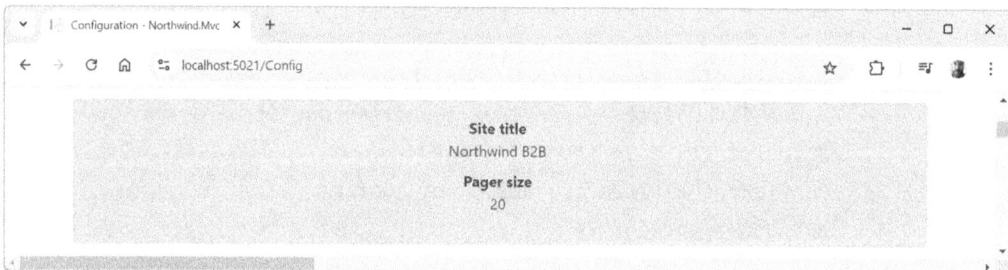

Figure 8.8: Options pattern values

Using IOptionsSnapshot and IOptionsMonitor

There are related classes that you can use:

- IOptionsSnapshot<T>: This is useful if you want the options to be reloaded when the configuration changes. This is typically used in scoped services.

- IOptionsMonitor<T>: Provides notifications when options change. It can be used to watch for changes in configuration at runtime and react accordingly.

Here's an example of using IOptionsMonitor:

```
public class HomeController : Controller
{
  private readonly ILogger<HomeController> _logger;
  private readonly NorthwindOptions _settings;

  public HomeController(ILogger<HomeController> logger,
    IOptionsMonitor<NorthwindOptions> optionsMonitor)
  {
    _logger = logger;
    _settings = optionsMonitor.CurrentValue;

    optionsMonitor.OnChange(changedSettings =>
    {
      _settings = changedSettings;
      _logger.LogInformation("Northwind settings have changed.");
    });
  }
}
```

Configuration validation

ASP.NET Core allows you to validate configuration options. This can be done by implementing the IValidateOptions<T> interface or using the Validate extension method, as shown in the following code:

```
builder.Services
  .AddOptions<NorthwindOptions>("Northwind")
  .Validate(settings => settings.PagerSize > 0,
    "PagerSize must be greater than zero.");
```

With the preceding validation rule, if PagerSize is less than or equal to 0, the application will throw an OptionsValidationException during startup.

Using custom configuration providers

If your application needs to load configuration from a custom source, you can create a custom configuration provider by inheriting from ConfigurationProvider and implementing an IConfigurationSource, as shown in the following code:

```
public class MyCustomConfigurationSource : IConfigurationSource
{
  public IConfigurationProvider Build(IConfigurationBuilder builder)
  {
    return new MyCustomConfigurationProvider();
  }
}

public class MyCustomConfigurationProvider : ConfigurationProvider
{
  public override void Load()
  {
    // Load custom settings into the Data dictionary.
    Data = new Dictionary<string, string?>
    {
      { "CustomSetting", "CustomValue" }
    };
  }
}
```

Then, add this custom provider to the configuration pipeline:

```
((IConfigurationBuilder)builder.Configuration).Add(new
MyCustomConfigurationSource());
```

ASP.NET Core provides a flexible configuration system that can load settings from a wide range of sources. The Options pattern is the recommended approach for managing configuration in a type-safe way, and advanced techniques like validation and custom providers extend its capabilities.

By structuring your application's configuration effectively, you can ensure that it is maintainable, scalable, and easy to manage as your project grows.

Now, let's see how you can prepare your web projects for deployment by containerizing them.

Containerizing ASP.NET Core projects

Containerization is a technology that is about making software development, deployment, and execution more efficient, consistent, and scalable.

How containers work and their benefits

Containers run on a single machine's OS kernel and share that kernel with other containers. They're lightweight because they don't need the extra load of a hypervisor that manages VMs. Containers run directly within the host machine's kernel. This makes them more efficient, faster, and less resource-intensive than traditional VMs that require a full-blown OS for each VM. This makes containers especially useful for hosting microservices.

The primary benefits of containerization are shown in the following list:

- **Portability**: Once a container is created, it can be run anywhere, making it easy to move applications across different operating system environments, like variations of Linux or Windows Server, with confidence. This allows you to switch container hosting providers with no issues so you are not tied to an expensive host if Microsoft, Amazon, or whoever you are paying increases their prices for container hosting services, like any of the following:

  - **Azure App Service**: `https://azure.microsoft.com/en-us/products/app-service`
  - **Azure Kubernetes Service** (AKS): `https://azure.microsoft.com/en-us/products/kubernetes-service`
  - **Elastic Kubernetes Service** (EKS): `https://aws.amazon.com/eks/`

- **Consistency**: Containers provide a consistent environment for applications from development through to production, reducing bugs and inconsistencies.
- **Isolation**: Each container is isolated, so it doesn't interfere with others or the host system.
- **Efficiency**: Containers use system resources more efficiently than VMs, allowing you to get more out of your hardware.
- **Scalability**: Containers can be easily scaled up or down, making it simple to adjust resources to meet demand.
- **Speedy deployments**: Containers can be created and destroyed in seconds, making it easier to dynamically adjust to workload demands.

No technology solution is perfect, so let's review some of the potential downsides to containerization:

- **Security concerns**: Since containers share the host OS kernel, a vulnerability in the kernel could potentially compromise all containers running on that host. Containers provide process isolation, but it is not as robust as the hardware-level isolation provided by VMs. This can increase the risk of container escape attacks, where a malicious container could access the host system. But overall, your container host provider should manage this better than you could on your own.
- **Management complexity**: In production, managing a large number of containers requires orchestration tools like Kubernetes, which add complexity and require significant expertise to configure and maintain. During development, managing containers can be significantly improved using Aspire. Container networking can become complex, especially when dealing with multi-host networking, service discovery, and network policies.

- **Persistent storage management:** Containers are designed to be ephemeral, which can make managing persistent storage challenging. Solutions like volume mounts and network-attached storage are available from any good container host provider but must be carefully implemented to ensure data persistence and consistency.
- **Compatibility issues:** Not all applications are easily containerized, particularly legacy applications that may depend on specific hardware or OS features.
- **Debugging challenges:** The layered nature of container images and the complexity of container orchestration can make debugging more challenging compared to traditional applications.

While containerization offers significant advantages in terms of efficiency, scalability, and consistency, you should consider the potential downsides.

Now, let's introduce you to some technologies that enable containerization.

Docker and Aspire

Docker is a platform that popularized containerization and made it accessible to developers by providing an open standard for packaging and distributing containerized applications. Building, shipping, and running applications are streamlined with Docker, making development workflows more predictable and scalable. It packages applications and their dependencies into a container, which can then be run on any Linux server or Windows that supports Docker. These containers are lightweight, ensuring that you can pack a lot of applications into a single host.

Beyond Docker, there's a whole ecosystem to support containerization, including orchestration tools like **Kubernetes**, which automates the deployment, scaling, and management of containerized applications in production. **Aspire** performs a similar role on a developer's computer during local development.

Docker and Kubernetes serve different but complementary roles in the world of containerization. If we consider containerization as organizing and shipping goods, Docker would be the packaging system that wraps up the goods (applications and their dependencies) into neat, transportable containers, while Kubernetes would be the shipping hub that manages where and how these containers are shipped, stored, and scaled.

Docker provides the tools for managing the lifecycle of containers: building images, running containers, moving them around, managing versions, and so on. It simplifies the process of creating containers, making it accessible even to those new to the technology.

Docker containers can be integrated into CI/CD pipelines to automate the deployment process, making it faster and reducing the chances of errors.

Aspire is a part of the broader .NET ecosystem, focusing on modernizing .NET with the latest technologies and practices. This includes embracing cloud-native practices, microservices architectures, and, notably, containerization technologies like Docker. Containerizing .NET applications with Docker enables developers to take full advantage of the portability, efficiency, and isolation that containers offer.

Installing Docker and using prebuilt images

If you've been using SQL Server locally or in the cloud to host the Northwind database, let's now install Docker and explore how to use it to manage containers:

1. Install **Docker Desktop** from the following page: `https://www.docker.com/products/docker-desktop/`.

2. Start Docker Desktop and note the user interface, including the **Containers** view, which will probably be empty if you have not run any containers yet, as shown in *Figure 8.9*:

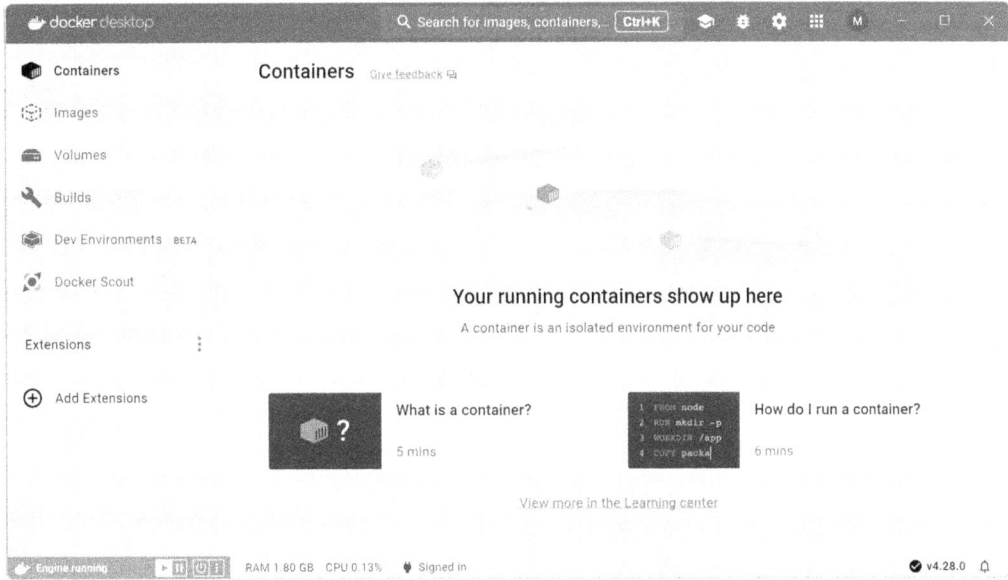

Figure 8.9: The Containers view in Docker Desktop

3. In the left navigation bar, click **Images**, as shown in *Figure 8.10*. Note that on my machine, I already have a Docker image for SQL Server 2025 downloaded:

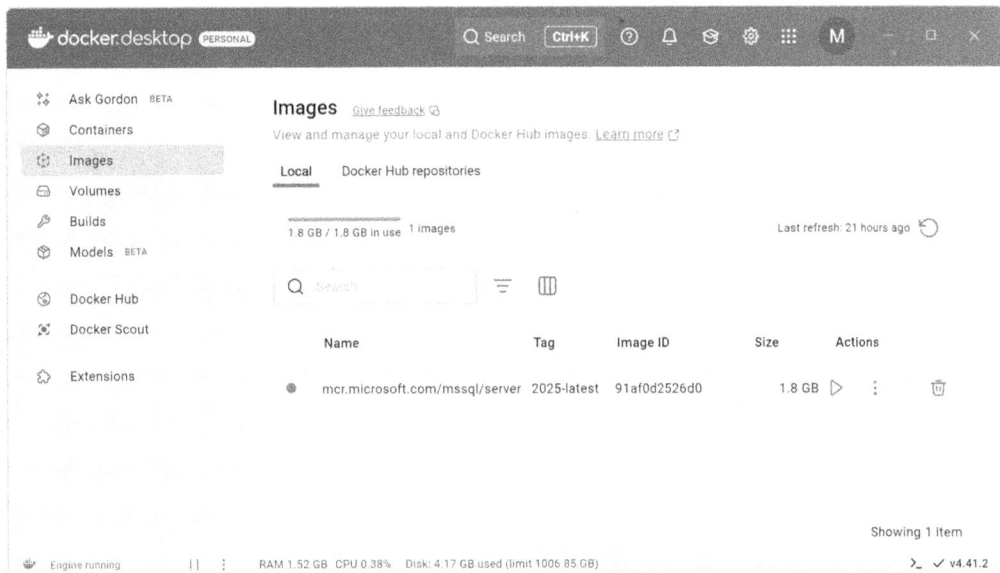

Figure 8.10: The Images view in Docker Desktop

In the table of images, note the **Tag** column, which is often used for version information. If you don't have any Docker images, then none will be listed, of course! For now, just look at my list and imagine the possibilities.

4. In a command prompt or terminal, list the Docker images using the following command:

```
docker images
```

5. Note the results on my computer, as shown in the following output, which matches *Figure 8.10*:

```
REPOSITORY                        TAG           IMAGE ID      CREATED
SIZE
mcr.microsoft.com/mssql/server    2025-latest   91af0d2526d0  7 days ago
1.81GB
```

6. In a terminal, download the Docker image for the sample ASP.NET Core project image and run it with external port 8000 mapped to internal port 8080, interactive TTY mode (-it), and remove it when the container stops (--rm), as shown in the following command:

```
docker run --rm -it -p 8000:8080 mcr.microsoft.com/dotnet/
samples:aspnetapp
```

7. Note the results, including downloading the image, starting the container, and outputting the console output from inside the container that is hosting the ASP.NET Core sample project, as shown in the following output:

```
Unable to find image 'mcr.microsoft.com/dotnet/samples:aspnetapp' locally
aspnetapp: Pulling from dotnet/samples
4abcf2066143: Pull complete
4e1692478f05: Pull complete
73df137ef55b: Pull complete
0ab1344a44f8: Pull complete
c9a33571af57: Pull complete
458c6e372327: Pull complete
d57ff6e481d4: Pull complete
Digest:
sha256:0bca5ff4b566b29c7d323efc0142ee506681efb31a7839cec91a9acbf760dfa8
Status: Downloaded newer image for mcr.microsoft.com/dotnet/
samples:aspnetapp
warn: Microsoft.AspNetCore.DataProtection.Repositories.
FileSystemXmlRepository[60]
      Storing keys in a directory '/root/.aspnet/DataProtection-Keys'
that may not be persisted outside of the container. Protected data will
be unavailable when container is destroyed. For more information go to
https://aka.ms/aspnet/dataprotectionwarning
```

```
warn: Microsoft.AspNetCore.DataProtection.KeyManagement.XmlKeyManager[35]
      No XML encryptor configured. Key {419c59e8-3d0b-43fa-bf2c-
4574734788c4} may be persisted to storage in unencrypted form.
info: Microsoft.Hosting.Lifetime[14]
      Now listening on: http://[::]:8080
info: Microsoft.Hosting.Lifetime[0]
      Application started. Press Ctrl+C to shut down.
info: Microsoft.Hosting.Lifetime[0]
      Hosting environment: Production
info: Microsoft.Hosting.Lifetime[0]
      Content root path: /appL
```

8. Leave your command prompt or terminal window running.

9. Start your preferred web browser, navigate to `http://localhost:8000/`, and you can see that the home page shows information about the ASP.NET Core app in the container, as shown in *Figure 8.11*:

Figure 8.11: An ASP.NET Core website hosted in a Docker container

The preceding screenshot was taken in June 2025, when the current sample app used .NET 9. By the time this book is published at the end of 2025, the sample app will use .NET 10.

10. In Docker Desktop, you can see that the container is running with a random name like **wizardly_yonath**, as shown in *Figure 8.12*:

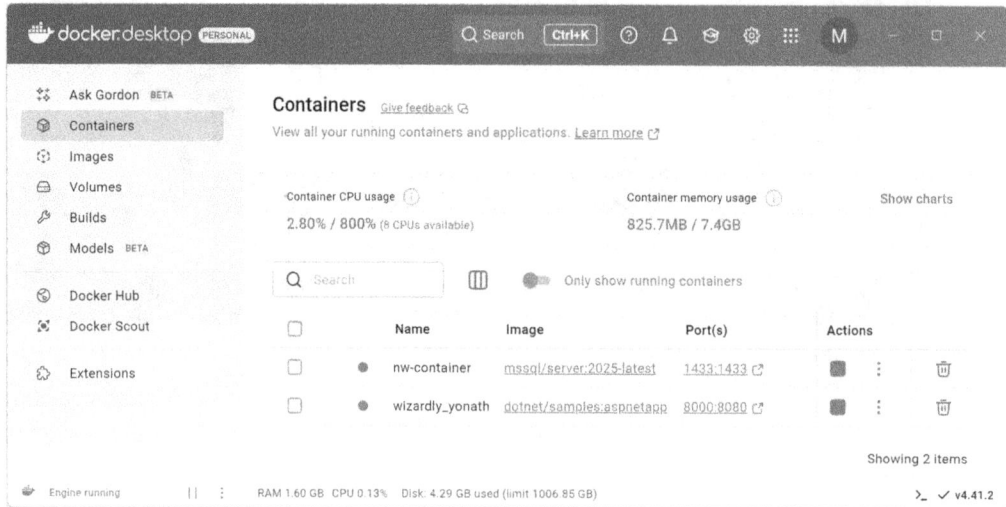

Figure 8.12: Randomly named running container

11. Close the browser and, at the command prompt or terminal, shut down the web server by pressing *Ctrl + C*.

12. In Docker Desktop, note that the container automatically removes itself due to the `--rm` switch but the image remains on the local disk; however, it shows in gray instead of black text because it is not being used.

Although Visual Studio does have support for working with Docker containers directly, the modern way of doing so is via Aspire.

Aspire for orchestrating projects

Let's review what Aspire does for ASP.NET Core developers. Aspire is a feature introduced with .NET 8 that improves the local development experience when building distributed cloud-native solutions.

From the announcement blog post (`https://devblogs.microsoft.com/dotnet/introducing-dotnet-aspire-simplifying-cloud-native-development-with-dotnet-8/`), "*.NET Aspire is an opinionated stack for building resilient, observable, and configurable cloud-native applications with .NET.*"

It is worth noting each carefully chosen phrase in that description:

- **Opinionated stack:** One of the trickier aspects of building modern distributed solutions is that there is too much choice. For each feature of your solution, there are multiple integrations that you could pick from. For each of those integrations, there are multiple ways to configure them based on your needs. Aspire has an opinion about which integrations you should use and how you should configure them, which is explained in the *Aspire integrations* section later in the chapter. If you concur with those opinions, then Aspire is especially great, and if not, you can always override the default configuration.

- **Resilient:** Aspire is designed to be resilient by implementing best practices for cloud solutions, like implementing caching or queuing, or fault tolerance using Polly.

> Using Polly to add fault tolerance to your apps and services is covered in my book *Apps and Services with .NET 10*, and you can read Polly's documentation using the following link: `https://www.pollydocs.org/`. But if you use Aspire, Polly is one of Aspire's integrations that Aspire includes by default and configures for you.

- **Observable:** Aspire enables tracing, logging, and metrics using the most popular telemetry framework for .NET and other platforms, OpenTelemetry. Aspire also includes a dashboard to monitor all activity across the many complex tiers of your solution.
- **Configurable:** Aspire has sensible defaults for configuring all its integrations but is open to be configured however you want. Of course, you can override the defaults, but if your needs are genuinely different, then you won't get as much out of Aspire as other developers who are happy to go along with the recommended integrations with the most popular configuration that works best for most distributed solutions.
- **Cloud-native:** Aspire projects assume they will eventually be deployed to the cloud in containers. For local testing, Aspire projects have a dependency on Docker Desktop or Podman. You learned about Docker earlier in this chapter. You can learn about Podman using the following link: `https://podman.io/`.

Aspire includes service discovery, telemetry, resilience, and health checks by default. Aspire simplifies the local developer experience and makes it easy to discover, acquire, and configure essential dependencies.

Aspire previews were first made available with the launch of .NET 8 in November 2023. Aspire 13 shipped alongside .NET 10 in November 2025. Aspire is versioned 13 to emphasize that it is no longer part of .NET. Aspire 13 is polyglot and fully-supports orchestrating projects written in languages like JavaScript and Python.

Aspire projects work best in their own solutions, because they require multiple projects, so when we come to create a practical example later in this chapter, we will create a new solution as well as multiple projects within it.

Aspire project types

To work, Aspire solutions need two special projects as well as any ASP.NET Core and other .NET projects:

- **AppHost:** This is a console app that starts all the other projects and ensures the correct configuration of all resources and endpoints.
- **ServiceDefaults:** This is a class library that centralizes the configuration of all the Aspire resources, including components like databases and .NET projects.

The AppHost project will run any projects, containers, or executables needed as part of your cloud-native distributed application. If you are using Visual Studio, then debugging will attach to all the running projects, allowing you to step into and across each service.

The `ServiceDefaults` project contains common service and component logic that applies to each of the projects in the app. This is where components like service discovery, telemetry, and health checks are configured. It is a centralized convention where you would go to customize configurations to be developer-friendly.

All Aspire solutions will have these two special projects, as well as any other projects that make up your complete distributed solution, as shown in *Figure 8.13*:

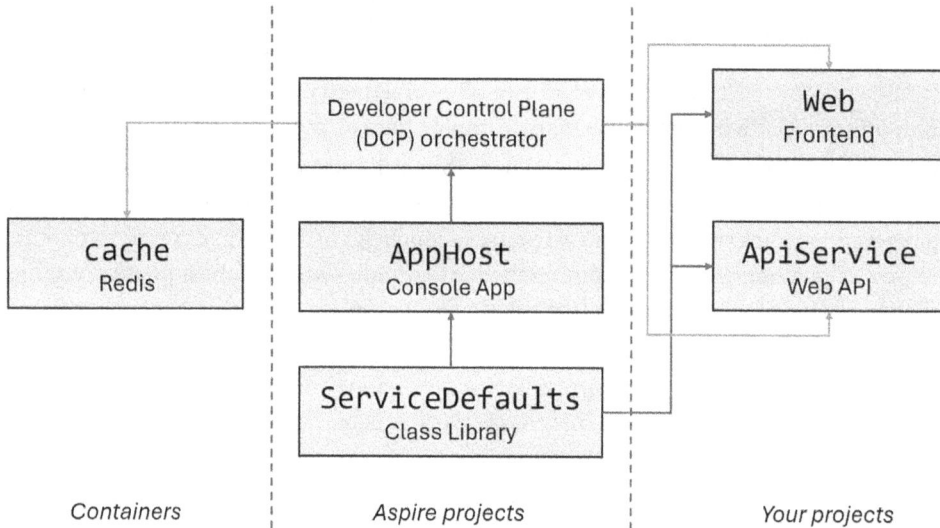

Figure 8.13: DCP, Aspire projects, your projects, and containers in an Aspire application model

> The **Developer Control Plane (DCP)** is a closed-source orchestrator used by Aspire. The team doesn't like to talk about it much because it is closed source and therefore not open to developers to customize. Everything else about Aspire is designed to be open and extendable.

The `AppHost` project reads configuration from the `ServiceDefaults` project and uses the DCP to orchestrate the startup of any containers and your projects. Your projects should read the configuration from the `ServiceDefaults` project too.

Aspire resource types

In Aspire, the built-in types of resources are:

- **Project:** A project, for example, an ASP.NET Core web service or a Python or JavaScript website
- **Container:** A container image, for example, a Docker image of Redis or RabbitMQ
- **Executable:** An executable file

For container resources, you can have Aspire either launch a container during development or connect to an existing resource via connection strings.

Developer dashboard for monitoring

Starting an Aspire project brings you to the developer dashboard. This is an essential tool for debugging distributed applications because it gives you a unified view of your services alongside their logs, metrics, and traces, as shown in *Figure 8.16*.

You can use it to see logs and traces across all projects, for example, a distributed trace showing a request to the weather page. Traces are very helpful for diagnosing problems in distributed applications.

The developer dashboard uses all the same open standards you would use in production when you configure production telemetry systems like Grafana and Prometheus.

The Aspire developer dashboard is visible while the AppHost project is running and will launch automatically when you start the project. The left navigation provides links to the different parts of the dashboard, as described in the following list:

- **Resources**: This is the home page of the dashboard, and it lists all the projects, containers, executables, and other resources in your Aspire solution. It shows the state of each resource and gives you links directly to parts of the solution, like web services and web user interfaces. It also highlights errors when they are logged so that you can easily jump to more details to zero in on problems.
- **Console**: This provides access to the logs of all the parts of your Aspire solution that write to the console or standard output using plain text.
- **Structured**: This provides a filterable view of your logs. The structured logs maintain the properties of your log messages so that they can be filtered and searched on, in contrast with the console log, which merges all properties into a single string message.
- **Traces**: This shows the path of a single action through all the layers of your solution as a distributed trace. This helps you to find the root cause of errors and performance bottlenecks, and diagnose other behaviors.
- **Metrics**: This shows all the metrics for your application.

> You can learn more about the Aspire dashboard at the following page: `https://aspire.dev/dashboard/overview/`.
>
> Information about how you can run the dashboard standalone without an Aspire solution can be found at the following page: `https://aspire.dev/dashboard/standalone/`.

Aspire support

The Aspire support policy is different from the .NET support policy. Aspire does not have LTS and STS releases. Every release immediately replaces the current release and only the current release is supported.

For example, when Aspire 9.3 was released on May 19, 2025, the previous release, Aspire 9.2, immediately reached its end-of-life. This is because Aspire is only used in development environments, never production environments.

To receive technical support from Microsoft, you also need to be on the latest servicing level update for the latest Aspire release. For example, Aspire 9.2.1 was released on April 24, 2025, two weeks after Aspire 9.2.0 was released on April 10, 2025. To maintain support, you would have needed to update to it immediately.

> You can learn more about Aspire's support policy at the following page: `https://dotnet.microsoft.com/en-us/platform/support/policy/aspire`.

Code editor and CLI support for Aspire

Support for Aspire is built into Visual Studio version 17.10 and later. Everything else, including VS Code, can use the CLI tools, and over time I expect support to be improved.

> You can learn more about Aspire's support in VS Code at the following page: `https://marketplace.visualstudio.com/items?itemName=microsoft-aspire.aspire-vscode`.

To use Aspire 13, you must have the following prerequisites:

1. .NET SDK 10 or later
2. An OCI-compliant container runtime, like Docker Desktop or Podman

To install the Aspire project templates manually, enter the following command:

```
dotnet new install Aspire.ProjectTemplates
```

> You can learn about the Rider plugin for Aspire at the following page: `https://blog.jetbrains.com/dotnet/2024/02/19/jetbrains-rider-and-the-net-aspire-plugin/`.

Starting an Aspire solution

To start an Aspire solution, you have three experiences to choose from, depending on your code editor:

- Press *F5* in Visual Studio or VS Code or Rider, which attaches the debugger to all projects. If you want to make a code change while running, you can use Hot Reload.
- Press *Ctrl + F5* in Visual Studio or VS Code or Rider, which runs the solution without debugging. You can make changes to individual projects and Visual Studio will automatically restart them.
- At the command prompt or terminal, enter `dotnet watch`. This has basic support for watching projects and restarting them when code files change. The Aspire team is working on improved Hot Reload support.

Aspire application model and orchestration

Aspire orchestration is designed to simplify and control the connections and configurations between all the integrations of a cloud-native solution.

Aspire orchestration assists with the following tasks:

- **Solution composition:** The AppHost project defines resources that make up the application, including .NET projects, containers, executables, and cloud resources.
- **Service discovery:** The AppHost project maps how the different resources communicate with each other.

In a similar manner to ASP.NET Core projects that use a class named WebApplication to build configuration for the website or web service, Aspire AppHost projects use a class named DistributedApplication, as shown in the following code:

```
var builder = DistributedApplication.CreateBuilder(args);
```

This builder object can then call methods to map the resources in a distributed Aspire application model, as shown in *Table 8.3*:

Method	Description
AddContainer	Adds a container resource to the Aspire application model. If you add a package reference to an Aspire package like Aspire.Hosting.Redis, then you can use extension methods like AddRedis that will add a container specifically for Redis.
AddExecutable	Adds an executable resource to the Aspire application model.
AddProject	Adds a project resource to the Aspire application model. This dynamically scans the referenced project for configuration in launchSettings.json like URLs.
AddResource	Adds a generic resource to the Aspire application model.

Table 8.3: Methods to map the resources in a distributed Aspire application model

For example, to add a Redis container, you call the AddRedis method, as shown in the following code:

```
var cache = builder.AddRedis("cache");
```

To add an ASP.NET Core Web API service project, you would call the AddProject method, as shown in the following code:

```
var apiService = builder.AddProject
  <Projects.AspireStarter_ApiService>("apiservice");
```

> **Good practice:** When you add an Aspire resource, you give it a short name like cache or apiservice. These are then used throughout your other projects to dynamically refer to that resource's endpoints and so on. For example, http://apiservice. Note that this is not a true URL. The actual URL and port numbers will be replaced dynamically during Aspire service discovery.

As well as methods for building the Aspire application model, there are methods to add settings, as shown in *Table 8.4*:

Method	Description
`AddConnectionString`	If you've already provisioned resources outside of the app host and want to use them.
`AddParameter`	Parameter values are read from the `Parameters` section of the app host's configuration and are used to provide values to the app while running locally. When deploying the app, the value will be asked for the parameter value. You can learn more about external parameters at the following page: `https://learn.microsoft.com/en-us/dotnet/aspire/fundamentals/external-parameters`.

Table 8.4: Methods to add settings for Aspire integrations

To connect the resources in an Aspire application model using service discovery, you call one of the `With` methods, as shown in *Table 8.5*:

Method	Description
`WithReference`	Links resources so they can use the correct configuration to communicate with each other by passing service discovery information for the referenced projects.
`WithExternalHttpEndpoints`	Configures a web project to have external HTTP endpoints that can be automatically configured for any related Aspire integrations and projects.
`WithHttpEndpoint,` `WithHttpsEndpoint`	Uses code to configure named endpoints.
`WithArgs`	Adds a callback to be executed with a list of command-line arguments when a container resource is started.
`WithEnvironment`	Adds an environment variable to the resource.

Table 8.5: Methods to connect and configure Aspire integrations

For example, to add a web frontend project that will call the web service and Redis container, you call the `AddProject` method and then connect to its dependencies by calling the `WithReference` method, as shown in the following code:

```
builder.AddProject<Projects.AspireStarter_Web>("webfrontend")
    .WithExternalHttpEndpoints()
    .WithReference(cache)
    .WithReference(apiService);
```

Any distributed solution needs the ability to call remote services. While building Aspire, the team created a new service discovery library named `Microsoft.Extensions.ServiceDiscovery`. This provides the core abstraction and several implementations of client-side service discovery and load balancing.

It enables integration with HttpClientFactory and **Yet Another Reverse Proxy (YARP)** (https://microsoft.github.io/reverse-proxy/) for local development, as well as Kubernetes in deployed environments.

> You can learn more about service discovery at the following page: https://learn.microsoft.com/en-us/dotnet/aspire/service-discovery/overview.

Aspire project templates

Aspire 13 for .NET has many dotnet CLI project templates to choose from:

- **Aspire Starter Application** / aspire-starter: A solution with four or five projects and an optional Redis container, depending on the options selected. This is used to learn about Aspire.
- **Aspire Python Starter App** / aspire-py-starter: An example solution using Python.
- **Aspire Empty App** / aspire: A solution with the two required projects, AppHost and ServiceDefaults. This is used for new greenfield projects that will use Aspire.
- **Aspire App Host** / aspire-apphost: A project with minimum setup for an app host. This is used to add Aspire to an existing solution when you do not use Visual Studio's tooling.
- **Aspire Single-File App Host** / aspire-apphost-singlefile: A project with minimal setup for an app host and no project file.
- **Aspire Service Defaults** / aspire-servicedefaults: A project with minimum setup for service defaults. This is used to add Aspire to an existing solution when you do not use Visual Studio's tooling.
- **Aspire Test Project (xUnit/NUnit/MSTest)** / aspire-xunit, aspire-nunit, aspire-mstest: A project to add integration tests to an Aspire solution
- **.NET MAUI for Aspire Service Defaults** / maui-aspire-servicedefaults: A project with setup for service defaults for .NET MAUI apps.

If you have previously installed old Aspire project templates, then you can install the latest using the following command:

```
dotnet new install Aspire.ProjectTemplates --force
```

You can list the project templates at the command prompt or terminal using the following command:

```
dotnet new list aspire
```

As well as the project templates, Visual Studio has tooling support to add Aspire orchestration and the two required projects to an existing solution.

Now let's use the starter project template to review some key concepts and implementation details of Aspire.

Exploring the Aspire starter template

The **Aspire Starter Application** project template is designed to get you started with a working Aspire solution that you can try out. It's a great way to initially understand how all the Aspire parts fit together.

The project template solution is made up of four or five projects and an optional Redis cache, as described in the following list:

- A **Blazor Web Application** project named `<Solution_Name>.Web` as the frontend user interface
- An **ASP.NET Core Web API** (using Minimal API) project named `<Solution_Name>.ApiService` as a backend weather information service
- A **Aspire App Host** project named `<Solution_Name>.AppHost`
- A **Aspire Service Defaults** project named `<Solution_Name>.ServiceDefaults`
- An optional **xUnit Test** project named `<Solution_Name>.Tests`
- An optional container for Redis hosted in Docker (by default) or hosted in Podman

Let's create an Aspire starter application using the project template:

1. If you have the `MatureWeb` solution open, close it.

> We will create the solution in the `web-dev-net10` folder so that it does not use CPM and the `Directory.Packages.props` file that is in the `MatureWeb` directory hierarchy.

2. Use your preferred code editor to create a new **Aspire Starter Application** / `aspire-starter` project with a solution named `AspireStarter` in the `web-dev-net10` folder, as shown in *Figure 8.14*:

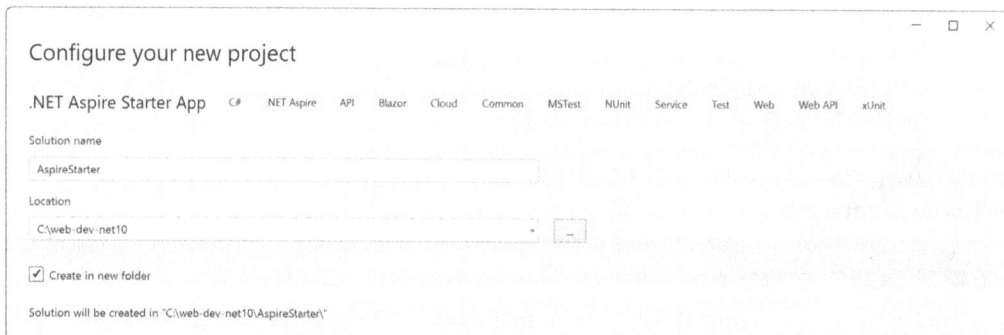

Figure 8.14: Configure your new project for the Aspire starter template

> **Warning!** This project template does not allow you to specify a project name because it creates multiple projects for you. Instead, you specify a solution name that is then used as a prefix for the names of all its projects. In this chapter, you will use the folder named `web-dev-net10` to contain multiple solutions, each of which contains multiple projects.

3. Click **Next**.

4. On the **Additional information** step, choose the following options:

   - **Framework: .NET 10.0 (Long Term Support)**
   - **Configure for HTTPS:** Selected
   - **Aspire version:** 13.0
   - **Use Redis for caching:** Selected (this will create the optional container for Redis)
   - **Create a test project: xUnit.net** (this will create the optional project for integration tests)
   - **xUnit.net version:** v2
   - **Use the .dev.localhost TLD in the application URL:** Cleared

5. Click **Create**.

6. In **Solution Explorer**, note the five projects and that the AspireStarter.AppHost project is set as the startup project (it's in bold), as shown in *Figure 8.15*:

   1. AspireStarter.ApiService: An ASP.NET Core Minimal API web service. In your own solution, it could be an ASP.NET Core Web API with controllers web service.

   2. AspireStarter.AppHost: One of the required Aspire projects. This is a console app that orchestrates all the other projects and resources, starting them up and connecting them as necessary.

   3. AspireStarter.ServiceDefaults: One of the required Aspire projects. This is a class library where you should centralize configuration for all the projects in the Aspire solution.

   4. AspireStarter.Tests: An xUnit.net project for writing unit and integration tests.

   5. AspireStarter.Web: A Blazor project for a web user interface. In your own solution, it could be an ASP.NET Core MVC website.

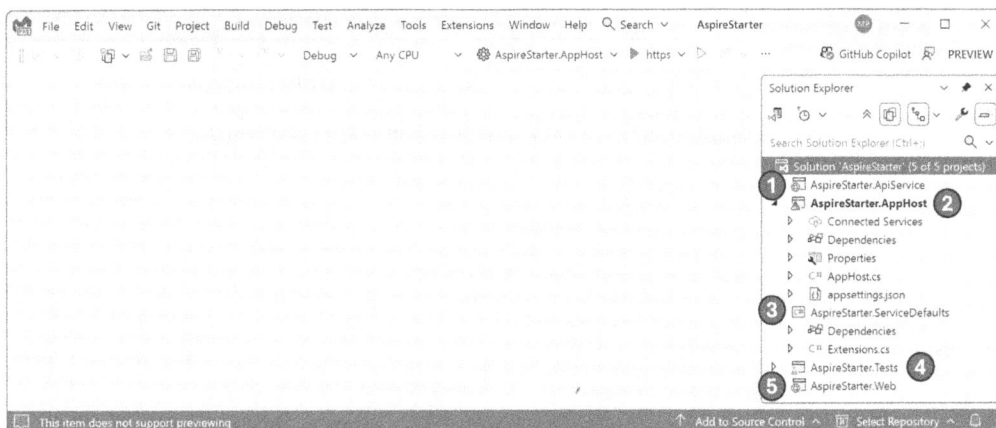

Figure 8.15: Aspire starter application solution with five projects

> Since we created this solution in the web-dev-net10 folder, it will not use **Central Package Management (CPM)**. We could move the Directory.Packages.props file up to the web-dev-net10 folder, but then we would need to remove all the version attributes from all the projects. Since we will only be using this Aspire solution in this section, it's probably not worth the time. But in your own Aspire solutions, you might want to use CPM.

7. Start Docker Desktop. This will also start the Docker daemon.

8. Start the AspireStarter.AppHost project with the debugger attached by navigating to **Debug | Start Debugging**, or clicking the **https** button, or pressing *F5*.

9. Note the successful launch of the app host console app and the Aspire dashboard on a random port, in my case 17143, as shown in the following output:

```
info: Aspire.Hosting.DistributedApplication[0]
      Aspire version: 13.0.0+0fcb1e9885266c1700c49c16513a6d97480bb058
info: Aspire.Hosting.DistributedApplication[0]
      Distributed application starting.
info: Aspire.Hosting.DistributedApplication[0]
      Application host directory is: C:\web-dev-net10\AspireStarter\
AspireStarter.AppHost
info: Aspire.Hosting.DistributedApplication[0]
      Now listening on: https://localhost:17143
info: Aspire.Hosting.DistributedApplication[0]
      Login to the dashboard at https://localhost:17143/
login?t=88c817f3679614a06778de42009aa624
info: Aspire.Hosting.DistributedApplication[0]
      Distributed application started. Press Ctrl+C to shut down.
```

Note the link to **Login to the dashboard** on the following page (with a unique GUID):

https://localhost:17143/login?t=88c817f3679614a06778de42009aa624.

Exploring the Aspire starter solution

Now that we've seen how to successfully create and start the Aspire starter solution, let's explore it:

1. Note that the dashboard in the browser shows that a Redis container named cache is running, as well as two projects, the Web API service named apiservice and the Blazor client named webfrontend, as shown in *Figure 8.16*:

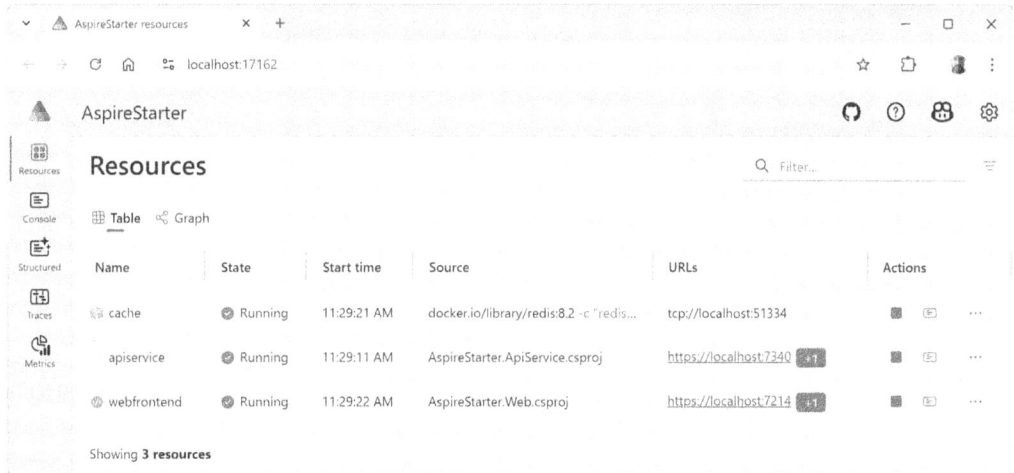

Figure 8.16: The Aspire dashboard shows one container and two projects

2. In the **apiservice** row, in the **URLs** column, click the +1 button to show the second endpoint with its port number, and then click the https link to call the web service. You will see the plain text: **API service is running**. Navigate to /weatherforecast to see sample data.

3. Append weatherforecast to the end of the address, and note the randomly-generated weather forecast that results, as shown in *Figure 8.17*:

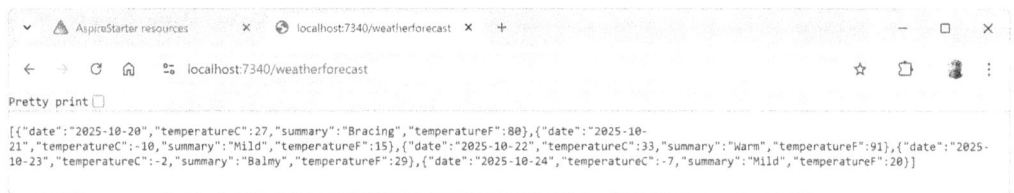

Figure 8.17: Randomly-generated weather forecast from the web service

4. In the Aspire dashboard, in the **webfrontend** row, in the **URLs** column, click the https link to open the Blazor client, then navigate to the **Weather** page, and note the table of weather forecasts, as shown in *Figure 8.18*:

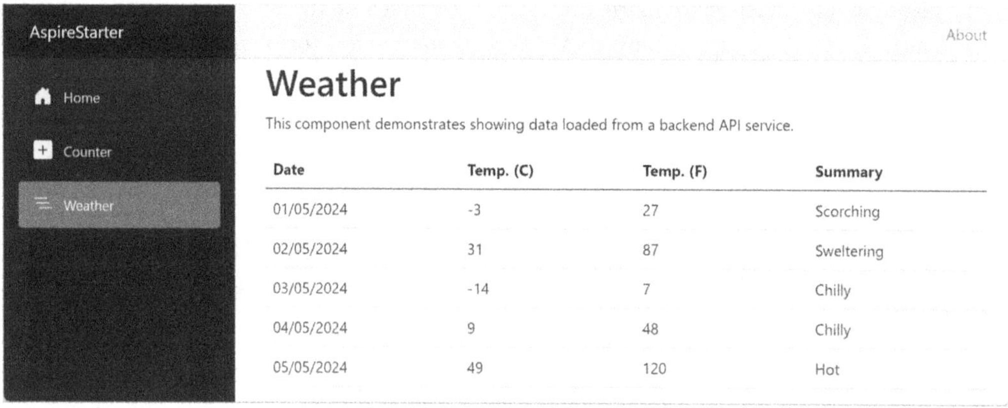

Figure 8.18: Blazor web frontend

5. In the Aspire dashboard, navigate to **Console**, and select each of the three resources in turn to view their console output, as shown in *Figure 8.19*:

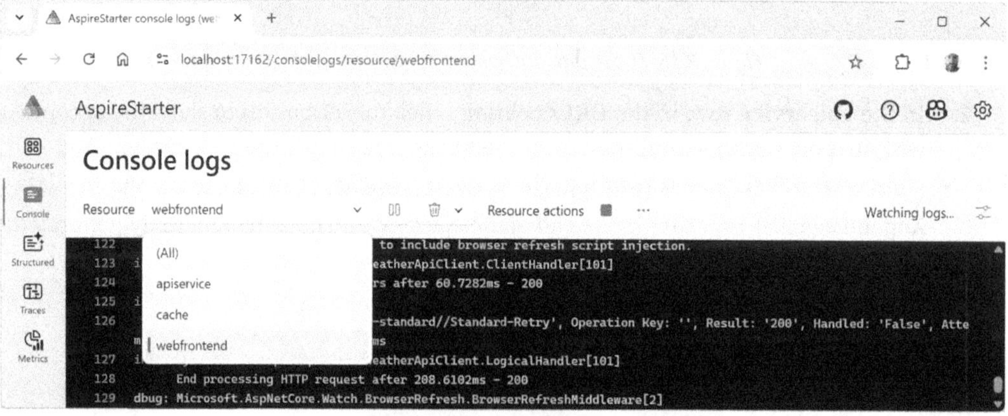

Figure 8.19: Console logs in the Aspire dashboard

6. Note that the console logs for webfrontend show that it successfully connected to the Redis container and made a successful request to the web service using Polly for retries, as shown in the following partial output:

```
info: StackExchange.Redis.ConnectionMultiplexer[0]
      Connecting (sync) on .NET 10.0.0 (StackExchange.Redis:
v2.8.31.52602)
...
info: StackExchange.Redis.ConnectionMultiplexer[0]
      localhost:58709/Interactive: Connected
```

```
...
info: System.Net.Http.HttpClient.WeatherApiClient.ClientHandler[100]
      Sending HTTP request GET https://localhost:7403/weatherforecast
info: System.Net.Http.HttpClient.WeatherApiClient.ClientHandler[101]
      Received HTTP response headers after 18.2274ms - 200
info: Polly[3]
      Execution attempt. Source: '-standard//Standard-Retry', Operation
Key: '', Result: '200', Handled: 'False', Attempt: '0', Execution Time:
'68.7295'
info: System.Net.Http.HttpClient.WeatherApiClient.LogicalHandler[101]
      End processing HTTP request after 178.3335ms - 200
```

7. Navigate to **Structured** to show the structured logs, as shown in *Figure 8.20*:

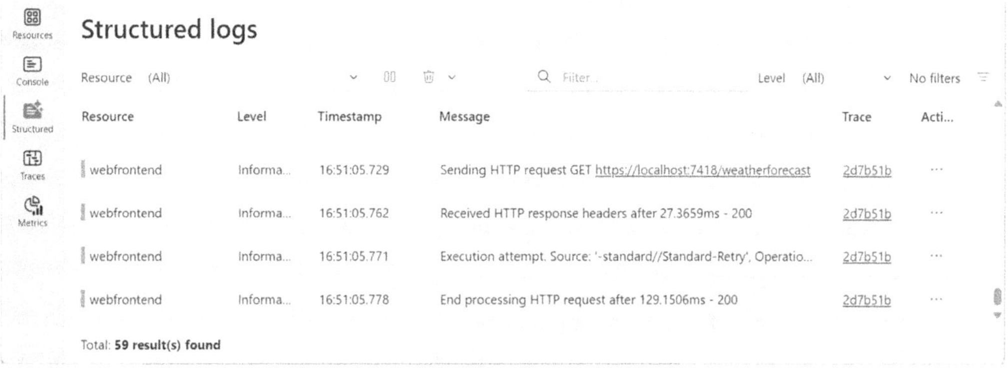

Figure 8.20: Structured logs in the Aspire dashboard

8. In the **Trace** column, click the GUID value, and note that the /weather route in the Blazor app triggered a request to the Redis cache, then to the web service because it hadn't been cached yet, and again to the Redis cache to store the data for the next request, as shown in *Figure 8.21*:

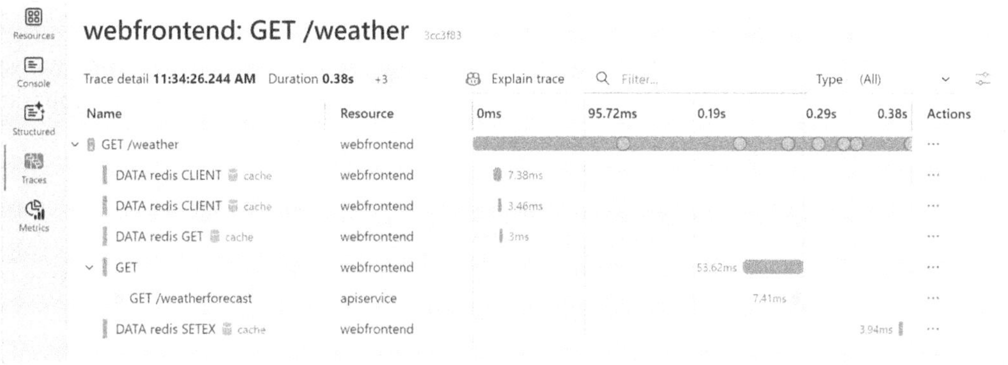

Figure 8.21: Details of a trace including calls between Aspire project resources

9. Navigate to **Metrics** and note you can select and see graphs and tables for data like process.runtime.dotnet.thread_pool.threads.count and http.server.request.duration.

10. In Docker Desktop, note the Redis container that was spun up for you automatically, as shown in *Figure 8.22*:

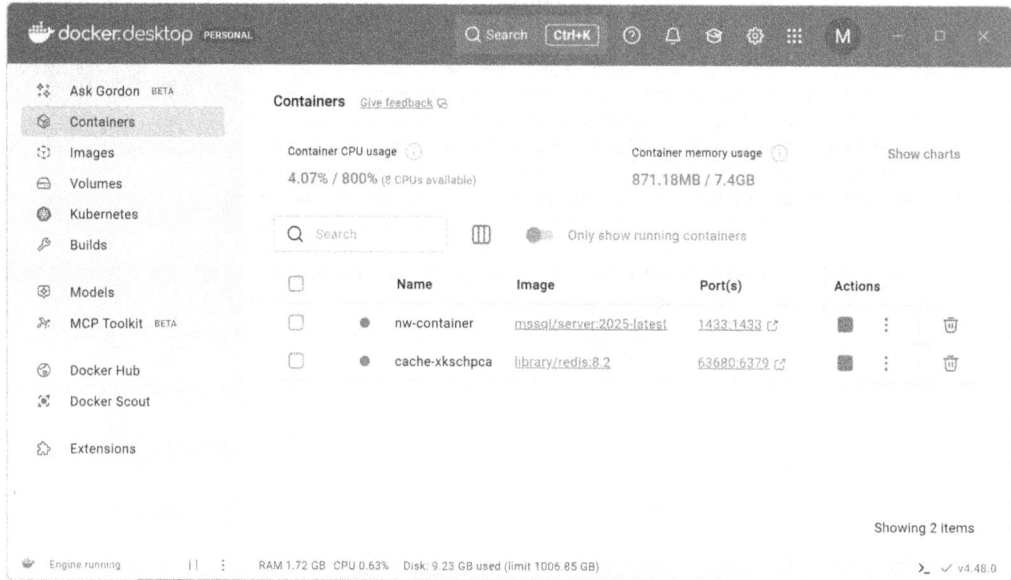

Figure 8.22: Redis container in Docker Desktop

11. Close the browser, and at the command prompt or terminal for the Aspire app host, press *Ctrl + C* to shut down the distributed application.

12. In Docker Desktop, note that the Redis container is automatically stopped and removed.

There are a lot of parts to Aspire. Let's dive in and see what role all the parts of Aspire play.

AppHost project for orchestrating resources

The `AppHost` project lets you express the needs of your solution, and it orchestrates the running of your app on your local developer computer.

Aspire provides abstractions that allow you to orchestrate service discovery, environment variables, and container configurations without having to manage the details manually (unless you want to).

Let's see how it works in the starter template:

1. In the `AspireStarter.AppHost.csproj` project file, note that the app host project is a console app that is configured as the Aspire `AppHost`, references the two functional projects, and references the `Aspire.Hosting.Redis` package, as shown highlighted in the following markup:

```
<Project Sdk="Aspire.AppHost.Sdk/13.0.0">

  <PropertyGroup>
    <OutputType>Exe</OutputType>
    <TargetFramework>net10.0</TargetFramework>
```

```xml
    <ImplicitUsings>enable</ImplicitUsings>
    <Nullable>enable</Nullable>
    <UserSecretsId>1d713f01-3bf2-4a15-9910-799f70fe499f</UserSecretsId>
  </PropertyGroup>

  <ItemGroup>
    <ProjectReference Include=
      "..\AspireStarter.ApiService\AspireStarter.ApiService.csproj" />
    <ProjectReference Include=
      "..\AspireStarter.Web\AspireStarter.Web.csproj" />
  </ItemGroup>

  <ItemGroup>
    <PackageReference Include="Aspire.Hosting.Redis" Version="13.0.0"/>
  </ItemGroup>

</Project>
```

> A `<ProjectReference>` in an Aspire host project is not like a traditional project reference to a class library. Instead of building the referenced project and copying the `.dll` to the local project `bin` folder where it will be found at runtime, a `<ProjectReference>` in an Aspire host project tells the tooling to manage connections via endpoints, including ports and paths, by processing any `launchSettings.json` files. We will explore this in more detail later in the chapter.

2. In the `Properties` folder, in the `launchSettings.json` file, note that it includes URLs to access the dashboard named `applicationUrl`, as well as the URL for the endpoint that hosts an **Open Telemetry Protocol (OTLP)** service and receives telemetry, and the URL for the gRPC endpoint to which the dashboard connects for its data, as shown highlighted in the following markup:

```json
{
  "$schema": "https://json.schemastore.org/launchsettings.json",
  "profiles": {
    "https": {
      "commandName": "Project",
      "dotnetRunMessages": true,
      "launchBrowser": true,
      "applicationUrl": "https://localhost:17143;http://localhost:15099",
      "environmentVariables": {
        "ASPNETCORE_ENVIRONMENT": "Development",
        "DOTNET_ENVIRONMENT": "Development",
        "ASPIRE_DASHBOARD_MCP_ENDPOINT_URL": "https://localhost:23240"
```

```
    "ASPIRE_DASHBOARD_OTLP_ENDPOINT_URL": "https://localhost:21184",
    "ASPIRE_RESOURCE_SERVICE_ENDPOINT_URL": "https://localhost:22057"
  }
},
```

3. In `AppHost.cs`, note that we orchestrate the container for Redis and the two web projects, including calling the `WaitFor` method introduced in Aspire 9 to make sure the Redis cache and the web service are running before showing them as ready in the Aspire dashboard, as shown in the following code:

```
var builder = DistributedApplication.CreateBuilder(args);

var cache = builder.AddRedis("cache");

var apiService = builder.AddProject<Projects
  .AspireStarter_ApiService>("apiservice")
  .WithHttpHealthCheck("/health");

builder.AddProject<Projects.AspireStarter_Web>("webfrontend")
  .WithExternalHttpEndpoints()
  .WithHttpHealthCheck("/health")
  .WithReference(cache)
  .WaitFor(cache)
  .WithReference(apiService)
  .WaitFor(apiService);

builder.Build().Run();
```

4. In the call to `AddProject`, click in the `AspireStarter_ApiService` type and press *F12* or right-click and select **Go To Definition**, and note the `ProjectPath` property, as shown in the following code:

```
// <auto-generated/>

namespace Projects;

[global::System.CodeDom.Compiler.GeneratedCode("Aspire.Hosting", null)]
[global::System.Diagnostics.CodeAnalysis.ExcludeFromCodeCoverage(
  Justification = "Generated code.")]
[global::System.Diagnostics.DebuggerDisplay(
  "Type = {GetType().Name,nq}, ProjectPath = {ProjectPath}")]
public class AspireStarter_ApiService : global::Aspire.Hosting.
IProjectMetadata
{
```

```
    public string ProjectPath => """C:\web-dev-net10\AspireStarter\
    AspireStarter.ApiService\AspireStarter.ApiService.csproj""";
}
```

This autogenerated code is created when you add a project reference to an Aspire host project. In effect, all it does is store the path to the other project so that the tooling can read information about the project and find related files like its launchSettings.json file to know how to connect endpoints using service discovery.

When you add a project to an AppHost project, either using Visual Studio's **Add Project Reference** or by calling AddProject<T>(), it is *not* the same as adding a usual .NET-to-.NET project reference! The SDK works magic to fake it and autogenerate code. You can add a reference to a .NET Framework project, and that project will get added to the dashboard, but it won't get any special integrations, and so on.

> Aspire resources are not .NET specific. They could be any executable or type of project. With Aspire 13, the AppHost project must be a .NET project. Future versions of Aspire will allow you to use other languages like Python or JavaScript, and Aspire will become fully polyglot with no requirement for .NET.

When you call AddProject, Aspire dynamically reads the launchSettings.json to discover URL and port numbers, and so on. An AppHost project has its own launchSettings.json file so it can have multiple URLs for all the projects it references.

You can pass an extra parameter to AddProject to specify an alternative profile, launchProfileName: "https". Setting it to null means disable, or for a port, it means generate a random port, as shown in the following code:

```
.WithEndpoint("https", e => e.Port = null) // Generate random port number.
```

ServiceDefaults project for centralized configuration

The ServiceDefaults project provides a central place to configure all the Aspire services and integrations. Let's review how it works:

1. In the AspireStarter.ServiceDefaults.csproj project file, note that it is a class library that is configured as an Aspire shared project, it has a framework reference to Microsoft.AspNetCore.App, and it references multiple packages for implementing features like resilience, service discovery, and instrumentation for OpenTelemetry, as shown in the following markup:

    ```
    <Project Sdk="Microsoft.NET.Sdk">

      <PropertyGroup>
        <TargetFramework>net10.0</TargetFramework>
        <ImplicitUsings>enable</ImplicitUsings>
        <Nullable>enable</Nullable>
        <IsAspireSharedProject>true</IsAspireSharedProject>
      </PropertyGroup>
    ```

```
<ItemGroup>
  <FrameworkReference Include="Microsoft.AspNetCore.App" />

  <PackageReference Include="Microsoft.Extensions.Http.Resilience"
Version="10.0.0" />
  <PackageReference Include="Microsoft.Extensions.ServiceDiscovery"
Version="10.0.0" />
  <PackageReference Include="OpenTelemetry.Exporter.
OpenTelemetryProtocol"
Version="1.13.1" />
  <PackageReference Include="OpenTelemetry.Extensions.Hosting"
Version="1.13.1" />
  <PackageReference Include="OpenTelemetry.Instrumentation.AspNetCore"
Version="1.13.0" />
  <PackageReference Include="OpenTelemetry.Instrumentation.Http"
Version="1.13.0" />
  <PackageReference Include="OpenTelemetry.Instrumentation.Runtime"
Version="1.13.0" />
  </ItemGroup>

</Project>
```

2. In `Extensions.cs`, note that the `Extensions` class is defined in the `Microsoft.Extensions.` `Hosting` namespace and defines extension methods for `IHostApplicationBuilder`, as shown in the following list:

    *   `AddServiceDefaults`: This method should be called within any project that wants to participate in the distributed application, like the web service and Blazor website. It calls the next method.
    *   `ConfigureOpenTelemetry`: This method sets up OpenTelemetry with sensible defaults for logging, adds metrics for ASP.NET Core, HTTP clients, and .NET runtime counters, and adds tracing for ASP.NET Core and HTTP clients. It calls the next method.
    *   `AddOpenTelemetryExporters`: This method reads configuration like the appropriate environment variable to know whether it should enable OTLP exporters.
    *   `AddDefaultHealthChecks`: This method adds a basic health check to ensure a service is responding to requests.
    *   `MapDefaultEndpoints`: This method maps the health checks endpoint to `/health` and the liveness endpoint to `/alive`.

> **Good practice:** If you have other shared functionality, put it in a separate class library. The Aspire service defaults class library project should only be used to configure Aspire services and integrations.

Participating functional projects

Now let's see what is different about your functional projects, the web service and web user interface, that allows them to participate in this Aspire distributed solution:

1. In the `ApiService` project, in its project file, note that it has a reference to the service defaults project. This is so the project can call the `AddServiceDefaults` method.

2. In the `ApiService` project, in `Program.cs`, note that it adds a call to `AddServiceDefaults`, as shown in the following code:

    ```
    // Add service defaults & Aspire client integrations.
    builder.AddServiceDefaults();
    ```

3. In the `Web` project, in its project file, note that it has a package reference to `Aspire.StackExchange.Redis.OutputCaching`, and it also has a reference to the service defaults project. This is so the project can call the `AddServiceDefaults` method.

    > The `Aspire.StackExchange.Redis.OutputCaching` package is an example of an **Aspire integration**. Aspire integrations are wrapper class libraries that configure a feature like Redis to operate well in a cloud-native environment. We will learn more about them later in this chapter.

4. In the `Web` project, in `Program.cs`, note that it adds a call to `AddServiceDefaults` and to add Redis for output caching, as shown in the following code:

    ```
    // Add service defaults & Aspire integrations.
    builder.AddServiceDefaults();
    builder.AddRedisOutputCache("cache");
    ```

    > The name `cache` comes from when Redis was registered as an Aspire resource in the app host project, as shown in the following code: `builder.AddRedis("cache")`.

5. In the `Web` project, in `Program.cs`, note the statement to configure the web frontend to be able to call the weather web service API, as shown in the following code:

    ```
    builder.Services.AddHttpClient<WeatherApiClient>(client =>
      {
        // This URL uses "https+http://" to indicate HTTPS is preferred over
    HTTP.
    ```

```
    // Learn more about service discovery scheme resolution at https://
aka.ms/dotnet/sdschemes.
    client.BaseAddress = new("https+http://apiservice");
});
```

> The name `apiservice` comes from when the web service was registered as an Aspire resource in the app host project, as shown in the following code:
>
> ```
> builder.AddProject<Projects.AspireStarter_ApiService>("apiservice")
> ```

Aspire runs your projects and their dependencies and configures them appropriately, allowing them to communicate. Aspire removes the need to know the ports and connection strings from the developer experience. This is achieved by a service discovery mechanism that allows you to use logical names like `apiservice` instead of IP addresses and ports when making HTTP calls.

In the preceding URL, you can use the name `apiservice` when making HTTP calls via `IHttpClientFactory`. The calls made using this method will also automatically retry and handle transient failures because Aspire preconfigures integration with Polly for resilience features.

Now let's learn more details about Aspire integrations.

Aspire integrations

Aspire integrations are designed to solve the biggest roadblock to getting started with cloud-native development. The roadblock is that there is too much configuration that you must get right, and it often is not obvious what path to start with.

Aspire helps this by being opinionated about what an integration needs to provide, mandating that all integrations at a minimum provide resiliency defaults, health checks, set up telemetry, and integrate with DI.

Every Aspire integration must comply with the following requirements:

- An Aspire integration must provide a JSON schema so that statement completion works when editing `appsettings.json`.
- An Aspire integration must have default but configurable resilience patterns such as retries, timeouts, and circuit breakers to maximize availability.
- An Aspire integration must have health checks that enable Aspire solutions to track and respond to its health.
- An Aspire integration must provide integrated logging, metrics, and tracing using modern .NET abstractions like `ILogger`, `Meter`, and `Activity`.
- An Aspire integration must provide extension methods that connect the services from the SDK to the DI container with the right lifetime for the types being registered.

Currently, Aspire provides the integrations shown in *Table 8.6*:

Integration	Description
Apache Kafka	Producing and consuming messages from an Apache Kafka broker.
Dapr	Modeling Dapr as an Aspire resource.
Docker	Deploying Aspire applications using Docker Compose.
Elasticsearch	Accessing Elasticsearch databases.
Keycloak	Accessing Keycloak authentication.
Milvus	Accessing Milvus databases.
MongoDB Driver	Accessing MongoDB databases.
MySqlConnector	Accessing MySQL databases.
NATS	Accessing NATS messaging.
Oracle EF Core	Accessing Oracle databases with Entity Framework Core.
OpenAI	Accessing OpenAI APIs.
Orleans	Modeling Orleans as an Aspire resource.
PostgreSQL EF Core	Accessing PostgreSQL databases using Entity Framework Core.
PostgreSQL	Accessing PostgreSQL databases.
Qdrant	Accessing Qdrant databases.
RabbitMQ	Accessing RabbitMQ.
Redis Distributed Caching	Accessing Redis caches for distributed caching.
Redis Output Caching	Accessing Redis caches for output caching.
Redis	Accessing Redis caches.
Seq	Logging to Seq.
SQL Server EF Core	Accessing SQL Server databases using Entity Framework Core.
SQL Server	Accessing SQL Server databases.

Table 8.6: Aspire integrations

> You can see the current list of Aspire integrations, including ones specific to Azure, at the following page: `https://learn.microsoft.com/en-us/dotnet/aspire/fundamentals/integrations-overview#official-integrations`.

Logging, tracing, and metrics for observability

For a solution to be observable:

- All integrations in the distributed solution need to provide data in a way you can consume. This includes .NET itself, any libraries that you use, and your own project code.
- The data needs to be sent somewhere that you can access.
- Tools to view, query, and analyze the data need to be set up.

Aspire solutions are observable by default. This means that you can see what is going on in your solution from all the data being collected from the running resources and their logs, metrics, and traces.

.NET teams have invested in OpenTelemetry as both the format of data by adopting OpenTelemetry naming and structure, and for getting data into tools by using OTLP.

Aspire provides the code to enable OpenTelemetry by default in the `ServiceDefaults` project. By using a shared code project instead of hardcoding this implementation, the conventions Aspire uses, like the names of health endpoints, can be customized if you need to. The alternative would have been to put them in a library with configuration settings for customization, which would ultimately be more complex.

Aspire presents all the logs, metrics, and traces from your solution in its developer dashboard. The **Traces** view makes finding things like user actions that cause inefficient paths through the solution easy.

You can see issues like multiple potentially unnecessary database calls or individual services that are slowing down other parts of the system. These types of issues can be difficult to discover without this type of data and a view of the data.

Docker versus Podman for containers

With the initial version of Aspire, you have two choices for hosting containers: Docker (the default) and Podman.

Docker pros:

- More established ecosystem
- Larger community
- More third-party integrations
- Features like Docker Compose to manage multi-container solutions

Podman pros:

- Lower cost of licenses

Unless you have a good reason to use Podman, like your team has already standardized on using it, I recommend that you use Docker because the Aspire team chose it as the default for the good reasons listed above.

Waiting for containers to be ready

If you're familiar with Docker Compose, then you might know that a common issue is that, during startup, the Docker Compose depends_on instruction does not wait until a container is "ready"; it only waits until it's "running." This can cause issues because if you have a relational database system that needs to start its own services before being able to handle incoming connections, then another service may call the database before it is truly ready.

Aspire had a similar issue because calling WithReference does something like the Docker Compose depends_on instruction. However, the Aspire team knows that the capability to truly make a resource depend on another resource is one of the top asks from the .NET community.

Aspire 9 introduced a WaitFor method that uses health checks to provide a better experience.

Alternatively, you can implement retries for automatic resiliency while the dependent resources get ready.

Adding Aspire to your existing .NET apps

You can add Aspire to your existing apps and get a dashboard, health checks, and more, all without changing how your apps work. You can read more at the following page: https://devblogs.microsoft. com/dotnet/adding-dotnet-aspire-to-your-existing-dotnet-apps/.

Deployment with Aspire

The AppHost project has two execution modes, run and publish:

- Run mode is used during the developer inner loop on your local computer
- Publish mode produces a manifest file that statically describes the application model that can be used in deployment scenarios

> **Warning!** The AppHost project itself is not deployed and does not run outside of local development and test scenarios.

Understanding Aspire manifests

The application model can produce a manifest definition that describes the solution's relationships and dependencies that tools can consume, augment, and build upon for deployment.

With this manifest, you can get your Aspire solution into Azure using Azure Container Apps in the simplest and fastest way possible. The Azure Developer CLI and Aspire work together to enable you to quickly provision and deploy the Azure resources in one step. The Azure Developer CLI can also create Bicep from the manifest to allow developers and platform engineers to audit or augment the deployment processes.

Bicep is a **domain-specific language** (DSL) that uses declarative syntax to deploy Azure resources.

Aspire cloud deployments

Although Aspire today works best for deploying to Azure, it is open to other deployment systems.

The final artifacts of an Aspire application are .NET apps and configurations that can be deployed to your cloud environments. With the strong container-first mindset of Aspire, the .NET SDK native container builds serve as a valuable tool to publish these apps to containers.

While Aspire itself doesn't natively provide a direct mechanism to deploy your applications to their final destinations, the Aspire application model that you build knows all about the dependencies, configurations, and connections to all the distributed solution's resources.

> You can learn about deploying to Azure Container Apps at the following page: `https://devblogs.microsoft.com/dotnet/how-to-deploy-dotnet-aspire-apps-to-azure-container-apps/`.

Aspir8 deployment YAML files

Another deployment tool is **Aspir8**, which can generate a deployment YAML file for an Aspire `AppHost` project, but be warned that it is still in preview so you can only install pre-release versions.

> You can learn more about Aspir8 at the following page: `https://prom3theu5.github.io/aspirational-manifests/getting-started.html`.
>
> Aspir8's GitHub repository can be found at the following page: `https://github.com/prom3theu5/aspirational-manifests`.

Practicing and exploring

Test your knowledge and understanding by answering some questions, getting some hands-on practice, and exploring this chapter's topics with deeper research.

Exercise 8.1 – Online material

You can read more about the **Options pattern in ASP.NET Core** at the following page:

`https://learn.microsoft.com/en-us/aspnet/core/fundamentals/configuration/options`.

The official ASP.NET Core documentation has useful pages about deployment:

- Deploy to IIS (Windows Internet Information Service): `https://learn.microsoft.com/en-us/aspnet/core/tutorials/publish-to-iis`
- Deploy to Azure Web App using Visual Studio: `https://learn.microsoft.com/en-us/aspnet/core/tutorials/publish-to-azure-webapp-using-vs`
- Deploy to Nginx on Linux: `https://learn.microsoft.com/en-us/aspnet/core/host-and-deploy/linux-nginx`

You can read official materials from Microsoft using the following links:

- Announcement: `https://devblogs.microsoft.com/dotnet/introducing-dotnet-aspire-simplifying-cloud-native-development-with-dotnet-8/`
- GA release: `https://devblogs.microsoft.com/dotnet/dotnet-aspire-general-availability/`
- Aspire 13 documentation: `https://aspire.dev/get-started/welcome/`
- Sample code: `https://github.com/dotnet/aspire-samples`
- Aspire Community Toolkit repository: `https://github.com/CommunityToolkit/Aspire`
- Introducing the .NET Aspire Community Toolkit: `https://devblogs.microsoft.com/dotnet/introducing-the-dotnet-aspire-community-toolkit/`

You can read more about Aspire from third-party sites using the following links:

- Dashboard: `https://anthonysimmon.com/dotnet-aspire-dashboard-best-tool-visualize-opentelemetry-local-dev/`
- Frequently asked questions: `https://learn.microsoft.com/en-us/dotnet/aspire/reference/aspire-faq`

In this book, we do not want any dependencies on Azure or AWS resources because they cost money. But you should know that there are Azure-specific methods for configuring Aspire, as shown in *Table 8.7*:

Package	Link
Azure hosting	`https://www.nuget.org/packages/Aspire.Hosting.Azure/`
AWS hosting	`https://www.nuget.org/packages/Aspire.Hosting.AWS/`

Table 8.7: Azure and AWS cloud hosting packages

Exercise 8.2 – Practice exercises

The following practice exercises help you to explore the topics in this chapter more deeply.

Learn how to run a custom container in Azure with the following Microsoft official tutorial:

`https://learn.microsoft.com/en-us/azure/app-service/quickstart-custom-container.`

Using Podman

Instead of using Docker, try using Podman for the coding tasks in this chapter.

You can tell Aspire to use Podman by setting the `DOTNET_ASPIRE_CONTAINER_RUNTIME` environment variable to podman, as shown in the following PowerShell command:

```
$env:DOTNET_ASPIRE_CONTAINER_RUNTIME = "podman"
```

Aspireify

You can find lots of articles and tutorials to practice with Aspire at **aspireify.net** by Jeff Fritz, @ csharpfritz, using the following link: `https://aspireify.net/`.

Exercise 8.3 – Test your knowledge

Answer the following questions:

1. What is the main idea of DI?
2. In .NET, you can register dependency services with different lifetimes. What are they?
3. What makes containers lightweight compared to VMs?
4. What is the relationship between a Docker registry, a Docker image, and a Docker container?
5. In a Dockerfile, how do you specify the base image?
6. What are the three main types of Aspire resource?
7. What role do the `AppHost` project and the `ServiceDefaults` project play in an Aspire solution?
8. What are the benefits of referencing an Aspire component package instead of the usual package for a component like Redis?
9. What container technologies are supported by Aspire?
10. What does the `AddProject` method do?

Exercise 8.4 – Explore topics

Use the links on the following page to learn more about the topics covered in this chapter:

`https://github.com/markjprice/web-dev-net10/blob/main/docs/book-links.md#chapter-8---configuring-and-containerizing-aspnet-core-projects`.

Summary

In this chapter, you learned how to:

*   Configure dependency services
*   Configure the HTTP pipeline
*   Configure options and override them in deployments
*   Containerize ASP.NET Core projects ready for deployments anywhere
*   Use Aspire to orchestrate local development

In the next five chapters, you will learn how to build and test web services. Unlike a website that will be used by a human visitor and therefore has a user interface, web services are called by code, so they have different requirements. For example, although the most common web service technologies use controllers and models, they do not need views.

Three of the five chapters review different technologies for building web services and two chapters cover how to build clients to web services and test and debug them:

*   *Chapter 9* covers **ASP.NET Core Web API using controllers:** This provides maximum flexibility and control, but it requires the most developer effort.
*   *Chapter 10* covers building **clients** for web services.
*   *Chapter 11* covers **testing and debugging** web services.

- *Chapter 12* covers **ASP.NET Core OData**: This provides maximum developer productivity but can be less performant and provides less control, especially over security, so it works best for internal websites like intranets.

- *Chapter 13* covers **FastEndpoints**: This provides good developer productivity and production performance but is not a standard part of ASP.NET Core because it relies on a third-party NuGet package.

By comparing three mechanisms for building web services, you will be able to choose the best for your needs.

Get This Book's PDF Version and Exclusive Extras

UNLOCK NOW

Scan the QR code (or go to `packtpub.com/unlock`). Search for this book by name, confirm the edition, and then follow the steps on the page.

Note: Keep your invoice handy. Purchases made directly from Packt don't require one.

9

Building Web Services Using ASP.NET Core Web API

This chapter is about learning how to build web services, aka **HTTP (Hypertext Transfer Protocol)** or **Representational State Transfer (REST)** services, using ASP.NET Core Web API with controllers.

While some developers use the terms HTTP and REST interchangeably when describing web services, it is worth highlighting that they are not directly synonymous. An HTTP service is any service that uses the HTTP protocol to communicate, regardless of architectural style. HTTP services therefore include SOAP services, **RPC (Remote Procedure Call)** over HTTP, and GraphQL APIs.

REST is an architectural style that typically uses HTTP as the underlying protocol, but is more specific in how the interactions and structures are designed. So, REST is a type of HTTP service, but not all HTTP services are RESTful.

REST follows a specific set of architectural constraints like statelessness, resource orientation, and having a uniform interface, while HTTP services don't necessarily follow these rules. HTTP is a protocol, while REST is an architectural style that can, but doesn't have to, use HTTP.

In this chapter, we will cover the following topics:

- Introducing web services
- Creating a web service for the Northwind database
- Documenting and trying out web services
- Caching responses and logging

> Building clients for web services will be covered in the next chapter, *Chapter 10, Building Clients for Web Services*.

Introducing web services

Before we build a modern web service, we need to cover some background to set the context for this chapter.

Aspects of RESTful services

REST is an architectural style for designing networked applications, particularly web services. It was introduced by Roy Fielding in his doctoral dissertation in 2000, and its principles are widely adopted today in web service development. Let's review REST's key architectural aspects.

Statelessness

RESTful services are stateless, meaning each request from a client to the server must contain all the information needed to understand and process the request. The server doesn't store any session information between requests.

For example, if a client sends a request to retrieve a user's profile, it must include everything the server needs, like authentication, user ID, and so on. The server doesn't rely on previous interactions to process the request.

The benefit of this aspect is scalability. Since the server doesn't need to remember the state of any client, it can handle multiple requests from multiple clients independently. This also makes REST suitable for distributed, large-scale systems.

Resource-based

In REST, everything is considered a resource. For example, a user, a blog post, and a comment are all resources. These resources are identified by URIs (**Uniform Resource Identifiers**).

For example, a user might be represented by the URI /users/123, and a blog post might be /posts/567.

The benefit of this aspect is that this creates a clean, structured API design, and resources can be manipulated through standard HTTP methods like GET, POST, PUT, and DELETE.

Uniform interface

The uniform interface is one of the most important principles of REST. It dictates that RESTful APIs must have a consistent, standardized way of interacting with resources regardless of the client type.

The main components of the RESTful uniform interface are as follows:

- Identification of resources through URIs
- Manipulation of resources using representations like JSON or XML to represent data
- Self-descriptive messages where the server response contains all the necessary information, including status, headers, and so on, for the client to interpret
- **Hypermedia as the engine of application state** (HATEOAS), meaning that the client should discover the actions they can take by following links provided by the server

For example, using the HTTP method GET to retrieve a resource, POST to create a new resource, PUT to update, and DELETE to remove it.

The benefit is that this uniformity ensures that clients and servers can communicate with minimal knowledge about each other, leading to flexibility and independent evolution.

Client-server architecture

The client and server are separated into distinct entities. The client handles the user interface and user interactions, while the server manages the resources and handles requests.

For example, a web browser makes a request to a web server to retrieve a resource. The client only needs to know how to interact with the API, and it doesn't need to know the server's inner workings.

The benefit is that this separation allows each to evolve independently, and the client-side technology can be completely different from the server-side technology. For example, you could build an Angular front end that consumes a Python Django web service API. But that'd be crazy! .NET is so much better.

Cacheability

Responses from the server should explicitly indicate whether they are cacheable or not. Caching can significantly improve performance, especially for read-heavy applications.

For example, if a request is sent to retrieve a user's public profile, the response can be cached so that subsequent requests don't need to go back to the server as long as the data remains valid.

The benefit is that properly using caching reduces the server's load, decreases latency, and improves user experience.

Layering

REST allows the architecture to be composed of multiple layers where each layer operates independently and handles specific responsibilities. For example, intermediaries such as load balancers, proxies, or gateways can sit between the client and the server.

For example, a client may make a request that is handled by a load balancer, which forwards it to a particular server in a server cluster.

The benefit is that this approach increases scalability, security, and flexibility. Intermediary layers can handle things like authentication, logging, and load balancing without affecting the client-server relationship.

Representation of resources

Resources in REST can have multiple representations, like JSON, XML, HTML, and so on. When a client requests a resource, the server can respond with the requested representation. Typically, REST services use JSON as it is lightweight and easier to parse for web clients. Specifically, REST services use JSON for the following reasons:

- The ability to negotiate the media type of content exchanged in requests and responses, such as XML and JSON. Content negotiation happens when the client specifies a request header like `Accept: application/xml,*/*;q=0.8`. This means: my preference for XML is weighted at `1.0` (the default), and my preference for all other formats is weighted at `0.8`.

- The default response format used by ASP.NET Core Web API is JSON, which means one of the response headers would be `Content-Type: application/json; charset=utf-8`.

Idempotency

Certain HTTP methods like `PUT`, `DELETE`, and `GET` are idempotent, meaning that making the same request multiple times will produce the same result without side effects.

For example, sending multiple `DELETE /posts/123` requests will always result in that one post being deleted (if it exists), and if it's already deleted, nothing else is affected.

Hypermedia as the Engine of Application State (HATEOAS)

This states that a RESTful service should not only return data but also provide links for the client to discover other actions they can take. The client navigates the application by following the links included in the server's response.

For example, when a client retrieves a user profile from /users/123, the response might include links to edit the profile or delete it, as shown in the following JSON:

```json
{
  "id": 123,
  "name": "John Doe",
  "links": {
    "edit": "/users/123/edit",
    "delete": "/users/123/delete"
  }
}
```

Why REST matters

Let's summarize why REST is a great architectural style for implementing web services:

- REST's simplicity is one of its greatest strengths. By leveraging existing web protocols and the HTTP standard, REST makes APIs more understandable and easier to implement.
- REST's stateless nature makes it inherently scalable, as servers can handle each request in isolation, enabling large systems to scale horizontally by adding more servers.
- The separation of client and server, combined with standardized communication, allows for the independent evolution of both sides.
- REST has become the de facto standard for designing web APIs, especially in environments that require interoperability between different systems or microservices.

Understanding HTTP versions

HTTP has evolved through multiple versions since its creation, each introducing improvements in performance, security, and functionality. The primary versions are HTTP/0.9, HTTP/1.0, HTTP/1.1, HTTP/2, and HTTP/3.

HTTP/0.9 (1991)

The very first version of HTTP was released in 1991 and developed for early web browsers and servers. It was a simple text-based protocol and only supported the GET method for retrieving HTML files. It didn't support HTTP headers, meaning there was no metadata like content type, status codes, or content length exchanged between the client and server. It had no support for multimedia like images, scripts, or different content types, and the connection closed after each request.

HTTP/1.0 (1996)

This was the first official version of HTTP, standardized by the IETF in RFC 1945. It introduced support for metadata through headers, including Content-Type and Content-Length. It introduced methods like GET, POST, and HEAD, and status codes like 200 OK and 404 Not Found.

A separate connection for each request made HTTP/1.0 inefficient and slow for complex web pages, where multiple resources are needed. It didn't define proper caching mechanisms, making every resource retrieval start from scratch, impacting performance.

HTTP/1.1 (1997, updated in 1999)

Standardized in RFC 2068 (and updated in RFC 2616), HTTP/1.1 brought many improvements over HTTP/1.0 and became the most widely used version for over a decade.

Some of its key features include the following:

- **Persistent connections**: Allowed the reuse of the same TCP connection for multiple requests and responses, reducing overhead.
- **Chunked transfer encoding**: Enabled servers to send data in chunks, which is especially useful for streaming and large files.
- **More methods**: Added methods like OPTIONS, PUT, DELETE, TRACE, and CONNECT.
- **Improved caching**: Introduced cache-control mechanisms through headers like ETag, Cache-Control, and Last-Modified, allowing better control over caching.
- **Content negotiation**: Servers could serve different versions of resources based on the client's capabilities, like language or format preferences.

HTTP/2 (2015)

HTTP/2 (based on Google's SPDY protocol) was standardized in RFC 7540, offering major performance improvements to address the inefficiencies of HTTP/1.1.

Some of its key improvements include the following:

- **Multiplexing**: Multiple requests and responses can be sent over a single TCP connection concurrently, eliminating head-of-line blocking and the need for multiple connections.
- **Header compression**: Uses HPACK header compression to reduce the overhead caused by large HTTP headers, improving performance for repeated requests.
- **Binary framing**: HTTP/2 uses a binary format instead of the text-based format of HTTP/1.x, making it more efficient to parse and transfer data.

- **Stream prioritization:** Clients can assign different priorities to streams, allowing the most important resources (like HTML) to be loaded first.

- **Improved security:** While not mandatory, HTTP/2 is often implemented over TLS (though it can also be used over plain TCP).

HTTP/2 dramatically reduces latency, improves page load speed due to multiplexing, and reduces overhead through header compression and persistent connections.

HTTP/3 (2020)

HTTP/3, based on Google's **QUIC (Quick UDP Internet Connections)** protocol, was standardized in RFC 9114. It represents a significant departure from previous versions by shifting from TCP to UDP.

Some of its key features include the following:

- **Uses QUIC over UDP:** Instead of relying on TCP, HTTP/3 uses QUIC, which is based on UDP, to improve latency and reliability.

- **Eliminates TCP head-of-line blocking:** By leveraging QUIC's stream multiplexing, each stream is independent. Packet loss in one stream does not block others, unlike TCP-based HTTP/2.

- **Zero Round-Trip Time (0-RTT) handshakes:** QUIC allows faster connections by reducing the number of round trips needed to establish a secure connection, significantly speeding up initial request times.

- **Built-in encryption:** HTTP/3 is always encrypted using TLS 1.3, meaning there is no unencrypted HTTP/3.

- **Stream multiplexing:** Similar to HTTP/2, but without the same head-of-line blocking issues at the transport layer.

- **Faster connection recovery:** If a connection drops, QUIC can recover without re-establishing the entire connection, improving resilience on unreliable networks.

The benefits of HTTP/3 include faster page loads and more resilient connections, especially over poor network conditions like mobile or wireless connections. It has reduced latency compared to HTTP/2, particularly for secure connections.

Since HTTP/3 uses UDP, it may face deployment issues in networks with firewalls or middleboxes that restrict UDP traffic. While HTTP/3 is rapidly being adopted (especially by major CDNs like Cloudflare), it still isn't as universally supported as HTTP/2.

Understanding HTTP requests and responses for web APIs

HTTP defines standard types of requests and standard codes to indicate a type of response. Most of them can be used to implement web API services.

GET requests

The most common type of request is GET, to retrieve a resource identified by a unique path, with additional options like what media type is acceptable set as a request header, such as Accept, as shown in the following example:

```
GET /path/to/resource
Accept: application/json
```

Common response status codes

Common responses include success and multiple types of failure, as summarized in the following list:

- 1xx: Information
- 2xx: Success
- 3xx: Redirect
- 4xx: Client Error
- 5xx: Server Error

Specific status codes and their meanings are shown in *Table 9.1*:

Status code	Description
`101 Switching Protocols`	The requester has asked the server to switch protocols and the server has agreed to do so. For example, it is common to switch from HTTP to **WebSockets (WS)** for more efficient communication.
`103 Early Hints`	This is used to convey hints that help a client make preparations to process the final response. For example, the server might send the following response before then sending a normal `200 OK` response for a web page that uses a stylesheet and JavaScript file: HTTP/1.1 103 Early Hints Link: </style.css>; rel=preload; as=style Link: </script.js>; rel=preload; as=script
`200 OK`	The path was correctly formed. The resource was successfully found, serialized into an acceptable media type, and then returned in the response body. The response headers specify the `Content-Type`, `Content-Length`, and `Content-Encoding`, for example, `GZIP`.
`301 Moved Permanently`	Over time, a web service may change its resource model, including the path used to identify an existing resource. The web service can indicate the new path by returning this status code and a response header named `Location` that has the new path. Any future requests for this resource should use the new URI.
`302 Found`	This is like `301`, but the resource is only temporarily located at a different URL. It tells the client that it should continue to use the original URL for future requests. Use this when you're temporarily redirecting traffic, such as during website maintenance, a temporary campaign, or A/B testing new features. It's also used for geographic redirection by redirecting users to different versions of a website based on their location, while still maintaining the original URL as canonical.
`304 Not Modified`	If the request includes the `If-Modified-Since` header, then the web service can respond with this status code. The response body is empty because the client should use its cached copy of the resource. You will see a fuller example later in this section.

307 Temporary Redirect	The requested resource has been temporarily moved to the URL in the `Location` header. The browser should make a new request using that URL. For example, this is what happens if you enable `UseHttpsRedirection` and a client makes an HTTP request.
400 Bad Request	The request was invalid; for example, it used a path for a product using an integer ID where the ID value is missing.
401 Unauthorized	The request was valid and the resource was found, but the client did not supply credentials or is not authorized to access that resource. Re-authenticating may enable access, for example, by adding or changing the `Authorization` request header.
403 Forbidden	The request was valid and the resource was found, but the client is not authorized to access that resource. Re-authenticating will not fix the issue.
404 Not Found	The request was valid, but the resource was not found. The resource may be found if the request is repeated later. To indicate that a resource will never be found, return `410 Gone`.
406 Not Acceptable	This is returned if the request has an `Accept` header that only lists media types that the web service does not support. For example, if the client requests JSON but the web service can only return XML.
429 Too Many Requests	The client has sent too many requests in a given amount of time. The client should reduce the rate due to this rate limiting. A `Retry-After` header may be included in this response to indicate how long a client should wait before making another request.
451 Unavailable for Legal Reasons	A website hosted in the USA might return this for requests coming from Europe to avoid having to comply with the **General Data Protection Regulation (GDPR)**. The number was chosen as a reference to the novel Fahrenheit 451, in which books are banned and burned.
500 Server Error	The request was valid, but something went wrong on the server side while processing the request. Retrying later might work.
503 Service Unavailable	The web service is busy and cannot handle the request. Trying again later might work.

Table 9.1: Common HTTP status code responses to the GET method

Caching requests example

Let's review a typical client-server interaction using caching and the `304 Not Modified` status, as shown in the following steps:

1. **Initial request:** The client requests a resource, `GET /index.html HTTP/1.1`, and the server returns a `200 OK` response with the resource and caching headers like `ETag` and `Last-Modified`, as shown in the following response:

```
HTTP/1.1 200 OK
Content-Type: text/html
```

```
ETag: "686897696a7c876b7e"
Last-Modified: Tue, 21 Oct 2024 07:28:00 GMT
Cache-Control: max-age=3600
```

The client stores the `ETag` and `Last-Modified` values along with the cached version of the resource. In subsequent requests, the client sends them back to the server to check whether the resource has been modified. The `ETag` value is typically a hash or a version number that uniquely identifies the resource at that particular state.

2. **Subsequent request:** The client makes another request for the same resource but includes conditional headers to check if the cached version is still valid, as shown in the following request:

```
GET /index.html HTTP/1.1
If-None-Match: "686897696a7c876b7e"
If-Modified-Since: Tue, 21 Oct 2024 07:28:00 GMT
```

`If-None-Match` contains the `ETag` from the previous response. `If-Modified-Since` contains the `Last-Modified` date from the previous response.

3. **304 Not Modified Response:** If the server determines that the resource has not changed, it returns a `304 Not Modified` status with relevant headers:

```
HTTP/1.1 304 Not Modified
Date: Wed, 23 Oct 2024 10:00:00 GMT
ETag: "686897696a7c876b7e"
Cache-Control: max-age=3600
```

HTTP's caching mechanism reduces bandwidth and speeds up web performance by avoiding the unnecessary transfer of unchanged resources. The headers in a 304 response provide information for managing the cache and ensuring that the client can continue to serve fresh content efficiently.

POST, PUT, and other requests and common responses

Other common types of HTTP requests include `POST`, `PUT`, `PATCH`, and `DELETE`, which create, modify, or delete resources.

To create a new resource, you might make a `POST` request with a body that contains the new resource, as shown in the following code:

```
POST /path/to/resource
Content-Length: 123
Content-Type: application/json
```

To create a new resource or update an existing resource, you might make a PUT request with a body that contains a whole new version of the existing resource, and if the resource does not exist, it is created, or if it does exist, it is replaced (sometimes called an **upsert** operation), as shown in the following code:

```
PUT /path/to/resource
Content-Length: 123
Content-Type: application/json
```

To update an existing resource more efficiently, you might make a PATCH request with a body that contains an object with only the properties that need changing, as shown in the following code:

```
PATCH /path/to/resource
Content-Length: 123
Content-Type: application/json
```

To delete an existing resource, you might make a DELETE request, as shown in the following code:

```
DELETE /path/to/resource
```

As well as the responses shown in the table above for a GET request, all the types of requests that create, modify, or delete a resource have additional possible common responses, as shown in *Table 9.2*:

Status code	Description
201 Created	The new resource was created successfully, the response header named Location contains its path, and the response body contains the newly created resource. Immediately GET-ting the resource should return 200.
202 Accepted	The new resource cannot be created immediately, so the request is queued for later processing, and immediately GET-ting the resource might return 404. The body can contain a resource that points to some form of status checker or an estimate of when the resource will become available.
204 No Content	This is commonly used in response to a DELETE request since returning the resource in the body after deleting it does not usually make sense! It's sometimes used in response to POST, PUT, or PATCH requests if the client does not need to confirm that the request was processed correctly.
405 Method Not Allowed	This is returned when the request used a method that is not supported. For example, a web service designed to be read-only may explicitly disallow PUT, DELETE, and so on.
415 Unsupported Media Type	This is returned when the resource in the request body uses a media type that the web service cannot handle. For example, if the body contains a resource in XML format, but the web service can only process JSON.

Table 9.2: Common HTTP status code responses to other methods like POST and PUT

Creating an ASP.NET Core Web API with controllers project

We will build a web service that provides a way to work with data in the Northwind database using ASP.NET Core so that the data can be used by any client application on any platform that can make HTTP requests and receive HTTP responses.

To do this, we will use the **ASP.NET Core Web API** / dotnet new webapi project template. This allows the creation of a sample weather web service implemented using either controllers like MVC or the newer Minimal APIs. Using controllers is still the most popular choice, although Microsoft has changed the default to Minimal APIs to encourage their use.

> **Warning!** With .NET 6 and .NET 7, the dotnet new webapi command creates a service implemented using controllers. To implement a service using Minimal APIs, you need to add the --use-minimal-apis switch to the command. Using .NET 8 and later, the dotnet new webapi command creates a service implemented using Minimal APIs. To implement the service using controllers, you need to add the --use-controllers switch.

> .NET 8 introduced the **ASP.NET Core Web API (native AOT)** / dotnet new webapiaot project template, which can only use Minimal API web services and supports native AOT publishing. AOT stands for Ahead-Of-Time compilation, which can further improve performance for specific use cases. I cover this in my books *C# 14 and .NET 10 – Modern Cross-Platform Development Fundamentals* and *Apps and Services with .NET 10*.

We will build on your experience with MVC by creating a Web API service using controllers. For simplicity, we will allow anonymous requests to the web service by selecting none for authentication.

Let's go:

1. Use your preferred code editor to open the MatureWeb solution.
2. Add a new project, as defined in the following list:

   - Project template: **ASP.NET Core Web API** / webapi --use-controllers
   - Solution file and folder: MatureWeb
   - Project file and folder: Northwind.WebApi

3. If you are using Visual Studio, then confirm the following defaults have been chosen:

   - **Framework: .NET 10.0 (Long Term Support)**
   - **Authentication type:** None
   - **Configure for HTTPS:** Selected
   - **Enable container support:** Cleared
   - **Enable OpenAPI support:** Selected
   - **Do not use top-level statements:** Cleared
   - **Use controllers:** Selected

> **Warning!** Make sure to select the **Use controllers** checkbox or your code will look very different because it will use Minimal API endpoints instead of Web API controllers!

4. If you are using VS Code or Rider, then in the `MatureWeb` directory, at the command prompt or terminal, enter the following commands:

```
dotnet new webapi --use-controllers -o Northwind.WebApi
dotnet sln add Northwind.WebApi
```

5. If you are using Visual Studio, set the `Northwind.WebApi` project to be your startup project.

6. In the `Northwind.WebApi.csproj` project file, delete the version attribute from the package reference, as shown in the following markup:

```
<Project Sdk="Microsoft.NET.Sdk.Web">

  <PropertyGroup>
    <TargetFramework>net10.0</TargetFramework>
    <Nullable>enable</Nullable>
    <ImplicitUsings>enable</ImplicitUsings>
  </PropertyGroup>

  <ItemGroup>
    <PackageReference Include="Microsoft.AspNetCore.OpenApi" />
  </ItemGroup>

</Project>
```

7. Build the `Northwind.WebApi` project.

Reviewing an ASP.NET Core Web API with controllers project

Now we can review the code in the project and note how it is different from an ASP.NET Core MVC project:

1. In the `Controllers` folder, open and review `WeatherForecastController.cs`, which was created by the project template, as shown in the following code:

```
using Microsoft.AspNetCore.Mvc;

namespace Northwind.WebApi.Controllers
{
  [ApiController]
  [Route("[controller]")]
```

```
public class WeatherForecastController : ControllerBase
{
  private static readonly string[] Summaries = new[]
  {
    "Freezing", "Bracing", "Chilly", "Cool", "Mild",
    "Warm", "Balmy", "Hot", "Sweltering", "Scorching"
  };

  [HttpGet(Name = "GetWeatherForecast")]
  public IEnumerable<WeatherForecast> Get()
  {
    return Enumerable.Range(1, 5).Select(index => new WeatherForecast
    {
      Date = DateOnly.FromDateTime(DateTime.Now.AddDays(index)),
      TemperatureC = Random.Shared.Next(-20, 55),
      Summary = Summaries[Random.Shared.Next(Summaries.Length)]
    })
    .ToArray();
  }
}
```

While reviewing the preceding code, note the following:

- The [ApiController] attribute was introduced with ASP.NET Core 2.1 and enables REST-specific behavior for controllers, like automatic HTTP 400 responses for invalid models, as you will see later in this chapter.

- The [Route] attribute registers the /weatherforecast relative URL for clients to use to make HTTP requests that will be handled by this controller. For example, an HTTP request for https://localhost:5001/weatherforecast/ would be handled by this controller. Some developers like to prefix the controller name with api/, which is a convention to differentiate between MVCs and Web APIs in mixed projects. If you use [controller] as shown, it uses the characters before Controller in the class name, in this case, WeatherForecast. You can also simply enter a different name without the square brackets, for example, [Route("api/forecast")].

> The Controller class registers a route using the [Route] attribute that starts with api/ and includes the name of the controller, that is, api/customers. The [controller] part is automatically replaced with the class name with the Controller suffix removed and with lowered casing. Therefore, the base address of the route to the CustomersController is api/customers. The constructor uses dependency injection to get the registered repository for working with customers.

> **Good practice:** Specifying a route using a literal string like this is poor practice. I am only doing so here to keep the example simple. It would be better in practice to define a static class with string constant values and use those instead. Then, you have a central place to change routes if needed in the future.

- The `Controller` class inherits from `ControllerBase`. This is simpler than the `Controller` class used in MVC because it does not have methods like `View` to generate HTML responses by passing a view model to a Razor file.
- The `[HttpGet]` attribute registers the `Get` method in the `Controller` class to respond to HTTP GET requests, and its implementation uses the shared `Random` object to return an array of `WeatherForecast` objects with random temperatures and summaries like `Bracing` or `Balmy` for the next five days of weather.

2. In `WeatherForecastController.cs`, declare a private field to store a logger, and set it in a constructor using dependency injection, as shown in the following code:

```
private readonly ILogger<WeatherForecastController> _logger;

public WeatherForecastController(ILogger<WeatherForecastController>
logger)
{
  _logger = logger;
}
```

> **Good practice:** This is a common pattern, and the old project template used to do it for you, but it means that to execute any action method within that controller, all DI services used in any of the action methods must be instantiated for every call. This would be a waste of time and resources if every action method did not need all the dependency services.

3. In `WeatherForecastController.cs`, add a second `Get` method that allows the call to specify how many days ahead the forecast should be by implementing the following:

   a. Add a comment above the original method to show the action method and URL path that it responds to.
   b. Add a new method with an integer parameter named `days`.
   c. Cut and paste the original `Get` method implementation code statements into the new `Get` method. We are cutting because we need to move the statements from the original method to the new method.
   d. Modify the new method to create an `IEnumerable` of integers up to the number of days requested.
   e. Modify the original `Get` method to call the new `Get` method and pass the value 5.
   f. Modify the registered name of the original `Get` method to `GetWeatherForecastFiveDays`.
   g. For both methods, log the action method called with any relevant parameter values.

Your modifications and additions should be as shown highlighted in the following code:

```
// GET /weatherforecast
[HttpGet(Name = "GetWeatherForecastFiveDays")]
public IEnumerable<WeatherForecast> Get()
{
  _logger.LogInformation("GetWeatherForecastFiveDays called.");
  return Get(days: 5); // Five-day forecast.
}

// GET /weatherforecast/7
[HttpGet(template: "{days:int}", Name = "GetWeatherForecast")]
public IEnumerable<WeatherForecast> Get(int days)
{
  _logger.LogInformation("GetWeatherForecast called with {days} days.",
days);

  return Enumerable.Range(1, days).Select(index => new WeatherForecast
    {
      Date = DateOnly.FromDateTime(DateTime.Now.AddDays(index)),
      TemperatureC = Random.Shared.Next(-20, 55),
      Summary = Summaries[Random.Shared.Next(Summaries.Length)]
    })
    .ToArray();
}
```

> In the [HttpGet] attribute, note the route template pattern {days:int} constrains the days parameter to int values.

Trying out the weather forecast web service's functionality

Now, we will try out the web service's functionality:

1. In the Properties folder, in launchSettings.json, set the https profile to launch the browser and navigate to the /weatherforecast relative URL path, as shown highlighted in the following markup:

```
"https": {
  "commandName": "Project",
  "dotnetRunMessages": true,
  "launchBrowser": true,
  "launchUrl": "weatherforecast",
```

```
  "applicationUrl": "https://localhost:7189;http://localhost:5249",
  "environmentVariables": {
    "ASPNETCORE_ENVIRONMENT": "Development"
  }
}
```

2. For the `http` profile, for its `applicationUrl`, change the random port number for HTTP to 5090, as shown highlighted in the following markup:

    ```
    "applicationUrl": "http://localhost:5090",
    ```

3. For the `https` profile, for its `applicationUrl`, change the random port number for HTTPS to 5091 and for HTTP to 5090, as shown highlighted in the following markup:

    ```
    "applicationUrl": "https://localhost:5091;http://localhost:5090",
    ```

4. Save changes to all modified files.

5. Start the `Northwind.WebApi` web service project using the `https` launch profile.

6. On Windows, if you see a **Windows Security Alert** dialog box saying **Windows Defender Firewall has blocked some features of this app**, then click the **Allow access** button.

7. Start Chrome, and navigate to `https://localhost:5091/`. Note that you will get a 404 status code response because we have not enabled static files and there is not an `index.html`, nor is there an MVC controller with a route configured. Remember that this project is not designed for a human to view and interact with, so this is expected behavior for a web service.

8. In Chrome, show **Developer Tools**.

9. Navigate to `https://localhost:5091/weatherforecast` and note that the Web API service should return a JSON document with five random weather forecast objects in an array, as shown in *Figure 9.1*:

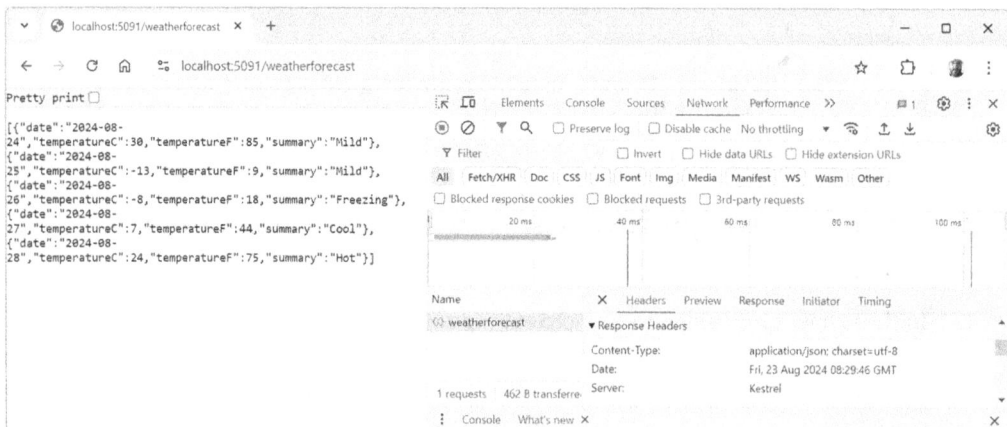

Figure 9.1: A request and response from a weather forecast web service

10. Recent versions of Chrome have a **Pretty print** checkbox, which formats data formats like JSON in a manner easier for humans to read. Try it out to see the effect.

> Your browser might request a `favicon.ico` file to show in the browser tab. If the
> `404` errors when this file is missing annoy you, then you could create one, but we
> are only using the browser for basic web service testing at this time.

11. Close **Developer Tools**.

12. Navigate to `https://localhost:5091/weatherforecast/14` and note that the response when requesting a two-week weather forecast contains 14 forecasts.

13. Note the requests are logged to the console, as shown in the following output:

```
info: Northwind.WebApi.Controllers.WeatherForecastController[0]
      GetWeatherForecastFiveDays called.
info: Northwind.WebApi.Controllers.WeatherForecastController[0]
      GetWeatherForecast called with 5 days.
info: Northwind.WebApi.Controllers.WeatherForecastController[0]
      GetWeatherForecast called with 14 days.
```

14. Close Chrome and shut down the web server.

Setting the new Description property in .NET 10

With .NET 10 and later, `ProducesAttribute`, `ProducesResponseTypeAttribute`, and `ProducesDefaultResponseType` now accept an optional `string` parameter, `Description`, that will set the description of the response in the generated OpenAPI document, as shown in the following code:

```
[HttpGet(Name = "GetWeatherForecast")]
[ProducesResponseType<IEnumerable<WeatherForecast>>(StatusCodes.Status200OK,
  Description = "The weather forecast for the next 5 days.")]
public IEnumerable<WeatherForecast> Get()
{
  ...
}
```

The preceding code would generate an OpenAPI response with the given description, as shown in the following JSON:

```
"responses": {
  "200": {
    "description": "The weather forecast for the next 5 days.",
    "content": { ... }
  }
}
```

> You will learn how to read the generated JSON documentation for a web service later in this chapter, in the section titled *Documenting and trying out web services*.

Minimal API web service and native AOT compilation

.NET 8 introduced the **ASP.NET Core Web API (native AOT)** / `dotnet new webapiaot` project template, which only uses Minimal API and supports native AOT publishing. More components of .NET will support AOT over time, as you can read in the following quote from `https://github.com/dotnet/aspnetcore/issues/51834#issuecomment-1913300365`:

> *"We expect to make progress investigating Native AOT support for MVC & Blazor in the .NET 9 timeframe, but we don't expect to deliver production ready Native AOT support for .NET 9 given the large amount of work involved." – Dan Roth*

A non-benefit of Minimal API

It is often said that a major benefit of Minimal API over a controller-based Web API is that each Minimal API endpoint only needs to instantiate the **dependency injection** (**DI**) services that it needs.

With controllers, to execute any action method within that controller, all DI services used in any of the action methods must be instantiated for every call. This is a waste of time and resources.

But this is only true if the controller follows the common pattern of getting dependency services in the constructor of the class and storing them in private fields, as shown in the following code:

```
// Base address: api/customers
[Route("api/[controller]")]
[ApiController]
public class CustomersController : ControllerBase
{
  private readonly ICustomerRepository _repo;
  private readonly ILogger<CustomersController> _logger;

  // Constructor injects repository registered in Program.cs.
  public CustomersController(ICustomerRepository repo,
    ILogger<CustomersController> logger)
  {
    _repo = repo;
    _logger = logger;
  }
}
```

```
  // GET: api/customers
  // GET: api/customers/?country=[country]
  // this will always return a list of customers (but it might be empty)
  [HttpGet]
  [ProducesResponseType(200, Type = typeof(IEnumerable<Customer>))]
  public async Task<IEnumerable<Customer>> GetCustomers(string? country)
  {
    if (string.IsNullOrWhiteSpace(country))
    {
      _logger.LogInformation("GetCustomers called for all countries.");
      return await _repo.RetrieveAllAsync();
    }
    else
    {
      _logger.LogInformation("GetCustomers called with country={country}",
country);
      return (await _repo.RetrieveAllAsync())
        .Where(customer => customer.Country == country);
    }
  }
  ... }
```

One of the reasons that the above pattern is common and assumed to be the only or best way to do dependency injection is that it is used by the ASP.NET Core Web API project template to define a logger, and many developers then follow that convention for their own dependency services.

A more flexible and efficient good practice is to use method injection, as shown in the following code:

```
// Base address: api/customers
[Route("api/[controller]")]
[ApiController]
public class CustomersController : ControllerBase
{
  // GET: api/customers
  // GET: api/customers/?country=[country]
  // this will always return a list of customers (but it might be empty)
  [HttpGet]
  [ProducesResponseType(200, Type = typeof(IEnumerable<Customer>))]
  public async Task<IEnumerable<Customer>> GetCustomers(string? country,
    ICustomerRepository _repo,
    ILogger<CustomersController> _logger)
  {
    if (string.IsNullOrWhiteSpace(country))
```

```
    {
      _logger.LogInformation("GetCustomers called for all countries.");
      return await _repo.RetrieveAllAsync();
    }
    else
    {
      _logger.LogInformation("GetCustomers called with country={country}",
  country);
      return (await _repo.RetrieveAllAsync())
        .Where(customer => customer.Country == country);
    }
  }
  ...
}
```

You can decorate the parameters with [FromServices] to explicitly indicate where those parameters will be set from, as shown in the following code: [FromServices] ICustomerRepository _repo, but this is optional.

Minimal API still has other benefits over a controller-based Web API, but dependency injection efficiency is not one of them!

Now that you've seen a simple example of a controller-based Web API service, let's build our own more real-world web service that exposes data from a typical database.

Creating a web service for the Northwind database

Unlike MVC controllers, Web API controllers do not call Razor Views to return HTML responses for website visitors to see in browsers. Instead, they use **content negotiation** with the client application that made the HTTP request to return data in formats such as XML, JSON, or X-WWW-FORM-URLENCODED in their HTTP response.

X-WWW-FORM-URLENCODED format looks like the following example:

```
firstName=Mark&lastName=Price&jobtitle=Author
```

The client application must then deserialize the data from the negotiated format. The most used format for modern web services is **JSON** because it is compact and works natively with JavaScript in a browser when building **Single-Page Applications** (**SPAs**) with client-side technologies like Angular, React, and Vue.

> One of the limitations of Minimal API compared to a controller-based Web API is that Minimal API does not support content negotiation with the client, so clients must understand JSON, or you must implement content negotiation yourself.

Integrating the Northwind entity model and enabling XML responses

We will reference the Entity Framework Core entity data model for the Northwind database that you created in *Chapter 1, Introducing Real-World Web Development Using .NET*:

1. In the `Northwind.WebApi.csproj` project file, add a project reference to the Northwind database context class library, and globally and statically import the `System.Console` class, as shown in the following markup:

    ```
    <ItemGroup Label="To use the Northwind entity models." >
      <ProjectReference Include=
        "..\Northwind.DataContext\Northwind.DataContext.csproj" />
    </ItemGroup>

    <ItemGroup Label="To simplify use of WriteLine.">
      <Using Include="System.Console" Static="true" />
    </ItemGroup>
    ```

2. Build the `Northwind.WebApi` project and fix any compile errors in your code.

3. In `Program.cs`, import namespaces for working with web media formatters and the Northwind entity model classes and extension methods, as shown in the following code:

    ```
    using Microsoft.AspNetCore.Mvc.Formatters; // To use IOutputFormatter.
    using Northwind.EntityModels; // To use AddNorthwindContext method.
    ```

4. In `Program.cs`, add a statement before the call to `AddControllers` to register the `Northwind` database context class, as shown in the following code:

    ```
    builder.Services.AddNorthwindContext();
    ```

5. In the call to `AddControllers`, add a lambda block with statements to write the names and supported media types of the default output formatters to the console, and then add XML serializer formatters, as shown highlighted in the following code:

    ```
    builder.Services.AddControllers(options =>
    {
      WriteLine("Default output formatters:");

      foreach (IOutputFormatter formatter in options.OutputFormatters)
      {
        OutputFormatter? mediaFormatter = formatter as OutputFormatter;

        if (mediaFormatter is null)
        {
          WriteLine($" {formatter.GetType().Name}");
    ```

```
    }
    else // OutputFormatter class has SupportedMediaTypes.
    {
      WriteLine("  {0}, Media types: {1}",
        arg0: mediaFormatter.GetType().Name,
        arg1: string.Join(", ",
        mediaFormatter.SupportedMediaTypes));
    }
  }
})
.AddXmlDataContractSerializerFormatters()
.AddXmlSerializerFormatters();
```

6. Start the `Northwind.WebApi` web service project using the `https` launch profile.

7. In the command prompt or terminal, note that there are four default output formatters, in-cluding ones that convert `null` values into `204 No Content` and ones to support responses that are plain text, byte streams, and JSON, as shown in the following output:

```
Default output formatters:
  HttpNoContentOutputFormatter
  StringOutputFormatter, Media types: text/plain
  StreamOutputFormatter
  SystemTextJsonOutputFormatter, Media types: application/json, text/
json, application/*+json
```

8. Close the browser (if necessary) and shut down the web server.

There are other output formatters that can be used in ASP.NET Core Web API services, and you can build your own custom ones. For example, CSV is a simple, lightweight format mainly used for tabular data export in APIs. It's human-readable but not suitable for complex or nested data structures, and is usually implemented via custom output formatters in ASP.NET Core.

Controlling XML serialization

In `Program.cs`, we added the `XmlSerializer` so that our Web API service can return XML as well as JSON if the client requests that.

However, the `XmlSerializer` cannot serialize interfaces, and our entity classes use `ICollection<T>` to define related child entities. This causes a warning at runtime, for example, for the `Customer` class and its `Orders` property, as shown in the following output:

```
warn: Microsoft.AspNetCore.Mvc.Formatters.XmlSerializerOutputFormatter[1]
An error occurred while trying to create an XmlSerializer for the type
'Northwind.EntityModels.Customer'.
System.InvalidOperationException: There was an error reflecting type
'Northwind.EntityModels.Customer'.
```

```
---> System.InvalidOperationException: Cannot serialize member 'Northwind.
EntityModels.Customer.Orders' of type 'System.Collections.Generic.
ICollection`1[[Northwind.EntityModels.Order, Northwind.EntityModels,
Version=1.0.0.0, Culture=neutral, PublicKeyToken=null]]', see inner exception
for more details.
```

We can prevent this warning by excluding the Orders property when serializing a Customer into XML:

1. In the Northwind.EntityModels project, in Customer.cs, import the namespace so that we can use the [XmlIgnore] attribute, as shown in the following code:

    ```
    using System.Xml.Serialization; // To use [XmlIgnore].
    ```

2. Decorate the Orders property with an attribute to ignore it when serializing, as shown highlighted in the following code:

    ```
    [InverseProperty(nameof(Order.Customer))]
    [XmlIgnore]
    public virtual ICollection<Order> Orders { get; set; } = new
    List<Order>();
    ```

3. Decorate the CustomerTypes property with [XmlIgnore] too, as shown highlighted in the following code:

    ```
    [ForeignKey("CustomerId")]
    [InverseProperty("Customers")]
    [XmlIgnore]
    public virtual ICollection<CustomerDemographic> CustomerTypes
      { get; set; } = new List<CustomerDemographic>();
    ```

> We use the [XmlIgnore] attribute because we are using XmlSerializerOutputFormatter. If you use alternatives like XmlDataContractSerializerOutputFormatter, then they will have different attributes like [DataContract] and [DataMember] to define the structure of the XML.

You will confirm that the web service can return XML as well as JSON later in this chapter.

For now, we will continue adding functionality to the service to access the Northwind database.

Routing web service requests to action methods

With MVC controllers, a route like /home/index tells us the controller class name and the action method name, for example, the HomeController class and the Index action method.

With Web API controllers, a route like /weatherforecast only tells us the controller class name, for example, WeatherForecastController. To determine the action method name to execute, we must map HTTP methods like GET and POST to methods in the controller class.

You should decorate controller methods with the following attributes to indicate the HTTP method that they will respond to:

- [HttpGet] and [HttpHead]: These action methods respond to GET or HEAD requests to retrieve a resource and return either the resource and its response headers or just the response headers.
- [HttpPost]: This action method responds to POST requests to create a new resource or perform some other action defined by the service.
- [HttpPut] and [HttpPatch]: These action methods respond to PUT or PATCH requests to update an existing resource either by replacing it or updating a subset of its properties.
- [HttpDelete]: This action method responds to DELETE requests to remove a resource.
- [HttpOptions]: This action method responds to OPTIONS requests.

As well as routing a web service request to a method within a controller, you can further control routing with constraints.

Route constraints

Route constraints allow us to control matches based on data types and other validation rules like numeric ranges and pattern matching. Route constraints are added in the attribute route like this:

```
[HttpGet("resource/{param:constraint}")]
```

In the preceding example, constraint is something like int, range(1,100), minlength(3), and so on.

Common route constraints are summarized in *Table 9.3*:

Constraint	Example	Parameter
required	{id:required}	Must be provided
int and long	{id:int}	Must be any integer of the correct size
decimal, double, and float	{unitprice:decimal}	Must be any real number of the correct size
bool	{discontinued:bool}	Must be a case-insensitive match on true or false
datetime	{hired:datetime}	Must be an invariant culture date/time
guid	{id:guid}	Must be a GUID value
minlength(n), maxlength(n), length(n), and length(n, m)	{title:minlength(5)}, {title:length(5, 25)}	Must have the defined minimum and/or maximum length
min(n), max(n), and range(n, m)	{age:range(18, 65)}	Must be within the defined minimum and/or maximum range
alpha, regex	{firstname:alpha}, {id:regex(^[A-Z] {{5}}$)}	Must match one or more alphabetic characters or the regular expression

Table 9.3: Route constraints with examples and descriptions

Use colons to separate multiple constraints, as shown in the following example:

```
[Route("employees/{years:int:minlength(3)}")]
public Employees[] GetLoyalEmployees(int years)
```

For regular expressions, `RegexOptions.IgnoreCase` | `RegexOptions.Compiled` | `RegexOptions.CultureInvariant` is added automatically. Regular expression tokens must be escaped (replace \ with \\, { with {{, and } with }}) or use verbatim string literals.

> **Warning!** If a route doesn't match the constraint, ASP.NET Core will return a `404`, not a `400`. This is by design because route matching happens before model binding or validation.

> You can create custom route constraints by defining a class that implements `IRouteConstraint`. This is beyond the scope of this book, but you can read about it at the following link: `https://learn.microsoft.com/en-us/aspnet/core/fundamentals/routing#custom-route-constraints`.

Understanding action method return types

An action method can return .NET types like a single `string` value; complex objects defined by a `class`, `record`, or `struct`; or collections of complex objects. ASP.NET Core will serialize them into the requested data format set in the HTTP request `Accept` header, for example, JSON, if a suitable serializer has been registered.

For more control over the response, there are helper methods that return an `ActionResult` wrapper around the .NET type.

For more flexibility, you can declare the action method's return type to be `IActionResult` if it could return different return types based on the input or other variables.

You can also declare the action method's return type to be `ActionResult<T>` if it will only return a single type, but with different status codes.

> **Good practice:** Decorate action methods with the `[ProducesResponseType]` attribute to indicate all the known types and HTTP status codes that the client should expect in a response. This information can then be publicly exposed to document how a client should interact with your web service. Think of it as part of your formal documentation. Later in this chapter, you will learn how you can install a code analyzer to give you warnings when you do not decorate your action methods like this.

For example, an action method that gets a product based on an `id` parameter will be decorated with three attributes – one to indicate that it responds to `GET` requests and has an `id` parameter and two to indicate what happens when it succeeds and when the client has supplied an invalid product ID, as shown in the following code:

```
[HttpGet("{id}")]
[ProducesResponseType(200, Type = typeof(Product))]
[ProducesResponseType(404)]
public IActionResult Get(string id)
```

The `ControllerBase` class has methods to make it easy to return different responses, as shown in *Table 9.4*:

Method	Description
Ok	This returns a 200 status code and a resource converted into the client's preferred format, like JSON or XML. It's commonly used in response to a GET request.
CreatedAtRoute	This returns a 201 status code and the path to the new resource. It's commonly used in response to a POST request to create a resource that can be performed quickly.
Accepted	This returns a 202 status code to indicate the request is being processed but has not been completed. It's commonly used in response to a POST, PUT, PATCH, or DELETE request that triggers a background process that takes a long time to complete.
NoContentResult	This returns a 204 status code and an empty response body. It's commonly used in response to a PUT, PATCH, or DELETE request when the response does not need to contain the affected resource.
BadRequest	This returns a 400 status code and an optional message string with more details.
NotFound	This returns a 404 status code and automatically populates the ProblemDetails body (and requires a compatibility version of 2.2 or later).

Table 9.4: ControllerBase helper methods that return a response

Configuring the customer repository and Web API controller

Now that you've learned enough theory, you will put it into practice to configure the Northwind repository that you created in *Chapter 6, Performance and Scalability Optimization Using Caching*, so that it can be called from within a Web API controller.

You will register a scoped dependency service implementation for the repository when the web service starts up, and then use constructor parameter injection to get it in a new Web API controller for working with customers.

It will have five action methods to perform CRUD operations on customers. Two GET methods (for all customers or one customer), and then POST (create), PUT (update), and DELETE:

1. In the Northwind.WebApi.csproj project file, add a package reference for hybrid caching, and add a reference to the Northwind repositories project, as shown highlighted in the following markup:

```
<ItemGroup>
  <PackageReference Include="Microsoft.AspNetCore.OpenApi" />
  <PackageReference Include="Microsoft.Extensions.Caching.Hybrid" />
</ItemGroup>

<ItemGroup Label="To use the Northwind entity models.">
  <ProjectReference Include=
  "..\Northwind.DataContext\Northwind.DataContext.csproj" />
  <ProjectReference Include=
    "..\Northwind.Repositories\Northwind.Repositories.csproj" />
</ItemGroup>
```

2. Build the Northwind.WebApi project to build dependencies and restore packages.

3. In Program.cs, import the namespaces for working with a hybrid cache and for working with our customer repository, as shown in the following code:

```
using Microsoft.Extensions.Caching.Hybrid; // To use
HybridCacheEntryOptions.
using Northwind.Repositories; // To use ICustomerRepository.
```

4. In Program.cs, before the call to builder.Build, in the section for configuring services, register the hybrid cache service with a default cache entry duration of 60 seconds overall, and 30 seconds for local in-memory caching. This is shown in the following code:

```
builder.Services.AddHybridCache(options =>
{
  options.DefaultEntryOptions = new HybridCacheEntryOptions
  {
    Expiration = TimeSpan.FromSeconds(60),
    LocalCacheExpiration = TimeSpan.FromSeconds(30)
  };
});
```

> **Good practice:** It would be better to create an extension method for WebApplicationBuilder to keep the Program.cs as uncluttered as possible, as we did in the Northwind.Mvc project, but I will leave that as an optional exercise for the reader.

5. In `Program.cs`, before the call to the `builder.Build` method, in the section for configuring services, add a statement that will register the `CustomerRepository` for use at runtime as a scoped dependency, as shown in the following code:

    ```
    builder.Services.AddScoped<ICustomerRepository, CustomerRepository>();
    ```

    > **Good practice:** Our repository uses a database context that is registered as a scoped dependency. You can only use scoped dependencies inside other scoped dependencies, so we cannot register the repository as a singleton. You can read more about this at the following link: `https://learn.microsoft.com/en-us/dotnet/core/extensions/dependency-injection#scoped`.

6. In the `Controllers` folder, add a new class named `CustomersController.cs`. If you are using Visual Studio, then you can choose the **API Controller - Empty** project item template.

7. In `CustomersController.cs`, add statements to define a Web API controller class to work with customers, as shown in the following code:

    ```
    // To use [Route], [ApiController], ControllerBase and so on.
    using Microsoft.AspNetCore.Mvc;
    using Northwind.EntityModels; // To use Customer.
    using Northwind.Repositories; // To use ICustomerRepository.

    namespace Northwind.WebApi.Controllers;

    // Base address: api/customers
    [Route("api/[controller]")]
    [ApiController]
    public class CustomersController : ControllerBase
    {
      private readonly ICustomerRepository _repo;

      // Constructor injects repository registered in Program.cs.
      public CustomersController(ICustomerRepository repo)
      {
        _repo = repo;
      }
    }
    ```

8. In `CustomersController.cs`, add statements to define an action method that responds to HTTP `GET` requests for all customers, as shown in the following code:

    ```
    // GET: api/customers
    // GET: api/customers/?country=[country]
    // this will always return a list of customers (but it might be empty)
    ```

```
[HttpGet]
[ProducesResponseType(200, Type = typeof(IEnumerable<Customer>))]
public async Task<IEnumerable<Customer>> GetCustomers(string? country)
{
  if (string.IsNullOrWhiteSpace(country))
  {
    return await _repo.RetrieveAllAsync();
  }
  else
  {
    return (await _repo.RetrieveAllAsync())
      .Where(customer => customer.Country == country);
  }
}
```

> The GetCustomers method can have a string parameter passed with a country name. If it is missing, all customers are returned. If it is present, it is used to filter customers by country.

9. In CustomersController.cs, add statements to define an action method that responds to HTTP GET requests for an individual customer, as shown in the following code:

```
// GET: api/customers/[id]
[HttpGet("{id}", Name = nameof(GetCustomer))] // Named route.
[ProducesResponseType(200, Type = typeof(Customer))]
[ProducesResponseType(404)]
public async Task<IActionResult> GetCustomer(string id)
{
  Customer? c = await _repo.RetrieveAsync(id, default);

  if (c == null)
  {
    return NotFound(); // 404 Resource not found.
  }

  return Ok(c); // 200 OK with customer in body.
}
```

> The GetCustomer method has a route explicitly named GetCustomer so that it can be used to generate a URL after inserting a new customer.

10. In `CustomersController.cs`, add statements to define an action method that responds to HTTP POST requests to insert a new customer entity, as shown in the following code:

```
// POST: api/customers
// BODY: Customer (JSON, XML)
[HttpPost]
[ProducesResponseType(201, Type = typeof(Customer))]
[ProducesResponseType(400)]
public async Task<IActionResult> Create([FromBody] Customer c)
{
  if (c == null)
  {
    return BadRequest(); // 400 Bad request.
  }

  Customer? addedCustomer = await _repo.CreateAsync(c);

  if (addedCustomer == null)
  {
    return BadRequest("Repository failed to create customer.");
  }
  else
  {
    return CreatedAtRoute( // 201 Created.
      routeName: nameof(GetCustomer),
      routeValues: new { id = addedCustomer.CustomerId.ToLower() },
      value: addedCustomer);
  }
}
```

11. In `CustomersController.cs`, add statements to define an action method that responds to HTTP PUT requests, as shown in the following code:

```
// PUT: api/customers/[id]
// BODY: Customer (JSON, XML)
[HttpPut("{id}")]
[ProducesResponseType(204)]
[ProducesResponseType(400)]
[ProducesResponseType(404)]
public async Task<IActionResult> Update(
  string id, [FromBody] Customer c)
{
  id = id.ToUpper();
  c.CustomerId = c.CustomerId.ToUpper();
```

```
    if (c == null || c.CustomerId != id)
    {
      return BadRequest(); // 400 Bad request.
    }

    Customer? existing = await _repo.RetrieveAsync(id, default);
    if (existing == null)
    {
      return NotFound(); // 404 Resource not found.
    }

    await _repo.UpdateAsync(c);

    return new NoContentResult(); // 204 No content.
  }
```

Note the following:

- The Create and Update methods both decorate the customer parameter with [FromBody] to tell the model binder to populate it with values from the body of the POST request.

- The Create method returns a response that uses the GetCustomer route so that the client knows how to get the newly created resource in the future. We are matching up two methods to create and then get a customer.

- In the past, the Create and Update methods would need to check the model state of the customer passed in the body of the HTTP request. If it is invalid, they should return a 400 Bad Request containing details of the model validation errors. This happens automatically now because the controller is decorated with [ApiController].

12. In CustomersController.cs, add statements to define an action method that responds to HTTP DELETE requests, as shown in the following code:

```
// DELETE: api/customers/[id]
[HttpDelete("{id}")]
[ProducesResponseType(204)]
[ProducesResponseType(400)]
[ProducesResponseType(404)]
public async Task<IActionResult> Delete(string id)
{
  Customer? existing = await _repo.RetrieveAsync(id, default);

  if (existing == null)
  {
    return NotFound(); // 404 Resource not found.
  }
```

```
  bool? deleted = await _repo.DeleteAsync(id);

  if (deleted.HasValue && deleted.Value) // Short circuit AND.
  {
    return new NoContentResult(); // 204 No content.
  }
  else
  {
    return BadRequest( // 400 Bad request.
      $"Customer {id} was found but failed to delete.");
  }
}
```

13. Save all the changes.

When an HTTP request is received by the service, it will create an instance of the Controller class, call the appropriate action method, return the response in the format preferred by the client, and release the resources used by the controller, including the repository and its database context.

Specifying problem details

A feature added in ASP.NET Core 2.1 and later is an implementation of a web standard for specifying problem details. In Web API controllers decorated with [ApiController] in a project where compatibility with ASP.NET Core 2.2 or later is enabled, action methods that return IActionResult and return a client error status code, that is, 4xx, will automatically include a serialized instance of the ProblemDetails class in the response body.

If you want to take control, then you can create a ProblemDetails instance yourself and include additional information.

Let's simulate a bad request that needs custom data returned to the client. At the top of the implementation of the Delete action method, add statements to check if the id matches the literal string value "bad", and if so, then return a custom ProblemDetails object, as shown in the following code:

```
// Take control of problem details.
if (id == "bad")
{
  ProblemDetails problemDetails = new()
  {
    Status = StatusCodes.Status400BadRequest,
    Type = "https://localhost:5091/customers/failed-to-delete",
    Title = $"Customer ID {id} found but failed to delete.",
    Detail = "More details like Company Name, Country and so on.",
    Instance = HttpContext.Request.Path
```

```
    };
    return BadRequest(problemDetails); // 400 Bad Request
}
```

You will document and try out this functionality in the next section.

Documenting and trying out web services

You can easily try out a web service by making HTTP GET requests using a browser. To try out other HTTP methods, we need a more advanced tool. But let's start by trying out GET requests using a browser.

Making GET requests using a browser

You will use Chrome to try out the three implementations of a GET request – for all customers, for customers in a specified country, and for a single customer using their unique customer ID:

1. In Northwind.WebApi, in the Properties folder, in launchSettings.json, for the https profile, change the launchUrl to request all customers, as shown highlighted in the following markup:

    ```
    "launchUrl": "api/customers",
    ```

2. Make sure that the Docker container hosting SQL Server and the Northwind database is running.

3. Start the Northwind.WebApi web service project using the https launch profile.

4. Start Chrome, navigate to https://localhost:5091/api/customers, and note the JSON document returned, containing all 91 customers in the Northwind database (unsorted), as shown in *Figure 9.2*:

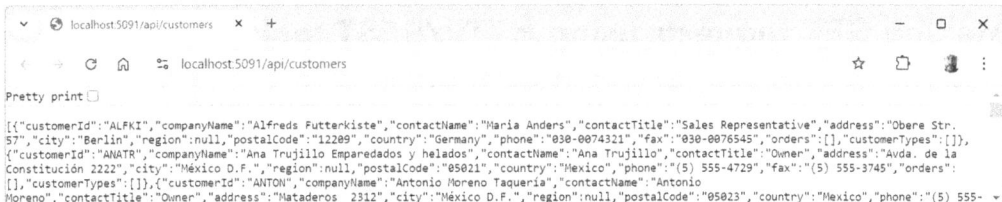

Figure 9.2: Customers from the Northwind database as a JSON document

5. Navigate to https://localhost:5091/api/customers?country=Germany and note the JSON document returned, containing only the customers in Germany.

> If you get an empty array returned, then make sure you have entered the country name using the correct casing, because the database query is case-sensitive. For example, compare the results of uk and UK. On a real-world website where visitors choose a country, you would provide a user interface that restricts their choice to the about 200 well-known countries to ensure country case correctness. To allow you to re-enter a country with its correct casing, in Chrome, navigate to **History** (or press *Ctrl + H*), find the wrong-cased entry, click its ... menu on the right, and then select **Remove from history**.

6. Navigate to `https://localhost:5091/api/customers/alfki` and note the JSON document returned containing only the customer named **Alfreds Futterkiste**.

Unlike country names, we do not need to worry about casing for the customer `id` value because, in the customer repository implementation, we normalized the `string` value as uppercase.

Trying out complex scenarios gets trickier with a browser. How can we try out the other HTTP methods, such as `POST`, `PUT`, and `DELETE`? And how can we document our web service so it's easy for anyone to understand how to interact with it?

> There are many tools for trying out Web APIs, for example, **Postman**. Although Postman is popular, I prefer tools like **HTTP Editor** in Visual Studio or **REST Client** in VS Code because they do not hide what is happening. I feel Postman is too GUI-y. But I encourage you to explore different tools and find the ones that fit your style. You can learn more about Postman at the following link: `https://www.postman.com/`. Postman is also available as an extension in VS Code: `https://marketplace.visualstudio.com/items?itemName=Postman.postman-for-vscode`.

To solve the first problem, we can use the **HTTP Editor** tool built into Visual Studio and install a VS Code extension named **REST Client**. Rider has its own equivalent. These are tools that allow you to send any type of HTTP request and view the response in your code editor.

To solve the second problem, the Web API project template uses **OpenAPI**, the world's most popular technology for documenting and trying out HTTP APIs.

But first, let's see what is possible with the code editor HTTP/REST tools.

Making GET requests using HTTP/REST tools

We will start by creating a file for trying out `GET` requests:

1. If you have not already installed REST Client by Huachao Mao (`humao.rest-client`), then install it in VS Code now.
2. In your preferred code editor, open the `MatureWeb` solution and then start the `Northwind.WebApi` project web service.
3. In **File Explorer**, **Finder**, or your favorite Linux file tool, in the `MatureWeb` folder, create a `HttpRequests` folder.
4. In the `HttpRequests` folder, create a file named `get-customers.http`, and open it in your preferred code editor, like Visual Studio or VS Code. They should recognize the file extension and provide a suitable editing experience.
5. In `get-customers.http`, modify its contents to contain an HTTP `GET` request to retrieve all customers, as shown in the following code:

```
### Configure a variable for the web service base address.
@base_address = https://localhost:5091/api/customers/

### Make a GET request to the base address.
GET {{base_address}}
```

6. Above the HTTP GET request, click **Send request**, and note that the response is shown in a new tabbed window, as shown in *Figure 9.3*:

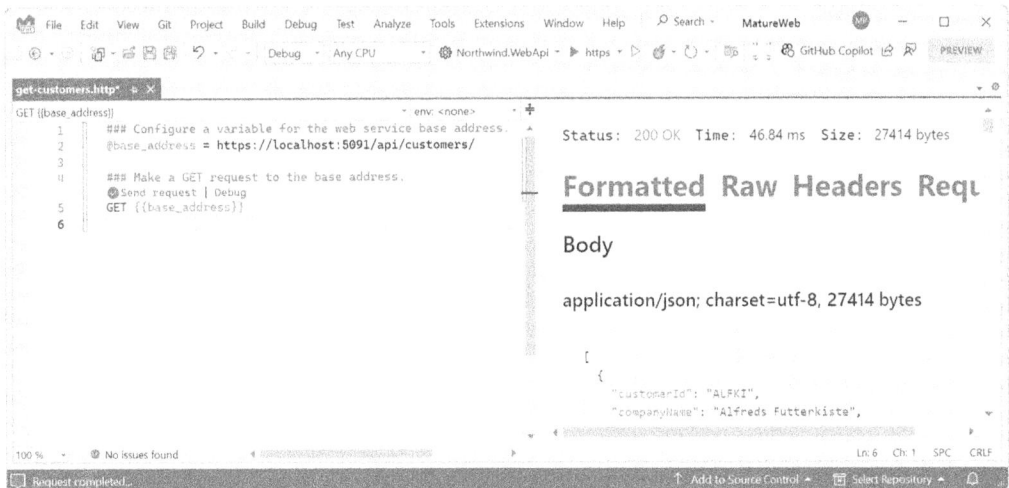

Figure 9.3: Sending an HTTP GET request using Visual Studio

> HTTP Editor in Visual Studio is designed to add REST Client-like capabilities, and its user interface is likely to evolve rapidly as it catches up. You can read its official documentation at the following link: `https://learn.microsoft.com/en-us/aspnet/core/test/http-files`.

7. In `get-customers.http`, add more GET requests, each separated by three hash symbols, to get customers in various countries and get a single customer using their ID, as shown in the following code:

```
### Get customers in Germany
GET {{base_address}}?country=Germany

### Get customers in USA in XML format
GET {{base_address}}?country=USA
Accept: application/xml

### Get Alfreds Futterkiste
GET {{base_address}}ALFKI

### Get a non-existent customer
GET {{base_address}}abcxy
```

> **Warning!** If a `.http` file contains multiple HTTP requests, if you do not separate the HTTP requests with ### comments, then they will not be recognized correctly.

8. Click the **Send Request** link above each request to send it; for example, the GET request that has a request header to request customers in the USA as XML instead of JSON using the VS Code extension REST Client, as shown in *Figure 9.4*:

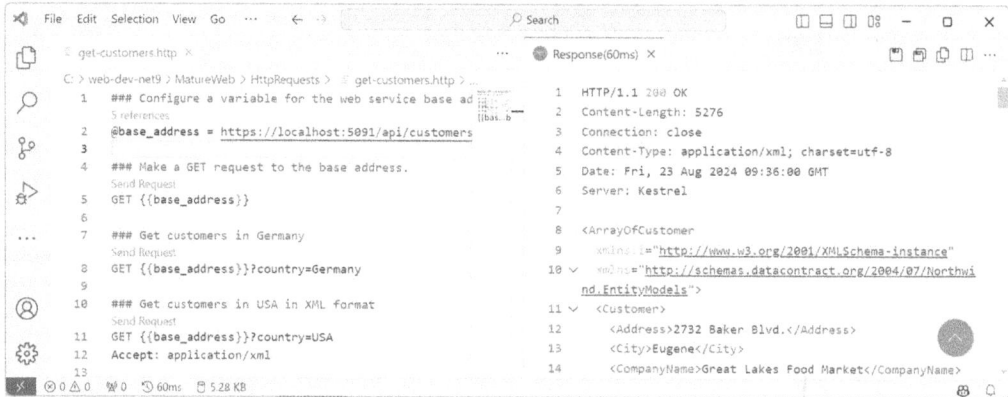

Figure 9.4: Sending a request for XML and getting a response using VS Code REST Client

Making other requests using HTTP/REST tools

Next, we will create a file for making other requests, like POST:

1. In the HttpRequests folder, create a file named create-customer.http and modify its contents to define a POST request to create a new customer, as shown in the following code:

```
### Configure a variable for the web service base address.
@base_address = https://localhost:5091/api/customers/

### Make a POST request to the base address.
POST {{base_address}}
Content-Type: application/json

{
  "customerID": "ABCXY",
  "companyName": "ABC Corp",
  "contactName": "John Smith",
  "contactTitle": "Sir",
  "address": "Main Street",
  "city": "New York",
  "region": "NY",
  "postalCode": "90210",
  "country":  "USA",
  "phone": "(123) 555-1234"
}
```

> **Warning!** If you have already sent this request, then you will get an exception on subsequent requests: `UNIQUE constraint failed: Customers.CustomerId`. This error means you are trying to insert a new customer with a `CustomerId` value that is already in use by an existing customer. To avoid this exception, change the `ABCXY` to a value that does not already exist in the table. Or delete the existing customer with the `CustomerId` of `ABCXY`.

2. Send the request and note the response is `201 Created`. Also, note that in the **Headers** section and the **Location** entry (that is, the URL) of the newly created customer is `https://localhost:5091/api/Customers/abcxy`, as shown in *Figure 9.5*:

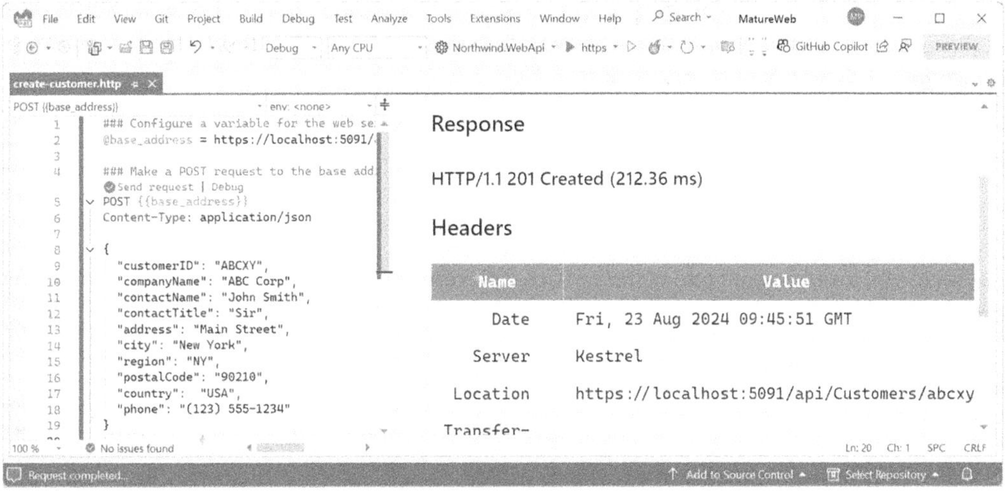

Figure 9.5: Adding a new customer by POSTing to the Web API service

I will leave you an optional challenge to create `.http` files that update a customer (using `PUT`) and delete a customer (using `DELETE`). Try them on customers that do exist (that you created) as well as customers that do not. Solutions are in the GitHub repository for this book at the following link: `https://github.com/markjprice/web-dev-net10/tree/main/code/MatureWeb/HttpRequests`.

> **Warning!** In this section, you implemented a data repository service that can create, update, and delete customers. This works if you create a new customer, then update that customer, and then delete that customer, because that customer does not have any related data. But if you run the project and attempt to delete a customer that has related orders (for example, any of the customers that are in the original database), then an exception is thrown because of a referential integrity constraint defined by a foreign key in the table. Do not try to delete a customer that has related orders. You could implement cascading deletes (either in the database or programmatically) that delete related orders before deleting a customer (but you would also need to delete all the related order details rows too). To simplify the example, we just throw an exception and fail to delete the customer.

Passing environment variables

To get an environment variable, use $processenv, as shown in the following command:

```
{{$processEnv [%]envVarName}}
```

For example, if you have set an environment variable to store a secret value like a password to connect to a SQL Server database that must be kept out of any files committed to a GitHub repository, you can use the following command:

```
{{$processEnv MY_SQL_PWD}}
```

> You can learn more about using environment variables with REST Client at `https://marketplace.visualstudio.com/items?itemName=humao.rest-client#environments`.
>
> You can learn more about using environment variables and Secret Manager with HTTP Editor at `https://devblogs.microsoft.com/visualstudio/safely-use-secrets-in-http-requests-in-visual-studio-2022/`.

A related tool for trying out and working with web services is Visual Studio's Endpoints Explorer. Let's briefly review its capabilities.

Visual Studio Endpoints Explorer

A useful tool in Visual Studio is the Endpoints Explorer, which you can access from the **View** menu.

It scans your current solution for projects that expose endpoints, like MVC and Web API projects, and then documents all the endpoints, showing their routes and parameters, as shown in *Figure 9.6*:

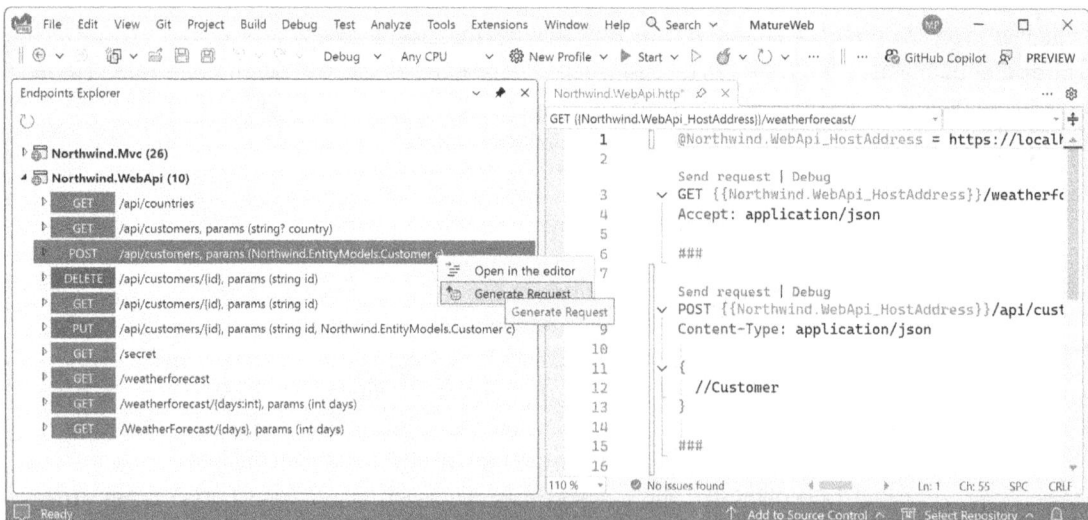

Figure 9.6: Visual Studio Endpoints Explorer

If you right-click on an endpoint and choose **Generate Request,** it will add a new request to the `<project_name>.http` file with skeleton code to make a request to that endpoint. For example, to POST to the `/api/customers` endpoint, as shown in *Figure 9.6*.

Now that we've seen a quick and easy way to try out our service, which also happens to be a great way to learn HTTP, what about external developers? We want it to be as easy as possible for them to learn and then call our service. For that purpose, we will use OpenAPI.

Documenting web services with Swagger, OpenAPI, and Swashbuckle

Let's start by explaining some terminology related to documenting web services:

- **Swagger**: Originally, Swagger was a framework for describing, documenting, and trying out REST APIs. It included tools like the Swagger UI and Swagger Editor. However, Swagger evolved into the **OpenAPI Specification (OAS)**, which is now the industry standard for defining RESTful APIs in a machine-readable format (YAML or JSON).

- **OpenAPI**: This is the formalized specification that defines how to describe and document REST APIs. The OAS provides a standardized way to describe API endpoints, request/response models, authentication, and more. OpenAPI is maintained by the **OpenAPI Initiative (OAI)** under the Linux Foundation.

- **Swashbuckle:** This is a .NET library that automatically generates OpenAPI documentation for ASP.NET Core Web API web services. It implements a Swagger UI, allowing you to visualize and test API endpoints directly in the browser.

It is easy to confuse Swashbuckle and Swagger because they start with similar letters: Swa. Try to remember that you shouldn't use either:

- When talking about the specification that defines how to describe and document REST APIs, replace Swagger with OpenAPI.

- When referencing a package to describe and document a web service project, replace Swashbuckle with a more modern package like Scalar or NSwag.

Recently, the ASP.NET Core team has changed how these technologies are used in ASP.NET Core projects:

- In ASP.NET Core 8 and earlier, the third-party `Swashbuckle.AspNetCore` package was used to generate an OpenAPI JSON document to formally describe the web service. Swashbuckle includes a Swagger UI that provides an interactive web page to explore and try out API endpoints. But the Swashbuckle package is third-party, so it is out of the control of Microsoft, and it has not been maintained well enough by its owner for Microsoft to want to use it anymore.

- In ASP.NET Core 9 and later, the first-party `Microsoft.AspNetCore.OpenApi` package is used to generate an OpenAPI JSON document to formally describe the web service. But this package does not provide an interactive UI for trying out the web service.

Here's a summary of recent versions of ASP.NET Core and how they document web services, as shown in *Table 9.5*:

Version	Packages	My Book
8	`Swashbuckle.AspNetCore`	The 8th edition describes (1) how to request a JSON document that documents a web service, (2) how to use the Swashbuckle package to try out a web service using a web user interface, and (3) how to try out a web service using REST Client in VS Code and HTTP Editor in Visual Studio.
9	`Microsoft.AspNetCore.OpenApi`	The 9th edition describes (1) how to request a JSON document that documents a web service and (2) how to try out a web service using REST Client in VS Code and HTTP Editor in Visual Studio.
10	`Microsoft.AspNetCore.OpenApi, Scalar.AspNetCore`	The 10th edition describes (1) how to request a JSON document that documents a web service, (2) how to try out a web service using REST Client in VS Code and HTTP Editor in Visual Studio, and (3) how to use the Scalar package to try out a web service using a web user interface.

Table 9.5: Recent versions of ASP.NET Core and how they document web services

> You can learn more about how to use OpenAPI documentation at the following link: https://learn.microsoft.com/en-us/aspnet/core/fundamentals/openapi/using-openapi-documents.

Implementing the OpenAPI Specification

It is important to version the OpenAPI documentation for your web service as you version its functionality. You should also put effort into adding quality descriptions and examples rather than just relying on the auto-generated files that are only based on your code.

Developers can use the OpenAPI Specification for a Web API to automatically generate strongly typed client-side code in their preferred language or library.

Let's review how OpenAPI is enabled for our web service using the Web API project template:

1. If the web service is running, shut down the web server.
2. In `Northwind.WebApi.csproj`, note the package reference for `Microsoft.AspNetCore.OpenApi` that was added by the project template, as shown in the following markup:

    ```
    <PackageReference Include="Microsoft.AspNetCore.OpenApi" />
    ```

> With .NET 8 and earlier, the Web API project template used a third-party package named Swashbuckle, but the developer has abandoned it, so Microsoft wrote its own. Microsoft's package is less functional; for example, it generates OpenAPI documentation but does not provide a user interface for trying out the web service.

3. In `Program.cs`, in the section for adding services to the container, note the services registered by the project template to use OpenAPI, as shown in the following code:

```
// Learn more about configuring OpenAPI at https://aka.ms/aspnet/openapi
builder.Services.AddOpenApi();
```

4. In the section that configures the HTTP request pipeline, note the statement for mapping an endpoint for an auto-generated OpenAPI document when in development mode, as shown highlighted in the following code:

```
// Configure the HTTP request pipeline.
if (builder.Environment.IsDevelopment())
{
    app.MapOpenApi();
}
```

5. Start the `Northwind.WebApi` web service project using the `https` launch profile.

6. Navigate to `https://localhost:5091/openapi/v1.json`, and note the JSON document that documents the service, including validation rules to post to the service, as shown in the following partial markup and in *Figure 9.7*:

```
{
  "openapi": "3.1.1",
  "info": {
    "title": "Northwind.WebApi | v1",
    "version": "1.0.0"
  },
  "servers": [
    {
      "url": "https://localhost:5091"
    }
  ],
  "paths": {
    "/api/Customers": {
      "get": {
        "tags": [
          "Customers"
        ],
        "parameters": [
          {
            "name": "country",
            "in": "query",
            "schema": {
              "type": "string",
```

```
                    "nullable": true
                }
            }
        ],
        "responses": {
          "200": {
            "description": "OK",
            "content": {
...
                "application/json": {
                  "schema": {
                    "type": "array"
                    "items": {
                      "$ref": "#/components/schemas/Customer"
                    }
                  }
                },
...
          },
          "post": {
            "tags": [
              "Customers"
            ],
            "requestBody": {
              "content": {
                "application/json": {
                  "schema": {
                    "$ref": "#/components/schemas/Customer",
...
    "components": {
        "schemas": {
          "Category": {
            "type": "object",
            "properties": {
              "categoryId": {
                "pattern": "^-?(?:0|[1-9]\\d*)$",
                "type": [
                  "integer",
                  "string"
                ],
                "format": "int32"
              },
```

```
              "categoryName": {
                "maxLength": 15,
                "minLength": 0,
                "type": "string"
              },
  ...
          "Customer": {
            "type": "object",
            "properties": {
              "customerId": {
                "maxLength": 5,
                "minLength": 0,
                "pattern": "[A-Z]{5}",
                "type": "string"
              },
              "companyName": {
                "maxLength": 40,
                "minLength": 0,
                "type": "string"
              },
```

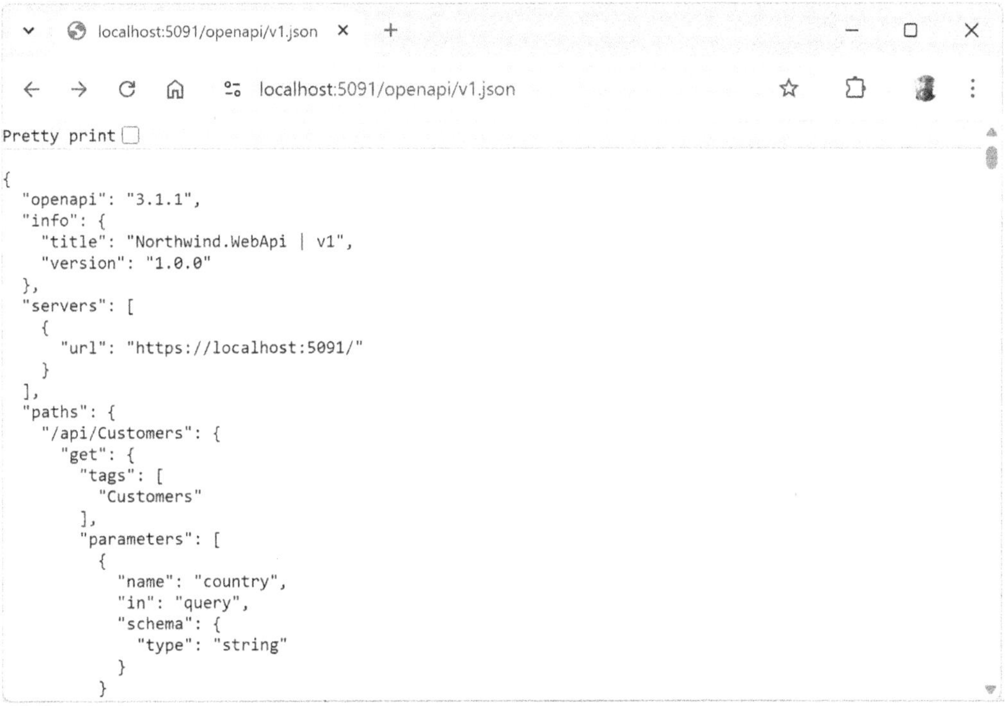

Figure 9.7: JSON documenting the Northwind web service

Note the following about the OpenAPI JSON document:

- It specifies all the relative paths for the service, like /api/Customers and /WeatherForecast/ {days}.
- For parameters like days, it specifies their type and default value, as shown in *Figure 9.8* and in the following JSON:

```
"parameters": [
  {
    "name": "days",
    "in": "path",
    "required": true,
    "schema": {
      "pattern": "^-?(?:0|[1-9]\\d*)$",
      "type": "integer",
      "format": "int32"
    }
  }
],
"responses": {
  "200": {
    "description": "OK",
    ...
```

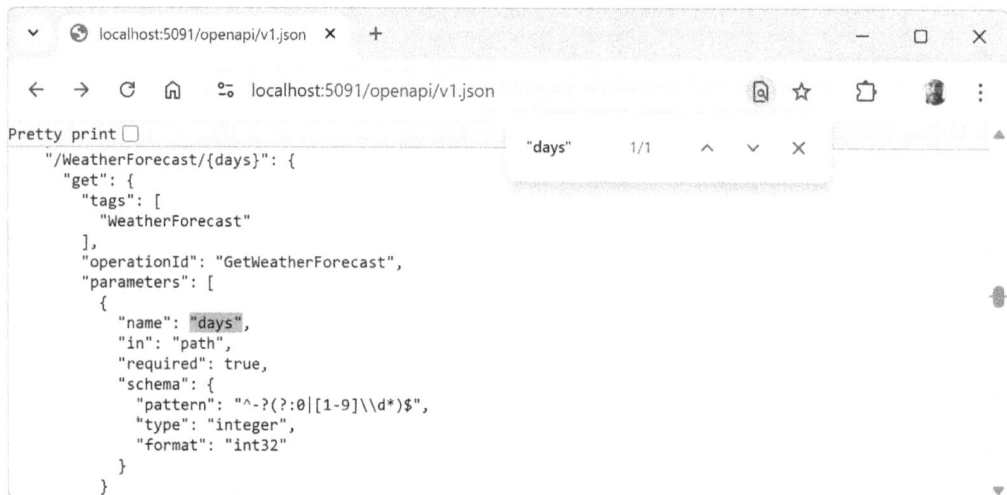

Figure 9.8: Searching for the days parameter in the OpenAPI document

1. Use the browser's find feature to search for the schema definition for a Customer, as shown in *Figure 9.9* and in the following JSON:

```json
"Customer": {
  "type": "object",
  "properties": {
    "customerId": {
      "maxLength": 5,
      "minLength": 0,
      "pattern": "[A-Z]{5}",
      "type": "string"
    },
    "companyName": {
      "maxLength": 40,
      "minLength": 0,
      "type": "string"
    },
    ...
    "orders": {
      "type": "array",
      "items": {
        "$ref": "#/components/schemas/Order"
      }
    },
    "customerTypes": { }
  }
},
...
```

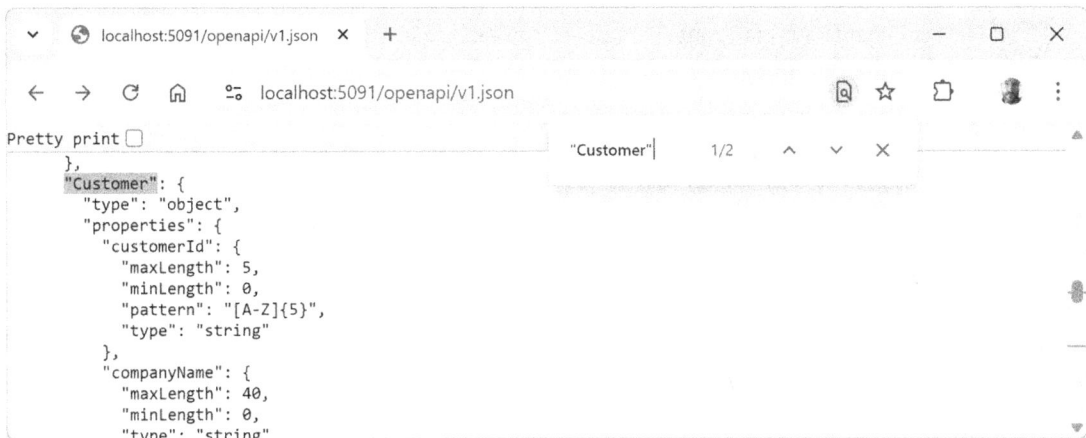

Figure 9.9: The schema for a Customer in JSON

Support for OpenAPI 3.1

With .NET 10, ASP.NET Core added support for generating OpenAPI version 3.1 documents. OpenAPI 3.1 is a significant update to the OpenAPI specification, with full support for JSON Schema draft 2020-12 that you can read about at the following link: `https://json-schema.org/specification-links#2020-12`.

The default OpenAPI version for generated documents is 3.1, but you can change this by setting the `OpenApiVersion` property of the `OpenApiOptions`, as shown in the following code:

```
builder.Services.AddOpenApi(options =>
{
    // Specify the OpenAPI version to use.
    options.OpenApiVersion = Microsoft.OpenApi.OpenApiSpecVersion.OpenApi3_0;
});
```

> You can learn more at the following link: `https://learn.microsoft.com/en-us/aspnet/core/fundamentals/minimal-apis/openapi#describe-endpoints`.

Generate OpenAPI documents in YAML format

ASP.NET Core supports generating the OpenAPI document in YAML format. YAML can be more concise than JSON, eliminating curly braces and quotation marks when these can be inferred. YAML also supports multi-line strings, which can be useful for long descriptions.

To configure your application to serve the generated OpenAPI document in YAML format, specify the endpoint in the `MapOpenApi` call with a ".yaml" or ".yml" suffix, as shown in the following code:

```
app.MapOpenApi("/openapi/{documentName}.yaml");
```

> The .yaml extension tells ASP.NET Core to serve the document in YAML instead of JSON. {documentName} is a route parameter. You can request different OpenAPI documents by changing the documentName in the request URL. For example: `https://localhost:5001/openapi/v1.yaml` or `https://localhost:5001/openapi/v2.yaml`.

Generating clients using an OpenAPI specification

One of the benefits of enabling your web service to automatically provide a JSON file to document itself is that there are many tools available that can generate clients to simplify interacting with the service.

One of the most popular ones for .NET is NSwag. NSwag is a powerful toolchain that allows you to generate C# clients from OpenAPI specifications. It integrates well with .NET projects and can be used in a variety of ways, including command-line tools, MSBuild, and directly within Visual Studio.

You can learn more about NSwag at `https://github.com/RicoSuter/NSwag`.

Implementing Scalar

Another choice for documenting and trying out web services is Scalar, and it is gaining popularity with ASP.NET Core developers.

Let's add a modern third-party package to provide a user interface to try out our web service:

1. In the `Northwind.WebApi.csproj` project file, add a package reference for Scalar's integration with ASP.NET Core, as shown in the following markup:

    ```
    <PackageReference Include="Scalar.AspNetCore" />
    ```

2. In `Program.cs`, import the Scalar namespace, as shown in the following code:

    ```
    using Scalar.AspNetCore; // To use MapScalarApiReference method.
    ```

3. In `Program.cs`, add statements so that when in the development environment, you enable Scalar's API reference capability, as shown highlighted in the following code:

    ```
    if (app.Environment.IsDevelopment())
    {
      app.MapOpenApi();
      app.MapScalarApiReference(options =>
      {
        options.AddDocuments(docs =>
        {
          docs.Add("v1", "/openapi/v1.json", isDefault: true);
          docs.Add("v2", "/openapi/v2.json");
        });
      });
    }
    ```

    You can also integrate Scalar with Swashbuckle and NSwag, as well as Microsoft's OpenAPI implementation.

4. Start the `Northwind.WebApi` web service project using the `https` launch profile.

5. Navigate to `https://localhost:5091/scalar/v1`, and note that the Scalar UI shows a list of endpoints like **/api/Customers/{id} GET** in the left navigation, as shown in *Figure 9.10*:

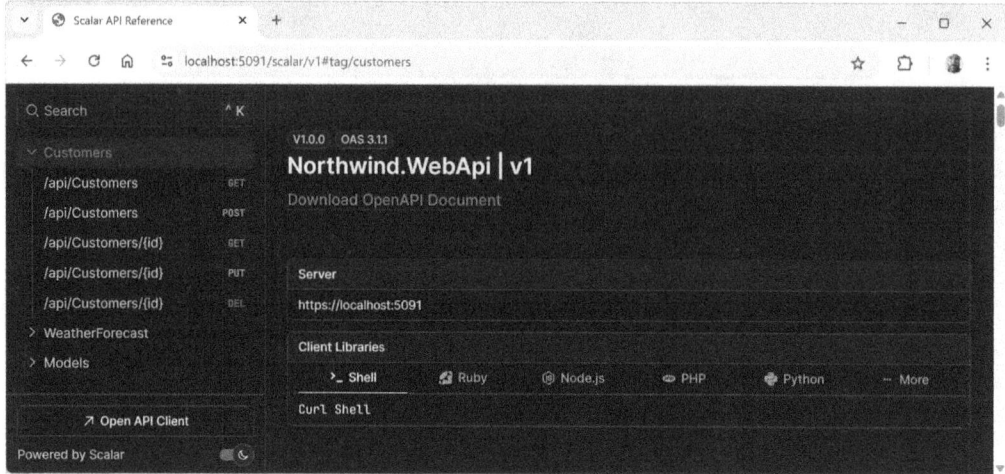

Figure 9.10: Scalar listing all endpoints in a web service

6. Click one of the endpoints and try calling it with appropriate parameter values.
7. Close the browser and shut down the web server.

> You can learn more about Scalar at the following link: `https://scalar.com/`.

Now that you've seen how to build a web service, document it, and try it out, let's see how we can improve its scalability and performance, as well as easing troubleshooting, by adding caching and logging.

Caching responses and logging

You can improve the performance and scalability of a web service by implementing caching. You can simplify troubleshooting a web service by enabling logging.

Caching HTTP responses for web services

Response (aka HTTP) caching is tied to HTTP `GET` requests and responses because it is based on HTTP headers. Therefore, it only works with websites and web services that use HTTP as their transport technology, like web services built using controller-based Web APIs and OData.

> You can read the official standard for HTTP caching at `https://www.rfc-editor.org/rfc/rfc9111`.

Requirements for HTTP, aka response, caching include the following:

- The request must be a GET or HEAD one. POST, PUT, and DELETE requests, and so on, are never cached by HTTP caching.
- The response must have a 200 OK status code.
- If the request has an Authorization header, then the response is not cached. When a user is logged in to a website, their requests will have an Authorization header.
- If the request has a Vary header, then the response is not cached when the values are not valid or *.

The web server sets response caching headers, and then intermediate proxies and clients should respect the headers to tell them how they should cache the responses.

> **Good practice:** Response, aka HTTP, caching is not typically useful for web user interfaces because web browsers often set request headers that prevent HTTP caching. For web user interfaces, output caching is better suited.

The Cache-Control HTTP header for requests and responses has some common directives, as shown in *Table 9.6*:

Directive	Description
public	Clients and intermediaries can cache this response.
private	Only a client should cache this response.
max-age	The client does not accept responses older than the specified number of seconds.
no-cache	A client request is asking for a non-cached response. A server is telling the client and intermediaries not to cache the response.
no-store	A cache must not store the request or response.

Table 9.6: Common Cache-Control HTTP header directives

As well as Cache-Control, there are other headers that might affect caching, as shown in *Table 9.7*:

Header	Description
Age	Estimated number of seconds old the response is.
Expires	An absolute date/time after which the response should be considered expired.
Vary	All fields must match for a cached response to be sent. Otherwise, a fresh response is sent. For example, a query string of color.

Table 9.7: Common HTTP headers for caching

For example, a client could ask for a fresh list of discontinued products, and the service should not use any cached version, as shown in the following HTTP response:

```
GET api/products/discontinued
Cache-Control: no-cache
```

A service could return some products as a JSON array, with a header to say that intermediaries should not cache the response but clients can, as shown in the following HTTP response:

```
content-type: application/json; charset=utf-8
date: Fri,09 Jun 2024 06:05:13 GMT
server: Kestrel
cache-control: private
[
  {
    "productId": 5,
    "productName": "Chef Anton's Gumbo Mix",
    ...
```

Decorate a controller or method with the [ResponseCache] attribute to control caching responses from the server (code to control caching requests has to go in the client code). This attribute has common parameters, as shown in *Table 9.8*:

Property	Description
Duration	How long to cache in seconds.
Location	Where the response can be cached: Any (cache-control: public), Client (cache-control: private), None (cache-control: no-cache).
NoStore	Sets cache-control: no-store.
VaryByHeader	Sets the Vary header.
VaryByQueryKeys	Query keys to vary by.

Table 9.8: Common parameters of the [ResponseCache] attribute

Let's apply response caching to the web service:

1. In the Northwind.WebApi project, in Program.cs, before the call to Build, add a statement to add response caching middleware as a dependency service, as shown in the following code:

    ```
    builder.Services.AddResponseCaching();
    ```

2. In Program.cs, after the call to use HTTPS redirection, add a statement to use response caching middleware, as shown in the following code:

    ```
    app.UseResponseCaching();
    ```

> **Warning!** If you are using CORS middleware, then UseCors must be called before UseResponseCaching.

3. In `CustomersController.cs`, decorate the `Get` method with a `string id` parameter with the `[ResponseCache]` attribute, as highlighted in the following code:

```
// GET: api/customers/[id]
[HttpGet("{id}", Name = nameof(GetCustomer))] // Named route.
[ProducesResponseType(200, Type = typeof(Customer))]
[ProducesResponseType(404)]
[ResponseCache(Duration = 5, // Cache-Control: max-age=5
  Location = ResponseCacheLocation.Any, // Cache-Control: public
  VaryByHeader = "User-Agent" // Vary: User-Agent
)]
public async Task<IActionResult> GetCustomer(string id)
{
  Customer? c = await _repo.RetrieveAsync(id, default);
  if (c == null)
  {
    return NotFound(); // 404 Resource not found.
  }
  return Ok(c); // 200 OK with customer in body.
}
```

4. Start the web service project, using the `https` profile without debugging.

5. In the `HttpRequests` folder, open the `get-customers.http` file.

6. Send the request for a specific customer, as shown in the following code:

```
GET {{base_address}}ALFKI
```

7. Note that the response includes headers to control caching, as shown in *Figure 9.11*:

Figure 9.11: Headers for response caching

8. Close the browser and shut down the web server.

> **Good practice:** Response caching will only be enabled for anonymous requests. Authenticated requests and responses will not be cached.

Caching is one of the best ways to improve the performance and scalability of your services. We covered invalidation strategies for cached data in *Chapter 6, Performance and Scalability Optimization Using Caching*.

Next, we will learn how to enable logging to help resolve issues.

Enabling HTTP logging

HTTP logging is an optional middleware component that is useful when trying out a web service. It logs information about HTTP requests and HTTP responses, including the following:

- Information about the HTTP request
- Headers
- Body
- Information about the HTTP response

This is valuable in web services for auditing and debugging scenarios, but beware because it can negatively impact performance. You might also log **Personally Identifiable Information (PII)**, which can cause compliance issues in some jurisdictions.

Log levels can be set to the following:

- `Error`: Only `Error` level logs.
- `Warning`: `Error` and `Warning` level logs.
- `Information`: `Error`, `Warning`, and `Information` level logs.
- `Verbose`: All level logs.

Log levels can be set for the namespace in which the functionality is defined. Nested namespaces allow us to control which functionality has logging enabled:

- `Microsoft`: Include all log types in the `Microsoft` namespace.
- `Microsoft.AspNetCore`: Include all log types in the `Microsoft.AspNetCore` namespace.
- `Microsoft.AspNetCore.HttpLogging`: Include all log types in the `Microsoft.AspNetCore.HttpLogging` namespace.

Let's see HTTP logging in action:

1. In the `Northwind.WebApi` project, in `appsettings.Development.json`, add an entry to set HTTP logging to `Information` level, as shown highlighted in the following code:

```
{
  "Logging": {
```

```
      "LogLevel": {
        "Default": "Information",
        "Microsoft.AspNetCore": "Warning",
        "Microsoft.AspNetCore.HttpLogging": "Information"
      }
    }
  }
```

> Although the `Default` log level might be set to `Information`, more specific configurations take priority. For example, any logging systems in the `Microsoft.AspNetCore` namespace will use the `Warning` level. By making the change we did, any logging systems in the `Microsoft.AspNetCore.HttpLogging.HttpLoggingMiddleware` namespace will now use `Information`.

2. In `Program.cs`, import the namespace for working with HTTP logging, as shown in the following code:

    ```
    using Microsoft.AspNetCore.HttpLogging; // To use HttpLoggingFields.
    ```

3. In the services configuration section, before the call to `builder.Build`, add a statement to add and configure HTTP logging, as shown in the following code:

    ```
    builder.Services.AddHttpLogging(options =>
    {
      options.LoggingFields = HttpLoggingFields.All;
      options.RequestBodyLogLimit = 4096; // Default is 32k.
      options.ResponseBodyLogLimit = 4096; // Default is 32k.
    });
    ```

4. In the HTTP pipeline configuration section, after the call to `builder.Build`, add a statement to add HTTP logging before the call to use routing, as shown in the following code:

    ```
    app.UseHttpLogging();
    ```

5. Start the `Northwind.WebApi` web service using the `https` launch profile.

6. Start Chrome and navigate to `https://localhost:5091/api/customers`.

7. At the command prompt or terminal hosting the web service, note the request and response have been logged, as shown in the following partial output:

    ```
    info: Microsoft.AspNetCore.HttpLogging.HttpLoggingMiddleware[1]
          Request:
          Protocol: HTTP/2
          Method: GET
          Scheme: https
          PathBase:
    ```

```
        Path: /api/customers
        Accept: text/html,application/xhtml+xml,application/
xml;q=0.9,image/avif,image/webp,image/apng,*/*;q=0.8,application/signed-
exchange;v=b3;q=0.7
        Host: localhost:5091
        User-Agent: Mozilla/5.0 (Windows NT 10.0; Win64; x64)
AppleWebKit/537.36 (KHTML, like Gecko) Chrome/128.0.0.0 Safari/537.36
        Accept-Encoding: gzip, deflate, br, zstd
        Accept-Language: en-GB,en;q=0.9,fr-FR;q=0.8,fr;q=0.7,en-US;q=0.6
        Upgrade-Insecure-Requests: [Redacted]
        sec-ch-ua: [Redacted]
...
info: Microsoft.AspNetCore.HttpLogging.HttpLoggingMiddleware[2]
        Response:
        StatusCode: 200
        Content-Type: application/json; charset=utf-8
info: Microsoft.AspNetCore.HttpLogging.HttpLoggingMiddleware[4]
        ResponseBody: [{"customerId":"ALFKI","companyName":"Alfreds
Futterkiste","contactName":"Maria Anders","contactTitle":"Sales
Representative",
...
info: Microsoft.AspNetCore.HttpLogging.HttpLoggingMiddleware[8]
        Duration: 925.24ms
```

8. Close Chrome and shut down the web server.

If you are hosting your web service in the cloud, then you can integrate logging with monitoring solutions like CloudWatch or Azure Application Insights.

Logging to the Windows-only Event Log

When configuring logging, you might want to enable logging to the Windows Event Log, as shown in the following code:

```
var builder = WebApplication.CreateBuilder(args);

// Option 1
builder.Services.AddLogging(logging =>
{
  logging.AddEventLog();
});

// Option 2
builder.Host.ConfigureLogging(logging =>
{
```

```
    logging.AddEventLog();
});
```

```
// Option 3: .NET 6 or later. Concise and recommended by Microsoft.
builder.Logging.AddEventLog();
```

You will see a code analyzer warning, `CA1416`, because enabling Event Log only works on Windows. If you run this code on any other OS, then a runtime exception will be thrown. To avoid the warning (and runtime error), you should wrap the call to `AddEventLog` with an OS check.

First, import a namespace, as shown in the following code:

```
using System.Runtime.InteropServices; // To use RuntimeInformation.
```

Then, wrap any calls to `AddEventLog`, as shown in the following code:

```
if (RuntimeInformation.IsOSPlatform(OSPlatform.Windows))
{
  // Call the AddEventLog method.
}
```

Support for logging additional request headers in W3CLogger

W3CLogger is a middleware that writes logs in the W3C standard format. You can do the following:

* Record details of HTTP requests and responses.
* Filter which headers and parts of the request and response messages are logged.

> **Warning!** W3CLogger can reduce the performance of an app.

> W3CLogger is like HTTP logging, so I will not cover details of how to use it in this book. You can learn more about W3CLogger at https://learn.microsoft.com/en-us/aspnet/core/fundamentals/w3c-logger/.

In ASP.NET Core 7 or later, you can specify that you want to log additional request headers when using W3CLogger. Call the `AdditionalRequestHeaders` method and pass the name of the header you want to log, as shown in the following code:

```
services.AddW3CLogging(options =>
{
  options.AdditionalRequestHeaders.Add("x-forwarded-for");
  options.AdditionalRequestHeaders.Add("x-client-ssl-protocol");
});
```

Logging and security principles

Logging sensitive or personal information can lead to security vulnerabilities, breaches of privacy, or even regulatory violations (such as GDPR or HIPAA). To maintain security, it's important to log responsibly, ensuring that sensitive data isn't inadvertently exposed.

Here are good practices for logging with security in mind, along with examples and explanations of what to avoid and how to implement safe logging.

Avoid logging sensitive information

Certain types of information should never be logged because they can be used maliciously if exposed. Examples of sensitive data include passwords, authentication tokens like **JSON Web Tokens** (**JWTs**) and OAuth tokens, and API keys.

You should avoid logging PII like names, addresses, phone numbers, Social Security numbers, credit card numbers, bank account numbers, medical records, insurance numbers, and so on.

If you need to log something related to a sensitive operation, only log non-sensitive metadata, like the username (without the password) or some indication of a request, without including sensitive details.

Mask or obfuscate sensitive data

Sometimes it's necessary to log sensitive data, but only in a masked or obfuscated form. For instance, you might need to log part of a credit card number for transaction purposes, as shown in the following code:

```
string creditCardNumber = "4111111111111111";
string maskedCardNumber = creditCardNumber.Substring(0, 4)
    + "****" + creditCardNumber.Substring(12);


_logger.LogInformation("Payment processed for card: {CardNumber}",
maskedCardNumber);
```

In this case, only the first four and last four digits of the credit card number are logged. This provides enough information to identify the transaction without exposing the full credit card number.

Avoid logging request and response bodies for sensitive endpoints

Logging HTTP request and response bodies can be useful for debugging, but it's risky for endpoints that handle sensitive data, such as authentication or payment endpoints. Logging these bodies may expose sensitive details like passwords, tokens, or credit card information.

Avoid logging bodies for sensitive endpoints or filter out sensitive information from the body before logging. If you must log request/response bodies, ensure that sensitive fields are removed.

Use structured logging for sensitive data management

Structured logging, whereby you log specific properties instead of free-form text, helps ensure that sensitive data is treated in a controlled manner.

With structured logging, sensitive properties like passwords can be controlled at the logging provider level, allowing you to redact or filter sensitive information. This helps you log actionable events without accidentally leaking sensitive data in free-form log messages.

Log security events without sensitive data

It's important to log security events like failed login attempts, unauthorized access, or errors in a secure manner, as shown in the following code:

```
_logger.LogWarning(
    "Failed login attempt for user {Username} from IP {IPAddress}",
    username, context.Connection.RemoteIpAddress);
```

This captures important metadata about a failed login attempt, like the username and IP address, which is useful for detecting security issues like brute-force attacks. However, it does not expose any sensitive data like passwords or tokens.

Beware of third-party library logging

Some third-party libraries may perform their own logging. Make sure you review their logging practices and configurations to ensure they aren't logging sensitive data. You may need to adjust their logging levels or configure logging settings to prevent accidental data leaks.

For example, when using Entity Framework Core, avoid logging SQL queries that might contain sensitive parameters like user passwords or personal information in query strings, as shown in the following code:

```
services.AddDbContext<ApplicationDbContext>(options =>
    options.UseSqlServer(connectionString)
    .EnableSensitiveDataLogging(false)); // Disable sensitive logging.
```

Disabling sensitive data logging ensures that personal data is not logged with SQL queries.

Log errors with caution

When logging exceptions, avoid logging detailed stack traces or error messages that might contain sensitive data, especially for publicly exposed services. This might inadvertently log sensitive details from the exception message, such as internal server paths or even data that was part of the exception.

Consider logging only generic error information and capturing detailed errors for internal use only.

You are now ready to build applications that consume your web service.

Practicing and exploring

Test your knowledge and understanding by answering some questions, getting some hands-on practice, and exploring this chapter's topics with deeper research.

Exercise 9.1 – Online material

Implementing advanced features for web services

If you would like to learn about web service health checks, OpenAPI analyzers, adding security HTTP headers, and enabling HTTP/3 support for `HttpClient`, then you can read the optional online-only section at the following link:

```
https://github.com/markjprice/web-dev-net10/blob/main/docs/ch09-advanced.md.
```

Improved route tooling

For .NET 8, Microsoft improved the tooling for working with routes for all ASP.NET Core technologies, including controller-based Web APIs, Minimal APIs, and Blazor. The features include the following:

- **Route syntax highlighting**: Different parts of routes are now highlighted in your code editor.
- Autocompletion of parameter and route names, and route constraints.
- **Route analyzers and fixers**: These address the common problems that developers have when implementing their routes.

You can read about them in the blog article *ASP.NET Core Route Tooling Enhancements in .NET 8*, found at

```
https://devblogs.microsoft.com/dotnet/aspnet-core-route-tooling-dotnet-8/.
```

Exercise 9.2 – Practice exercise

Add a `ShippersController` to handle CRUD operations for the `Shippers` table. To test your web service endpoints, use the following HTTP requests.

To get all shippers:

```
### Configure a variable for the web service base address.
@base_address = https://localhost:5091/api/v1/shippers/


### Make a GET request to the base address.
GET {{base_address}}
```

To get a specific shipper:

```
GET {{base_address}}1
```

To add a new shipper:

```
POST {{base_address}}
Content-Type: application/json

{
  "companyName": "ABC Shipping",
  "phone": "(123) 555-1234"
}
```

To update an existing shipper:

```
PUT {{base_address}}4
Content-Type: application/json

{
  "shipperId": 4,
  "companyName": "XYZ Shipping",
  "phone": "(123) 555-9999"
}
```

To delete a shipper (you can only delete shippers that you've created because the three existing shippers all have related data):

```
DELETE {{base_address}}4
```

Exercise 9.3 – Test your knowledge

Answer the following questions:

1. Which class should you inherit from to create a controller class for an ASP.NET Core Web API service?
2. What must you do to specify which controller action method will be executed in response to an HTTP request?
3. What must you do to specify what responses should be expected when calling an action method?
4. List three methods that can be called to return responses with different status codes.
5. List four ways that you can try out a web service.

Exercise 9.4 – Explore topics

Use the links in the following GitHub repository to learn more details about the topics covered in this chapter:

https://github.com/markjprice/web-dev-net10/blob/main/docs/book-links.md#chapter-9---building-web-services-using-aspnet-core-web-api.

Summary

In this chapter, you learned the following:

- How to build an ASP.NET Core Web API service that can be called by any app on any platform that can make an HTTP request and process an HTTP response.
- How to try out and document web service APIs with OpenAPI.
- How to enable caching and logging in a web service.

In the next chapter, you will learn how to build clients for web services and how to configure CORS.

Learn more on Discord

To join the Discord community for this book – where you can share feedback, ask questions to the author, and learn about new releases – follow this QR code:

```
https://packt.link/RWWD10
```

Join .NETPro – It's Free

Staying sharp in .NET takes more than reading release notes. It requires real-world tips, proven patterns, and scalable solutions. That's what .NETPro, Packt's new newsletter, is all about.

Scan the QR code or visit the link to subscribe:

```
https://landing.packtpub.com/dotnetpronewsletter/
```

10

Building Clients for Web Services

This chapter is about learning how to consume web services using HTTP clients, which could be any other type of .NET app, including a website, mobile, or desktop app, or any other platform that can make HTTP requests.

In this chapter, we will cover the following topics:

- Consuming web services using HTTP clients
- Consuming web services using Refit
- Relaxing the same-origin security policy using **Cross-Origin Resource Sharing (CORS)**
- Understanding identity services
- Principles of Web API design
- Implementing URI versioning

Consuming web services using HTTP clients

Now that we have built and tried calling our Northwind service using tools, we will learn how to call it from any .NET app using the `HttpClient` class and its factory.

Understanding HttpClient

The official way to consume a web service is to use the `HttpClient` class. However, many people use it incorrectly because it implements `IDisposable`, and Microsoft's own documentation shows poor usage of it. See the book links in the GitHub repository for articles with more discussion of this, found at the following link: `https://github.com/markjprice/web-dev-net10/blob/main/docs/book-links.md`.

Usually, when a type implements `IDisposable`, you should create it inside a `using` statement to ensure that it is disposed of as soon as possible. `HttpClient` is different because it is shared, reentrant, and partially thread-safe.

The problem has to do with how the underlying network sockets must be managed. The bottom line is that you should use a single instance of it for each HTTP endpoint that you consume during the life of your application. This will allow each HttpClient instance to have defaults set that are appropriate for the endpoint it works with, while managing the underlying network sockets efficiently.

Configuring HTTP clients using HttpClientFactory

Microsoft is aware of the issue of .NET developers misusing HttpClient, and in ASP.NET Core 2.1, it introduced HttpClientFactory to implement best practices for you; that is the technique we will use.

In the following example, we will use the Northwind MVC website as a client for the Northwind Web API service. Let's configure an HTTP client:

1. In the Northwind.Mvc project, in the Extensions folder, in WebApplicationBuilderExtensions.cs, import the namespace for setting a media type header value, as shown in the following code:

    ```
    using System.Net.Http.Headers; // To use MediaTypeWithQualityHeaderValue.
    ```

2. In WebApplicationBuilderExtensions.cs, add a method to enable HttpClientFactory with a named client to make calls to the Northwind Web API service using HTTPS on port 5091 and request JSON as the default response format, as shown in the following code:

    ```
    public static WebApplicationBuilder AddNorthwindWebApiClient(
      this WebApplicationBuilder builder)
    {
      builder.Services.AddHttpClient(name: "Northwind.WebApi",
        configureClient: options =>
        {
          options.BaseAddress = new Uri("https://localhost:5091/");
          options.DefaultRequestHeaders.Accept.Add(
            new MediaTypeWithQualityHeaderValue(
            mediaType: "application/json", quality: 1.0));
        });

      return builder;
    }
    ```

3. In Program.cs, before calling the builder.Build method, call the extension method, as shown in the following code:

    ```
    builder.AddNorthwindWebApiClient();
    ```

Getting customers as JSON in the controller

When a client makes a request to the web service, the client can only deserialize the JSON response into strongly-typed objects if it has a reference to an assembly that defines the models. The client project doesn't need the database context class, but in this simplified task, the client project does need all the entity models, like the Customer class.

Instead of reusing the entity models in both the client and service, you might define **data transfer object** (DTO) classes, and then that would be a shared assembly referenced by the client and the service. But then the service would have to convert entity models into DTO models, serialize them to JSON, and return them in a response to the client, and then the client would have to deserialize the DTO models and display them. Any two client/server projects will always have some shared assemblies to define the "shape" of any data that needs to be transferred between them.

In the simple examples used in this book, we want all the data from the entity models, so it'd be a waste to define DTOs that have the same "shape" as the entity models. I made a decision not to define separate DTO classes. In your real-world projects, you might choose differently.

Getting distinct country names

First, we will add an endpoint to the web service to get a list of valid country names:

1. In the `Northwind.WebApi` project, in the `Controllers` folder, add a new controller class named `CountriesController.cs`.

2. In `CountriesController.cs`, add an action method to get sorted, distinct country names used in the `Customers` table, as shown in the following code:

```
using Microsoft.AspNetCore.Mvc; // To use [ApiController] and so on.
using Microsoft.EntityFrameworkCore; // To use ToArrayAsync.
using Northwind.EntityModels; // To use Customer and NorthwindContext.

namespace Northwind.WebApi.Controllers;

[Route("api/[controller]")]
[ApiController]
public class CountriesController : ControllerBase
{
  // GET: api/countries
  // This will always return an array of country names (but it might be
empty).
  [HttpGet]
  [ProducesResponseType(200, Type = typeof(IEnumerable<Customer>))]
  public async Task<string?[]> GetCountries([FromServices]
NorthwindContext db)
  {
    return await db.Customers
      .Select(customer => customer.Country)
      .Distinct()
      .Order()
      .ToArrayAsync();
  }
}
```

Implementing an MVC action method for calling the web service

Now we can create an MVC controller action method that does the following:

- Uses the factory to create an HTTP client
- Makes a GET request for customers
- Deserializes the JSON response using convenient extension methods introduced with .NET 5 in the System.Net.Http.Json assembly and namespace

Let's go:

1. In the Northwind.Mvc project, in the Controllers folder, in HomeController.cs, declare a field for storing the HTTP client factory, as shown in the following code:

   ```
   private readonly IHttpClientFactory _clientFactory;
   ```

2. Set the field in the constructor, as shown highlighted in the following code:

   ```
   public HomeController(
       ILogger<HomeController> logger,
       NorthwindContext db, IMemoryCache memoryCache,
       IDistributedCache distributedCache,
       IHttpClientFactory httpClientFactory)
   {
       _logger = logger;
       _db = db;
       _memoryCache = memoryCache;
       _distributedCache = distributedCache;
       _clientFactory = httpClientFactory;
   }
   ```

3. In the Index action method, add statements for calling the Northwind Web API service, fetching all countries, and storing them in the ViewData dictionary, as shown in the following code:

   ```
   HttpClient client = _clientFactory.CreateClient(
       name: "Northwind.WebApi");

   HttpRequestMessage request = new(
       method: HttpMethod.Get, requestUri: "api/countries");

   try
   {
       HttpResponseMessage response = await client.SendAsync(request);

       string[]? countries = await response.Content
   ```

```
      .ReadFromJsonAsync<string[]>();

  if (countries is not null)
  {
    ViewData["Countries"] = countries;
  }
  else
  {
    _logger.LogWarning("No countries were returned from the web
service.");
  }
}
catch (Exception ex)
{
  _logger.LogError(
    $"Exception when calling countries web service: {ex.Message}");
}
```

4. At the bottom of the controller class, add a new action method for calling the Northwind Web API service, fetching all customers, and passing them to a view, as shown in the following code:

```
public async Task<IActionResult> Customers(string country)
{
  string uri;

  if (string.IsNullOrEmpty(country))
  {
    ViewData["Title"] = "All Customers Worldwide";
    uri = "api/customers";
  }
  else
  {
    ViewData["Title"] = $"Customers in {country}";
    uri = $"api/customers/?country={country}";
  }

  HttpClient client = _clientFactory.CreateClient(
    name: "Northwind.WebApi");

  HttpRequestMessage request = new(
    method: HttpMethod.Get, requestUri: uri);
```

```
    HttpResponseMessage response = await client.SendAsync(request);

    IEnumerable<Customer>? model = await response.Content
      .ReadFromJsonAsync<IEnumerable<Customer>>();

    return View(model);
}
```

5. In the `Views`/`Home` folder, create a Razor View file named `Customers.cshtml`.

6. Modify the Razor file to render the customers, as shown in the following markup:

```
@model IEnumerable<Customer>
<h2>@ViewData["Title"]</h2>
<table class="table">
  <thead>
    <tr>
      <th>Company Name</th>
      <th>Contact Name</th>
      <th>Address</th>
      <th>Phone</th>
    </tr>
  </thead>
  <tbody>
    @if (Model is not null)
    {
      @foreach (Customer c in Model)
      {
        <tr>
          <td>
            @Html.DisplayFor(modelItem => c.CompanyName)
          </td>
          <td>
            @Html.DisplayFor(modelItem => c.ContactName)
          </td>
          <td>
            @Html.DisplayFor(modelItem => c.Address)
            @Html.DisplayFor(modelItem => c.City)
            @Html.DisplayFor(modelItem => c.Region)
            <strong>@Html.DisplayFor(modelItem => c.Country)</strong>
            @Html.DisplayFor(modelItem => c.PostalCode)
```

```
            </td>
            <td>
              @Html.DisplayFor(modelItem => c.Phone)
            </td>
          </tr>
        }
      }
    </tbody>
  </table>
```

7. In the `Views/Home` folder, in `Index.cshtml`, after the form to query products by price, add a form to allow visitors to enter a country and see the customers, as shown in the following markup:

```
<h3>Query customers from a service</h3>
<form asp-action="Customers" method="get">
  @{
    string[]? countries = ViewData["Countries"] as string[];
  }
  @if (countries is null)
  {
    <input name="country" placeholder="Enter a country" />
  }
  else
  {
    <select name="country" class="form-select">
      <option value="">Worldwide</option>
      @foreach (string country in countries)
      {
        <option value="@country">@country</option>
      }
    </select>
  }
  <input type="submit" />
</form>
```

Starting multiple projects

Up to this point, we have only started one project at a time. Now we have two projects that need to be started: a web service and an MVC website. In the step-by-step instructions, I will only tell you to start individual projects one at a time, but you should use whatever technique you prefer to start them.

If you are using Visual Studio and want to start projects manually

Visual Studio can start multiple projects manually, one by one, if the debugger is not attached, as described in the following steps:

1. In **Solution Explorer,** right-click on the solution or any project and then select **Configure Startup Projects...,** or select the solution and navigate to **Project | Configure Startup Projects....**

2. In the **Solution '<name>' Property Pages** dialog box, select **Current selection.**

3. Click **OK.**

4. Select a project in **Solution Explorer** so that its name becomes bold to indicate the current selection.

5. Navigate to **Debug | Start Without Debugging** or press *Ctrl + F5.*

6. Repeat *steps 4* and *5* to select and then start as many projects as you need.

> If you need to debug the projects, then you must start multiple instances of Visual Studio. Each instance can start a single project with debugging.

If you are using Visual Studio and want to start projects automatically

You can also configure multiple projects to start up at the same time using the following steps:

1. In **Solution Explorer,** right-click the solution or any project and then select **Configure Startup Projects...,** or select the solution and navigate to **Project | Configure Startup Projects....**

2. In the **Solution '<name>' Property Pages** dialog box, select **Multiple startup projects,** and for any projects that you want to start, select either **Start** or **Start without debugging,** and then use the up and down arrows to order them appropriately, for example, start the web service before the website, as shown in *Figure 10.1*:

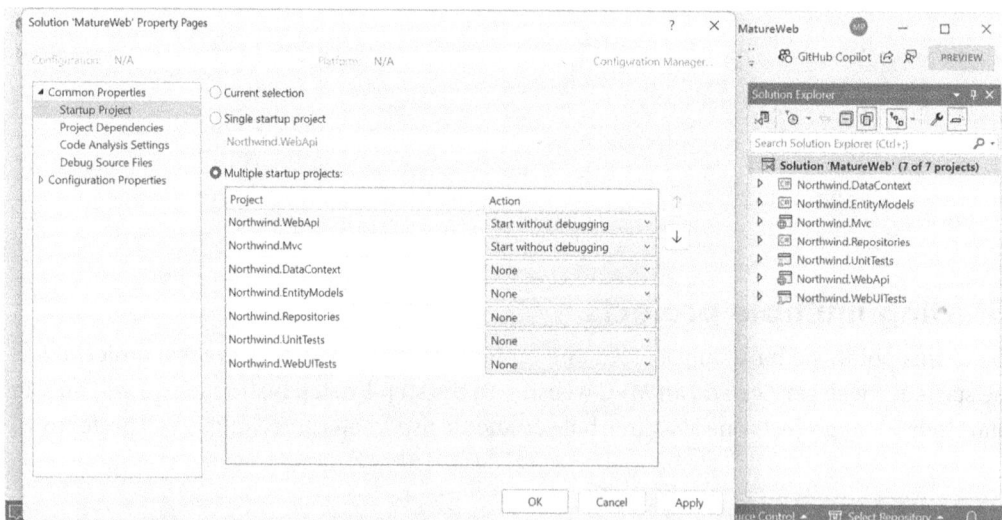

Figure 10.1: Selecting multiple projects to start up in Visual Studio

3. Click **OK**.

4. Navigate to **Debug | Start Debugging** or **Debug | Start Without Debugging** or click the equivalent buttons in the toolbar to start all the projects that you selected.

> You can learn more about multi-project startup using Visual Studio at the following link: `https://learn.microsoft.com/en-us/visualstudio/ide/how-to-set-multiple-startup-projects`.

If you are using VS Code

If you need to start multiple projects at the command line with `dotnet`, then write a script or batch file to execute multiple `dotnet run` commands, or open multiple command prompt or terminal windows.

If you need to debug multiple projects using VS Code, then after you've started the first debug session, you can just launch another session. Once the second session is running, the user interface switches to multi-target mode. For example, in **CALL STACK**, you will see both named projects with their own threads, and then the debug toolbar shows a drop-down list of sessions with the active one selected. Alternatively, you can define compound launch configurations in `launch.json`.

> You can learn more about multi-target debugging using VS Code at `https://code.visualstudio.com/Docs/editor/debugging#_multitarget-debugging`.

Starting the web service and MVC client projects

Now we can try calling the web service with the MVC client:

1. Start the `Northwind.WebApi` project and confirm that the web service is listening on ports `5091` and `5090`, as shown in the following output:

```
info: Microsoft.Hosting.Lifetime[14]
   Now listening on: https://localhost:5091
info: Microsoft.Hosting.Lifetime[14]
   Now listening on: http://localhost:5090
```

2. Start the `Northwind.Mvc` project and confirm that the website is listening on ports `5021` and `5020`, as shown in the following output:

```
info: Microsoft.Hosting.Lifetime[14]
   Now listening on: https://localhost:5021
info: Microsoft.Hosting.Lifetime[14]
   Now listening on: http://localhost:5020
```

3. Start Chrome and navigate to `https://localhost:5021/`.

4. On the home page, in the **Query customers from a service** drop-down list, select a country, click **Submit**, and note the list of customers, as shown in *Figure 10.2* for Argentina:

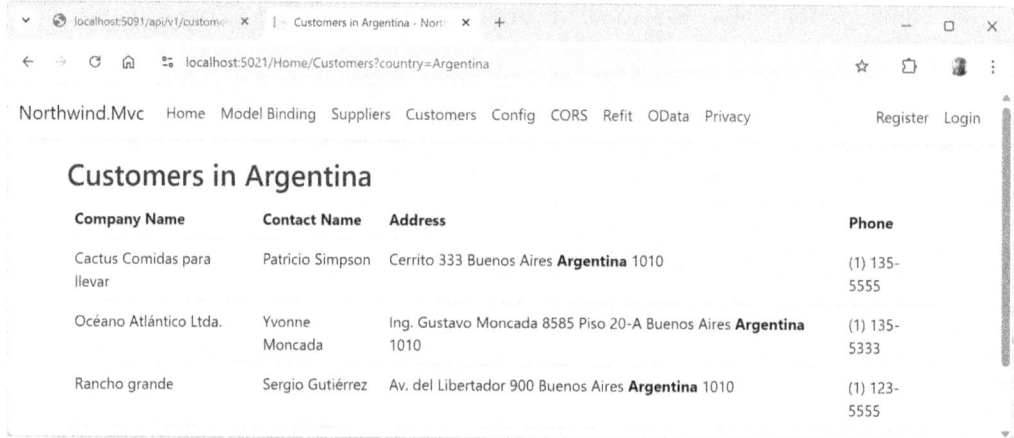

Figure 10.2: Customers in Argentina

5. Click the **Back** button in your browser, select **Worldwide**, click **Submit**, and note the worldwide list of customers.

6. At the command prompt or terminal hosting the web service, note that the `HttpClient` writes each HTTP request that it makes and each HTTP response that it receives, as shown in the following output:

```
info: System.Net.Http.HttpClient.Northwind.WebApi.LogicalHandler[100]
      Start processing HTTP request GET https://localhost:5091/api/customers
info: System.Net.Http.HttpClient.Northwind.WebApi.ClientHandler[100]
      Sending HTTP request GET https://localhost:5091/api/customers
info: System.Net.Http.HttpClient.Northwind.WebApi.ClientHandler[101]
      Received HTTP response headers after 91.829ms - 200
info: System.Net.Http.HttpClient.Northwind.WebApi.LogicalHandler[101]
      End processing HTTP request after 92.4345ms - 200
```

7. Close Chrome and shut down the two web servers.

Consuming web services using Refit

Using Refit in .NET is one of the cleanest and most convenient ways to define and consume HTTP APIs using a strongly-typed interface. Refit generates REST API calls for you behind the scenes, eliminating boilerplate code for HTTP requests. It's heavily inspired by Retrofit from the Android world.

Let's use Refit to make a client to the customers endpoint in our Web API service:

1. In the Northwind.Mvc.csproj project file, add references to the Refit packages for core functionality and integration with HttpClientFactory, as shown in the following configuration:

    ```
    <PackageReference Include="Refit" />
    <PackageReference Include="Refit.HttpClientFactory" />
    ```

2. In the Northwind.Mvc project, add a new folder named Clients.
3. In the Clients folder, add a new interface file named ICustomersClient.cs.
4. In ICustomersClient.cs, add statements to define an interface that matches the endpoints to get customers, as shown in the following code:

    ```csharp
    using Northwind.EntityModels; // To use Customer.
    using Refit; // To use [Get] attribute.

    namespace Northwind.Mvc.Clients;

    public interface ICustomersClient
    {
      [Get("/api/customers")]
      Task<List<Customer>> GetCustomersAsync();

      [Get("/api/customers?country={country}")]
      Task<List<Customer>> GetCustomersAsync(string? country);

      [Get("/api/customers/{id}")]
      Task<List<Customer>> GetCustomerAsync(string id);

      [Post("/api/customers")]
      Task<Customer> CreateCustomerAsync([Body] Customer customer);

      [Put("/api/customers/{id}")]
      Task UpdateCustomerAsync(string id, [Body] Customer customer);

      [Delete("/api/customers/{id}")]
      Task DeleteCustomerAsync(string id);
    }
    ```

5. In `Program.cs`, import the namespace to work with Refit, as shown in the following code:

    ```
    using Refit; // To use AddRefitClient and so on.
    ```

6. In `Program.cs`, after the call to `CreateBuilder`, add a statement to register a Refit client with a base address of the web service, as shown in the following code:

    ```
    builder.Services
      .AddRefitClient<ICustomersClient>()
      .ConfigureHttpClient(c =>
      {
        c.BaseAddress = new Uri("https://localhost:5091");
      });
    ```

7. In the `Controllers` folder, add a new empty MVC controller class named `RefitController.cs`.

8. In `RefitController.cs`, define a controller that uses dependency injection to get the registered Refit client and use it to get customers, and then pass the list of customers to the same Razor View that we previously created for the customers controller, as shown in the following code:

    ```
    using Microsoft.AspNetCore.Mvc; // To use Controller and IActionResult.
    using Northwind.EntityModels; // To use Customer.
    using Northwind.Mvc.Clients; // To use ICustomersClient.

    namespace Northwind.Mvc.Controllers;

    public class RefitController : Controller
    {
      public async Task<IActionResult> Index([FromServices] ICustomersClient
    client)
      {
        List<Customer> model = await client.GetCustomersAsync();

        // Reuse the same view as the CustomersController.
        return View("Views/Customers/Index.cshtml", model);
      }
    }
    ```

9. In the `Northwind.Mvc` project, in the `Views\Shared` folder, in `_Layout.cshtml`, add a navigation menu item to go to the Refit controller and its `Index` action method, as shown in the following markup:

    ```
    <li class="nav-item">
      <a class="nav-link text-dark" asp-area="" asp-controller="Refit"
        asp-action="Index">Refit</a>
    </li>
    ```

10. Start the `Northwind.WebApi` project.

11. Start the `Northwind.Mvc` project.

12. Start Chrome and navigate to `https://localhost:5021/`.

13. In the navigation menu, click **Refit**, and note that customers are retrieved using Refit.

14. Close Chrome and shut down the two web servers.

> You can learn more about Refit at the following link: `https://github.com/reactiveui/refit`.

You've now seen ways to build clients for a web service. One of the most common clients of your web services will be web pages on other websites. When this happens, you must take extra precautions due to web browsers' security policies.

Relaxing the same-origin security policy using CORS

Modern web browsers support multiple tabs, so users can visit multiple websites at the same time efficiently. If code executing in one tab could access resources in another tab, then that could be a vector of attack.

Understanding the same-origin policy in web browsers

All web browsers implement a security feature called the **same-origin policy**. This means that only requests that come from the same origin are allowed. For example, if a block of JavaScript is served from the same origin that hosts a web service or serves an `<iframe>` element, then that JavaScript can call the service and access the data in the `<iframe>`. If a request is made from a different origin, then the request fails. But what counts as the "same origin?"

An origin is defined by the following:

- **Scheme**, a.k.a. **protocol**, for example, `http` or `https`.
- **Port**, for example, `801` or `5081`. The default port for `http` is `80`, and for `https`, it is `443`.
- **Host/domain/subdomain**, for example, `www.example.com`, `www.example.net`, or `example.com`.

If the origin is `https://www.example.com/about-us/`, then the following are *not* the same origin:

- **Different scheme**: `http://www.example.com/about-us/`
- **Different host/domain**: `https://www.example.co.uk/about-us/`
- **Different subdomain**: `https://careers.example.com/about-us/`
- **Different port**: `https://www.example.com:444/about-us/`

It is the web browser that sets the `Origin` header automatically when making a request. This cannot be overridden.

Warning! The same-origin policy does *not* apply to any requests that come from a non-web browser because, in those cases, the programmer could change the Origin header anyway. If you create a console app or even an ASP.NET Core project that uses .NET classes such as HttpClient to make a request, the same-origin policy does not apply unless you explicitly set the Origin header.

Let's see some examples of calling the web service from a web page with a different origin and from a .NET app.

Configuring HTTP logging for the web service

First, let's customize HTTP logging for the web service to configure it to show the origin of requests, and then let's create a web page client that will attempt to use JavaScript to call the web service:

1. In the Northwind.WebApi project, in Program.cs, in the call to AddHttpLogging, add a statement to include the Origin header, as shown in the following code:

```
builder.Services.AddHttpLogging(options =>
{
  // Add the Origin header so it will not be redacted.
  options.RequestHeaders.Add("Origin");
  options.LoggingFields = HttpLoggingFields.All;
  options.RequestBodyLogLimit = 4096; // Default is 32k.
  options.ResponseBodyLogLimit = 4096; // Default is 32k.
});
```

2. In the Northwind.Mvc project, in the Views\Shared folder, in _Layout.cshtml, add a navigation menu item to go to a CORS controller with a JavaScript action method, as shown in the following markup:

```
<li class="nav-item">
  <a class="nav-link text-dark" asp-area="" asp-controller="Cors"
     asp-action="JavaScript">CORS</a>
</li>
```

3. In the Northwind.Mvc project, in the Controllers folder, add a new **MVC Controller – Empty** file named CorsController.cs.

4. In CorsController.cs, define a controller class with a JavaScript action method, as shown in the following code:

```
using Microsoft.AspNetCore.Mvc;

namespace Northwind.Mvc.Controllers;

public class CorsController : Controller
```

```
{
  public IActionResult JavaScript()
  {
    return View();
  }
}
```

5. In the Views folder, add a new folder named Cors.

6. In the Views/Cors folder, add a new **Razor View** - **Empty** file named JavaScript.cshtml.

> If you are using Visual Studio, then you can right-click the **JavaScript** action method and select **Add View....** This will create both the Cors folder and the JavaScript. cshtml file.

7. In JavaScript.cshtml, replace the existing markup with the markup that follows, which has a link to a route that has not been defined yet, a textbox and button, and a JavaScript block that makes a call to the web service to get customers that contain a partial name, as shown in the following code:

```
@{
  ViewData["Title"] = "Customers using JavaScript";
}
<div class="text-center">
  <h1 class="display-4">@ViewData["Title"]</h1>
  <div>
      Go to <a href="/cors/net">Customers using .NET</a>
  </div>
  <div>
    <input id="country" placeholder="Enter a country" />
    <input id="getCustomersButton" type="button" value="Get Customers" />
  </div>
  <div>
    <table id="customersTable" class="table">
      <thead>
        <tr>
          <th scope="col">Company Name</th>
          <th scope="col">City</th>
          <th scope="col">Country</th>
        </tr>
      </thead>
      <tbody id="tableBody">
        <!-- This will be populated from the web service. -->
```

```
        </tbody>
      </table>
    </div>
    <script>
    var baseaddress = "https://localhost:5091/";

    function xhr_load() {
      console.log(this.responseText);
      var customers = JSON.parse(this.responseText);
      var out = "";
      var i;

      for (i = 0; i < customers.length; i++) {
        out += '<tr><td><a href="' + baseaddress + 'api/customers/' +
        customers[i].customerId + '">' +
        customers[i].companyName + '</a></td><td>' +
        customers[i].city + '</td><td>' +
        customers[i].country + '</td></tr>';
      }

      document.getElementById("tableBody").innerHTML = out;
    }

    function getCustomersButton_click() {
      xhr.open("GET", baseaddress + "api/customers/?country=" +
      document.getElementById("country").value);
      xhr.send();
    }

    document.getElementById("getCustomersButton")
      .addEventListener("click", getCustomersButton_click);

    var xhr = new XMLHttpRequest();
    xhr.addEventListener("load", xhr_load);
    </script>
  </div>
```

The preceding ASP.NET Core MVC Razor View mixes Razor, HTML, and JavaScript to display a customer list dynamically:

- `<div>` contains a text input where the user types a country name. It also has a button that, when clicked, triggers JavaScript to fetch customers, and the button is wired to a click event later in the script.

- `<table>` is used to display the returned customers. `<thead>` defines the column headers. `<tbody>` is initially empty. JavaScript populates `<tbody id="tableBody">` dynamically after fetching data from the API.

- In `<script>`, a hardcoded base URL is used for the backend API. Normally, you'd use `appsettings.json` or Razor to inject this, as you learned in *Chapter 8*, but for simplicity, here it's static.

- The `xhr_load()` function is used to handle to API response. First, it converts the response text from the API into a JavaScript object using `JSON.parse()`. It loops through customers and builds table rows (`<tr>`) for each customer. Each company name becomes a clickable link to `api/customers/{id}`. Finally, it updates the DOM by injecting the built HTML string into the table body.

- When the button is clicked, it calls `xhr.open()` to prepare an HTTP GET request to the API. The country comes from the input field. It sends the request via `xhr.send()`.

Trying out the JavaScript call to the web service

Now we are ready to try out what happens when a web page uses JavaScript to call our web service:

1. Start the `Northwind.WebApi` project using the `https` profile without debugging.
2. Start the `Northwind.Mvc` project using the `https` profile without debugging.
3. In Chrome, show **Developer Tools** and **Console**.
4. On the home page, in the top navigation menu, click **CORS**.
5. On the **Customers using JavaScript** web page, in the text box, enter USA, click the **Get Customers** button, and note the error, as shown in the following output and in *Figure 10.3*:

```
Access to XMLHttpRequest at 'https://localhost:5091/api/
customers/?country=USA' from origin 'https://localhost:5021' has been
blocked by CORS policy: No 'Access-Control-Allow-Origin' header is
present on the requested resource.
```

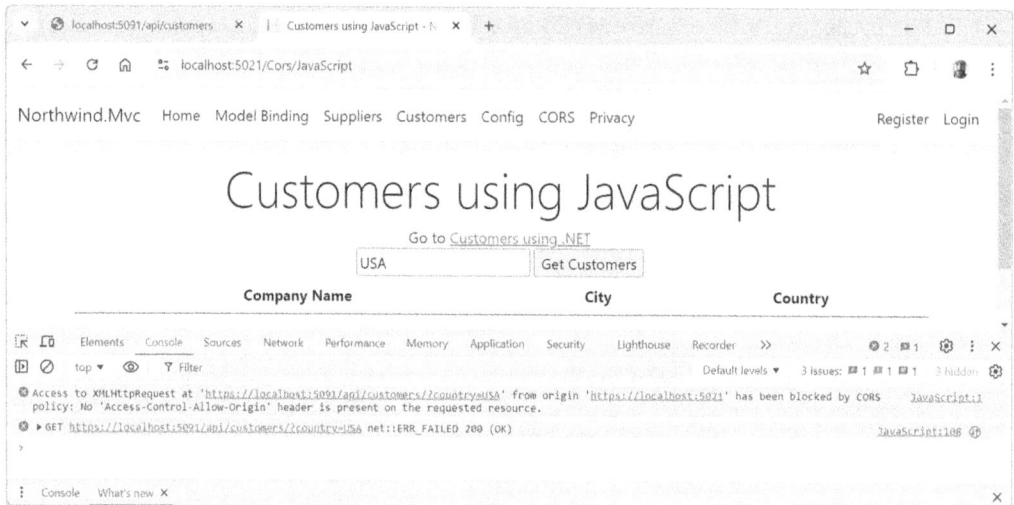

Figure 10.3: CORS error in the Chrome Developer Tools console

6. At the command prompt or terminal for the `Northwind.WebApi` project, note the HTTP log for the request and that `Host` is on a different port number (5091) to `Origin` (5021), so they are not the same origin, as shown in the following output:

```
info: Microsoft.AspNetCore.HttpLogging.HttpLoggingMiddleware[1]
      Request:
      Protocol: HTTP/2
      Method: GET
      Scheme: https
      PathBase:
      Path: /api/customers
      Accept: */*
      Host: localhost:5091
      User-Agent: Mozilla/5.0 (Windows NT 10.0; Win64; x64)
AppleWebKit/537.36 (KHTML, like Gecko) Chrome/113.0.0.0 Safari/537.36
      Accept-Encoding: gzip, deflate, br
      Accept-Language: en-US,en;q=0.9,sv;q=0.8
      Origin: https://localhost:5021
      Referer: [Redacted]
      ...
```

7. Also, note that the output shows that the web service executed the database query and returned the USA customers in a JSON document response to the browser, as shown in the following output:

```
info: Microsoft.AspNetCore.HttpLogging.HttpLoggingMiddleware[2]
      Response:
      StatusCode: 200
      Content-Type: application/json; charset=utf-8
info: Microsoft.AspNetCore.HttpLogging.HttpLoggingMiddleware[4]
      ResponseBody: [{"customerId":"GREAL","companyName":"Great
Lakes Food Market","contactName":"Howard
Snyder","contactTitle":"Marketing Manager","address":"2732 Baker
Blvd.","city":"Eugene","region":"OR","postalCode":"97403",
"country":"USA","phone":"(503)
555-7555","fax":null,"orders":[],"customerTypes":[]},
...
,{"customerId":"WHITC","companyName":"White Clover Markets",
"contactName":"Karl Jablonski","contactTitle":"Owner","address":
"305 - 14th Ave. S. Suite 3B","city":"Seattle","region":"WA",
"postalCode":"98128","country":"USA","phone":"(206) 555-4112",
"fax":"(206) 555-4115","orders":[],"customerTypes":[]}]
```

> Although the browser receives a response containing the data requested, it is the browser that enforces the same-origin policy by refusing to reveal the HTTP response to the JavaScript. The web service is not "secured" by CORS.

8. Close the browser(s) and shut down the web servers.

You previously saw on the home page that if it is the .NET HTTP client that is calling the web service, the same-origin policy does not apply. If you were to check the logs at the command line or terminal as you did before, you would see the ports are different, but it does not matter.

Understanding CORS

CORS is an HTTP header-based feature that asks the browser to *disable* its same-origin security policy in specific scenarios. The HTTP headers indicate which origins should be allowed in addition to the same origin.

> CORS is not about strengthening security; it is about weakening security to allow the sharing of resources across different origins!

Let's enable CORS in the web service so that it can send extra headers to indicate to the browser that it is allowed to access resources from a different origin:

1. In the `Northwind.WebApi` project, in `Program.cs`, after creating `builder`, add CORS support to the web service, as shown in the following code:

    ```
    builder.Services.AddCors(options =>
    {
      options.AddPolicy(name: "Northwind.Mvc.Policy",
        policy =>
        {
          policy.WithOrigins("https://localhost:5021");
        });
    });
    ```

2. In `Program.cs`, after the call to `UseHttpsRedirection`, add a statement to use the CORS policy, as shown in the following code:

    ```
    app.UseCors(policyName: "Northwind.Mvc.Policy");
    ```

3. Start the `Northwind.WebApi` project using the `https` profile without debugging.
4. Start the `Northwind.Mvc` project using the `https` profile without debugging.
5. Show **Developer Tools** and **Console**.

6. On the home page, click **CORS**, and then in the text box, enter USA, click **Get Customers**, and note that the console shows the JSON document returned from the web service, and the table is filled with the 13 customers, as shown in *Figure 10.4*:

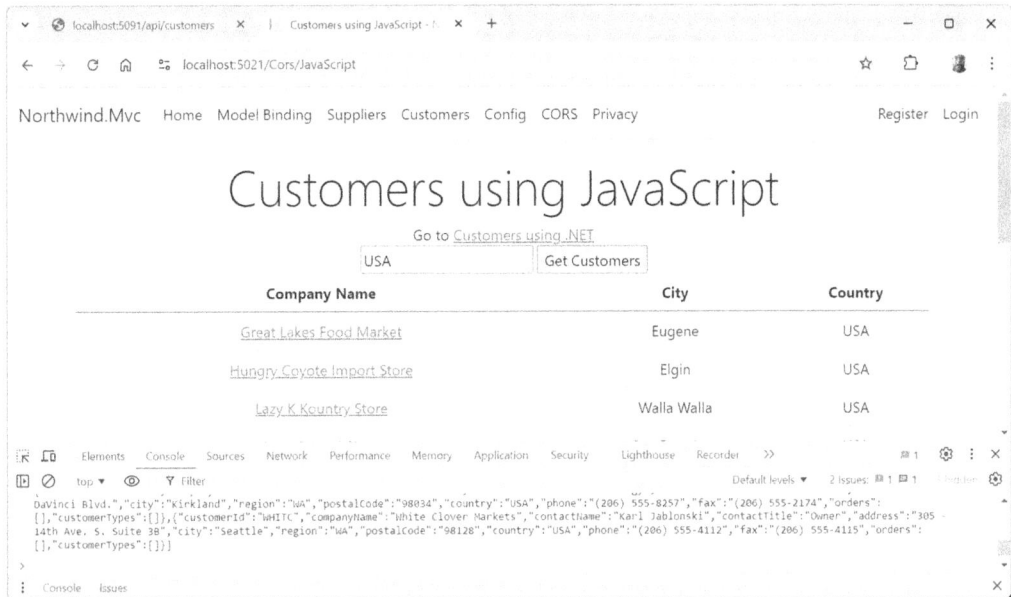

Figure 10.4: A successful cross-origin request to the web service using JavaScript

7. Close the browser and shut down the web servers.

Understanding other CORS policy options

You can control the following:

- Allowed origins, for example, `https://*.example.com/`
- Allowed HTTP methods, for example, `GET`, `POST`, `DELETE`, and so on
- Allowed HTTP request headers, for example, `Content-Type`, `Content-Language`, `x-custom-header`, and so on
- Exposed HTTP response headers, meaning which headers to include unredacted in a response (because, by default, response headers are redacted), for example, `x-custom-header`

> You can learn more about options for CORS policies at the following link: https://learn.microsoft.com/en-us/aspnet/core/security/cors#cors-policy-options.

Now that you know that CORS does not secure a web service, let's look at how you can actually identify, authenticate, and authorize requests.

Understanding identity services

In *Chapter 5, Authentication and Authorization,* you learned about security in the context of an ASP.NET Core MVC website. You saw an example of a local authentication database that a visitor could register with and then used it to authorize visitors identified as administrators to access protected areas of the website. But what if we don't want to authenticate using a local database?

Identity services are used to identify, authenticate, and authorize requests. It is important for these services to implement open standards so that you can integrate disparate systems. Common standards include **OpenID Connect** and **OAuth 2.0**.

> Microsoft has no plans to officially support third-party authentication servers like **Identity-Server4** because *"creating and sustaining an authentication server is a full-time endeavor, and Microsoft already has a team and a product in that area, Azure Active Directory, which allows 500,000 objects for free."* This quote is from an ASP.NET Core GitHub repository issue that you can find at the following link: https://github.com/dotnet/aspnetcore/issues/32494.

JWT bearer authorization

JSON Web Token (JWT) is a standard that defines a compact and secure method to transmit information as a JSON object. The JSON object is digitally signed, so it can be trusted. The most common scenario for using a JWT is authorization.

A user logs in to a trusted party using credentials like a username and password, a biometric scan, or two-factor authentication, and the trusted party issues a JWT. This is then sent with every request to the secure web service.

In their compact form, JWTs consist of three parts separated by dots. These parts are the *header,* *payload,* and *signature,* as shown in the following format: aaa.bbb.ccc. The header and payload are Base64 encoded.

Authenticating service clients using JWT bearer authentication

During local development, the dotnet user-jwts command-line tool is used to create and manage local JWTs. The values are stored in a JSON file in the local machine's user profile folder.

Let's secure the web service using JWT bearer authentication and try it with a local token:

1. In the Northwind.WebApi project, add a reference to the package for JWT bearer authentication, as shown in the following markup:

   ```
   <PackageReference Include=
     "Microsoft.AspNetCore.Authentication.JwtBearer" />
   ```

2. Build the Northwind.WebApi project to restore packages.

3. In Program.cs, import the namespace for security claims, as shown in the following code:

   ```
   using System.Security.Claims; // To use ClaimsPrincipal.
   ```

4. In Program.cs, after creating the builder, add statements to add authorization and authentication using JWT, as shown highlighted in the following code:

   ```
   var builder = WebApplication.CreateBuilder(args);

   builder.Services.AddAuthorization();
   builder.Services.AddAuthentication(defaultScheme: "Bearer")
     .AddJwtBearer();
   ```

5. In Program.cs, after mapping controllers, add a statement to map an HTTP GET request for the secret path to return the authenticated user's name if they are authorized, as shown in the following code:

   ```
   app.MapControllers();

   app.MapGet("/secret", (ClaimsPrincipal user) =>
     string.Format("Welcome, {0}. The secret ingredient is love.",
     user.Identity?.Name ?? "secure user"))
     .RequireAuthorization();
   ```

6. In the Northwind.WebApi project folder, at the command prompt or terminal, create a local JWT, as shown in the following command:

   ```
   dotnet user-jwts create
   ```

7. Note the automatically assigned ID, Name, and Token, as shown in the following output:

```
New JWT saved with ID 'f2d14dfa'.
Name: markj
Token: eyJhbGciOiJIUzI1NiIsInR5cCI6IkpXVCJ9.
eyJ1bmlxdWVfbmFtZSI6Im1hcmtqIiwic3ViIjoibWFya2oiLCJqdGkiOiJmMmQxNGRmYSIs
ImF1ZCI6WyJodHRwOi8vbG9jYWxob3N0OjUwOTAiLCJodHRwczovL2xvY2FsaG9zdDo1MDkxI
l0sIm5iZiI6MTcyNDUwMzE5NCwiZXhwIjoxNzMyNDUxOTk0LCJpYXQiOjE3MjQ1MDMxOTUs
ImlzcyI6ImRvdG5ldC11c2VyLWp3dHMifQ.grLo3oRI2j2-
LuF7IEZSLxjVFOh57FcRWO9SyC4se2M
```

8. At the command prompt or terminal, print all the information for the ID that was assigned, as shown in the following command:

```
dotnet user-jwts print f2d14dfa --show-all
```

9. Note that the scheme is Bearer, so the token must be sent with every request; the audience(s) lists the authorized client domains and port numbers, and the token expires after three months. Also note the JSON objects that represent the header and payload, and finally, the compact token with its Base64-encoded three parts separated by dots, as shown in the following partial output:

```
Found JWT with ID 'f2d14dfa'.
ID: f2d14dfa
Name: markj
Scheme: Bearer
Audience(s): http://localhost:5090, https://localhost:5091
Not Before: 2025-08-24T12:39:54.0000000+00:00
Expires On: 2025-11-24T12:39:54.0000000+00:00
Issued On: 2025-08-24T12:39:55.0000000+00:00
Scopes: none
Roles: [none]
Custom Claims: [none]
Token Header: {"alg":"HS256","typ":"JWT"}
Token Payload: {"unique_
name":"markj","sub":"markj","jti":"f2d14dfa","aud":
["http://localhost:5090","https://
localhost:5091"],"nbf":1724503194,"exp":
1732451994,"iat":1724503195,"iss":"dotnet-user-jwts"}
Compact Token: eyJhbGciOiJIUzI1NiIsInR5cCI6IkpXVCJ9.
eyJ1bmlxdWVfbmFtZSI6Im
1hcmtqIiwic3ViIjoibWFya2oiLCJqdGkiOiJmMmQxNGRmYSIsIm
F1ZCI6WyJodHRwOi8vbG9jYWxob3N0OjUwOTAiLCJodHRwczovL2xvY2FsaG9zdDo1MDkxIl0s
Im5
iZiI6MTcyNDUwMzE5NCwiZXhwIjoxNzMyNDUxOTk0LCJpYXQiOjE3MjQ1MDMxOTUsImlzcyI6Im
RvdG5ldC11c2VyLWp3dHMifQ.grLo3oRI2j2-LuF7IEZSLxjVFOh57FcRWO9SyC4se2M
```

10. In your preferred browser, navigate to `https://jwt.ms/`, then copy and paste your JWT compact token into the box to decode it, as shown in *Figure 10.5*:

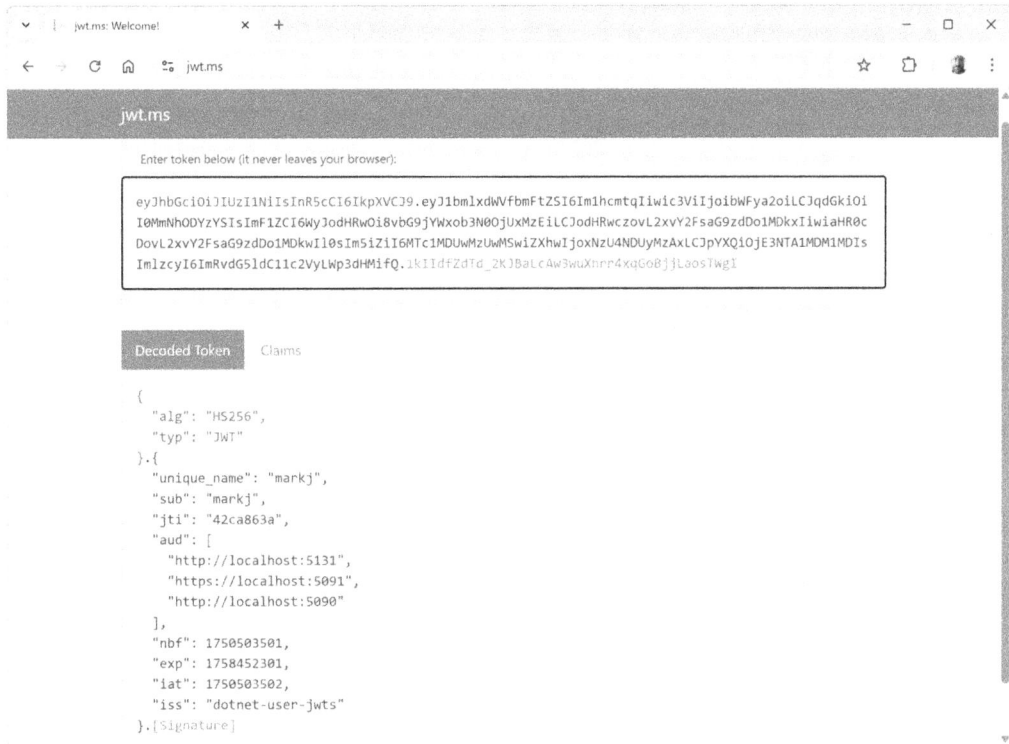

Figure 10.5: Decoding a JWT

11. Click the **Claims** tab and note the claims like sub or subject and exp or expiration time, as shown in *Figure 10.6*:

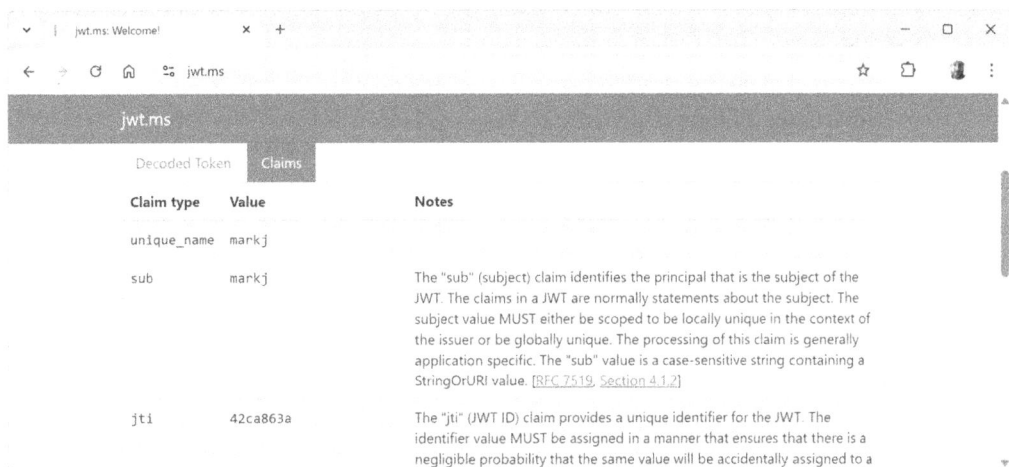

Figure 10.6: Descriptions of the JWT claims

12. In the Northwind.WebApi project, in appsettings.Development.json, note the new section named Authentication, as shown highlighted in the following configuration:

```
{
  "Logging": {
    "LogLevel": {
      "Default": "Information",
      "Microsoft.AspNetCore": "Warning",
      "Microsoft.AspNetCore.HttpLogging": "Information"
    }
  },
  "Authentication": {
    "Schemes": {
      "Bearer": {
        "ValidAudiences": [
          "http://localhost:5090"
          "https://localhost:5091"
        ],
        "ValidIssuer": "dotnet-user-jwts"
      }
    }
  }
}
```

Trying out the token

Now we can try out the web service and its token for authentication:

1. Start the Northwind.WebApi project using the https profile without debugging.

2. In the browser, in the tab that has called the web service and received a JSON document of customers, change the relative path to /secret and note that the response is rejected with a 401 status code, as shown in *Figure 10.7*:

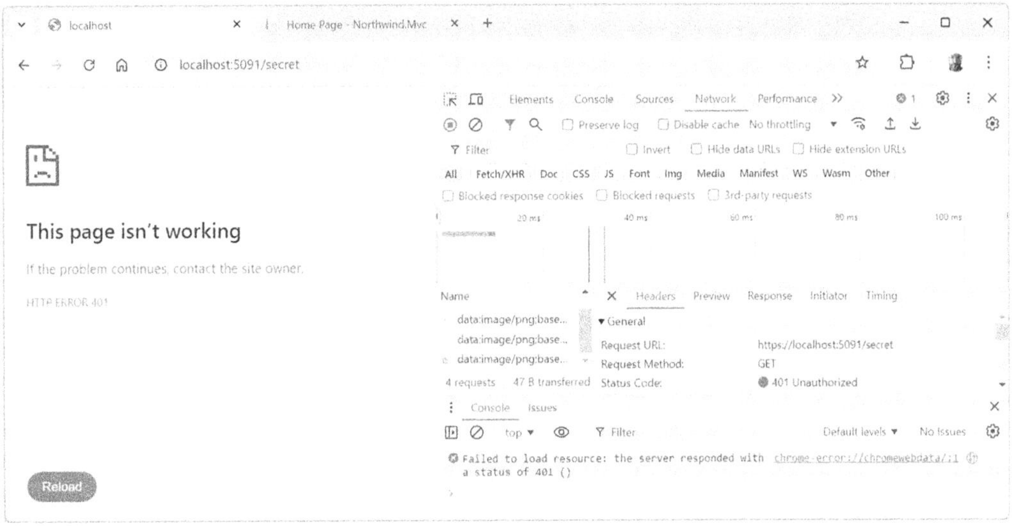

Figure 10.7: A failed request to a protected resource

3. In the `HttpRequests` folder, create a file named `webapi-secure-request.http` and modify its contents to contain a request to get the secret ingredient, as shown in the following code (but use your `Bearer` token, of course):

```
### Get the secret ingredient.
GET https://localhost:5091/secret/
Authorization: Bearer eyJhbGciOiJIUzI1NiIsInR5cCI6IkpXVCJ9.
eyJ1bmlxdWVfbmFtZSI6Im1hcmtqIiwic3ViIjoibWFya2oiLCJqdGkiOiJmMmQxNGRmYSIs
ImF1ZCI6WyJodHRwOi8vbG9jYWxob3N0OjUwOTAiLCJodHRwczovL2xvY2FsaG9zdDo1MDkx
Il0sIm5iZiI6MTcyNDUwMzE5NCwiZXhwIjoxNzMyNDUxOTk4LCJpYXQiOjE3MjQ1MDMxOTUs
ImlzcyI6ImRvdG5ldC11c2VyLWp3dHMifQ.grLo3oRI2j2-
LuF7IEZSLxjVFOh57FcRWO9SyC4se2M
```

4. Click **Send Request**, and note the response, as shown in *Figure 10.8* and in the following output:

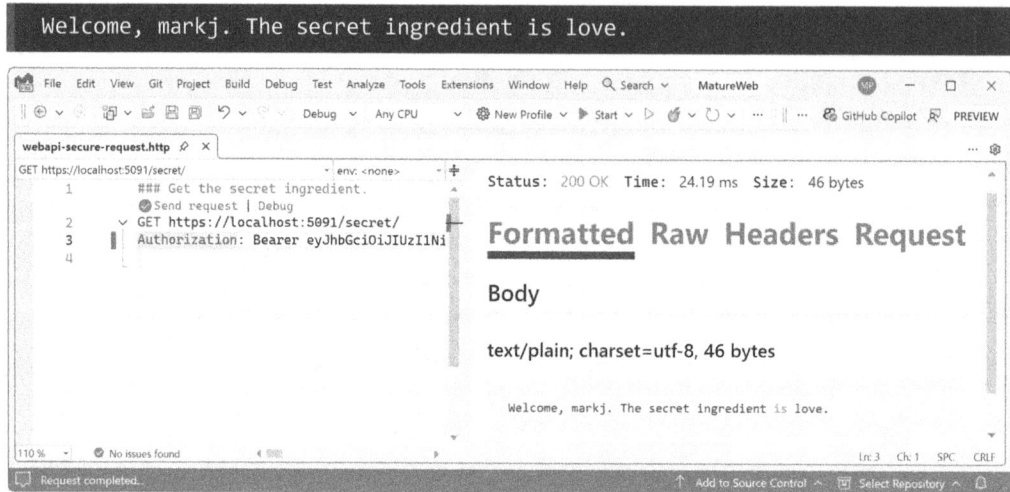

Figure 10.8: Making a successful secure request

5. Close the browser and shut down the web service.

JWT in production

Developers often understand JWTs as a "token you add to a header," but the source and validation model of those tokens changes drastically once you leave your localhost comfort zone. Let's review what's happening behind the scenes and how it transitions from development to production.

When you're building your Web API locally, you typically don't have a full-fledged identity infrastructure running. You configure ASP.NET Core to trust a fixed or generated JWT, or you mock an identity provider.

In this mode, the token is usually created in one of three ways:

*   A hardcoded "development token." This is what we did.
*   A self-contained test identity server. Sometimes you spin up a local `IdentityServer`, or use ASP.NET Core's `AddTestServer()` helper, which produces JWTs signed by a local key pair.
*   An embedded "fake" bearer scheme. You can even plug in a middleware that skips token validation entirely for local debugging.

Any of these setups is fast and convenient because both token issuance and validation happen inside your solution. There's no network call to an identity service. But it's not secure and doesn't scale to multiple environments or clients. That's why production deployments must integrate with a real issuer.

Common identity providers

When you go to production, the API must stop trusting self-signed or locally issued tokens. Instead, it must validate tokens issued by a trusted identity provider, typically one of the following shown in *Table 10.1*:

Provider	Common Usage	Notes
Entra ID	Microsoft ecosystem	Tokens signed with RS256 using Microsoft's public keys (JWKS)
Auth0	Multi-tenant apps	Easy setup for custom APIs and SPAs
Okta	Enterprise SSO	Same model: JWTs signed with asymmetric keys
AWS Cognito	Serverless and cloud-native apps	Uses OpenID Connect discovery
IdentityServer (self-hosted)	Roll-your-own identity	You control signing keys and claims

Table 10.1: Common identity providers

The central idea is that your API trusts JWTs not because it generated them, but because it knows how to verify that they were issued by the correct authority.

When an external identity service issues a JWT:

1. It signs the token using a private key.
2. It publishes the matching public key at a well-known endpoint (often /jwks).
3. It exposes metadata through an OpenID Connect discovery document, typically at https://<tenant>/.well-known/openid-configuration.
4. Your API retrieves this document automatically (or periodically caches it) to validate tokens.

Configuring authentication with an identity provider

In Program.cs, you configure the authentication, as shown in the following code:

```
builder.Services
  .AddAuthentication(JwtBearerDefaults.AuthenticationScheme)
  .AddJwtBearer(options =>
  {
    options.Authority = "https://login.microsoftonline.com/<tenant-id>/v2.0";
    options.Audience = "api://<your-api-client-id>";
  });
```

ASP.NET Core's JwtBearerHandler will then:

1. Fetch the signing keys (JWKS) from the authority.
2. Validate the token's signature using those keys.
3. Ensure that the aud (audience) matches your API.
4. Check the iss (issuer) claim and expiry time.

You no longer store or know the signing key locally; only the identity provider does. In production, the API doesn't need to (and shouldn't) mint tokens itself. That job belongs to the identity service. Your API just validates them.

Registering with an identity provider

You register your Web API with the identity provider so that it's recognized as a resource that clients can request access to. This creates a logical binding between your project and the IdP.

For example, in Entra ID:

1. You register an "app" for your API.
2. You register a second "app" for your client (e.g., SPA or mobile app).
3. You configure your API's app ID URI, like api://f51a9b27-....
4. Clients request tokens for that audience.
5. Entra ID issues a JWT with aud = "api://f51a9b27-...".
6. Your API's JWT Bearer middleware checks for that aud and trusts the signature from the Azure tenant's public keys.

That's the production trust chain.

In real-world setups, you often need both development and production token validation, without changing the entire code base. The best practice is to configure the authentication handler conditionally, as shown in the following code:

```
if (app.Environment.IsDevelopment())
{
  builder.Services.AddAuthentication("Bearer")
    .AddJwtBearer("Bearer", options =>
    {
      options.TokenValidationParameters = new TokenValidationParameters
      {
        ValidateIssuer = false,
        ValidateAudience = false,
        ValidateLifetime = false,
        IssuerSigningKey = new SymmetricSecurityKey(
          Encoding.UTF8.GetBytes("dev-super-secret-key"))
      };
    });
```

```
  }
  else
  {
    builder.Services.AddAuthentication("Bearer")
      .AddJwtBearer("Bearer", options =>
      {
        options.Authority = "https://login.microsoftonline.com/<tenant-id>/v2.0";
        options.Audience = "api://<your-client-id>";
      });
  }
```

In the preceding code:

- Locally, your API trusts a simple shared secret for convenience.
- In production, it only accepts tokens that are verifiably issued by your real IdP.

> **Good practice:** Never reuse your dev keys or mock tokens in production.

Now that you've seen how to use JWT during development to secure your web service, let's look at some principles that you should follow when designing your web service APIs.

Principles of Web API design

Designing a web service API is about structuring a system that is predictable, consistent, and maintainable for its consumers. Whether it's a RESTful API, GraphQL, or something custom, good design matters far more than which web framework or backend language you use.

Use resource-oriented URIs

Web APIs should expose resources using URIs that are nouns, not verbs.

Here's a good example:

```
GET /users/123
POST /orders
PATCH /products/456
```

Here's a bad example:

```
GET /getUser?id=123
POST /createOrder
PATCH /updateProduct/456
```

Why?

- Resource URIs follow REST principles.
- HTTP verbs already describe the action, so don't duplicate it in the path.

HTTP methods semantics

HTTP methods and how they should be used in a web service are summarized in *Table 10.2*:

Verb	Action	Use case
GET	Read	Retrieve a resource or collection
POST	Create	Create a new resource
PUT	Replace	Replace a resource completely
PATCH	Update	Partially update a resource
DELETE	Delete	Remove a resource

Table 10.2: HTTP methods and how they should be used in a web service

Here's an example:

```
[HttpGet("users/{id}")]
public IActionResult GetUser(int id) { ... }


[HttpPost("users")]
public IActionResult CreateUser(User user) { ... }


[HttpPut("users/{id}")]
public IActionResult ReplaceUser(int id, User user) { ... }


[HttpPatch("users/{id}")]
public IActionResult UpdateUser(int id, JsonPatchDocument<User> patch) { ... }


[HttpDelete("users/{id}")]
public IActionResult DeleteUser(int id) { ... }
```

Good practice: Use PUT only if you're replacing all fields. Prefer PATCH for partial updates. Don't overload POST with non-creation logic, for example, search.

Response status codes

Your API should respond with meaningful HTTP status codes, as shown in *Table 10.3*:

Code	Meaning	When to use
200	OK	Successful GET or PUT
201	Created	Successful POST
204	No Content	Successful DELETE or PATCH
400	Bad Request	Validation or input error
401	Unauthorized	No valid authentication
403	Forbidden	Auth present, but not allowed
404	Not Found	Resource doesn't exist
409	Conflict	Duplicate or business rule error
500	Internal Server Error	Unexpected error

Table 10.3: HTTP status codes and when to return them

> **Good practice:** Avoid using 200 for everything, especially for failures.

Here's an example:

```
if (user == null)
  return NotFound(); // Returns 404 Missing resource.

return Ok(user); // Returns 200 OK.
```

Versioning web services

APIs change over time. Versioning ensures backward compatibility. There are several ways to implement versioning in a web service, as shown in the following list:

- **URI versioning** (most common) puts a version number in the relative path, which is easy to route, clear to clients, but pollutes the URIs, as shown in the following examples:

    ```
    GET /v1/users/123
    GET /v2/users/123
    ```

- **Header versioning** puts a version number in the HTTP request headers, which keeps your URIs clean, but is harder to discover and leads to more complex tooling, as shown in the following example:

```
GET /users/123
Header: X-API-Version: 2
```

- **Query string versioning** puts a version number in the query string, which is simple to implement but is not semantically clean, as shown in the following example:

```
GET /users/123?api-version=2
```

> **Good practice:** Use URI versioning for public APIs. Use header versioning only if you have very advanced versioning needs and clients that can support it.

Resource nesting

Reflect relationships using nested routes only when the child can't exist without the parent.

Here's a good example:

```
GET /users/123/orders          // Orders belong to a user.
GET /users/123/orders/456
```

Here's a bad example:

```
GET /users/123/orders/456/items/999     // Too deeply nested.
```

> **Good practice:** No more than two levels of nesting. Beyond that, use filters or IDs.

Filtering, sorting, and paging

Use query parameters for optional behavior like search, filter, sort, or page, as shown in the following code:

```
GET /products?category=books&sort=price_asc&page=2&pageSize=10
```

Common query string parameters include:

- `filter=`
- `sort=`
- `page=`
- `pageSize=`
- `sort=price_asc`

Good practice: Avoid POST for search unless the payload is very complex, for example, large JSON filters.

Request and response shapes

Use consistent naming and casing, as shown in the following bullets and JSON:

- Use camelCase for JSON (standard in JavaScript)
- Include only necessary fields
- Avoid leaking internal data structures

```
{
  "id": 123,
  "firstName": "John",
  "lastName": "Doe"
}
```

Hypermedia as the Engine of Application State (HATEOAS)

HATEOAS is a REST API design principle where the server provides not just data but also hyperlinks that tell the client what actions are possible next. The client doesn't need to hardcode API paths. Instead, the API itself guides the client on what to do. This makes APIs self-descriptive, discoverable, and easier to evolve.

This is optional and mostly useful in complex hypermedia-driven APIs:

```
{
  "id": 123,
  "name": "John",
  "links": [
    { "rel": "self", "href": "/users/123" },
    { "rel": "orders", "href": "/users/123/orders" }
  ]
}
```

These are the pros:

- Self-discoverable API
- Better for clients that navigate the API

These are the cons:

- Extra links make responses heavier
- Web service must generate correct links for each resource
- Often overkill for typical REST APIs

Error handling and standard errors

Use a consistent error response schema. For example, as shown in the following JSON:

```json
{
  "error": "Invalid input",
  "details": [
    { "field": "email", "message": "Email is invalid" }
  ]
}
```

> 💡 **Good practice:** Use HTTP 400 for validation issues, not 500. Avoid returning stack traces.

Authentication and authorization

Not a design topic in terms of routing, but this affects how endpoints are accessed:

- Use 401 Unauthorized if no credentials are provided
- Use 403 Forbidden if credentials are valid but access is denied

Use attribute-based security in ASP.NET Core:

```
[Authorize(Roles = "Admin")]
public IActionResult DeleteUser(int id) { ... }
```

Design summary

Designing an API isn't just about slapping routes and methods together – it's a contract between you and your clients. A well-designed API:

- Uses consistent, resource-oriented URIs
- Applies HTTP methods and status codes semantically
- Supports discoverability, extensibility, and versioning
- Maintains clarity, minimalism, and consistency

> 💡 **Good practice:** When it comes to API design, be boring, be predictable, and stick to conventions.

One of the design principles is to implement versioning since your web service API is likely to change over time. Let's look into that in more detail and see how you might implement versioning in practice.

Implementing URI versioning

URI versioning can be implemented either manually via route templates or formally using the Asp.Versioning.Mvc package (a replacement for the deprecated Microsoft.AspNetCore.Mvc.Versioning package). Asp.Versioning.Mvc is widely used and maintained by the same author (Chris Martinez) and is fully aligned with current .NET ecosystem best practices.

Using this package gives you a cleaner, extensible, and industry-standard way to manage API versions with features like:

- Version negotiation (via URI, query string, or header)
- Automatic version discovery
- Versioned controllers

It works by decorating the controller class with [ApiVersion] and specifying versioned route templates with {version:apiVersion}.

Adding versions to the customers web service

Let's see a practical example:

1. In the Northwind.WebApi project, add a reference to the packages for versioning and its integration with API Explorer, as shown in the following markup:

    ```
    <PackageReference Include="Asp.Versioning.Mvc" />
    <PackageReference Include="Asp.Versioning.Mvc.ApiExplorer" />
    ```

2. Build the Northwind.WebApi project to restore packages.
3. In the Northwind.WebApi project, add a new folder named Extensions.
4. In the Extensions folder, add a new class named IServiceCollectionExtensions.cs.
5. In IServiceCollectionExtensions.cs, add statements to define an extension method that adds versioning support, as shown in the following code:

    ```
    using Asp.Versioning; // To use ApiVersion.

    namespace Northwind.WebApi.Extensions;

    public static class IServiceCollectionExtensions
    {
      public static IServiceCollection AddUriVersioning(
        this IServiceCollection services)
      {
        services.AddApiVersioning(options =>
        {
          options.DefaultApiVersion = new ApiVersion(1, 0);
          options.AssumeDefaultVersionWhenUnspecified = true;
          options.ReportApiVersions = true;
    ```

```
            // Use URL segment for versioning: /api/v1/customers
            options.ApiVersionReader = new UrlSegmentApiVersionReader();

            // Use query string for versioning: /api/customers?api-version=1.0
            // options.ApiVersionReader = new QueryStringApiVersionReader("api-
        version");

            // Use header for versioning: X-Version: 1.0
            // options.ApiVersionReader = new HeaderApiVersionReader("X-
        Version");

            // Use multiple versioning schemes.
            // options.ApiVersionReader = ApiVersionReader.Combine(
            //    new QueryStringApiVersionReader("api-version"),
            //    new HeaderApiVersionReader("X-API-Version"));
        })
        .AddApiExplorer(options =>
        {
            // Group names like "v1", "v2".
            options.GroupNameFormat = "'v'VVV";

            // If you use URL segment versioning.
            options.SubstituteApiVersionInUrl = true;
        });

        return services;
    }
}
```

6. In `Program.cs`, import the namespace to use the extension method, as shown in the following code:

```
using Northwind.WebApi.Extensions;
```

7. In `Program.cs`, after the call to `CreateBuilder`, call the extension method, as shown in the following code:

```
builder.Services.AddUriVersioning();
```

8. In `Program.cs`, duplicate the call to `AddOpenApi` for both versions, as shown in the following code:

```
builder.Services.AddOpenApi("v1");
builder.Services.AddOpenApi("v2");
```

9. In the `Controllers` folder, in `CustomersController.cs`, decorate the controller class, change the route to use versioning, change [controller] to customers, and change the class name, as shown highlighted in the following code:

```
[ApiVersion("1.0")]
// Base address: api/v1/customers
[Route("api/v{version:apiVersion}/customers")]
[ApiController]
public class CustomersV1Controller : ControllerBase
{
  private readonly ICustomerRepository _repo;

  // Constructor injects repository registered in Program.cs.
  public CustomersV1Controller(ICustomerRepository repo)
```

10. In the `Controllers` folder, copy and paste the `CustomersController.cs` file, and then rename the copy to `CustomersV2Controller.cs`.

11. Optionally, rename the filename `CustomersController.cs` to `CustomersV1Controller.cs`. The filename has no effect on compilation.

12. In `CustomersV2Controller.cs`, renumber to version 2, as shown in the following code:

```
[ApiVersion("2.0")]
// Base address: api/v2/customers
[Route("api/v{version:apiVersion}/customers")]
[ApiController]
public class CustomersV2Controller : ControllerBase
{
  private readonly ICustomerRepository _repo;

  // Constructor injects repository registered in Program.cs.
  public CustomersV2Controller(ICustomerRepository repo)
```

13. In the `GetCustomer` action method, append " (v2)" to the company name before returning it to the client, as shown highlighted in the following code:

```
public async Task<IActionResult> GetCustomer(string id)
{
  Customer? c = await _repo.RetrieveAsync(id, default);

  if (c == null)
  {
    return NotFound(); // 404 Resource not found.
  }
```

```
    c.CompanyName += " (v2)"; // Add v2 to CompanyName.


    return Ok(c); // 200 OK with customer in body.
}
```

14. In the `Properties` folder, in `launchSettings.json`, add the version number to the launch URL, as shown highlighted in the following configuration:

    ```
    "launchUrl": "api/v1/customers",
    ```

Trying out the versioning

Now we can try both v1 and v2 versions of the `customers` web service and compare the company names returned:

1. Start the `Northwind.WebApi` project using the `https` profile without debugging.

2. Start Chrome and navigate to `https://localhost:5091/api/v1/customers/alfki`. Note the last segment to request a specific customer with the `CustomerId` of `ALFKI`. Note the company name is `Alfreds Futterkiste`, as shown in *Figure 10.9*:

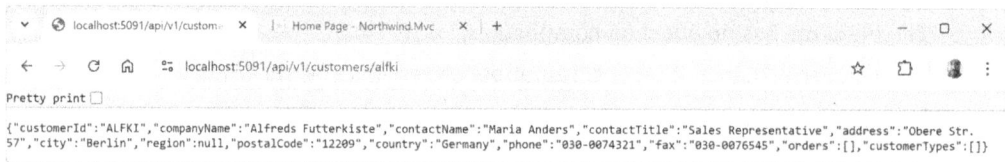

Figure 10.9: Company names are untouched in version 1

3. In Chrome, change the version number in the address bar to navigate to `https://localhost:5091/api/v2/customers/alfki`.

4. Note the company name is suffixed with `(v2)`, as shown in *Figure 10.10*:

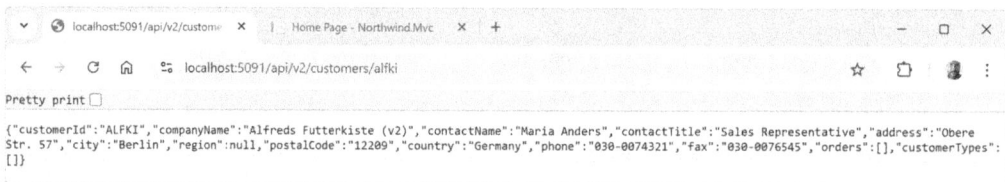

Figure 10.10: Company names are suffixed in version 2

Updating clients to use versioning

You will also need to update the paths used by clients to add the version number.

For example, in the `Northwind.Mvc` project, the following files need updating:

*   `Clients\ICustomersClient.cs`
*   `Controllers\HomeController.cs`: Customers action method
*   `Views\Cors\JavaScript.cshtml`

> **Good practice:** Implement versioning from the very start of your web service projects.

Manual versioning without a package

If you prefer not to use a package, you can just define the version in the route, as shown in the following code:

```
[ApiController]
[Route("api/v1/users")]
public class UsersV1Controller : ControllerBase
{
    [HttpGet]
    public IActionResult Get() => Ok("This is v1");
}

[ApiController]
[Route("api/v2/users")]
public class UsersV2Controller : ControllerBase
{
    [HttpGet]
    public IActionResult Get() => Ok("This is v2");
}
```

The drawbacks of this manual approach include the following points:

- No version negotiation
- You have to handle versioning manually
- Harder to manage as the number of versions grows

Practicing and exploring

Test your knowledge and understanding by answering some questions, getting some hands-on practice, and exploring this chapter's topics with deeper research.

Exercise 10.1 – Online material

JSON Web Tokens are an open, industry-standard RFC 7519 method for representing claims securely between two parties. JWT.IO allows you to decode, verify, and generate JWTs: `https://jwt.io/introduction`.

Exercise 10.2 – Practice exercise

Creating and deleting customers with HttpClient

Extend the Northwind.Mvc website project to have pages where a visitor can fill in a form to create a new customer, or search for a customer and then delete them. The MVC controller should make calls to the Northwind web service to create and delete customers.

Exercise 10.3 – Test your knowledge

Answer the following questions:

1. When configuring an HTTP client, how do you specify the format of data that you prefer in the response from the web service?
2. Why should you not wrap your use of HttpClient in a using statement to dispose of it when you are finished, even though it implements the IDisposable interface, and what should you use instead?
3. What is CORS?
4. What is a JWT?
5. What are the three parts of a JWT?

Exercise 10.4 – Explore topics

Use the links in the following GitHub repository to learn more details about the topics covered in this chapter:

https://github.com/markjprice/web-dev-net10/blob/main/docs/book-links.md#chapter-10---building-clients-for-web-services.

Summary

In this chapter, you learned the following:

*   How to consume services efficiently
*   How to relax the same-origin policy using CORS
*   How to authenticate service clients using JWT bearer authentication
*   How to design your web services APIs
*   How to implement versioning in a web service

In the next chapter, you will learn how to test and debug web services.

Learn more on Discord

To join the Discord community for this book – where you can share feedback, ask questions to the author, and learn about new releases – follow this QR code:

`https://packt.link/RWWD10`

Join .NETPro — It's Free

Staying sharp in .NET takes more than reading release notes. It requires real-world tips, proven patterns, and scalable solutions. That's what .NETPro, Packt's new newsletter, is all about.

Scan the QR code or visit the link to subscribe:

`https://landing.packtpub.com/dotnetpronewsletter/`

11

Testing and Debugging Web Services

This chapter is about testing and debugging your web services. Unit tests are good at detecting errors in business logic in a class or method, but you also need to verify that larger parts of your codebase work together with each other and external systems. This is where integration testing becomes important for web services.

Some external systems should be used directly in integration tests, and some should be replaced with a test double. Integration tests commonly call out-of-process systems like databases, event buses, and message queues. This makes integration tests slower than unit tests, but integration tests cover more code, both in your codebase and external libraries. Integration tests are more likely to catch regressions.

One tool available at the command line and in Visual Studio that makes it easier to perform debugging on web services is dev tunnels. Dev tunnels are incredibly useful for testing web services, especially in team environments where you might be a developer writing and debugging code, and writing and running unit tests, but someone else on the team is a tester, running the more complex cross-functional tests like integrating components, including web services. Dev tunnels solve the problem of accessing local development environments from external networks, like the internet, which is particularly useful for services that need to interact with external APIs, webhooks, or remote clients.

Many APIs, like payment gateways and messaging platforms, send HTTP requests to your web service. Using a dev tunnel, you can easily receive these requests on your local machine without deploying your service to a live production environment. If you are developing a backend for a mobile app, you can point your app to the dev tunnel's public URL, which routes requests to your locally running web service.

One of the biggest advantages of using dev tunnels is the ability to run and debug your code in a familiar local development environment while simultaneously interacting with remote services. Since the requests are routed directly to your local server, you can hit breakpoints, inspect variables, and analyze logs in real time as your service responds to external requests. When you make changes to your local code, you don't have to redeploy it to a remote server to test those changes. You can simply reload or restart your local environment, and the dev tunnel will continue routing traffic to it.

This chapter covers the following topics:

- Introducing all types of testing
- Basics of integration testing
- Testing web services using xUnit
- Mocking in tests
- Debugging web services using dev tunnels

Introducing all types of testing

Testing is one of the most critical phases in the software development process. Good tests will ensure that your application is robust, reliable, and ready for production. But bad tests have a big cost. It is vital to spend the effort you put into writing tests effectively. What represents a good or bad test is one of the most important topics.

Your testing strategy should cover various aspects of the application to catch bugs, avoid regressions, alleviate performance issues, and fix usability problems before they reach the end users. Let's review each of the major types of testing.

Unit testing

The purpose of a **unit test** is to verify individual units of behavior of your project in isolation to ensure that they work as expected. You should focus on business logic, algorithms, and individual functions or methods. Every method that is part of a public API should ideally have at least one corresponding unit test. Note, I do not say *every* method!

Non-public methods typically do not require direct unit testing because:

- Testing through public interfaces naturally covers non-public methods
- Non-public methods have implementation details that are subject to change
- Focusing on behavior rather than implementation leads to more robust and maintainable tests
- Simpler test suites are easier to manage
- Higher-level testing, like integration and end-to-end testing, can provide necessary coverage for complex interactions

By concentrating on public methods, you ensure that your tests remain meaningful, resilient to change, and focused on the class's intended behavior, promoting a more effective and maintainable testing strategy.

Now that you know what methods to test, it's worth emphasizing what makes a good unit test.

A good unit test should meet the following criteria:

- It verifies a single unit of behavior, for example, a method that implements some business logic.
- It executes as fast as possible. For example, it may use an in-memory data store instead of the production database to increase speed while testing business logic. A good test framework will allow you to set a timeout to stop a test from running for too long.

- It performs its work isolated from other tests (and optionally from its dependencies).

Common tools for unit testing .NET code include xUnit, NUnit, and MSTest. In this book, we will focus on xUnit, but the others are similar enough that you will still benefit from this chapter even if you use alternative tools.

Integration, end-to-end, and security testing

Higher-level types of testing include integration, end-to-end, and security testing.

An **integration test** can look like a unit test and use the same tools, like xUnit, but it does not meet one or more of the stricter criteria for a unit test. For example, they can test more than just a small piece of code, they often take longer to execute, and they are not isolated from other parts of the system.

The purpose of integration testing is to verify that different components, modules, or services of the project work together as intended. Integration tests should test database interactions, API integrations, and the interaction between different layers of the project. For example, they should test the interaction between the data access layer and the business logic layer.

An **end-to-end test** is a subtype of integration tests, and it verifies a part of the system from the end user's point of view.

The purpose of a **security test** is to identify vulnerabilities in your apps and services and ensure that data is protected against unauthorized access. You should test authentication and authorization mechanisms, data encryption, as well as protection against common security threats, for example, SQL injection, cross-site scripting, and so on.

Common tools for integration testing include the same ones as for unit testing. The difference is what the tests do. Common tools for security testing include OWASP checklists and .NET security analyzers.

Performance, load, and stress testing

The purpose of performance, load, and stress testing is to ensure the application performs well under expected load conditions. You should test the response times of services, system throughput, and the ability to handle concurrent users or requests without degradation in performance.

Common tools include Apache JMeter, BenchmarkDotNet, and k6.

Functional and usability testing

The purpose of **functional testing** is to ensure the application meets specified requirements and behaves correctly in all scenarios. You should test user scenarios, workflows, and end-to-end tasks. This includes testing form inputs and navigation flows.

The purpose of **usability testing** is to evaluate the application's user interface and overall user experience. You should test the ease of use, design consistency, navigation flow, and accessibility of your apps by getting user feedback, implementing A/B testing, and running usability testing sessions.

Common tools for functional testing include Playwright and Selenium for web apps and Appium for mobile applications.

Testing terminology

Let's review some of the common terms used in testing, as shown in *Table 11.1*:

Term	Definition
System Under Test (SUT), Method Under Test (MUT)	**SUT** is a type, like a class, being tested. You often create a test class with multiple test methods to group all the test methods for the SUT. **MUT** is a method within an SUT being tested.
Test double	An object that has the same public API as a dependency but with simplified and predictable behavior. The name is derived from the concept of a stunt double in film production. It has nothing to do with the `double` number type. It is an umbrella term for any non-production test-only dependencies.
Mock	A subtype of test double that is used to verify interactions between objects by setting up expectations and behaviors on the mock object and then asserting that these expectations were met during the test.
Regression	When code stops working as intended after a code modification.
Coverage metric	Measures how much code a test project executes. This can be 0% to 100%. It's good practice to have a high level of coverage in the core business logic of your project, but do not make this a requirement, especially in non-core parts. A good separation of business logic helps to make it clear what requires testing.
Test fixture	An object the test needs to run, like a dependency. It could be an argument passed to the test, or some state in a file or database. The key point is that the value should be *fixed* so the test produces the same result each time it runs, hence the name *fixture*.

Table 11.1: Common testing terms

Attributes of all good tests

All good tests must have the following attributes:

1. **Verifies the most important parts of the codebase:** For unit tests, this is typically the domain model and business logic algorithms. For integration tests, it is typically controllers or orchestrators for a process that spans as many external systems as possible. But code coverage for tests does not need to be 100%. Tests should verify the end result of a process, not its implementation's technical details.

2. **Integrates automatically into the development process:** Set up your continuous integration and deployment system to run tests automatically.

3. **Avoids regressions**: As you add more features and your codebase becomes more complex, bugs can be introduced that break your code. Good tests will highlight these regressions so you can immediately fix them. They are an early warning system.

4. **Resistant to refactoring**: This means that if you refactor the implementation of a feature, its tests continue to pass. Tests that fail after refactoring lack resistance. They are false positives, aka false alarms.

5. **Balances costs and benefits**: Strikes a balance between the maintenance cost and the benefit gained from tests. Testing trivial code, like setting and getting properties on a model, is not worth the effort.

> **Good practice:** It is always better not to write a test than to write a bad test! Every statement adds to the maintenance costs of a project. If those statements do not provide value, that test is bad.

Test outcomes

When discussing test outcomes, we use the terms *positive* and *negative*, which refer to whether a test indicates the presence or absence of a defect or error. Like testing negative for a disease, a negative outcome is a good thing!

We also use the terms *true* and *false*, which refer to the correctness of the test result in relation to the actual condition of the code being tested. True is good and false is bad!

To summarize, by combining these terms, there are four possible test outcomes, as shown in *Table 11.2*:

	Positive	Negative
True	**True Positive (TP)**: The test correctly identifies a defect. This means the code is faulty, and the test detects it. This is a good outcome. The test finds a defect that actually exists in the code.	**True Negative (TN)**: The test correctly identifies that there is no defect. This means the code is correct, and the test confirms it. This is a good outcome. The test confirms that there are no defects in the code.
False	**False Positive (FP)**: The test incorrectly identifies a defect. This means the code is correct, but the test mistakenly reports a defect. This is a bad outcome. The test reports a defect, but the code is actually correct.	**False Negative (FN)**: The test fails to identify a defect. This means the code is faulty, but the test mistakenly reports that there are no defects. This is a bad outcome. The test fails to report a defect that exists in the code.

Table 11.2: Four possible test outcomes

Let's review some scenarios for a method to help you understand, as shown in *Table 11.3*:

	Scenario	Test	Outcome
TP	There's a bug in the method.	A unit test runs and fails, indicating an error.	The test correctly identifies the bug.
TN	The method is bug-free.	A unit test runs and passes, indicating no errors.	The test correctly confirms the method has no bugs.
FP	The method is bug-free.	A unit test runs and fails, indicating an error.	The test incorrectly reports a bug in the method.
FN	There's a bug in the method.	A unit test runs and passes, indicating no errors.	The test fails to identify the bug.

Table 11.3: Test outcome scenarios

Test doubles, mocks, and stubs

A **test double** is the umbrella term for any fake dependency in a test. They are used in tests in place of real dependencies that would be harder to set up consistently than a double.

There are multiple types of double. The most common are mocks and **stubs**:

- **Mocks** are doubles for outgoing interactions. For example, the test could call a mocked dependency that fakes sending an email during user registration. State could be changed in the external system. Mocks are usually created using a mocking framework. When they are manually created, they are sometimes called **spies**.
- **Stubs** are doubles for incoming interactions. For example, the test could call a stubbed dependency that retrieves product information from a database. No state is changed in the external system. When the dependency does not yet exist, for example, if using TDD, then a stub is known as a **fake**. When a stub is a simple value and does not affect the outcome, then it is known as a **dummy**.

> The separation of mocks and stubs is related to the **Command Query Separation (CQS)** principle. Every method should be either a command or a query. Mocks are for methods that could have side effects and do not return a value. Stubs are for methods that do not have side effects and return a value.

To improve your chances of success with testing, you and your team will need to commit to adopting a testing mindset.

Adopting a testing mindset

To get the best from testing, you will need to adopt a testing mindset. A comprehensive testing strategy will help in identifying and fixing bugs early in the development cycle. It will make sure that your projects meet the performance, security, and usability standards expected by users. As a .NET developer, investing time in learning about and implementing a broad range of testing methodologies will pay off in the form of more reliable, efficient, and user-friendly applications.

One of the strategies that you should consider is adopting **Test-Driven Development** (TDD). This is where you write tests before writing the code itself. This approach can encourage better design and more maintainable code.

> This book focuses on the most useful types of testing for web development: web user interface testing of websites and integration testing of web services. For more types of testing, including unit testing, performance, stress and load testing, and functional testing, please read the companion book, *Tools and Skills for .NET 10*.

Basics of integration testing

Integration testing is a phase of software testing where individual modules or components of an application are combined and tested as a group to ensure they work together correctly. This type of testing focuses on detecting issues that arise from the interaction between integrated units, such as data transfer errors, interface mismatches, and communication failures.

By validating the combined functionality of these interconnected components, integration testing helps ensure that the overall system operates seamlessly and meets specified requirements. It typically follows unit testing and precedes other types of high-level testing, like security and performance testing, in the software development lifecycle.

Integration testing uses similar tools to unit testing. For example, you can write integration tests using xUnit.

To better understand integration tests, it is helpful to remember that unit tests must be:

- A single unit of behavior.
- As fast-executing as possible.
- Isolated from other tests.

The simplest definition of an integration test is any coded test that does not meet the criteria for a unit test!

One other difference between the two types of testing is how many tests you typically write. One way of visually comparing integration testing to unit testing (and **end-to-end** (**E2E**) testing) is the test pyramid, as shown in *Figure 11.1*:

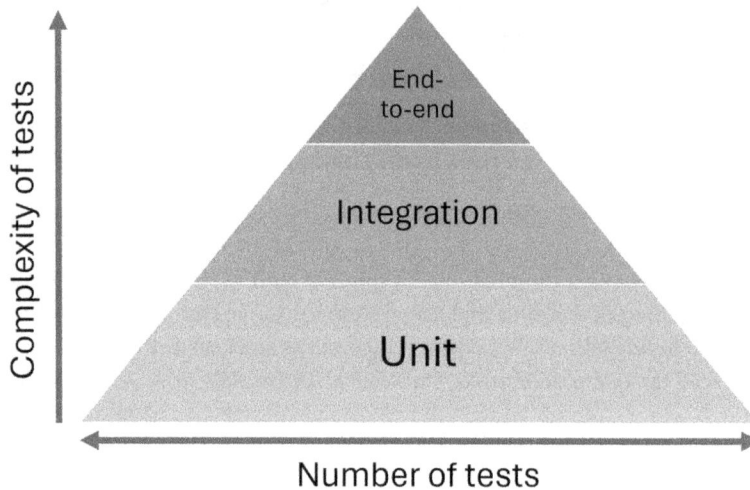

Figure 11.1: The test pyramid shows the weighting of test types

Lower-level tests like unit tests should have a higher number of tests than higher-level tests like E2E tests. Integration tests should have a number of tests in the middle.

> **Good practice:** Define integration tests for the most common scenarios that occur in the real-life usage of your projects. Write enough integration tests to interact with every external system used. Edge cases are scenarios that result in errors and should mostly be covered by unit tests. Only define integration tests for edge cases that cannot be covered by unit tests.

Which external systems to test

External systems come in two types: ones under your control and ones outside your control. External systems under your control include data stores that only your project accesses. No other system updates the data. External systems outside your control include email systems and public services like weather or government systems.

As you can probably already guess, you should directly use external systems under your control, but mock external systems that you don't control.

What if the database is used by other systems? You might start with a database that's only used by your system, but over time, other systems might want the convenience of direct access to it too. This breaks the design principles of microservices and leads to problems later, but it is very common in the real world. In this case, you will have to treat the database as out of your control and mock it.

Sharing fixtures in integration tests

There is a common scenario where you might want to initialize a fixture because it is genuinely shared between all tests: when using a database or EF Core model, especially when creating integration tests.

But in this case, use inheritance so that your unit test class does not need a constructor, as shown in the following code:

```
public class NorthwindStoreTests : DatabaseIntegrationTests
{
  [Fact]
  public void Checkout_ShouldFailWhenLowInventory()
  {
    // Use the _db fixture here.
  }
  ...
}

public abstract class DatabaseIntegrationTests : IDisposable
{
  protected readonly NorthwindContext _db;

  protected DatabaseIntegrationTests(NorthwindContext db)
  {
    _db = db;
  }

  public void Dispose()
  {
    _db.Dispose();
  }
}
```

If `NorthwindContext` requires additional setup or teardown steps, like seeding or clearing data, then you can implement these in the base class or a separate fixture setup/teardown method.

Understanding web service functional and end-to-end testing

Functional testing verifies that individual components or features of an application work as intended by comparing actual outcomes against specified requirements. It is granular, often automated, and tests inputs and expected outputs without delving into the system's internals.

E2E testing simulates real user scenarios by testing the entire application flow from start to finish, encompassing multiple integrated components to ensure that they work properly together. This type of testing validates the complete system, identifying issues that may arise from interactions between different parts of the application, thus providing a more holistic assurance of software functionality and reliability.

Imagine you have an ASP.NET Core Web API service that serves as the backend for a task management application. The API includes endpoints to create, retrieve, update, and delete tasks.

End-to-end test scenario

A user creates a new task, updates it, marks it as completed, and then retrieves it to confirm the changes:

1. Call the POST endpoint to create a new task with specific details.
2. Call the PUT endpoint to update the task's title and description.
3. Call another PUT endpoint to mark the task as completed.
4. Call the GET endpoint to retrieve the task and verify that all changes have been applied correctly.

Tools: You could use Postman for manual testing, create these tests with their AI assistant named Postbot, or write automated tests using RestSharp or your own client library along with xUnit.

Functional test scenario

Ensure that the task creation endpoint correctly handles input validation:

1. Call the POST endpoint with invalid input, for example, missing required fields.
2. Verify that the API returns a 400 Bad Request status code with a descriptive error message, usually generated using the ProblemDetails class in the .NET service.

Tools: You could use xUnit to write the test, FluentAssertions for more expressive assertions, and NSubstitute for mocking.

Test automation

Test automation is recommended in both functional and E2E testing for several reasons. It enhances the efficiency, reliability, and scalability of the testing process while ensuring that tests are repeatable, consistent, and easily maintainable.

Automated tests run consistently with the same inputs, reducing the likelihood of human error and ensuring repeatable results across multiple test cycles. Running automated functional tests is faster than manual testing, allowing for frequent and quick feedback during development. Test automation enables the execution of thousands of tests quickly, something that's impractical manually. This is essential for regression testing, ensuring that bug fixes or updates don't break existing functionality.

Automated E2E tests simulate how users interact with the system, making sure real-life use cases work across the entire workflow. With multiple services, APIs, and microservices interacting, automation is key in catching integration bugs early. It also helps test external systems or APIs that may not always be available during manual testing. While writing E2E automation tests can be time-consuming upfront, it saves significant effort in the long term. This is especially true for projects with frequent releases, as automated tests can be reused in every build cycle, reducing the need for manual regression testing.

As you have seen in the preceding examples, E2E tests are more complex and involve multiple features, whereas functional tests focus more on testing a single feature.

Now, let's look at the biggest challenge with integration testing, which is managing data stores.

Integration testing with data stores

One of the most common systems that will interact with integration tests is data stores, and they require special handling.

The schema for your data stores should be treated like code and be tracked in a source control system like Git. This allows you to keep all the schema changes over time in sync with changes to code that works on data in that structure.

The database schema includes table structure, index definitions, views, and stored procedures. For a SQL-based database, these are defined in SQL script files. You should also consider **reference data**, which is data that should be inserted into the database to prepopulate it. For example, you might need to add about 200 rows to a `CountryRegion` table used by your project for location lookups.

NoSQL databases like MongoDB and Couchbase are designed to handle unstructured or semi-structured data. Unlike SQL databases, they don't enforce strict schemas. Data can be stored in formats like JSON, and records (documents) can differ from one another in structure.

Since NoSQL databases are schema-less or schema-flexible, integration tests should focus more on the data structure validation within each document rather than relying on predefined schemas. The structure of the data, for example, required fields in a document, can be validated using tools like JSON Schema. Validation often occurs at the application level, where models are expected to conform to certain structures, even if the database itself doesn't enforce it.

You may need to set up specific collections and populate them with the necessary test data before running tests. While migrations are less of a concern, you still need to ensure that data models are aligned with the codebase's expectations.

Many NoSQL databases offer in-memory testing capabilities. For example, the MongoDB memory server makes integration tests faster without the need for a full database instance.

Many integration tests for SQL databases rely on transaction rollbacks. The test framework starts a transaction, executes the test, and then rolls back the transaction to leave the database in its original state.

Developer instances of the database and migrations

Each developer in a team should have their own instance of the database to work with locally. This is so that tests run by different developers do not interfere with each other. Doing this also maximizes performance during test executions.

Over time, the database structure will change. New tables will be added. Columns will be added to tables. The best way to handle this is to use migrations.

These are schema changes represented by the SQL statements that make the change, for example, `CREATE TABLE` and `ALTER TABLE`. **Object-Relational Mappers (ORMs)** like EF Core support migrations with classes with equivalent commands, as shown in the following code:

```
using Microsoft.EntityFrameworkCore.Migrations; // To use Migration.

namespace YourApp.Migrations;

public partial class AddPosts : Migration
{
  protected override void Up(MigrationBuilder migrationBuilder)
  {
    migrationBuilder.CreateTable(name: "Posts", columns: table => new
      {
        PostId = table.Column<int>(nullable: false)
          .Annotation("SqlServer:ValueGenerationStrategy",
            SqlServerValueGenerationStrategy.IdentityColumn),
        Title = table.Column<string>(nullable: true),
        Content = table.Column<string>(nullable: true),
        DateCreated = table.Column<DateTime>(nullable: false)
      },
      constraints: table =>
      {
        table.PrimaryKey("PK_Posts", x => x.PostId);
      });
  }

  protected override void Down(MigrationBuilder migrationBuilder)
  {
    migrationBuilder.DropTable(name: "Posts");
  }
 }
}
```

Note the following about the preceding code:

- The `Up` method creates a new table called `Posts` with four columns: `PostId`, `Title`, `Content`, and `DateCreated`. The `PostId` column is configured as an identity column, which means its value will be automatically generated by the database when a new row is inserted. The `table.PrimaryKey` method is used to specify `PostId` as the primary key of the `Posts` table.
- The `Down` method reverses the changes made by the `Up` method. In this case, it simply drops the `Posts` table. This method ensures that you can revert your database schema to its previous state if needed.

The actual SQL commands executed by these methods depend on the database provider you're using. EF Core translates the methods into the appropriate SQL commands for the configured database provider, like SQL Server, SQLite, or PostgreSQL.

A migration class can be auto-generated by the EF Core tools based on your model definitions and `DbContext` configuration. Whenever you make changes to your models that affect the database schema, you should create a new migration, as shown in the following command:

```
dotnet ef migrations add <MigrationName>
```

Here, `<MigrationName>` would be something like `AddPosts`.

This technique allows you to version your database schema alongside your application code, making it easier to manage changes and deployments.

To run any outstanding migrations, which call their `Up` methods, use the following command:

```
dotnet ef database update
```

To revert to a specified migration point, which calls the `Down` methods on the migration classes after that point, use the following command:

```
dotnet ef database update <MigrationName>
```

This will revert all migrations applied after the specified migration, so the database schema will match the state defined by the specified migration.

To revert all migrations so that the database returns to its original state, which calls all the `Down` methods of each migration in order, use the following command:

```
dotnet ef database update 0
```

Good practice: It is important to include the database migration scripts in the application's source control system to ensure that schema changes are tracked and can be easily reverted or shared.

Data lifecycle

Tests should not depend on the state of the database. Your tests should initialize the state of the database themselves to ensure consistency and remove data between test runs.

If you cannot do this, then your tests will need to execute sequentially so that the state of the database is known. If you execute tests in parallel, then you are more likely to get the state out of sync.

There are common ways to reset data between tests:

- Restore a database backup before each test. This can be slow depending on the size of the database.

- Create a database transaction and then roll it back at the end of the test. If the transaction is only used in the test, then production behavior is different.
- Scripting the cleanup of data after each test. This is fast, but if a test fails without performing the cleanup, it will cause problems for other tests.
- Scripting the cleanup of data before each test. This is fast and less likely to leave the database in an unknown state if a test fails.

You should define a base class for integration tests that share a common database and the same initial state. Call a SQL script to clean up and initialize the database state, as shown in the following code:

```csharp
using Microsoft.Data.SqlClient; // To use SqlConnection and so on.
using System.Data; // To use CommandType.

public abstract class DatabaseIntegrationTests
{
  private const string _connectionString;

  protected DatabaseIntegrationTests()
  {
    ResetDatabase();
  }

  public void ResetDatabase()
  {
    string sql = "DELETE FROM ...;" +
                 "DELETE FROM ...;" +
                 "INSERT INTO ...;";

    // Or load the SQL statements from a script file.
    using SqlConnection con = new(_connectionString);
    SqlCommand cmd = new(sql, con);
    cmd.CommandType = CommandType.Text;
    con.Open();
    cmd.ExecuteNonQuery();
  }
}
```

Good practice: Avoid in-memory database replacements. Although they are faster, modern databases are almost as fast, and only an integration test that uses a real database is a true integration test. Use the same data store system in tests as you will use in production.

You should define factory methods in a helper class to create entities, as shown in the following code:

```
public static class ObjectMother
{
  public static Category CreateCategory(
    int categoryId = 1,
    string categoryName = "Beverages",
    string description = "...")
  {
    using NorthwindContext db = new();

    Category category = new Category()
    {
      CategoryId = categoryId,
      CategoryName = categoryName,
      Description = description
    };

    db.Categories.Add(category);
    db.SaveChanges();

    return category;
  }
}
```

You should use the factory method in a test, as shown in the following code:

```
using static ObjectMother;

Category c1 = CreateCategory(); // Create Beverages.
Category c2 = CreateCategory(2, "Condiments", "..."); // Create Condiments.
```

Improvements to integration testing of apps with top-level statements

In .NET 10, Microsoft has introduced a significant enhancement to streamline integration testing for ASP.NET Core applications utilizing top-level statements.

Top-level statements simplify the entry point of C# applications by eliminating the need for an explicit `Main` method. For example, the `Program.cs` file might only contain the following code:

```
var builder = WebApplication.CreateBuilder(args);
var app = builder.Build();
app.MapGet("/", () => "Hello World!");
app.Run();
```

Under the hood, the compiler generates an internal `Program` class to encapsulate these statements. However, this internal designation poses a problem for integration testing. Testing frameworks often require access to the `Program` class to configure the test host or access services, which isn't possible if the class is `internal`.

Previously, developers had to manually add a `public partial class Program` declaration to expose the class for testing purposes:

```
public partial class Program { }
```

This workaround, while effective, was an extra step that could be easily overlooked, leading to confusion and potential errors.

To address this, .NET 10 introduces a source generator that automatically creates a `public partial class Program` when one isn't explicitly defined. This means that the compiler-generated `Program` class becomes accessible to test projects without any additional code from the developer.

We have covered a lot of theory; now let's get practical and implement testing for a web service.

Testing web services using xUnit

There are multiple ways to test web services:

- Automatically using testing frameworks like xUnit, NUnit, and MSTest.
- Manually using HTTP request editors like REST Client for VS Code or HTTP Editor in Visual Studio.
- Manually using GUI tools like Postman, NSwag, or Swagger UI.

> **Warning!** Swagger UI integration using the Swashbuckle package has been removed from the ASP.NET Core 9 and later project templates. You can learn more about this at the following link: `https://github.com/dotnet/aspnetcore/issues/54599`.

The ASP.NET Core team has replaced the OpenAPI document generation with a built-in feature, but they have no plans to replace the Swagger UI for testing.

Unit testing using xUnit

xUnit.net, often simply referred to as **xUnit**, is a popular unit testing framework for the .NET ecosystem. xUnit has been specifically designed to address some of the limitations found in older testing frameworks like NUnit and MSTest.

Even internal Microsoft teams avoid MSTest in favor of xUnit. For example, the ASP.NET Core team uses xUnit, as shown at the following link: `https://github.com/dotnet/aspnetcore/tree/main/src/Testing/src/xunit`.

If you are familiar with other testing frameworks, then you can review summary comparison tables at the following links:

https://code-maze.com/csharp-testing-framework-differences-between-nunit-xunit-and-mstest/

https://www.browserstack.com/guide/nunit-vs-xunit-vs-mstest

https://daily.dev/blog/nunit-vs-xunit-vs-mstest-net-unit-testing-framework-comparison

xUnit utilizes a range of .NET attributes to define and control the behavior of tests within your test suite. These attributes are crucial for organizing tests, specifying test behaviors, and managing test data. Let's review them next.

Common xUnit attributes

The most common xUnit attributes with examples of usage and descriptions are shown in *Table 11.4*:

Attribute example	Description

`[Fact]`
 	
`public void TestAdding2and2()`
	`[Fact]` declares a test method that does not take any parameters and is run once by the test runner.

`[Theory]`
 	
`[...]`
 	
`public void TestAdding(`
 	
`  double expected,`
 	
`  double number1,`
 	
`  double number2)`
	`[Theory]` declares a test method that has one or more parameters that are run multiple times with different data. It must be used in conjunction with data-providing attributes like `[InlineData]`, `[ClassData]`, or `[MemberData]`.

`[InlineData(4, 2, 2)]`
 	
`[InlineData(5, 2, 3)]`
	`[InlineData]` supplies fixed values for parameters in the defined order for an MUT decorated with `[Theory]`.

`[ClassData(`
 	
`  typeof(AddingNumbersData))]`
	`[ClassData]` supplies enumerated values for parameters in the defined order for an MUT decorated with `[Theory]`. The class can implement `IEnumerable<object[]>`. To provide strongly typed data, the class must derive from `TheoryData`.

`[MemberData(`
 	
`  nameof(GetTestData))]`
	`[MemberData]` supplies enumerated values for parameters in the defined order for an MUT decorated with `[Theory]`. The method must be `static` and return `IEnumerable<object[]>`.

`[Trait("Feature",`
 	
`  "Shopping Cart")]`
	This allows the addition of metadata to tests, categorizing them for filtering during test runs.

Table 11.4: Common xUnit attributes

[Fact] and [Theory] both allow you to change the display name of the test shown in results and set a timeout as an integer in milliseconds, as shown in the following code:

```
[Fact(Timeout = 3000)] // Test will timeout after 3 seconds.
```

If you want to temporarily skip running a [Fact] or [Theory] test, you can just set the Skip parameter to a text reason for skipping it, as shown in the following code:

```
[Fact(Skip = "Skipping this test for now.")]
```

Now, let's see how we can host a web service during testing.

Web service hosting with WebApplicationFactory

One of the trickier aspects of testing web services is how to host the web service during testing and how to simulate an HTTP context. Integration tests for ASP.NET Core projects require the following:

- A test project to contain and execute the tests. The test project has a reference to the website or web service project, aka the SUT.
- The test project creates a test web host for the SUT and uses a test server client to handle requests and responses with the SUT.

The Microsoft.AspNetCore.Mvc.Testing package handles the following tasks:

- It sets the content root to the SUT's project root so that static files and pages/views are found when the tests are executed
- It provides the WebApplicationFactory class to streamline bootstrapping the SUT with the TestServer class

We will create an example weather service using the built-in project template. Then, we will write integration tests for it.

WebApplicationFactory<Program> is used to create an instance of the application under test, where Program is the class that contains your minimal API's Main method. The CreateClient method of WebApplicationFactory<T> creates an HttpClient configured to send requests to this instance.

The first test will send a GET request to the /weatherforecast endpoint and assert that the response is successful by checking for a status code in the range 200–299. The second test will make the same request and check that there are five weather forecasts in the deserialized JSON response.

By using WebApplicationFactory<T>, the tests will automatically handle the setup and teardown of the test server for you. This means you get to test your application in an environment very close to production, without the overhead of deploying and hosting the web service.

Enabling an ASP.NET Core 9 and earlier project to be tested

By default, ASP.NET Core projects use top-level statements, meaning the Program class is generated automatically. With .NET 9 and earlier, it will not be a public class. An improvement in .NET 10 is that a source generator is used to define the Program class, and it will be public if needed.

If you are using .NET 9 or earlier, to automate integration tests, we need the Program class to be public so that we can reference it in a separate testing project.

If you're using .NET 10 or later, then you do not need to perform the following steps:

1. In the Northwind.WebApi project, in Program.cs, add an explicit declaration of the Program class and its Main method, as shown highlighted in the following code:

```
public class Program
{
  public static void Main(string[] args)
  {
    var builder = WebApplication.CreateBuilder(args);
    ...
  }
}
```

2. Build the Northwind.WebApi project.

Creating the test project

Now, we can create a test project that references the web service project:

1. Use your preferred code editor to add a new **xUnit Test Project** / xunit project named Northwind. IntegrationTests to the MatureWeb solution.

2. In the Northwind.IntegrationTests.csproj project file, remove all the version attributes for the default packages, and add a package reference for ASP.NET Core testing, as shown in the following markup:

```
<PackageReference Include="Microsoft.AspNetCore.Mvc.Testing" />
```

3. In the Northwind.IntegrationTests.csproj project file, add a project reference to the web service, as shown in the following markup:

```
<ItemGroup>
  <ProjectReference Include="..\Northwind.WebApi\Northwind.WebApi.csproj"
/>
</ItemGroup>
```

4. In the Northwind.IntegrationTests project, rename UnitTest1.cs to WeatherForecastTests. cs.

5. In WeatherForecastTests.cs, define a class with test methods, as shown in the following code:

```
using Microsoft.AspNetCore.Mvc.Testing; // To use
WebApplicationFactory<T>.
using System.Net.Http.Json; // To use ReadFromJsonAsync.
using Northwind.WebApi; // To use Program.

namespace Northwind.IntegrationTests;
```

```csharp
public class WeatherForecastTests :
  IClassFixture<WebApplicationFactory<Program>>
{
  private readonly WebApplicationFactory<Program> _factory;
  private const string relativePath = "/weatherforecast";

  public WeatherForecastTests(WebApplicationFactory<Program> factory)
  {
    _factory = factory;
  }

  [Fact]
  public async Task Get_WeatherForecasts_ReturnsSuccessStatusCode()
  {
    // Arrange
    HttpClient client = _factory.CreateClient();

    // Act
    HttpResponseMessage response =
      await client.GetAsync(relativePath);

    // Assert
    Assert.True(response.IsSuccessStatusCode); // Status Code 200-299.
  }

  [Fact]
  public async Task Get_WeatherForecasts_ReturnsFiveForecasts()
  {
    // Arrange
    HttpClient client = _factory.CreateClient();

    // Act
    HttpResponseMessage response = await client.GetAsync(relativePath);
    WeatherForecast[]? forecasts = await response.Content
      .ReadFromJsonAsync<WeatherForecast[]>();

    // Assert
    Assert.NotNull(forecasts);
    Assert.True(forecasts.Length == 5);
  }
}
```

6. Run the tests in the `WebServiceTests` project and note that they succeed without needing to start the web service project because the web service is hosted in a `TestServer` instance in the test project.

You've now written some simple integration tests. More complex tests will require you to isolate dependencies. You do this with mocking.

Mocking in tests

Mocking in unit tests is a technique used to isolate the unit of code being tested by replacing its dependencies with controlled, pre-configured substitutes known as "mocks." This allows the developer to focus on testing the specific functionality of the unit without interference from its dependencies.

The key concepts of mocking include the following:

- **Isolation**: The primary purpose of mocking is to isolate the unit of code under test. This isolation ensures that the test is focused only on the behavior of the unit itself, rather than on the behavior of its dependencies. By using mocks, you create a controlled environment where you can precisely control the inputs and outputs of the dependencies.
- **Substitutes for real objects:**
    - **Mocks** are stand-ins for the real objects that the unit under test interacts with. They mimic the behavior of real objects but are configured to return specific values or perform specific actions.
    - **Fakes** are simpler implementations of interfaces or classes used in the test environment. Unlike mocks, they provide working implementations but may not be as configurable or detailed.
    - **Stubs** provide predefined responses to specific calls, without implementing the entire behavior of the dependency. They are typically used for providing fixed inputs to the unit under test.
    - **Spies** are like mocks but also record information about how they were called, which can be useful for verifying interactions.
    - **Dummies** are objects passed around but never actually used. They are typically used to fill parameter lists.
- **Verification of interactions**: Mocks can be set up with expectations about how they should be used, such as which methods should be called, how many times they should be called, and with what arguments. After the test runs, the mock framework verifies whether these expectations were met. This helps ensure that the unit under test interacts with its dependencies as expected.

There are many benefits of mocking, such as:

- **Isolation and focus:** By isolating the unit under test from its dependencies, you can focus on testing its specific behavior without interference.
- **Control over your test environment:** Mocks allow you to simulate various scenarios by controlling the inputs and outputs of the dependencies.

- **Improved test reliability**: By removing the dependencies, you reduce the chance of flaky tests caused by external factors such as network issues or database states.
- **Faster tests**: Mocking often leads to faster tests since mocks usually run in memory and do not involve time-consuming operations like database access or network communication.
- **Better coverage**: Mocks allow you to simulate edge cases and error conditions that might be difficult or impossible to reproduce with real dependencies.

A use case for mocking is mocking an interface to test a service method that depends on a repository layer without hitting the actual database. Another is creating a substitute for a logging service to verify that error logging occurs for a given input without actually writing to a log file.

Libraries for mocking

The choice of mocking framework often comes down to personal or team preference, the specific needs of the project, and the existing technological stack. **Moq**, **NSubstitute**, and **FakeItEasy** each offer a modern, developer-friendly approach to mocking, with active communities and ongoing development, making them excellent choices for most .NET projects today. When selecting a mocking framework, consider experimenting with a few to see which one best fits your development style and project requirements.

Moq is widely regarded as one of the easiest-to-use mocking libraries for .NET. It's particularly known for its straightforward syntax and ability to quickly set up mocks without needing to manage complex configurations or setups.

Moq supports a wide range of features, including the ability to mock interfaces, abstract classes, and concrete classes, as well as setting up returns, verifying method calls, and handling properties. It uses lambda expressions for setting up mocks in a strongly typed manner, which helps with refactoring and code readability.

> **Warning!** Moq developer kzu courted controversy by adding a component known as **SponsorLink** in version 4.20.0 on August 7, 2023. You can read the pull request at the following link: `https://github.com/devlooped/moq/pull/1363`.
>
> Moq "now ships with a closed-source obfuscated dependency that scrapes your Git email and phones it home" and was considered by many developers to be unacceptable, as you can read at the following link: `https://www.reddit.com/r/programming/comments/15m2q0o/moq_a_net_mocking_library_now_ships_with_a/`.
>
> Four days later, kzu removed SponsorLink from Moq version 4.20.69, but the damage had already been done. Many organizations have switched to alternatives like NSubstitute, as you can read at the following link: `https://www.reddit.com/r/dotnet/comments/173ddyk/now_that_the_controversy_from_moqs_dependencies/`.

NSubstitute is designed with a focus on simplicity and ease of use, offering a concise API that can reduce the amount of mock-related code you need to write. It's a great choice for developers who prioritize readability and efficiency. Like Moq, NSubstitute allows for mocking interfaces and classes. It also supports argument matching and checking calls to specific methods and has a unique feature for automatically creating substitute instances for dependencies when constructing an object.

> You can learn more about NSubstitute at the following link: `https://github.com/nsubstitute/NSubstitute`.

FakeItEasy aims to be the most user-friendly mocking library for .NET, with a syntax that's designed to be easy to read and write. It's a good choice for teams looking for a balance between functionality and simplicity. It allows for easy creation of fake objects for interfaces and classes, with straightforward methods for configuring behavior, returns, and exceptions. FakeItEasy also supports advanced scenarios like calls to specific methods with certain arguments.

> You can learn more about FakeItEasy at the following link: `https://fakeiteasy.github.io/`.

It doesn't matter much which mocking framework we use because the principles are the same. I picked NSubstitute for this book, but the others would work equally well.

Using NSubstitute to create test doubles

NSubstitute is designed to make it easy to create test doubles like mocks, stubs, and so on for unit testing. This allows you to test components in isolation from their dependencies.

To create a mock, call the `Substitute.For<T>` method, where `T` is the interface or class that you need to mock, as shown in the following code:

```
ICalculator calc = Substitute.For<ICalculator>();
```

You can pass parameters if the class has a constructor, as shown in the following code:

```
var substitute = Substitute.For<ClassWithConstructor>(5, "Error");
```

The `substitute` object will not just have the members of the type it substitutes for, like `Add` for `ICalculator`. It will also have extension methods used to configure how the substitute should work, as shown in *Table 11.5*:

Extension method	Description
`Returns`	To set a return value for a method call on a substitute, call the method as normal, then follow it with a call to the `Returns()` extension method. For example: `calc.Add(2, 3).Returns(5)`. Instead of specifying a literal value to return, you can execute any lambda block, for example, to throw an exception.
`Received`	To check that a method has been called on a substitute, call the `Received()` extension method, followed by the call being checked. For example: `calc.Received().Add()`.
`When`	Used to specify a condition or an action you want to monitor or react to. It's often used when you don't just want to return a specific value from a method but want to perform additional behavior when a method is called.
`Do`	Used to define the custom behavior that should be executed when the specified condition (in the `When` method) is met. This is where you write the logic that the mock should perform. `Do` accepts a lambda expression, which provides access to the arguments of the intercepted method call. These arguments are available via the `CallInfo` parameter.

Table 11.5: NSubstitute extension methods

For example:

```
substitute.When(x => x.SomeMethod(Arg.Any<int>()))
  .Do((CallInfo info) =>
  {
    // Could also use info.Args(0)
    Console.WriteLine($"SomeMethod called with argument: {info[0]}");
  });
```

You can match arguments using `Args.Any<T>`. For example, when adding any integer to 5, you could specify to return 7, as shown in the following code:

```
calc.Add(Arg.Any<int>(), 5).Returns(7);
```

You can match specific arguments using `Args.Is<T>`. For example, when adding any integer greater than 3 to 5, you could specify to return 9, as shown in the following code:

```
calc.Add(Arg.Is<int>(x => x > 3), 5).Returns(9);
```

You can throw exceptions, as shown in the following code:

```
calc.Add(-1, -1).Returns(x => { throw new Exception(); });
```

Mocking with NSubstitute example

We will create a class library and then an xUnit project that uses mocking to test it.

Creating a class library to mock

Let's explore:

1. Use your preferred code editor to add a new **Class Library** / classlib project named Mocking. BusinessLogic to the MatureWeb solution.

2. In the Mocking.BusinessLogic.csproj project file, treat warnings as errors and statically and globally import the Console class.

3. In the Mocking.BusinessLogic project, delete the Class1.cs file, and then add a new interface file named IEmailSender.cs.

4. In IEmailSender.cs, define an interface for sending emails, as shown in the following code:

```
namespace Mocking.BusinessLogic;

public interface IEmailSender
{
  bool SendEmail(string to, string subject, string body);
}
```

5. In the Mocking.BusinessLogic project, add a new class file named UserService.cs.

6. In UserService.cs, define a class for creating a user that sends an email as part of its process, as shown in the following code:

```
namespace Mocking.BusinessLogic;

public class UserService
{
  private readonly IEmailSender _emailSender;

  public UserService(IEmailSender emailSender)
  {
    _emailSender = emailSender;
  }

  public bool CreateUser(string email, string password)
  {
    // Create user.
    bool successfulUserCreation = true;

    // Send email to user.
    bool successfulEmailSend = _emailSender.SendEmail(
```

```
            to: email,
            subject: "Welcome!",
            body: "Your account is created.");

        return successfulEmailSend && successfulUserCreation;
    }
}
```

7. Build the Mocking.BusinessLogic project.

Creating a test project with mocking

Now we can create an xUnit project to test the class library using mocking:

1. Use your preferred coding tool to add a new **xUnit Test Project [C#]** / xunit project named
    Mocking.BusinessLogicUnitTests to the MatureWeb solution. For example, at the command
    prompt or terminal in the Chapter11 folder, enter the following commands:

    ```
    dotnet new xunit -o Mocking.BusinessLogicUnitTests
    dotnet sln add Mocking.BusinessLogicUnitTests
    ```

2. In the Mocking.BusinessLogicUnitTests.csproj project file, remove all the version attributes
    from package references, and then add a project reference to the Mocking.BusinessLogic
    project, as shown in the following markup:

    ```
    <ItemGroup>
      <ProjectReference Include=
        "..\Mocking.BusinessLogic\Mocking.BusinessLogic.csproj" />
    </ItemGroup>
    ```

    > The path for a project reference can use either forward (/) or back (\) slashes
    > because the paths are processed by the .NET SDK and changed if necessary for
    > the current operating system.

3. In the Mocking.BusinessLogicUnitTests project, add a package reference for NSubstitute,
    as shown in the following markup:

    ```
    <PackageReference Include="NSubstitute" />
    ```

4. Build the Mocking.BusinessLogicUnitTests project to restore packages.

5. In the Mocking.BusinessLogicUnitTests project, delete UnitTest1.cs.

6. In the Mocking.BusinessLogicUnitTests project, add a new class file named
    EmailSenderUnitTests.cs.

7. In `EmailSenderUnitTests.cs`, define a class with a test method that uses NSubstitute to create a mock of the `IEmailSender` interface, as shown in the following code:

```
using NSubstitute; // To use Substitute.
using Mocking.BusinessLogic; // To use IEmailSender.
using Xunit.Abstractions; // To use ITestOutputHelper.

namespace Mocking.BusinessLogicUnitTests;

public class EmailSenderUnitTests
{
  private readonly ITestOutputHelper _output;

  public EmailSenderUnitTests(ITestOutputHelper output)
  {
    _output = output;
  }

  [Fact]
  public void SendEmailTest()
  {
    #region Arrange
    IEmailSender emailSender = Substitute.For<IEmailSender>();

    emailSender.SendEmail(
      to: Arg.Any<string>(),
      subject: Arg.Any<string>(),
      body: Arg.Any<string>())
      .Returns(true);

    emailSender.When(x => x.SendEmail(
        to: Arg.Is<string>(s => s.EndsWith("example.com")),
        subject: Arg.Any<string>(),
        body: Arg.Any<string>()))
      .Do(x => _output.WriteLine("Email sent to example domain."));

    UserService sut = new(emailSender);
    #endregion

    #region Act
    bool result = sut.CreateUser("user@example.com", "password");
    #endregion
```

```
#region Assert
Assert.True(result);

emailSender.Received(requiredNumberOfCalls: 1)
  .SendEmail(to: "user@example.com",
    subject: Arg.Any<string>(), body: Arg.Any<string>());
#endregion
  }
}
```

8. Navigate to **Test | Test Explorer**, right-click **Mocking.BusinessLogicUnitTests**, run the test, and note that it succeeds.

Note the following about the code for the test method:

- `Substitute.For<IEmailSender>()` creates a mock object for the `IEmailSender` interface.
- The `Returns` method is used to specify the return value when the `SendEmail` method is called with any arguments.
- The `When` and `Do` methods are used to specify an action that executes only when the email is sent to an address in the `example.com` domain, and if so, a message is written to the test output.
- The `Received` method checks that `SendEmail` was called exactly once with the expected arguments.

We've spent most of this chapter looking at testing. It's now time to look at debugging.

Debugging web services using dev tunnels

Dev tunnels are a technology concept that's gained traction among web service developers. Dev tunnels create a secure, public URL that maps to a local server on your machine. This means you can share your local development environment with anyone in the world, without deploying the web service to a public server.

Imagine you're working on a web application on your laptop. Normally, the app would only be accessible to you, since it's running on your local server as `localhost`. If you, the developer, wanted someone else, like a tester, to try it out, you'd have to deploy it to a public server, which can be a hassle, especially for quick feedback loops.

Dev tunnels work by establishing a secure connection between your local server and a service that creates a publicly accessible URL. This URL points directly back to your local server. When someone accesses this URL, the dev tunnel service routes that traffic to your machine, letting others interact with your local development project as if it were hosted online.

Dev tunnels provide several benefits, as shown in the following list:

- **Simplified collaboration:** Dev tunnels make it easy to share your work with clients, testers, or colleagues without the need to deploy it to a public staging environment. This is especially handy for quick reviews or collaborative debugging.
- **Real-world testing:** Dev tunnels allow for testing webhooks, third-party integrations, and mobile apps that require a public URL to function correctly, directly from your local environment.
- **Learning:** For learners and educators, dev tunnels provide a straightforward way to work on projects, experiment with new technologies, and share progress without the complexities of server management.
- **Mobile development:** Dev tunnels are essential if you are developing a mobile app. If we want to try out a web service called from the app running in a mobile emulator, then we must go through a dev tunnel since the emulator is running in a separate environment and cannot connect to localhost.

There is some dev tunnel terminology that you should be familiar with, as shown in *Table 11.6*:

Term	Description
Tunnel	This provides secure remote access to one host through a relay service. A dev tunnel has a unique DNS name, multiple ports, access controls, and other associated metadata.
Tunnel relay service	This facilitates secure connections between a dev tunnel host and clients via a cloud service, even when the host may be behind a firewall and unable to accept incoming connections directly.
Tunnel host	This accepts client connections to a dev tunnel via the dev tunnel relay service and forwards those connections to local ports.
Tunnel port	This is an IP port number (1-65535) that is allowed through a dev tunnel. A dev tunnel only allows connections on ports that have been added. One dev tunnel can support multiple ports, and different ports within a dev tunnel may use different protocols (HTTP, HTTPS, etc.) and may have different access controls.

Table 11.6: Dev tunnel terminology

While dev tunnels are secure, exposing your local environment to the public internet always comes with risks. It's important to use these tools judiciously, ensure that any sensitive data is protected, and possibly limit access using authentication or IP whitelisting. Also, think carefully if your dev tunnel should be configured to be temporary or permanent, limiting the lifetime of the assigned URL, thereby improving security. Access can also be limited to members of your organization.

The performance seen through a dev tunnel might not accurately reflect the performance of a fully deployed application, due to the overhead of tunneling and the specifics of your local development setup.

Installing the dev tunnel CLI

Before you can use dev tunnels, you must install the dev tunnel CLI:

- On Windows, use `winget`, as shown in the following command:

```
winget install Microsoft.devtunnel
```

- On macOS, use Homebrew, as shown in the following command:

```
brew install --cask devtunnel
```

- On Linux, use `curl`, as shown in the following command:

```
curl -sL https://aka.ms/DevTunnelCliInstall | bash
```

> You will need to restart your command prompt or terminal before the `devtunnel` CLI will be available on your computer path.

> **Warning!** This feature is currently in public preview. The CLI might have bugs that are introduced and fixed over time. Command names and options may change in future releases. The preview version is provided without a service-level agreement, and it's not recommended for production workloads. Certain features might not be supported or might have constrained capabilities. Read the latest about the CLI at the following link: `https://learn.microsoft.com/en-us/azure/developer/dev-tunnels/cli-commands`.

Exploring a dev tunnel with the CLI and an echo service

An echo service is a simple server or endpoint that receives HTTP requests and sends back the same data in the response. It is often used for testing, debugging, and educational purposes because it allows developers to see exactly what data is being sent to the server and verify that it is correctly received and processed.

Let's explore how to use dev tunnels with an echo service to do a basic "sanity check" that it is working:

1. Before you can create a dev tunnel, you must log in with a Microsoft Entra ID, Microsoft, or GitHub account, as shown in the following command:

```
devtunnel user login
```

2. Select your account and note the result, as shown in the following output:

```
Logged in as <your-email-account> using Microsoft.
```

> If you get an error, `Missing wamcompat_id_token in WAM case`, then try using device flow to log in instead, as shown in the following command: `devtunnel login -d`

3. Start hosting a simple service on port 8080 that just echoes any HTTP requests to it, as shown in the following command:

```
devtunnel echo http -p 8080
```

4. In another command prompt or terminal window, start hosting a dev tunnel for port 8080, as shown in the following command:

```
devtunnel host -p 8080
```

5. Note the result, as shown in the following output:

```
Hosting port: 8080
Connect via browser: https://40bhwxgp.uks1.devtunnels.ms:8080,
https://40bhwxgp-8080.uks1.devtunnels.ms
Inspect network activity: https://40bhwxgp-8080-inspect.uks1.devtunnels.
ms
Ready to accept connections for tunnel: happy-hill-zw1k7n8
```

6. Start your preferred web browser and navigate to the URL specified in the output. For example, for me, it was the following link: `https://40bhwxgp.uks1.devtunnels.ms:8080`.

7. Log in using the same account as you used to host the dev tunnel because, by default, dev tunnels are only accessible to you. Note the warning that confirms that you are about to connect to your dev tunnel, as shown in *Figure 11.2*:

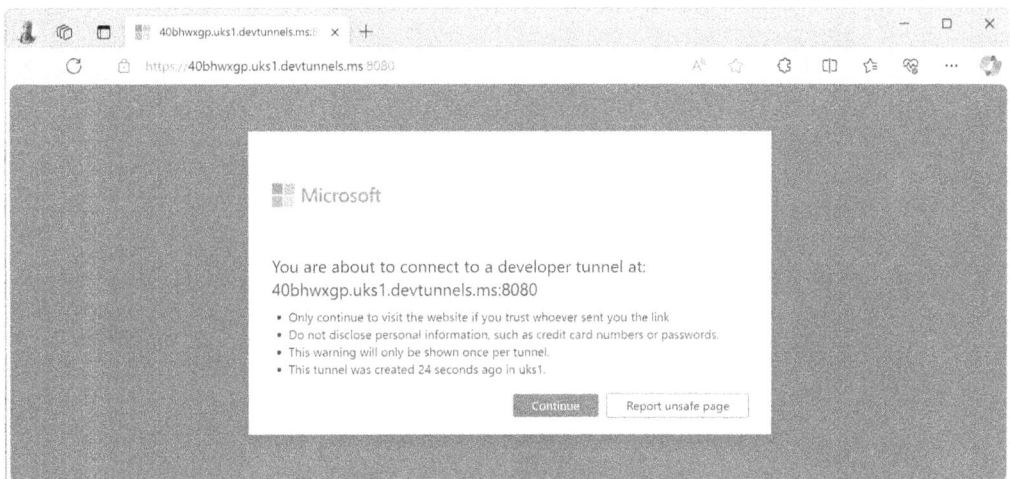

Figure 11.2: Connecting to a dev tunnel

8. Close the browser, because we don't actually need to connect to it at this point. We are just confirming that it's there.

9. At the command prompt or terminal, press *Ctrl + C* to shut down the dev tunnel host.

10. At the command prompt or terminal, press *Ctrl + C* to shut down the echo service.

Now, let's see how to use a dev tunnel with an ASP.NET Core project.

Exploring a dev tunnel with an ASP.NET Core project

Now, let's look at a more practical example of how to use a dev tunnel with an ASP.NET Core project.

Let's explore:

1. In the `Northwind.WebApi` project, in `Program.cs`, before the call to `app.Run()`, add statements to output the tunnel URL, as shown in the following code:

    ```
    string? tunnelUrl = Environment.GetEnvironmentVariable("VS_TUNNEL_URL");

    if (tunnelUrl is not null)
    {
      WriteLine($"Tunnel URL: {tunnelUrl}");
    }
    ```

2. Start the `Northwind.WebApi` project using the `https` launch profile without debugging.

3. Try out the weather service by navigating to `https://localhost:5091/weatherforecast/10` and note it returns random weather, as shown in *Figure 11.3*:

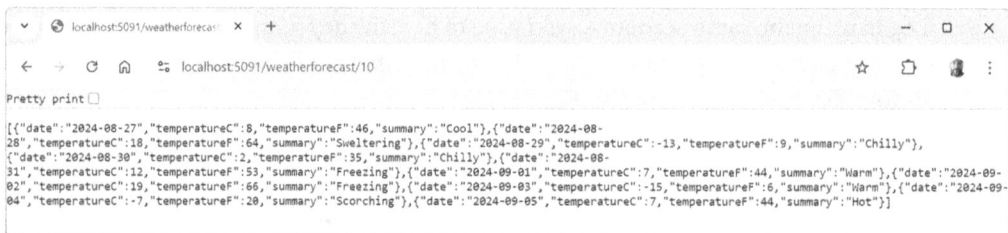

Figure 11.3: Random weather from a service in localhost

4. At the command prompt or terminal, note the web service is hosted on `localhost` and listening on ports `5091` and `5090`, as shown highlighted in the following output:

    ```
    Default output formatters:
        HttpNoContentOutputFormatter
        StringOutputFormatter, Media types: text/plain
        StreamOutputFormatter
        SystemTextJsonOutputFormatter, Media types: application/json, text/
    json, application/*+json
    info: Microsoft.Hosting.Lifetime[14]
    ```

```
         Now listening on: https://localhost:5091
info: Microsoft.Hosting.Lifetime[14]
         Now listening on: http://localhost:5090
info: Microsoft.Hosting.Lifetime[0]
         Application started. Press Ctrl+C to shut down.
info: Microsoft.Hosting.Lifetime[0]
         Hosting environment: Development
info: Microsoft.Hosting.Lifetime[0]
         Content root path: C:\web-dev-net9\MatureWeb\Northwind.WebApi
```

5. Close the browser and shut down the web service.

Configuring a dev tunnel in Visual Studio

Let's configure a dev tunnel in Visual Studio:

1. If you have multiple startup projects configured, then navigate to **Project | Configure Startup Project...**, select **Single startup project**, select **Northwind.WebApi**, and click **OK**. (We need to do this so we can access the user interface for dev tunnels in the next step. You can reset back to multiple startup projects once we've done that.)

2. In Visual Studio, in the standard toolbar, navigate to **https | Dev Tunnels (no active tunnel) | Create a Tunnel...**, as shown in *Figure 11.4*:

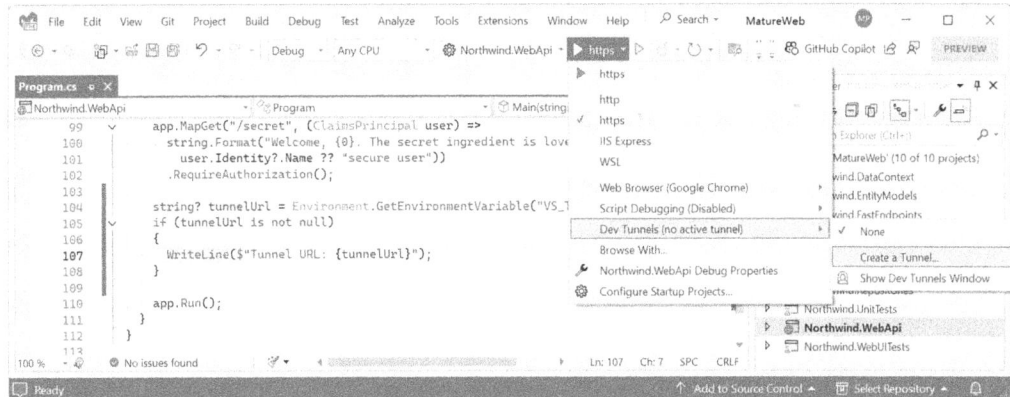

Figure 11.4: Creating a dev tunnel in Visual Studio

3. In the dialog box, select a Microsoft or GitHub account, enter a name for the tunnel, like `Northwind Web API`, select **Temporary** for the tunnel type, select **Private** for the access level, and click **OK**, as shown in *Figure 11.5*:

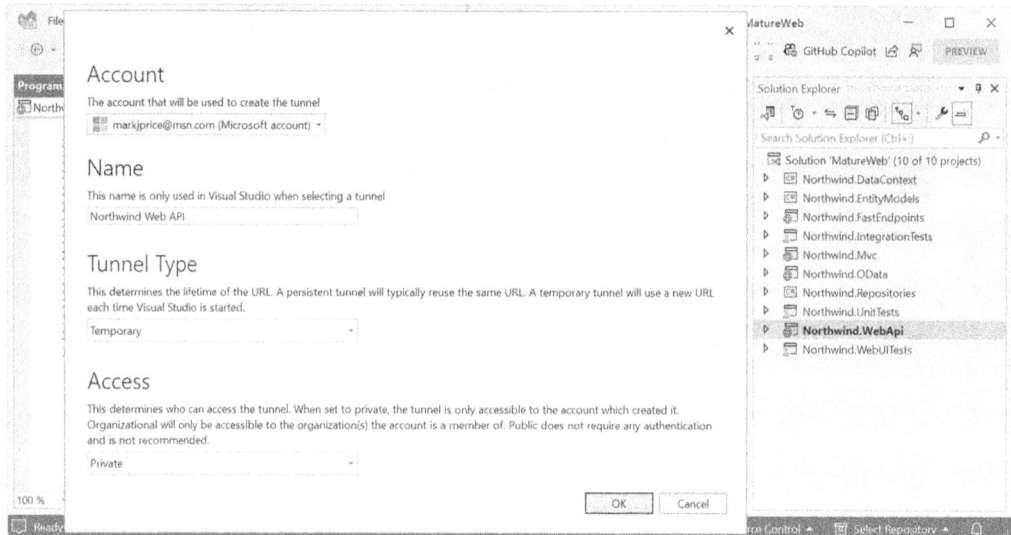

Figure 11.5: Creating a dev tunnel in Visual Studio

4. At this point, if you want to go back to multiple startup projects, you can, but we are only going to start the `Northwind.WebApi` project anyway.

5. Start the `Northwind.WebApi` project using the `https` profile without debugging.

6. If you are using a GitHub account, then you may need to authorize dev tunnels to verify your identity.

7. Try out the weather service and note that it returns random weather, as shown in *Figure 11.6*:

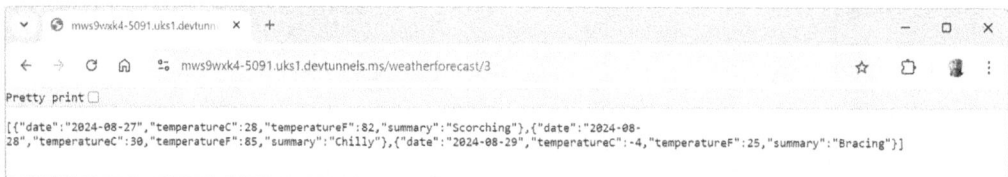

Figure 11.6: Random weather from a web service callable on the public internet

8. At the command prompt or terminal, note that the web service is still hosted on `localhost` and listening on ports 5091 and 5090. But now, a dev tunnel is redirecting public HTTP requests via the public URL to your local web service, so the environment variable containing the tunnel URL is available, as shown in the following output and *Figure 11.7*:

```
Tunnel URL: https://mds6pvxg-5091.uks1.devtunnels.ms/
```

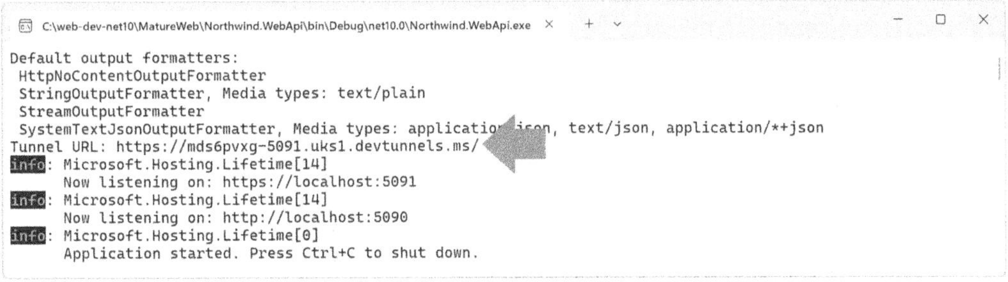

```
 C:\web-dev-net10\MatureWeb\Northwind.WebApi\bin\Debug\net10.0\Northwind.WebApi.exe    ×    +  ∨                    —    □    ×

Default output formatters:
  HttpNoContentOutputFormatter
  StringOutputFormatter, Media types: text/plain
  StreamOutputFormatter
  SystemTextJsonOutputFormatter, Media types: application/json, text/json, application/*+json
Tunnel URL: https://mds6pvxg-5091.uks1.devtunnels.ms/
info: Microsoft.Hosting.Lifetime[14]
      Now listening on: https://localhost:5091
info: Microsoft.Hosting.Lifetime[14]
      Now listening on: http://localhost:5090
info: Microsoft.Hosting.Lifetime[0]
      Application started. Press Ctrl+C to shut down.
```

Figure 11.7: The tunnel URL shown in the output

9. In Visual Studio, navigate to **View** | **Output**, select **Show output from: Dev Tunnels**, and note the results, as shown in the following output and in *Figure 11.8*:

```
Getting dev tunnels for account 'Mark Price (markjprice@msn.com)':
Succeeded
Getting dev tunnels for account 'markjprice (GitHub)': Failed to get the
list of dev tunnels. Tunnel service response status code: Unauthorized
Request ID: 0c27c229-0843-4d16-9dab-01382ae77890 Response status code
does not indicate success: 401 (Unauthorized).
Dev tunnel 'Northwind Web API' was created successfully
Successfully configured the following urls on dev tunnel 'Northwind Web
API':
        https://localhost:5091  ->  https://mws9wxk4-5091.uks1.
devtunnels.ms/
```

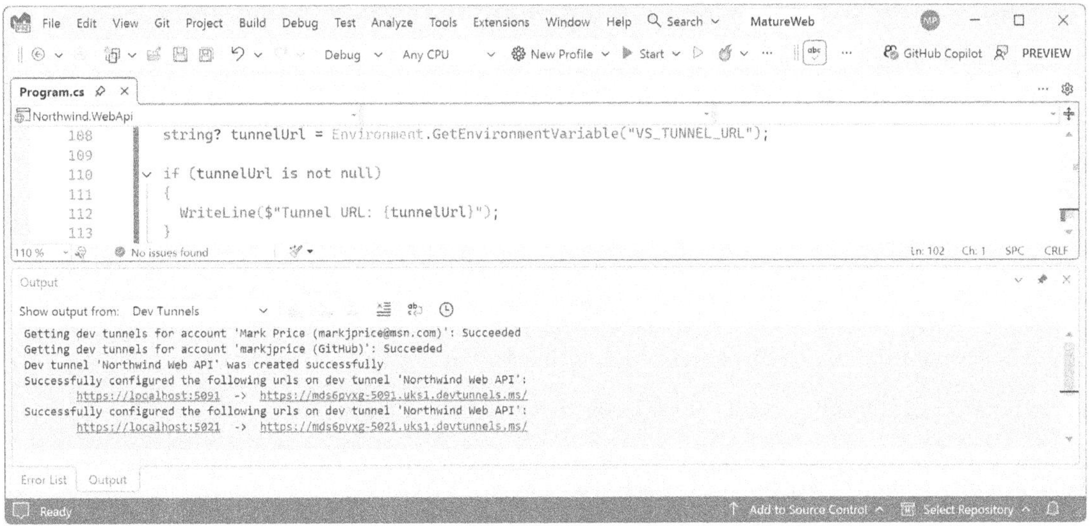

Figure 11.8: Dev Tunnels output in Visual Studio

Disabling dev tunnels

When you have finished using dev tunnels, in Visual Studio, in the standard toolbar, navigate to **https | Dev Tunnels (Northwind Web API) | None**.

Dev tunnels summary

Whether you're a solo developer working on a side project or part of a team iterating rapidly on a complex application, dev tunnels offer a flexible, powerful way to bridge the gap between local development and public accessibility. Just remember to consider the implications of exposing your local environment and to use these tools wisely.

> Popular alternatives to Microsoft dev tunnels include Cloudflare Tunnels (`https://developers.cloudflare.com/cloudflare-one/connections/connect-networks/`) and ngrok (`https://ngrok.com/`). While ngrok is dev-first, Cloudflare is infra-first, aimed at both developers and ops. They solve similar problems but for different audiences. ngrok is the MacBook of tunnels: polished, premium, good UX. Cloudflare Tunnel is more like a high-performance Linux server: powerful, free, but requires more effort to set up.

Practicing and exploring

Test your knowledge and understanding by answering some questions, getting some hands-on practice, and exploring the topics covered in this chapter with deeper research.

Exercise 11.1 – Online-only material

For a good official overview of all types of testing with .NET, view the following link:

`https://learn.microsoft.com/en-us/dotnet/core/testing/`.

You can learn more about integration tests in ASP.NET Core at the following link:

`https://learn.microsoft.com/en-us/aspnet/core/test/integration-tests`.

You can review common questions about ASP.NET Core and integration testing on Stack Overflow at the following link:

`https://stackoverflow.com/questions/tagged/asp.net-core+integration-testing`.

You can learn more about testing web services using dev tunnels at the following link:

`https://learn.microsoft.com/en-us/aspnet/core/test/dev-tunnels`.

Exercise 11.2 – Practice exercises

Create integration tests for three web service technologies

In *Chapters 9*, *12*, and *13*, you will have created projects that implement web services to work with customers in the Northwind database with the following technologies:

1. Web API using controllers

2. OData

3. FastEndpoints

Create a new xUnit project and then write integration tests to retrieve a single customer and all customers in Germany from each of these three projects once you have completed those chapters.

Exercise 11.3 – Test your knowledge

Answer the following questions. If you get stuck, try googling the answers, while remembering that if you get totally stuck, the answers are in the appendix:

1. What is a MUT?

2. What is a test double?

3. What is the most dangerous test outcome from the following: TN, TP, FN, and FP? Why?

4. For integration testing, what types of external systems should you test, and which should you mock?

5. What are the benefits of automating tests?

6. What should you consider when integration testing with data stores?

7. How are tests in xUnit configured?

8. Why would you use the `WebApplicationFactory` class in an integration test?

9. Using NSubstitute, how do you configure the return value of a faked method?

10. What are dev tunnels and how are they useful to .NET developers?

Exercise 11.4 – Explore topics

Use the following link to learn more details about the topics covered in this chapter:

```
https://github.com/markjprice/web-dev-net10/blob/main/docs/book-links.md#chapter-11--
-testing-and-debugging-web-services.
```

Summary

In this chapter, you learned:

• The basic concepts of integration testing

• Considerations about integration testing with data stores

• How to test web services using xUnit

• How to mock dependencies in tests

• How to test web services using dev tunnels

In the next chapter, you will learn how to build web services using OData.

Learn more on Discord

To join the Discord community for this book – where you can share feedback, ask questions to the author, and learn about new releases – follow this QR code:

```
https://packt.link/RWWD10
```

Join .NETPro — It's Free

Staying sharp in .NET takes more than reading release notes. It requires real-world tips, proven patterns, and scalable solutions. That's what .NETPro, Packt's new newsletter, is all about.

Scan the QR code or visit the link to subscribe:

```
https://landing.packtpub.com/dotnetpronewsletter/
```

12

Building Web Services Using ASP.NET Core OData

Websites often need to display data, and that data often comes from relational databases. To improve modularity and reuse, instead of a website directly calling the database, it should call a web service. That web service can then be called by other clients, like mobile and desktop apps, as well as the website itself or even other web services.

If you already have a well-structured relational database, instead of manually defining controllers with action methods that query the database and return responses, as you learned to do with ASP.NET Core Web API in *Chapter 9*, *Building Web Services Using ASP.NET Core Web API*, it would be even better if you could just wrap an EF Core entity model with a web service that automatically supports complex querying using HTTP standards.

Guess what? That's exactly what ASP.NET Core OData does for you!

In this chapter, you will be introduced to OData, a standard that makes it easy to expose data via the web to make it accessible to any client that can make an HTTP request. OData is great for scenarios where a standardized, flexible data protocol is needed, especially for internal enterprise environments that integrate with Microsoft products like Excel and Power BI. It simplifies the development of data-driven applications by offering built-in querying, CRUD operations, and deep integration with many tools.

While there are performance considerations that we will consider, OData's strengths lie in its standardization, metadata-driven model, and ease of integration with complex relational data systems.

This chapter will cover the following topics:

- Understanding OData
- Building a web service that supports OData
- Exploring OData services using HTTP/REST tools
- Implementing versions and data modifications
- Building clients for OData services

Understanding OData

One of the most common uses of a web service is to expose a database to clients that do not know how to work directly with the native database, or cannot for security reasons. Another common use is to provide a simplified or abstracted API that exposes an authenticated interface to a subset of the data to control access.

In *Chapter 1, Introducing Real-World Web Development Using .NET*, you created an EF Core model to expose an SQL Server database to any .NET project. But what about non-.NET projects? I know it's crazy to imagine, but not every developer uses .NET! Non-.NET developers cannot use our EF Core entity model class libraries.

Luckily, all development platforms support HTTP, so all development platforms can call web services, and ASP.NET Core has a package for making that easy and powerful using a standard named OData.

Understanding the OData standard

OData (Open Data Protocol) is an ISO/IEC-approved, OASIS standard that defines a set of best practices for building and consuming RESTful APIs. Microsoft created it in 2007 and released versions 1.0, 2.0, and 3.0 under its Microsoft Open Specification Promise. Version 4.0 was then standardized at OASIS and released in 2014. OData is based on HTTP and has multiple endpoints to support multiple versions and entity sets.

> ASP.NET Core OData implements OData version 4.0. You can learn more about the OData standard at the following link: `https://www.odata.org/`.

Benefits of OData

OData has many benefits when it comes to simplifying data access over HTTP.

Standardized querying

Unlike traditional ASP.NET Core Web API services, where the service defines all the methods and what gets returned, OData uses **URL query strings** to define its queries. This enables the client to have more control over what is returned and minimizes round trips. Of course, the OData service controls the scope of those queries, but within that scope, the client has complete control.

For example, with a Web API controller-based web service, an endpoint defined by a controller action might always return all columns from the `Products` table in the HTTP response, but only data from the `Products` table, not from related tables like `Categories`. If a client app needs to show a list of product names with their category names, then the client app might have to make two round trips to call two Web API endpoints and then match up the response data at the client side, throwing away the unneeded data. With OData, the client can request just the columns it needs and from multiple related tables in a single round trip.

OData uses familiar HTTP methods (`GET`, `POST`, `PUT`, and `DELETE`) and supports rich querying features like filtering, sorting, paging, and projections, which make it easy to interact with data from any OData-compliant service.

OData comes with built-in query options that save developers time in implementing filtering, sorting, and pagination logic. These features are easily enabled, and clients can pass query options directly in the URL, like `$filter`, `$select`, `$top`, and so on, reducing the need for custom server-side logic for such tasks.

For example, the following request retrieves products with a price greater than 100, sorted by price in descending order, and limited to 10 results, as shown in the following URL relative path:

```
/products?$filter=Price gt 100&$orderby=Price desc&$top=10
```

As another example, when querying the Northwind database, a client might only need two fields of data, `ProductName` and `UnitPrice`, and the related `Supplier` object, and only for products where the `ProductName` contains the word `burger` and the cost is less than `4.95`, with the results sorted by country and then cost. The client would construct their query as a URL query string using standard named parameters, as shown in the following request:

```
GET https://example.com/v1/products?$filter=contains(ProductName,
'burger') and UnitPrice lt 4.95&$orderby=Supplier/
Country,UnitPrice&$select=ProductName,UnitPrice&$expand=Supplier
```

Cross-platform interoperability and integration with the Microsoft ecosystem

OData is designed to be platform-agnostic, meaning it can be used across various environments and technologies. Whether you are using .NET, Java, Python, or any other platform, you can interact with an OData service using standard HTTP methods, making it easy to integrate systems that may otherwise not communicate smoothly.

Being an open standard with wide adoption ensures that OData services and clients can be easily integrated with existing tools, reducing the overhead of building custom data access layers. This also means you can take advantage of a wealth of community support and documentation.

As well as supporting maximum interoperability with almost any developer platform, OData is well supported within the Microsoft ecosystem. Technologies like Power BI, Excel, and EF Core can natively consume OData endpoints, making it particularly useful for businesses that rely on Microsoft tools, as shown in *Figure 12.1*:

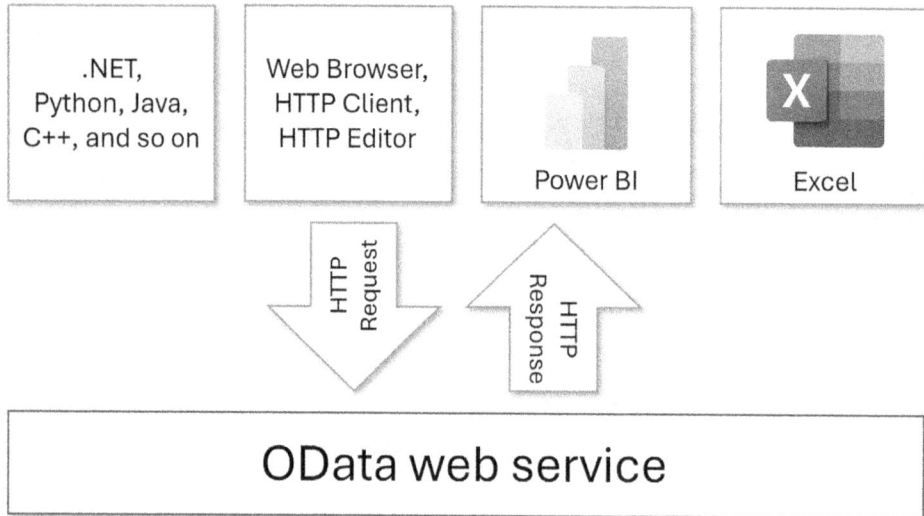

Figure 12.1: Any client that can make an HTTP request can call an OData web service

This integration allows users to easily connect to data sources, create reports, and perform data analysis with minimal setup. Because OData is built for querying and manipulating data, it's particularly useful for applications that are heavily data-driven, such as reporting systems, dashboards, and analytics tools. Its ability to represent relationships between entities, like in relational databases, makes it a great fit for applications needing to work with complex data models.

Self-describing and rich metadata

One of OData's strengths is its ability to expose rich metadata about the data service it offers. OData includes a standardized way of describing the schema of the data, which clients can read to understand the structure of the underlying data model. For example, OData documents the available entities and their types, relationships, and so on. This allows dynamic, client-side tools to work effectively without prior knowledge of the schema.

An OData metadata document, which describes the entire data model, makes it easier for clients to dynamically discover and consume the service without needing external documentation. The client can use this document to understand what entities are available, their relationships, and the operations that can be performed.

Supports RESTful principles and CRUD operations

OData is built on top of REST principles, which makes it familiar to developers accustomed to REST APIs. It uses HTTP methods like GET for retrieving, POST for creating, and so on, in a predictable manner, and its stateless interactions align with standard web service design patterns.

OData allows for full **CRUD (Create, Read, Update, Delete)** operations, which makes it more than just a query language. You can use it to not only fetch data but also modify data on the server, providing a comprehensive data access layer over HTTP.

Supports multiple data formats

OData supports multiple data formats, like JSON, XML, and AtomPub, giving it flexibility based on client needs. JSON is particularly valuable for web and mobile applications due to its lightweight nature, while XML and AtomPub can be useful for enterprise-level integrations.

Built-in support for data relationships

OData naturally supports data relationships, a.k.a. navigation properties, making it easy to traverse and query related data. This is particularly useful when working with relational databases, as you can retrieve entities and their related data with minimal effort.

For example, you can retrieve an order and its related customer information in a single query, as shown in the following URL relative path:

```
/Orders?$expand=Customer
```

Extensibility

OData is flexible and can be extended. For instance, you can add custom actions and functions that go beyond basic CRUD operations to provide additional behaviors, such as custom workflows, without breaking the RESTful nature of the protocol. This makes it more powerful and adaptable to different business needs.

Standard security features

OData leverages existing web security standards like OAuth, OpenID Connect, and HTTPS. While not exclusive to OData, the protocol doesn't require creating a custom security solution and can fit into existing security models.

Disadvantages of OData

This chapter would not be complete without a discussion of when it is not appropriate to use OData to build a web service.

OData can introduce additional complexity and overhead compared to simpler web services, especially for developers unfamiliar with its structure and metadata format. The learning curve can be steep for those accustomed to traditional REST APIs or other simpler alternatives.

If implemented poorly, OData can have performance concerns:

- **Over-fetching data:** By default, OData may return large datasets when only a small portion is needed. Although you can fine-tune queries, the default behavior can result in significant performance overhead if not properly managed.

- **Query complexity:** OData supports complex queries, including filtering and sorting, which can impact server performance if users make unoptimized queries. This complexity also puts more burden on the server to process these queries.

While the flexibility of OData queries is one of its strengths, it can also be a drawback. Client developers can craft complex queries that might be inefficient or hard to optimize, causing unpredictable performance issues. This is especially concerning when exposing public endpoints that allow developers to run extensive filtering and sorting operations on large datasets.

OData services may struggle when working with large datasets or high concurrency, as the query structure can introduce processing overhead. Other APIs built around simpler REST principles can be more efficient and easier to scale because they often don't need to process complex queries directly within the URL.

OData can be difficult to version over time. REST APIs are typically versioned by the endpoint, but OData services are generally designed around a single, large API surface. Adding new functionality or making changes can become challenging without breaking existing clients.

OData doesn't provide robust mechanisms for fine-grained security control. It may be difficult to restrict access to certain parts of data or prevent certain query types. Because it supports a wide array of querying options, you have to manually enforce many security measures, making it more prone to exposing sensitive data unintentionally.

OData's adherence to strict standards like the AtomPub (XML) and JSON formats can result in bloated responses, particularly when metadata is included by default. This can be especially problematic for mobile or low-bandwidth environments, where minimizing payload size is important for performance.

While OData simplifies querying for the client, it can also add complexity on the client side to process the responses. Clients need to understand the OData protocol and how to construct complex queries, and this can be cumbersome in environments where the primary goal is simplicity, such as lightweight mobile apps.

While there are OData libraries and support outside of Microsoft, its popularity tends to wane when working in non-Microsoft environments, leading to fewer resources, documentation, and community support if you're not primarily working within Microsoft tools.

OData works best with relational data, as it was designed with SQL databases in mind. When working with NoSQL databases or unstructured data, OData can become cumbersome.

While OData is a powerful tool for specific use cases, particularly in enterprise environments or where data interoperability is important, OData does have drawbacks related to performance, complexity, security, and scalability. If you're building services where interoperability, simplicity, speed, or lightweight interactions are more important than maturity, then simpler REST or GraphQL alternatives might be more appropriate than OData.

> I cover modern options for building web services with Minimal API and GraphQL in my book *Apps and Services with .NET 10*. That book also covers efficient non-web microservices using gRPC.

Building a web service that supports OData

There is no dotnet new project template for ASP.NET Core OData, but it uses controller classes, so we will use the ASP.NET Core Web API using controllers project template and then add package references to add the OData capabilities:

1. Use your preferred code editor to add a new project, as defined in the following list:

    - **Project template: ASP.NET Core Web API** / `webapi --use-controllers`
    - **Solution file and folder:** `MatureWeb`
    - **Project file and folder:** `Northwind.OData`

2. If you are using Visual Studio, then confirm that the following defaults have been chosen:

    - **Framework: .NET 10.0 (Long Term Support)**
    - **Authentication type: None**
    - **Configure for HTTPS:** Selected
    - **Enable container support:** Cleared
    - **Enable OpenAPI support:** Selected
    - **Do not use top-level statements:** Cleared
    - **Use controllers:** Selected
    - **Enlist in Aspire orchestration:** Cleared

    > **Warning!** Make sure to select the **Use controllers** checkbox, or your code will look very different because it will use Minimal API instead of controllers!

3. If you are using VS Code or Rider, then in the `MatureWeb` directory, at the command prompt or terminal, you can enter the following commands:

    ```
    dotnet new webapi --use-controllers -o Northwind.OData
    dotnet sln add Northwind.OData
    ```

4. In the `Northwind.OData.csproj` project file, delete the version attribute from the OpenAPI package reference, add a package reference for OData integration with ASP.NET Core, and add a project reference to the Northwind database context project, as shown highlighted in the following markup:

    ```
    <Project Sdk="Microsoft.NET.Sdk.Web">

      <PropertyGroup>
    ```

```
        <TargetFramework>net10.0</TargetFramework>
        <Nullable>enable</Nullable>
        <ImplicitUsings>enable</ImplicitUsings>
    </PropertyGroup>

    <ItemGroup>
        <PackageReference Include="Microsoft.AspNetCore.OpenApi" />
        <PackageReference Include="Microsoft.AspNetCore.OData" />
    </ItemGroup>

    <ItemGroup>
        <ProjectReference Include=
        "..\Northwind.DataContext\Northwind.DataContext.csproj" />
    </ItemGroup>

</Project>
```

> **Warning!** Although it is the most popular downloaded package for OData, do *not* reference `Microsoft.Data.OData` because it only supports versions 1 to 3, and it is not being maintained. The other popular packages for OData are `Microsoft.OData.Core` and `Microsoft.OData.Edm`, which are both dependencies of the package you just referenced, so they will be included in your project automatically.

5. In the `Northwind.OData` project folder, delete `WeatherForecast.cs`.
6. In the `Controllers` folder, delete `WeatherForecastController.cs`.
7. Build the `Northwind.OData` project to compile dependencies and restore packages.

Defining OData models for the EF Core models

The first task is to define what we want to expose as OData models in the web service. You have complete control, so if you have an existing EF Core model, as we do for Northwind, you do not have to expose all of it.

You do not even have to use EF Core models. The data source can be anything. In this book, we will only look at using it with EF Core because that is the most common use for .NET developers.

Traditionally, if you only had a single data model, then you would use odata as the name (but this is just a convention), as shown in *Table 12.1*:

Endpoint	Description	Response
/odata	Retrieve the service document.	JSON-based representation of the service document listing all the top-level entity sets
/odata/$metadata	Retrieve service metadata.	Service metadata XML document describing the **Entity Data Model (EDM)** for the service
/odata/<entityset> /odata/Products	Retrieve all entities in an entity set.	Collection of products
/odata/<entityset>/$count /odata/Products/$count	Retrieve the number of entities in an entity set.	Count of products
/odata/<entityset>(<key>) /odata/<entitytset>/<key> /odata/Products(77) /odata/Products/77	Retrieve entity by ID.	Entity object, for example, the product with an ID of 77

Table 12.1: Conventions for OData endpoints

Defining OData models in the project

Let's define two OData models – one to expose the Northwind product catalog named catalog, includ-ing the Categories and Products tables, and one to expose the customers, their orders, and related tables, named ordersystem:

1. In the Northwind.OData project folder, add a new folder named Extensions.
2. In the Extensions folder, add a new class named IServiceCollectionExtensions.cs.
3. In IServiceCollectionExtensions.cs, import the namespace for working with OData and the namespace for the database context registration extension method, and then register the Northwind database context and chain a call to the AddOData extension method to define two OData models and enable features like projection, filtering, and sorting, as shown in the following code:

```csharp
using Microsoft.AspNetCore.OData; // To use AddOData.
using Microsoft.OData.Edm; // To use IEdmModel.
using Microsoft.OData.ModelBuilder; // ODataConventionModelBuilder
using Northwind.EntityModels; // To use AddNorthwindContext.

namespace Northwind.OData.Extensions;

public static class IServiceCollectionExtensions
{
```

```csharp
private static IEdmModel GetEdmModelForCatalog()
{
  ODataConventionModelBuilder builder = new();
  builder.EntitySet<Category>("Categories");
  builder.EntitySet<Product>("Products");
  builder.EntitySet<Supplier>("Suppliers");
  return builder.GetEdmModel();
}

private static IEdmModel GetEdmModelForOrderSystem()
{
  ODataConventionModelBuilder builder = new();
  builder.EntitySet<Customer>("Customers");
  builder.EntitySet<Order>("Orders");
  builder.EntitySet<Employee>("Employees");
  builder.EntitySet<Product>("Products");
  builder.EntitySet<Shipper>("Shippers");
  return builder.GetEdmModel();
}

public static IServiceCollection AddNorthwindODataControllers(
  this IServiceCollection services)
{
  services.AddNorthwindContext();

  services.AddControllers()
    // Register OData models.
    .AddOData(options => options

      // GET /catalog and /catalog/$metadata
      .AddRouteComponents(routePrefix: "catalog",
        model: GetEdmModelForCatalog())

      // GET /ordersystem and /ordersystem/$metadata
      .AddRouteComponents(routePrefix: "ordersystem",
        model: GetEdmModelForOrderSystem())

      // Enable query options:
      .Select() // $select for projection
      .Expand() // $expand to navigate to related entities
      .Filter() // $filter
```

```
            .OrderBy() // $orderby
            .SetMaxTop(100) // $top
            .Count() // $count
        );

    return services;
    }
}
```

4. In `Program.cs`, replace the call to `AddControllers` with a call to `AddNorthwindODataControllers`, as shown in the following code:

    ```
    // builder.Services.AddControllers();

    builder.Services.AddNorthwindODataControllers();
    ```

5. In the `Properties` folder, open `launchSettings.json`.

6. In the `https` profile, modify `applicationUrl` to use port 5121 for HTTPS and 5120 for HTTP, as shown in the following markup:

    ```
    "applicationUrl": "https://localhost:5121;http://localhost:5120",
    ```

7. In the `https` profile, add a `launchUrl` entry to request the `catalog` service document, and set `launchBrowser` to `true`, as shown in the following markup:

    ```
    "launchBrowser": true,
    "launchUrl": "catalog",
    ```

8. Save the changes.

Testing the OData models

Now we can check that the OData models have been defined correctly:

1. Set the `Northwind.OData` project as the startup project.

2. Start the `Northwind.OData` project with the `https` launch profile.

3. Start Chrome if it does not start automatically.

4. Navigate to `https://localhost:5121/catalog` and note the `Northwind.OData` service catalog entity sets are included in a JSON document, as shown in the following markup:

    ```
    {
      "@odata.context": "https://localhost:5121/catalog/$metadata",
      "value": [
        {
          "name": "Categories",
          "kind": "EntitySet",
          "url": "Categories"
    ```

```
    },
    {
      "name": "Products",
      "kind": "EntitySet",
      "url": "Products"
    },
    {

      "name": "Suppliers",
      "kind": "EntitySet",
      "url": "Suppliers"

    }
  ]
}
```

> The `@odata.context` value tells us the URL to request a complete XML file that documents the catalog model. The `url` values tell us the relative path to access the entities in those entity sets. For example, to retrieve all suppliers, you would use `https://localhost:5121/catalog/Suppliers`.

5. Navigate to `https://localhost:5121/catalog/$metadata` and note the `Northwind.OData` service catalog entity model is fully documented in an XML document, as shown in *Figure 12.2*:

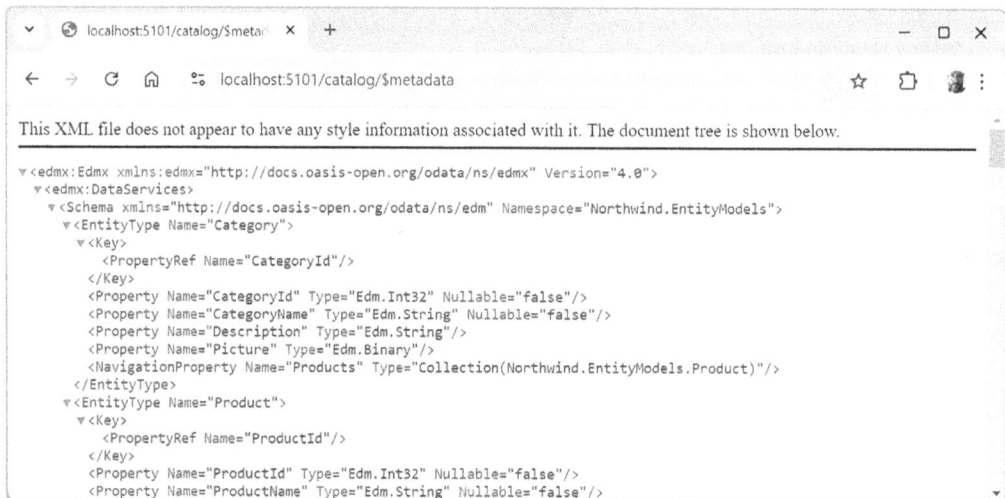

Figure 12.2: Documentation for the Northwind.OData project catalog

6. Navigate to `https://localhost:5121/ordersystem` and `https://localhost:5121/ordersystem/$metadata`, and note that the `Northwind.OData` service order system entity model is also documented.

7. Close Chrome and shut down the web server.

At this point, we have documented the two models, but if we try to access the entities in those models, they fail. The next step is to create an OData controller for each entity set with code to read and write to the data.

Creating and testing OData controllers

Next, we must create OData controllers, one for each type of entity, to retrieve data:

1. In the `Controllers` folder, add an empty controller class file named `CategoriesController.cs`.
2. Modify its contents to inherit from `ODataController`, get an instance of the Northwind database context using constructor parameter injection, and define two `Get` methods to retrieve all categories or one category using a unique key, as shown in the following code:

```
using Microsoft.AspNetCore.Mvc; // To use IActionResult.
using Microsoft.AspNetCore.OData.Query; // To use [EnableQuery].
using Microsoft.AspNetCore.OData.Routing.Controllers; // ODataController
using Northwind.EntityModels; // To use NorthwindContext.

namespace Northwind.OData.Controllers;

public class CategoriesController : ODataController
{
  private readonly NorthwindContext _db;

  public CategoriesController(NorthwindContext db)
  {
    _db = db;
  }

  [EnableQuery]
  public IActionResult Get()
  {
    return Ok(_db.Categories);
  }

  [EnableQuery]
  public IActionResult Get(int key)
  {
    return Ok(_db.Categories.Where(
      category => category.CategoryId == key));
  }
}
```

> **Good practice:** Make sure that your Get methods are decorated with [EnableQuery]
> so that OData can work its magic and extend the LINQ query so that the generated
> SQL statement is optimized.

3. Repeat the above step for Products and Suppliers.

> I will leave it as an optional task for you to do the same for the other entities to
> enable the order system OData model. Note that the CustomerId is a string
> instead of an int. The solution code for all OData controllers can be found at the
> following link: https://github.com/markjprice/web-dev-net10/tree/main/
> code/MatureWeb/Northwind.OData/Controllers.

4. Start the Northwind.OData web service using the https launch profile.

5. Start Chrome, navigate to https://localhost:5121/catalog/Products, and note the response
    body that shows a JSON document containing all products in the entity set, as partially shown
    in the following output and in *Figure 12.3*:

```json
{
    "@odata.context": "https://localhost:5121/catalog/$metadata#Products",
    "value": [
        {
            "ProductId": 1,
            "ProductName": "Chai",
            "SupplierId": 1,
            "CategoryId": 1,
            "QuantityPerUnit": "10 boxes x 20 bags",
            "UnitPrice": 18,
            "UnitsInStock": 39,
            "UnitsOnOrder": 0,
            "ReorderLevel": 10,
            "Discontinued": false
        },
        {
            "ProductId": 2,
            "ProductName": "Chang",
            "SupplierId": 1,
            "CategoryId": 1,
            "QuantityPerUnit": "24 - 12 oz bottles",
            "UnitPrice": 19,
            "UnitsInStock": 17,
            "UnitsOnOrder": 40,
            "ReorderLevel": 25,
            "Discontinued": false
```

```
        },
        ...
    ]
}
```

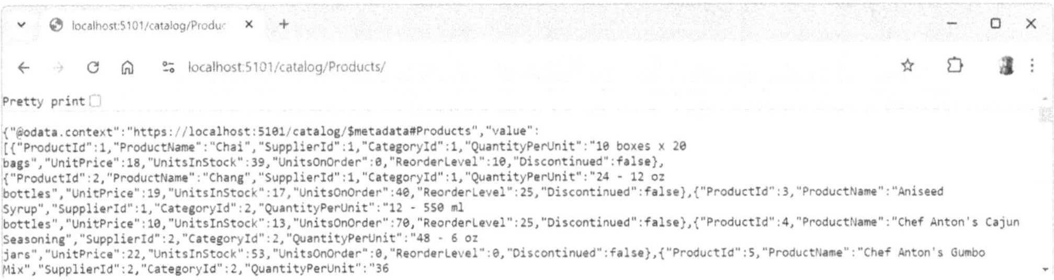

```
localhost:5101/catalog/Produ    ×    +                                    —  □  ×

←  →  C  ⌂  🔒  localhost:5101/catalog/Products/                        ☆  ⟳  👤  :

Pretty print ☐

{"@odata.context":"https://localhost:5101/catalog/$metadata#Products","value":
[{"ProductId":1,"ProductName":"Chai","SupplierId":1,"CategoryId":1,"QuantityPerUnit":"10 boxes x 20
bags","UnitPrice":18,"UnitsInStock":39,"UnitsOnOrder":0,"ReorderLevel":10,"Discontinued":false},
{"ProductId":2,"ProductName":"Chang","SupplierId":1,"CategoryId":1,"QuantityPerUnit":"24 - 12 oz
bottles","UnitPrice":19,"UnitsInStock":17,"UnitsOnOrder":40,"ReorderLevel":25,"Discontinued":false},{"ProductId":3,"ProductName":"Aniseed
Syrup","SupplierId":1,"CategoryId":2,"QuantityPerUnit":"12 - 550 ml
bottles","UnitPrice":10,"UnitsInStock":13,"UnitsOnOrder":70,"ReorderLevel":25,"Discontinued":false},{"ProductId":4,"ProductName":"Chef Anton's Cajun
Seasoning","SupplierId":2,"CategoryId":2,"QuantityPerUnit":"48 - 6 oz
jars","UnitPrice":22,"UnitsInStock":53,"UnitsOnOrder":0,"ReorderLevel":0,"Discontinued":false},{"ProductId":5,"ProductName":"Chef Anton's Gumbo
Mix","SupplierId":2,"CategoryId":2,"QuantityPerUnit":"36
```

Figure 12.3: The Products entity set

6. At the command prompt or terminal, note the output from logging the SQL command that was executed, as shown in the following output:

```
info: Microsoft.EntityFrameworkCore.Database.Command[20101]
      Executed DbCommand (5ms) [Parameters=[], CommandType='Text',
CommandTimeout='30']
      SELECT [p].[ProductId], [p].[CategoryId], [p].[Discontinued],
[p].[ProductName], [p].[QuantityPerUnit], [p].[ReorderLevel], [p].
[SupplierId], [p].[UnitPrice], [p].[UnitsInStock], [p].[UnitsOnOrder]
      FROM [Products] AS [p]
```

> We are noting the SQL statement now so that you can see that all the columns and rows are requested by the OData service when it receives a **GET** request to the catalog/Products path. Later, we will use EF Core logs again to see how OData queries are automatically translated into efficient SQL queries. OData services do not have to return all columns and rows from the database to the service and then perform the filtering inside the service.

7. Close Chrome and shut down the web server.

Exploring OData services using HTTP/REST tools

Instead of a browser, a better tool for exploring your OData service is the VS Code extension named **REST Client** or the HTTP editor built into Visual Studio.

Creating an HTTP file for making requests

Let's explore the many types of queries that your OData web service can automatically handle by creating an .http file:

1. In your preferred code editor, start the Northwind.OData project web service and leave it running.

2. In the `HttpRequests` folder, create a file named `odata-catalog.http` and modify its contents
    to contain some basic requests to the catalog model, as shown in the following code:

```
### Configure a variable for the web service base address.
@base_address = https://localhost:5121/catalog/


### Make a GET request to the base address.
GET {{base_address}}


### Make a GET request to the base address for metadata.
GET {{base_address}}$metadata


### Make a GET request to get all categories.
GET {{base_address}}categories


### Make a GET request to get all products.
GET {{base_address}}products


### Make a GET request to get all suppliers.
GET {{base_address}}suppliers
```

3. For each request, click **Send request**, and note the response, for example, a JSON document
    containing all categories, as shown in *Figure 12.4*:

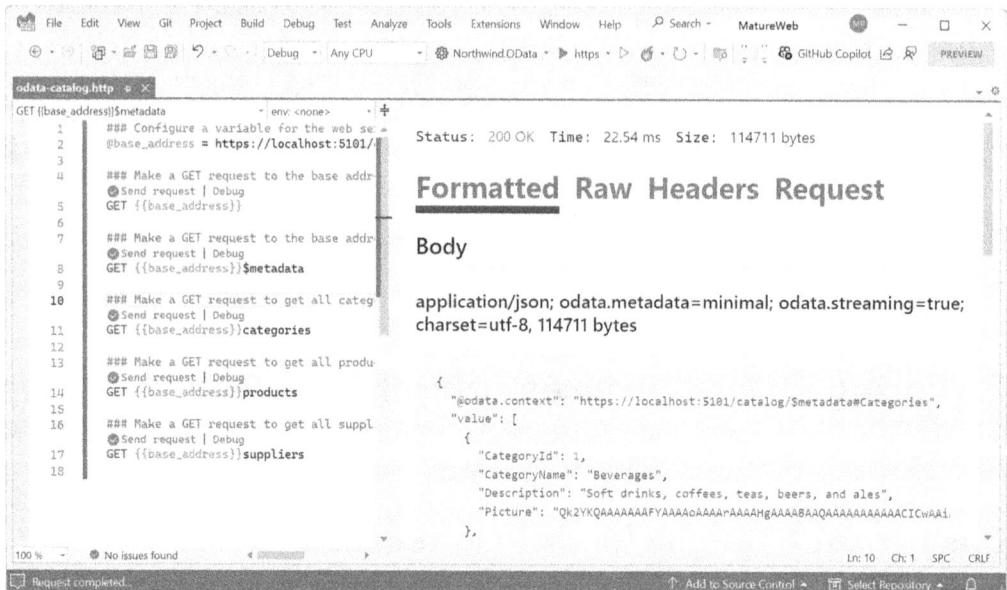

Figure 12.4: Visual Studio's HTTP editor getting the categories from the OData service

4. In odata-catalog.http, add more requests separated by ###, as shown in *Table 12.2* (remember to prefix it with {{base_address}}):

Relative request	Response

categories(3)	```
	{
	  "@odata.context":
	"https://localhost:5121/catalog/$metadata#Categories/$entity",
	  "CategoryId": 3,
	  "CategoryName": "Confections",
	  "Description": "Desserts, candies, and sweet breads",
	  "Picture": "FRwvAA..."
	}
	``

categories/3	Same as above
categories/$count	8
products/$count	77
suppliers/$count	29

products(77)	```
	{
	  "@odata.context": "https://localhost:5121/
	catalog/$metadata#Products",
	  "value": [
	  {
	  "ProductId": 77,
	  "ProductName": "Original Frankfurter grüne Soße",
	  "SupplierId": 12,
	  "CategoryId": 2,
	  "QuantityPerUnit": "12 boxes",
	  "UnitPrice": 13.0000,
	  "UnitsInStock": 32,
	  "UnitsOnOrder": 0,
	  "ReorderLevel": 15,
	  "Discontinued": false
	  }
	  ]
	}
	``

Table 12.2: Additional requests to the OData service

Understanding OData queries

Let's review some of the common features of OData queries.

Note that OData queries use the standard query string features of URLs. In other words, they start with a ? at the end of the relative path, and if you specify multiple query options, they must be separated by the & character.

> I strongly recommend using VS Code and its REST Client extension to write your OData queries because it allows you to split an HTTP request over multiple lines, and you can use normal spaces in them. Visual Studio's HTTP editor does not support multiple lines or spaces. You can learn more about its limitations at the following link: https://learn. microsoft.com/en-us/aspnet/core/test/http-files?#unsupported-syntax.

OData standard query options

One of the benefits of OData is that it defines standard query options, as shown in *Table 12.3*:

Option	Description	Example
$select	Selects properties for each entity.	$select=CategoryId,CategoryName
$expand	Selects related entities via navigation properties.	$expand=Products
$filter	The expression is evaluated for each resource, and only entities where the expression is true are included in the response. Use parentheses to wrap expressions to explicitly specify priority.	$filter=startswith(ProductName, 'ch') or (UnitPrice gt 50)
$orderby	Sorts the entities by the comma-separated properties listed in ascending (default) or descending order.	$orderby=UnitPrice desc,ProductName
$skip $top	Skips the specified number of items. Takes the specified number of items.	$skip=40&$top=10

Table 12.3: OData query options

OData operators

OData has operators for use with the $filter option, as shown in *Table 12.4*:

Operator	Description
eq	Equal to
ne	Not equal to
lt	Less than
gt	Greater than

le	Less than or equal to
ge	Greater than or equal to
and	And
or	Or
not	Not
add	Arithmetic addition for numbers and date/time values
sub	Arithmetic subtraction for numbers and date/time values
mul	Arithmetic multiplication for numbers
div	Arithmetic division for numbers
mod	Arithmetic modulus division for numbers

Table 12.4: OData query operators

OData functions

OData has functions for use with the `$filter` option, as shown in *Table 12.5*:

Operator	Description
startswith(stringToSearch, stringToSearchFor)	Text values that start with the specified value
endswith(stringToSearch, stringToSearchFor)	Text values that end with the specified value
concat(string1, string2)	Concatenate two text values
contains(stringToSearch, stringToSearchFor)	Text values that contain the specified value
indexof(stringToSearch, stringToSearchFor)	Returns the position of a text value
length(string)	Returns the length of a text value
substring(string, index[, length])	Extracts a substring from a text value
tolower(string)	Converts to lowercase
toupper(string)	Converts to uppercase
trim(string)	Trims whitespace before and after text value
now	The current date and time
day(datetime), month(datetime), year(datetime)	Extracts date components
hour(datetime), minute(datetime), second(datetime)	Extracts time components

Table 12.5: OData query functions

Exploring OData queries

Let's experiment with some OData queries:

1. In the `HttpRequests` folder, create a file named `odata-catalog-queries.http` and modify its contents to contain a request to get all categories, as shown in the following code:

    ```
    ### Configure a variable for the web service base address.
    @base_address = https://localhost:5121/catalog/


    ### Make a GET request for two columns for categories.
    GET {{base_address}}categories/?$select=CategoryId,CategoryName
    ```

2. Arrange the command prompt or terminal window so that you can see it alongside the HTTP file.

3. Click **Send request** and note that the response is a JSON document containing all categories, but only the ID and name properties, and the OData service used the EF Core model to execute a dynamically generated SQL statement that efficiently requested only those two columns, as shown in *Figure 12.5*:

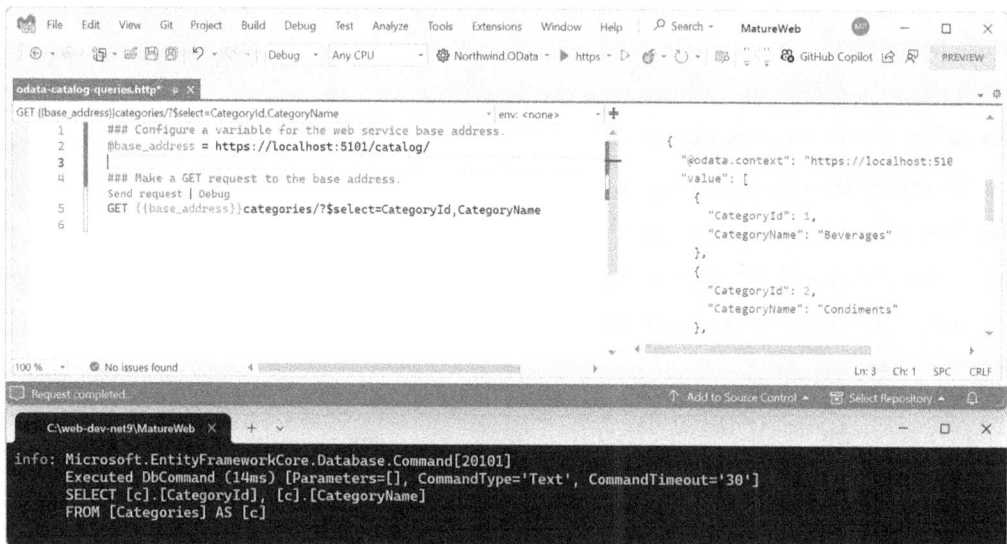

Figure 12.5: OData service efficiently executing SQL against the Northwind database

4. Add and send a request to get the names and prices of products with names that start with `Ch`, like `Chai` and `Chef Anton's Gumbo Mix`, or have a unit price of more than 50, like `Mishi Kobe Niku` or `Sir Rodney's Marmalade`, as shown in the following request and in *Figure 12.6*:

    ```
    ### Make a GET request for products that start with Ch or cost more than
    $50.
    GET {{base_address}}products/
      ?$select=ProductName,UnitPrice
      &$filter=startswith(ProductName,'Ch') or (UnitPrice gt 50)
    ```

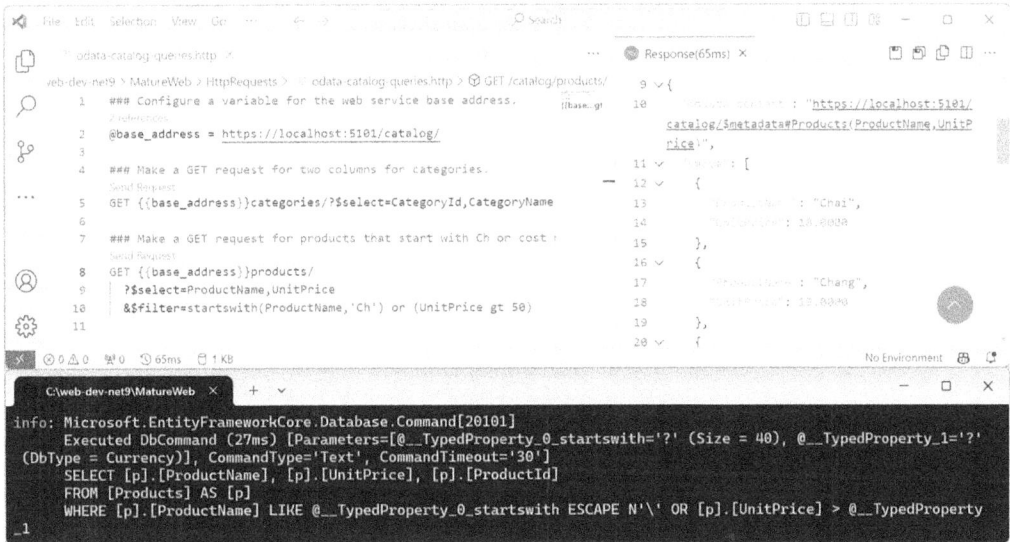

Figure 12.6: VS Code and the REST Client extension executing a multi-line OData request

Visual Studio's HTTP editor cannot execute multi-line HTTP requests, nor does it support spaces in paths. To use it, you must encode the URL. For example, replace each space character with %20, as shown in the following request and in *Figure 12.7*: GET {{base_address}}products/?$select=ProductName,UnitPrice& $filter=startswith(ProductName,'Ch')%20or%20(UnitPrice%20gt%2050).

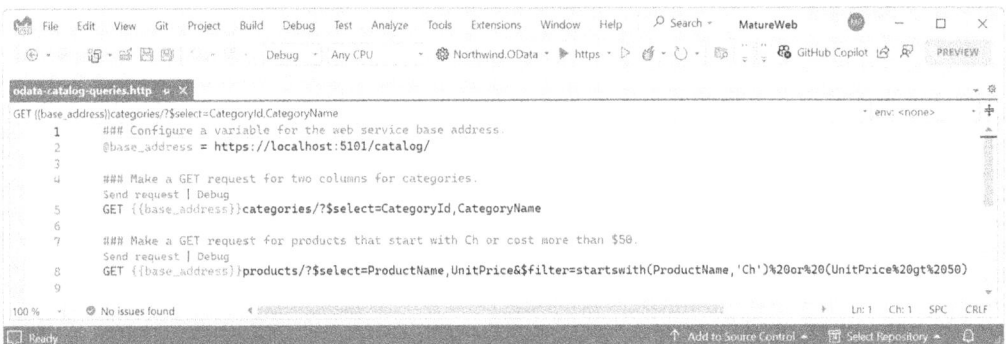

Figure 12.7: Visual Studio's HTTP editor executing an encoded request

5. Add and send a request to get products sorted with the most expensive at the top, and then for each price, sorted by product name, only including the ID, name, and price properties, as shown in the following request:

```
### Make a GET request for products sorted by price.
GET {{base_address}}products/
  ?$orderby=UnitPrice desc,ProductName
  &$select=ProductId,ProductName,UnitPrice
```

6. Add and send a request to get a specific product, and only include the ID, name, and price properties, as shown in the following request:

    ```
    ### Make a GET request for a subset of properties for product 77.
    GET {{base_address}}products(77)/
        ?$select=ProductId,ProductName,UnitPrice
    ```

7. Add and send a request to get categories and their related products, as shown in the following request:

    ```
    ### Make a GET request for categories and their related products.
    GET {{base_address}}categories/
        ?$select=CategoryId,CategoryName
        &$expand=Products
    ```

8. Add and send a request to get a specific category and its related products, as shown in the following request:

    ```
    ### Make a GET request for category 8 and its related products.
    GET {{base_address}}categories(8)/
        ?$select=CategoryId,CategoryName
        &$expand=Products
    ```

9. Add and send a request to get a specific category and a count of its related products, as shown in the following request:

    ```
    ### Make a GET request for categories and a count of their related
    products.
    GET {{base_address}}categories/
        ?$select=CategoryId,CategoryName
        &$expand=Products($count=true)
    ```

10. Shut down the web server.

> For the official documentation of OData URL conventions and standard queries, use the following link: `http://docs.oasis-open.org/odata/odata/v4.01/odata-v4.01-part2-url-conventions.html#_Toc31360954`.

Using logs to review the efficiency of OData requests

How does OData querying work? Let's find out by using logging in the Northwind database context to see the actual SQL statements that are executed:

1. Start the `Northwind.OData` web service.

2. Start Chrome and navigate to `https://localhost:5121/catalog/products/?$filter=startswith(ProductName,'Ch') or (UnitPrice gt 50)&$select=ProductId,ProductName,UnitPrice`.

3. In Chrome, note the result, as shown in the following output:

```
{"@odata.context":"https://localhost:5121/
catalog/$metadata#Products(ProductId,ProductName,UnitPrice)","value":
[{"ProductId":1,"ProductName":"Chai","UnitPrice":18.0000},{"ProductId":2,
"ProductName":"Chang","UnitPrice":19.0000},{"ProductId":4,"ProductName":
"Chef Anton's Cajun
Seasoning","UnitPrice":22.0000},{"ProductId":5,"ProductName":"Chef
Anton's Gumbo
Mix","UnitPrice":21.3500},{"ProductId":9,"ProductName":"Mishi Kobe
Niku","UnitPrice":97.0000},{"ProductId":18,"ProductName":"Carnarvon
Tigers","UnitPrice":62.5000},{"ProductId":20,"ProductName":"Sir Rodney's
Marmalade","UnitPrice":81.0000},{"ProductId":29,"ProductName":"Th\
u00fcringer
Rostbratwurst","UnitPrice":123.7900},{"ProductId":38,"ProductName":"C\
u00f4te de
Blaye","UnitPrice":263.5000},{"ProductId":39,"ProductName":"Chartreuse
verte","UnitPrice":18.0000},{"ProductId":48,"ProductName":"Chocolade",
"UnitPrice":12.7500},{"ProductId":51,"ProductName":"Manjimup Dried
Apples","UnitPrice":53.0000},{"ProductId":59,"ProductName":"Raclette
Courdavault","UnitPrice":55.0000}]}
```

4. At the command prompt or terminal, note the logged SQL statement that was executed, as shown in the following output:

```
info: Microsoft.EntityFrameworkCore.Database.Command[20101]
      Executed DbCommand (57ms) [Parameters=[@__TypedProperty_0='?' (Size
= 4000), @__TypedProperty_0_1='?' (Size = 40), @__TypedProperty_1='?'
(Precision = 2) (DbType = Decimal)], CommandType='Text',
CommandTimeout='30']
      SELECT [p].[ProductId], [p].[ProductName], [p].[UnitPrice]
      FROM [Products] AS [p]
      WHERE @__TypedProperty_0 = N'' OR LEFT([p].[ProductName],
LEN(@__TypedProperty_0_1)) = @__TypedProperty_0 OR [p].[UnitPrice] >
@__TypedProperty_1
```

5. Close the browser and shut down the web server.

It might look like the Get action method on the ProductsController returns the entire Products table with a 200 OK status code, but it actually returns an IQueryable<Products> object.

In other words, it returns a LINQ query, not the results. We decorated the Get action method with the [EnableQuery] attribute. This enables OData to extend the LINQ query with filters, projections, sorting, and so on, and only then does it execute the query, serialize the results, and return them to the client with the 200 OK status code (or the 404 Missing Resource status code in the case where an ID was passed that does not exist).

This makes OData services as flexible *and* efficient as possible when it translates from its query language to LINQ and then into SQL statements.

Implementing versions and data modifications

Now, let's look at how you can implement some more features, including versioning and enabling data modifications.

Versioning OData controllers

It is good practice to plan for future versions of your OData models that might have different schemas and behavior.

To maintain backward compatibility, you can use OData URL prefixes to specify a version number:

1. In the `Northwind.OData` project, in the `Extensions` folder, in `IServiceCollectionExtensions.cs`, after adding the two OData models for `catalog` and `orders`, add a third OData model that has a version number and uses the same `GetEdmModelForCatalog` method, as shown in the following code:

   ```
   // GET /catalog/v1, /catalog/v2, and so on.
   .AddRouteComponents(routePrefix: "catalog/v{version}",
     model: GetEdmModelForCatalog())
   ```

2. In `ProductsController.cs`, modify the `Get` methods to add a `string` parameter named `version` that defaults to `"1"`, and use it to change the behavior of the methods if version 2 is specified in a request, as shown highlighted in the following code:

   ```
   [EnableQuery]
   public IActionResult Get(string version = "1")
   {
       Console.WriteLine($"*** ProductsController version {version}.");
       return Ok(db.Products);
   }

   [EnableQuery]
   public IActionResult Get(int key, string version = "1")
   {
       Console.WriteLine($"*** ProductsController version {version}.");
       IQueryable<Product> products = _db.Products.Where(
         product => product.ProductId == key);

       Product? p = products.FirstOrDefault();
       if ((products is null) || (p is null))
       {
           return NotFound($"Product with id {key} not found.");
   ```

```
    }

    if (version == "2")
    {
      p.ProductName += " version 2.0";
    }

    return Ok(p);
  }
```

3. In your preferred code editor, start the `Northwind.OData` project web service.

4. In `odata-catalog-queries.http`, add a request to get the product with ID 50 using the v2 OData model, as shown in the following code:

```
### GET product 50 using version 2 of the implementation.
GET {{base_address}}v2/products(50)
```

5. Click **Send request**, and note the response is the product with its name appended with version 2.0, as shown highlighted in the following output:

```
{
  "@odata.context": "https://localhost:5121/
v2/$metadata#Products/$entity",
  "ProductId": 50,
  "ProductName": "Valkoinen suklaa version 2.0",
  "SupplierId": 23,
  "CategoryId": 3,
  "QuantityPerUnit": "12 - 100 g bars",
  "UnitPrice": 16.2500,
  "UnitsInStock": 65,
  "UnitsOnOrder": 0,
  "ReorderLevel": 30,
  "Discontinued": false
}
```

6. At the command prompt or terminal, note that `version 2` is used, as shown in the following output:

```
*** ProductsController version 2.
```

7. In `odata-catalog-queries.http`, add a request to get the product with ID 50 using the default (v1) OData model, as shown in the following code:

```
### GET product 50 using the default version 1 of the implementation.
GET {{base_address}}products(50)
```

8. Click **Send request**, and note that the response is the product with its name unmodified.

9. At the command prompt or terminal, note that version 1 is used, as shown in the following output:

```
*** ProductsController version 1.
```

10. Shut down the web server.

Matching HTTP requests to controller action methods

In ASP.NET Core OData, the framework determines which HTTP methods are supported by a controller class primarily by inspecting the presence of action methods whose names and parameters match expected OData patterns. It does not use attributes like [HttpGet] or [HttpPost] in the same way that traditional Web API controllers do.

Routing conventions

ASP.NET Core OData uses routing conventions to map incoming OData requests to controller actions. These conventions examine:

*   The HTTP method (GET, POST, PUT, PATCH, or DELETE)
*   The OData path (for example, /Products(78))
*   The controller name (should match the entity set name)
*   The action method name and signature

For example:

*   GET /Products → ProductsController.Get()
*   GET /Products(78) → ProductsController.Get(int key)
*   POST /Products → ProductsController.Post(Product product)
*   PUT /Products(78) → ProductsController.Put(int key, Product update)
*   PATCH /Products(78) → ProductsController.Patch(int key, Delta<Product> delta)
*   DELETE /Products(78) → ProductsController.Delete(int key)

The supported HTTP methods depend entirely on which matching methods are implemented in your controller.

If you make a call like PUT /Products(78) and your OData controller does not define a method with a matching name and signature (Put(int key, Product product)), then ASP.NET Core OData returns 405 Method Not Allowed. The framework concludes that the resource exists, but that the HTTP method is not allowed on it. The HTTP response also includes an Allow header that explicitly lists the HTTP methods supported for the requested resource based on the routes the framework has matched, as shown in the following HTTP response:

```
HTTP/1.1 405 Method Not Allowed
Allow: GET, DELETE
```

The `Allow` header is generated by the OData routing middleware. When a request matches a route pattern but not the HTTP method, ASP.NET Core injects the `Allow` header and lists only the HTTP methods for which your controller implements a matching action method.

Method signatures

The framework uses convention-based method names, so you do not have to decorate methods with `[HttpGet]`, `[HttpPost]`, and so on. The key method names the OData looks for are shown in *Table 12.6*:

HTTP method	Controller method signature	Description
GET	Get(), Get([key])	Returns entities or an entity by key
POST	Post([entity])	Creates a new entity
PUT	Put([key], [entity])	Full update (replacement)
PATCH	Patch([key], Delta<T>)	Partial update
DELETE	Delete([key])	Deletes an entity

Table 12.6: Key method names that OData looks for

You can decorate action method parameters with `[FromRoute]`, `[FromODataUri]`, `[FromBody]`, and other parameter binding attributes, but they do not determine HTTP support. They just clarify how parameters should be resolved.

Delta and partial updates

OData supports partial updates via HTTP PATCH using the `Delta<T>` class. If you want to support PATCH, you must write a method like:

```
public IActionResult Patch(int key, [FromBody] Delta<Product> delta)
```

`Delta<T>` is explicitly designed for PATCH requests, not PUT, because PATCH represents a partial update, whereas PUT represents a full replacement of the resource.

With PUT, you send the entire entity; any missing properties are assumed to be reset to null or default, and the action method parameter must be the full `Product` object. To perform the update to the entity, you can either find the existing entity and manually set each property (which gives you more control), or you can use a single statement to update the full product:

```
_context.Entry(updatedProduct).State = EntityState.Modified;
```

With PATCH, the `Delta<T>` type is a partial representation of the entity. It's designed to track which properties were set and only update those. That's ideal for PATCH, where you're not replacing the full resource, as shown in the following code:

```
public IActionResult Patch(int key, [FromBody] Delta<Product> delta)
{
    Product? productToUpdate = _context.Products.Find(key);
    if (productToUpdate is null) return NotFound();
```

```
        delta.Patch(productToUpdate);
        _context.SaveChanges();

        return Updated(productToUpdate);
    }
```

In the HTTP PATCH request, you only include the properties you want to change (any omitted properties remain unchanged on the server):

```
### Update an existing product unit price and units in stock.
PATCH {{base_address}}products/78
Content-Type: application/json

{
  "UnitPrice": 60.25,
  "UnitsInStock": 75
}
```

Delta<T> internally tracks which properties were set in the incoming JSON. You can inspect it via delta.GetChangedPropertyNames() or delta.TryGetPropertyValue(...). This can be useful for validation, logging, or change auditing.

Overriding OData routing conventions with attribute routing

Starting with OData 8 and later, ASP.NET Core supports attribute routing for more precise control, which can override the default routing conventions. To make [HttpPut] work with a custom method name, you need to switch to attribute routing in your OData configuration, as shown in the following code:

```
services.AddControllers()
  .AddOData(opt =>
  {
    opt.EnableAttributeRouting()
    ...
```

Next, map the route to the non-conventionally named method, as shown in the following code:

```
[Route("odata/Products({key})")]
[HttpPut]
public IActionResult UpdateProduct(int key, [FromBody] Product product)
{
  ...
}
```

In the preceding code, UpdateProduct will correctly respond to PUT /odata/Products(78), because you're explicitly telling ASP.NET Core which path and method it handles. This is more common when you want to support complex custom routes or go beyond the OData conventions. But for basic CRUD with entity sets, you typically don't need this. Using attributes is much more work:

- You must specify the exact OData path in the [Route] attribute.
- The method must still match the expected signature conventions, like (int key, [FromBody] Product product) for a PUT method handler.
- You lose the automatic conventions, so everything must be mapped manually.
- You still need to define your entity data model correctly; otherwise, the OData middleware won't understand your entity types or routing logic.

Enabling entity inserts, updates, and deletes

Although the most common use for OData is to provide a Web API that supports custom queries, you might also want to support CRUD operations like inserts.

Let's see how to do that:

1. In ProductsController.cs, import the namespace for tracking entity state, as shown in the following code:

   ```
   using Microsoft.EntityFrameworkCore; // To use EntityState.
   ```

2. In ProductsController.cs, add an action method to respond to POST requests, as shown in the following code:

   ```
   public IActionResult Post([FromBody] Product product)
   {
     _db.Products.Add(product);
     _db.SaveChanges();
     return Created(product);
   }
   ```

3. In ProductsController.cs, add an action method to respond to PUT requests, as shown in the following code:

   ```
   public IActionResult Put(int key, [FromBody] Product product)
   {
       Product? productToUpdate = _db.Products.Find(key);

       if (productToUpdate is null)
       {
         return NotFound($"Product with id {key} not found.");
       }
   ```

```
    // Individually set each property to avoid overwriting other
properties.
        productToUpdate.ProductName = product.ProductName;
        productToUpdate.SupplierId = product.SupplierId;
        productToUpdate.CategoryId = product.CategoryId;
        productToUpdate.QuantityPerUnit = product.QuantityPerUnit;
        productToUpdate.UnitPrice = product.UnitPrice;
        productToUpdate.UnitsInStock = product.UnitsInStock;
        productToUpdate.UnitsOnOrder = product.UnitsOnOrder;
        productToUpdate.ReorderLevel = product.ReorderLevel;
        productToUpdate.Discontinued = product.Discontinued;

        // Or overwrite the entire object.
        // _db.Entry(productToUpdate).State = EntityState.Modified;


    _db.SaveChanges();
    return Updated(product);
}
```

4. In `ProductsController.cs`, add an action method to respond to `DELETE` requests, as shown in the following code:

```
public IActionResult Delete(int key)
{
    Product? productToDelete = _db.Products.Find(key);

    if (productToDelete is null)
    {
      return NotFound($"Product with id {key} not found.");
    }

    _db.Products.Remove(productToDelete);

  _db.SaveChanges();
  return NoContent();
}
```

5. Set a breakpoint on the open brace of the `Post` method.

6. Start the `Northwind.OData` web service project using the `https` launch profile with debugging, so it will pause when it hits the breakpoint.

7. In the `HttpRequests` folder, create a new file named `odata-catalog-modify-product.http`, as shown in the following HTTP request:

```
### Configure a variable for the web service base address.
@base_address = https://localhost:5121/catalog/


### Insert a new product.
POST {{base_address}}products
Content-Type: application/json


{
  "ProductName": "Impossible Burger",
  "SupplierId": 7,
  "CategoryId": 6,
  "QuantityPerUnit": "Pack of 4",
  "UnitPrice": 40.25,
  "UnitsInStock": 50,
  "UnitsOnOrder": 0,
  "ReorderLevel": 30,
  "Discontinued": false
}
```

> **Warning!** You do not specify a `ProductId` value because the SQL Server database will assign one automatically. Make a note of the value assigned. In this book, I will assume that it is **78** because there were 77 existing products, but if you have added more products, then the number could be higher!

8. Click **Send request**.

9. In your code editor, note that the breakpoint is hit, and you can use the debugging tools to see the product parameter successfully deserialized from the body of the HTTP POST request, as shown in *Figure 12.8*:

Figure 12.8: Debugging the OData POST request method handler

10. Allow the code to continue executing.

> 📝 If you get an error response saying, **The request was canceled due to the configured timeout of 20 seconds elapsing,** then click **Send request** again, and this time, immediately allow the code to continue after hitting the breakpoint, or remove the breakpoint.

11. Note the successful response, as shown in *Figure 12.9*:

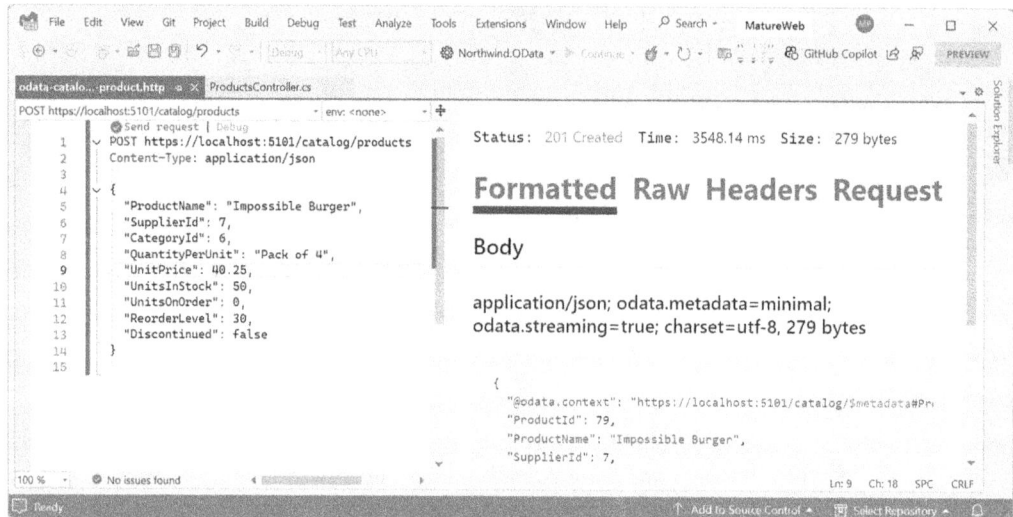

Figure 12.9: A successful POST response

12. Confirm that the new product was inserted by retrieving it:

```
### Get an existing product.
GET {{base_address}}products/78
```

> 💡 **Warning!** Change the `ProductId` value if necessary.

13. Try updating an existing entity:

```
### Update an existing product.
PUT {{base_address}}products/78
Content-Type: application/json

{
  "ProductId": 78,
  "ProductName": "Unpossible Burger",
```

```
    "SupplierId": 7,
    "CategoryId": 6,
    "QuantityPerUnit": "Pack of 4",
    "UnitPrice": 50.25,
    "UnitsInStock": 50,
    "UnitsOnOrder": 0,
    "ReorderLevel": 30,
    "Discontinued": false
}
```

14. Try deleting an existing entity (but only one that you created, because the existing products 1 to 77 have related data, so they cannot be deleted!):

```
### Delete an existing product.
DELETE {{base_address}}products/78
```

15. Optionally, implement a method to enable updates using an HTTP PATCH request, as shown in the following code:

```
public async Task<IActionResult> Patch(int key, [FromBody] Delta<Product>
patch)
{
  if (!ModelState.IsValid)
    return BadRequest(ModelState);

  Product? existingProduct = await _db.Products.FindAsync(key);
  if (existingProduct is null)
    return NotFound();

  patch.Patch(existingProduct); // Apply changes.

  _db.SaveChanges();

  return Updated(existingProduct); // Returns 200 with updated entity.
}
```

16. Optionally, try patching an existing entity, as shown in the following command:

```
### Update an existing product with PATCH.
PATCH {{base_address}}products/78
Content-Type: application/json

{
  "ProductName": "Subpossible Burger",
  "UnitPrice": 29.99
}
```

The solution code can be found at the following link: `https://github.com/markjprice/`
`web-dev-net10/blob/main/code/MatureWeb/Northwind.OData/Controllers/`
`ProductsController.cs`.

Building clients for OData services

Finally, let's see how a .NET client might call the OData web service. Let's review how clients interact with an OData service.

If we wanted to query the OData service for products that start with the letters Cha, then we would need to send a GET request with a relative URL path similar to the following:

```
catalog/products/?$filter=startswith(ProductName,
'Cha')&$select=ProductId,ProductName,UnitPrice
```

OData returns data in a JSON document with a property named value that contains the resulting products as an array, as shown in the following JSON document:

```
{
  "@odata.context": "https://localhost:5121/catalog/$metadata#Products",
  "value": [
    {
      "ProductId": 1,
      "ProductName": "Chai",
      "UnitPrice": 18
    },
```

We will use our Northwind.Mvc project as a client and define a model class to make it easy to deserialize the HTTP response:

1. In the Northwind.Mvc project, in the Models folder, add a new class file named ODataProducts. cs, as shown in the following code:

```
using Northwind.EntityModels; // To use Product.

namespace Northwind.Mvc.Models;

public class ODataProducts
{
  public Product[]? Value { get; set; }
}
```

2. In the `Extensions` folder, in `WebApplicationBuilderExtensions.cs`, define an extension method to register an HTTP client for the OData service that will request JSON for the response data format, as shown in the following code:

```
public static WebApplicationBuilder AddNorthwindODataClient(
  this WebApplicationBuilder builder)
{
  builder.Services.AddHttpClient(name: "Northwind.OData",
    configureClient: options =>
    {
      options.BaseAddress = new Uri("https://localhost:5121/");
      options.DefaultRequestHeaders.Accept.Add(
        new MediaTypeWithQualityHeaderValue(
        "application/json", 1.0));
    });

  return builder;
}
```

3. In `Program.cs`, before the call to `builder.Build()`, call the extension method, as shown in the following code:

```
builder.AddNorthwindODataClient();
```

Calling services in the Northwind MVC website

Next, we will call the service in a new controller:

1. In the `Northwind.Mvc` project, in the `Views\Shared` folder, in `_Layout.cshtml`, add a navigation menu item to go to `ODataClientController` with an `Index` action method, as shown in the following markup:

```
<li class="nav-item">
  <a class="nav-link text-dark" asp-area=""
  asp-controller="ODataClient" asp-action="Index">OData</a>
</li>
```

2. In the `Controllers` folder, add a new **MVC Controller – Empty** file named `ODataClientController.cs`.

3. In `ODataClientController.cs`, define a controller class with an `Index` action method, declare fields to store a logger and the registered HTTP client factory service, and then add statements that call the OData service to get products that start with `Cha` and store the result in the `ViewData` dictionary, as shown in the following code:

```
using Microsoft.AspNetCore.Mvc; // To use Controller.
using Northwind.EntityModels; // To use Product.
using Northwind.Mvc.Models; // To use ODataProducts.

namespace Northwind.Mvc.Controllers;

public class ODataClientController : Controller
{
  private readonly ILogger<ODataClientController> _logger;
  private readonly IHttpClientFactory _httpClientFactory;

  public ODataClientController(
    ILogger<ODataClientController> logger,
    IHttpClientFactory httpClientFactory)
  {
    _logger = logger;
    _httpClientFactory = httpClientFactory;
  }

  public async Task<IActionResult> Index(string startsWith = "Cha")
  {
    IEnumerable<Product>? model = Enumerable.Empty<Product>();

    try
    {
      HttpClient client = _httpClientFactory.CreateClient(
        name: "Northwind.OData");

      HttpRequestMessage request = new(
        method: HttpMethod.Get, requestUri:
        "catalog/products/?$filter=startswith(ProductName," +
        $"'{startsWith}')&$select=ProductId,ProductName,UnitPrice");

      HttpResponseMessage response = await client.SendAsync(request);

      ViewData["startsWith"] = startsWith;
```

```
        model = (await response.Content
          .ReadFromJsonAsync<ODataProducts>())?.Value;
    }
    catch (Exception ex)
    {
      _logger.LogWarning(
        $"Northwind.OData exception: {ex.Message}");
    }
    return View(model);
  }
}
```

4. In a `Views/ODataClient` folder, add a new **Razor View - Empty** file named `Index.cshtml`. If you are using Visual Studio, then you can right-click the **Index** action method and select **Add View....**

5. In `Views/ODataClient`, in `Index.cshtml`, delete its existing markup and then add markup to render the products with a form for the visitor to enter the start of a product name, as shown in the following markup:

```
@model IEnumerable<Product>?
@{
  ViewData["Title"] = "OData Products";
}
<div class="text-center">
  <h1 class="display-4">@ViewData["Title"]</h1>
  @if (Model is not null)
  {
    <h2>Products that start with '@ViewData["startsWith"]' using OData</
h2>
    <p>
      @if (!Model.Any())
      {
        <span class="badge rounded-pill bg-danger">No products found.</
span>
      }
      else
      {
        @foreach (Product p in Model)
        {
          <span class="badge rounded-pill bg-info text-dark">
            @p.ProductId
            @p.ProductName
            @(p.UnitPrice is null ? "" : p.UnitPrice.Value.ToString("c"))
```

```
              </span>
          }
        }
      </p>
    }
    <form method="get">
      Product name starts with:
      <input name="startsWith" value="@ViewData["startsWith"]" />
      Press ENTER to search.
    </form>
  </div>
```

Trying out the OData client

Now we can try out the MVC client with the OData service:

1. Start the `Northwind.OData` project using the `https` profile without debugging.

2. Start the `Northwind.WebApi` project using the `https` profile without debugging.

3. Start the `Northwind.Mvc` project using the `https` profile without debugging.

4. Start Chrome and navigate to `https://localhost:5021/`.

5. On the home page, in the top navigation menu, click **OData**.

6. Note that three products are returned from the OData service, as shown in *Figure 12.10*:

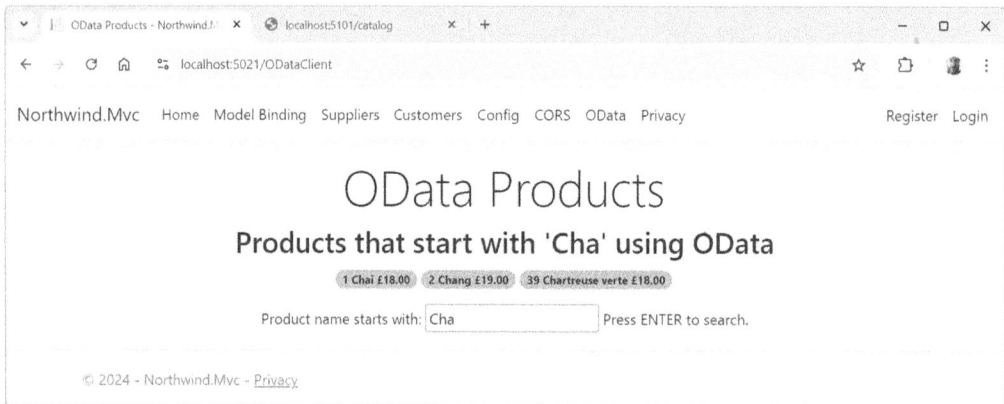

Figure 12.10: Three product names starting with Cha returned from the OData service

7. At the command line or terminal for the OData service, note the SQL command used, as shown in the following output:

```
info: Microsoft.EntityFrameworkCore.Database.Command[20101]
      Executed DbCommand (43ms) [Parameters=[@__TypedProperty_0_
startswith='?' (Size = 40)], CommandType='Text', CommandTimeout='30']
      SELECT [p].[ProductId], [p].[ProductName], [p].[UnitPrice]
```

```
            FROM [Products] AS [p]
            WHERE [p].[ProductName] LIKE @__TypedProperty_0_startswith ESCAPE
   N'\'
```

8. At the command line or terminal for the MVC website, note the HTTP request made and its response, as shown in the following output:

```
info: System.Net.Http.HttpClient.Northwind.OData.LogicalHandler[100]
      Start processing HTTP request GET https://localhost:5121/catalog/
products/?*
info: System.Net.Http.HttpClient.Northwind.OData.ClientHandler[100]
      Sending HTTP request GET https://localhost:5121/catalog/products/?*
info: System.Net.Http.HttpClient.Northwind.OData.ClientHandler[101]
      Received HTTP response headers after 1587.4018ms - 200
info: System.Net.Http.HttpClient.Northwind.OData.LogicalHandler[101]
      End processing HTTP request after 1609.3402ms - 200
```

9. Type b in the text box, press *Enter*, and note that the results only include the one product that starts with the letter *b*, Boston Crab Meat.

10. Type d in the text box, press *Enter*, and note the error message saying that no products were found.

11. Close Chrome and shut down both web servers.

LINQ to OData

LINQ to OData means using standard C# LINQ queries that a library translates into OData query options like $filter, $select, $orderby, $top, and so on. On the client, your LINQ gets turned into an HTTP URL. On the server, those OData query options get turned back into a LINQ expression over your data source, usually EF Core. Same LINQ on both sides, clean URLs in the middle:

- **Client side:** The OData Client for .NET exposes entity sets as IQueryable<T>. When you write Where, Select, OrderBy, Skip, Take, and other LINQ extension methods, the client converts your expression tree into an OData URI and issues an HTTP GET. You can inspect the exact URI it will call.

- **Server side:** In ASP.NET Core OData, the [EnableQuery] filter parses the incoming OData query options, validates them, then builds a LINQ expression and applies it to your IQueryable result. If you are using EF Core, that ends up as an SQL query.

Think of it like this:

```
Client LINQ  ->  OData URL  ->  Server parses URL -> Server LINQ -> DB query
```

Installing LINQ to OData in a client project

In your client app project, add the LINQ to OData package, as shown in the following command:

```
dotnet add package Microsoft.OData.Client
```

This gives you the `DataServiceContext`, `DataServiceQuery<T>`, and expression-to-OData translator.

Generating typed classes for LINQ to OData

To use the Visual Studio user interface:

1. Right-click the project and click **Add** | **Connected Service**.
2. Choose **OData Connected Service**.
3. Enter the metadata URL of your service (for example):

```
https://localhost:5001/odata/$metadata
```

4. Choose a namespace, for example: `NorthwindODataClient`
5. Click **Finish**.

It scaffolds:

- A subclass of `DataServiceContext`: Create an instance of this in a similar way to instantiating an instance of the `NorthwindContent` database context.
- Entity classes like `Product` and `Category`.
- Navigation properties matching your OData metadata.

This is Microsoft's officially supported tooling for typed OData clients.

To use the CLI:

1. Install the CLI:

```
dotnet tool install --global Microsoft.OData.ConnectedService.Cli
```

2. Execute the CLI against the OData endpoint:

```
odata-codegen --endpoint "https://localhost:5001/odata/$metadata"
--output-dir ./Generated
```

3. Include the generated `.cs` files in your client project.

Querying with LINQ to OData

A typical console app client-side query would look something like the following code:

```
using Microsoft.OData.Client;
using NorthwindODataClient; // Namespace created by the Connected Service.

Uri serviceRoot = new("https://localhost:5121/odata/");
Container context = new(serviceRoot);

// Example 1: Simple LINQ filter and ordering.
var productsOver20 =
  from p in context.Products
```

```
  where p.UnitPrice > 20
  orderby p.ProductName
  select new { p.ProductId, p.ProductName, p.UnitPrice };

// See the generated OData URL
DataServiceQuery dsq1 = (DataServiceQuery)productsOver20;
WriteLine("OData URL:\n" + dsq1.ToString());
WriteLine();

/* Example URL output from dsq1:
https://localhost:5001/odata/Products?$filter=UnitPrice gt
20&$orderby=ProductName&$select=ProductId,ProductName,UnitPrice
*/

foreach (var item in productsOver20.Take(5))
{
  WriteLine($"{item.ProductId}: {item.ProductName,-40} {item.UnitPrice,8:C}");
}

// Example 2: Expanding navigation properties.
var productsCategories = context.Products
  .Expand(p => p.Category)
  .Where(p => p.Category.CategoryName == "Beverages")
  .Select(p => new { p.ProductName, Category = p.Category.CategoryName,
p.UnitPrice });

DataServiceQuery dsq2 = (DataServiceQuery)productsCategories;
WriteLine("\nExpanded OData URL:\n" + dsq2.ToString());
WriteLine();
foreach (var item in productsCategories.Take(3))
{
  WriteLine($"{item.ProductName} ({item.Category}) - {item.UnitPrice:C}");
}

// Example 3: Paging.
var pagedOrders = context.Orders
  .OrderByDescending(o => o.OrderDate)
  .Skip(0)
  .Take(10)
  .Select(o => new { o.OrderId, o.OrderDate, o.Freight });
```

```
DataServiceQuery dsq3 = (DataServiceQuery)pagedOrders;
WriteLine("\nPaged Orders URL:\n" + dsq3.ToString());
WriteLine();


foreach (var order in pagedOrders)
{
  WriteLine($"Order {order.OrderId} on {order.OrderDate:d} freight {order.
Freight:C}");
}
```

Note the following about the preceding code:

- The LINQ expression tree is parsed.
- The OData Client library builds an OData query URI (you can inspect it via .ToString()).
- It sends an HTTP GET request.
- The server applies [EnableQuery] to interpret $filter, $orderby, $expand, and so on as a LINQ query against EF Core.
- EF Core generates efficient SQL and returns JSON.
- The OData Client deserializes that JSON into your entity objects.

To summarize, here are some notes about LINQ to OData:

- context.Products and other sets are DataServiceQuery<T>, which implement IQueryable<T>.
- Expand() works like EF Core's Include(), and it adds $expand in the URI.
- You can chain Skip() and Take(), which are translated into $skip and $top.
- To enable $count, call .IncludeTotalCount() before executing, or use .Count() with QueryOptions.IncludeCount = true.
- The OData Client supports ExecuteAsync() too.
- Only simple LINQ constructs are translated (comparisons, Boolean operators, and basic string functions). Complex client-side logic runs locally after retrieval.

> LINQ to OData (a.k.a. OData Client) is documented at the following link: https://learn.
> microsoft.com/en-us/odata/client/getting-started.

Revisiting the introductory query

At the start of this chapter, I introduced an example of a query you could run against an OData service. Let's see if it works with our service:

1. In the `HttpRequests` folder, create a new file named `odata-final-query.http`, as shown in the following HTTP request:

    ```
    ### Configure a variable for the web service base address.
    @base_address = https://localhost:5121/catalog/

    ### Make a complex GET request for products.
    GET {{base_address}}products
        ?$filter=contains(ProductName, 'ch') and UnitPrice lt 44.95
        &$orderby=Supplier/Country,UnitPrice
        &$select=ProductName,UnitPrice
        &$expand=Supplier
    ```

2. Make sure the OData web service project has been started.

3. Click **Send request** and note that the response contains products and their suppliers, sorted by country first and then, within each country, sorted by unit price, as shown in the following partial output and in *Figure 12.11*:

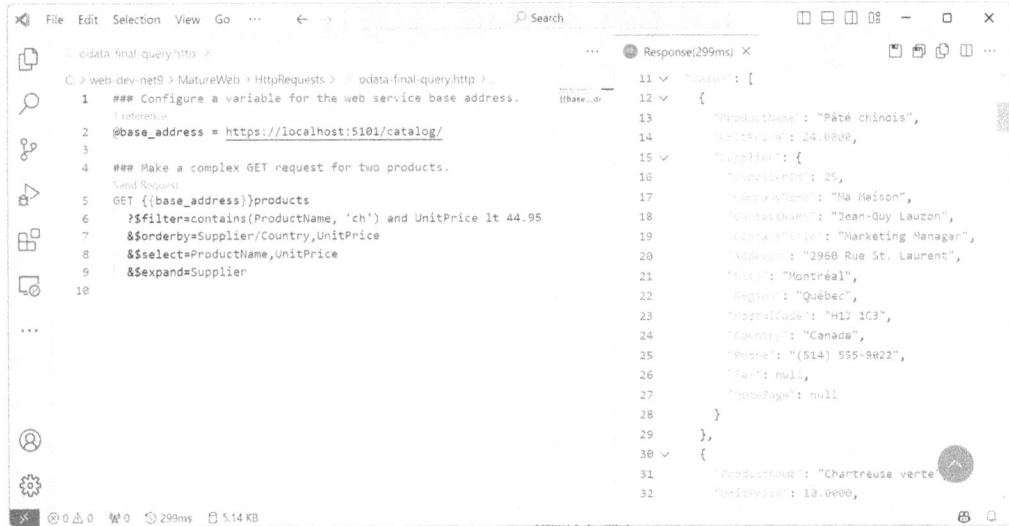

Figure 12.11: A complex OData query in VS Code and REST Client

The parts of the output that I clipped out to save space are indicated with ellipses (…):

```
HTTP/1.1 200 OK
Connection: close
Content-Type: application/json; odata.metadata=minimal; odata.
streaming=true
Date: Sun, 25 Aug 2024 11:53:13 GMT
Server: Kestrel
Transfer-Encoding: chunked
OData-Version: 4.0
{
  "@odata.context": "https://localhost:5121/
catalog/$metadata#Products(ProductName,UnitPrice,Supplier())",
  "value": [
    ...
    {
      "ProductName": "Chartreuse verte",
      "UnitPrice": 18.0000,
      "Supplier": {
        ...
        "Country": "France",
        ...
      }
    },
    ...
    {
      "ProductName": "Gnocchi di nonna Alice",
      "UnitPrice": 38.0000,
      "Supplier": {
        ...
        "Country": "Italy",
        ...
      }
    },
    {
      "ProductName": "Chocolade",
      "UnitPrice": 12.7500,
      "Supplier": {
        ...
        "Country": "Netherlands",
        ...
      }
```

```
    },
    ...
    {
      "ProductName": "Chai",
      "UnitPrice": 18.0000,
      "Supplier": {

        ...
        "Country": "UK",
        ...

      }
    },
    {
      "ProductName": "Chang",
      "UnitPrice": 19.0000,
      "Supplier": {

        ...
        "Country": "UK",
        ...

      }
    },
    ...

  ]
}
```

Practicing and exploring

Test your knowledge and understanding by answering some questions, getting some hands-on practice, and exploring this chapter's topics with deeper research.

Exercise 12.1 — Online material

You can learn more about OData at the following links:

- OData documentation: `https://learn.microsoft.com/en-us/odata/`
- ASP.NET Core OData documentation: `https://learn.microsoft.com/en-us/odata/webapi-8/overview`
- ASP.NET Core OData GitHub repository: A server library built upon ODataLib and ASP.NET Core: `https://github.com/OData/AspNetCoreOData`
- ASP.NET Core OData blog: `https://devblogs.microsoft.com/odata/`

Exercise 12.2 – Practice exercises

The following practice exercises help you to explore the topics in this chapter more deeply.

Make sure that you have implemented controllers for the entity sets in the order system, and then write queries that will return the following results:

1. The company names, cities, and countries of customers in Germany, sorted by city
2. The contact names and phone numbers of customers in the USA
3. The number of orders made by customer ALFKI

Exercise 12.3 – Test your knowledge

Answer the following questions:

1. What transport protocol does an OData service use?
2. Why is an OData service more flexible than a traditional ASP.NET Core Web API service?
3. What must you do to an action method in an OData controller to enable query strings to customize what it returns?
4. What URL path would return customers in Germany who have made more than one order?
5. How do you get related entities?

Exercise 12.4 – Explore topics

Use the links on the following page to learn more details about the topics covered in this chapter:

https://github.com/markjprice/web-dev-net10/blob/main/docs/book-links.md#chapter-12--
-building-web-services-using-aspnet-core-odata.

Summary

In this chapter, you learned:

*   The concepts around OData services
*   How to build an OData service using ASP.NET Core and a Microsoft NuGet package
*   How to query an OData service
*   How to perform data modifications
*   How to build an OData client

In the next chapter, you will learn about FastEndpoints, a third-party package for building performant web services.

Get This Book's PDF Version and Exclusive Extras

UNLOCK NOW

Scan the QR code (or go to packtpub.com/unlock). Search for this book by name, confirm the edition, and then follow the steps on the page.

Note: Keep your invoice handy. Purchases made directly from Packt don't require one.

13

Building Web Services Using FastEndpoints

This chapter is about building web services using FastEndpoints, a popular third-party package that shuns controllers in favor of a more efficient way of defining web service endpoints. While 95% of this book is about controller-based technologies, real-world web development shouldn't be dogmatic about technology choices. This chapter is the only one that doesn't use controllers, to show an alternative way to build web services that is popular with .NET developers.

ASP.NET Core Web API, ASP.NET Core OData, and FastEndpoints are all options for building web services (mostly for developers to call using HTTP, although user apps like Excel and Power BI can also pull data from web services, especially those built using OData, due to its flexible nature).

All web services can be interacted with using the same tools like VS Code's REST Client and Visual Studio's HTTP Editor, and web services can be called by a developer in your own apps in the same way. For example, a .NET developer would typically use HttpClient to call any web service regardless of how it was built.

You learned how to build a client to a web service in *Chapter 10, Building Clients for Web Services*, so you already know how to do the same with a web service built using FastEndpoints.

This chapter will cover the following topics:

- Introducing FastEndpoints
- Implementing FastEndpoints
- Configuring FastEndpoints

Introducing FastEndpoints

FastEndpoints is a high-performance, open-source library designed to simplify and speed up the development of HTTP/REST APIs using .NET. It provides an alternative to ASP.NET Core Web API, focusing on ease of use, performance, and a streamlined development process.

FastEndpoints embraces the concept of "endpoint-first" development, where developers define the endpoints of their API explicitly, without the need for the controllers and actions typical in traditional ASP.NET Core Web API services.

Pros and cons of FastEndpoints

There are a few benefits of using FastEndpoints:

- **Performance:** FastEndpoints is optimized for speed, providing better performance out of the box compared to ASP.NET Core Web API. This is achieved through streamlined request processing, reduced middleware overhead, and a minimalist approach to endpoint execution.
- **Simplicity:** It simplifies the development process by eliminating the need for controllers and actions. Instead, you define your endpoints directly, making the codebase more straightforward and easier to maintain.
- **Minimal boilerplate:** FastEndpoints minimizes the amount of boilerplate code typically required in ASP.NET Core Web API projects. This allows developers to focus more on writing business logic rather than repetitive setup code.
- **Flexibility:** FastEndpoints provides flexibility in how you structure your endpoints, allowing you to define them as classes with specific request and response types, middleware, and other components. This can lead to cleaner, more organized code.
- **Customizability:** You can easily customize various aspects of the request pipeline, including validation, authorization, and serialization, without having to dig deep into the ASP.NET Core infrastructure.

FastEndpoints has some cons compared to ASP.NET Core Web API:

- **Learning curve:** Developers familiar with the traditional ASP.NET Core Web API might find the FastEndpoints approach unconventional, requiring some time to get used to it. The endpoint-first approach might not align with every team's preferred architectural style, especially those deeply ingrained in the controller paradigm.
- **Ecosystem:** ASP.NET Core Web API has a more extensive ecosystem, including documentation, community support, and third-party libraries. FastEndpoints, while growing, does not yet have the same level of resources. ASP.NET Core Web API has a much larger user base and community support, which might make it easier to find help and resources compared to FastEndpoints.

What makes it "fast"?

FastEndpoints is "fast" due to several optimizations and design choices:

- **Direct endpoint mapping**: Instead of routing requests through controllers and actions, FastEndpoints maps requests directly to endpoints, reducing the complexity and time involved in routing and handling requests.

- **Optimized request processing with minimal middleware overhead**: FastEndpoints reduces the number of middleware components involved in the request processing pipeline, leading to faster request handling. Developers can fine-tune the request pipeline to remove unnecessary steps, leading to performance gains specific to their application needs.

- **Reduced reflection usage**: By minimizing the use of reflection and other costly operations, FastEndpoints can improve runtime performance.

The TechEmpower benchmarks that can be found at `https://fast-endpoints.com/benchmarks#techempower-benchmark-preliminary` rank FastEndpoints at #2, after ASP.NET Core Minimal API, and well above ASP.NET Core MVC/Web API at #8, as shown in *Figure 13.1*:

	Best JSON responses per second, Citrine (19 tests)							
Rnk Framework	Best performance (higher is better)		Errors	Cls	Lng	Plt	FE	Aos	IA
1 asp.net core [minimal apis, pg, dapper]	1,977,242	100.0% (53.4)	0	Mcr	c#	.ne	kes	lin	rea
2 fastendpoints	1,949,552	98.6% (52.6)	0	Mcr	c#	.ne	kes	lin	rea
3 reaper [aot,slim]	1,885,326	95.4% (50.9)	0	Mcr	c#	.ne	kes	lin	rea
4 netcoreserver	1,702,922	86.1% (46.0)	0	ful	c#	.ne	net	lin	rea
5 zysocket-v	1,420,376	71.8% (38.3)	0	ful	c#	.ne	zys	lin	rea
6 ben [kestrel]	1,353,272	68.4% (36.5)	0	Mcr	c#	.ne	kes	lin	rea
7 genhttp	1,280,871	64.8% (34.6)	0	ful	c#	.ne	gen	lin	rea
8 asp.net core [mvc, pg, ef]	1,260,876	63.8% (34.0)	0	ful	c#	.ne	kes	lin	rea
9 easyrpc	1,185,284	59.9% (32.0)	0	ful	c#	.ne	kes	lin	rea
10 carter	1,013,617	51.3% (27.4)	0	Mcr	c#	.ne	kes	lin	rea
11 asp.net core [middleware, mono]	762,923	38.6% (20.6)	0	Mcr	c#	.ne	kes	lin	rea
12 servicestack-v6	701,073	35.5% (18.9)	0	Mcr	c#	.ne	kes	lin	rea
13 nancy [asp.net core, my]	458,637	23.2% (12.4)	0	Mcr	c#	.ne	kes	lin	rea
14 asp.net core [mvc, mono]	197,354	10.0% (5.3)	0	ful	c#	.ne	kes	lin	rea
15 beetlex	76,476	3.9% (2.1)	0	ful	c#	.ne	bee	lin	rea
16 nancy [asp.net core, mono, my]	19,509	1.0% (0.5)	0	Mcr	c#	.ne	kes	lin	rea
17 embedio	13,057	0.7% (0.4)	0	ful	c#	.ne	emb	lin	rea
18 sisk framework	11,601	0.6% (0.3)	0	ful	c#	.ne	sis	lin	rea
19 tetsu.web	11,435	0.6% (0.3)	0	Mcr	c#	.ne	tet	lin	rea

Figure 13.1: TechEmpower benchmarks comparing FastEndpoints with Core MVC/Web API

FastEndpoints is a good choice if you are looking for a high-performance, simple, and flexible alternative to ASP.NET Core Web API with controllers. However, it might not be the best fit for every project, especially those deeply integrated into the broader ASP.NET Core ecosystem or those with teams more comfortable with traditional controller-based Web API patterns.

FastEndpoints does not and likely will never support AOT-native compilation. To take advantage of AOT, you will need to switch to ASP.NET Core Minimal API until the ASP.NET Core team enables AOT with controllers.

Introducing the REPR pattern

The REPR pattern in the context of FastEndpoints stands for:

Request → Endpoint → Processor → Response

This pattern is a conceptual and architectural flow model used by FastEndpoints to structure and simplify HTTP endpoint handling. It formalizes the steps from receiving a request to sending a response, while offering hooks for customization and extension at each step.

Like many acronyms, REPR is a simplification because FastEndpoints actually supports PreProcessors as well as PostProcessors:

Request → PreProcessor → Endpoint → PostProcessor → Response

Request

This is the incoming HTTP request, and it's represented by a request **DTO** (**Data Transfer Object**), usually a C# class or record, as shown in the following code:

```
public class CreateUserRequest
{
  public string Email { get; set; }
  public string Password { get; set; }
}
```

The CreateUserRequest class represents the shape of the incoming data that an endpoint will process.

FastEndpoints binds this automatically from the incoming HTTP payload. It handles parsing from:

- Query parameters
- Route values
- Form data
- JSON body
- Headers

Endpoint

This is the actual handler for the request, which is your business logic entry point.

To define one, you typically subclass the `Endpoint<TRequest>` or `Endpoint<TRequest, TResponse>` base class, as shown in the following code:

```
public class CreateUserEndpoint : Endpoint<CreateUserRequest, UserResponse>
{
  public override async Task HandleAsync(CreateUserRequest req,
CancellationToken ct)
  {
    // Business logic goes here.
    var user = await CreateUserInDbAsync(req.Email, req.Password);
    await Send.OkAsync(new UserResponse { Id = user.Id });
  }
}
```

In the preceding code:

- `CreateUserRequest` is the request
- `UserResponse` is the response
- `HandleAsync` is where you process the input and return an output

The endpoint is where you do validation, orchestrate services, and determine what the result should be.

Processor

Processor is a broader term referring to pre-processing and post-processing behaviors. FastEndpoints supports both:

- PreProcessors: Run before the endpoint logic
- PostProcessors: Run after the endpoint logic, before the response is sent

Processors provide a neat way to implement cross-cutting concerns like logging, validation, authorization, caching, and so on. Processors are analogous to filters or middleware but more tightly scoped to an endpoint.

An example PreProcessor is shown in the following code:

```
public class AuthPreProcessor : PreProcessor<CreateUserRequest>
{
  public override Task PreProcessAsync(
    CreateUserRequest req, HttpContext ctx)
  {
    if (!ctx.User.Identity.IsAuthenticated)
      throw new UnauthorizedAccessException();

    return Task.CompletedTask;
  }
}
```

An example PostProcessor is shown in the following code:

```
public class LoggingPostProcessor : PostProcessor<CreateUserRequest,
UserResponse>
{
  public override Task PostProcessAsync(
    CreateUserRequest req, UserResponse res, HttpContext ctx)
  {
    Console.WriteLine($"User created with ID: {res.Id}");
    return Task.CompletedTask;
  }
}
```

Response

This is the output DTO sent back to the client. It's serializable (usually JSON) and defined explicitly, as shown in the following code:

```
public class UserResponse
{
  public string Id { get; set; }
}
```

You use Send.OkAsync() to return this from the endpoint.

The explicitness of the REPR flow helps keep your endpoint logic clean, testable, and deterministic. Unlike traditional ASP.NET Core Web API controllers, which can become overloaded with responsibilities, FastEndpoints enforces separation of concerns naturally via this model.

How REPR differs from controllers

I have highlighted the difference between controllers and REPR in *Table 13.1*:

Concept	ASP.NET Core Web API	FastEndpoints REPR
Request binding	Attributes like [FromBody]	Auto-bound from request DTO
Endpoint	Controller action methods	Strongly typed endpoint class
Middleware	Global pipeline	Per-endpoint processors
Response	Return object, or use IActionResult	Strongly typed response DTOs

Table 13.1: Comparing REPR to controllers

The REPR pattern is the backbone of FastEndpoints' design. It structures the API pipeline as:

Request DTO → PreProcessor(s) → Endpoint logic → PostProcessor(s) → Response DTO

This leads to cleaner, more maintainable code with better separation of concerns compared to traditional ASP.NET patterns.

How to define an endpoint

An endpoint in FastEndpoints is a class that inherits from one of the base classes shown in *Table 13.2*:

Base class	Description
`Endpoint<TRequest>`	An endpoint with no response model.
`Endpoint<TRequest, TResponse>`	An endpoint with both a request model and a response model.
`Endpoint<TRequest, TResponse, TMapper>`	An endpoint with both a request model and a response model, and a class that implements the `IMapper` interface to handle complex mappings.
`EndpointWithoutRequest`	An endpoint with no request model or response model. You could also inherit from `Endpoint<EmptyRequest, EmptyResponse>` to achieve the same effect.
`EndpointWithoutRequest<TResponse>`	An endpoint with no request model.
`EndpointWithoutRequest<TResponse, TMapper>`	An endpoint with no request model and a class that implements the `IMapper` interface.

Table 13.2: Base classes of an endpoint in FastEndpoints

The FastEndpoints system scans all referenced assemblies for classes that derive from one of the `Endpoint` base classes and maps their routes.

In your class implementation, you override one or more methods, as shown in *Table 13.3*:

Method to override	Description
`Configure`	Called once during initial registration at service startup, not every time the endpoint is executed. Common configuration includes what actions the endpoint responds to (for example, `GET` and `POST`) and authentication and authorization requirements.
`ExecuteAsync(string, CancellationToken)`	Called every time the endpoint is executed. It returns the response.
`HandleAsync(string, CancellationToken)`	Called every time the endpoint is executed.
`OnBeforeHandle, OnBeforeHandleAsync, OnAfterHandle, OnAfterHandleAsync`	Event handlers if you need to run code before and after handling an endpoint request.
`OnBeforeValidate, OnBeforeValidateAsync, OnAfterValidate, OnAfterValidateAsync`	Event handlers if you need to run code before and after validation.
`OnValidationFailed, OnValidationFailedAsync`	Event handlers if you need to run code if the validation fails.

Table 13.3: Common Endpoint methods to override

By deriving from one of the `Endpoint` base classes, your class can call any of the following methods to configure and implement the endpoint that your class represents, as shown in *Table 13.4*:

Member	Description
`Verbs`	Specifies which HTTP methods (verbs) the endpoint will handle. Without this, an endpoint will default to handling all HTTP methods. For example: `Verbs(Http.POST, Http.PUT);`
`Routes`	Specifies the URL route(s) that the endpoint responds to. It simplifies route definition directly in the endpoint class. For example: `Routes("/api/products", "/api/items");`
`ResponseCache`	Enables caching for the endpoint response, reducing load and improving performance by serving cached responses to repeated requests. For example: `ResponseCache(60);`
`AllowAnonymous`	Specifies an endpoint as publicly accessible, bypassing any authentication mechanism that may otherwise be required for accessing it. When this method is used, no authentication (like OAuth, JWT, or other mechanisms) is required to access the endpoint.
`Roles`	This method restricts access to the endpoint based on user roles. You specify one or more roles that users must have to access the endpoint. For example: `Roles("Admin", "Manager");`
`Authorize`	This method enforces authorization policies on the endpoint. You can specify a policy that needs to be satisfied for access to be granted. It requires callers to pass specific authorization rules, allowing more fine-grained access control than just role-based checks. For example: `Authorize("MyCustomPolicy");`

`PreProcessors`, `PostProcessors`	These are methods that can be used to inject logic before or after the request is processed by the `HandleAsync` method. They allow you to perform common tasks such as validation, logging, and so on. For example:
	
	`PreProcessors(new MyRequestValidator());`
	
	`PostProcessors(new MyResponseLogger());`

`Send.OkAsync`	This is a helper method to send an HTTP 200 status code response asynchronously. You can use it to send a response back to the client with optional data. It handles the serialization of objects and ensures the response is returned asynchronously to avoid blocking the thread.
`Send.CreatedAtAsync`	This is a helper method to send an HTTP 201 status code response asynchronously. You can use it to send a response back to the client with the newly created entity.

Table 13.4: Common inherited methods

In FastEndpoints, methods like Verbs, Routes, AllowAnonymous, and Send.OkAsync simplify configuring web endpoints, defining how they should behave and interact with HTTP requests. Other common members such as HandleAsync, Roles, and Authorize further enhance the security and control over endpoints.

This declarative and minimal approach is designed to reduce boilerplate while ensuring high performance and scalability.

Example FastEndpoints endpoint implementation

Here's some example code for a basic FastEndpoints endpoint implementation.

First, set up an endpoint in a class that derives from one of the Endpoint<T> base classes, perhaps in a file named HelloEndpoint.cs, as shown in the following code:

```csharp
using FastEndpoints; // To use Endpoint<TRequest, TResponse>.

namespace Northwind.FastEndpoints.Endpoints;

public class HelloEndpoint : Endpoint<HelloRequest, HelloResponse>
{
  public override void Configure()
  {
    Verbs(Http.GET);
    Routes("/hello");
    AllowAnonymous();
  }

  public override async Task HandleAsync(HelloRequest req, CancellationToken ct)
  {
    HelloResponse response = new($"Hello, {req.Name
      }. You're looking great for {req.Age}!");

    await Send,OkAsync(response, cancellation: ct);
  }
}

public record HelloRequest(string Name, int Age);

public record HelloResponse(string Message);
```

Finally, set up FastEndpoints in `Program.cs`, as shown in the following code:

```
using FastEndpoints; // To use AddFastEndpoints and so on.

var builder = WebApplication.CreateBuilder(args);

builder.Services.AddFastEndpoints();

var app = builder.Build();

app.MapFastEndpoints();

app.Run();
```

Implementing FastEndpoints

Let's build a web service using FastEndpoints that provides endpoints to work with customers in Northwind, so that you can see the differences between FastEndpoints or Web API and OData.

Adding FastEndpoints to an empty ASP.NET Core project

To see how to implement FastEndpoints, we will start with the simplest ASP.NET Core project:

1. Use your preferred code editor to open the MatureWeb solution and then add a new project, as defined in the following list:

    *   Project template: **ASP.NET Core Empty** / web
    *   Solution file and folder: MatureWeb
    *   Project file and folder: Northwind.FastEndpoints

2. If you are using Visual Studio, then confirm the following defaults have been chosen:

    *   **Framework: .NET 10.0 (Long Term Support)**
    *   **Configure for HTTPS:** Selected
    *   **Enable container support:** Cleared
    *   **Do not use top-level statements:** Cleared

3. If you are using VS Code or Rider, then in the MatureWeb directory, at the command prompt or terminal, enter the following commands:

    ```
    dotnet new web -o Northwind.FastEndpoints
    dotnet sln add Northwind.FastEndpoints
    ```

4. In the `Northwind.FastEndpoints.csproj` project file, globally and statically import the `Console` class, add a reference to the Northwind database context project, and add a reference to the FastEndpoints package, as shown highlighted in the following markup:

```xml
<Project Sdk="Microsoft.NET.Sdk.Web">

  <PropertyGroup>
    <TargetFramework>net10.0</TargetFramework>
    <Nullable>enable</Nullable>
    <ImplicitUsings>enable</ImplicitUsings>
  </PropertyGroup>

  <ItemGroup Label="To simplify use of WriteLine.">
    <Using Include="System.Console" Static="true" />
  </ItemGroup>

  <ItemGroup Label="To use the Northwind entity models.">
    <ProjectReference Include=
      "..\Northwind.DataContext\Northwind.DataContext.csproj" />
  </ItemGroup>

  <ItemGroup>
    <PackageReference Include="FastEndpoints" />
  </ItemGroup>

</Project>
```

5. Build the `Northwind.FastEndpoints` project.

6. In the `Properties` folder, in `launchSettings.json`, for the `https` profile, for its `applicationUrl`, change the random port number for HTTPS to 5131 and for HTTP to 5130, as shown highlighted in the following markup:

```
"applicationUrl": "https://localhost:5131;http://localhost:5130",
```

7. Save changes to all modified files.

Enabling FastEndpoints and defining endpoints

It is easy to enable FastEndpoints in any ASP.NET Core project by adding its dependency service and mapping any endpoints defined in the current and any referenced assemblies:

1. In `Program.cs`, import the `FastEndpoints` namespace. Then add statements to add the `FastEndpoints` middleware and use it in the HTTP pipeline, and register the Northwind database context as a dependency service, as shown in the following code:

    ```csharp
    using FastEndpoints; // To use AddFastEndpoints and so on.
    using Northwind.EntityModels; // To use AddNorthwindContext method.

    var builder = WebApplication.CreateBuilder(args);

    builder.Services.AddFastEndpoints();
    builder.Services.AddNorthwindContext();

    var app = builder.Build();

    app.MapGet("/", () => """
      Hello FastEndpoints!
      GET /hello?Name=<string>&Age=<int>
      GET /hello/<name>/<age>

      GET /customers/
      GET /customers/<country>
      """);

    app.MapFastEndpoints();

    app.Run();
    ```

2. In the `Northwind.FastEndpoints` project, add a new folder named `Endpoints`.
3. In the `Endpoints` folder, add a new class file named `HelloEndpoint.cs`.
4. In `HelloEndpoint.cs`, define an endpoint to say hello in response to a request with a name and age, as shown in the following code:

    ```csharp
    using FastEndpoints; // To use Endpoint<TRequest, TResponse>.

    namespace Northwind.FastEndpoints.Endpoints;

    #region DTOs for Request and Response in HelloEndpoint

    public record HelloRequest(string Name, int Age);
    ```

```
public record HelloResponse(string Message);

#endregion

public class HelloEndpoint : Endpoint<HelloRequest, HelloResponse>
{
  public override void Configure()
  {
    // Automatically supports query strings, for example:
    // GET /hello?Name=Bob&Age=50
    // Explicitly specify route parameters:
    // GET /hello/Bob/50
    Verbs(Http.GET);
    Routes("/hello", "/hello/{Name}/{Age}");
    AllowAnonymous();
  }

  public override async Task HandleAsync(
    HelloRequest req, CancellationToken ct)
  {
    HelloResponse response = new($"Hello, {req.Name
      }. You're looking great for {req.Age}!");

    await Send.OkAsync(response, cancellation: ct);
  }
}
```

5. In the `Endpoints` folder, add a new class file named `CustomersEndpoint.cs`.

6. In `CustomersEndpoint.cs`, define an endpoint to get all customers or customers in a named country, as shown in the following code:

```
using FastEndpoints; // To use Endpoint<TRequest, TResponse>
using Northwind.EntityModels; // To use Customer.

namespace Northwind.FastEndpoints.Endpoints;

#region DTO for Request in CustomersEndpoint (Response is Customer[])

public record CustomersRequest(string Country);

#endregion
```

```csharp
public class CustomersEndpoint : Endpoint<CustomersRequest, Customer[]>
{
  private readonly NorthwindContext _db;

  public CustomersEndpoint(NorthwindContext db) => _db = db;

  public override void Configure()
  {
    Verbs(Http.GET);
    Routes("/customers", "/customers/{Country}");
    AllowAnonymous();
  }

  public override async Task HandleAsync(
    CustomersRequest request, CancellationToken ct)
  {
    IQueryable<Customer> query = _db.Customers;

    if (!string.IsNullOrWhiteSpace(request.Country))
    {
      query = query.Where(customer => customer.Country == request.
Country);
    }

    Customer[] response = query.ToArray();

    await Send.OkAsync(response, cancellation: ct);
  }
}
```

Trying out the FastEndpoints web service

Now we can try out the FastEndpoints web service and its two endpoints:

1. Set the Northwind.FastEndpoints web service as the startup project.
2. Start the Northwind.FastEndpoints web service project using the https launch profile.

3. Note the plain text documentation for the web service, as shown in *Figure 13.2*:

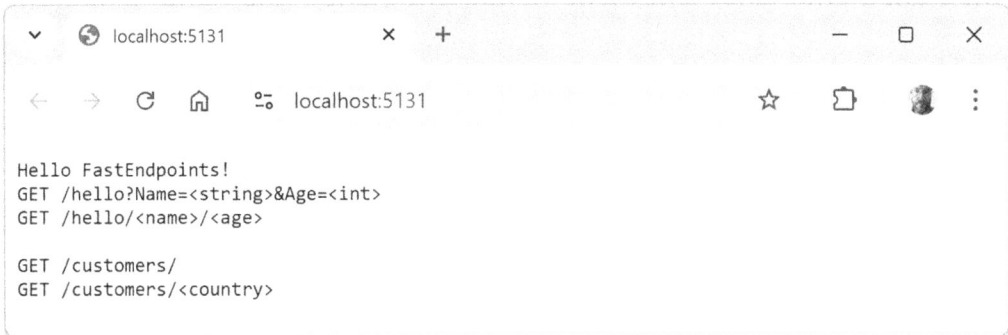

Figure 13.2: Plain text documentation for the FastEndpoints web service

4. At the end of the address bar, add a relative path and parameters to call the `hello` endpoint, as shown in the following text and in *Figure 13.3*:

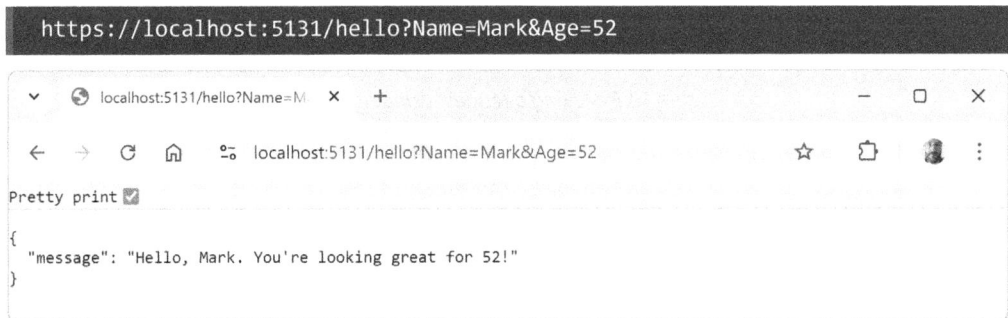

```
https://localhost:5131/hello?Name=Mark&Age=52
```

Figure 13.3: Making a request using query string parameters

5. Enter a relative path to call the `hello` endpoint, as shown in the following text and in *Figure 13.4*:

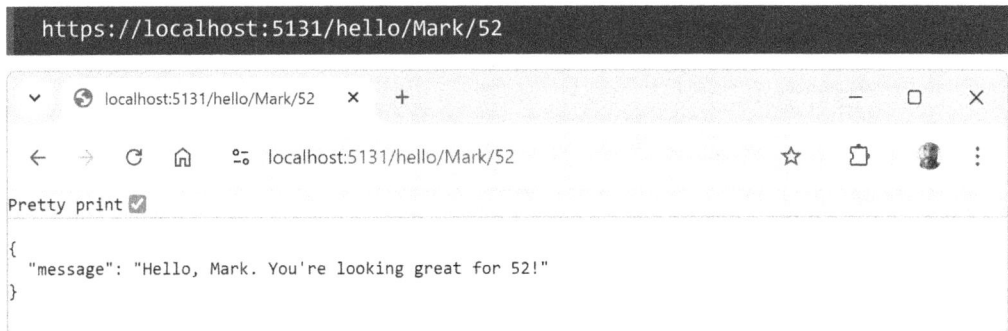

```
https://localhost:5131/hello/Mark/52
```

Figure 13.4: Making a request using route parameters

6. Enter a relative path to call the `customers` endpoint, as shown in the following text and in *Figure 13.5*:

```
https://localhost:5131/customers
```

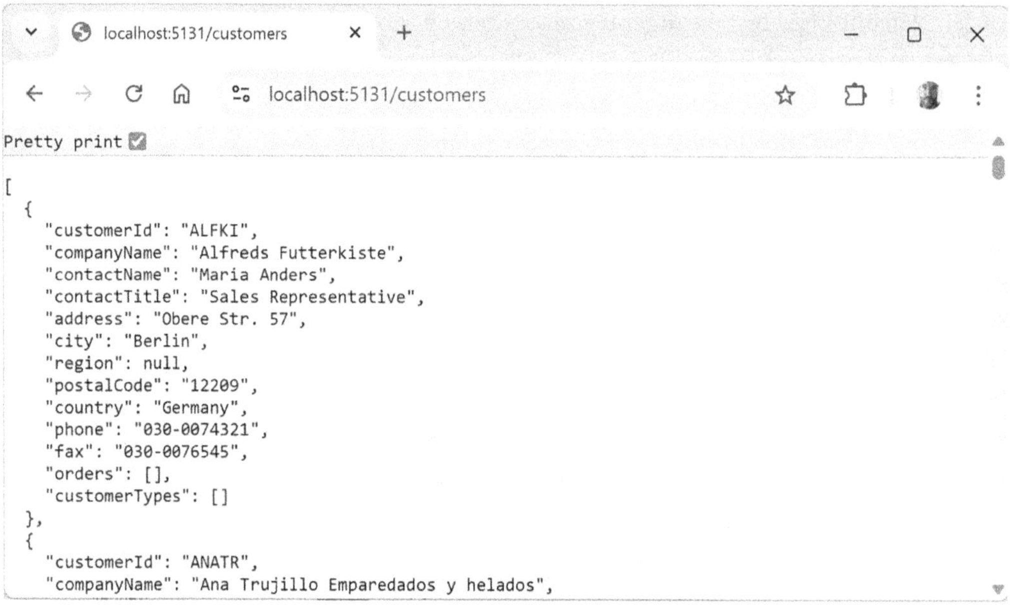

Figure 13.5: Making a request using query string parameters

7. Enter a relative path to call the customers endpoint and return only customers in a specified country, like UK, as shown in the following text and in *Figure 13.6*:

```
https://localhost:5131/customers/UK
```

Figure 13.6: Making a request using query string parameters

8. Close the browser and shut down the web server.

Configuring FastEndpoints

You configure how an endpoint should listen to incoming requests in your overridden `Configure()` method. You call inherited methods like `Get()`, `Post()`, `AllowAnonymous()`, and so on.

Configuration methods and properties

A more complete list of configuration methods is shown in *Table 13.5*:

Methods	Description
`Get, Head, Post, Patch, Put, Delete`	All these methods can have a comma-separated list of string values passed, `params string[] routePatterns`. You cannot configure multiple verbs using these methods.
`Verbs, Routes`	Pass a comma-separated list of HTTP verbs, and pass a comma-separated list of string values, `params string[] routePatterns`. Often used together as an alternative to the preceding individual HTTP verb methods.
`AllowAnonymous`	Allow unauthenticated requests to this endpoint.
`Claims`	Allow access if any of the listed claims are valid for the current user's request.
`Description`	Add metadata for OpenAPI documentation.
`EnableAntiforgery`	Enables anti-forgery verification for this endpoint.

`Options(builder => builder`
 	
`.RequireCors(x =>`
`x.AllowAnyOrigin())`
 	
`.RequireHost("domain.com")`
 	
`.ProducesProblem(404));`
	Use this method to customize aspects of endpoint registration like CORS and documentation. The builder object is a `RouteHandlerBuilder`.

`Version`	Specify the version of the endpoint.

Table 13.5: Methods to configure FastEndpoints

A more complete list of configuration properties is shown in *Table 13.6*:

Properties	Description
`BaseURL`	The base URL for the current request.
`Config`	Provides access to the project configuration via the standard `IConfiguration` interface. If you need to access this property from within your `Configure` method, you must pass the configuration explicitly, as shown in the following code: `.AddFastEndpoints(config: builder.Configuration)`.
`Definition`	Represents the configuration settings of an endpoint.

Env	Represents the environment of an endpoint. For example, `Env.EnvironmentName` and `Env.IsDevelopment()`.
Files	The files sent with the request.
Form	The `<form>` sent with the request.
HttpContext	A standard `HttpContext` object that encapsulates the HTTP-specific information about an individual request.
HttpMethod	An enum value of `FastEndpoints.Http` that specifies a verb like GET or POST.
Logger	An `ILogger` implementation.
Response	The response object sent to the client. Its type is `TResponse`.
User	A standard `ClaimsPrincipal` object.
ValidationFailures	A collection of validation failures, for example, when model binding.

Table 13.6: Methods to configure FastEndpoints

Mapping requests and responses to entity models

Sometimes the default mapping system cannot work out how to map between an incoming request and entity models, or how to construct a response model from entity models. This is particularly relevant when your internal domain model differs from the structure of your external API contracts. In these scenarios, you can define a mapper class.

Suppose you're building a web service to work with `Product` entities. In the domain entity model, the `Product` class might have more properties or a different structure than what you expose through your web service API.

The `Product` class might be defined as shown in the following code:

```
public class Product
{
  public Guid Id { get; set; }
  public string Name { get; set; }
  public string Description { get; set; }
  public decimal Price { get; set; }
  public DateTime CreatedAt { get; set; }
  public DateTime UpdatedAt { get; set; }
}
```

The request and response DTO models for an endpoint used to create a new product and add it to the database might be defined as shown in the following code:

```
public class CreateProductRequest
{
  public string Name { get; set; }
  public string Description { get; set; }
```

```
    public decimal Price { get; set; }
}


public class ProductResponse
{
  public Guid Id { get; set; }
  public string Name { get; set; }
  public string Description { get; set; }
  public decimal Price { get; set; }
  public DateTime CreatedAt { get; set; }
}
```

You then define a mapper class to handle the conversion between your DTOs and domain models, as shown in the following code:

```
public class ProductMapper :
  Mapper<CreateProductRequest, ProductResponse, Product>
{
  // This method maps the request DTO to the domain model.
  public override Product ToEntity(CreateProductRequest req)
  {
    return new Product
    {
      Id = Guid.NewGuid(),
      Name = req.Name,
      Description = req.Description,
      Price = req.Price,
      CreatedAt = DateTime.UtcNow,
      UpdatedAt = DateTime.UtcNow
    };
  }


  // This method maps the domain model to the response DTO
  public override ProductResponse FromEntity(Product entity)
  {
    return new ProductResponse
    {
      Id = entity.Id,
      Name = entity.Name,
      Description = entity.Description,
      Price = entity.Price,
      CreatedAt = entity.CreatedAt
```

```
    };
  }
}
```

Now you can use the `ProductMapper` in your endpoint to handle the transformation seamlessly, as shown in the following code:

```
public class CreateProductEndpoint :
  Endpoint<CreateProductRequest, ProductResponse, ProductMapper>
{
  public override void Configure()
  {
    Post("/products");
    AllowAnonymous();
  }

  public override async Task HandleAsync(
    CreateProductRequest req, CancellationToken ct)
  {
    Product product = Map.ToEntity(req); // Maps request DTO to domain model.

    // Assume we successfully save the product to the database here.
    // Maps domain model to response DTO.
    ProductResponse response = Map.FromEntity(product);

    await Send.CreatedAtAsync(
      $"/products/{added.Entity.ProductId}",
      added.Entity, cancellation: ct);
  }
}
```

To summarize:

- **The domain model** – `Product`: Represents your internal business object with full properties
- **DTO models** – `CreateProductRequest` and `ProductResponse`: Represent the data structures exposed through your web service API
- **Mapper** – `ProductMapper`: Handles the transformation between the domain model and DTOs
- **Endpoint** – `CreateProductEndpoint`: Uses the mapper to handle data conversion and implements the business logic

This structure is useful because it separates concerns, ensuring that your business logic isn't tightly coupled with how data is transmitted over the wire. By using a mapper, you can easily adapt your API to changing requirements without affecting the core logic of your application.

Validating with FluentValidation

FastEndpoints integrates well with FluentValidation. Let's create an endpoint for creating a new customer:

1. In the `Northwind.FastEndpoints` project, add a package reference for `FluentValidation`, as shown in the following markup:

    ```
    <PackageReference Include="FluentValidation" />
    ```

2. Build the `Northwind.FastEndpoints` project to restore packages.

3. In the `Northwind.FastEndpoints` project, add a new folder named `Validators`.

4. In the `Validators` folder, add a new class named `CreateCustomerValidator.cs`.

5. In `CreateCustomerValidator.cs`, define a validator for a customer, as shown in the following code:

    ```
    using FastEndpoints; // To use Validator<T>.
    using FluentValidation; // To use NotEmpty, MaximumLength, and so on.
    using Northwind.EntityModels; // To use Customer.

    namespace Northwind.FastEndpoints.Validators;

    public class CreateCustomerValidator : Validator<Customer>
    {
      public CreateCustomerValidator()
      {
        RuleFor(x => x.CustomerId)
          .NotEmpty().WithMessage("Customer ID is required.")
          .MaximumLength(5).WithMessage(
            "Customer ID must be exactly 5 characters long.")
          .Matches(@"^[A-Z0-9]{5}$").WithMessage(
            "Customer ID must consist of 5 uppercase letters or digits.");

        RuleFor(x => x.CompanyName)
          .NotEmpty().WithMessage("Company name is required.")
          .MaximumLength(40).WithMessage(
            "Company name must be at most 40 characters long.");

        RuleFor(x => x.ContactName)
          .NotEmpty().WithMessage("Contact name is required.")
          .MaximumLength(30).WithMessage(
            "Contact name must be at most 30 characters long.");

        RuleFor(x => x.ContactTitle)
    ```

```
      .MaximumLength(30).WithMessage(
        "Contact title must be at most 30 characters long.");

    RuleFor(x => x.Country)
      .NotEmpty().WithMessage("Country is required.")
      .MaximumLength(15).WithMessage(
        "Country must be at most 15 characters long.");
  }
}
```

6. In the `Endpoints` folder, add a new class named `CreateCustomerEndpoint.cs`.

7. In `CreateCustomerEndpoint.cs`, define an endpoint for adding a customer, as shown in the following code:

```
using FastEndpoints; // To use Endpoint<TRequest, TResponse>.
using FluentValidation.Results; // To use ValidationResult.
using Northwind.EntityModels; // To use Customer.
using Northwind.FastEndpoints.Validators; // To use
CreateCustomerValidator.

namespace Northwind.FastEndpoints.Endpoints;

public class CreateCustomerEndpoint : Endpoint<Customer, Customer>
{
  private readonly NorthwindContext _db;

  public CreateCustomerEndpoint(NorthwindContext db) => _db = db;

  public override void Configure()
  {
    Verbs(Http.POST);
    Routes("/customers");
    AllowAnonymous();
  }

  public override async Task HandleAsync(Customer request,
CancellationToken ct)
  {
    CreateCustomerValidator validator = new();
    ValidationResult? validationResult =
      await validator.ValidateAsync(request, ct);
```

```
    if (!validationResult.IsValid)
    {
      await Send.ErrorsAsync(cancellation: ct);
      return;
    }

    EntityEntry<Customer> added = _db.Customers.Add(request);
    await _db.SaveChangesAsync(ct);

    await Send .CreatedAtAsync(
      $"/customers/{added.Entity.CustomerId}",
      added.Entity, cancellation: ct);
  }
}
```

8. In the `Endpoints` folder, add a new class named `ReplaceCustomerEndpoint.cs`.

9. In `ReplaceCustomerEndpoint.cs`, define an endpoint for adding a customer, as shown in the following code:

```
using FastEndpoints; // To use Endpoint<TRequest, TResponse>.
using Northwind.EntityModels; // To use Customer.

namespace Northwind.FastEndpoints.Endpoints;

public class ReplaceCustomerEndpoint : Endpoint<Customer, Customer>
{
  private readonly NorthwindContext _db;

  public ReplaceCustomerEndpoint(NorthwindContext db) => _db = db;

  public override void Configure()
  {
    Verbs(Http.PUT);
    Routes("/customers/{Id}");
    AllowAnonymous();
  }

  public override async Task HandleAsync(
    Customer req, CancellationToken ct)
  {
    Customer? customer = await _db.Customers.FindAsync([ req.CustomerId
], ct);
```

```
    if (customer is null)
    {
      await Send.NotFoundAsync(ct);
      return;
    }

    customer.CompanyName = req.CompanyName;
    customer.ContactName = req.ContactName;
    customer.ContactTitle = req.ContactTitle;
    customer.Address = req.Address;
    customer.City = req.City;
    customer.Region = req.Region;
    customer.PostalCode = req.PostalCode;
    customer.Country = req.Country;
    customer.Phone = req.Phone;
    customer.Fax = req.Fax;

    await _db.SaveChangesAsync(ct);
    await Send.NoContentAsync(ct);
  }
}
```

10. In the `Endpoints` folder, add a new class named `DeleteCustomerEndpoint.cs`.

11. In `DeleteCustomerEndpoint.cs`, define an endpoint for deleting a customer, as shown in the following code:

```
using FastEndpoints; // To use EndpointWithoutRequest.
using Northwind.EntityModels; // To use Customer.

namespace Northwind.FastEndpoints.Endpoints;

public class DeleteCustomerEndpoint : EndpointWithoutRequest
{
  private readonly NorthwindContext _db;

  public DeleteCustomerEndpoint(NorthwindContext db) => _db = db;

  public override void Configure()
  {
    Verbs(Http.DELETE);
    Routes("/customers/{id}");
```

```
    AllowAnonymous();
  }

  public override async Task HandleAsync(CancellationToken ct)
  {
    string? id = Route<string>("id");

    Customer? customer = await _db.Customers.FindAsync(
      [ id ], cancellationToken: ct);

    if (customer is null)
    {
      await Send.NotFoundAsync(cancellation: ct);
      return;
    }

    _db.Customers.Remove(customer);
    await _db.SaveChangesAsync(ct);

    await Send.NoContentAsync(cancellation: ct);
  }
}
```

Trying out creating, updating, and deleting

Now we can try out the CRUD operations using FastEndpoints:

1. Start the `Northwind.FastEndpoints` web service project using the `https` launch profile.

2. In the `HttpRequests` folder, create a file named `customer-fastendpoints.http` and modify its contents to contain a request to `POST` a customer, as shown in the following code:

```
### Configure a variable for the web service base address.
@base_address = https://localhost:5131/customers/

### Make a GET request for all UK customers.
GET {{base_address}}UK

### Make a POST request to the base address.
POST {{base_address}}
Content-Type: application/json

{
  "customerID": "XYZAB",
```

```
  "companyName": "XYZ Corp",
  "contactName": "Jill Takodo",
  "contactTitle": "Ms",
  "address": "St James Street",
  "city": "Brighton",
  "region": "West Sussex",
  "postalCode": "BN1 4AH",
  "country":  "UK",
  "phone": "(0) 794 3490 2365"
}

### Make a PUT request to the base address.
PUT {{base_address}}xyzab
Content-Type: application/json

{
  "customerID": "XYZAB",
  "companyName": "XYZ Corp",
  "contactName": "Joe",
  "contactTitle": "Ms",
  "address": "St James Street",
  "city": "Brighton",
  "region": "West Sussex",
  "postalCode": "BN1 4AH",
  "country":  "UK",
  "phone": "(0) 794 3490 2365"
}

### Delete the customer with ID XYZAB.
DELETE https://localhost:5131/customers/xyzab
```

3. Above the POST request, click **Send request**, and note the response, as shown in *Figure 13.7*:

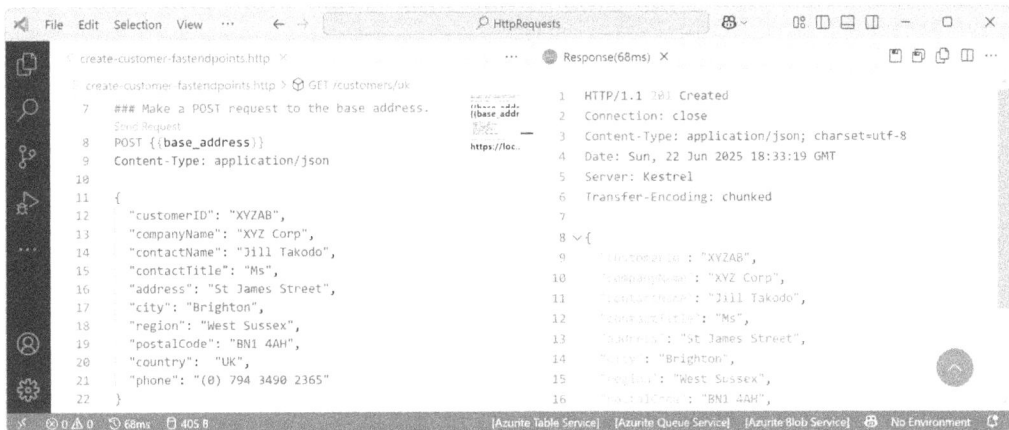

Figure 13.7: Using POST to add a new customer

4. Above the GET request for UK customers, click **Send Request**, and confirm that the new customer has been added.

5. Try out the PUT and DELETE requests and confirm that they work.

FastEndpoint versioning

FastEndpoints supports API versioning in a clean and declarative way using the Version() method in the Configure() method of each endpoint. This is a great feature when you're evolving your API and want to keep older versions running without breaking existing clients.

Let's walk through a complete example of versioned Customer endpoints with:

- v1 – original, basic version
- v2 – enhanced version with more fields

The directory structure might look something like this:

```
/Endpoints
  /Customers
    GetCustomersV1.cs
    GetCustomersV2.cs
/DTOs
  /Customers
    CustomersRequest.cs
    CustomersResponseV1.cs
    CustomersResponseV2.cs
```

Both versions might use the same request model, as shown in the following code:

```
namespace Northwind.FastEndpoints.DTOs.Customers;


public record CustomersRequest(string? Country);
```

But v1 might have a simpler response model, as shown in the following code:

```
namespace Northwind.FastEndpoints.DTOs.Customers;


public record CustomersResponseV1(
  string Id, string CompanyName);
```

And v2 might add some more properties, as shown in the following code:

```
namespace Northwind.FastEndpoints.DTOs.Customers;


public record CustomersResponseV2(
  string Id, string CompanyName, string ContactName, string Country);
```

The v1 endpoint, as shown in the following code:

```
using FastEndpoints; // To use Endpoint<T, T>.
using Microsoft.EntityFrameworkCore; // To use ToArrayAsync.
using Northwind.EntityModels; // To use NorthwindContext.
using Northwind.FastEndpoints.DTOs.Customers;


namespace Northwind.FastEndpoints.Endpoints.Customers;


public class GetCustomersV1 : Endpoint<CustomersRequest, CustomersResponseV1[]>
{
  private readonly NorthwindContext _db;

  public GetCustomersV1(NorthwindContext db) => _db = db;

  public override void Configure()
  {
    Verbs(Http.GET);
    Routes("/customers");
    Version(1); // <-- Version 1
    AllowAnonymous();
  }


  public override async Task HandleAsync(CustomersRequest req,
CancellationToken ct)
```

```
  {
    var query = _db.Customers.AsQueryable();

    if (!string.IsNullOrWhiteSpace(req.Country))
    {
      query = query.Where(c => c.Country == req.Country);
    }

    var result = await query
      .Select(c => new CustomersResponseV1(
        c.CustomerId,
        c.CompanyName))
      .ToArrayAsync(ct);

    await Send.OkAsync(result, cancellation: ct);
  }
}
```

The v2 endpoint, as shown in the following code:

```
using FastEndpoints; // To use Endpoint<T, T>.
using Microsoft.EntityFrameworkCore; // To use ToArrayAsync.
using Northwind.EntityModels; // To use NorthwindContext.
using Northwind.FastEndpoints.DTOs.Customers;

namespace Northwind.FastEndpoints.Endpoints.Customers;

public class GetCustomersV2 : Endpoint<CustomersRequest, CustomersResponseV2[]>
{
  private readonly NorthwindContext _db;

  public GetCustomersV2(NorthwindContext db) => _db = db;

  public override void Configure()
  {
    Verbs(Http.GET);
    Routes("/customers");
    Version(2); // <-- Version 2
    AllowAnonymous();
  }
```

```
    public override async Task HandleAsync(CustomersRequest req,
CancellationToken ct)
    {
      var query = _db.Customers.AsQueryable();

      if (!string.IsNullOrWhiteSpace(req.Country))
      {
        query = query.Where(c => c.Country == req.Country);
      }

      var result = await query
        .Select(c => new CustomersResponseV2(
          c.CustomerId,
          c.CompanyName,
          c.ContactName ?? string.Empty,
          c.Country ?? string.Empty))
        .ToArrayAsync(ct);

      await Send.OkAsync(result, cancellation: ct);
    }
}
```

FastEndpoints automatically exposes both versions under distinct routes:

*   `GET /customers/v1`
*   `GET /customers/v2`

There is no need to manually suffix routes with `/v1` or `/v2`. FastEndpoints takes care of that based on `.Version(n)`.

In REST Client or HTTP Editor, you can call the different version endpoints, as shown in the following code:

```
### V1
GET https://localhost:5131/customers/v1?Country=USA

### V2 with more fields
GET https://localhost:5131/customers/v2?Country=USA
```

Practicing and exploring

Test your knowledge and understanding by answering some questions, getting some hands-on practice, and exploring this chapter's topics with deeper research.

Exercise 13.1 – Online material

Read the official documentation for FastEndpoints at `https://fast-endpoints.com/`.

Learn how to add OpenAPI, *aka* Swagger, support using NSwag to your FastEndpoints web services at the following link:

`https://fast-endpoints.com/docs/swagger-support`

FastEndpoints recommends xUnit, WebApplicationFactory, and FluentAssertions for unit and integration testing.

Exercise 13.2 – Practice exercises

FastEndpoints has an extensive tutorial for learning it in more depth that can be found at the following link:

`https://dev.to/djnitehawk/building-rest-apis-in-net-6-the-easy-way-3h0d`

Exercise 13.3 – Test your knowledge

Answer the following questions:

1. Why is a web service built using FastEndpoints "fast"?
2. How do you define an endpoint that has complex request and response models using FastEndpoints?
3. If you do not call the `Verbs` method in the overridden `Configure` method of a FastEndpoints endpoint class, which HTTP methods does the endpoint respond to?
4. Why would you call the `Authorize` method rather than the `Roles` method to control access to a FastEndpoints endpoint?
5. Why might you call the `PreProcessors` and `PostProcessors` methods?

Exercise 13.4 – Explore topics

Use the links on the following page to learn more about the topics covered in this chapter:

`https://github.com/markjprice/web-dev-net10/blob/main/docs/book-links.md#chapter-13--`
`-building-web-services-using-fastendpoints`.

Summary

In this chapter, you learned how to build a web service using the FastEndpoints third-party package. You learned about the following:

- The benefits of the FastEndpoints package
- How to implement an endpoint using FastEndpoints
- How to configure an endpoint using FastEndpoints

You learned that FastEndpoints is designed with performance in mind. You further learned that it leverages the .NET runtime's performance optimizations to minimize overhead and improve request/response times. Compared to controller-based frameworks like ASP.NET Core Web API, FastEndpoints has a lower footprint and faster execution times, which is particularly beneficial for high-load applications and microservices that require minimal latency.

FastEndpoints focuses on reducing the amount of boilerplate code needed to define and handle API endpoints, as you learned in this chapter. You learned that you don't need controllers, attributes, or complex configurations. The framework simplifies the process by letting developers define routes, HTTP methods, and request/response handling in a clear and concise manner. This allows you to focus more on business logic rather than configuration and setup.

You learned that FastEndpoints uses a declarative approach to defining endpoints, including HTTP verbs, routes, roles, and authentication/authorization policies. The Configure method centralizes the setup for each endpoint, making it easy to see and manage how the endpoint behaves, as you learned in this chapter. This style reduces ambiguity and allows developers to understand the behavior of an endpoint at a glance without searching through annotations and configurations.

This chapter established that these benefits make FastEndpoints ideal for developers who want high-performance, clear, and maintainable web services with minimal setup and maximum flexibility.

In the next chapter, you will learn about Umbraco CMS, a .NET web content management system.

14

Web Content Management Using Umbraco CMS

This chapter is about building ASP.NET Core website projects that integrate with Umbraco CMS, a popular third-party web **content management system** (**CMS**). However, it is important to understand what this chapter does and does not cover with regard to Umbraco CMS.

The audience for this book is .NET developers. This chapter focuses on covering what a .NET developer needs to know about Umbraco CMS. That includes knowing how to integrate Umbraco CMS with an ASP.NET Core project and knowing what features are built in and therefore do not need to be created by the developer.

This chapter is *not* about how a senior marketer might use Umbraco CMS to design the branding of a website or how a junior marketer might use Umbraco CMS to create or edit web pages of content. (I provide links to external documentation for that.)

As a .NET developer tasked with enabling and probably extending Umbraco CMS, you should know some of the basic capabilities that are built in so that if you are asked to add a feature, you will know if that feature already exists, or if you will need to write custom code to extend Umbraco CMS to add that capability.

To understand the limits of what this chapter covers, it helps to understand that there are three main roles that work with a CMS, as described in the following list:

- **CMS developer:** This role does the technical work to enable the CMS on a development platform, like Umbraco on .NET or Django on Python. Once the website with a CMS is deployed, a CMS developer rarely needs to perform user tasks, like creating content and uploading images, or administering content types and assigning user permissions. One of the major benefits of implementing a CMS is that non-technical users can do that work without developer involvement. But if the built-in CMS features are not enough, then a developer might be asked to write code to implement a custom feature. You will learn about this in *Chapter 15, Customizing and Extending Umbraco CMS*.

- **CMS editor:** This role typically works in the marketing department of an organization and manages content for a website. They create web pages, upload images and other documents for use on the website, and update existing pages when changes occur in the organization, like when a C-level executive moves on. Often, CMS editors are trained internally for an hour or two about the available content types designed for the organization and how to use the basic CMS tools, like the HTML editor. This education includes how to add images and links to other pages. The CMS features for editors are as easy to learn as a word processor, so it shouldn't take long. Sometimes, a group of CMS editors will be trained together by a professional CMS expert training provider. Some CMSs have additional specialized types of editors. For example, Umbraco defines translators and writers as well as editors. These groups have slightly different permissions within the CMS.

> The official *Umbraco CMS Editor's Manual* is available at the following link: https://docs.umbraco.com/umbraco-cms/tutorials/editors-manual.
>
> This chapter shows enough of the built-in editor features that a developer can then scan through the rest of the functionality to know what's built in. This chapter does not teach you how to use all the editor tools. So, please read the manual if you do need that. For example, some organizations do seem to expect developers to train marketers on how to use the CMS to manage their content!

- **CMS administrator:** This role has complete access to all features of the CMS and typically defines the content types, assigns user permissions to areas of the website, and so on. CMS administrators need to know more details about how the CMS works, so they are more often trained by a professional CMS expert training provider.

These days, many CMSs only exist in the cloud as a **software-as-a-service (SaaS)** solution, like Squarespace, Wix, and the many WordPress hosts. For a small organization or a department within a large organization, these are good choices, despite their potential limitations in not having total control.

There are also many choices of CMS that integrate with web development platforms and therefore provide complete flexibility and customization. For cross-platform C# and .NET web developers, the best for learning about the important principles is Umbraco CMS. It was one of the first CMSs to support modern .NET.

In the real world, if you are a .NET developer working on a web development project, 99% of the time you will *not* be working *only* with ASP.NET Core, even ignoring the many frontend frameworks you might have to work with. You will almost certainly be working with another server-side platform built on top of ASP.NET Core. In this book, I wanted to emphasize that fact by including a chapter about a third-party platform for web development with .NET. I decided to use Umbraco CMS for this purpose, but I could equally have chosen Piranha CMS (`https://piranhacms.org/`), ABP Framework (`https://abp.io/`), nopCommerce (`https://www.nopcommerce.com/`), or any of dozens of others. By the end of this book, I want you to have an appreciation of how a typical real-life web platform extends ASP.NET Core. The goal is not to cover in depth any particular platform. I know that only a fraction of my readers will actually work with Umbraco CMS, but I believe that all my readers will find value in seeing how Umbraco extends ASP.NET Core as a common example.

Umbraco has three related products: Umbraco CMS, Umbraco Cloud, and Umbraco Heartcore. Umbraco Heartcore is a headless system. Umbraco Cloud is a hosted CMS.

We will look at Umbraco CMS because that provides its functionality as NuGet packages that can be integrated with any ASP.NET Core project and therefore gives you control over where you host it.

This chapter will cover the following topics:

- Understanding the benefits of a CMS
- Introducing Umbraco CMS
- Defining document types
- Working with media
- Structuring and navigating hierarchical content

Understanding the benefits of a CMS

To understand the benefits of a CMS, it helps to remember the two main roles that provide content for a website: one part of a website is managed by developers, and the other part is managed by editors.

In previous chapters, you learned how developers can create static HTML web pages and configure ASP.NET Core to serve them when requested by a visitor's browser.

You also learned how ASP.NET Core MVC Razor Views can add C# code that executes on the server side to generate HTML dynamically, including from information loaded live from a database, like a product catalog grouped into categories, as in the Northwind database, as shown in *Figure 14.1*. Additionally, you learned how ASP.NET Core MVC provides a separation of technical concerns to make building more complex websites more manageable.

Developers typically also build specialized web pages that are more like tools or apps. These have complex processing requirements that are best implemented by programmers and updated only when a new website deployment occurs.

On its own, ASP.NET Core does not solve the problem of managing website content. In those previous websites, the person creating and managing the content would have to have programming and HTML editing skills, or the ability to edit the data in the Northwind database, to change what visitors see on the website.

This is where a CMS becomes useful. A CMS separates the content (data values) from templates (layout, format, and style). Most CMSs generate web responses like HTML for humans viewing the website with a browser.

Some CMSs generate open data formats, like JSON and XML, to be processed by a web service or rendered in a browser using client-side technologies, like Angular, React, or Vue. This is often called a **headless CMS**.

Non-technical CMS administrators, often senior marketers within the organization, define the structure of data stored in the CMS using content type classes for different purposes, like a product page, with content templates that render the content data loaded from the CMS database into HTML, JSON, or other formats.

Non-technical CMS editors (a.k.a. content owners) can log into the CMS and use a simple user interface to create, edit, delete, and publish content that will fit the structure defined by the content type classes, without needing the involvement of developers or tools like Visual Studio.

For example, most websites have a section for important people in the organization, like biographies of the CEO, an **About Us** section with contact information and location maps, and a **News** or **Blog** section, as shown in *Figure 14.1*. All these need to be manually managed, typically by a member of the marketing or HR department, all non-technical people.

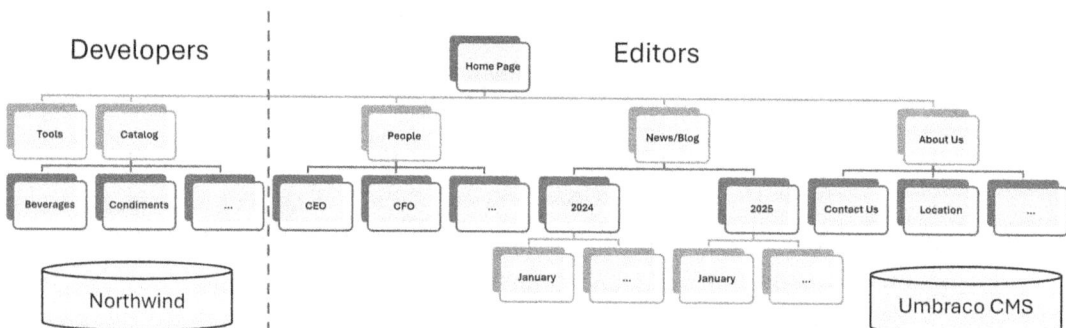

Figure 14.1: One part of a website is managed by developers, and the other part is managed by editors

Reviewing basic CMS features

Any decent basic CMS will include the following core features:

- A user interface that allows non-technical content owners to log in and manage their content
- Media asset management of images, videos, documents, and other files
- Sharing and reuse of pieces of content, often named *blocks*
- Saved drafts of content that are hidden from website visitors until they are published
- Search engine optimized URLs, page titles and related metadata, sitemaps, and so on
- Authentication and authorization, including management of users, groups, and their access rights to content
- A content delivery system that converts the content from simple data into one or more formats, like HTML and JSON

Reviewing enterprise CMS features

Any decent commercial enterprise-level CMS would add the following additional features:

- Forms designer for gathering input from visitors
- Marketing tools, like tracking visitor behavior and A/B testing of content
- Personalization of content based on rules, like geographic location or machine learning processing of tracked visitor behavior
- Retaining multiple versions of content and enabling the re-publishing of old versions
- Translation of content into multiple human languages, like English and German

Reviewing CMS platforms

CMSs exist for most development platforms and languages, as shown in *Table 14.1*:

Development platform	Content management systems
PHP	WordPress, Drupal, Joomla!, Magento
Python	Django CMS
Java	Adobe Experience Manager, Bloomreach Experience Manager (formerly Hippo CMS)
.NET	Umbraco CMS, Optimizely CMS, Sitecore, Kentico CMS, Piranha CMS, Orchard Core CMS

Table 14.1: CMS for different development platforms

Winning against WordPress

Ah, WordPress. It's the cockroach of the web. It seems impossible to kill, absurdly adaptable, and somehow it still thrives despite being ancient in web terms. WordPress owns the low-to-mid-tier website market. It powers over 40% of all websites globally (`https://w3techs.com/`), and there are reasons for that:

- Installation takes 5 minutes on a $3/month shared host, and you get a GUI immediately. For a small business, this feels like a godsend compared to installing .NET, configuring SQL Server, and setting up Umbraco CMS manually.

- Non-technical users can build feature-rich sites with zero code. Need an online shop? WooCommerce. Need SEO tools? Yoast. Need a drag-and-drop page builder? Elementor, Divi, and so on.

- Millions of freelancers and small agencies offer WordPress services. A company can hire someone on Fiverr or Upwork for $50 to fix a WordPress site. No lock-in to one expensive developer or agency.

- Cheap, ubiquitous hosting choices. No expensive Azure App Service or DevOps pipeline required.

Sounds great, right? But why am I highlighting WordPress in a book about web development with .NET?

> *"We must not belittle the saying in the book of Sun Wu Tzu, the great military expert of ancient China, 'Know your enemy and know yourself and you can fight a thousand battles without disaster.'"* – Mao

My book is about the real world, and in the real world, you need to be prepared to answer the question, "Why don't we just use WordPress?".

Here's how you push back strategically, not emotionally, as shown in *Table 14.2*:

WordPress vulnerability	Umbraco strength
WordPress is the #1 most targeted platform for automated hacking attempts. It has frequent plugin vulnerabilities, and out-of-date plugins and themes are a common attack vector. WordPress admins are often inexperienced at security and use weak passwords.	With Umbraco (especially on LTS), you're using fewer third-party packages and a modern, secure framework. Security practices are consistent with enterprise expectations.
WordPress is fine until you need something custom, then it's PHP spaghetti. Custom logic often means awkward plugin overrides or hacks. Plugin conflicts are common, where one plugin update can break others.	With Umbraco, custom features are written in clean, testable C# with dependency injection, logging, and proper architecture.

"We want marketing to be able to edit the site." Yes, and with WordPress, they will edit a plugin and break the theme, install new plugins without understanding performance and security implications, and overwrite page templates via a WYSIWYG builder. Every editor may lay out content differently unless tightly constrained.	Umbraco enforces structured content with document types and template constraints, making layout and branding consistent. Editors work inside a sandbox, so they can't inject arbitrary PHP or HTML.
WordPress can barely talk to serious APIs without writing PHP. WordPress has no native support for Entra ID, proper REST APIs, or a clean DI-based service architecture.	Umbraco integrates easily with any .NET system, Azure, REST API, or modern CI/CD pipeline.
WordPress feels "cheap." If the client is a law firm, healthcare provider, or major nonprofit, they may actually want to distance themselves from WordPress: "Isn't that what food bloggers use?"	Offer Umbraco as a professional, .NET-native CMS that aligns with enterprise development standards, scalability needs, and long-term maintainability.

Table 14.2: WordPress weaknesses versus Umbraco strengths

Sometimes WordPress is the right tool for a brochure site with 5 pages and no integrations: if the client already has in-house WordPress editors, the budget is under $1,000, and the timeline is "yesterday." In those cases, give them WordPress, and walk away.

But in the following scenarios, you need something serious like Umbraco CMS:

- The site needs custom data structures, integrations, or workflows.
- The dev team is C#/.NET-centric.
- You're building a multilingual or headless CMS setup.
- The client wants content authors to have guardrails.
- You need Entra ID, OAuth, or other enterprise features.

Now that you know all the good reasons to use Umbraco CMS, let's review what it can do for you and how it works in more detail.

Introducing Umbraco CMS

Umbraco CMS is an open-source CMS built on the Microsoft .NET framework. It's designed to be flexible, scalable, and user-friendly, making it a popular choice for developers and businesses that require a robust yet customizable platform for managing web content.

The key features of Umbraco CMS include the following:

- **Built on .NET**: Being based on .NET, Umbraco integrates with Microsoft technologies, which is a significant advantage for businesses already invested in the Microsoft ecosystem. It offers strong support for C# and .NET, making it a natural choice for developers familiar with these technologies.

- **Open source:** Umbraco is open source, which means that it is free to use and benefits from contributions from a large community of developers. This also ensures that the platform is continuously improved and updated.

- **Ecosystem:** Umbraco has a vibrant community of developers, designers, and users who contribute plugins and extensions and provide support. There's also a commercial arm, Umbraco HQ, which offers professional support, cloud hosting, and additional tools, like Umbraco Forms and Umbraco Cloud.

- **Flexibility:** Developers can create custom content types, layouts, and workflows tailored to the specific needs of a project. This makes it suitable for everything from simple websites to complex, enterprise-level applications.

- **User-friendly:** The backend interface of Umbraco is designed with usability in mind. Content editors and non-technical users can easily navigate the system to manage and publish content without needing extensive technical knowledge.

- **Scalability:** Umbraco is highly scalable, making it suitable for a wide range of projects, from small blogs by .NET developers who want to host their own websites to large corporate websites. Its architecture allows it to handle large amounts of content and traffic without sacrificing performance.

- **API-first:** Umbraco is designed to be API-driven, making it easier to integrate with other systems, develop custom applications, or serve as a headless CMS, where content is managed centrally and delivered to various platforms like websites, mobile apps, and IoT devices.

Why is Umbraco popular?

Umbraco is particularly popular among developers because of its flexibility, extensibility, and the fact that it's built on .NET. The ability to use familiar tools and languages makes it an attractive choice for .NET developers.

Unlike some other CMS platforms that might be more rigid or opinionated, Umbraco offers a high degree of customization. Developers can build exactly what they need without being constrained by the CMS.

The open-source nature of Umbraco means there's a large, active community that contributes plugins, extensions, and themes. This community also offers support, documentation, and regular updates, which help keep the platform modern and secure.

Umbraco strikes a good balance between making it easy for non-technical users to manage content and providing powerful tools for developers to create complex, dynamic websites.

For businesses that need more than what the open-source community can provide, Umbraco HQ offers commercial support, which includes service-level agreements, cloud hosting, and advanced features. This blend of open-source flexibility with optional enterprise-level support is a significant draw for larger organizations.

Organizations that are heavily invested in Microsoft technologies find Umbraco particularly appealing because it integrates well with other .NET applications, Azure services, and SQL Server.

With the increasing need for content to be delivered across multiple platforms (web, mobile, and IoT), Umbraco's support for headless CMS architecture makes it future-proof and adaptable to modern web development trends.

Umbraco is used across various industries, including corporate websites, e-commerce, government portals, and more. Its flexibility allows it to serve different purposes, from simple content management to complex, multi-site setups with extensive custom functionality.

Umbraco versions

Since Umbraco version 10, it has had a major release every six months. Umbraco has a **Long Term Support** (**LTS**) release every two years that aligns with .NET LTS releases. Like .NET, LTS releases are supported for three years. But unlike .NET, **Short Term Support** (**STS**) Umbraco releases are only supported for one year.

Umbraco has current and future versions planned, as shown in *Table 14.3*:

Version	Released	End of life	.NET
13 LTS	December 14, 2023	December 14, 2026	8 LTS
14 STS	May 30, 2024	May 30, 2025	8 LTS
15 STS	November 14, 2024	November 14, 2025	8 LTS
16 STS	June 12, 2025	June 12, 2026	8 LTS
17 LTS	**November 27, 2025**	**November 27, 2028**	**10 LTS**
18 STS	May 2026	May 2027	10 LTS
19 STS	November 2026	November 2027	10 LTS
20 STS	May 2027	May 2028	10 LTS
21 LTS	November 2027	November 2030	12 LTS

Table 14.3: Umbraco versions and support summary

This chapter was written using Umbraco 17 (LTS). You should be able to target future versions of Umbraco CMS, like Umbraco 18 to 20 (all STS), and complete all the same tasks in this book. With Umbraco 17, the Umbraco team focused on targeting .NET 10 to support LTS rather than adding new features.

If you need to target an LTS version for support, then target Umbraco 17 on .NET 10, and then upgrade to Umbraco 21 on .NET 12 in November 2027.

> Learn more about Umbraco versions and support at the following link: `https://umbraco.com/products/knowledge-center/long-term-support-and-end-of-life/`.
>
> Learn more about Umbraco requirements at the following link: `https://docs.umbraco.com/umbraco-cms/fundamentals/setup/requirements`.

Installing Umbraco CMS

Umbraco CMS is installed as .NET SDK project templates. Let's do that now:

1. At a command prompt or terminal, install the Umbraco project templates, as shown in the following command:

    ```
    dotnet new install Umbraco.Templates@17.0.0
    ```

    > If you do not specify the version number explicitly, then it will install the latest version. Since Umbraco releases new major versions every six months, and I want to make sure you have the same experience that I did while writing this book, I recommend explicitly using the latest patched version 17. Also note that the double-colon separator (::) has been deprecated in favor of the *at* symbol (@) for separating the package from the version in `dotnet new install`.

2. Note the three new project templates, as shown in the following output:

    ```
    Templates                Short Name          Language  Tags
    --------------------------------------------------------------------------
    Umbraco Project          umbraco             [C#]      Web/CMS/Umbraco
    Umbraco Extension        umbraco-extension   [C#]      Web/CMS/Umbraco/...
    Umbraco Docker Compose   umbraco-compose     [C#]      Web/CMS/Umbraco
    ```

3. In future, you can confirm that the project templates are installed using the `list` switch, as shown in the following command:

    ```
    dotnet new list umbraco
    ```

4. In Visual Studio (after a restart if necessary), the project templates should be found automatically, or you can type umbraco in the search box, as shown in *Figure 14.2*:

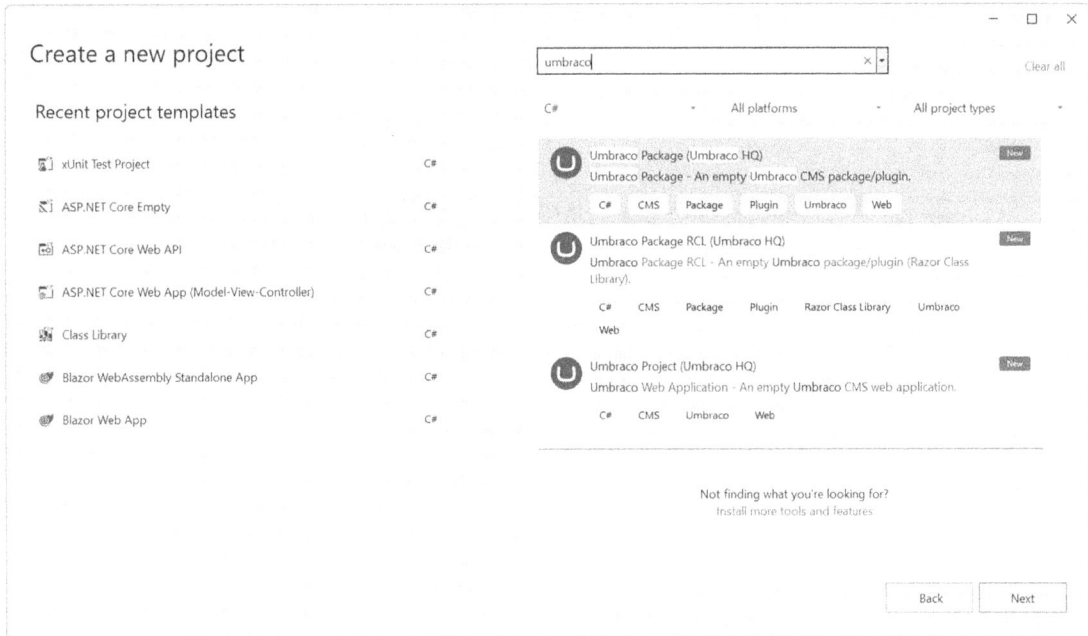

Figure 14.2: Searching for Umbraco project templates in Visual Studio

Creating a new Umbraco project

Now, let's set up a new Umbraco project with example content to easily explore its features. Later, we will see how to add Umbraco capabilities to an existing ASP.NET Core project.

Let's go:

1. Use your preferred code editor to open the `MatureWeb` solution and then add a new project, as defined in the following list:

    - **Project template: Umbraco Project (Umbraco HQ)** / umbraco
    - **Solution file and folder:** MatureWeb
    - **Project file and folder:** Northwind.Cms

2. If you are using Visual Studio, then confirm that the following defaults have been chosen:

    - **Framework: .NET 10.0 (Long Term Support)**
    - **Umbraco version:** Latest
    - **Use HTTPS redirect:** Selected
    - **Use Delivery API:** Selected
    - **Add Docker file:** Cleared
    - **Exclude .gitignore:** Cleared
    - **Minimal .gitignore:** Cleared

- **Connection string:** <empty>
- **Connection string provider name:** `Microsoft.Data.SqlClient`
- **Others:** Leave as defaults

> **Warning!** The options area is scrollable, so there are a lot more than are initially visible. For example, you can set an unattended username, password, and email.

3. In `Northwind.Cms.csproj`, delete the version numbers for any package references, as shown in the following markup:

```
<Project Sdk="Microsoft.NET.Sdk.Web">

  <PropertyGroup>
    <TargetFramework>net10.0</TargetFramework>
    <ImplicitUsings>enable</ImplicitUsings>
    <Nullable>enable</Nullable>
    <CompressionEnabled>false</CompressionEnabled>
  </PropertyGroup>

  <ItemGroup>
    <PackageReference Include="Umbraco.Cms" />
  </ItemGroup>

  <ItemGroup>
    <PackageReference Include="Microsoft.ICU.ICU4C.Runtime" />
    ...
```

4. Build the `Northwind.Cms` project to restore packages.
5. In the `Properties` folder, in `launchSettings.json`, for the `Umbraco.Web.UI` profile's `applicationUrl`, change the random port number for HTTPS to **5141** and for HTTP to **5140**, as shown highlighted in the following markup:

```
"applicationUrl": "https://localhost:5141;http://localhost:5140",
```

6. Save the changes to all modified files.
7. In `Program.cs`, note the differences with an empty or MVC project so that you can understand what is needed to integrate Umbraco CMS with an ASP.NET Core project, as shown highlighted in the following code and explained below the code:

```
WebApplicationBuilder builder = WebApplication.CreateBuilder(args);

builder.CreateUmbracoBuilder()
```

```
    .AddBackOffice()
    .AddWebsite()
    .AddDeliveryApi()
    .AddComposers()
    .Build();

WebApplication app = builder.Build();

await app.BootUmbracoAsync();

app.UseHttpsRedirection();

app.UseUmbraco()
    .WithMiddleware(u =>
    {
        u.UseBackOffice();
        u.UseWebsite();
    })
    .WithEndpoints(u =>
    {
        u.UseBackOfficeEndpoints();
        u.UseWebsiteEndpoints();
    });

await app.RunAsync();
```

Note the following about the preceding code:

- After creating an Umbraco builder, the `AddBackOffice`, `AddWebsite`, `AddDeliveryApi`, and `AddComposers` methods register dependency services that provide the following features to the project: a back office for admin functions, a frontend website for visitors, a headless delivery API for content distribution, and custom components to extend functionality.

- The `BootUmbracoAsync` method performs actions like initiating the database connection to verify connectivity and confirming that the database is ready for CRUD operations. It might also include running any outstanding database migrations to ensure schema compatibility with the code. Many CMS applications, including Umbraco, need background services for tasks like content caching, scheduled publishing, or running scheduled jobs.

- In the configuration of the HTTP pipeline, the `UseUmbraco` method registers endpoints for the back office at the `/umbraco` relative path and other endpoints.

Initializing a new Umbraco project

Now we can start the project to initialize it and its database (be patient!):

1. Set the `Northwind.Cms` project as the startup project.

2. Start the `Northwind.Cms` project using the `Umbraco.Web.UI` launch profile without debugging, as shown in *Figure 14.3*:

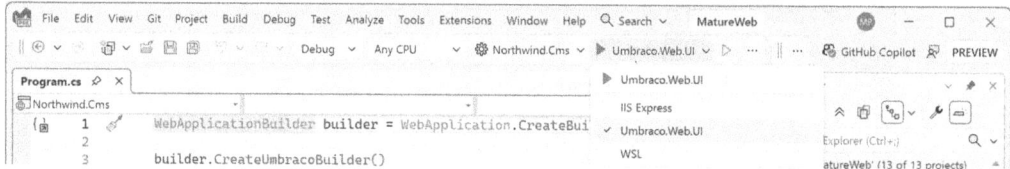

Figure 14.3: Selecting the Umbraco.Web.UI launch profile

> **Be patient!** It can take a few moments for an Umbraco CMS project to start the first time.

3. At the command prompt or terminal hosting the web server, note the background services started so that you understand what extra work must be completed for an ASP.NET Core project with Umbraco CMS integrated compared to an empty or basic MVC project, as shown in the following output:

```
[11:12:16 INF] Acquiring MainDom.
[11:12:16 INF] Acquired MainDom.
[11:12:16 INF] Starting recurring background jobs hosted services
[11:12:16 INF] Starting background hosted service for
OpenIddictCleanupJob
[11:12:16 INF] Starting background hosted service for
HealthCheckNotifierJob
[11:12:16 INF] Starting background hosted service for LogScrubberJob
[11:12:16 INF] Starting background hosted service for
ContentVersionCleanupJob
[11:12:16 INF] Starting background hosted service for
ScheduledPublishingJob
[11:12:16 INF] Starting background hosted service for TempFileCleanupJob
[11:12:16 INF] Starting background hosted service for
TemporaryFileCleanupJob
[11:12:16 INF] Starting background hosted service for
InstructionProcessJob
[11:12:16 INF] Starting background hosted service for TouchServerJob
[11:12:16 INF] Starting background hosted service for WebhookFiring
```

```
[11:12:16 INF] Starting background hosted service for
WebhookLoggingCleanup
[11:12:16 INF] Starting background hosted service for ReportSiteJob
[11:12:16 INF] Completed starting recurring background jobs hosted
services
[11:12:17 INF] Now listening on: https://localhost:5141
[11:12:17 INF] Now listening on: http://localhost:5140
[11:12:17 INF] Application started. Press Ctrl+C to shut down.
[11:12:17 INF] Hosting environment: Development
[11:12:17 INF] Content root path: C:\web-dev-net10\MatureWeb\Northwind.
Cms
```

4. In your browser, note the **Install Umbraco** page that appears the first time that you start a fresh Umbraco project, as shown in *Figure 14.4*:

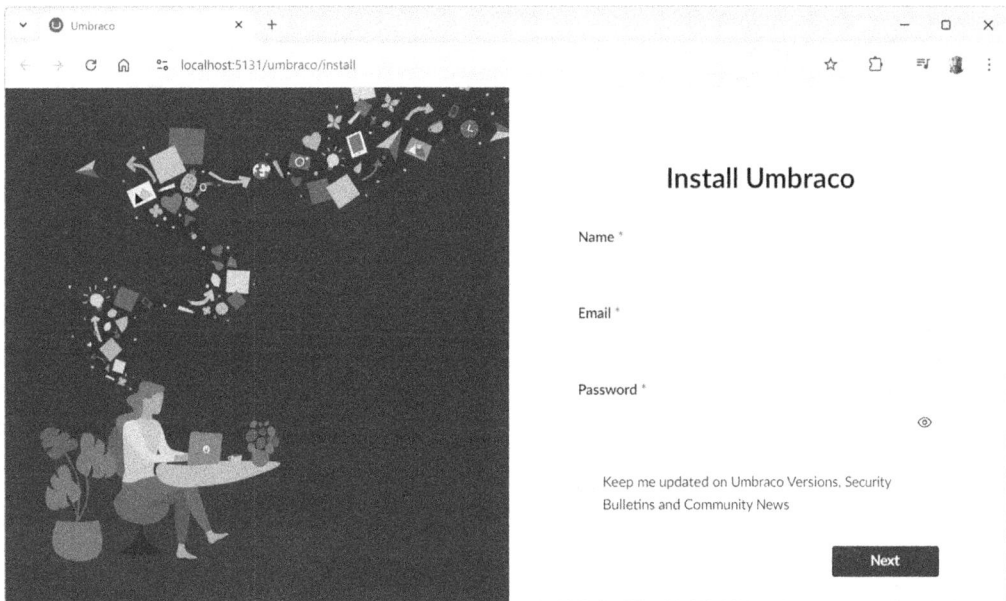

Figure 14.4: Installation page

5. Enter your name and email, type a strong password, and then click **Next**.
6. On the **Consent for telemetry data** page, select **1 Minimal**, and then click **Next**.
7. On the **Database Configuration** page, select a **Database type**, complete any other necessary information, like the connection string, and then click **Next**.

> Since we are just learning about Umbraco CMS functionality rather than building a production system, I recommend that you leave it on the default of **SQLite** with a database name of Umbraco.

8. On the **Welcome** login page, enter your email and password, and then click **Login**.

Exploring Umbraco back office

The Umbraco CMS back office is the web-based administrative interface where developers, content editors, designers, and site managers manage all aspects of an Umbraco-powered website or application. It's essentially the control panel for Umbraco, similar to WordPress's Dashboard but more flexible and developer-friendly.

Now let's review some of the important features of the Umbraco back office:

1. On the Umbraco back office home page, note the top menu to navigate between sections (**Content, Media, Settings, Packages, Users, Members,** and **Translation**) and the left navigation bar labeled **Content** with no content yet, as shown in *Figure 14.5*:

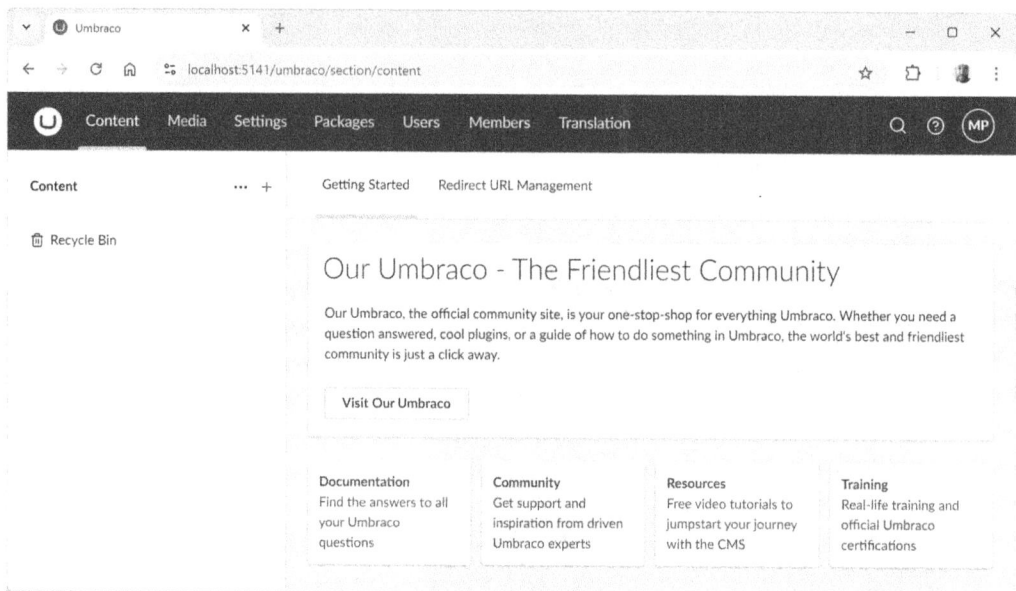

Figure 14.5: Umbraco back office home page

> The Umbraco back office is accessed through the `/umbraco` relative path, so for our project, it is at the following link:
>
> `https://localhost:5141/umbraco`

2. Click **Users**, and then click **User groups**, and note that different groups have access to different sections, as shown in *Figure 14.6*:

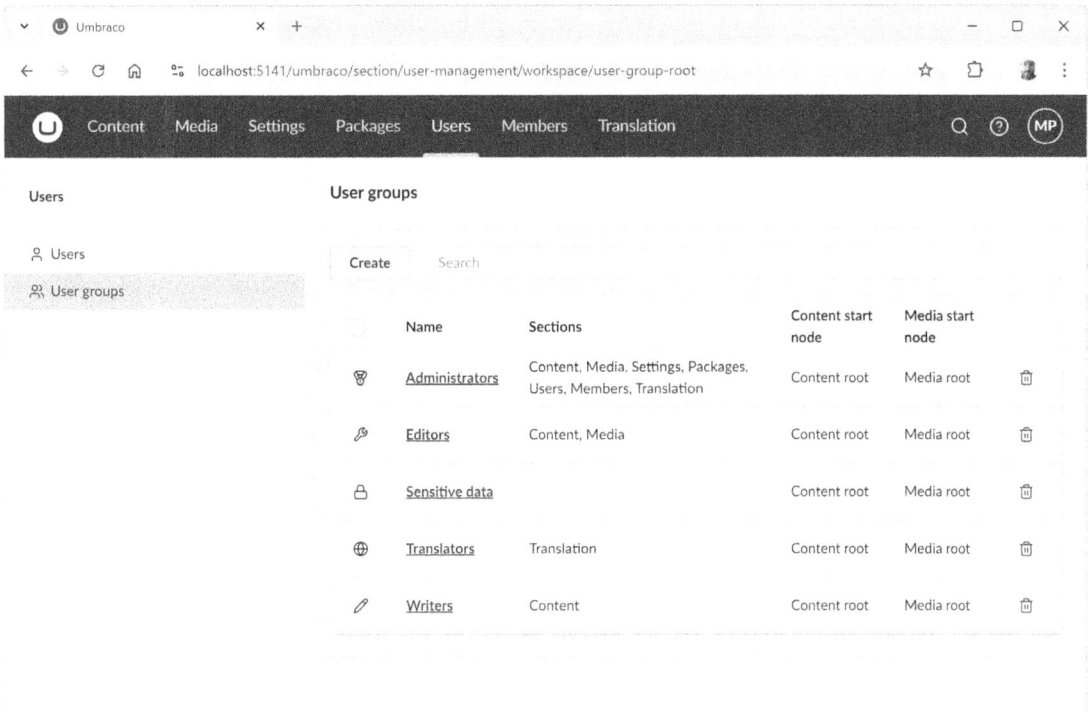

Figure 14.6: User groups and the sections they have access to

Setting up languages

By default, your website will support English (US). Let's enable some other languages:

1. In **Settings**, in the left navigation, click **Languages**.
2. On the **Languages** page, note that, by default, the CMS already has **English (United States)** enabled, it has a code of **en-US**, and it is the default language for the website, and then click **Create**, as shown in *Figure 14.7*:

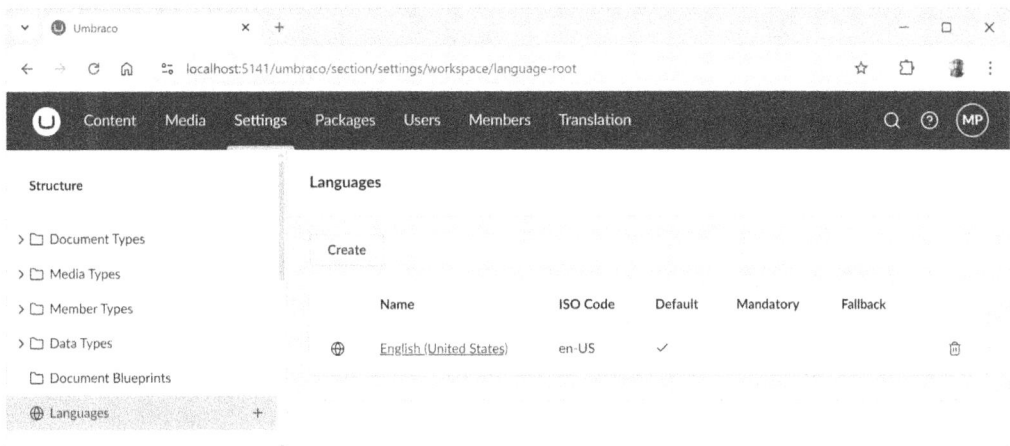

Figure 14.7: Listing languages enabled in the CMS website

3. In the **Language** box, enter `english`, select **English (United Kingdom)**, and note:

   • The ISO culture code is **en-GB**. This has two parts: *en* (language is English) and *GB* (region is Great Britain). This is known as a **specific culture**.

   • We could switch the default language for the website from English (US) to English (GB).

   • We can force editors to provide property values in English (GB) by setting it to be a mandatory language. We will leave that optional.

4. In the **Fallback language** section, click **Choose**, select **English (US)**, and then click **Submit**.

5. Click **Save**.

6. Click the back arrow button to return to the list of languages.

7. Click **Create** and add the **French** language, and note:

   • The ISO culture code is **fr**. French (without a region like France) is known as a **neutral culture**.

   • We will not set a fallback, so we must always supply translations to French of any required properties in a content type.

8. Click **Save**.

9. Click the back arrow button to return to the list of languages.

10. On the **Languages** page, note the table of three languages, as shown in *Figure 14.8*:

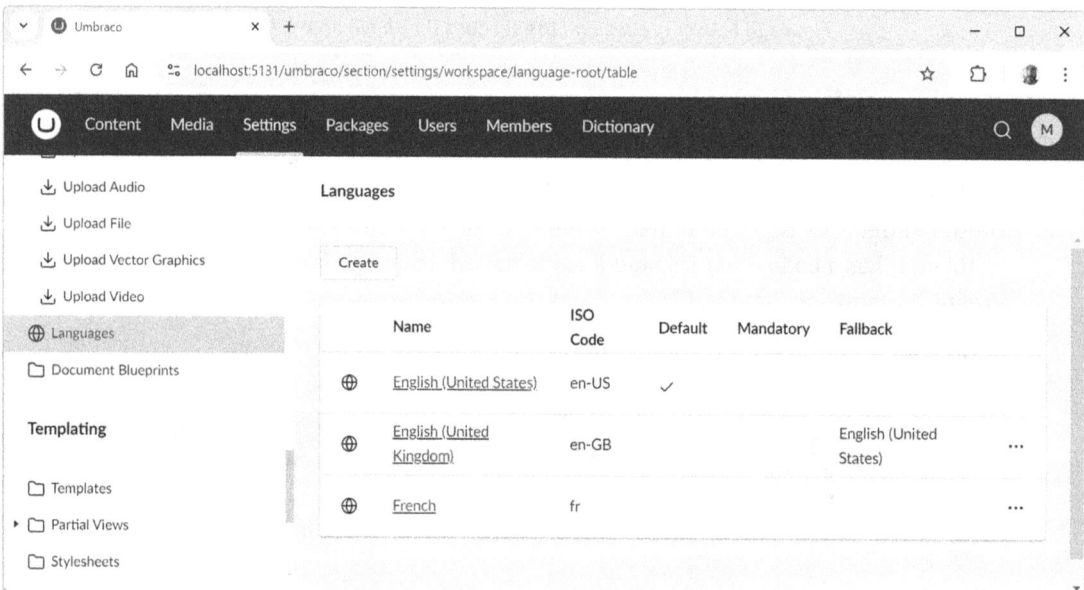

Figure 14.8: Managing languages in Umbraco

Note the following about the language configuration:

• **English (United States)** is the default language.

- **English (United Kingdom)** will fall back to using **English (United States)** if a UK version of the content is not found.

- **French** will not fall back to **English (United States)**, so when publishing instances of this page type, we must supply values for mandatory properties like Title; otherwise, publishing will fail (although saving will work).

Unattended installs

Umbraco has a feature that allows it to install without manually using the step-by-step user interface that you just used. But this means that if you need to customize an installation task, you cannot use an unattended install.

It's important to know that the install feature will only work if there is a connection string configured pointing to an empty database. A configuration for an unattended install is shown in the following code:

```
{
  "$schema": "https://json.schemastore.org/appsettings.json",
  "ConnectionStrings": {
    "umbracoDbDSN": "Server=.;Database=UmbracoDb;Integrated Security=true"
  },
  "Umbraco": {
    "CMS": {
      "Unattended": {
        "InstallUnattended": true,
        "PackageMigrationsUnattended": true,
        "UpgradeUnattended": true,
        "UnattendedUserName": "<administrators_name>",
        "UnattendedUserEmail": "<administrators_email>",
        "UnattendedUserPassword": "<administrators_password>"
      }
    }
  }
}
```

When you start the project with an unattended install configuration like the preceding one, this will automatically install Umbraco to the UmbracoDb database on the local SQL Server, and will also automatically upgrade whenever there is an upgrade to install.

> **Good practice:** You should not store user credentials in config files. I recommend that you use environment variables for these settings.

So, you now know the most important benefits and features of Umbraco CMS. Let's see how to use it, starting with defining the types of document (content) that you want the editors to be able to create, and then we will see how to manage multiple human languages for that content, like English and French.

Defining document types

In Umbraco, a document type is a blueprint for content on your site. It defines the structure and properties of a piece of content, such as a page or a component of a page.

Document types allow you to manage and organize content consistently across a website by setting up rules and templates that content editors follow when creating new pages or elements.

There are several key aspects of document types, as shown in *Table 14.4*:

Component	Description
Properties	These are the individual fields within a document type, like Title, Body Text, Image, Meta Description, and so on. Each property has a specific data type, such as Text, Rich Text, Media Picker, or Date Picker.
Templates	Templates define how the content of a particular document type is presented on the website. A document type can be associated with one or more templates, providing flexibility in how content is displayed.
Relationships	Document types can have hierarchical relationships. For example, a Blog Post document type might be a child of a Blog document type, reflecting the structure of content on the site.

Table 14.4: Components of document types

Example document types

Some common examples of document types that you might define on a typical website are shown in *Table 14.5*:

Name and purpose	Common properties	Template
Home page: The main landing page of the website	**Hero image:** Media picker to select the main banner image **Intro text:** Rich text editor for the welcome message or tagline **Featured articles:** Content picker to highlight specific articles or blog posts **Call to action buttons:** Text fields or content pickers for buttons leading to key pages	Custom layout for the home page, with designated areas for the hero image, intro text, and featured articles

Blog post: To create individual blog entries	**Title:** Text string for the blog post title **Body:** Rich text editor for the main content of the post **Author:** Text string or content picker for the author's name or profile **Publish date:** Date picker for when the post should be published **Tags:** Multiple text strings or tags for categorizing the post **Featured image:** Media picker for the main image associated with the post	A layout that presents the title, author, publish date, body text, and featured image in a blog format
Product page: To display information about a product	**Product name:** Text string for the name of the product **Description:** Rich text editor for the product description **Price:** Numeric field for the product's price **Image gallery:** Media picker for adding multiple images of the product **Specifications:** Text string or rich text for listing the technical specs **Related products:** Content picker to link to other products	A detailed product layout with areas for images, descriptions, and pricing
Contact page: A page where users can find contact information or submit inquiries	**Address:** Text string or rich text for the company's address **Phone number:** Text string for contact phone numbers **Email:** Text string for contact email addresses **Contact form:** Rich text or a form picker for embedding a contact form **Map:** Media picker or a Google Maps integration for displaying the location	A straightforward layout with sections for contact details, a form, and a map

Landing page: A customizable page often used for marketing campaigns	**Title:** Text string for the page title **Main content:** Rich text editor for detailed content or promotional information **Call to action:** Text field or content picker for buttons or links **Banner image:** Media picker for a top-of-the-page image **SEO metadata:** Text fields for meta descriptions and keywords	Flexible layout options to accommodate various marketing needs, often with sections that can be toggled on or off depending on the campaign

Table 14.5: Examples of document types

Document types in Umbraco matter because they ensure that content is consistent and manageable, regardless of who creates it. They enforce structure and provide a clear framework that content editors can follow, minimizing errors and maintaining the design integrity of the site.

In practice, a well-organized set of document types can greatly improve the efficiency of managing a website, especially as it grows in complexity. They also enable developers to create modular and reusable templates, which can be applied across multiple pages or sections of a site.

When you create a new document type, you have four choices:

- **Document type:** This is the data definition for a content component that can be created by editors in the content tree and be picked on other pages, but has no direct URL.
- **Document type with template:** This is the data definition for a content page that can be created by editors in the content tree and is directly accessible via a URL.
- **Element type:** This defines the schema for a repeating set of properties, for example, in a Block List or Block Grid property editor.
- **Folder:** This is used to organize the document types, compositions, and element types created in this document type tree.

Creating a document type for the home page

Let's define a few document types for our website:

1. In the Umbraco back office, navigate to **Settings | Document Types**.
2. Click the **+**, or click **...** and then click **+ Create**. In the **Create an item under Document Types** pane, click **Document Type with Template**. Or click the **Create >** button and then choose **Document Type with Template**.
3. Enter a name and description for your content type, as shown in the following bullets and *Figure 14.9*:
   - Name: Home Page
   - Description: The main landing page of the website.

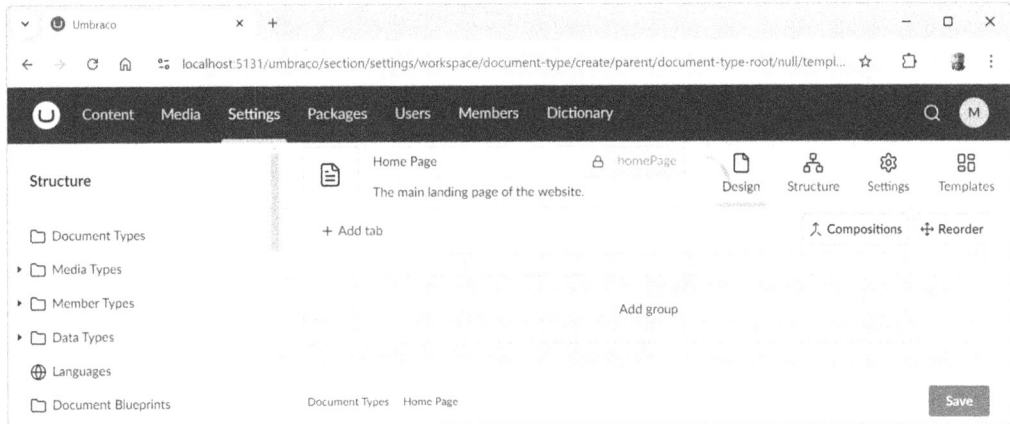

Figure 14.9: Entering a name and description for a content type

4. Click **Save**.

5. Click **Structure** and select **Allow at root**. This will allow editors to create content of this type in the root of the content tree.

> You control which page types are allowed at various points within the content tree hierarchy by selecting this option and by selecting **Allowed child node types**. For example, you might choose to only allow Blog Article document types to be created under a Blog document type.

6. Click **Settings** and select **Allow vary by culture**. This will allow editors to create content in different languages. For example, later in this chapter, you will create an English (US) home page, an English (GB) home page, and a French (France) home page.

7. Click **Design**, click + **Add tab**, and enter the tab name SEO.

8. Click **Add group**, and enter the group name Head section.

9. In **Head section**, click **Add property**.

10. In the **Add property** pane, fill in the following values, as shown in the following bullets and *Figure 14.10*:

    *   **Enter a name:** Title
    *   **Enter a description:** The page title. Should be between 5 and 50 characters.
    *   **Type: Text Box | Textstring** (click **Select Property Editor**, select **Text Box**, then **Text-string**)
    *   **Field is mandatory:** Selected (meaning we must supply a value for this property for all language variations before we can publish)
    *   **Custom validation: No validation**
    *   **Variation | Shared across cultures:** Cleared (so that we can provide different titles for different languages/cultures like US and UK English, or French)
    *   **Appearance: Label to the left**

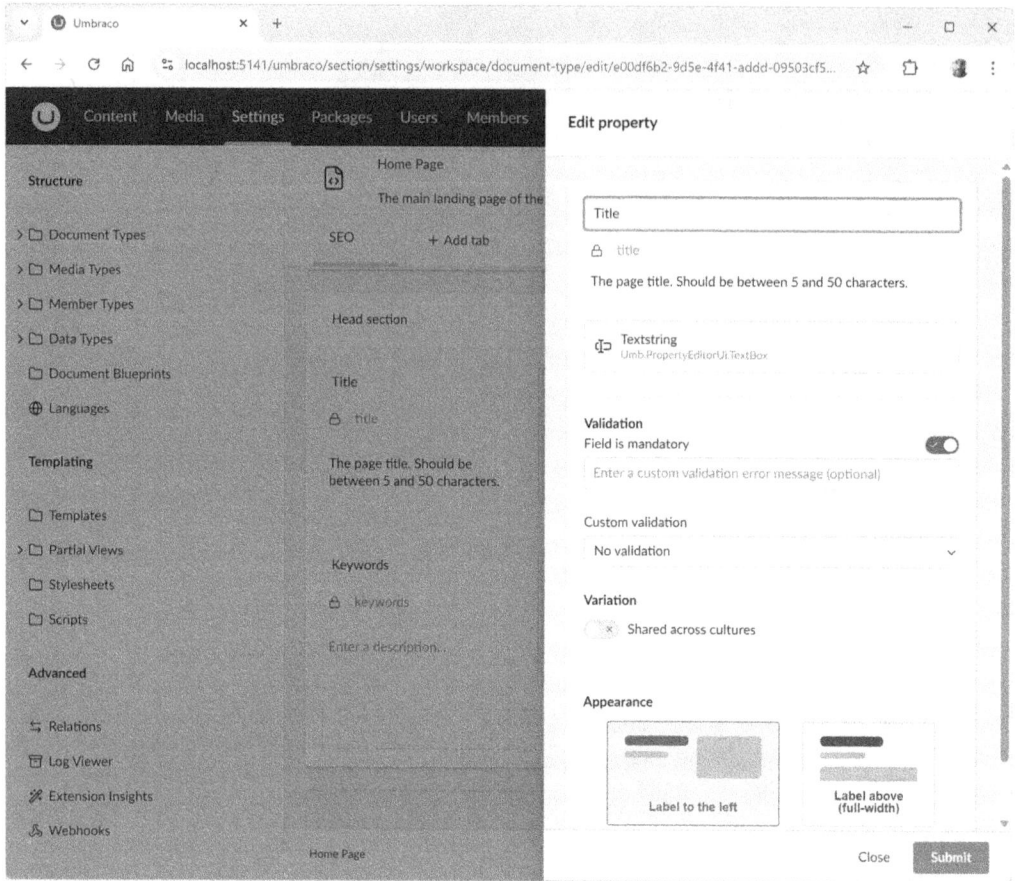

Figure 14.10: Setting properties for a content type property

11. Click **Submit**.

12. In **Head section**, click **Add property**.

13. In the **Add property** pane, fill in the values as shown in the following bullets:

    • **Enter a name:** Keywords

    • **Select Property Editor: Text Area | Textarea**

    • **Variation | Shared across cultures:** Cleared

    • **Appearance: Label to the left**

14. Click **Submit**.

15. Click + **Add tab**, and enter the name Body.

16. Click **Add property**.

17. In the **Add property** pane, fill in the values as shown in the following bullets:

    • **Enter a name:** Main Content

    • **Select Property Editor: Rich Text Editor [TipTap] | Richtexteditor**

- • **Variation | Shared across cultures:** Cleared
- • **Appearance:** Label above (full-width)

18. Click **Submit**.
19. Click **Save**.

There are many element types that you can choose to use in a content type. I encourage you to explore all of them in your own time so that you know what capabilities are built into Umbraco CMS that you, as a developer, do not need to implement. You can learn more about them at the following link:

`https://docs.umbraco.com/umbraco-cms/fundamentals/data/data-types/default-data-types`.

> **Good practice:** You might have to help a CMS administrator or marketer define content types. For example, you might have to work with a web designer who gives you a static web page and CSS file, and then you will be expected to create the content types. I recommend that you encourage them to do it themselves. They don't need to know that the markup is actually a Razor View file. To them, it's just HTML with a few @ symbols to insert fields.

Defining a document template

When we created the content type, we chose **Document Type with Template**. We have added properties to the document type. Now, we need to define the template so that content can be rendered into HTML:

1. In the **Home Page** document type, in its top navigation, click **Templates**, and note that you can choose which templates editors are allowed to use, as shown in *Figure 14.11*:

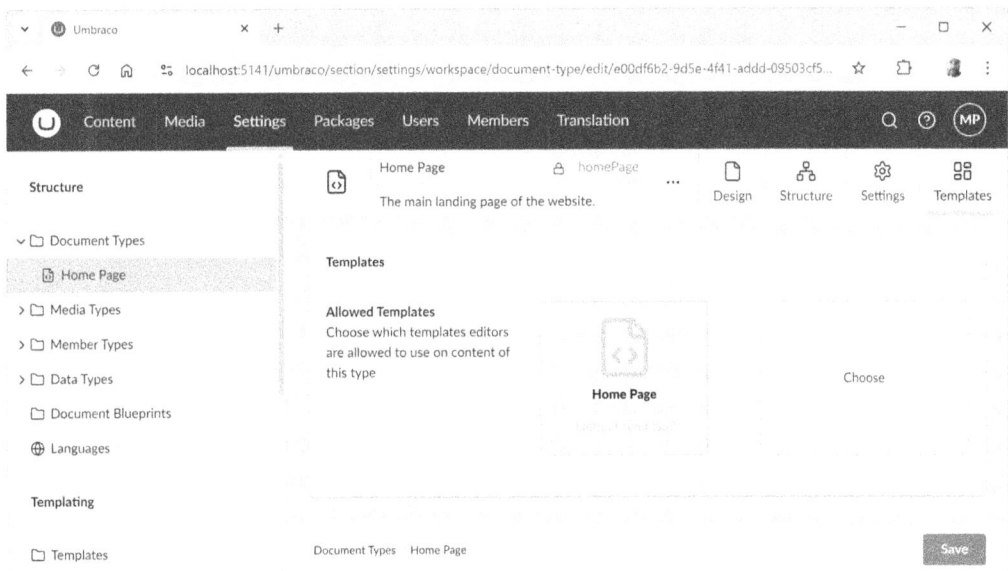

Figure 14.11: Selecting allowed templates

2. Select **Home Page,** and note that an Umbraco template is an MVC Razor View so it can use layouts, and that it inherits from an Umbraco class named UmbracoViewPage and imports any published models that you have defined, as shown in *Figure 14.12*:

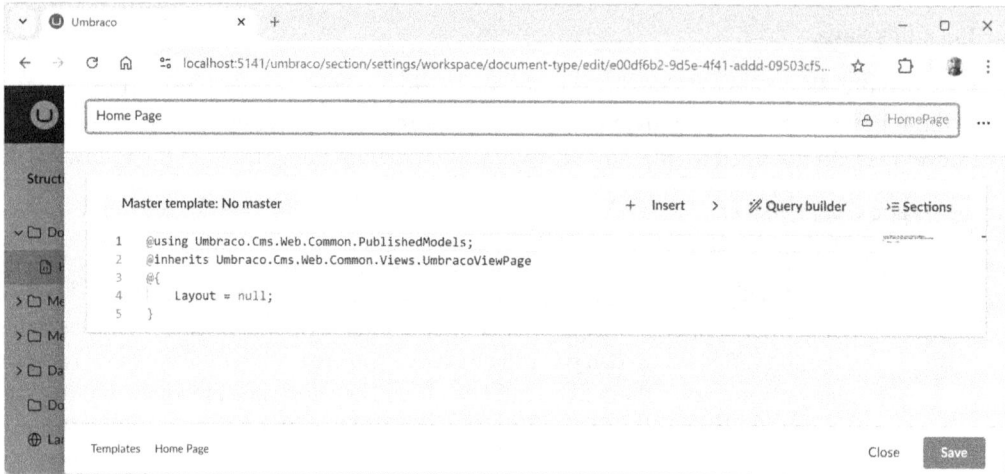

Figure 14.12: Editing the Home Page template

3. Click **Save.**

4. In the left navigation bar, in the **Templating** section, hover your mouse pointer over the Templates folder and then click the + icon, or click the **...** menu and then click **+ Create.**

5. Enter the name NorthwindCMS, and note the suggested internal name is northwindCms.

6. In the editing area, change the contents to use Razor syntax to define a layout that renders a standard web page with a collapsible Bootstrap navbar with menu items to go to the Umbraco back office and to switch between English (the default) and French languages, as shown in the following markup:

```
@using Umbraco.Cms.Web.Common.PublishedModels;
@inherits Umbraco.Cms.Web.Common.Views.UmbracoViewPage
<!doctype html>
<html lang="en">
<head>
  <meta charset="utf-8" />
  <meta name="viewport" content=
 "width=device-width, initial-scale=1, shrink-to-fit=no" />
  <meta name="keywords" content="@ViewData["keywords"]" />
  <link href="https://cdn.jsdelivr.net/npm/bootstrap@5.3.3/dist/css/
bootstrap.min.css" rel="stylesheet" integrity="sha384-QWTKZyjpPEjISv5WaRU
9OFeRpok6YctnYmDr5pNlyT2bRjXh0JMhjY6hW+ALEwIH" crossorigin="anonymous">
  <title>@ViewData["title"]</title>
</head>
```

```
<body>
  <nav class="navbar navbar-expand-lg bg-body-tertiary">
  <div class="container-fluid">
    <a class="navbar-brand" href="#">Northwind CMS</a>
    <button class="navbar-toggler" type="button" data-bs-
toggle="collapse" data-bs-target="#navbarNavAltMarkup" aria-
controls="navbarNavAltMarkup" aria-expanded="false" aria-label="Toggle
navigation">
      <span class="navbar-toggler-icon"></span>
    </button>
    <div class="collapse navbar-collapse" id="navbarNavAltMarkup">
      <div class="navbar-nav">
        <a class="nav-link active" aria-current="page" href="/
umbraco">Admin</a>
        <a class="nav-link active" aria-current="page" href="/">English</
a>
        <a class="nav-link active" aria-current="page" href="/
fr">French</a>
      </div>
    </div>
  </div>
  </nav>
  @RenderBody()
</body>
</html>
```

7. Click **Save**.

8. In the left navigation, in the **Templating** section, expand the `Templates` folder, and select **Home Page**.

9. Click **Master template: No master**, select **NorthwindCMS**, click the **Choose** button, and note that this changes the layout for this MVC Razor view: `Layout = "northwindCms.cshtml";`.

10. Under the code block, add HTML to define the page, as shown in the following markup and *Figure 14.13*:

```
@using Umbraco.Cms.Web.Common.PublishedModels;
@inherits Umbraco.Cms.Web.Common.Views.UmbracoViewPage
@{
  Layout = "northwindCms.cshtml";
  ViewData["title"] = Model.Value("title");
  ViewData["keywords"] = Model.Value("keywords");
}
<div class="container">
```

```
<div class="jumbotron">
  <h1 class="display-3">@Model.Value("title")</h1>
  <p class="lead">@Model.Value("mainContent")</p>
</div>
</div>
```

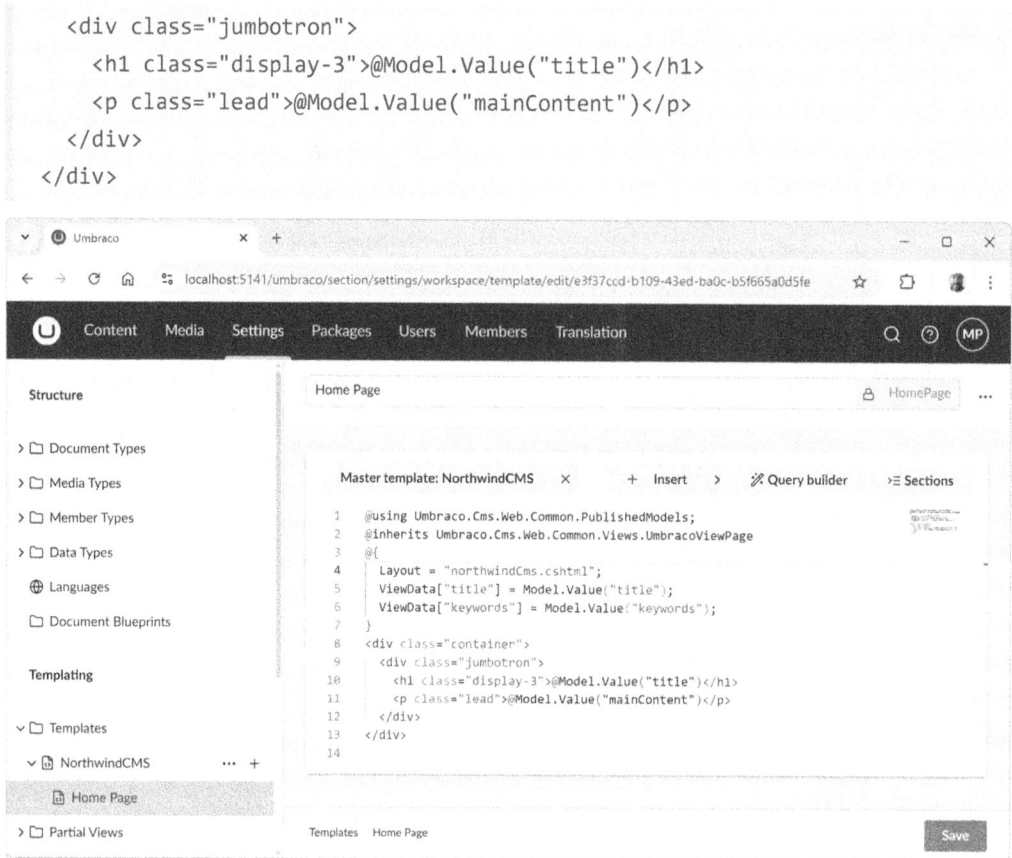

Figure 14.13: Editing the Home Page template

11. Click **Save**.

12. Optionally, when entering field values from the defined content type, instead of typing the expressions like Model.Value("title") manually, you can click the **Insert** button and complete a form, as shown in *Figure 14.14*:

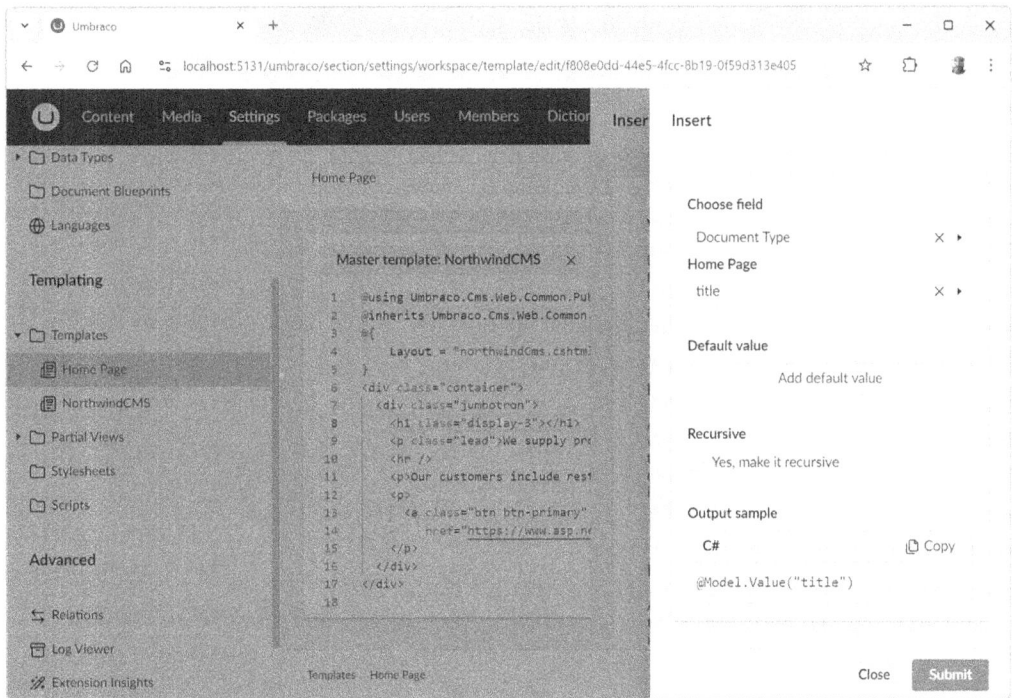

Figure 14.14: Insert feature building an expression to get a model property value

13. Click **Submit**.

Reviewing the website

I spent many years teaching developers how to implement a CMS, and you'd be surprised how many developers forget to publish their content when trying out their website, and then get confused when they view the website as a visitor and do not see their content. You are about to see this common mistake so that you recognize it and can fix it when you make the same mistake in the future.

So, let's review what a visitor would see at this point so that you can experience that and then know what we should have done:

1. In your browser, navigate to `https://localhost:5141/`, and note that the website does not yet have any published content, so it shows a standard page with a button to log in to the Umbraco back office, as shown in *Figure 14.15*:

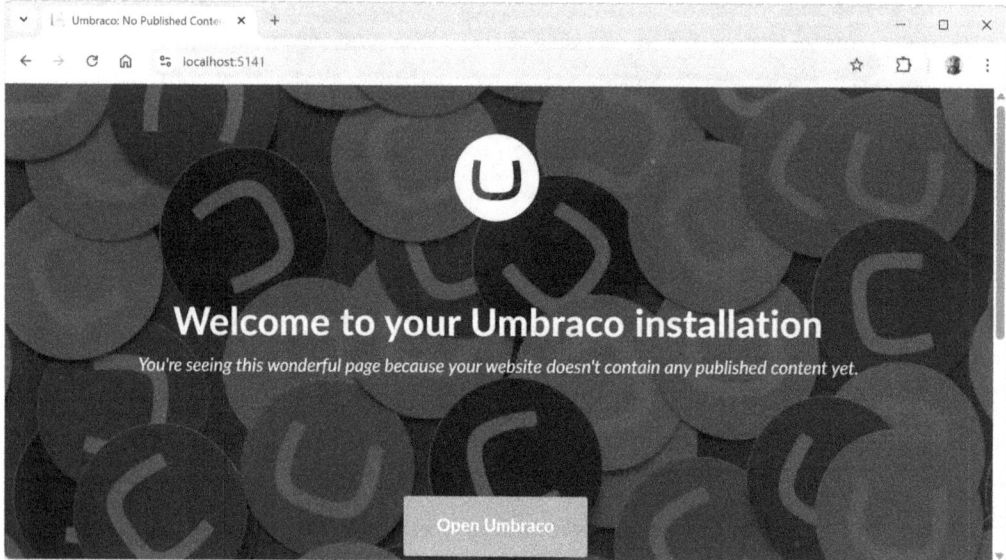

Figure 14.15: The website home page without published content

2. Click the **Open Umbraco** button.
3. If prompted to, enter your email and password and click **Login**.

Adding a home page as content

Now, we can add a home page for the default language, a.k.a. English (United States):

1. In the top navigation menu, click **Content**.
2. In the left navigation menu, click **+** or click **...** and then click **+ Create**.
3. In the **Create item under Content** pane, click **Home Page**.

4. Enter the name Home, and then set the following property values, as shown in the following list and *Figure 14.16*:

- **Title:** Hello World
- **Keywords:** home;welcome;northwind

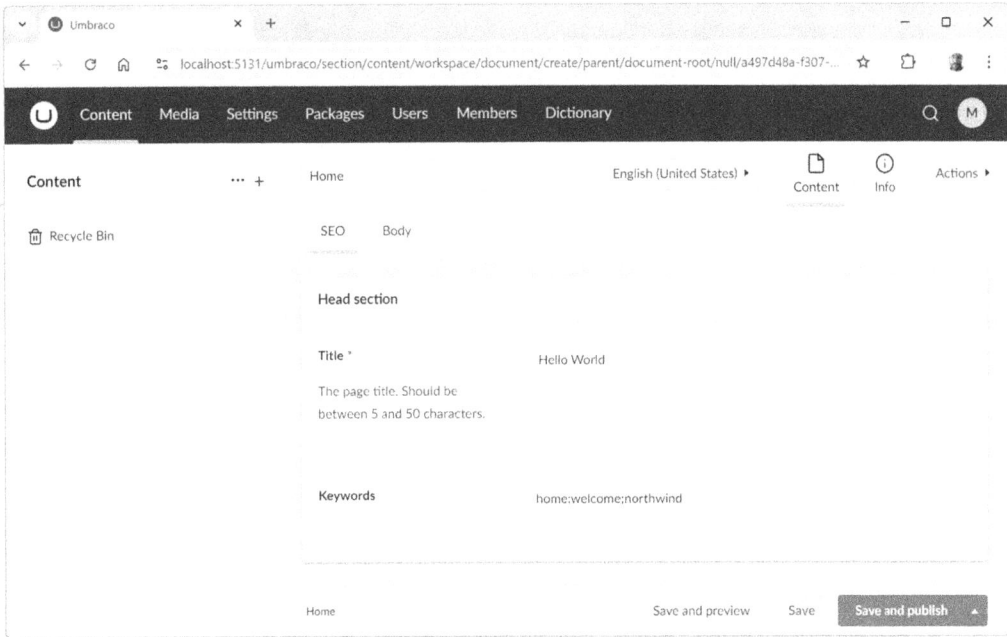

Figure 14.16: Creating a home page as content

5. Click the **Body** tab, and then enter some rich text in the **Main Content** property, as shown in *Figure 14.17*.

> You can learn more about Umbraco Rich Text Editor capabilities at the following link: https://docs.umbraco.com/umbraco-cms/tutorials/editors-manual/working-with-content.

6. In the top bar to the right side of the document name, **Home**, click **English (United States)**, and then select **+ French Not created**, as shown in *Figure 14.17*:

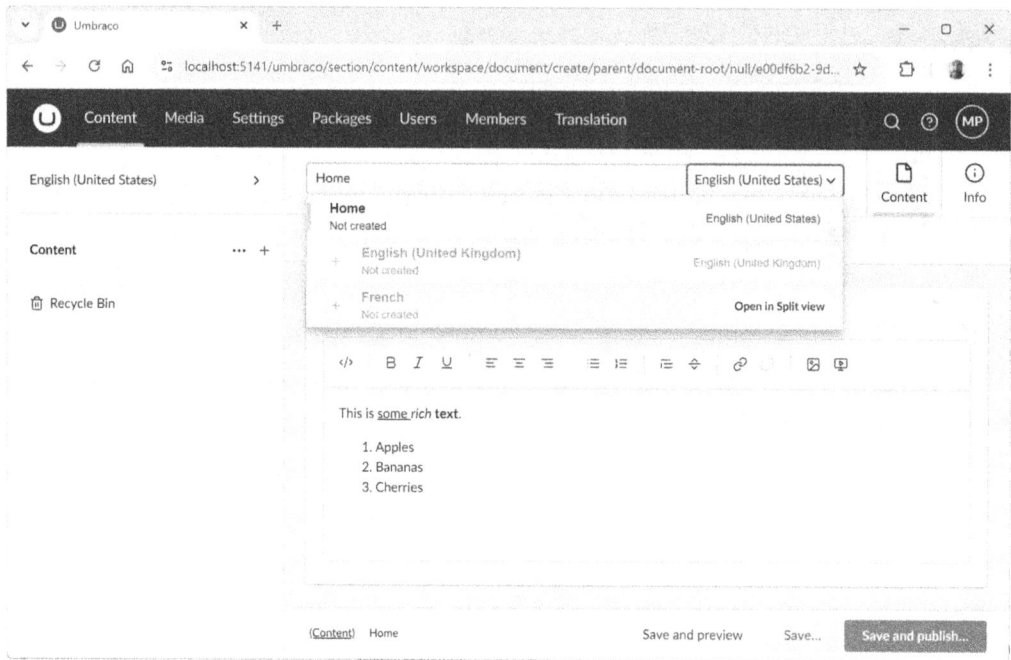

Figure 14.17: Creating a language variant

7. Set the document name to `Maison`, set **Title** to `Bonjour Monde`, and set **Main Content** to `C'est un texte riche`, with the word *riche* in bold and italics.

8. Click **Save and publish....**

9. In the **Save and publish** dialog box, note that the home page will have two languages published, US English and French, as shown in *Figure 14.18*:

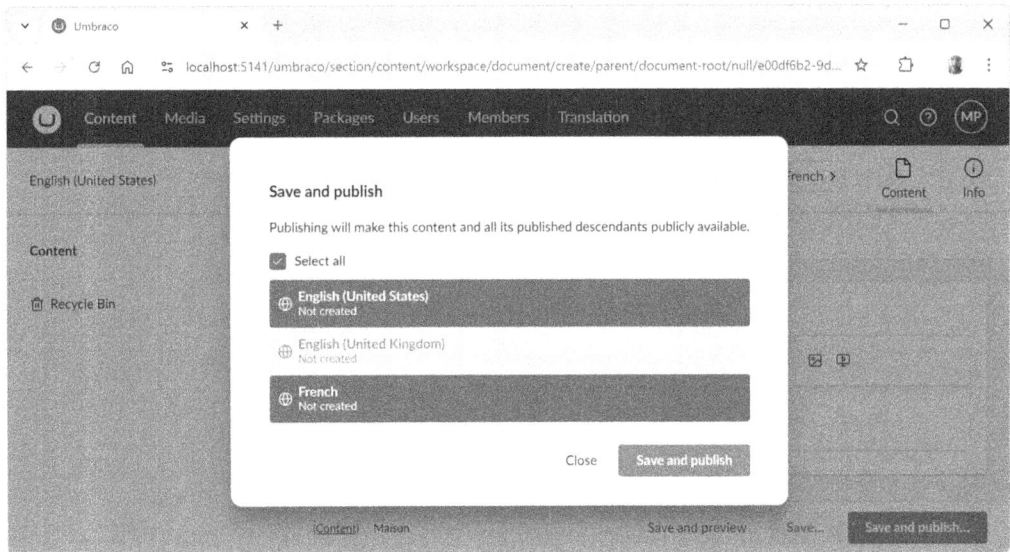

Figure 14.18: Saving and publishing English and French variants of the home page

10. Click **Save and publish**.

Configuring the French variant home page

Now, let's see how to configure the French variant of the home page:

1. In the top navigation, click **Content**.

2. In the left navigation, in the **Content** section, hover your mouse pointer over **Home**, click the
   ... button, and then in the menu, select **Culture and Hostnames**.

3. In the **Domains** section, click **Add new domain**.

4. Enter /fr and select **French**.

5. In the **Domains** section, click **Add new domain**.

6. Enter /en-gb and select **English (United Kingdom)**.

7. Confirm that you have defined two explicit domains using relative paths, as shown in *Figure 14.19*, and then click **Save**:

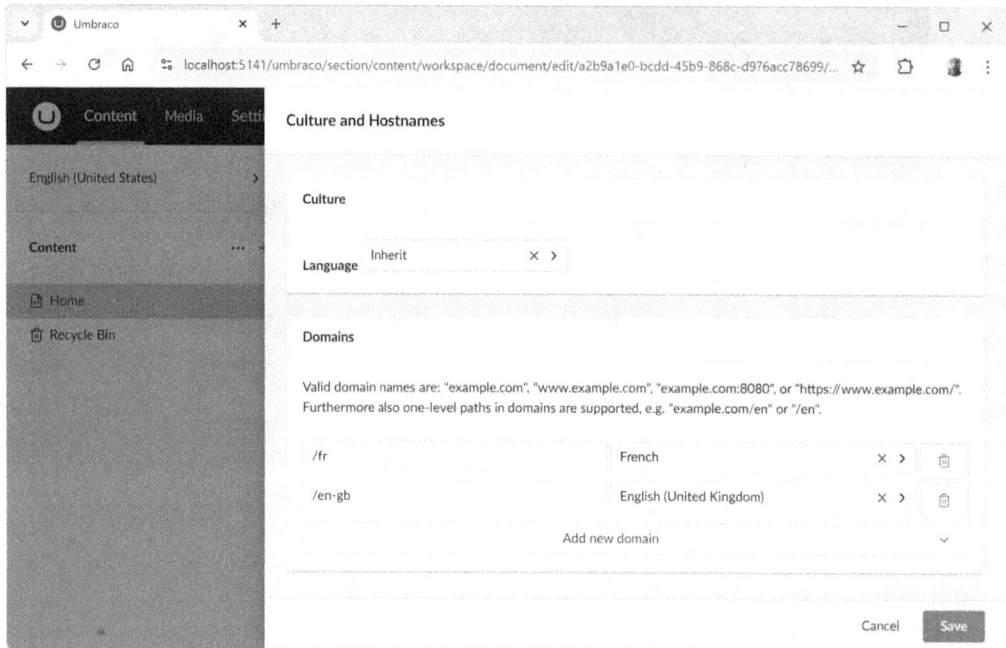

Figure 14.19: Two explicit domains using relative paths

8. In the **Content** section, click **Home**, click **Info**, and note that the **Home** page has been saved and published, and you can access it by clicking the / in the **Links** section, as shown in *Figure 14.20*:

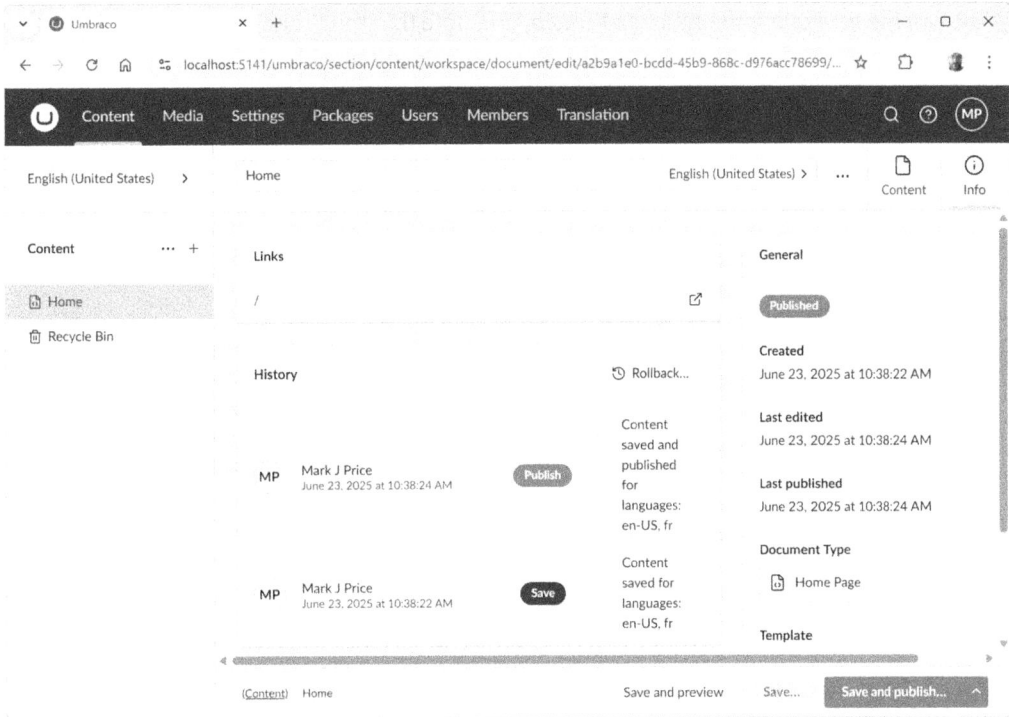

Figure 14.20: Links for multiple languages

9. Click the / link and note that a new table opens showing the English (United States) variant of the home page, as shown in *Figure 14.21*:

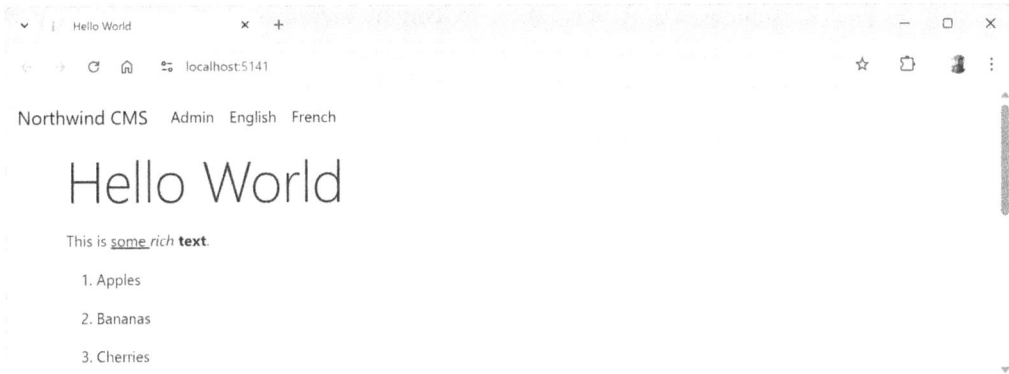

Figure 14.21: The home page content is published and visible to public visitors

10. In the navigation menu, click **French**, and note that the French language variant of the home page appears, and the address bar has been appended with /fr, as shown in *Figure 14.22*:

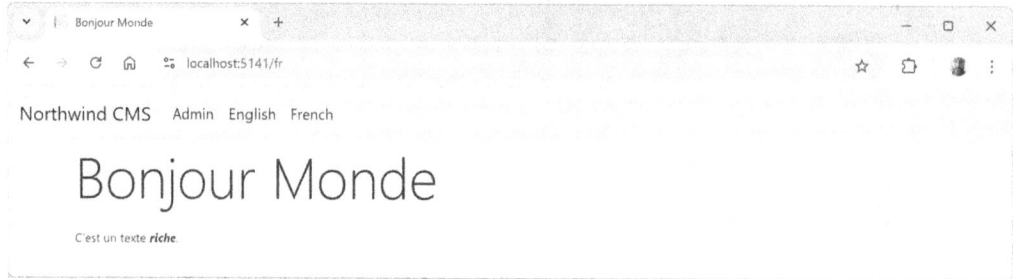

Figure 14.22: French variant of the home page

11. Optionally, create a British variant of the home page that says something like, *"Oi, Dizzy whirl, how's your pearl?"*

Making it easy for non-technical editors to create and manage their own content that conforms to nicely structured document types is very important. Just as important is to enable those editors to upload media and organize it well.

Working with media

Before we look at how to upload media to Umbraco, let's review some good practices for working with media.

Good media practices

Effective media management in Umbraco CMS keeps content organized, optimizes performance, and provides a consistent user experience. Here's some solid advice for editors and suggestions for custom features that a developer could implement to get the most out of Umbraco's media library.

Organizing media using folders

Organize media into folders by content type, year, project, or department. For instance, use separate folders for products, team photos, blogs, and so on. This structure will save editors time in locating files later.

But while folders are helpful, too many nested folders can make navigation cumbersome. Aim for a balance by using 1–2 levels of categorization. Developers could implement custom validation to enforce this.

Using tags to enhance searchability

Umbraco allows tagging media, which can make files easier to locate later. Tags like Product, Team, or Event help in filtering files when browsing the media library.

Administrators should establish a set of tags relevant to your content, and then editors should use them consistently to improve the searchability of assets across the team. Developers could implement custom validation to enforce rules to do this.

Optimizing image sizes before uploading

Avoid uploading full-resolution images directly from a camera or stock site. Instead, resize them to the actual display size you need, which reduces load times and saves storage.

Use tools like TinyPNG (https://tinypng.com/) or ImageOptim (https://imageoptim.com/) to compress images before uploading. Optimized images reduce bandwidth usage and load faster on the user end. As a developer, you may be asked to implement automatic image optimization, although it's usually better for the editors to have manual control.

Using meaningful filenames and alt text

Editors should name media files descriptively before uploading, for example, team-photo-john-doe. jpg instead of IMG_1234.jpg. This makes it easier to find files and is better for SEO. As a developer, you could write custom validation rules to enforce this.

Editors should always include alternative text for images to improve accessibility. In Umbraco, this can be done in the media properties. Alt text also helps search engines understand image content, boosting SEO. Again, a developer could enforce this.

Leveraging image cropping and variants

Umbraco allows you to set image crops for different aspect ratios, which is helpful for using the same image across various screen sizes and layouts. You can define crops like square, landscape, and portrait, and use them in different templates without needing separate files.

The cropper tool in Umbraco allows editors to preview how an image will appear in each variant. They should check each preview to ensure critical parts of the image remain in focus.

Avoiding duplicate media uploads

Duplicate images and files can clutter the media library and consume unnecessary storage. Always search the media library before uploading a new file to prevent duplicates. A developer could write an extension that integrates modern LLM-based image search to automate this process.

When images are used across multiple pages or documents, editors should link to the existing media rather than re-uploading it. This also helps maintain consistency across the site.

Removing unused media regularly

Editors should periodically review and delete unused or outdated files to keep the media library clean. Umbraco's media cleanup tools can help identify and remove orphaned media files.

Before deleting any media file, the editor should confirm it's not in use on any live page. Umbraco's media usage report can be useful here, as it identifies where each file is used across the site.

Using Umbraco's built-in permissions for media access

If certain teams or roles need access to specific folders, administrators should use Umbraco's permissions to limit access. This prevents accidental changes and reduces clutter for editors who don't need access to all media files.

Training editors on best practices and providing resources

Encourage all editors to follow these media guidelines and ensure they know how to use Umbraco's tools effectively. Regular training sessions can help reinforce good habits and introduce new features.

Uploading images to Umbraco CMS

Now, let's upload some images for use with our content:

1. In the top navigation menu, click **Media**.
2. Click **Create**, and then **Image**.
3. Enter the name Categories.
4. Click the **Click to upload** icon and browse to select categories.jpeg.
5. Click **Save**.

> All the category images are downloadable from the following link: https://github.com/markjprice/web-dev-net10/tree/main/code/images/Categories.

6. Repeat for the following names and files:
    *   **Beverages:** category1.jpeg
    *   **Condiments:** category2.jpeg
    *   **Confections:** category3.jpeg
    *   **Dairy Products:** category4.jpeg
    *   **Grains/Cereals:** category5.jpeg
    *   **Meat/Poultry:** category6.jpeg
    *   **Produce:** category7.jpeg
    *   **Seafood:** category8.jpeg

> These images are not named descriptively because they were used earlier in the book to render categories programmatically based on the `CategoryId` primary key value.

7. Navigate to **Content** and select **Home**.

8. Edit the **Body** | **Main Content**, and add the **Categories** image into the Rich Text Editor, as shown in *Figure 14.23*:

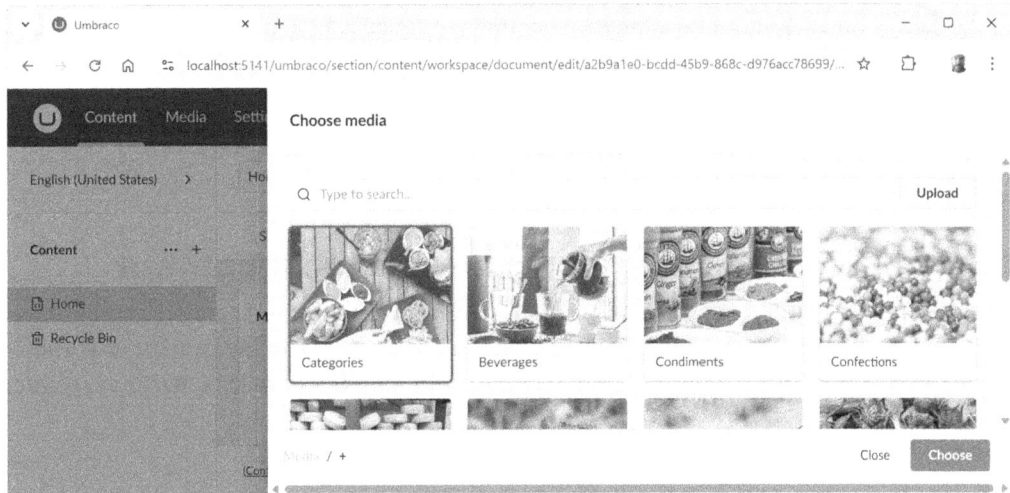

Figure 14.23: Adding an image to the Rich Text Editor

9. Click **Save and publish....**

10. View the home page on the website.

11. Right-click the image, select **Open image in new tab**, and note the path, as shown in *Figure 14.24*:

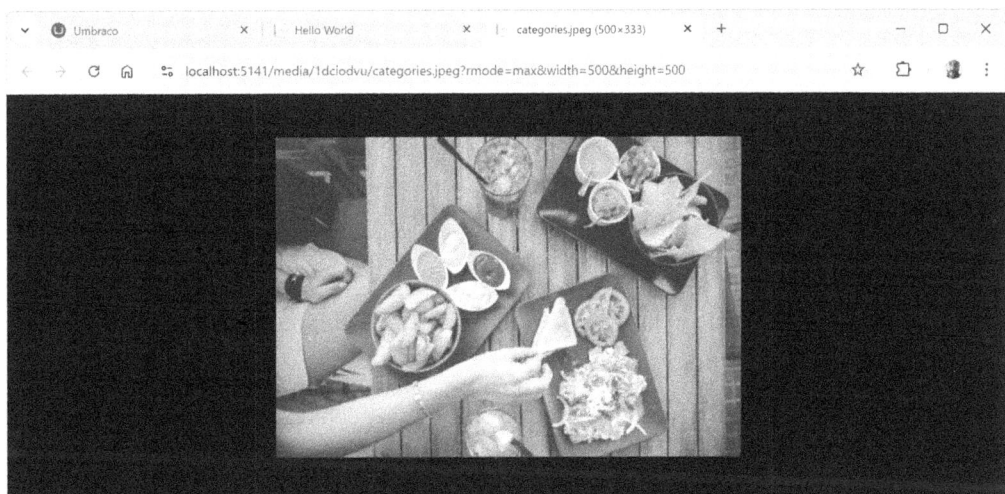

Figure 14.24: The path to an uploaded media file

12. Close the browser and shut down the web server.

> **Good practice:** Consider applying security access control or permissions to your uploaded media files to prevent misuse.

> Image optimization, like resizing and compressing, is important for faster website load times. You can learn more about these techniques in Ben Frain's *Responsive Web Design with HTML5 and CSS*.

Complex websites need a well-organized structure and easy navigation. Websites usually provide this via a content hierarchy.

Structuring and navigating hierarchical content

To generate a navigation menu in Umbraco CMS based on the structure defined by the content editor, you typically build a Razor partial view that reflects the hierarchy in the content tree. Here's how it works, step by step, using standard Umbraco APIs in an ASP.NET Core MVC Razor view setup.

Generating a navigation menu from structure

Let editors use the **Content** section to define pages like this:

```
- Home (allowed at root)
  - About Us
  - Services
    - Consulting
    - Training
  - Blog
  - Contact
```

Each of these pages is a content node of a document type that is allowed under **Home**. This hierarchy is exactly what we want to turn into a menu.

To be included in navigation, each page should:

- Have a template assigned.
- Be marked as "Visible in navigation" (optional but useful, more on this below).
- Be published.

You can add a Boolean property called something like hideFromNavigation to document types to give editors control over visibility.

Creating a document type for standard pages

Let's define a document type for the majority of pages on our website:

1. In the Umbraco back office, navigate to **Settings | Document Types**.

2. Click the **+**, or click **...** and then click **+ Create**. In the **Create an item under Document Types** pane, click **Document Type with Template**. Or click the **Create >** button and then choose **Document Type with Template**.

3. Enter a name and description for your content type, as shown in the following bullets:

   - Name: Standard Page
   - Description: The most commonly used page of the website.

4. Click **Save**.

5. Click **Settings** and select **Allow vary by culture**.

6. Click **Design**, click **+ Add tab**, and enter the name Body.

7. Click **Add property**.

8. In the **Add property** pane, fill in the values as shown in the following bullets:

   - **Enter a name:** Main Content
   - **Select Property Editor: Rich Text Editor (TipTap) | Richtexteditor**
   - **Variation | Shared across cultures:** Cleared
   - **Appearance: Label above (full-width)**

9. Click **Submit**.

10. Click **Add property**.

11. In the **Add property** pane, fill in the values as shown in the following bullets:

    - **Enter a name:** Is visible in menu
    - **Select Property Editor: Toggle | True/false**
    - **Variation | Shared across cultures:** Selected
    - **Appearance: Label above (full-width)**

12. Click **Submit**.

13. Click **Save**.

14. In the **Standard Page** toolbar, click **Structure**.

15. In the **Allow child node types** section, click **Choose**.

16. Select **Standard Page** and then click **Choose**.

17. Click **Save**.

18. Navigate to **Settings | Structure | Document Types | Home Page**.

19. In the **Home Page** toolbar, click **Structure**.

20. In the **Allow child node types** section, click **Choose**.

21. Select **Standard Page** and then click **Choose**.

22. Click **Save**.

23. Navigate to **Settings | Templating | Templates | Standard Page**.

24. Set the **Master template** to **NorthwindCMS**, and provide a basic template to render the page name and body, as shown in the following markup:

```
@using Umbraco.Cms.Web.Common.PublishedModels;
@inherits Umbraco.Cms.Web.Common.Views.UmbracoViewPage
@{
        Layout = "northwindCms.cshtml";
}
<div class="container">
  <div class="jumbotron">
    <h1 class="display-3">@Model.Value("name")</h1>
    <p class="lead">@Model.Value("mainContent")</p>
  </div>
</div>
```

25. Click **Save**.

Adding standard pages as content

Now, we can add a home page for the default language, a.k.a. English (United States):

1. In the top navigation menu, click **Content**.

2. In the left navigation menu, hover your mouse pointer over **Home**, click + or click **...**, and then click **+ Create**.

3. In the **Create item under Home** pane, click **Standard Page**, as shown in *Figure 14.25*:

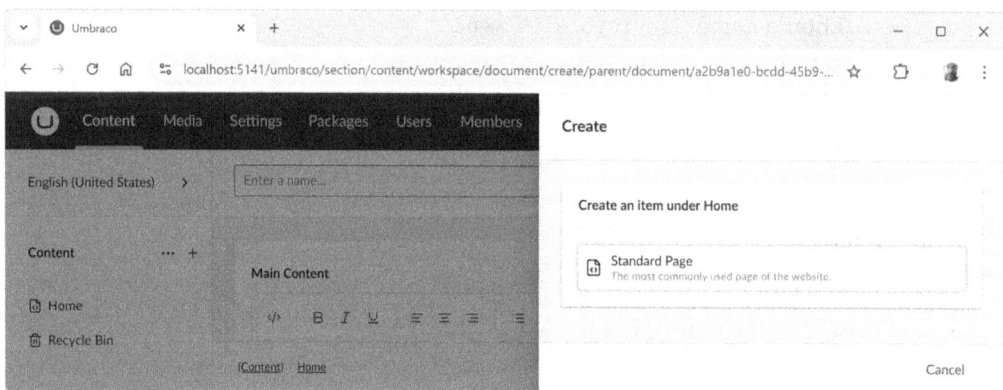

Figure 14.25: Creating a standard page under Home

4. Enter the name About Us, and then enter some rich text in the **Main Content** property.

5. Select the French page, set its name to À propos de nous, and enter some rich text.

6. Click **Save and publish....**

7. Review the two languages that will be published and then click **Save and publish**.

8. Create a few more standard pages directly under **Home**:

   - **Products / Produits**
   - **Blog / Bloguer**
   - **Contact Us / Contactez-nous**

9. Close the browser and shut down the web server.

Creating a Razor Partial View for navigation

Now we can add a basic Razor partial view to render the main navigation menu:

1. In the Northwind.Cms project, in the Views\Partials folder, add a new folder named Navigation.

2. In the Navigation folder, add a new **Razor View - Empty** named _Menu.cshtml.

3. In _Menu.cshtml, add statements to get the direct child content nodes of the **Home** page and then render them as clickable hyperlinks, as shown in the following code:

```
@using Umbraco.Cms.Web.Common.PublishedModels
@inherits Umbraco.Cms.Web.Common.Views.UmbracoViewPage<IPublishedContent>
@{
  IPublishedContent root = Model.Root(); // Usually "Home".

  IEnumerable<IPublishedContent> level1Items =
    root.Children().Where(x => x.IsVisible());
}
@if (level1Items is not null)
{
  foreach (IPublishedContent item in level1Items)
  {
    <a class="nav-link active" aria-current="page"
       href="@item.Url()">@item.Name</a>
  }
}
```

4. In the Views folder, in northwindCms.cshtml, render the menu after the Admin and language menu items, as shown highlighted in the following markup:

```
<div class="navbar-nav">
  <a class="nav-link active" aria-current="page" href="/umbraco">Admin</
a>
  <a class="nav-link active" aria-current="page" href="/">English</a>
  <a class="nav-link active" aria-current="page" href="/fr">French</a>
  @await Html.PartialAsync("Partials/Navigation/_Menu", Model)
</div>
```

5. Start the `Northwind.Cms` project using the `Umbraco.Web.UI` launch profile without debugging.

6. Use the navigation menu to switch between the pages, as shown in *Figure 14.26*:

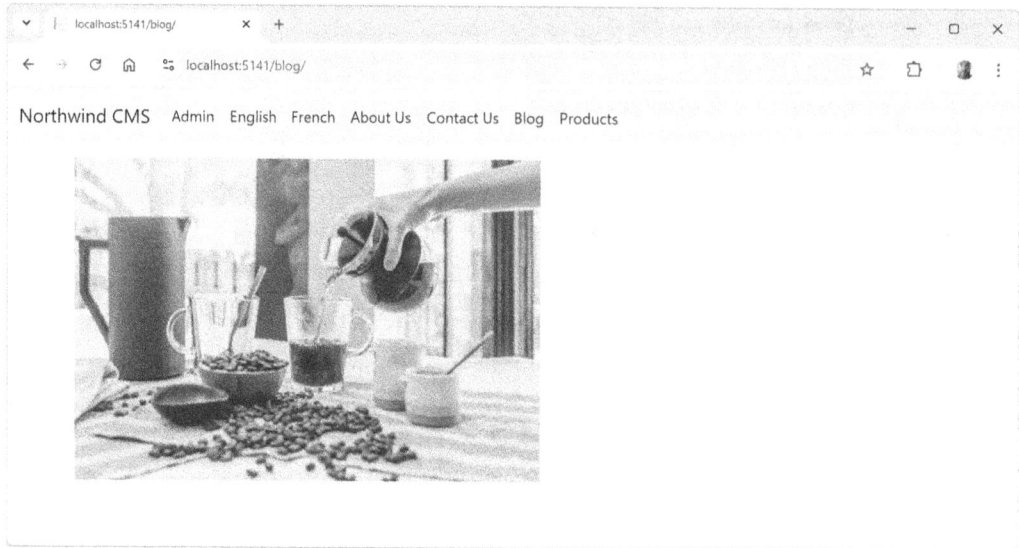

Figure 14.26: Switching between pages using the navigation menu

Practicing and exploring

Test your knowledge and understanding by answering some questions, getting some hands-on practice, and exploring this chapter's topics with deeper research.

Exercise 14.1 – Online material

You can learn more about Umbraco CMS at the following links:

- Umbraco CMS documentation: `https://docs.umbraco.com/umbraco-cms`

- Editor's Manual: `https://docs.umbraco.com/umbraco-cms/tutorials/editors-manual`

- Learn about scheduled publishing: `https://docs.umbraco.com/umbraco-cms/fundamentals/data/scheduled-publishing`

- Learn about dictionary items for translating text into different languages: `https://docs.umbraco.com/umbraco-cms/fundamentals/data/dictionary-items`

- Learn about relations for structuring the content tree: `https://docs.umbraco.com/umbraco-cms/fundamentals/data/relations`

Exercise 14.2 – Practice exercises

The following practice exercises help you to explore the topics in this chapter more deeply.

Define a document type for a blog entry with the following properties:

- **Title:** Text string for the blog post title
- **Body Text:** Rich Text Editor for the main content of the post
- **Author:** Text string or content picker for the author's name or profile
- **Publish Date:** Date picker for when the post should be published
- **Tags:** Multiple text strings or tags for categorizing the post
- **Featured Image:** Media picker for the main image associated with the post

Exercise 14.3 – Test your knowledge

Answer the following questions:

1. What are some basic features that every CMS would have?
2. For how long are Umbraco LTS releases supported?
3. How do you make Umbraco CMS available as a .NET project template?
4. What does the `BootUmbracoAsync` method do?
5. What is the relative path to the Umbraco back office?
6. What sections of the Umbraco back office can a member of the `Editors` user group access?
7. In Umbraco, what is a document type, and what are its three main components or aspects?
8. In the settings for a content type, why might you select the **Allow vary by culture** checkbox?
9. What syntax is used to define an Umbraco content template?
10. What are two ways of organizing media?

Exercise 14.4 – Explore topics

Follow this link to learn more about the topics covered in this chapter:

`https://github.com/markjprice/web-dev-net10/blob/main/docs/book-links.md#chapter-14--web-content-management-using-umbraco-cms`.

Summary

In this chapter, you learned how to:

- Create an Umbraco project
- Define a document type with properties
- Define a document template that renders properties in HTML
- Set up multiple languages and create language variants of content

In the next chapter, you will learn how to customize Umbraco websites.

15

Customizing and Extending Umbraco CMS

This chapter is about customizing and extending Umbraco. There are many examples of doing this because almost every project needs some kind of customization beyond what's built in. But it's therefore also tricky to provide examples that do not get too complex and obscure for an intermediate-level book.

I am keen to get feedback from readers about the Umbraco CMS content in this book. Please either raise an issue in the book's GitHub repository or leave a message in the Discord channel. I want to hear if you use Umbraco or other third-party platforms, and if I should go even deeper into Umbraco or cover something else.

This chapter will cover the following topics:

- Techniques for customizing and extending Umbraco
- Customizing Umbraco behavior using settings
- Working with MVC views and Razor syntax
- The UmbracoHelper class
- Headless mode with Delivery API

Techniques for customizing and extending Umbraco

Let's review, in theory, a few real-life advanced example techniques that illustrate the flexibility and scalability that Umbraco offers.

Building custom property editors for enhanced content creation

Imagine a media company that needs to manage a vast library of multimedia assets, like videos, images, and audio, within Umbraco. Standard property editors are too limited for this purpose, as the media company needs advanced metadata tagging, file categorization, and asset previews right within the editor.

A potential solution would be to build custom property editors using Blazor (or another client framework like React) and Umbraco's APIs, allowing content editors to add metadata tags, preview files, and categorize assets easily. These custom editors could dramatically improve the efficiency of the content team at a low cost by centralizing asset management and minimizing the need for third-party tools.

The company streamlines its workflow, improves content discoverability, and maintains consistency across its platform, demonstrating the power of customization in simplifying complex tasks.

Integrating third-party APIs to enhance functionality

Imagine an e-commerce website using Umbraco where the company wants to integrate real-time currency conversion for international customers, which isn't available in the standard Umbraco setup.

The solution could be to develop a custom plugin that integrates with a third-party currency conversion API, so the team can enable real-time currency updates directly within Umbraco's backend. The developers would build the plugin using .NET, leveraging Umbraco's extension points to manage configurations and update rates.

This integration would provide a seamless user experience for international customers and reduce manual data entry for editors. This example shows how external services can be woven into Umbraco to expand its capabilities.

Custom workflow automation for content approval

A large organization with a layered content approval process might need a customized workflow where different roles would approve specific content types before they go live.

Using Umbraco's workflow customization capabilities, a developer could build a custom workflow to handle multiple stages of content approval. This might involve creating a content approval plugin that incorporates notifications, conditional approvals, and escalation rules. It could use Umbraco's Events API and additional .NET code to automate role-specific approvals and notify the relevant team members.

The custom workflow would reduce approval time, minimize errors, and ensure that content is reviewed by the correct teams, and is a great example of Umbraco's adaptability for large-scale enterprise needs.

Multilingual capabilities with custom language switching

A tourism board needs a multi-language site where visitors can easily switch between languages without losing their place on a page, which is not fully supported by default in Umbraco.

The development team could create a language-switching module that saves a user's location on the page and then dynamically loads the equivalent content in the selected language. They extend Umbraco's language management capabilities and incorporate session handling to maintain the current page state as users switch languages.

This custom approach provides a smooth multilingual experience, deemed crucial for the tourism board's diverse audience, keeping visitors on the site and booking holidays.

Each of these examples highlights the ways Umbraco can be customized and extended to solve unique business problems. But all the preceding examples are advanced, requiring quite deep knowledge of Umbraco and how it works, and are therefore beyond the scope of this book. So now, let's see some built-in settings that can tweak the behavior of Umbraco with minimal effort.

Customizing Umbraco behavior using settings

Umbraco has hundreds of settings that can be configured to customize its behavior. Settings are grouped into categories, including the following main ones:

- **Content settings**: For example, allowed upload file types, allowed image file types or autofill image properties, visuals like the background image shown on the login page, and so on.
- **Security settings**: For example, whether to keep users logged in, password rules, and so on.
- **Imaging settings**: Configure the browser cache and resize settings for processed images on your project.
- **Global settings**: Configure the default UI language, reserved links, and so on.

Content settings

Content settings include settings such as allowed upload file types, image settings, and more. All the values in the content settings have default values, so all configuration is optional.

An `appsettings.json` file that shows the default values of content settings in Umbraco is shown in the following file:

```
"Umbraco": {
  "CMS": {
    "Content": {
      "ContentVersionCleanupPolicy": {
        "EnableCleanup": false,
        "KeepAllVersionsNewerThanDays": 7,
        "KeepLatestVersionPerDayForDays": 90
      },
      "AllowEditInvariantFromNonDefault": true,
      "AllowedUploadFiles": [],
      "AllowedMediaHosts":  [],
      "AllowedUploadedFileExtensions": [],
      "DisableDeleteWhenReferenced": false,
```

```
      "DisableUnpublishWhenReferenced": false,
      "DisallowedUploadFiles": ["ashx", "aspx", "ascx", "config", "cshtml",
"vbhtml", "asmx", "air", "axd", "xamlx"],
      "DisallowedUploadedFileExtensions": ["ashx", "aspx", "ascx", "config",
"cshtml", "vbhtml", "asmx", "air", "axd", "xamlx"],
      "Error404Collection": [],
      "HideBackOfficeLogo": false,
      "Imaging": {
        "ImageFileTypes": ["jpeg", "jpg", "gif", "bmp", "png", "tiff", "tif"],
        "AutoFillImageProperties": [
          {
            "Alias": "umbracoFile",
            "ExtensionFieldAlias": "umbracoExtension",
            "HeightFieldAlias": "umbracoHeight",
            "LengthFieldAlias": "umbracoBytes",
            "WidthFieldAlias": "umbracoWidth"
          }
        ]
      },
      "LoginBackgroundImage": "login/login.jpg",
      "LoginLogoImage": "login/logo_light.svg",
      "LoginLogoImageAlternative": "login/logo_dark.svg",
      "Notifications": {
        "DisableHtmlEmail": false,
        "Email": null
      },
      "PreviewBadge": "<![CDATA[<b>My HTML here</b>]]>",
      "ResolveUrlsFromTextString": false,
      "ShowDeprecatedPropertyEditors": false,
      "ShowDomainWarnings": true
    }
  }
}
```

Some of the content settings are shown in *Table 15.1*:

Setting	Description
Content version cleanup policy	The global settings for the scheduled job that cleans historic content versions. These settings can be overridden per document type. Current draft and published versions will never be removed, nor will individual content versions that have been marked as `preventCleanup`.
	If you don't wish to retain any content versions except for the current draft and those currently published, you can set both of the `keep` settings values to 0. After doing this, the next time the scheduled job runs (hourly), all non-current versions (except those marked `preventCleanup`) will be removed.
Allow edit invariant from non-default	Invariant properties are properties on a multilingual site that are not varied by culture. This means that they share the same value across all languages added to the website.
	When the setting is set to `false`, the invariant properties that are shared between all languages can only be edited from the default language. This means you need access to the default language in order to edit the property.
	When set to `true` (default), the invariant properties will need to be unlocked before they can be edited. The lock exists in order to make it clear that this change will affect more languages.
Allowed upload files	If provided, only files with these extensions can be uploaded via the backoffice.
Allowed media hosts	By default, only relative URLs are allowed when getting URLs for resized images or thumbnails using `ImagesController`. If you need absolute URLs, you will have to add the allowed hosts to this list. For example, the value could be `["northwind.com", "www.northwind.com", "images.northwind.com"]`.
Disable delete when referenced	This allows you to specify whether a user can delete content or media items that depend on other items. This also includes any descendants that have dependencies. Setting this to `true` will remove or disable the delete button.
Disable unpublish when referenced	This allows you to specify whether or not users can unpublish content items that depend on other items or have descendants that have dependencies. Setting this to `true` will disable the unpublish button.
Disallowed upload files	This setting consists of a list of file extensions that editors shouldn't be allowed to upload via the backoffice. This is important to prevent users from uploading malicious files. By default, it lists extensions for dynamically executable ASP.NET Core files, like Web Forms and Razor files.

Error 404 collection	In case of a 404 error (page not found), Umbraco can return a default page instead. This is set here. Notice you can also set a different error page, based on the current culture, so a 404 page can be returned in the correct language.
	
	`"Error404Collection": [ { "ContentId": 1, "Culture": "en-US" },`
	
	`{ "ContentId": 34, "Culture": "fr-CA" } ]`

Login background image and logo image	You can specify your own background image and the small logo in the top-left corner of the login screen, which is a common requirement for organizations with strong brands. These paths are relative to the `wwwroot/umbraco` path.
Show domain warnings	If you do not configure domains for each language on a multilingual site, then every time you publish your content, you get a warning.

Table 15.1: Content settings

Security settings

This allows you to configure all matters related to security, for example, whether to keep users logged in, password rules, and more.

An `appsettings.json` file that shows the default values of security settings in Umbraco is shown in the following file:

```json
"Umbraco": {
  "CMS": {
    "Security": {
      "KeepUserLoggedIn": false,
      "HideDisabledUsersInBackOffice": false,
      "AllowPasswordReset": true,
      "AuthCookieName": "UMB_UCONTEXT",
      "AuthCookieDomain": "",
      "UsernameIsEmail": true,
      "UserPassword": {
        "RequiredLength": 10,
        "RequireNonLetterOrDigit": false,
        "RequireDigit": false,
        "RequireLowercase": false,
        "RequireUppercase": false,
        "HashAlgorithmType": "PBKDF2.ASPNETCORE.V3",
        "MaxFailedAccessAttemptsBeforeLockout": 5
      },
      "MemberPassword": {
        "RequiredLength": 10,
        "RequireNonLetterOrDigit": false,
        "RequireDigit": false,
```

```
        "RequireLowercase": false,
        "RequireUppercase": false,
        "HashAlgorithmType": "PBKDF2.ASPNETCORE.V3",
        "MaxFailedAccessAttemptsBeforeLockout": 5
    },
    "UserDefaultLockoutTimeInMinutes": 43200,
    "MemberDefaultLockoutTimeInMinutes": 43200,
    "AllowConcurrentLogins": false
  }
 }
}
```

Some of the security settings are shown in *Table 15.2*:

Setting	Description
Keep user logged in	When set to false, a user will be logged out after a specific amount of time has passed with no activity. You can specify this time span in the global settings with the `TimeOut` key.
Hide disabled users in the backoffice	When this is set to true, it's not possible to see disabled users. This means it's not possible to re-enable their access to the backoffice again. It also means you can't create an identical username if the user was disabled by mistake.
Allow password reset	This feature allows users to reset their passwords if they have forgotten them. By default, this is enabled. It can be disabled at both the UI and API level by setting this value to `false`.
Username is email	This setting specifies whether the username and email address are separate fields in the backoffice editor. When set to `false`, you can specify an email address and username, but only the username can be used to log on. When set to `true` (the default value), the username is hidden and always the same as the email address.
User and member password settings	This lets you define the password rules for users and members; for example, the minimum length a user password is allowed to be, the required special characters, and the maximum amount of failed password attempts allowed before the user is locked out of the site.
User and member default lockout time	Use this setting to configure how long a user is locked out of the Umbraco backoffice when a lockout occurs. The setting accepts an integer, which defines the lockout in minutes. The default lockout time for users is 30 days (43,200 minutes).
Allow concurrent logins	When set to `false`, any user account is prevented from having multiple simultaneous sessions. In this mode, only one session per user can be active at any given time. This enhances security and prevents concurrent logins with the same user credentials.

Table 15.2: Security settings

Imaging settings

The options in the imaging section allow you to configure the cache and resize settings for processed images on your project (using `ImageSharp.Web` as the default implementation). If you need to configure allowed image file types or autofill image properties, you want to use content settings instead.

An `appsettings.json` file that shows the default values of imaging settings in Umbraco is shown in the following file:

```
"Umbraco": {
  "CMS": {
    "Imaging": {
      "Cache": {
        "BrowserMaxAge": "7.00:00:00",
        "CacheMaxAge": "365.00:00:00",
        "CacheFolderDepth": 8,
        "CacheHashLength": 12,
        "CacheFolder": "~/umbraco/Data/TEMP/MediaCache"
      },
      "Resize": {
        "MaxWidth": 5000,
        "MaxHeight": 5000
      }
    }
  }
}
```

Some of the imaging settings are shown in *Table 15.3*:

Setting	Description
Cache	This contains configuration for browser and server caching. When changing these cache headers, it is recommended to clear your media cache. This is due to the data being stored in the cache and not updated when the configuration is changed.
Browser max age	This specifies how long a requested processed image may be stored in the browser cache by using this value in the `Cache-Control` response header. The default is seven days (formatted as a timespan).
Cache max age	This specifies how long a processed image may be used from the server cache before it needs to be re-processed again. The default is one year (365 days, formatted as a timespan).
Cache folder depth	This gets or sets the depth of the nested cache folder structure to store the images. Defaults to eight.

Cache hash length	This gets or sets the length of the filename to use (minus the extension) when storing images in the image cache. Defaults to 12 characters.
Cache folder	This allows you to specify the location of the cached images folder. By default, the cached images are stored in ~/umbraco/Data/TEMP/MediaCache. The tilde (~) resolves to the content root of your project/application.
Resize | Max width/max height	This specifies the maximum width and height an image can be resized to. If the requested width and height are both above the configured maximums, no resizing will be performed. This adds basic security to prevent resizing to big dimensions and using a lot of server CPU/memory to do so.

Table 15.3: Imaging settings

Global settings

The options in the global section allow you to configure the default UI language, reserved links, and much more. All of these, except for SMTP settings, contain default values, meaning that all configuration is optional unless you wish to send emails from your site.

An appsettings.json file that shows the default values of global settings in Umbraco is shown in the following file:

```
"Umbraco": {
  "CMS": {
    "Global": {
      "ReservedUrls": "~/.well-known,",
      "ReservedPaths": "~/app_plugins/,~/install/,~/mini-profiler-resources/,~/
umbraco/,",
      "TimeOut": "00:20:00",
      "DefaultUILanguage": "en-US",
      "HideTopLevelNodeFromPath": true,
      "UseHttps": false,
      "VersionCheckPeriod": 7,
      "IconsPath": "~/umbraco/assets/icons",
      "UmbracoCssPath": "~/css",
      "UmbracoScriptsPath": "~/scripts",
      "UmbracoMediaPath": "~/media",
      "UmbracoMediaPhysicalRootPath": "X:/Shared/Media",
      "InstallMissingDatabase": false,
      "DisableElectionForSingleServer": false,
      "DatabaseFactoryServerVersion": "SqlServer.V2019",
      "MainDomLock": "FileSystemMainDomLock",
      "MainDomKeyDiscriminator": "",
      "Id": "184a8175-bc0b-43dd-8267-d99871eaec3d",
      "NoNodesViewPath": "~/umbraco/UmbracoWebsite/NoNodes.cshtml",
```

```
        "Smtp": {
          "From": "person@umbraco.dk",
          "Host": "localhost",
          "Port": 25,
          "SecureSocketOptions": "Auto",
          "DeliveryMethod": "Network",
          "PickupDirectoryLocation": "",
          "Username": "person@umbraco.dk",
          "Password": "SuperSecretPassword"
        },
        "DatabaseServerRegistrar": {
          "WaitTimeBetweenCalls": "00:01:00",
          "StaleServerTimeout": "00:02:00"
        },
        "DatabaseServerMessenger": {
          "MaxProcessingInstructionCount": 1000,
          "TimeToRetainInstructions": "2.00:00:00",
          "TimeBetweenSyncOperations": "00:00:05",
          "TimeBetweenPruneOperations": "00:01:00"
        },
        "DistributedLockingMechanism": "",
        "DistributedLockingReadLockDefaultTimeout": "00:01:00",
        "DistributedLockingWriteLockDefaultTimeout": "00:00:05",
      }
    }
  }
```

Some of the global settings are shown in *Table 15.4*:

Setting	Description
Reserved URLs	A comma-separated list of files or URLs to be left alone by Umbraco; these files will be served and the Umbraco request pipeline will not be triggered.
Reserved paths	A comma-separated list of all the folders in your directory to be left alone by Umbraco. If you have folders with custom files, add them to this setting to make sure Umbraco leaves them alone.
Timeout	Configure the session timeout to determine how much time without a request being made can pass before the user is required to log in again. The session timeout format needs to be set as HH:MM:SS. Any activity within the backoffice will reset the timer.
Version check period	This controls how frequently the system checks for updates or new versions of Umbraco CMS. By default, Umbraco will check for a new version every 7 days.

Umbraco icon resources, CSS, scripts, and media paths	By adding this, you can specify a new/different folder for storing your CSS, script, and media files, and still be able to edit them within Umbraco. By default, static content will only be served from the wwwroot folder.
No nodes view path	This specifies what view to render when there is no content on the site.
SMTP settings	This enables you to be able to send out emails from your Umbraco installation. This could be notification emails if you are using content workflow, or, if you are using Umbraco Forms, you also need to specify SMTP settings to be able to use the email workflows. The forgot password function from the backoffice also needs an SMTP server to send the email with the reset link.
Database server registrar settings, messenger, and distributed locking mechanism	It's unlikely that you will have to change these settings unless you're using a load-balanced setup.

Table 15.4: Global settings

Content version cleanup

Whenever you save and publish a content item in Umbraco, a new version is generated. This allows you to roll back to any previous version when needed. Each saved version creates an entry in the database, not just for the version itself but also for each property of the content item in that version. In a multi-lingual site, additional rows are added for each cultural variation.

Over time, this accumulation of data can grow significantly, consuming your SQL Server's resources and potentially impacting the performance of the Umbraco backoffice, although the performance of the website from a visitor's perspective should not be affected.

The default cleanup policy follows these rules:

- It retains all versions created within the last seven days, preserving recent version history. This is controlled by the KeepAllVersionsNewerThanDays setting.
- After seven days, it prunes older versions, keeping only the last version saved each day while deleting earlier versions from that day.
- Versions older than 90 days are deleted. This is governed by the KeepLatestVersionPerDayForDays setting.
- Published versions are never deleted.
- Versions specifically marked with preventCleanup in the backoffice version history are also never deleted.

For an individual content type, you can override the global settings.

Cleanup is performed by a scheduled job. Scheduled jobs are typically triggered at defined intervals, such as every hour, daily, or weekly. The timing can be managed directly in Umbraco for some tasks or configured more precisely using custom code.

You can learn more about scheduled jobs at the following link: `https://docs.umbraco.com/umbraco-cms/reference/scheduling`.

Working with views and Razor syntax

All Umbraco views inherit from `UmbracoViewPage<ContentModels.NameOfYourDocType>` in the `Umbraco.Cms.Web.Common.Views` namespace. If you use the following statement:

```
@using ContentModels = Umbraco.Cms.Web.Common.PublishedModels
```

This gives you access to various properties that can be used in Razor. You can access the properties of the document type in several ways:

- `@Model` (of type `Umbraco.Web.Mvc.ContentModel`): This is the model for the view, which contains the standard list of `IPublishedContent` properties and gives access to the strongly typed current page (of the type you defined in the angled brackets).
- `@Umbraco` (of type `UmbracoHelper`): Provides many useful methods, such as rendering fields or retrieving content by ID, along with many other helpful features.
- `@Html` (of type `HtmlHelper`): This is the familiar `HtmlHelper` in ASP.NET Core, enhanced with additional extension methods like `@Html.BeginUmbracoForm`.
- `@UmbracoContext` (of type `Umbraco.Cms.Web.Common.UmbracoContext`): This provides context for Umbraco within the current session.

Learn more about the `UmbracoContext` helper at the following link: `https://docs.umbraco.com/umbraco-cms/reference/querying/umbraco-context`.

What is IPublishedContent?

`IPublishedContent` is a core interface in Umbraco CMS that represents a piece of content or media in a structured, strongly typed way. It's one of the main ways that developers interact with content within Umbraco, allowing you to access fields, properties, and metadata of pages, media items, or members directly in their Razor views or custom code.

Core functionality of IPublishedContent

`IPublishedContent` represents a published version of content, meaning that it only deals with content that has been published, but not draft or unpublished versions of content. `IPublishedContent` is used across the board in Umbraco for content types like pages, posts, media items (images, videos), and members (registered visitors on a website).

IPublishedContent provides several properties and methods that allow you to access various parts of the content item. Here are some of the most commonly used ones:

- Name: The name or title of the content item. This property is useful for displaying page titles, media names, and so on. If you call the Name() method, then you can pass a culture to get the name in alternative languages.
- Url: The link to the content item. This is useful for linking to pages or media directly. You can pass a culture to get the link in alternative languages.
- Id: An int unique identifier for the content item within Umbraco CMS.
- ContentType: This represents the type of content, like Article, BlogPost, and so on. This is useful so that you can know what fields or properties might be available.
- CreateDate, UpdateDate: This returns the DateTime that the content was created/last updated.
- Children: A collection of child items, which allows you to retrieve and iterate over items that are nested under the current item in the content tree.
- Parent: The parent node, which lets you traverse back up the content hierarchy.
- Level: The tree level (depth) of the content item.
- Properties: A collection of all properties associated with the content, including custom fields defined in the Umbraco backoffice, like bodyText, heroImage, and so on.
- Value<T>(propertyAlias): This method retrieves the value of a specific property on the content item in a strongly typed way. This is particularly helpful for accessing custom properties.

Let's see some example usage that gets the name, link, and a custom field containing the rich text body of a content page, as shown in the following code:

```
string title = Model.Name; // Or Model.Name("fr-FR").
string url = Model.Url();
string bodyText = Model.Value<string>("bodyText");
```

IPublishedContent provides a strongly typed, consistent interface for content retrieval, minimizing the risk of runtime errors. Since it has properties for accessing parent and child items, it's straightforward to navigate through nested structures like page hierarchies.

Umbraco's caching system uses IPublishedContent to efficiently load published content, improving page load speeds and performance by reducing the need for database lookups.

Using IPublishedContent with ModelsBuilder

When using ModelsBuilder (Umbraco's code-generation tool), IPublishedContent is automatically extended with strongly typed models, meaning you can access properties directly without needing Value<T>(). ModelsBuilder generates classes for each content type, making code easier to read and maintain:

```
@Model.Title // Using ModelsBuilder-generated property directly.
```

You can learn more about `IPublishedContent` at the following link: `https://docs.umbraco.com/umbraco-cms/reference/querying/ipublishedcontent`.

Rendering fields in a strongly typed view

Rendering the content of a field using its alias is one of the most common tasks. For example, to render the content of a bodyContent field, write the following code:

```
@Model.Value("bodyContent")
```

If you're working within a partial view, you'll need to inherit the context to ensure the correct type is used for retrieving values. You can do this at the top of the partial view, as shown in the following code:

```
@inherits UmbracoViewPage<HomePage>
@Model.BodyContent
```

When looping over a collection of items, perhaps from a multi-item content picker, as shown in the following code:

```
@{
    IEnumerable<IPublishedContent> collection = Model.ItemList;
}
<ul>
    @foreach(IPublishedContent item in collection)
    {
        <li>@item.Name</li>
    }
</ul>
```

If you need to work with a specific type and conversion is possible, you can cast a property to a custom type, as shown in the following code:

```
@foreach (TeamMember person in Model.TeamMembers)
{
    <a href="@person.Url()">
        <span>@person.Name</span>
    </a>
}
```

In this case, we are looping through a collection of TeamMember objects, allowing access to strongly typed properties on each item.

Rendering complex field types

When rendering fields of a content type model in a Razor View with Umbraco, there are specific considerations for certain field types, like Rich Text and **Multinode Tree Picker** (MNTP). These fields require particular handling to display properly, especially given their complex data structures.

Rendering Rich Text Editor (RTE) fields

RTE fields store HTML content, so you don't need to encode the content when rendering it in a Razor View. If you use @Html.Raw, the HTML will render as intended in the view. Encoding it with @Model. MyRichTextField (without Html.Raw) will escape the HTML tags and show the raw HTML code instead, which is usually undesirable for rich text fields:

```
@Html.Raw(Model.Content.GetPropertyValue<string>("myRichTextField"))
```

If you want to display a preview or excerpt of the Rich Text content without HTML tags, consider using UmbracoHelper.StripHtml. This method removes HTML tags and allows you to limit the text length.

Rendering MNTP fields

MNTP fields allow selecting multiple content nodes (pages), returning an IEnumerable<IPublishedContent> if you have set it up to allow multiple selections, or a single IPublishedContent if only one item is allowed. You must check which type is returned in your view to avoid runtime errors.

If the MNTP is configured to allow multiple selections, loop through the IEnumerable<IPublishedContent> collection to access each selected item. Use properties on each item, such as Url, Name, or custom fields, to render content from the selected nodes, as shown in the following code:

```
@foreach (IPublishedContent content in Model.Content
   .GetPropertyValue<IEnumerable<IPublishedContent>>("myMultiNodePickerField"))
{
  <a href="@content.Url">@content.Name</a>
}
```

If the MNTP only allows a single node selection, you can render it directly without looping, as shown in the following code:

```
IPublishedContent content = Model.Content
   .GetPropertyValue<IPublishedContent>("mySingleNodePickerField");

if (content is not null)
{
  <a href="@content.Url">@content.Name</a>
}
```

Handling Media Picker fields

When using Media Picker, Umbraco will return IPublishedContent objects for selected media items. You can access members like Url, Name, and AltText (if available) on these items, as shown in the following code:

```
IPublishedContent mediaItem = Model.Content
   .GetPropertyValue<IPublishedContent>("myMediaPickerField");
```

```
if (mediaItem is not null)
{
  <img src="@mediaItem.Url" alt="@mediaItem.Name" />
}
```

Handling Nested Content and Block List editors

If your content model includes Nested Content or Block List fields, Umbraco returns an `IEnumerable<IPublishedElement>`, allowing you to iterate over nested items.

Each `IPublishedElement` represents a Nested Content item, and you can access its properties using `Value<T>()` or similar methods. This is especially useful for creating reusable components, as each Nested Content item can be rendered using partial views, as shown in the following code:

```
@foreach (IPublishedElement block in Model.Content
  .GetPropertyValue<IEnumerable<IPublishedElement>>("myNestedContentField"))
{
  <div>@block.Value<string>("nestedContentProperty")</div>
}
```

Common considerations

Always check for `null` when working with optional fields to avoid runtime errors, particularly when using Media Picker, MNTPs, or Nested Content.

Using lazy loading for large MNTP collections can help improve performance. Consider caching complex MNTP lookups or heavy RTE content if they don't change often.

Accessing member data

Members are registered visitors or users of the website or CMS. To work with member-related data, you can use the `IMemberManager` service. It provides a gateway to member management features. For example, you can check if a member is logged in, as shown in the following code:

```
@using Umbraco.Cms.Core.Security;
@inject IMemberManager _memberManager;
@if (_memberManager.IsLoggedIn())
{
  <p>A Member is logged in</p>
}
else
{
  <p>No member is logged in</p>
}
```

Learn more about `IMemberManager`, including how to find a member by ID, name, or email, at the following link: `https://docs.umbraco.com/umbraco-cms/reference/querying/imembermanager`.

Using Models Builder

The **Models Builder** feature allows you to work with strongly typed models in your views. For example, if you have a document type with the property `BodyText`, you can access it, as shown in the following code:

```
@Model.BodyText
```

Models Builder also utilizes value converters to automatically convert data into more usable forms, making it easier to work with nested objects in a strongly typed way, reducing potential errors that could arise from using dynamic types.

Learn more about Models Builder at the following link: `https://docs.umbraco.com/umbraco-cms/reference/templating/modelsbuilder`.

The UmbracoHelper class

The `UmbracoHelper` class is designed to provide various helper methods for working with content, media, members, and other components of an Umbraco-powered website. It simplifies common tasks, such as retrieving content by ID, rendering field values, and working with media files.

Some examples of uses of `UmbracoHelper` include the following list:

- Fetching content and media items by ID or GUID.
- Rendering field values from content items using the property aliases.
- Querying for published content using LINQ-like syntax.
- Working with members for user login and registration.
- Utility functions for URL generation, and so on.

The most common methods in `UmbracoHelper` are shown in *Table 15.5*:

Method	Description
TypedContent	This returns an `IPublishedContent` item based on an ID or GUID.
TypedMedia	This returns an `IPublishedContent` item from the media section.
RenderTemplate	This renders a specific template for a given content item.
GetDictionaryValue	This retrieves values from the dictionary (used for multilingual sites).
Query	This allows querying content using LINQ-like syntax.
IsMemberAuthorized	This checks if the current member is authorized based on permissions.

Table 15.5: Common methods in UmbracoHelper

Retrieving content by ID

This method fetches a published content item, like the CEO biography web page, by its unique ID. The content is returned as an `IPublishedContent` object, which gives you access to its properties, as shown in the following code:

```
@using Umbraco.Cms.Web.Common.PublishedModels;
@inject UmbracoHelper _umbracoHelper;
@{
    // Fetch content by its content node ID: 1234.
    IPublishedContent? content = _umbracoHelper.Content(1234);
}
@if (content is not null)
{
    <h1>@content.Name</h1>
    <p>@content.Value("bodyText")</p> <!-- Renders a property called "bodyText"
-->
}
else
{
    <p>Content not found.</p>
}
```

In this example, the `UmbracoHelper.Content(1234)` method retrieves the content node with ID 1234. You can then access properties using the `@content.Value("propertyAlias")` method.

Retrieving media by ID

To get a media item, for example, an image or document, by its ID, you can use the `TypedMedia` method, as shown in the following code:

```
@{
    IPublishedContent? media = _umbracoHelper.Media(5678); // 5678 is the media
ID.
}
@if (media is not null)
{
    <img src="@media.Url()" alt="@media.Name" />
}
else
{
    <p>Media not found.</p>
}
```

In the preceding code, `UmbracoHelper.Media(5678)` returns a media item, for example, an image, and we display the image's URL using the `@media.Url()` method.

Rendering a content template

You can use the `RenderTemplate` method to render a specific template for a given content item, as shown in the following code:

```
@{
    IPublishedContent? content = _umbracoHelper.Content(1234);
    IHtmlEncodedString renderedTemplate =
        await _umbracoHelper.RenderTemplateAsync(1234);
}
@if (!string.IsNullOrEmpty(renderedTemplate))
{
    @Html.Raw(renderedTemplate)
}
else
{
    <p>Template could not be rendered.</p>
}
```

In this example, `RenderTemplateAsync(1234)` renders the template assigned to the content item with ID 1234.

Getting dictionary values

For multilingual sites, Umbraco allows you to define dictionary items. You can retrieve their values using `GetDictionaryValue`, as shown in the following code:

```
@{
    string? welcomeText = _umbracoHelper.GetDictionaryValue("WelcomeText");
}
<p>@welcomeText</p>
```

This will fetch the dictionary value for the key `WelcomeText` based on the current language.

Querying content using LINQ

You can retrieve content based on more complex queries, like fetching all descendant content of a specific document type, as shown in the following code:

```
@{
    IEnumerable<IPublishedContent> articles = Model
        .DescendantsOrSelf("articlePage")
        .Where(x => x.IsVisible());
}
```

```
<ul>
@foreach (IPublishedContent article in articles)
{
  <li>
    <a href="@article.Url()">@article.Name</a>
  </li>
}
</ul>
```

This example retrieves all content items of type `articlePage` that are descendants and filters only the visible ones.

Checking member authorization

The `IsMemberAuthorized` method allows you to verify if the current member has the required permissions to access certain content, as shown in the following code:

```
@{
  bool isAuthorized = _umbracoHelper.IsMemberAuthorized("someSection");
}
@if (isAuthorized)
{
  <p>Welcome, authorized member!</p>
}
else
{
  <p>You do not have permission to view this content.</p>
}
```

This checks if the currently logged-in member is authorized to access a specific section of the site.

UmbracoHelper summary

The `UmbracoHelper` class is a central tool for developers working with content, media, and members in Umbraco. Its methods simplify common tasks such as fetching content and media, rendering templates, working with multilingual dictionary values, and ensuring correct member permissions.

You can read more about `UmbracoHelper` at the following link: `https://docs.umbraco.com/umbraco-cms/reference/querying/umbracohelper`.

Headless mode with Delivery API

Headless usage keeps rising because it lets teams ship faster across multiple frontends, improves performance by decoupling rendering, and scales cleanly as channels multiply. SPAs and native apps benefit most because they can request exactly the data they need and cache it aggressively. Industry guides and platform docs keep returning to the same benefits: omnichannel delivery, flexibility, performance, and team independence.

SPAs and native clients shouldn't be scraping HTML web pages. They want clean JSON with predictable shapes, culture-aware text, and media that works everywhere. Umbraco's built-in content Delivery API delivers exactly that at the relative link: `/umbraco/delivery/api`.

It's production-grade, versioned, and extensible, so you can keep editors in Umbraco and let React, Angular, Next.js, Swift, Blazor, or .NET MAUI clients consume pure data.

The Umbraco CMS Delivery API gives you:

- Opt-in, versioned REST endpoints for content and media, for example: `/umbraco/delivery/api/v2/content` and `/umbraco/delivery/api/v2/media`.
- Filtering, sorting, pagination, and structural selectors (children, ancestors, descendants) baked in.
- Localization via HTTP headers with `Accept-Language` to resolve language variants.
- Secured preview using an API key for draft content, plus support for protected content when configured.

If you select the **Delivery API** option in the project template, then the feature is enabled by default, as shown highlighted in the following code:

```
// Program.cs
builder.CreateUmbracoBuilder()
    .AddBackOffice()
    .AddWebsite()
    .AddDeliveryApi()
    .AddComposers()
    .Build();
```

You must also enable Delivery API in configuration, as shown in the following markup:

```
{
  "Umbraco": {
    "CMS": {
      "DeliveryApi": {
        "Enabled": true
      }
    }
  }
}
```

Rebuilding the indexes

Once the Delivery API is enabled, the next step is to rebuild the Delivery API content index (`DeliveryApiContentIndex`). This can be done using the **Examine Management** dashboard in the **Settings** section of the Umbraco backoffice:

1. Navigate to the Umbraco backoffice.
2. Navigate to the **Settings** section.
3. Open the **Examine Management** dashboard.
4. Scroll down to find **Tools**.
5. Click the **Rebuild index** button.

Once the index is rebuilt, the API can serve the latest content from the multiple-items endpoint.

Consuming content via Delivery API

Umbraco's "language variants" model surfaces neatly through the Delivery API. Clients specify their preferred culture via `Accept-Language`, and the API resolves variant values for you.

Common requests to the Delivery API:

- Get one item by key (use HTTP request headers to specify the content language and if you want draft, aka preview, content):

```
GET /umbraco/delivery/api/v2/content/item/{guid}
Accept-Language: en-US
Preview: true
```

- Get by route (path):

```
GET /umbraco/delivery/api/v2/content/item/{path}
```

- Get multiple by IDs:

```
GET /umbraco/delivery/api/v2/content/items?id={guid}&id={guid}
```

All of the above support fields and expand to shape the payload.

- Media has equivalent endpoints, for example:

```
GET /umbraco/delivery/api/v2/media/item/{guid}
GET /umbraco/delivery/api/v2/
media?fetch=children:/&filter=mediaType:Image&skip=0&take=10
```

Filtering and querying content

The content endpoint is where most clients start their queries:

```
GET /umbraco/delivery/api/v2/content
```

Key parameters include the following:

- Structural selectors with `fetch`

  - `fetch=children:{idOrPath}`
  - `fetch=descendants:{idOrPath}`
  - `fetch=ancestors:{idOrPath}`

- Filters with `filter`

  - `filter=contentType:article`
  - `filter=name:guide`

- Date ranges, for example:

  - `filter=createDate>:2025-01-01&filter=createDate<:2026-01-01`

- Sorting with `sort`

  - `sort=updateDate:desc&sort=name:asc`

- Paging with `skip` and `take`

For example, to get the latest ten articles under a section, where `name` contains guide, newest first:

```
GET /umbraco/delivery/api/v2/content
  ?fetch=descendants:dc1f43da-49c6-4d87-b104-a5864eca8152
  &filter=contentType:article
  &filter=name:guide
  &sort=updateDate:desc
  &skip=0&take=10
```

Handling media via API

You can enable the Media Delivery API and fetch items by `id` or `path`. You can filter by `mediaType`, page with `skip` and `take`, and select immediate children of a path with `fetch=children:/...`. The JSON shape includes URLs, dimensions, file sizes, focal points, and crop data, which frontends love for responsive images.

If you need absolute URLs or a CDN pattern change, the Delivery API uses a provider model for media URLs that you can swap with your own implementation.

To use the Delivery API for media, you must first enable it. Even if the Delivery API is enabled, the Delivery API for media remains disabled by default. The Delivery API for media is enabled by adding the `Media` section to the `DeliveryApi` configuration in `appsettings.json`, as shown in the following configuration:

```
{
  "Umbraco": {
    "CMS": {
      "DeliveryApi": {
```

```
      "Enabled": true,
      "PublicAccess": true,
      "Media": {
        "Enabled": true,
        "PublicAccess": false
      }
    }
  }
 }
}
```

Learn more about Delivery API at the following link: `https://docs.umbraco.com/umbraco-cms/reference/content-delivery-api`.

Practicing and exploring

Test your knowledge and understanding by answering some questions, getting some hands-on practice, and exploring this chapter's topics with deeper research.

Exercise 15.1 – Online material

You can find tutorials for Umbraco at the following link:

`https://docs.umbraco.com/umbraco-cms/tutorials/overview`.

Exercise 15.2 – Practice exercises

The following practice exercises help you to explore the topics in this chapter more deeply.

The Starter Kit

The Starter Kit is the name of one of the starter kit builds for Umbraco by Umbraco HQ. It is a great way to familiarize yourself with Umbraco CMS.

The Starter Kit will install sample content for a small site. You can edit the content or delete it and build your content from scratch. The sample content includes:

- **Home:** The home (or front page) of the site.
- **Text pages:** Generic text page with multi-column layout options.
- **Blog:** Blog section for the site, with blog overview and blog posts.
- **Products:** Product section, with featured products ready for shop integration.
- **People:** People section, with people profiles. Can be used for an employee section, for example.
- **Contact page:** The contact page contains a customizable map and contact form.

Here is a link to the Starter Kit: `https://docs.umbraco.com/umbraco-cms/tutorials/starter-kit`.

Extending Umbraco

Extending Umbraco often involves TypeScript and Lit, which are beyond the scope of this book. You can learn more about them at the following links:

- TypeScript documentation: `https://www.typescriptlang.org/docs/`
- Lit documentation: `https://lit.dev/docs/`

To complete tutorials about customizing the Umbraco editing experience, use the following link:

`https://docs.umbraco.com/umbraco-cms/tutorials/overview#customize-the-editing-experience`.

Exercise 15.3 – Test your knowledge

Answer the following questions:

1. Why might you build a custom property editor for Umbraco CMS?
2. What file types are disallowed for uploads by default?
3. By default, does Umbraco CMS follow the modern security good practice of enforcing password minimum length without enforcing special characters?
4. What is the difference between the `KeepAllVersionsNewerThanDays` and `KeepLatestVersionPerDayForDays` settings?
5. What are the two most commonly rendered properties of a published content item?
6. What does the Models Builder feature allow you to do?
7. How can you programmatically load media?
8. How can you programmatically render content using a template?
9. What are dictionary values used for?
10. In Umbraco CMS, what is a member?

Exercise 15.4 – Explore topics

Use the links on the following page to learn more about the topics covered in this chapter:

`https://github.com/markjprice/web-dev-net10/blob/main/docs/book-links.md#chapter-15--customizing-and-extending-umbraco-cms`.

Summary

In this chapter, you learned some of the techniques that can be used to customize and extend the behavior of Umbraco CMS. You learned about:

- Suggestions for advanced techniques for customizing and extending Umbraco
- How to customize Umbraco behavior using settings
- How to render published content in Razor views
- How to use `UmbracoHelper` for common tasks

In the *Epilogue*, I will make some suggestions for books to take you further with real-life web development using .NET.

Get This Book's PDF Version and Exclusive Extras

UNLOCK NOW

Scan the QR code (or go to `packtpub.com/unlock`). Search for this book by name, confirm the edition, and then follow the steps on the page.

Note: Keep your invoice handy. Purchases made directly from Packt don't require one.

Epilogue

I wanted this book to be different from others on the market. I hope that you found it to be a brisk, fun read, packed with practical, hands-on walk-throughs of each subject.

This epilogue contains the following short sections:

- Next steps on your web development learning journey
- The next edition
- Good luck!

Next steps on your web development learning journey

For subjects that I didn't have space to include in this book, but you might want to learn more about, I hope that the notes, good practice tips, and links in the GitHub repository point you in the right direction:

`https://github.com/markjprice/web-dev-net10/blob/main/docs/book-links.md`.

Companion books to continue your learning journey

I have written four books about .NET that further your journey with .NET 10. The other books act as companions to this book, and together they all form a .NET 10 quartet of books, as described in the following list and shown in *Figure 16.1*:

1. The first book covers the fundamentals of C#, .NET, and ASP.NET Core for modern web development. The 10th edition for .NET 10 contains changes from the 9th edition, including fixes for all errata, implementation of suggested improvements, and coverage of new .NET 10 features relevant to beginners, like partial members and extensions. The errata and improvements listed since the publishing of the 9th edition can be found at the following link: `https://github.com/markjprice/cs13net9/blob/main/docs/errata/README.md`.

2. The second book (the one you're reading now) covers real-world web development with .NET 10. This means it covers technologies that are mature and proven and are based on controller architecture. This includes MVC, Web APIs using controllers, OData, and the most popular .NET content management system, Umbraco CMS.

3. The third book covers more specialized topics, like internationalization and popular third-party packages, including Serilog and Noda Time. You will learn how to build native AOT-compiled services with ASP.NET Core minimal APIs and how to improve performance, scalability, and reliability using caching, queues, and background services. You will implement more services using GraphQL, gRPC, and SignalR. Finally, you will learn how to build graphical user interfaces for websites and desktop and mobile apps with Blazor and .NET MAUI.

4. The fourth book covers important tools and skills you should learn to become a well-rounded professional .NET developer. These include design patterns and solution architecture, debugging, memory analysis, all the important types of testing, from unit and integration to performance and web UI testing, and then topics like Docker and Aspire. Finally, it looks at how to prepare for an interview to get the .NET developer job that you want.

A summary of the companion .NET 10 books to this one and their most important topics is shown in *Figure E.1*:

C# language, including new C# 14 features, debugging, unit testing, and object-oriented programming.

.NET libraries, including number types, text, regular expressions, collections, file I/O, and data with EF Core and SQLite.

Modern websites and web services with ASP.NET Core, Blazor, and Minimal API web services.

Mature websites using ASP.NET Core MVC and Umbraco CMS, including defining routes, controllers, models, and views.

Mature web services using Web API controllers, OData, and FastEndpoints, including authentication, authorization, and integration testing.

Caching, web testing, configuration, and containerizing for deployment.

Modern apps: .NET MAUI mobile apps, Avalonia desktop apps, and Blazor WebAssembly web apps.

Modern services: Minimal API web services, caching, queuing, GraphQL, gRPC, and SignalR.

Libraries: Popular third-party packages, integrating LLMs and MCP, and internationalization.

Data: SQL Server, ADO.NET SqlClient, Dapper, and EF Core.

Tools: IDEs, debugging, memory analysis, and AI assistants.

Libraries: Cryptography, multi-tasking and concurrency.

Tests: Unit, integration, performance, security, and web.

Develop: Docker and Aspire.

Design: Patterns, principles, software and solution architecture.

Career: Teamwork and interviews.

Figure E.1: Companion books for learning .NET 10

To see a list of all the books that I have published with Packt, you can use the following link: `https://subscription.packtpub.com/search?query=mark+j.+price`.

Other books to take your learning further

If you are looking for other books from my publisher that cover related subjects, there are many to choose from, as shown in *Figure E.2*:

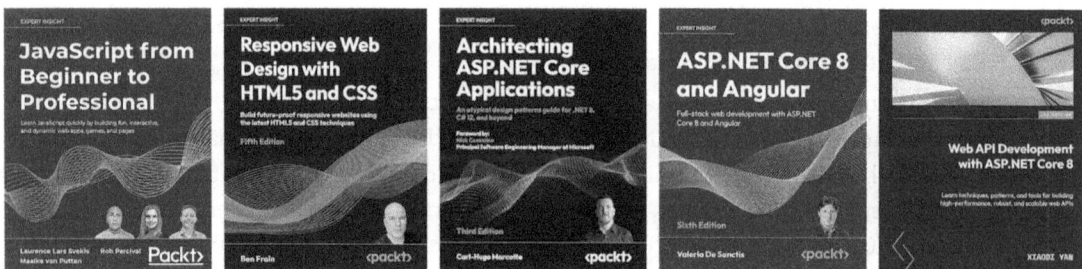

Figure E.2: Packt books to take your web development with .NET learning further

- *JavaScript from Beginner to Professional* (December 2021): This book demonstrates the capabilities of JavaScript for web application development by combining theoretical learning with code exercises and fun projects that you can challenge yourself with. The guiding principle of the book is to show how straightforward JavaScript techniques can be used to make web apps ranging from dynamic websites to simple browser-based games: `https://www.amazon.com/dp/1800562527/`.

- *Responsive Web Design with HTML5 and CSS* (October 2025): The fifth edition is the very latest, up-to-date version of one of the bestselling books on HTML5 and CSS. It emphasizes pragmatic application, teaching the approaches needed to build websites and applications, with downloadable examples. Written in Ben's friendly and easy-to-follow style, this title can be read as a complete guide or used as a reference for each topic: `https://www.amazon.com/dp/1837028230/`.

- *Architecting ASP.NET Core Applications* (March 2024): This unique ASP.NET Core book will fill in the gaps in your REST API and backend designs. Learn how to build robust, maintainable, and flexible apps using **Gang of Four (GoF)** design patterns and modern architectural principles. This new edition is updated for .NET 8 and focuses exclusively on the backend, with new content on REST APIs, the **Request-Endpoint-Response (REPR)** pattern, and building modular monoliths: `https://www.amazon.com/dp/1805123386/`.

- *ASP.NET Core 8 and Angular* (February 2024): If you want to learn how to use ASP.NET Core with Angular effectively, this hands-on guide is for you. Improve the way you create, debug, and deploy web applications while keeping up to date with the latest developments in .NET 8 and modern Angular, including ASP.NET Core Minimal API web services and the new Angular standalone API defaults: `https://www.amazon.com/dp/1805129937/`.

- *Web API Development with ASP.NET Core 8* (April 2024): By providing a deeper understanding of the various protocols implemented by ASP.NET Core, including RESTful, SignalR (WebSocket), gRPC, and GraphQL, supplemented by practical examples and optimization techniques, such as using middleware, testing, caching, and logging, this book offers invaluable insights for both newcomers as well as seasoned developers to meet modern web development requirements. Additionally, you'll discover how to use cloud platforms such as Azure and Azure DevOps to enhance the development and operational aspects of your application: `https://www.amazon.com/dp/B0C7GW84WD/`.

> Some of the preceding books may have been updated to later versions of ASP.NET Core. Check before ordering.

You will also find a list of Packt books in the GitHub repository at the following link:

`https://github.com/markjprice/web-dev-net10/blob/main/docs/book-links.md#additional-packt-books`.

The next edition

If you have suggestions for topics that you would like to see covered or expanded upon, or you spot mistakes that need fixing in the text or code, then please let me know the details via chat in the Discord channel or the GitHub repository for this book, found at the following link:

```
https://github.com/markjprice/web-dev-net10.
```

Good luck!

I wish you the best of luck with all your .NET web development projects!

Learn more on Discord

To join the Discord community for this book – where you can share feedback, ask questions to the author, and learn about new releases – follow this QR code:

```
https://packt.link/RWWD10
```

Join .NETPro — It's Free

Staying sharp in .NET takes more than reading release notes. It requires real-world tips, proven patterns, and scalable solutions. That's what .NETPro, Packt's new newsletter, is all about.

Scan the QR code or visit the link to subscribe:

```
https://landing.packtpub.com/dotnetpronewsletter/
```

Share Your Thoughts

Now you've finished *Real-World Web Development with .NET 10, Second Edition*, we'd love to hear your thoughts! Scan the QR code below to go straight to the Amazon review page for this book and share your feedback or leave a review on the site that you purchased it from.

https://packt.link/r/1-835-88893-3

Your review is important to us and the tech community and will help us make sure we're delivering excellent quality content.

Unlock Your Exclusive Benefits

Your copy of this book includes the following exclusive benefits:

- ☁ Next-gen Packt Reader
- 🖼 DRM-free PDF/ePub downloads

Follow the guide below to unlock them. The process takes only a few minutes and needs to be completed once.

Unlock this book's free benefits in 3 easy steps

Step 1

Keep your purchase invoice ready for *Step 3*. If you have a physical copy, scan it using your phone and save it as a PDF, JPG, or PNG.

For more help on finding your invoice, visit `https://www.packtpub.com/unlock-benefits/help`.

> **Note:** If you bought this book directly from Packt, no invoice is required. After *Step 2*, you can access your exclusive content right away.

Step 2

Scan the QR code or go to `packtpub.com/unlock`.

On the page that opens (similar to *Figure 16.1* on desktop), search for this book by name and select the correct edition.

Figure 16.1: Packt unlock landing page on desktop

Step 3

After selecting your book, sign in to your Packt account or create one for free. Then upload your invoice (PDF, PNG, or JPG, up to 10 MB). Follow the on-screen instructions to finish the process.

Need help?

If you get stuck and need help, visit `https://www.packtpub.com/unlock-benefits/help` for a detailed FAQ on how to find your invoices and more. This QR code will take you to the help page.

Note: If you are still facing issues, reach out to `customercare@packt.com`.

Index

www.ingramcontent.com/pod-product-compliance
Lightning Source LLC
Chambersburg PA
CBHW081208220326
41598CB00037B/6714